CADENCE BOOKS GRAPHIC NOVEL

ADOLF™
An Exile in Japan

CADENCE BOOKS GRAPHIC NOVEL

ADOLF™
An Exile in Japan

STORY & ART BY
OSAMU TEZUKA

STORY & ART BY
OSAMU TEZUKA

Translation/Yuji Oniki

Touch-up Art & Lettering/Viz Graphics
Cover Design/Viz Graphics
Editor/Annette Roman

Marketing Manager/Renée Solberg
Sales Representative/Mike Roberson
Director of Sales & Marketing/Dallas Middaugh
Publisher/Seiji Horibuchi
Editor-In-Chief/Hyoe Narita

Originally published as *Adolf ni Tsugu* by Bungei Shunju, Inc. in Japan in 1985.

Printed in Canada

Published by Cadence Books, Inc.
P.O. Box 77010 • San Francisco, CA 94107

10 9 8 7 6 5 4 3 2
First printing, February 1996
Second printing, August 2001

*

Osamu Tezuka's *ADOLF* Series:
A Tale of the Twentieth Century
An Exile in Japan
The Half-Aryan
Days of Infamy
1945 and All That Remains

CONTENTS

INTRODUCTION

TEZUKA'S TWENTIETH CENTURY

By Yuji Oniki

How can this century be remembered? On the one
hand, the modern technologies of photography, film, and
audio recording provide us with thorough documentation
of the past, on the other, as these points of view prolifer-
ate, we seem unable to agree on any coherent account of
this century. The recent controversies surrounding both
Holocaust revisionism theories and justifications of the
atomic bombings of Hiroshima and Nagasaki reveal how
little consensus we have about this century we call ours.
Osamu Tezuka's *Adolf*, in contrast to these conflicting
versions of the past, invites us to reconsider World War II
as a story that can no longer be confined to a particular
nation, culture, or, quite simply, point of view.

Stanislaw Lem, the postwar science fiction writer, once
remarked that he wrote science fiction because it was the only
literature he considered to be written primarily in the interest of
the human species. Similarly, the simplicity of Tezuka's pictures
and words suggests not only an attempt to reach a wider audi-
ence beyond Japan, but also an effort to tell a history that has
no allegiance to any particular nationality. It hardly seems sur-
prising that both Lem and Tezuka were survivors and witnesses

of the same world war.

Like words, images are lost in translation as they become increasingly complex. *Adolf* takes place all over the European continent, as well as Japan, switching constantly between characters speaking German, Japanese, Hebrew, and other languages, and it's largely due to Tezuka's spare images and drawing style that this story can take place nation to nation, city to city, and face to face without losing its focus.

As Lem resorts to science fiction to gain a futuristic perspective beyond the everyday prosaic dimensions of culture and nationality, Tezuka finds a new "language" in *manga* (Japanese comics) to portray a century in which we have yet to define ourselves as a unified species instead of dividing ourselves in terms of race. *Adolf,* spanning the course of several decades, unfolds into an account of racism rippling through the century both during and after World War II. World War II was unfinished business for Tezuka, not because he still felt victimized but because he was convinced that the remnants and "fallout," of racism expressed during the war lingered on into the present. World War II didn't mark the closing chapter of twentieth century racism, it marked the beginning. That's why I named the first volume of *Adolf* "A Tale of the Twentieth Century," for, whether we like it or not, no other fear continues to haunt this century more than that of racial difference.

As Americans, we often refer to World War II as the "Good War," which preceded the messiness of later conflicts like the Korean War and the Vietnam War. The story of World War II was told in terms of simple oppositions between good and evil, democracy and fascism, Nazis and Jews. To many it was the last war worth fighting for, because one could draw clear lines between cause and effect, oppressor and oppressed, and justice and injustice.

In the world of *Adolf*, however, these lines are obscured, mapped out as a tangled web of racial conflicts, myths, and secrets, all overlapping to such an extent that racism can no longer be accounted for within a single ideology or culture, whether Nazi, Jewish, or Japanese. "Pure" individuals don't exist in *Adolf*, but myths of purity do, and the conflicting emotions produced as a result of this incongruity shape and form the lives of everyone during the war.

Witness, for example, the three Adolfs. The story revolves around the secret of Adolf Hitler's Jewish ancestry. The historical validity of this premise is less important than the fact that each Adolf in Tezuka's story represents not a particular race or nationality, but a particular "mixed" circumstance. In *Adolf*, no one, not even Hitler, and no race, not even the Japanese, can claim a pure racial identity without being defined against other races.

We are all too familiar with Hitler's attempts to resolve his conflict over his racial identity by eradicating racial difference on a global scale. Now we find Tezuka's two other Adolfs pursuing their personal agendas at first in tandem and then separately as they try to decipher not only Hitler's secret, but their own confused circumstances of mixed racial and national identities. Adolf Kamil and Adolf Kaufmann grow up in Kobe, Japan, speaking Japanese as their native language, yet they are excluded by Japanese children because they are white.

Adolf Kamil, a Jew, insists he is just as Japanese as everyone around him, only to realize he will never be recognized as a fellow Japanese citizen because he is not, racially speaking, *one of them*. Of all the three Adolfs, Kamil is the most optimistic, believing that race should have nothing to do with nationality. Yet World War II confronts him with a confusing network of racial divisions drawn on the one hand between whites and Asians in the Asian arena, and on the other, between Jews and Aryans in the European arena. Kamil's final allegiance is just as much a consequence of the racism he suffers as a non-Asian in Japan as it is a reaction against the Holocaust in Europe.

Nothing could be more diametrically opposed to Kamil's struggle as a Japanese Jew than Adolf Kaufmann's evolution as a "half-Aryan" in Germany, but in many ways their experiences mirror each other. Just as Kamil spends most of his life trying to prove how Japanese he is, Kaufmann equals his friend's drive with his own efforts, at the Adolf Hitler Schule, to become a shining example of the "Aryan" race, despite the fact that his mother and native language are Japanese. While Kamil's skin prevents him from becoming Japanese in Japan,

Kaufmann's secret language, the Japanese he writes in his letters to his mother and best friend, protects him from becoming a full-fledged Nazi. As if to end this conflict between acting as a German and hiding his other "pre-German" self in the Japanese language, Kaufmann gives up his Japanese origins in the name of his surrogate father, Adolf Hitler. But by then, as we shall see in the concluding volume, Kaufmann's "final solution" hardly matters.

What matters most in *Adolf* isn't how right or wrong we determine each character to be. In *Adolf*, one is never quite sure where justice begins and ends. Although the story itself might be read as a mystery-thriller, the greatest mystery for Tezuka was finding where justice lay in the twentieth century. *Adolf* doesn't pretend to be a morality play, and Tezuka's characters don't work well as pawns in the service of social critique. The world of *Adolf* instead is a world of collisions where people, ideas, and races are constantly at odds. *Adolf* only provides the first chapters to this century. Whatever remains to be told is entirely up to each reader of this tale of the twentieth century.

Yuji Oniki, translator of Cadence Books' Adolf *series, is earning his Ph.D. in comparative literature at the University of California at Berkeley. He is currently writing his dissertation on the cultural production of mass media, film, and comics in contemporary Japan.*

CHAPTER
ONE

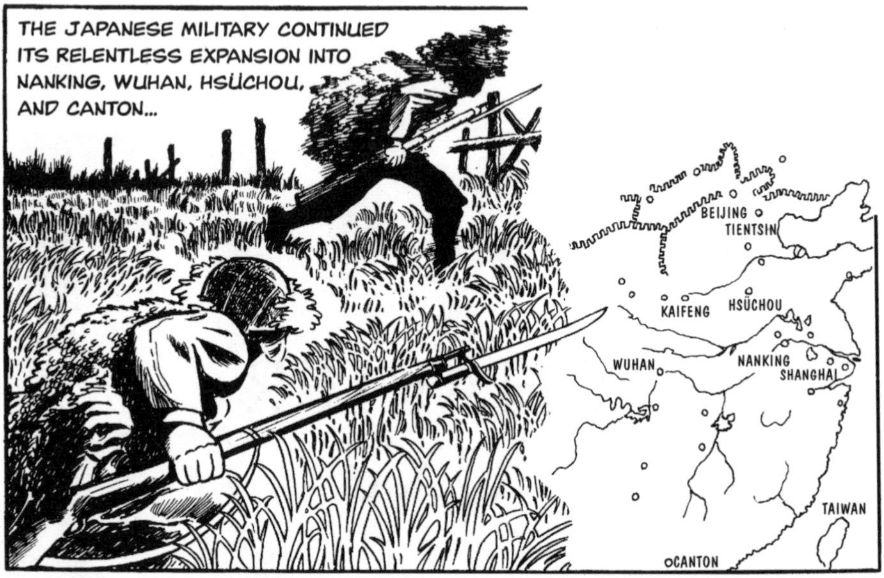
THE JAPANESE MILITARY CONTINUED ITS RELENTLESS EXPANSION INTO NANKING, WUHAN, HSÜCHOU, AND CANTON...
BEIJING
TIENTSIN
KAIFENG
HSÜCHOU
WUHAN
NANKING
SHANGHAI
TAIWAN
CANTON

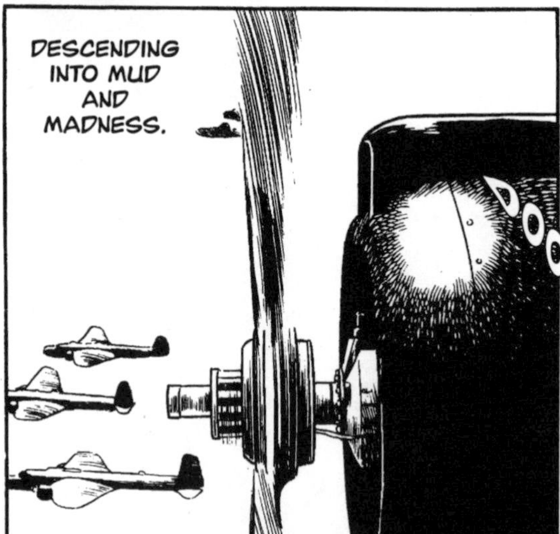
DESCENDING INTO MUD AND MADNESS.
DOOOM

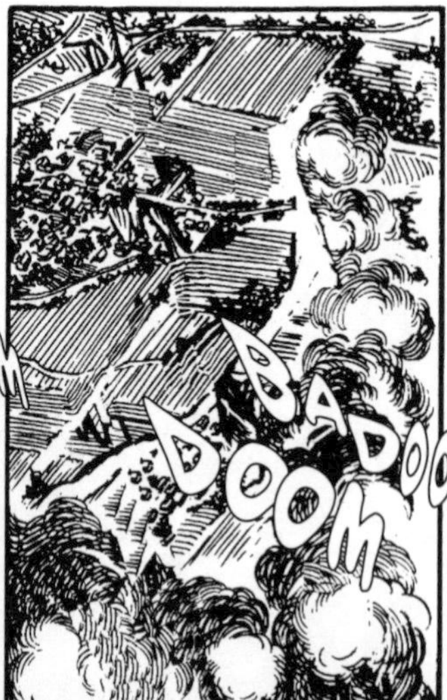
BADOOM
DOOM

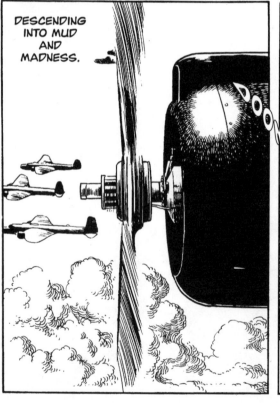

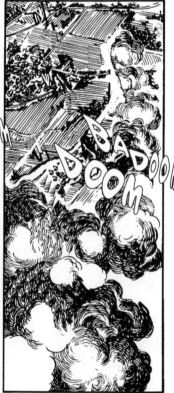

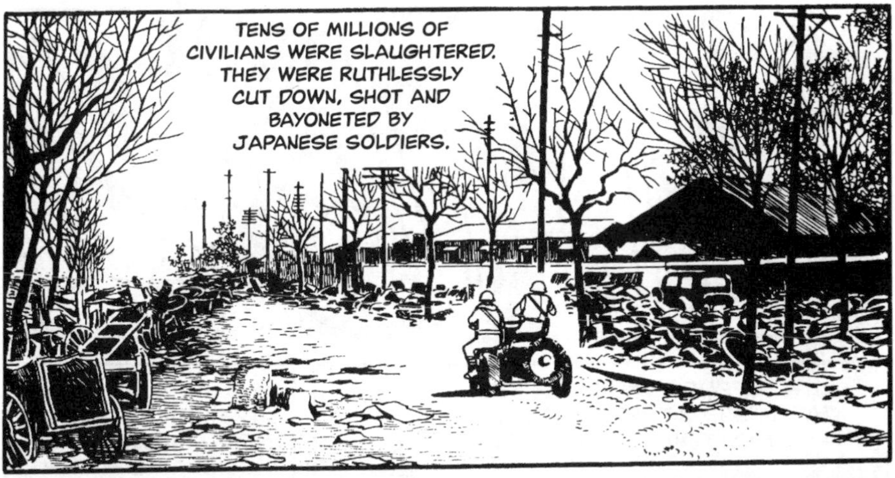
TENS OF MILLIONS OF CIVILIANS WERE SLAUGHTERED. THEY WERE RUTHLESSLY CUT DOWN, SHOT AND BAYONETED BY JAPANESE SOLDIERS.

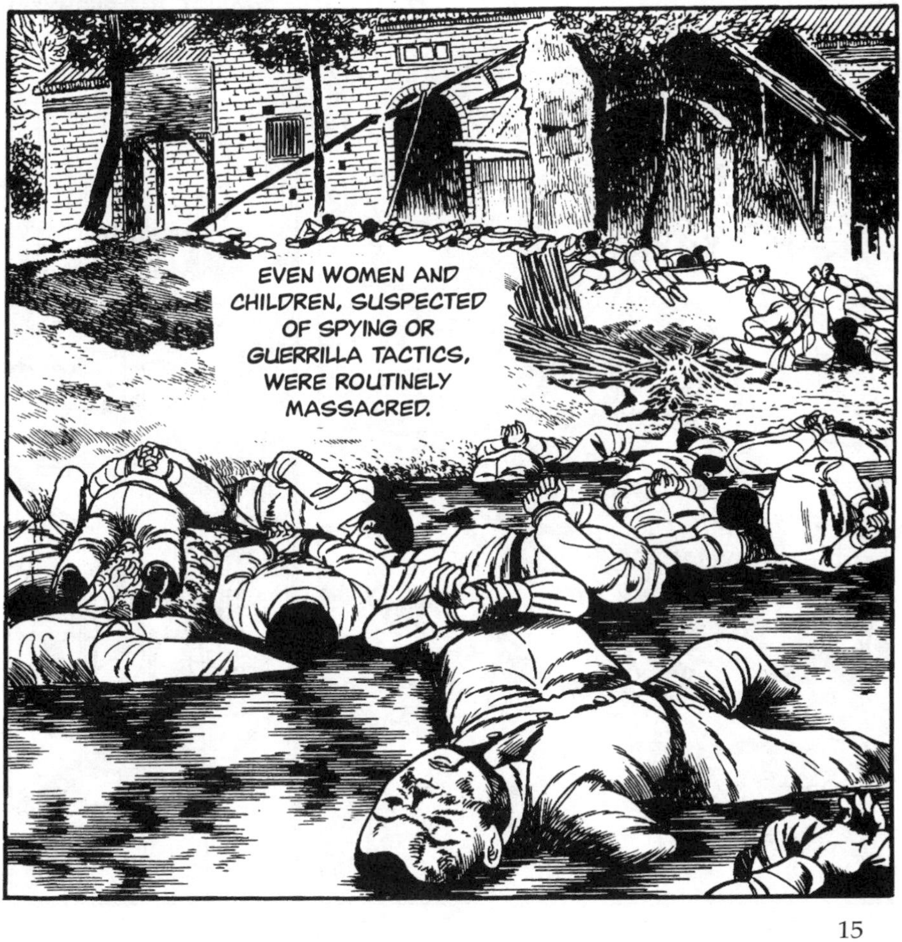
EVEN WOMEN AND CHILDREN, SUSPECTED OF SPYING OR GUERRILLA TACTICS, WERE ROUTINELY MASSACRED.

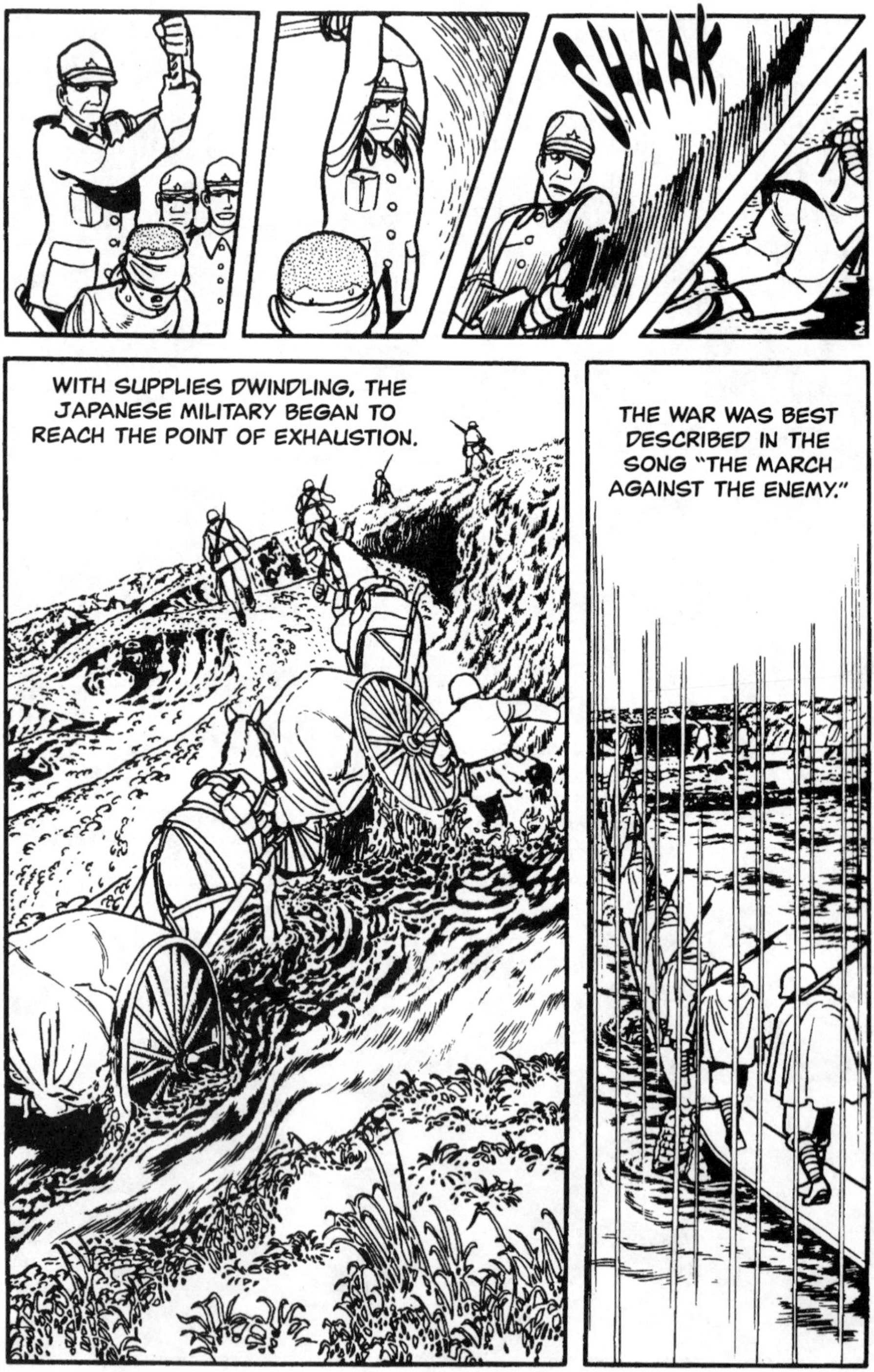
SHAAK
WITH SUPPLIES DWINDLING, THE JAPANESE MILITARY BEGAN TO REACH THE POINT OF EXHAUSTION.
THE WAR WAS BEST DESCRIBED IN THE SONG "THE MARCH AGAINST THE ENEMY."

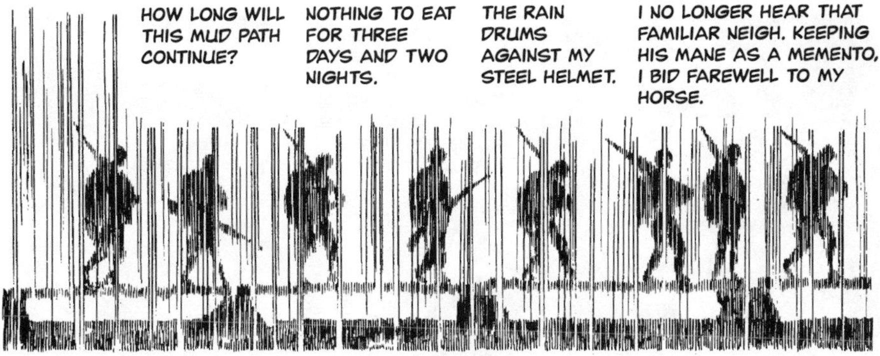
HOW LONG WILL THIS MUD PATH CONTINUE?
NOTHING TO EAT FOR THREE DAYS AND TWO NIGHTS.
THE RAIN DRUMS AGAINST MY STEEL HELMET.
I NO LONGER HEAR THAT FAMILIAR NEIGH. KEEPING HIS MANE AS A MEMENTO, I BID FAREWELL TO MY HORSE.

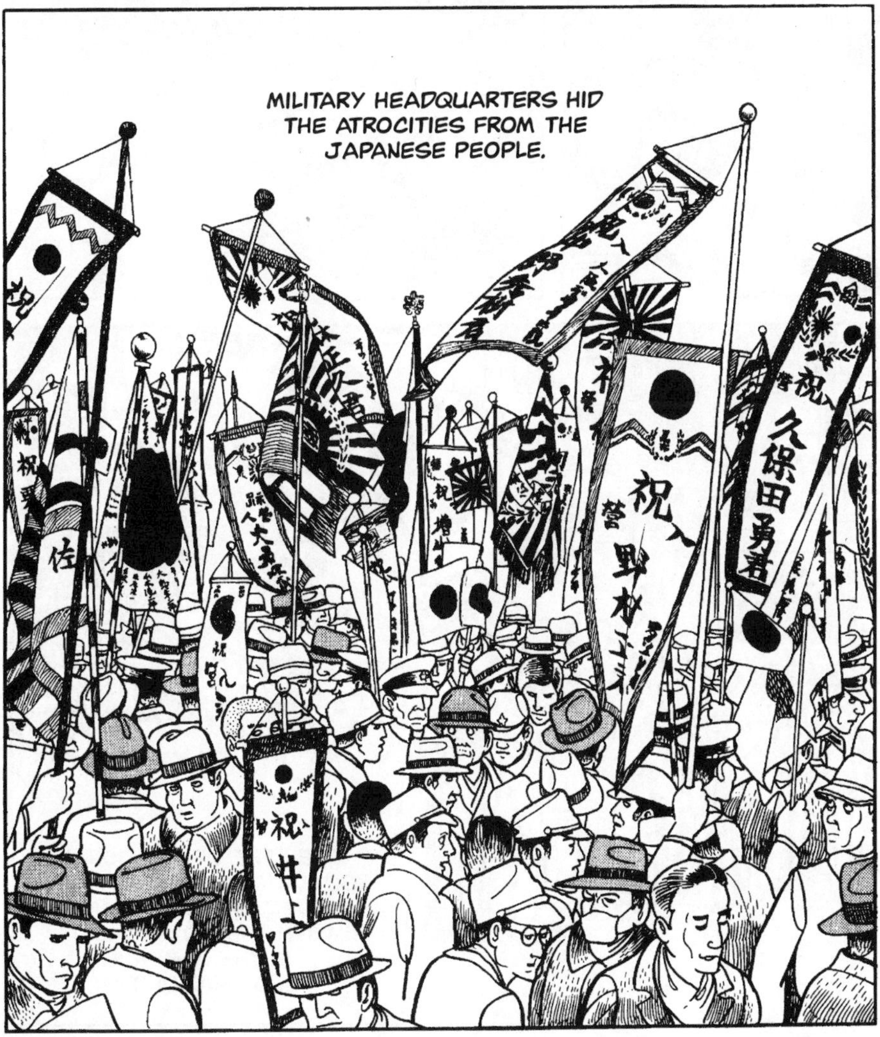
MILITARY HEADQUARTERS HID THE ATROCITIES FROM THE JAPANESE PEOPLE.

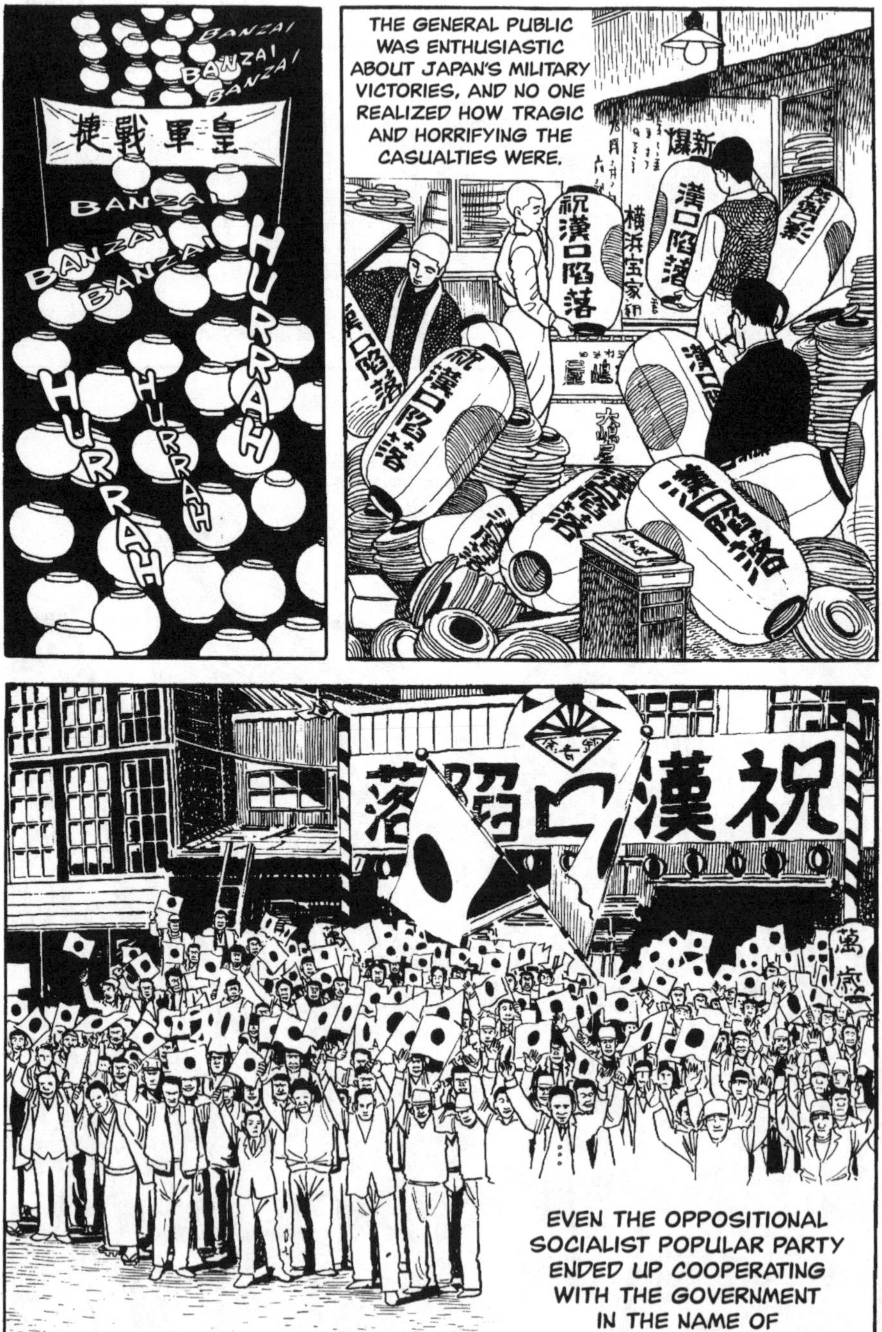
BANZAI
BANZAI
BANZAI
皇軍戰捷
BANZAI
BANZAI
BANZAI
BANZAI
HURRAH
HURRAH
HURRAH
THE GENERAL PUBLIC WAS ENTHUSIASTIC ABOUT JAPAN'S MILITARY VICTORIES, AND NO ONE REALIZED HOW TRAGIC AND HORRIFYING THE CASUALTIES WERE.
新爆
祝漢口陥落
漢口陥落
横浜宝家行
漢口陥落
祝漢口陥落
漢口陥落
祝漢口陥落
EVEN THE OPPOSITIONAL SOCIALIST POPULAR PARTY ENDED UP COOPERATING WITH THE GOVERNMENT IN THE NAME OF "NATIONAL UNITY."

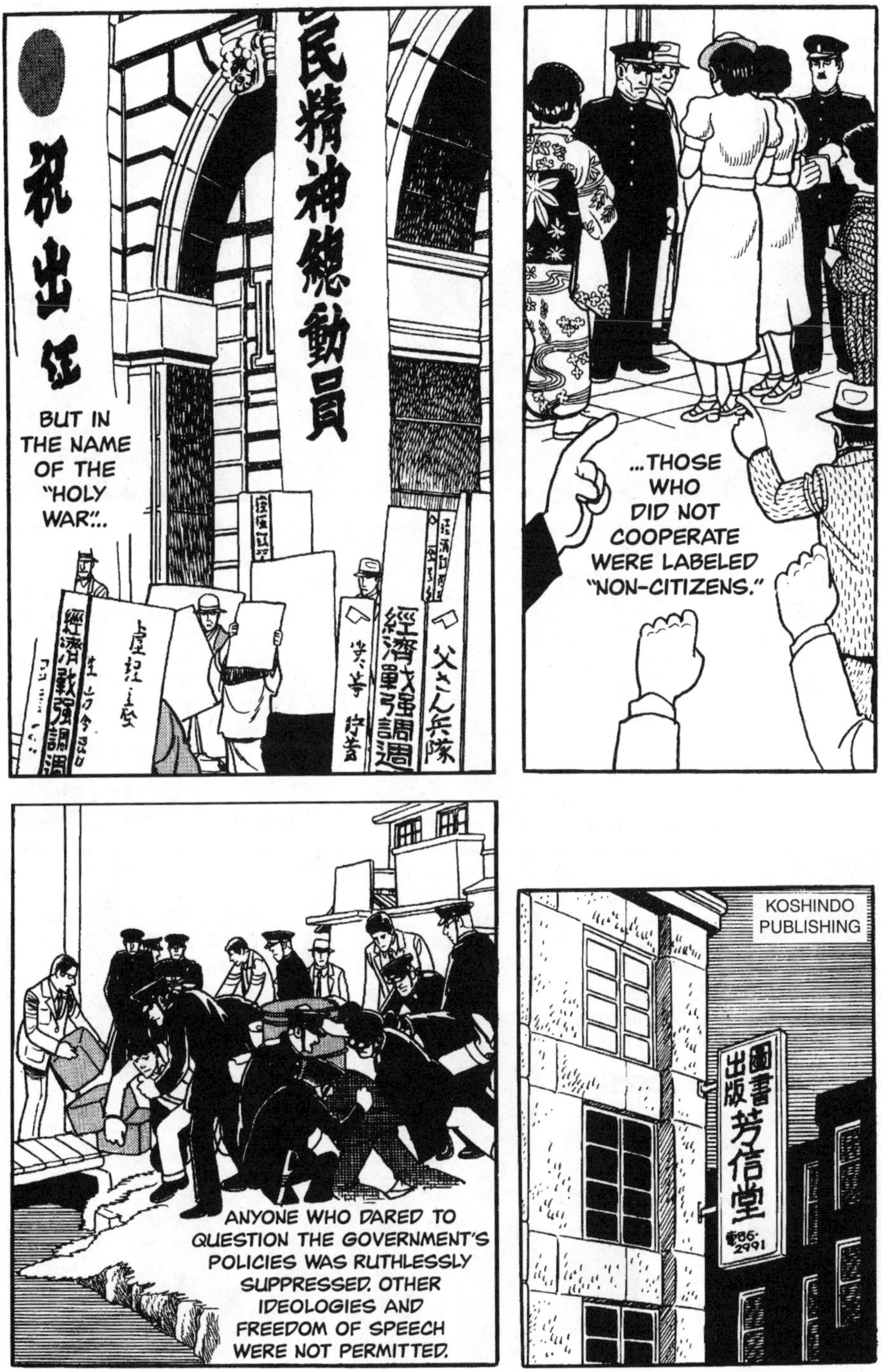
祝出征
民精神總動員
BUT IN THE NAME OF THE "HOLY WAR"...
經濟戰強調週
父さん兵隊
...THOSE WHO DID NOT COOPERATE WERE LABELED "NON-CITIZENS."
ANYONE WHO DARED TO QUESTION THE GOVERNMENT'S POLICIES WAS RUTHLESSLY SUPPRESSED. OTHER IDEOLOGIES AND FREEDOM OF SPEECH WERE NOT PERMITTED.
KOSHINDO PUBLISHING
圖書出版芳信堂

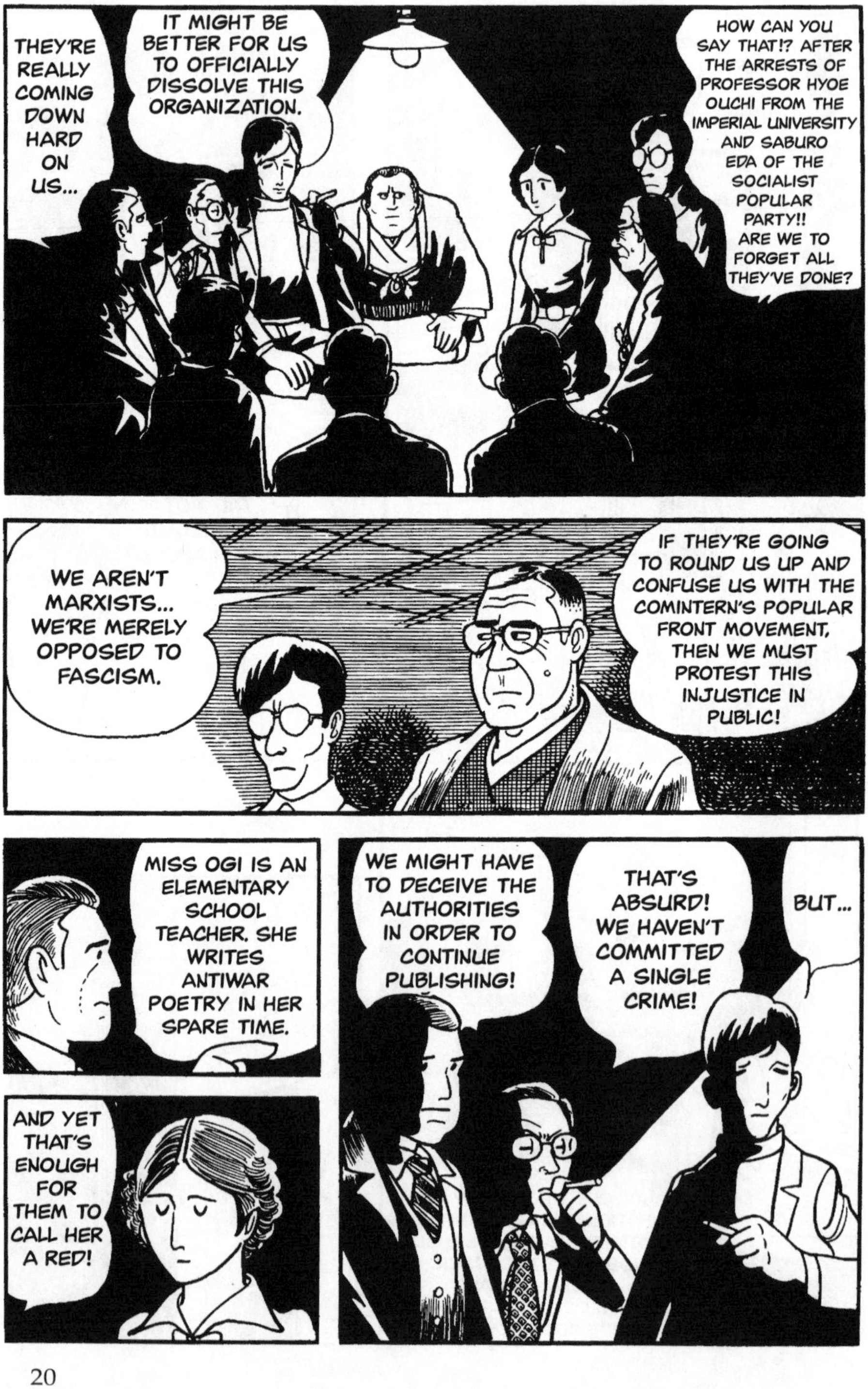
THEY'RE REALLY COMING DOWN HARD ON US...
IT MIGHT BE BETTER FOR US TO OFFICIALLY DISSOLVE THIS ORGANIZATION.
HOW CAN YOU SAY THAT!? AFTER THE ARRESTS OF PROFESSOR HYOE OUCHI FROM THE IMPERIAL UNIVERSITY AND SABURO EDA OF THE SOCIALIST POPULAR PARTY!! ARE WE TO FORGET ALL THEY'VE DONE?
WE AREN'T MARXISTS... WE'RE MERELY OPPOSED TO FASCISM.
IF THEY'RE GOING TO ROUND US UP AND CONFUSE US WITH THE COMINTERN'S POPULAR FRONT MOVEMENT, THEN WE MUST PROTEST THIS INJUSTICE IN PUBLIC!
MISS OGI IS AN ELEMENTARY SCHOOL TEACHER. SHE WRITES ANTIWAR POETRY IN HER SPARE TIME.
AND YET THAT'S ENOUGH FOR THEM TO CALL HER A RED!
WE MIGHT HAVE TO DECEIVE THE AUTHORITIES IN ORDER TO CONTINUE PUBLISHING!
THAT'S ABSURD! WE HAVEN'T COMMITTED A SINGLE CRIME!
BUT...

IF LIBERAL PROFESSORS LIKE OUCHI AND MINOBE ARE BEING ARRESTED, I DOUBT WE CAN DO MUCH PROTESTING.

EXCUSE ME FOR CHANGING THE SUBJECT...

...BUT I HAVE SOMETHING I MUST SHOW YOU.

I RECEIVED THIS LETTER FROM ONE OF MY FORMER PUPILS.

HE'S STUDYING AT BERLIN UNIVERSITY NOW.

THE DOCUMENTS ARE ALL WRITTEN IN GERMAN. THERE'S A DUPLICATE OF A BIRTH CERTIFICATE, SOME OTHER KIND OF CERTIFICATE, AND TWO OLD LETTERS.

I CAN'T READ GERMAN, BUT I THOUGHT PERHAPS PROFESSOR KUWAYAMA WOULD LIKE TO EXAMINE IT.

LET'S SEE.

HMM...

21

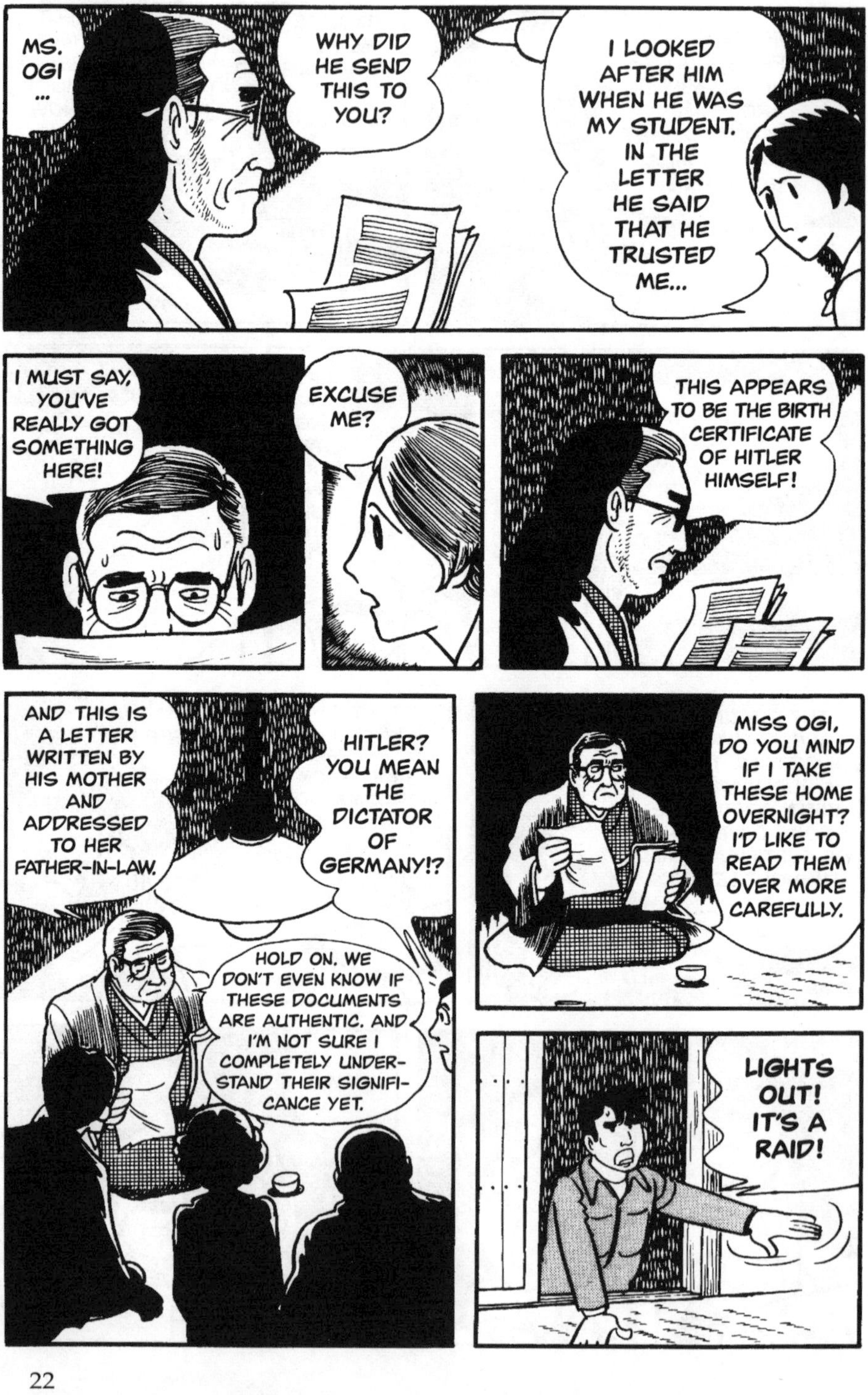
MS. OGI ...
WHY DID HE SEND THIS TO YOU?
I LOOKED AFTER HIM WHEN HE WAS MY STUDENT. IN THE LETTER HE SAID THAT HE TRUSTED ME...
I MUST SAY, YOU'VE REALLY GOT SOMETHING HERE!
EXCUSE ME?
THIS APPEARS TO BE THE BIRTH CERTIFICATE OF HITLER HIMSELF!
AND THIS IS A LETTER WRITTEN BY HIS MOTHER AND ADDRESSED TO HER FATHER-IN-LAW.
HITLER? YOU MEAN THE DICTATOR OF GERMANY!?
HOLD ON. WE DON'T EVEN KNOW IF THESE DOCUMENTS ARE AUTHENTIC. AND I'M NOT SURE I COMPLETELY UNDER-STAND THEIR SIGNIFI-CANCE YET.
MISS OGI, DO YOU MIND IF I TAKE THESE HOME OVERNIGHT? I'D LIKE TO READ THEM OVER MORE CAREFULLY.
LIGHTS OUT! IT'S A RAID!

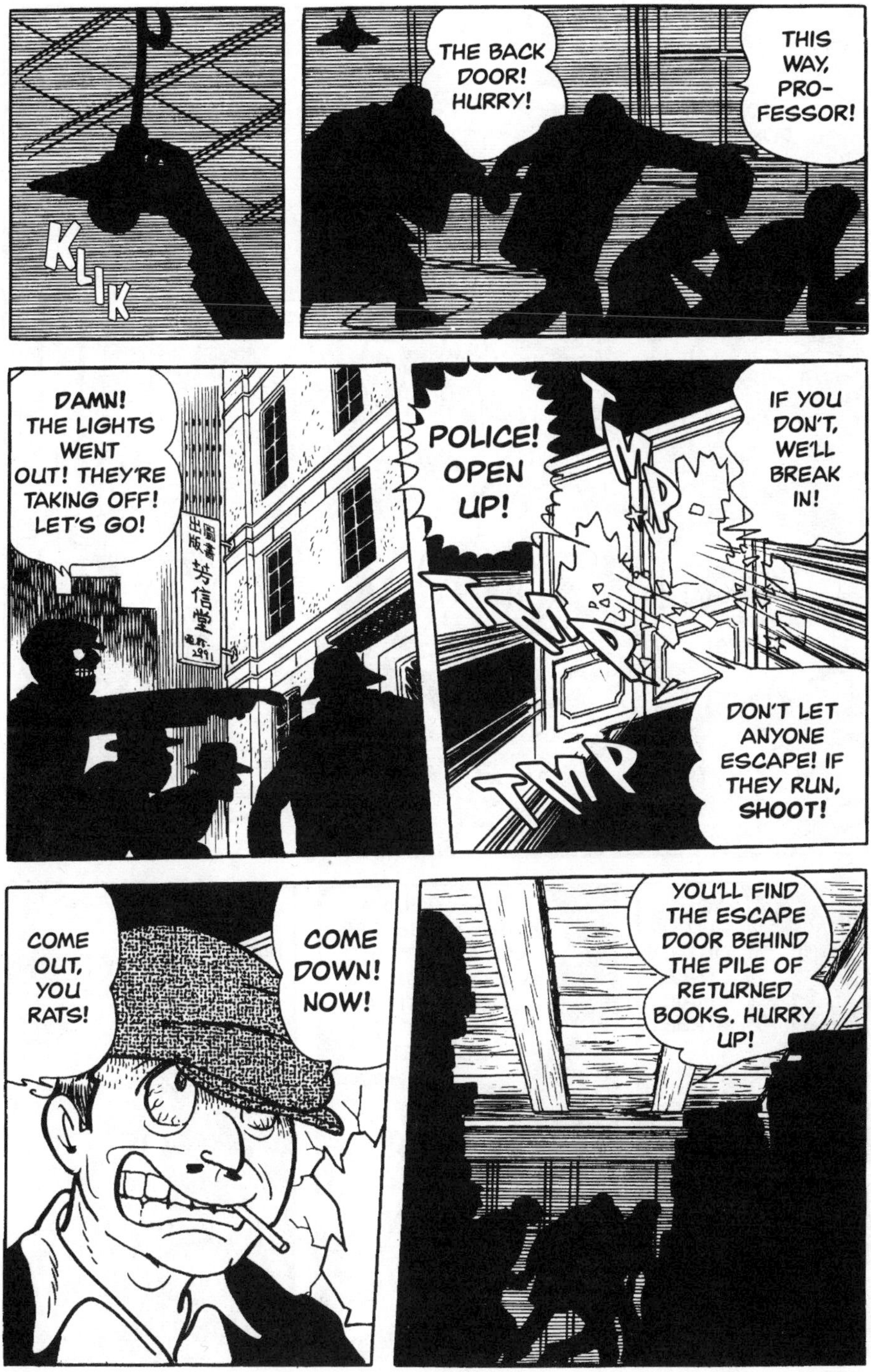
KLIK
THE BACK DOOR! HURRY!
THIS WAY, PRO-FESSOR!
DAMN! THE LIGHTS WENT OUT! THEY'RE TAKING OFF! LET'S GO!
圖書出版
芳信堂
POLICE! OPEN UP!
TMP
IF YOU DON'T, WE'LL BREAK IN!
TMP
TMP
DON'T LET ANYONE ESCAPE! IF THEY RUN, SHOOT!
COME OUT, YOU RATS!
COME DOWN! NOW!
YOU'LL FIND THE ESCAPE DOOR BEHIND THE PILE OF RETURNED BOOKS. HURRY UP!

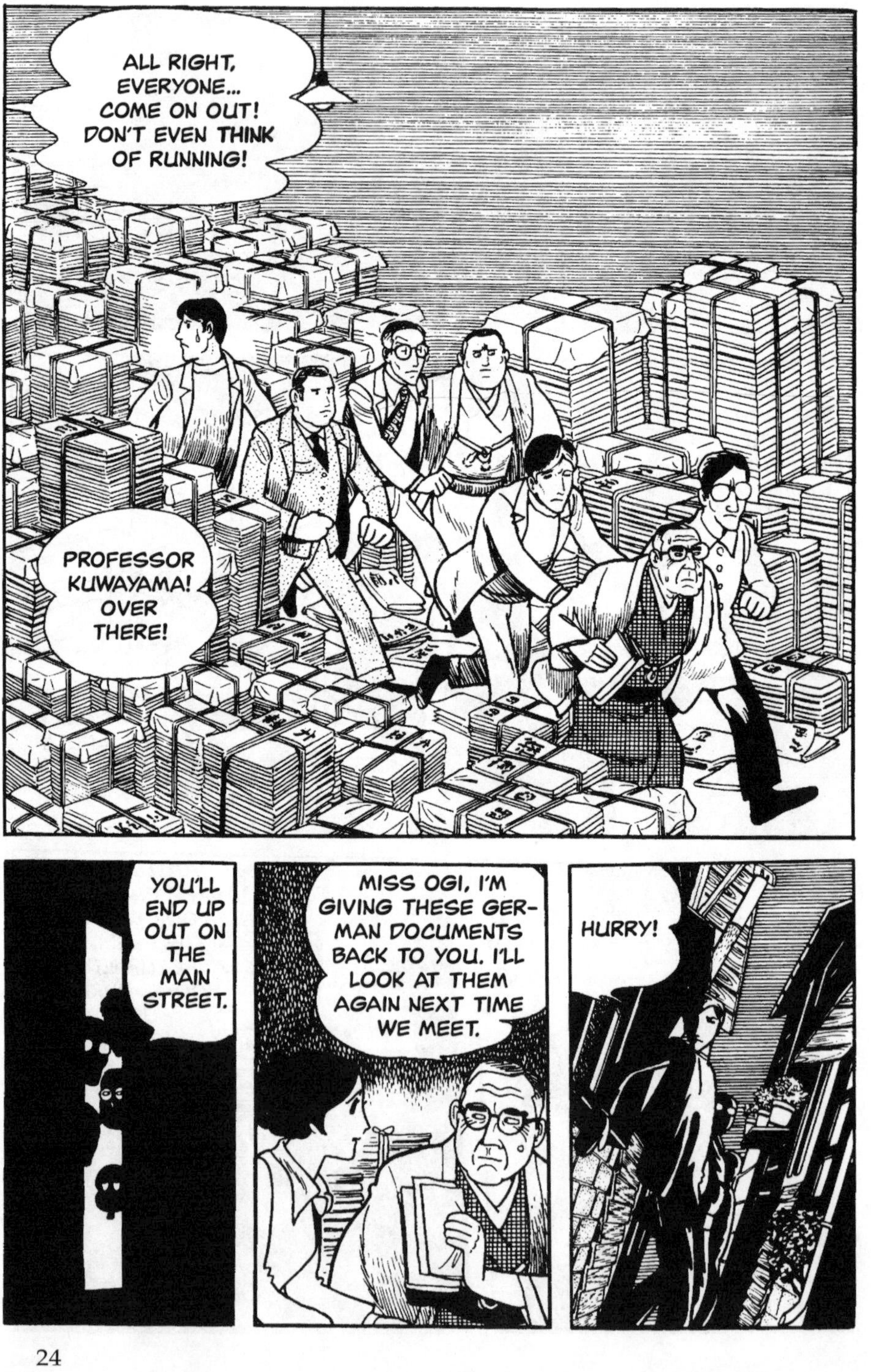
ALL RIGHT, EVERYONE... COME ON OUT! DON'T EVEN THINK OF RUNNING!
PROFESSOR KUWAYAMA! OVER THERE!
YOU'LL END UP OUT ON THE MAIN STREET.
MISS OGI, I'M GIVING THESE GER-MAN DOCUMENTS BACK TO YOU. I'LL LOOK AT THEM AGAIN NEXT TIME WE MEET.
HURRY!

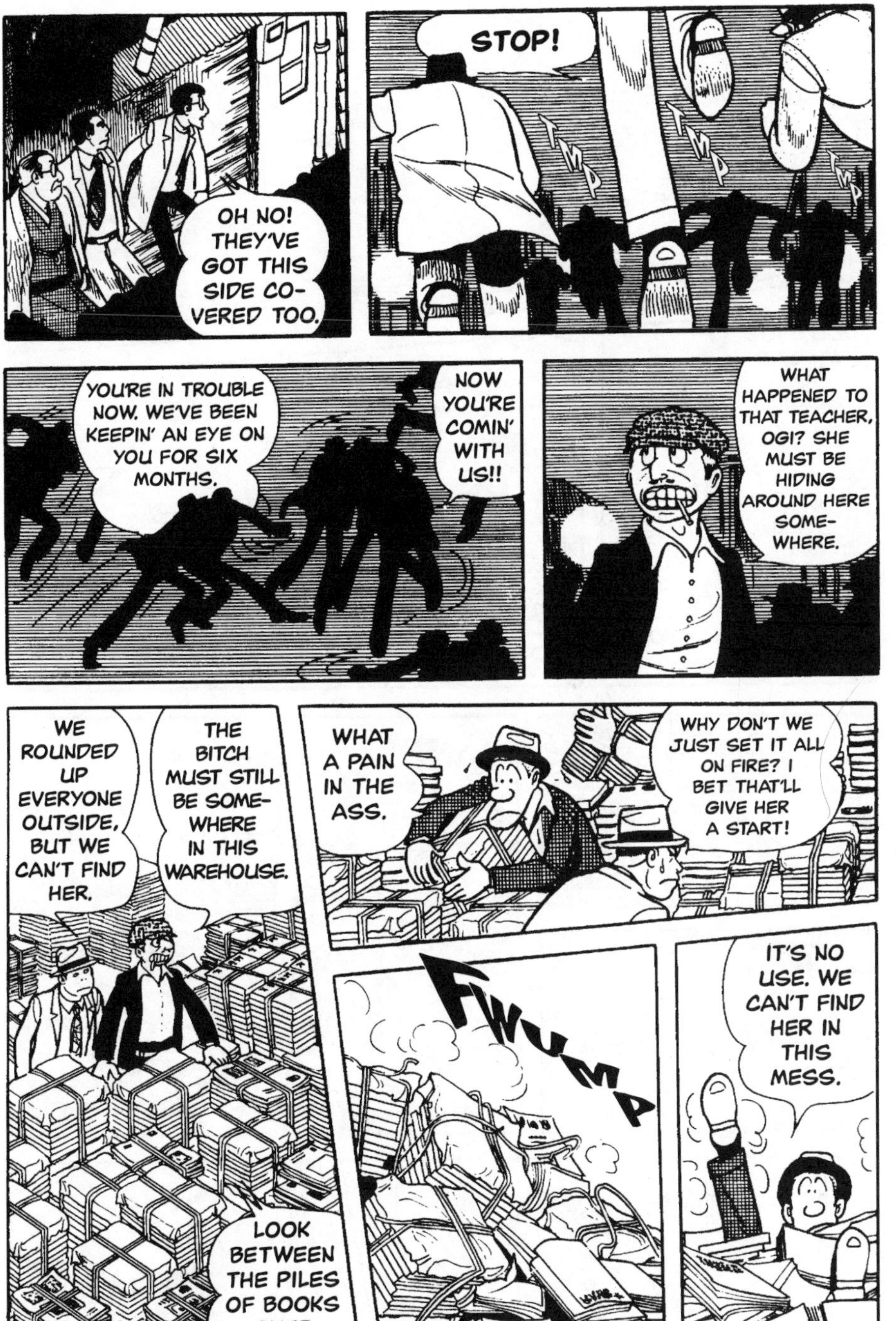
OH NO! THEY'VE GOT THIS SIDE CO- VERED TOO.
STOP!
TMP
TMP
TMP
YOU'RE IN TROUBLE NOW. WE'VE BEEN KEEPIN' AN EYE ON YOU FOR SIX MONTHS.
NOW YOU'RE COMIN' WITH US!!
WHAT HAPPENED TO THAT TEACHER, OGI? SHE MUST BE HIDING AROUND HERE SOME- WHERE.
WE ROUNDED UP EVERYONE OUTSIDE, BUT WE CAN'T FIND HER.
THE BITCH MUST STILL BE SOME- WHERE IN THIS WAREHOUSE.
LOOK BETWEEN THE PILES OF BOOKS OVER THERE.
WHAT A PAIN IN THE ASS.
WHY DON'T WE JUST SET IT ALL ON FIRE? I BET THAT'LL GIVE HER A START!
FWUMP
IT'S NO USE. WE CAN'T FIND HER IN THIS MESS.

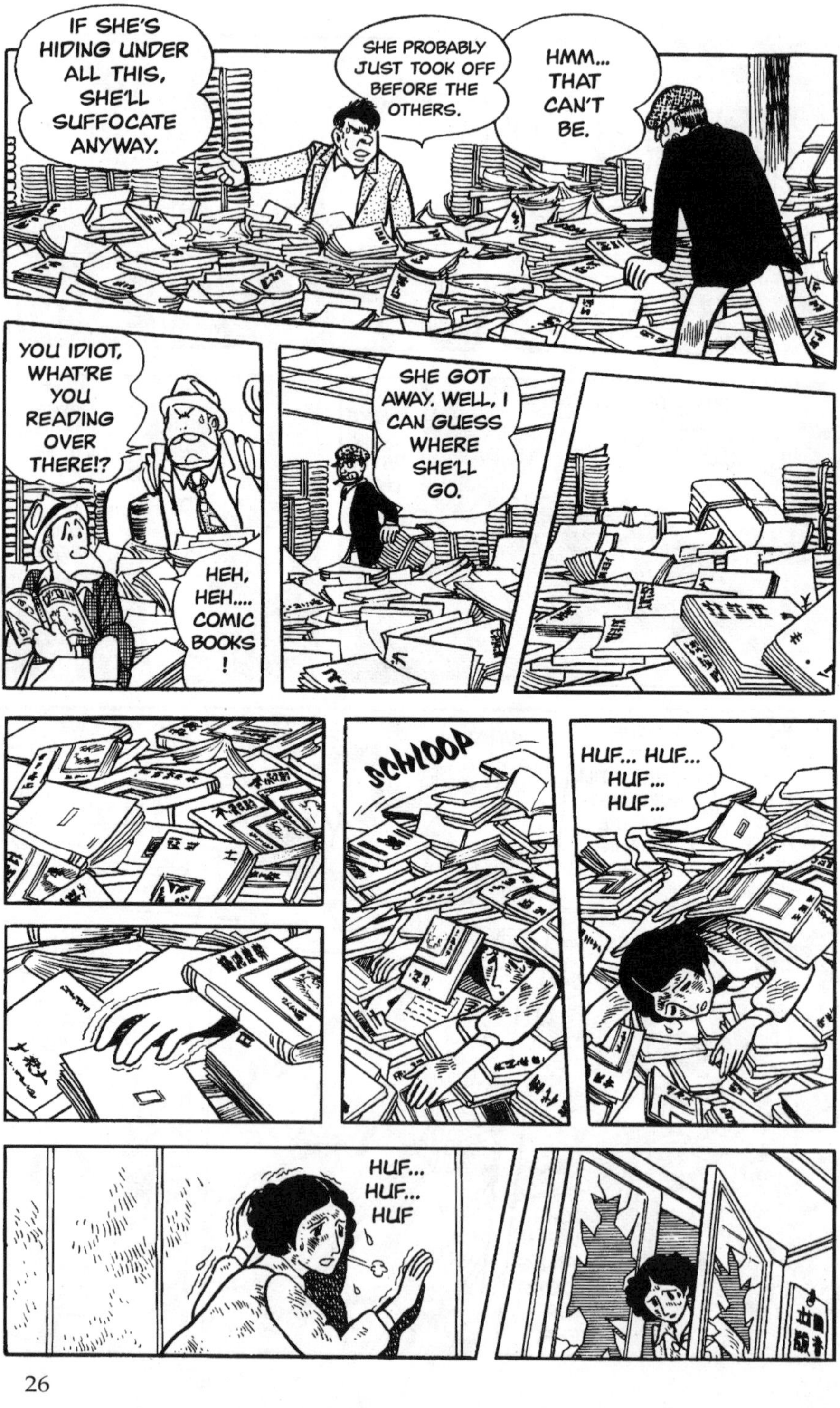
IF SHE'S HIDING UNDER ALL THIS, SHE'LL SUFFOCATE ANYWAY.
SHE PROBABLY JUST TOOK OFF BEFORE THE OTHERS.
HMM... THAT CAN'T BE.
YOU IDIOT, WHAT'RE YOU READING OVER THERE!?
HEH, HEH.... COMIC BOOKS !
SHE GOT AWAY. WELL, I CAN GUESS WHERE SHE'LL GO.
SCHLOOP
HUF... HUF... HUF... HUF...
HUF... HUF... HUF

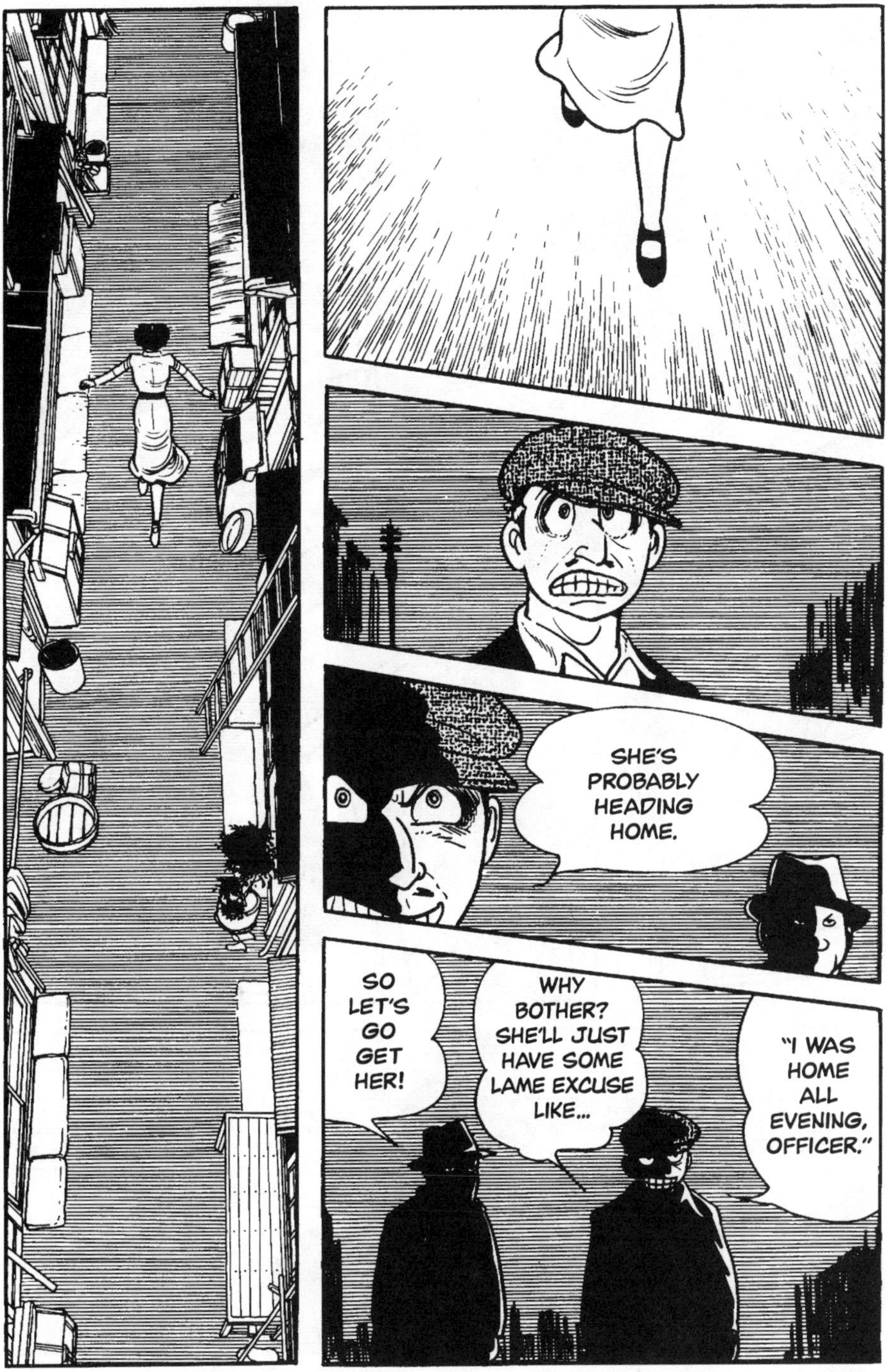
SHE'S PROBABLY HEADING HOME.
SO LET'S GO GET HER!
WHY BOTHER? SHE'LL JUST HAVE SOME LAME EXCUSE LIKE...
"I WAS HOME ALL EVENING, OFFICER."

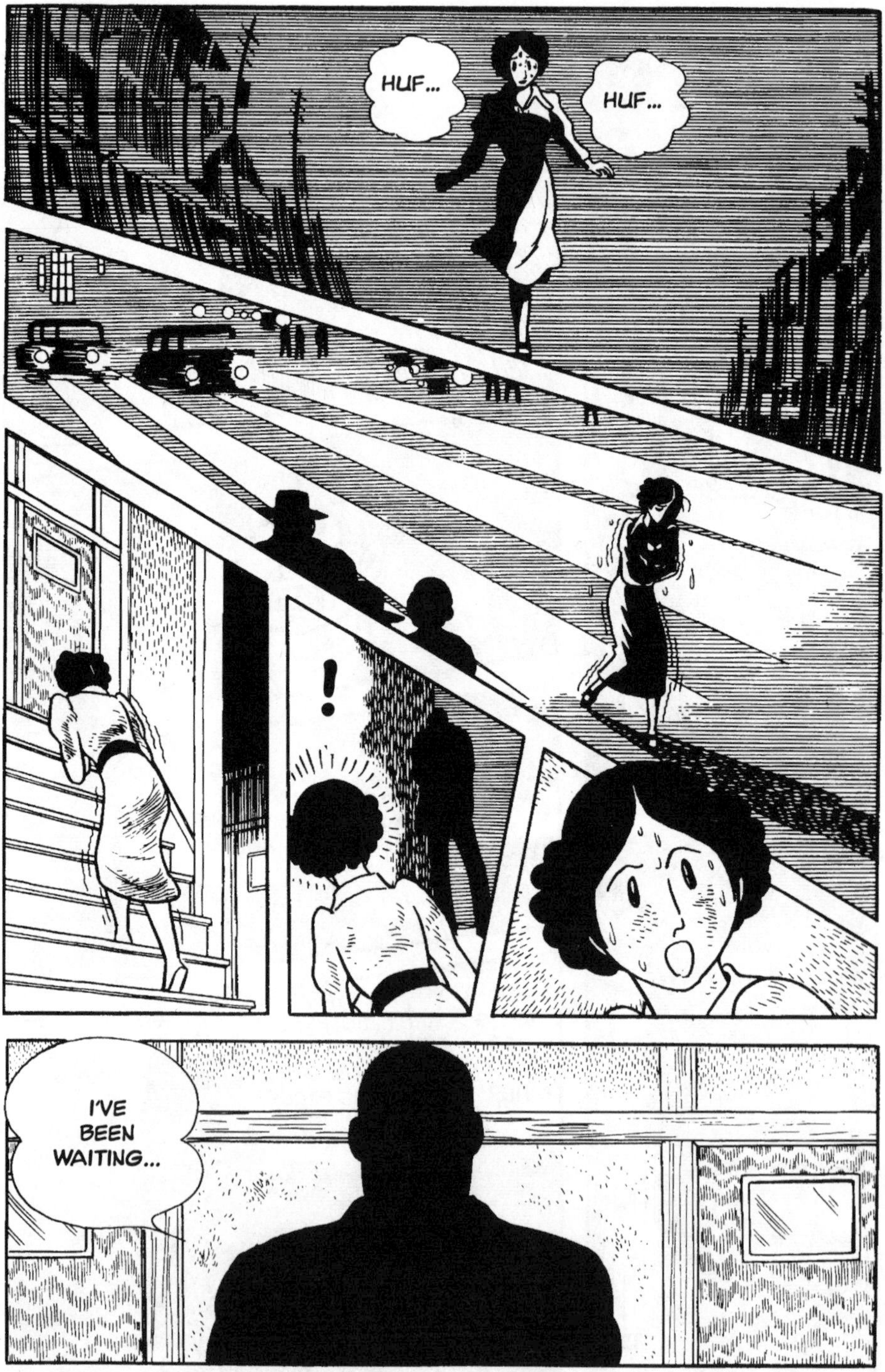
HUF...
HUF...
!
I'VE BEEN WAITING...

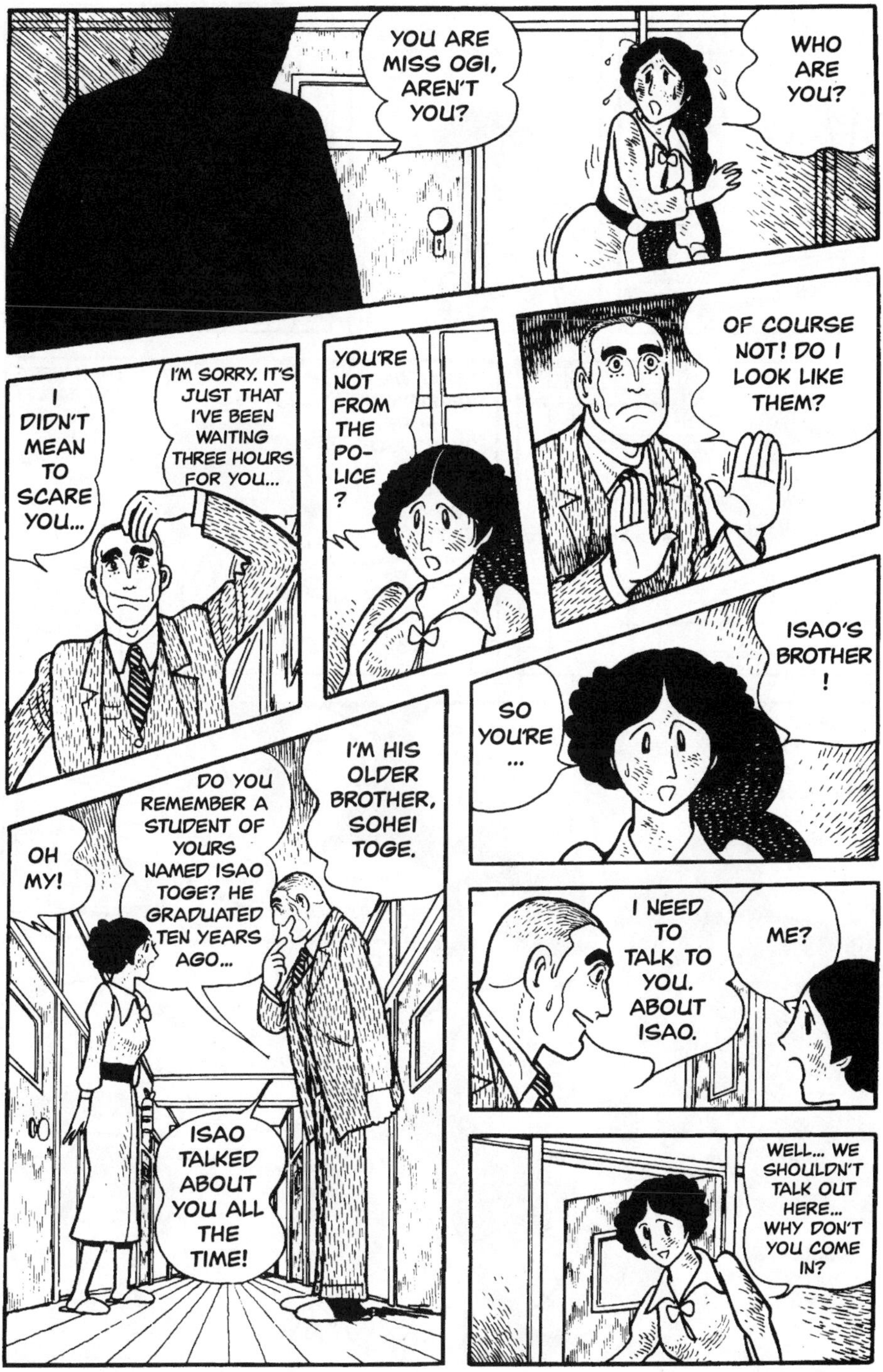
YOU ARE MISS OGI, AREN'T YOU?
WHO ARE YOU?
I DIDN'T MEAN TO SCARE YOU...
I'M SORRY. IT'S JUST THAT I'VE BEEN WAITING THREE HOURS FOR YOU...
YOU'RE NOT FROM THE PO-LICE?
OF COURSE NOT! DO I LOOK LIKE THEM?
DO YOU REMEMBER A STUDENT OF YOURS NAMED ISAO TOGE? HE GRADUATED TEN YEARS AGO...
I'M HIS OLDER BROTHER, SOHEI TOGE.
OH MY!
ISAO TALKED ABOUT YOU ALL THE TIME!
SO YOU'RE ...
ISAO'S BROTHER!
I NEED TO TALK TO YOU. ABOUT ISAO.
ME?
WELL... WE SHOULDN'T TALK OUT HERE... WHY DON'T YOU COME IN?

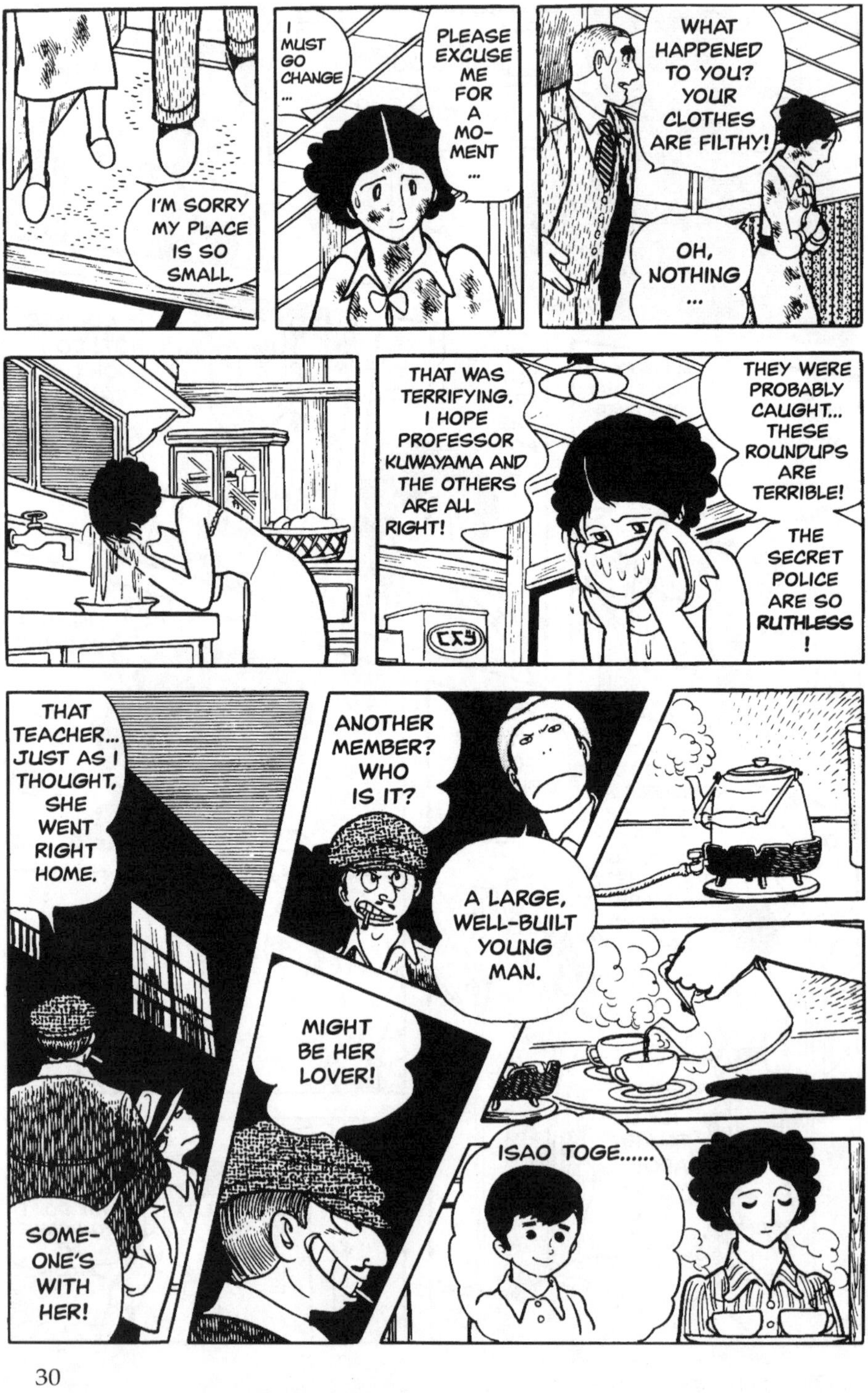
I'M SORRY MY PLACE IS SO SMALL.
I MUST GO CHANGE ...
PLEASE EXCUSE ME FOR A MOMENT ...
WHAT HAPPENED TO YOU? YOUR CLOTHES ARE FILTHY!
OH, NOTHING ...
THAT WAS TERRIFYING. I HOPE PROFESSOR KUWAYAMA AND THE OTHERS ARE ALL RIGHT!
THEY WERE PROBABLY CAUGHT... THESE ROUNDUPS ARE TERRIBLE!
THE SECRET POLICE ARE SO RUTHLESS!
THAT TEACHER... JUST AS I THOUGHT, SHE WENT RIGHT HOME.
SOME-ONE'S WITH HER!
ANOTHER MEMBER? WHO IS IT?
A LARGE, WELL-BUILT YOUNG MAN.
MIGHT BE HER LOVER!
ISAO TOGE......

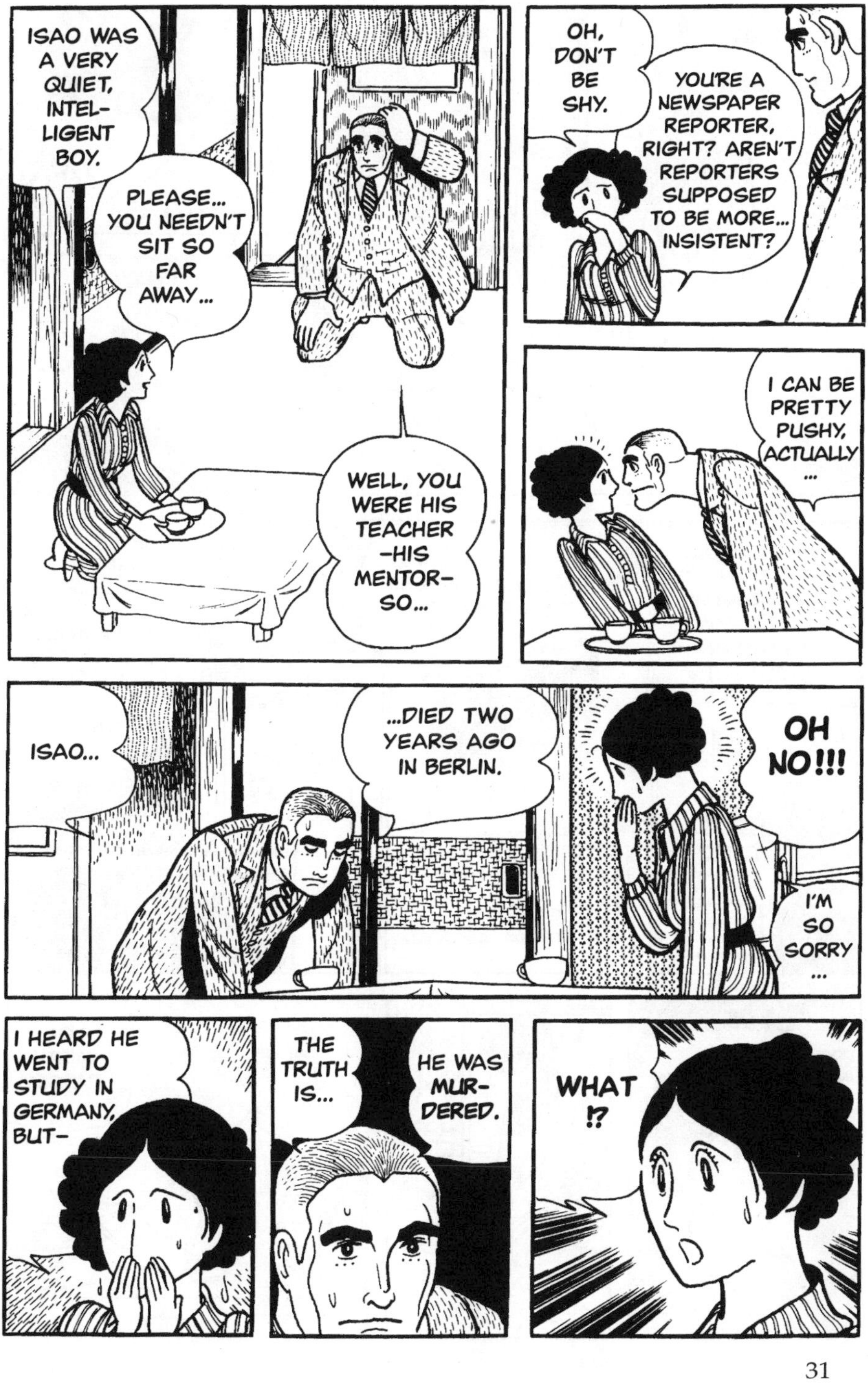
ISAO WAS A VERY QUIET, INTEL-LIGENT BOY.
PLEASE... YOU NEEDN'T SIT SO FAR AWAY...
WELL, YOU WERE HIS TEACHER -HIS MENTOR- SO...
OH, DON'T BE SHY.
YOU'RE A NEWSPAPER REPORTER, RIGHT? AREN'T REPORTERS SUPPOSED TO BE MORE... INSISTENT?
I CAN BE PRETTY PUSHY, ACTUALLY ...
ISAO...
...DIED TWO YEARS AGO IN BERLIN.
OH NO!!!
I'M SO SORRY ...
I HEARD HE WENT TO STUDY IN GERMANY, BUT–
THE TRUTH IS...
HE WAS MUR-DERED.
WHAT !?

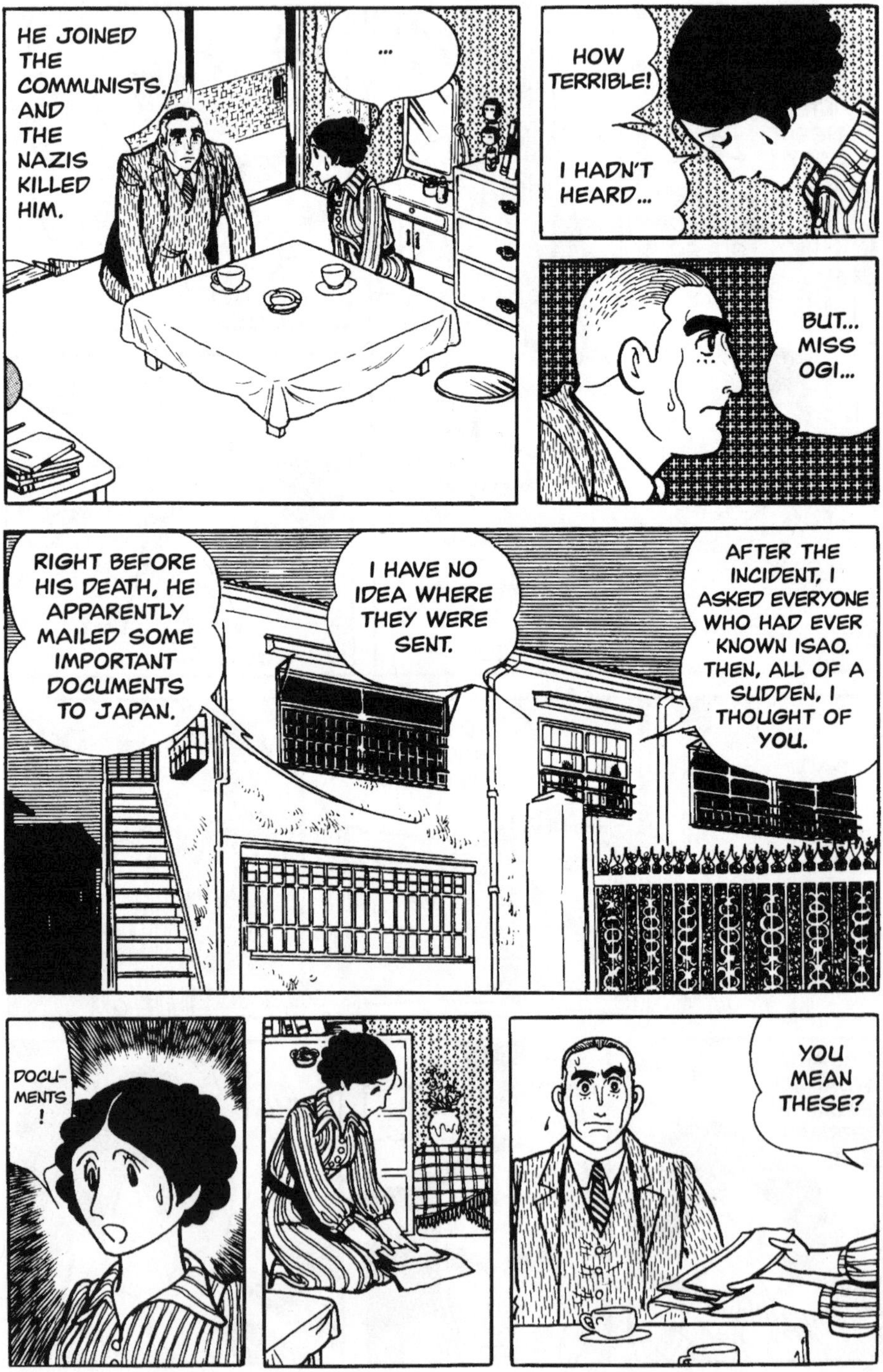
HE JOINED THE COMMUNISTS. AND THE NAZIS KILLED HIM.
...
HOW TERRIBLE!
I HADN'T HEARD...
BUT... MISS OGI...
RIGHT BEFORE HIS DEATH, HE APPARENTLY MAILED SOME IMPORTANT DOCUMENTS TO JAPAN.
I HAVE NO IDEA WHERE THEY WERE SENT.
AFTER THE INCIDENT, I ASKED EVERYONE WHO HAD EVER KNOWN ISAO. THEN, ALL OF A SUDDEN, I THOUGHT OF YOU.
DOCU-MENTS!
YOU MEAN THESE?

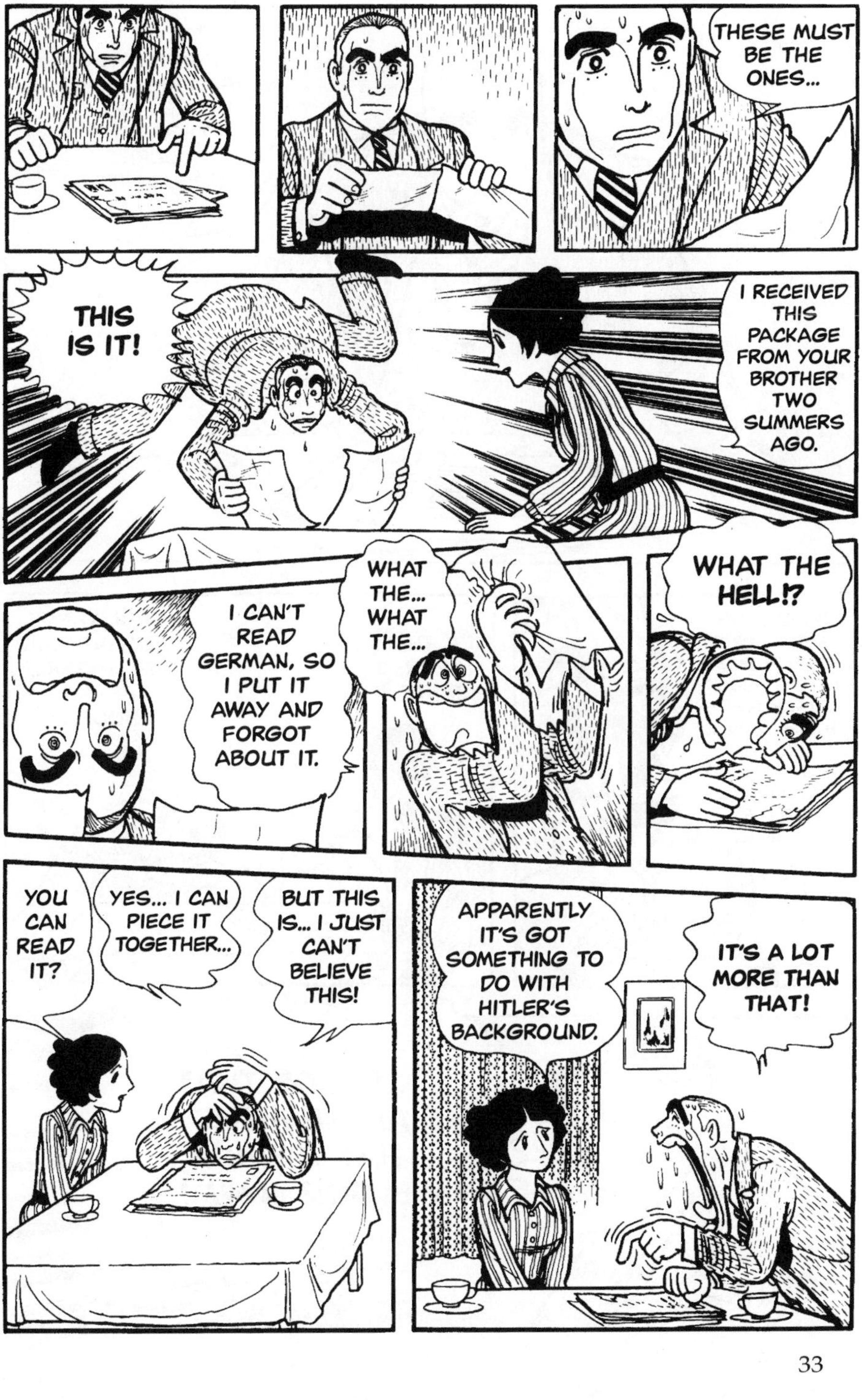
THESE MUST BE THE ONES...
THIS IS IT!
I RECEIVED THIS PACKAGE FROM YOUR BROTHER TWO SUMMERS AGO.
I CAN'T READ GERMAN, SO I PUT IT AWAY AND FORGOT ABOUT IT.
WHAT THE... WHAT THE...
WHAT THE HELL!?
YOU CAN READ IT?
YES... I CAN PIECE IT TOGETHER...
BUT THIS IS... I JUST CAN'T BELIEVE THIS!
APPARENTLY IT'S GOT SOMETHING TO DO WITH HITLER'S BACKGROUND.
IT'S A LOT MORE THAN THAT!

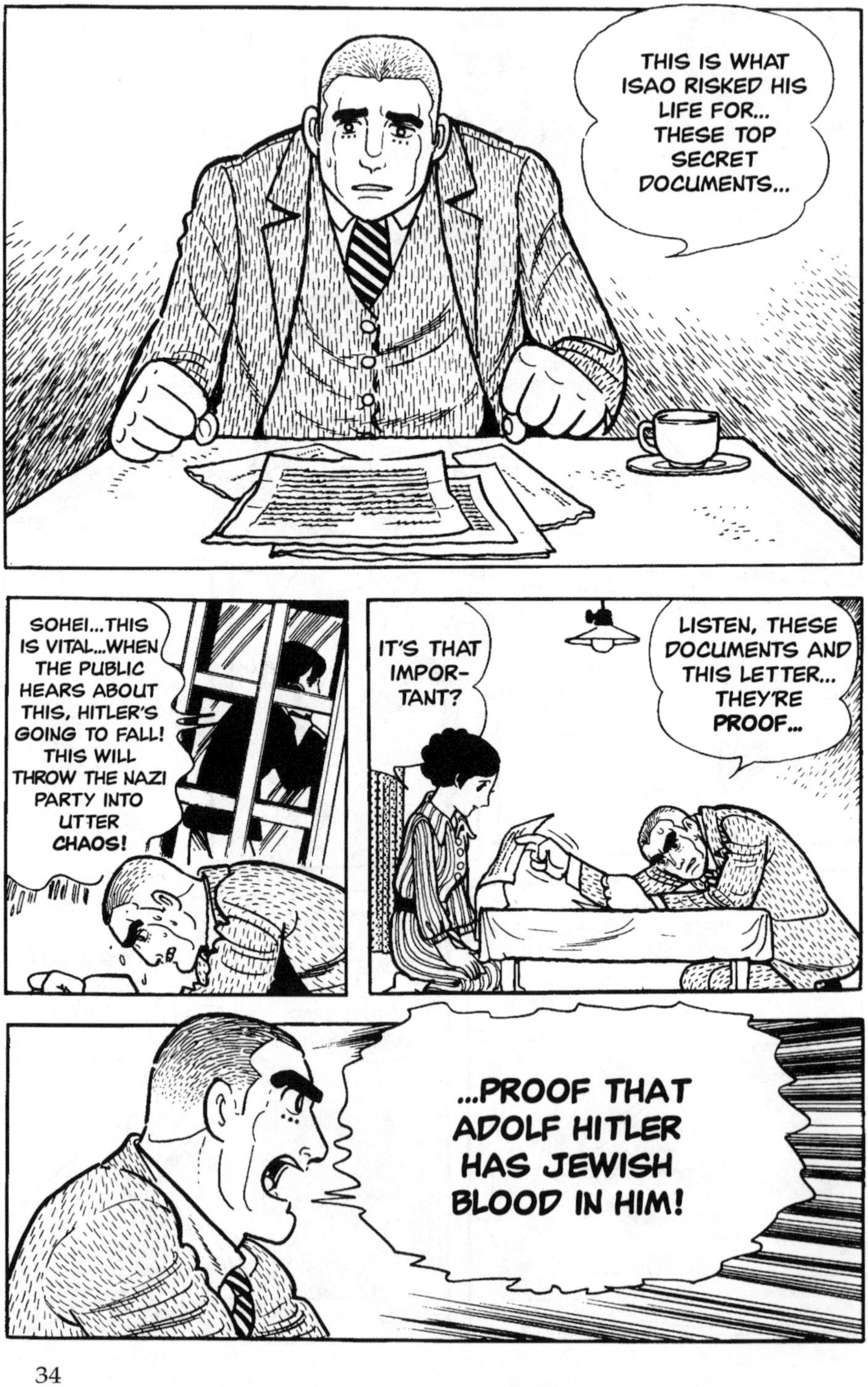
THIS IS WHAT ISAO RISKED HIS LIFE FOR... THESE TOP SECRET DOCUMENTS...
SOHEI...THIS IS VITAL...WHEN THE PUBLIC HEARS ABOUT THIS, HITLER'S GOING TO FALL! THIS WILL THROW THE NAZI PARTY INTO UTTER CHAOS!
IT'S THAT IMPOR-TANT?
LISTEN, THESE DOCUMENTS AND THIS LETTER... THEY'RE PROOF...
...PROOF THAT ADOLF HITLER HAS JEWISH BLOOD IN HIM!

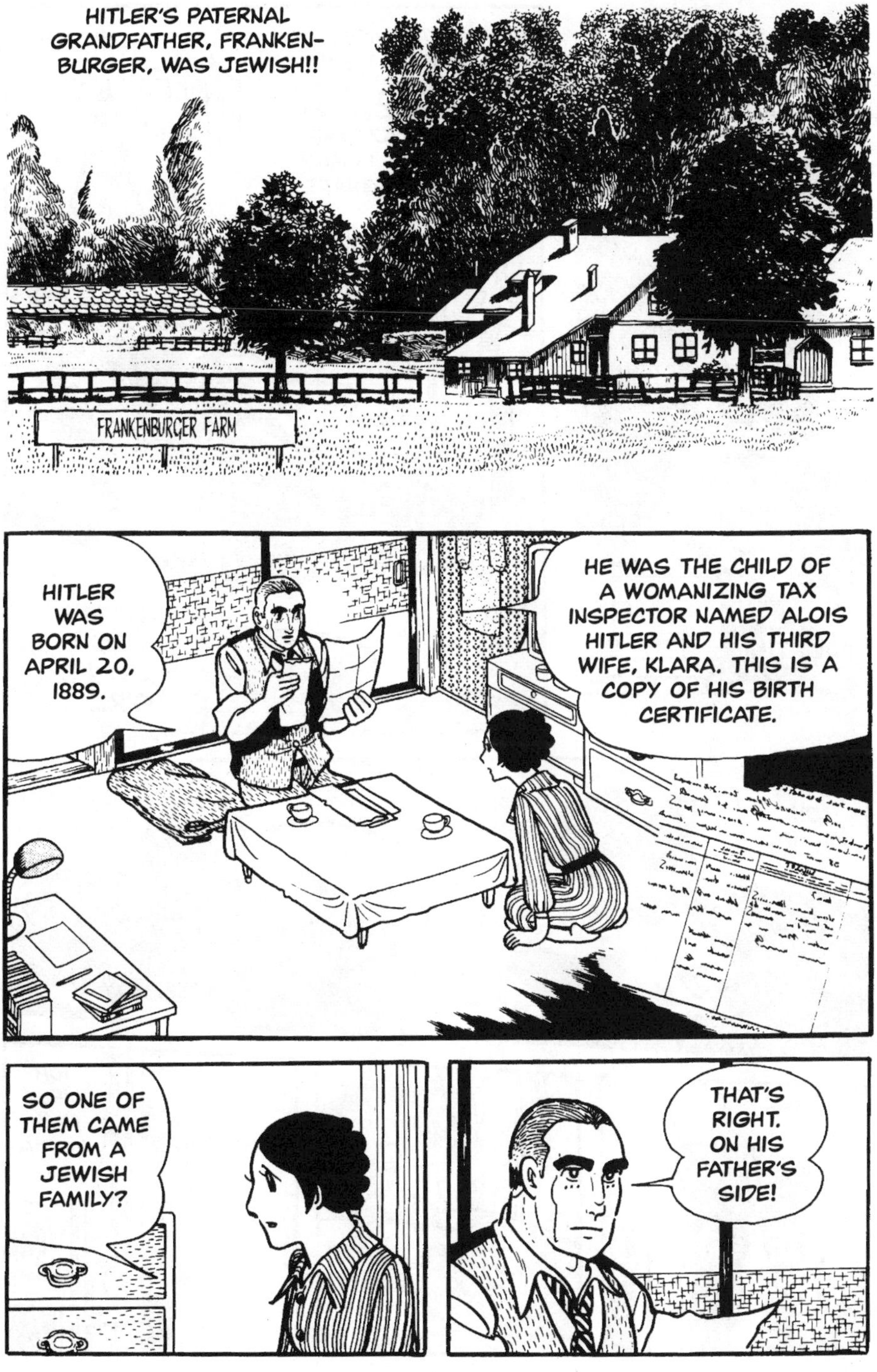
HITLER'S PATERNAL GRANDFATHER, FRANKENBURGER, WAS JEWISH!!
FRANKENBURGER FARM
HITLER WAS BORN ON APRIL 20, 1889.
HE WAS THE CHILD OF A WOMANIZING TAX INSPECTOR NAMED ALOIS HITLER AND HIS THIRD WIFE, KLARA. THIS IS A COPY OF HIS BIRTH CERTIFICATE.
SO ONE OF THEM CAME FROM A JEWISH FAMILY?
THAT'S RIGHT. ON HIS FATHER'S SIDE!

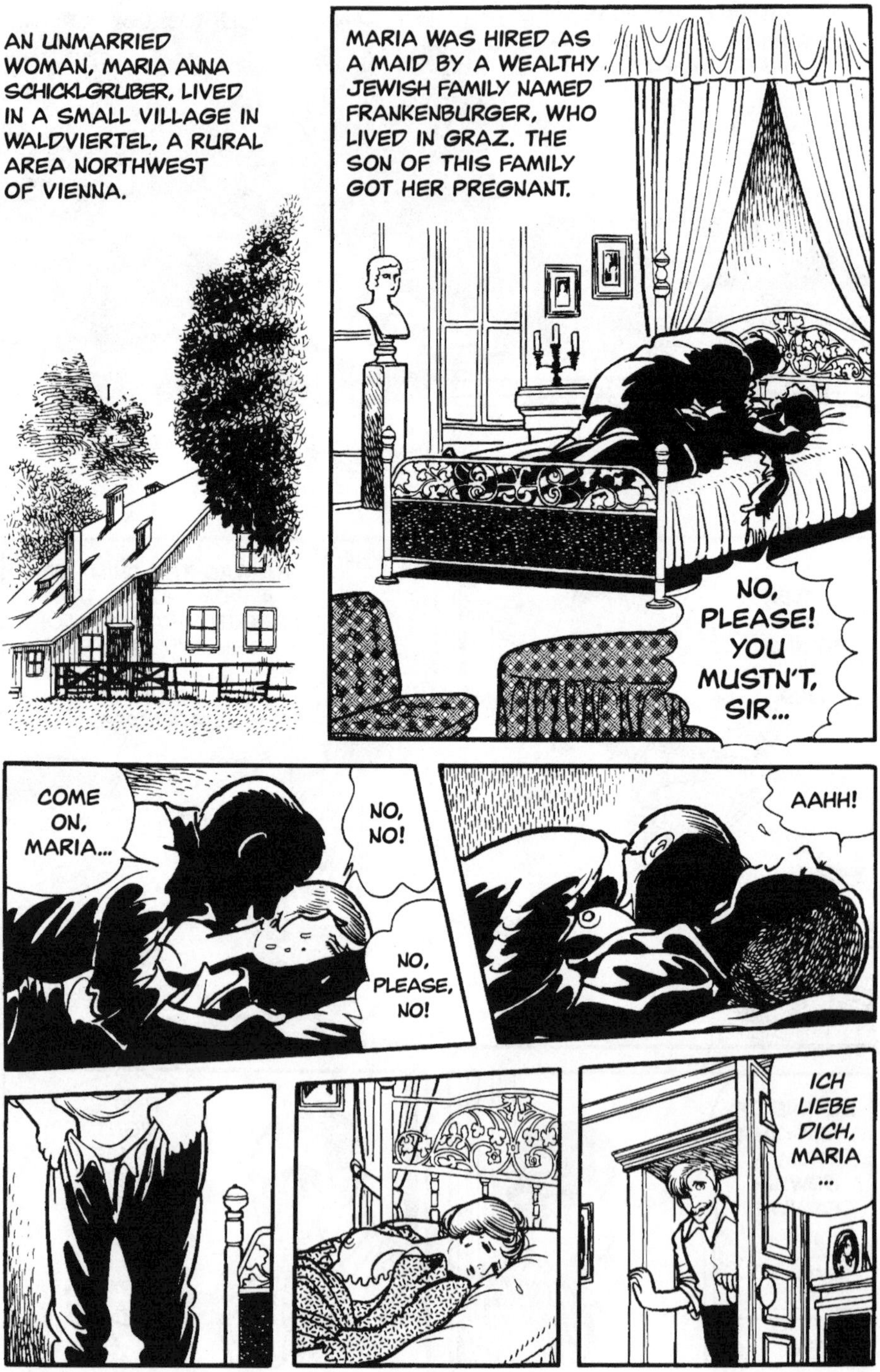
AN UNMARRIED WOMAN, MARIA ANNA SCHICKLGRUBER, LIVED IN A SMALL VILLAGE IN WALDVIERTEL, A RURAL AREA NORTHWEST OF VIENNA.
MARIA WAS HIRED AS A MAID BY A WEALTHY JEWISH FAMILY NAMED FRANKENBURGER, WHO LIVED IN GRAZ. THE SON OF THIS FAMILY GOT HER PREGNANT.
NO, PLEASE! YOU MUSTN'T, SIR...
COME ON, MARIA...
NO, NO!
NO, PLEASE, NO!
AAHH!
ICH LIEBE DICH, MARIA ...

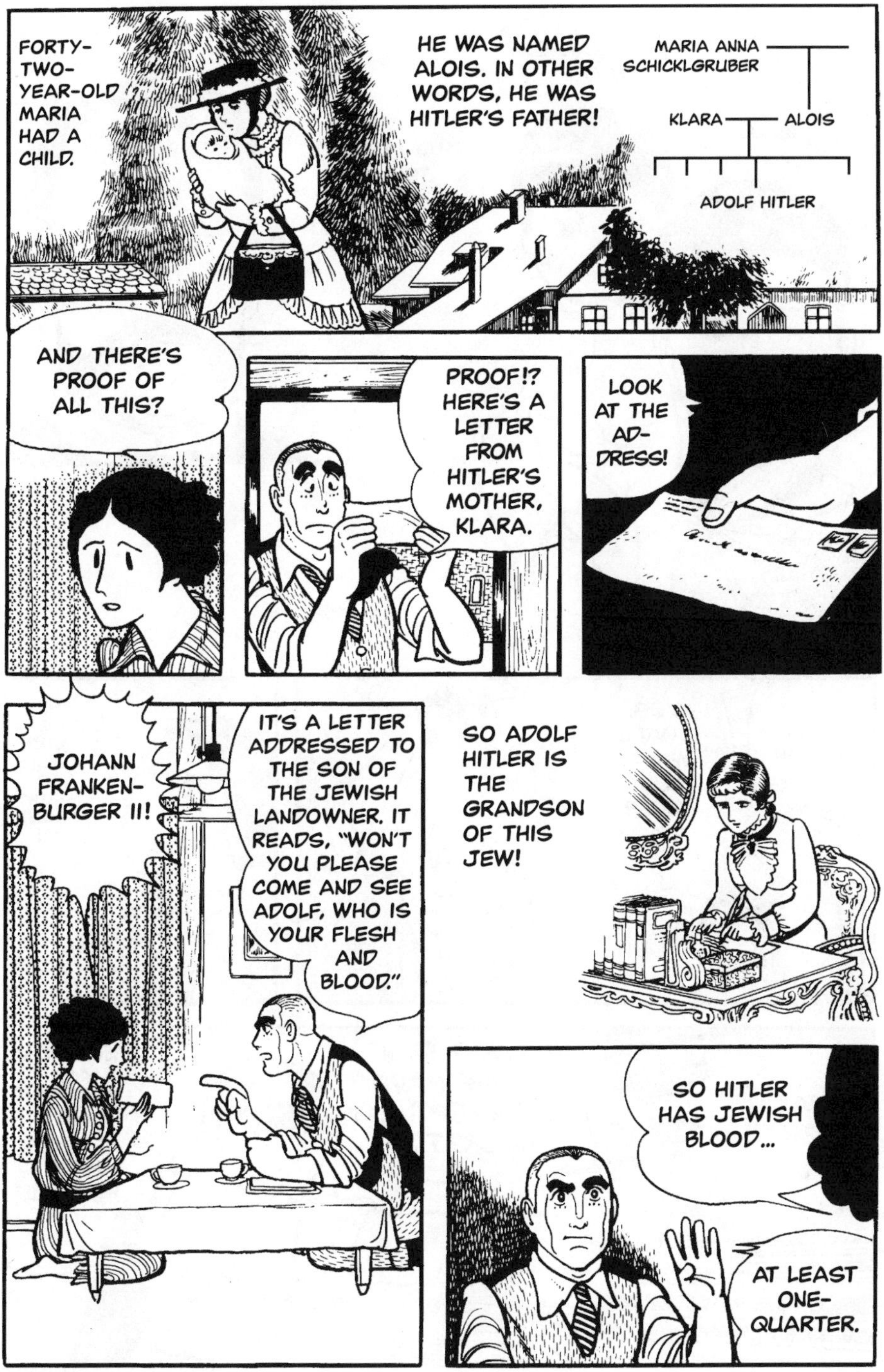
FORTY-TWO-YEAR-OLD MARIA HAD A CHILD.
HE WAS NAMED ALOIS. IN OTHER WORDS, HE WAS HITLER'S FATHER!
MARIA ANNA SCHICKLGRUBER
KLARA
ALOIS
ADOLF HITLER
AND THERE'S PROOF OF ALL THIS?
PROOF!? HERE'S A LETTER FROM HITLER'S MOTHER, KLARA.
LOOK AT THE AD-DRESS!
JOHANN FRANKEN-BURGER II!
IT'S A LETTER ADDRESSED TO THE SON OF THE JEWISH LANDOWNER. IT READS, "WON'T YOU PLEASE COME AND SEE ADOLF, WHO IS YOUR FLESH AND BLOOD."
SO ADOLF HITLER IS THE GRANDSON OF THIS JEW!
SO HITLER HAS JEWISH BLOOD...
AT LEAST ONE-QUARTER.

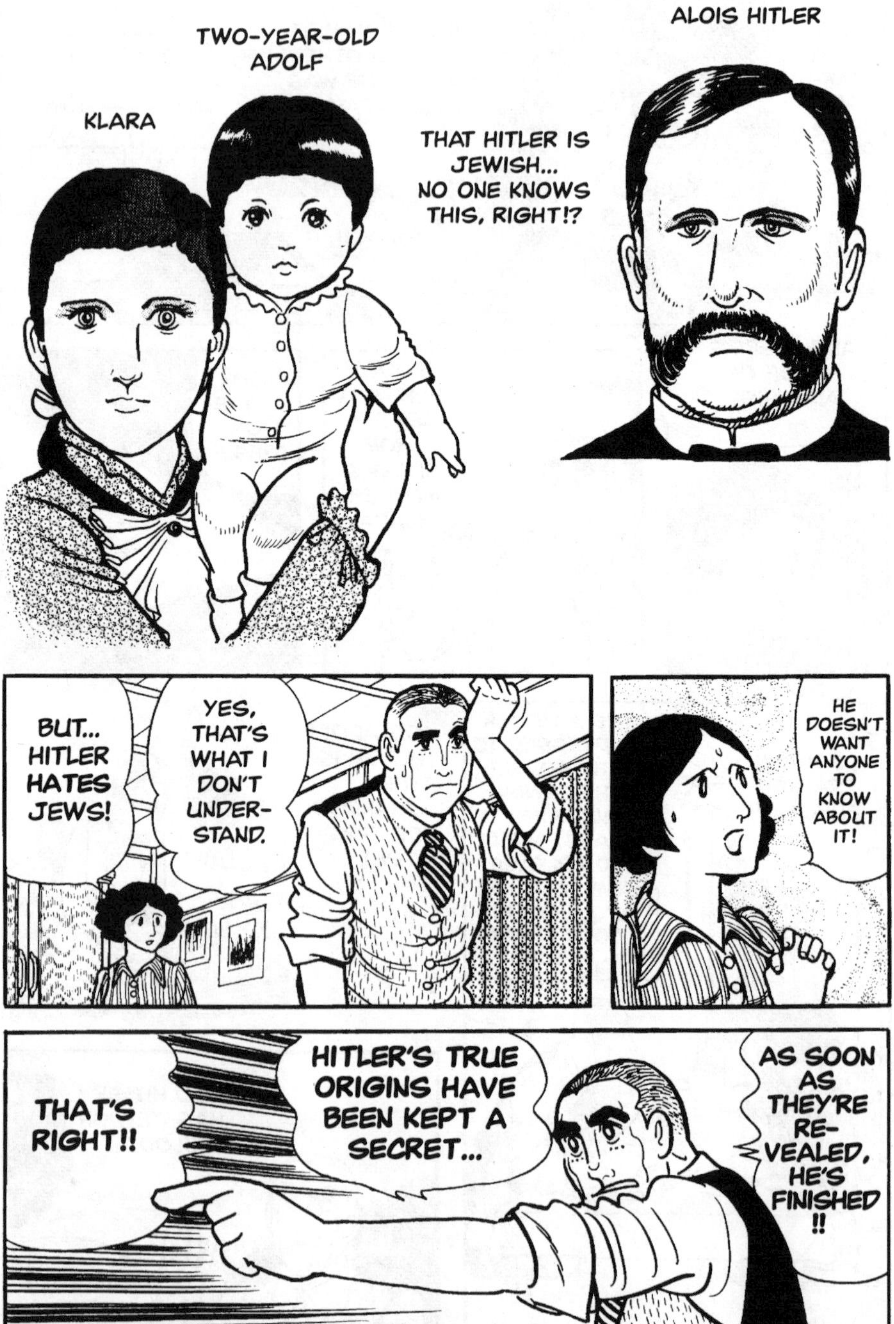
KLARA
TWO-YEAR-OLD ADOLF
THAT HITLER IS JEWISH... NO ONE KNOWS THIS, RIGHT!?
ALOIS HITLER
BUT... HITLER HATES JEWS!
YES, THAT'S WHAT I DON'T UNDER-STAND.
HE DOESN'T WANT ANYONE TO KNOW ABOUT IT!
THAT'S RIGHT!!
HITLER'S TRUE ORIGINS HAVE BEEN KEPT A SECRET...
AS SOON AS THEY'RE RE-VEALED, HE'S FINISHED!!

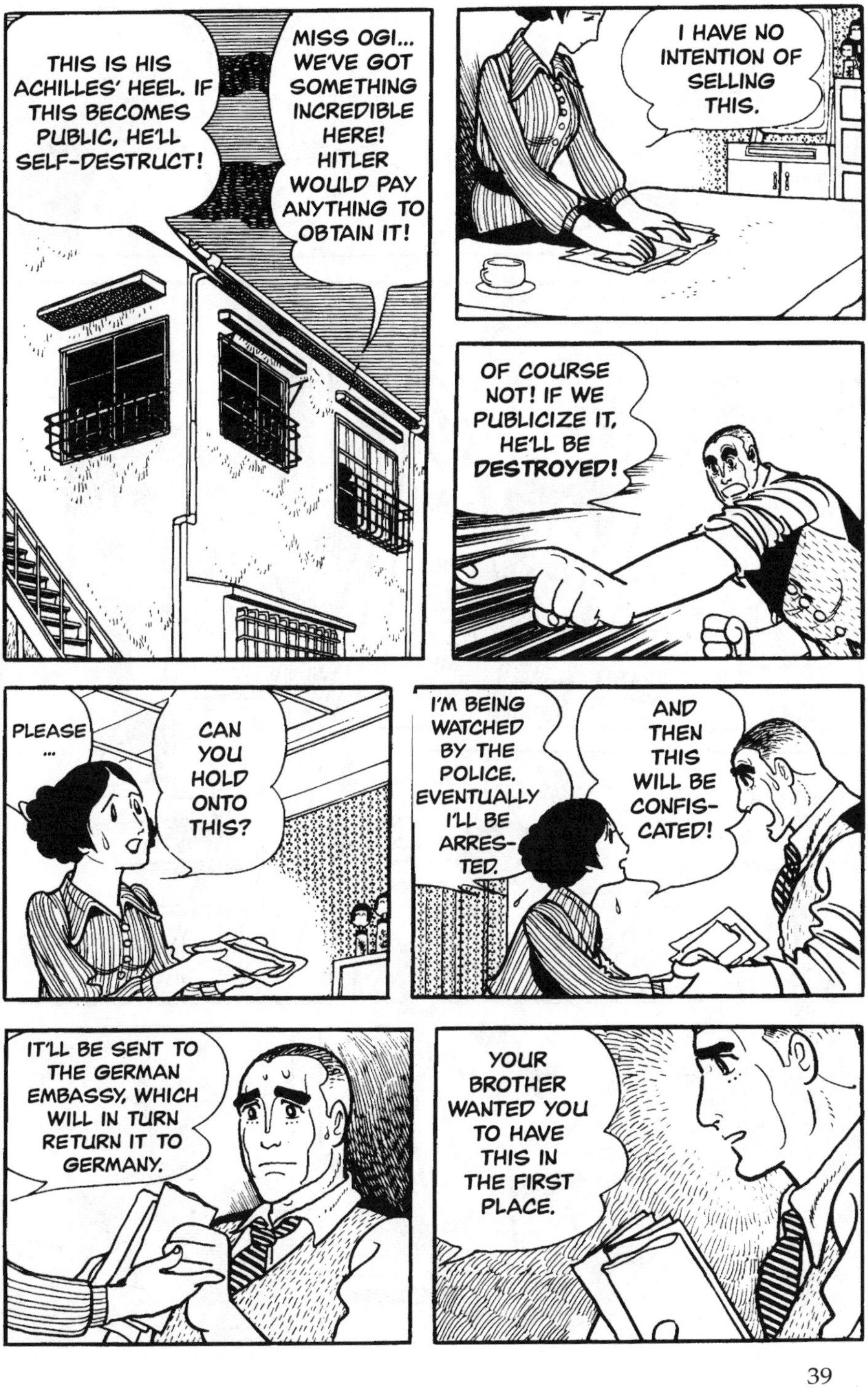
THIS IS HIS ACHILLES' HEEL. IF THIS BECOMES PUBLIC, HE'LL SELF-DESTRUCT!
MISS OGI... WE'VE GOT SOMETHING INCREDIBLE HERE! HITLER WOULD PAY ANYTHING TO OBTAIN IT!
I HAVE NO INTENTION OF SELLING THIS.
OF COURSE NOT! IF WE PUBLICIZE IT, HE'LL BE DESTROYED!
PLEASE ...
CAN YOU HOLD ONTO THIS?
I'M BEING WATCHED BY THE POLICE. EVENTUALLY I'LL BE ARRES-TED.
AND THEN THIS WILL BE CONFIS-CATED!
IT'LL BE SENT TO THE GERMAN EMBASSY, WHICH WILL IN TURN RETURN IT TO GERMANY.
YOUR BROTHER WANTED YOU TO HAVE THIS IN THE FIRST PLACE.

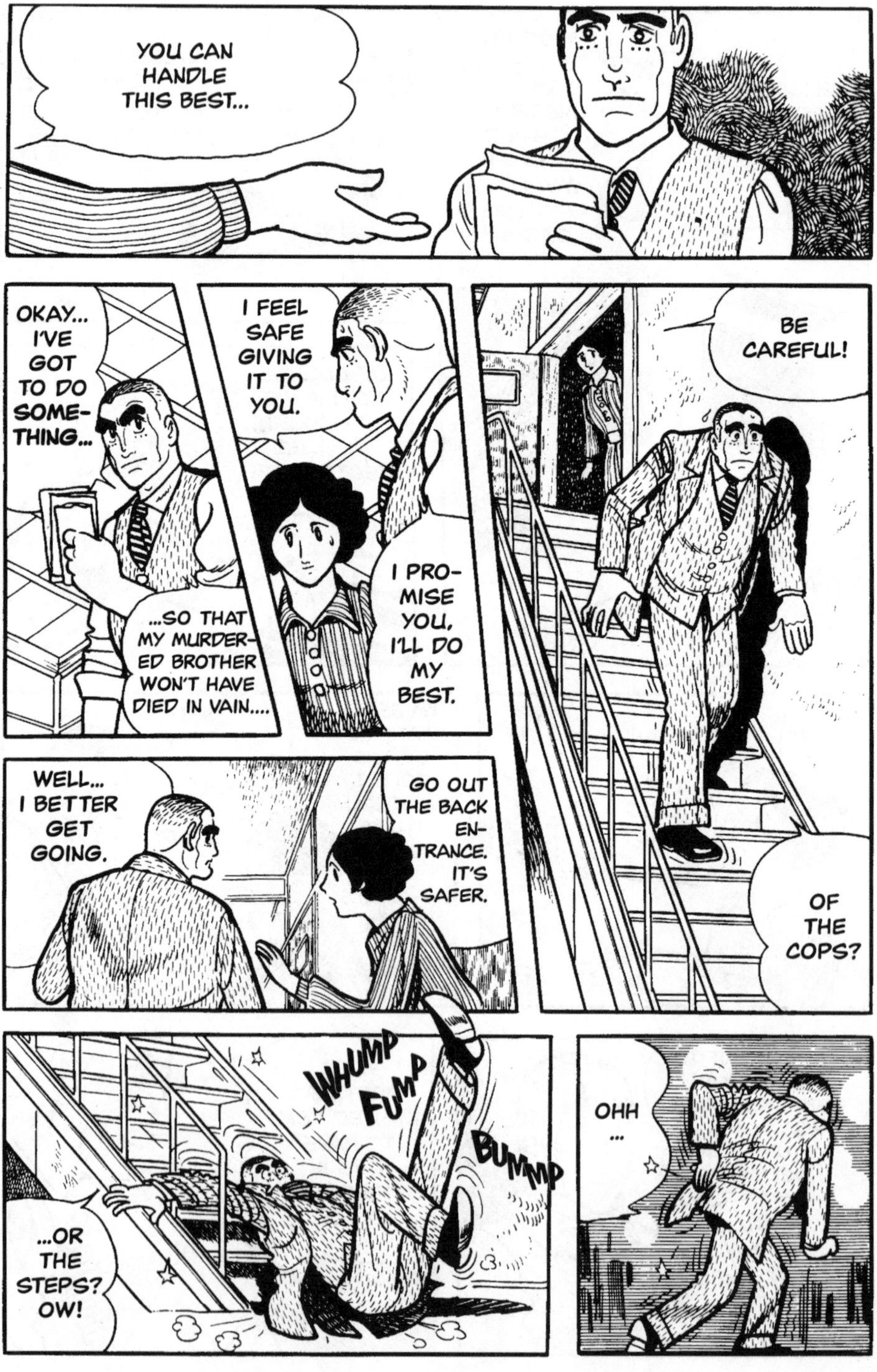
YOU CAN HANDLE THIS BEST...
OKAY... I'VE GOT TO DO SOMETHING...
...SO THAT MY MURDERED BROTHER WON'T HAVE DIED IN VAIN....
I FEEL SAFE GIVING IT TO YOU.
I PROMISE YOU, I'LL DO MY BEST.
WELL... I BETTER GET GOING.
GO OUT THE BACK ENTRANCE. IT'S SAFER.
BE CAREFUL!
OF THE COPS?
WHUMP
FUMP
BUMMP
...OR THE STEPS? OW!
OHH ...

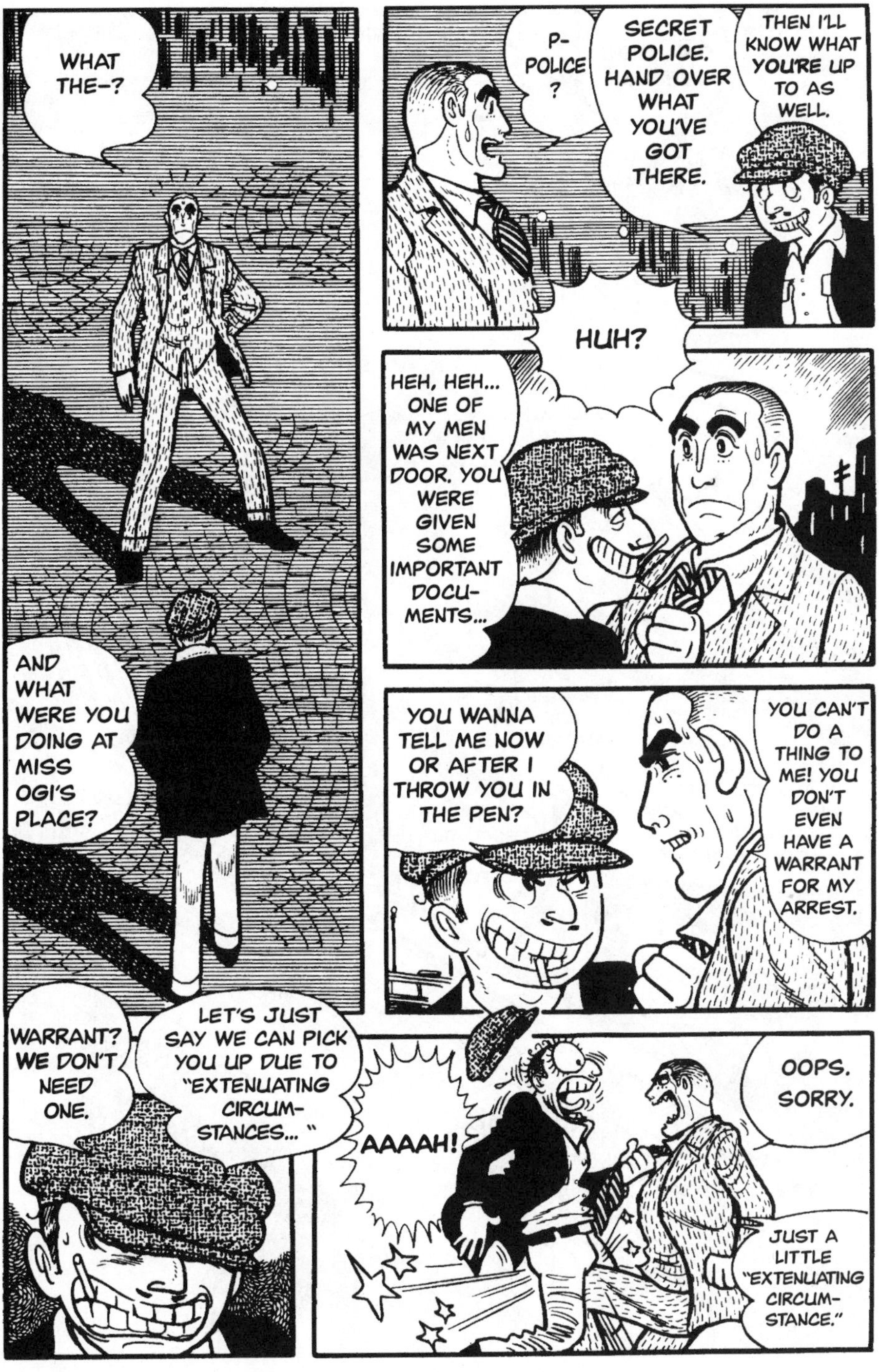
WHAT THE–?
AND WHAT WERE YOU DOING AT MISS OGI'S PLACE?
P-POLICE?
SECRET POLICE. HAND OVER WHAT YOU'VE GOT THERE.
THEN I'LL KNOW WHAT YOU'RE UP TO AS WELL.
HUH?
HEH, HEH... ONE OF MY MEN WAS NEXT DOOR. YOU WERE GIVEN SOME IMPORTANT DOCU-MENTS...
YOU WANNA TELL ME NOW OR AFTER I THROW YOU IN THE PEN?
YOU CAN'T DO A THING TO ME! YOU DON'T EVEN HAVE A WARRANT FOR MY ARREST.
WARRANT? WE DON'T NEED ONE.
LET'S JUST SAY WE CAN PICK YOU UP DUE TO "EXTENUATING CIRCUM-STANCES... "
AAAAH!
OOPS. SORRY.
JUST A LITTLE "EXTENUATING CIRCUM-STANCE."

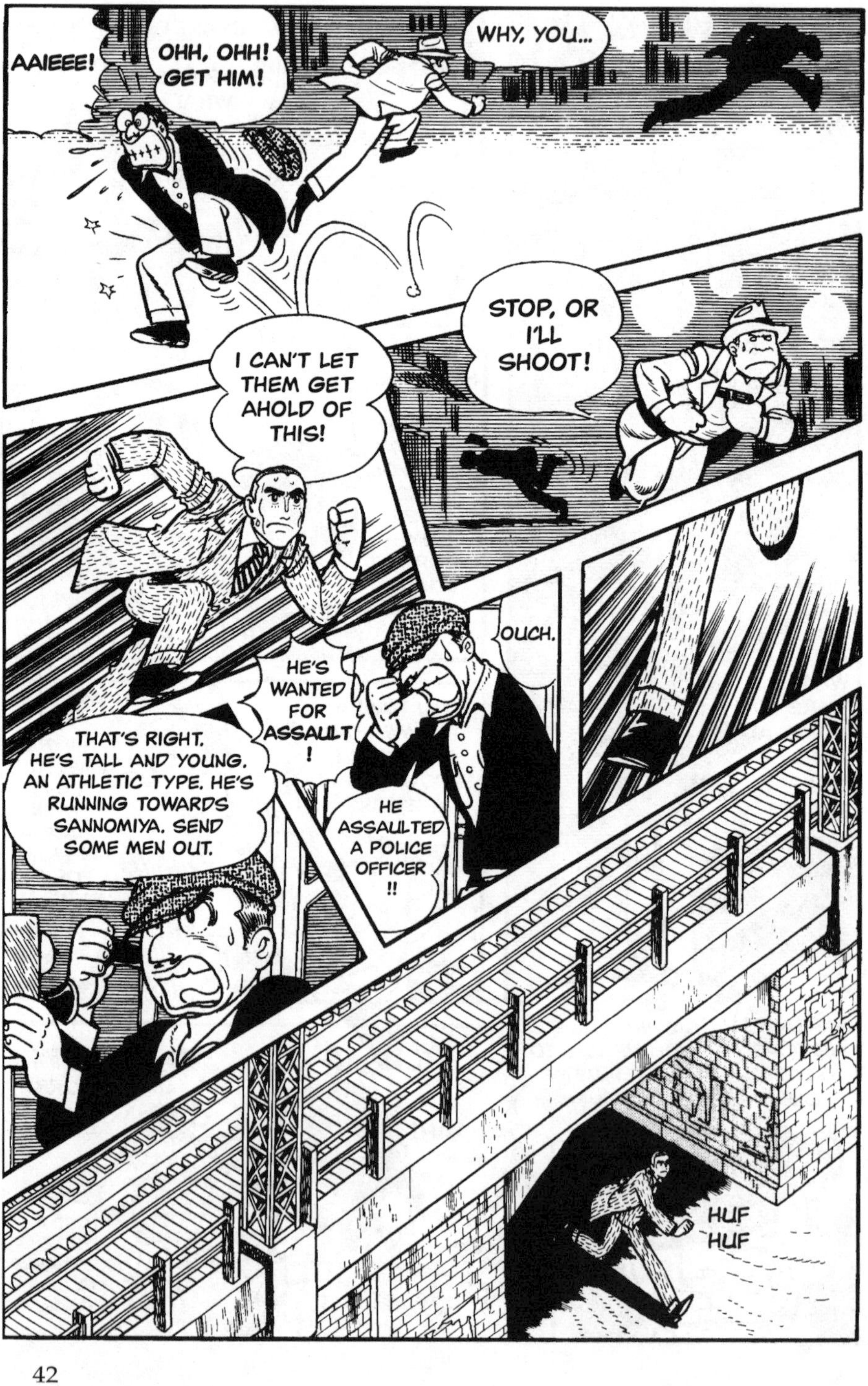
AAIEEE!
OHH, OHH! GET HIM!
WHY, YOU...
I CAN'T LET THEM GET AHOLD OF THIS!
STOP, OR I'LL SHOOT!
THAT'S RIGHT. HE'S TALL AND YOUNG. AN ATHLETIC TYPE. HE'S RUNNING TOWARDS SANNOMIYA. SEND SOME MEN OUT.
OUCH.
HE'S WANTED FOR ASSAULT!
HE ASSAULTED A POLICE OFFICER!!
HUF HUF

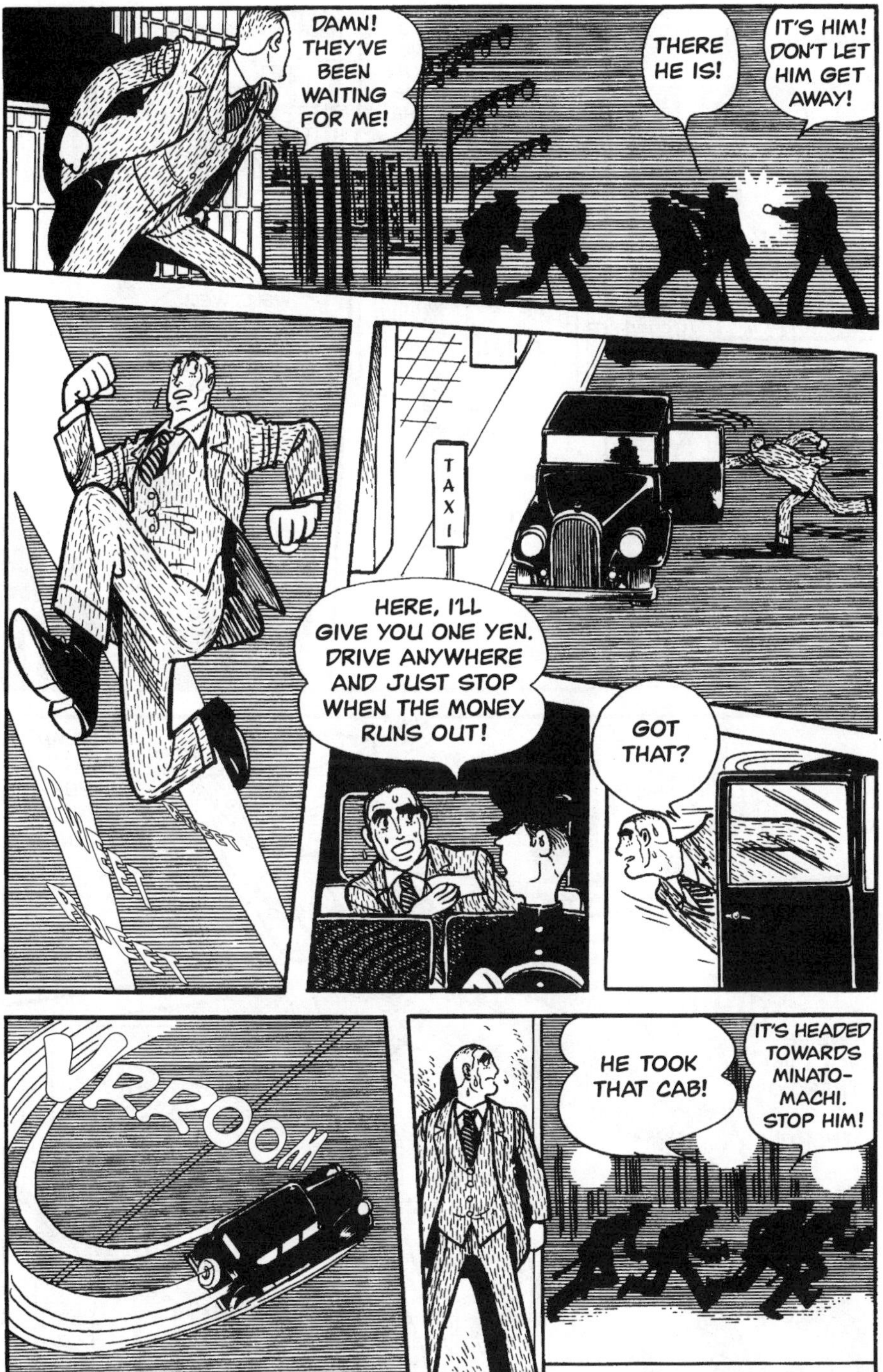
DAMN! THEY'VE BEEN WAITING FOR ME!
THERE HE IS!
IT'S HIM! DON'T LET HIM GET AWAY!
T A X I
HERE, I'LL GIVE YOU ONE YEN. DRIVE ANYWHERE AND JUST STOP WHEN THE MONEY RUNS OUT!
GOT THAT?
VRROOM
HE TOOK THAT CAB!
IT'S HEADED TOWARDS MINATO-MACHI. STOP HIM!

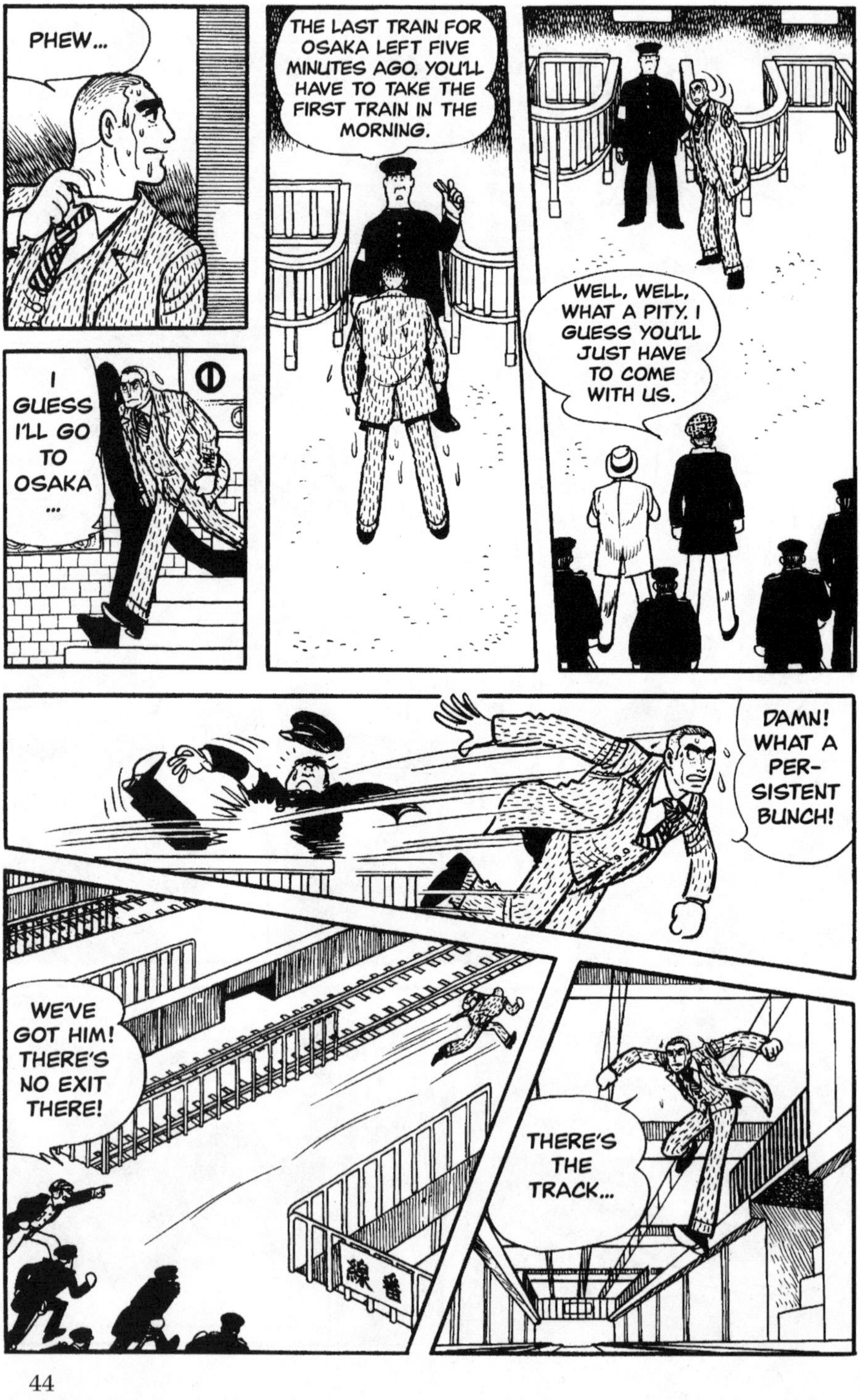
PHEW...
I GUESS I'LL GO TO OSAKA...
THE LAST TRAIN FOR OSAKA LEFT FIVE MINUTES AGO. YOU'LL HAVE TO TAKE THE FIRST TRAIN IN THE MORNING.
WELL, WELL, WHAT A PITY. I GUESS YOU'LL JUST HAVE TO COME WITH US.
DAMN! WHAT A PER-SISTENT BUNCH!
WE'VE GOT HIM! THERE'S NO EXIT THERE!
番線
THERE'S THE TRACK...

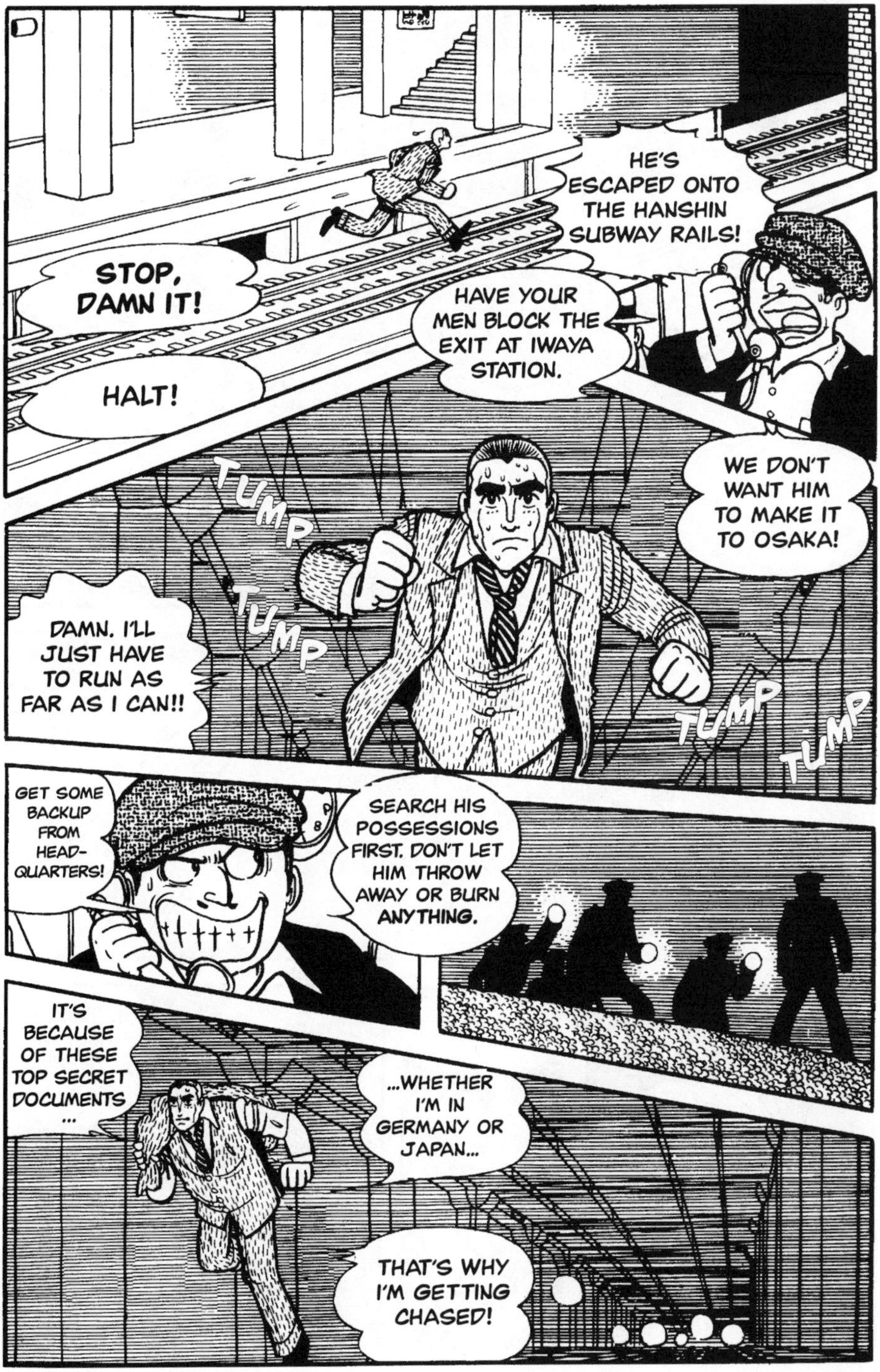
STOP, DAMN IT!
HALT!
HE'S ESCAPED ONTO THE HANSHIN SUBWAY RAILS!
HAVE YOUR MEN BLOCK THE EXIT AT IWAYA STATION.
WE DON'T WANT HIM TO MAKE IT TO OSAKA!
DAMN. I'LL JUST HAVE TO RUN AS FAR AS I CAN!!
TUMP
TUMP
TUMP
TUMP
GET SOME BACKUP FROM HEAD-QUARTERS!
SEARCH HIS POSSESSIONS FIRST. DON'T LET HIM THROW AWAY OR BURN ANYTHING.
IT'S BECAUSE OF THESE TOP SECRET DOCUMENTS ...
...WHETHER I'M IN GERMANY OR JAPAN...
THAT'S WHY I'M GETTING CHASED!

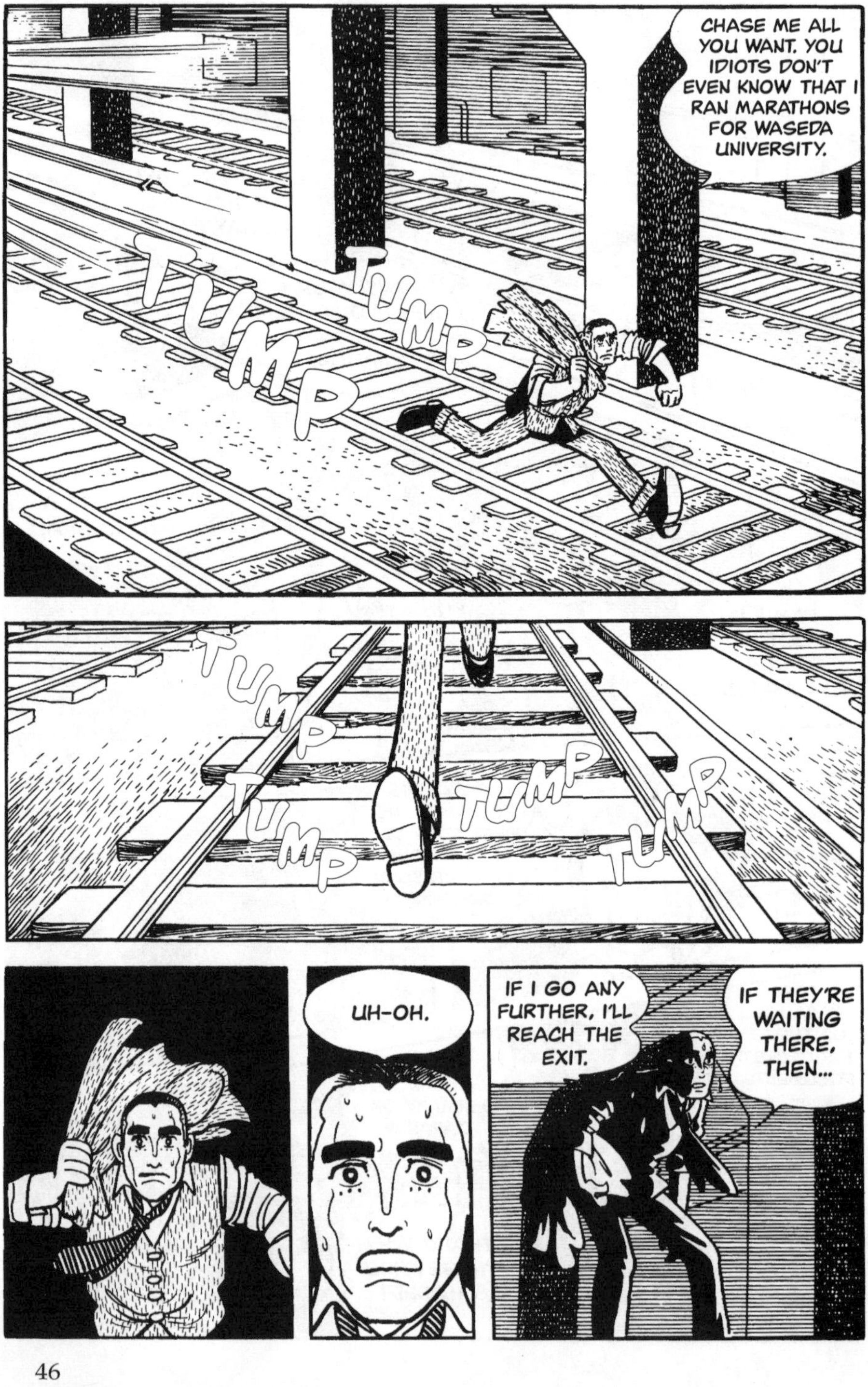
CHASE ME ALL YOU WANT. YOU IDIOTS DON'T EVEN KNOW THAT I RAN MARATHONS FOR WASEDA UNIVERSITY.
TUMP TUMP
TUMP
TUMP
TUMP
TUMP
TUMP
TUMP
UH-OH.
IF I GO ANY FURTHER, I'LL REACH THE EXIT.
IF THEY'RE WAITING THERE, THEN...

...I'M SANDWICHED IN.

IT'LL BE ALL OVER.

MAYBE THERE'S AN EMERGENCY EXIT SOMEWHERE.

HERE THEY COME!!

TUMP

TUMP

TUMP

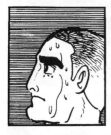

IF I'M CAUGHT AND THE DOCUMENTS ARE CONFISCATED, ISAO'S DEATH WILL HAVE BEEN FOR NOTHING!

WHAT'S THAT NOISE?

IT'S THE SOUND OF A TRAIN!

BUT THE LAST TRAIN ALREADY LEFT...

THIS MUST BE THE FREIGHT TRAIN!

IT'S THE RIGHT TIME FOR IT!

RRRUMMMBLE

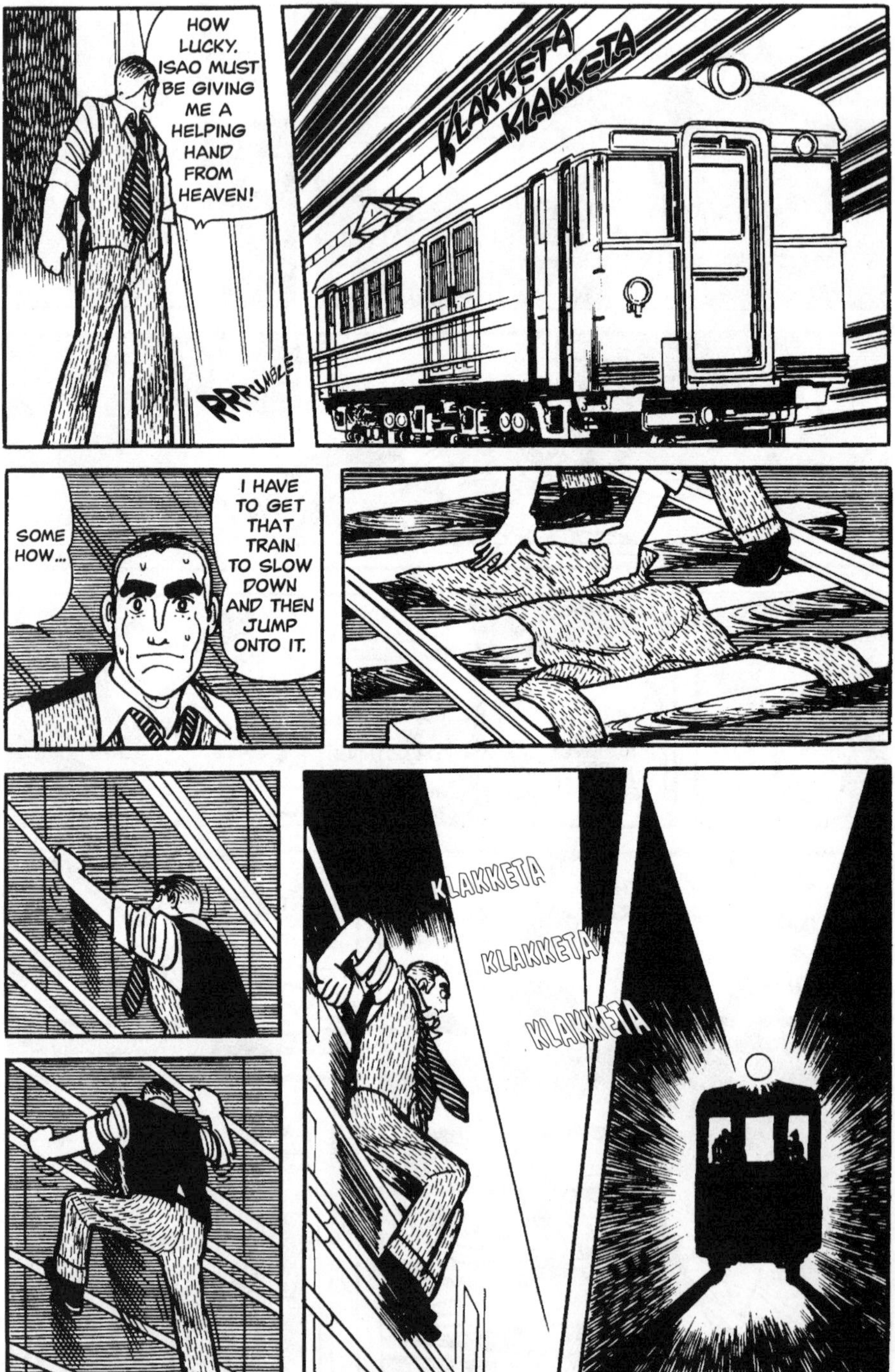
HOW LUCKY. ISAO MUST BE GIVING ME A HELPING HAND FROM HEAVEN!
RRRUMBLE
KLAKKETA KLAKKETA
SOME HOW...
I HAVE TO GET THAT TRAIN TO SLOW DOWN AND THEN JUMP ONTO IT.
KLAKKETA
KLAKKETA
KLAKKETA

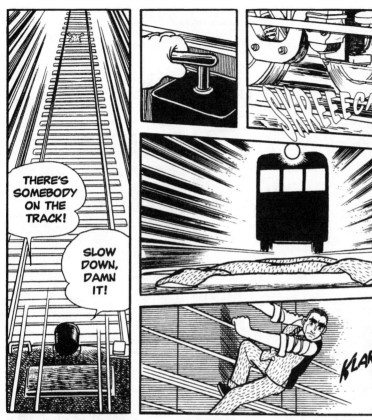

THERE'S SOMEBODY ON THE TRACK!

SLOW DOWN, DAMN IT!

SHREEECH

KLAKKETA KLAKKETA

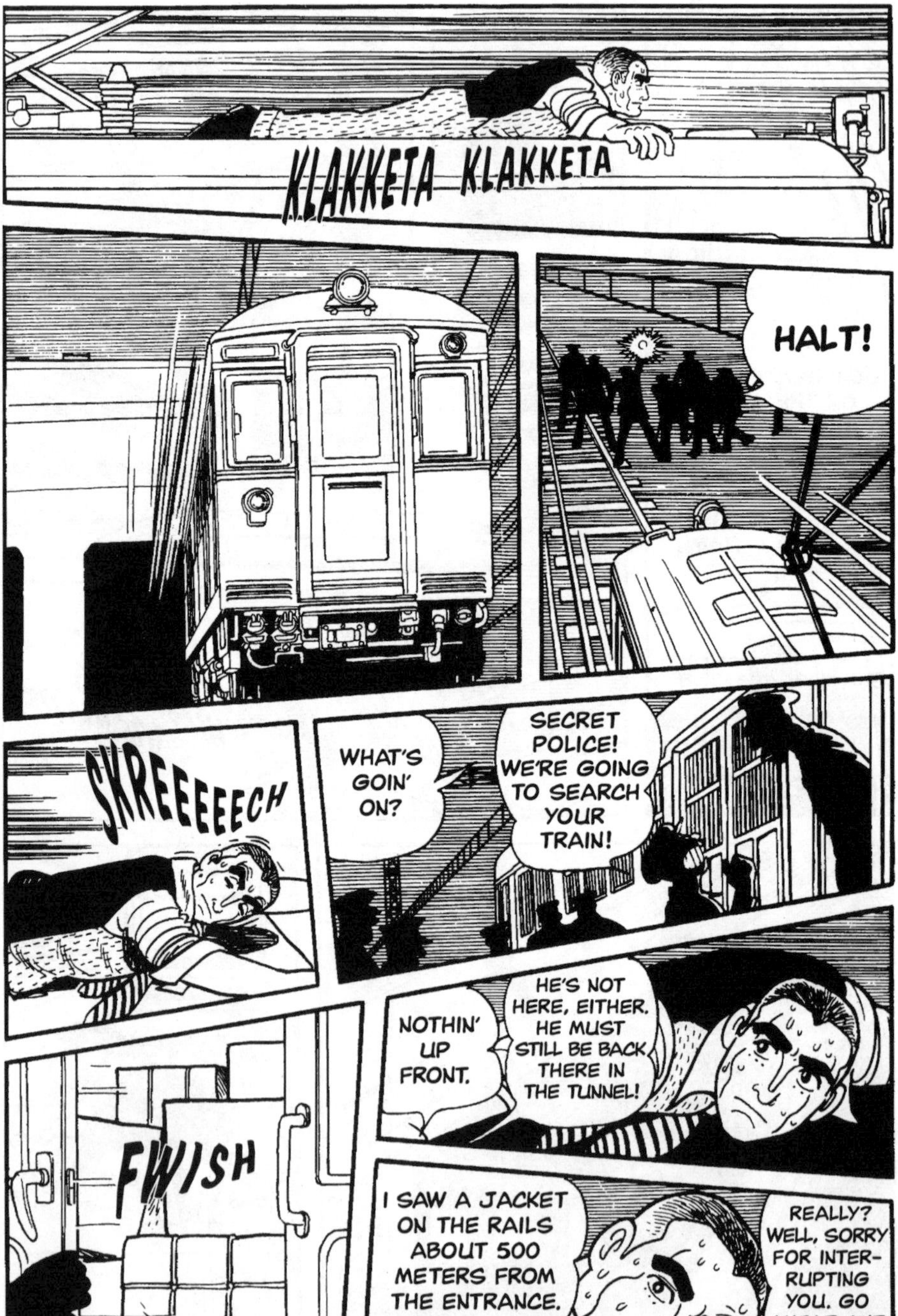
KLAKKETA KLAKKETA
HALT!
SKREEEEEECH
WHAT'S GOIN' ON?
SECRET POLICE! WE'RE GOING TO SEARCH YOUR TRAIN!
FWISH
NOTHIN' UP FRONT.
HE'S NOT HERE, EITHER. HE MUST STILL BE BACK THERE IN THE TUNNEL!
I SAW A JACKET ON THE RAILS ABOUT 500 METERS FROM THE ENTRANCE.
REALLY? WELL, SORRY FOR INTER-RUPTING YOU. GO AHEAD AND MOVE ON.

WAIT!

LET'S CHECK THE ROOF, JUST IN CASE.

LET'S HAVE A LOOK.

THERE'S NOTHIN' UP HERE.

ALL RIGHT, THEN.

WE'LL JUST HAVE TO GO BACK AND SEARCH THE SUBWAY RAILS.

WE'RE PULLING OUT, THEN.

WHAT'S THE MATTER WITH THOSE GUYS?

DRAGGING US INTO THIS...

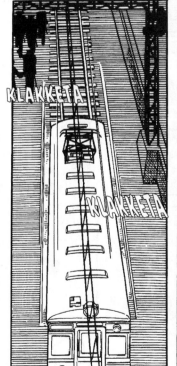

KLAKKETA

KLAKKETA

I HEARD THERE WAS A HUNT FOR REDS IN KYOMACHI.

OH YEAH? ONE OF 'EM MUST HAVE ESCAPED.

GUESS SO.

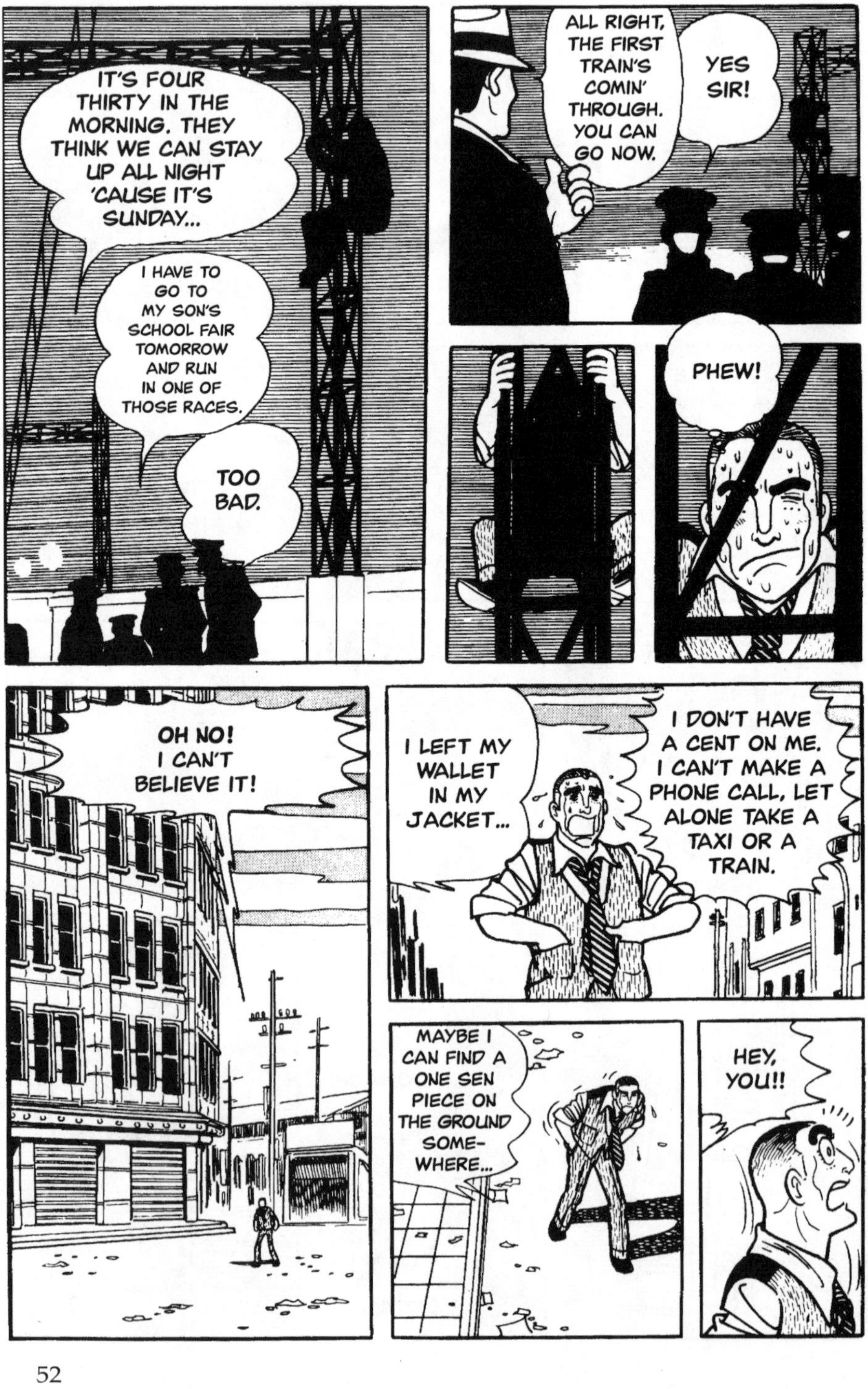
IT'S FOUR THIRTY IN THE MORNING. THEY THINK WE CAN STAY UP ALL NIGHT 'CAUSE IT'S SUNDAY...
I HAVE TO GO TO MY SON'S SCHOOL FAIR TOMORROW AND RUN IN ONE OF THOSE RACES.
TOO BAD.
ALL RIGHT, THE FIRST TRAIN'S COMIN' THROUGH. YOU CAN GO NOW.
YES SIR!
PHEW!
OH NO! I CAN'T BELIEVE IT!
I LEFT MY WALLET IN MY JACKET...
I DON'T HAVE A CENT ON ME. I CAN'T MAKE A PHONE CALL, LET ALONE TAKE A TAXI OR A TRAIN.
MAYBE I CAN FIND A ONE SEN PIECE ON THE GROUND SOME-WHERE...
HEY, YOU!!

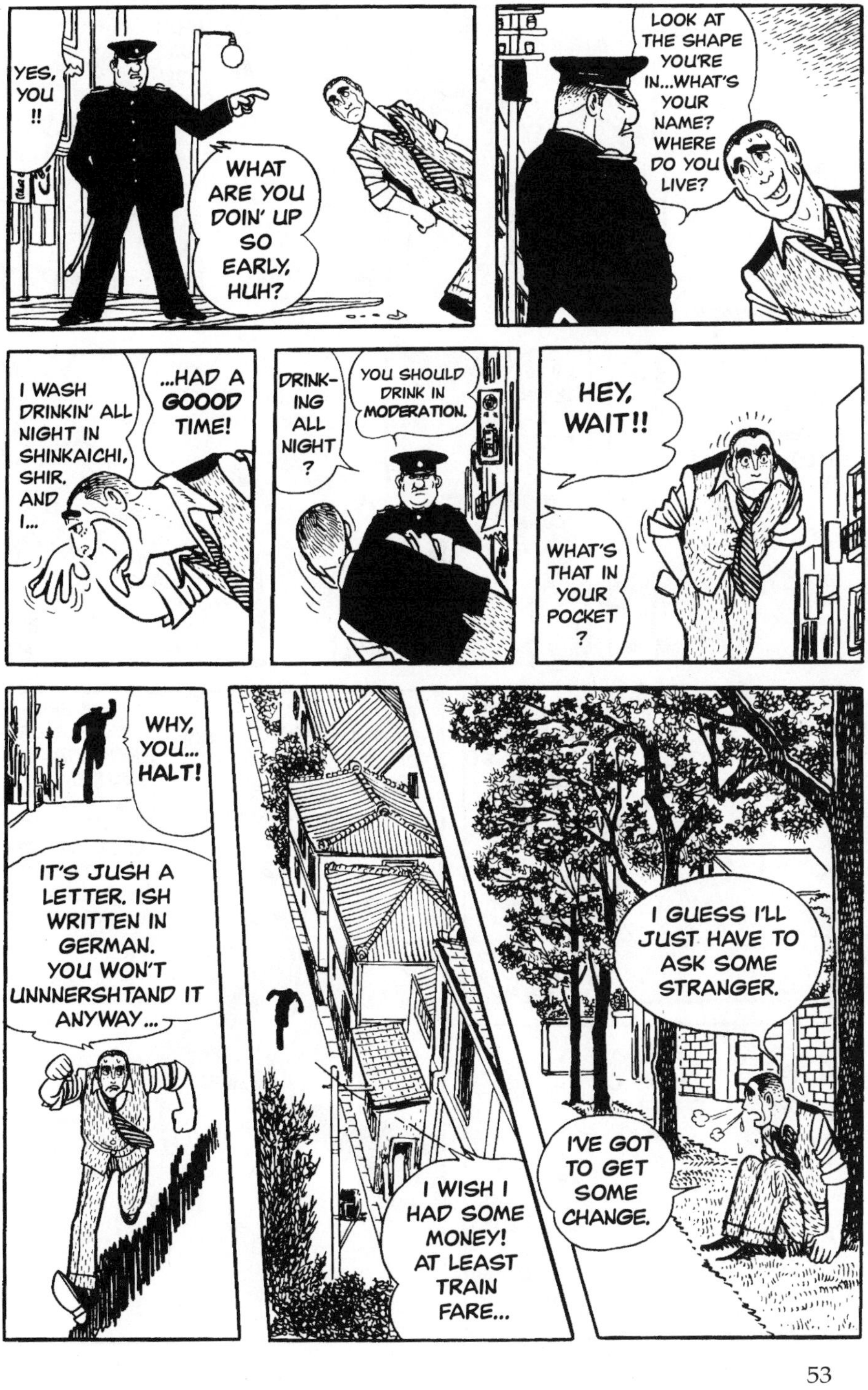
YES, YOU !!
WHAT ARE YOU DOIN' UP SO EARLY, HUH?
LOOK AT THE SHAPE YOU'RE IN...WHAT'S YOUR NAME? WHERE DO YOU LIVE?
I WASH DRINKIN' ALL NIGHT IN SHINKAICHI, SHIR. AND I...
...HAD A GOOOD TIME!
DRINK-ING ALL NIGHT ?
YOU SHOULD DRINK IN MODERATION.
HEY, WAIT!!
WHAT'S THAT IN YOUR POCKET ?
WHY, YOU... HALT!
IT'S JUSH A LETTER. ISH WRITTEN IN GERMAN. YOU WON'T UNNNERSHTAND IT ANYWAY...
I WISH I HAD SOME MONEY! AT LEAST TRAIN FARE...
I GUESS I'LL JUST HAVE TO ASK SOME STRANGER.
I'VE GOT TO GET SOME CHANGE.

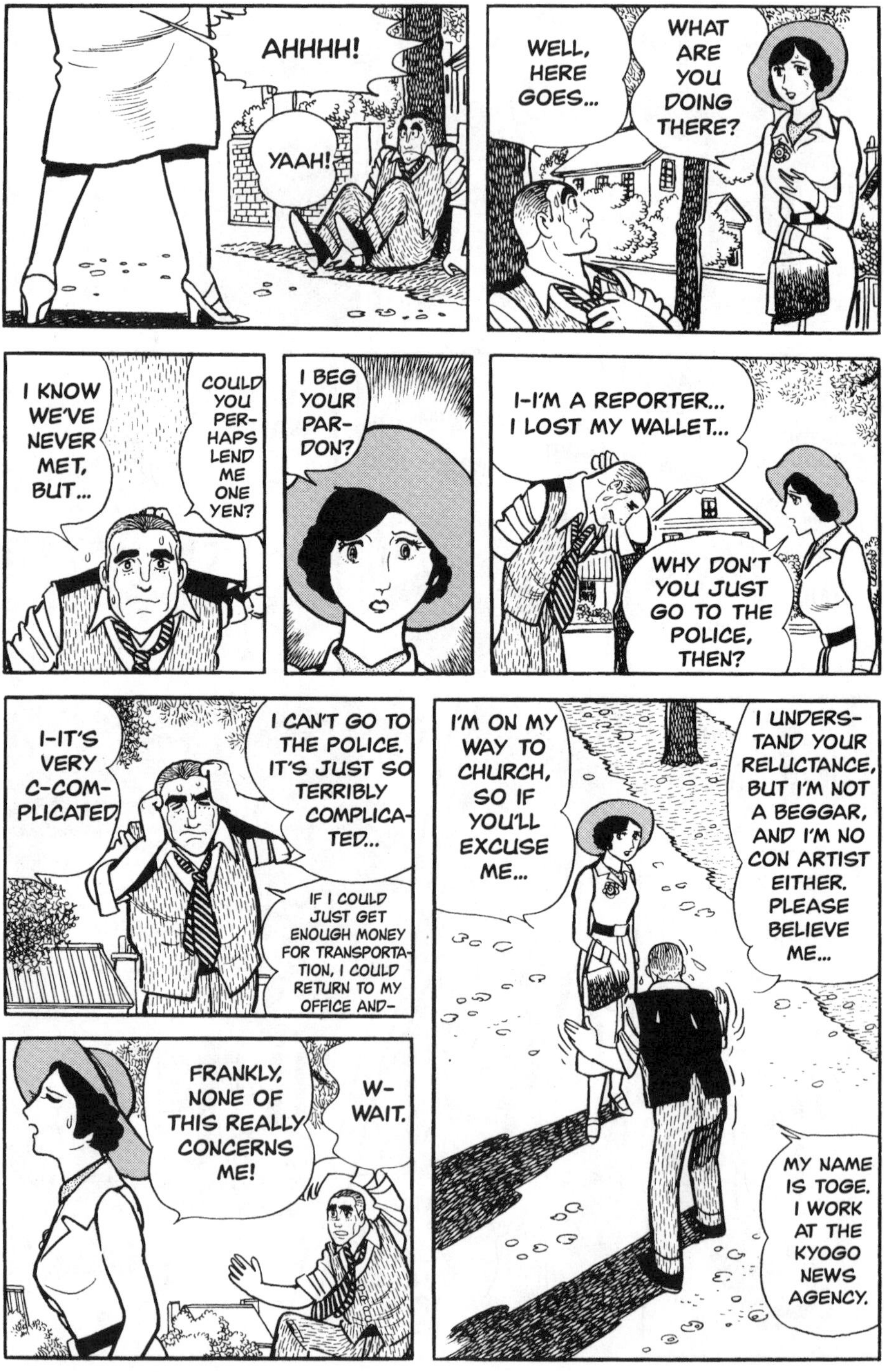
AHHHH!
YAAH!
WELL, HERE GOES...
WHAT ARE YOU DOING THERE?
I KNOW WE'VE NEVER MET, BUT...
COULD YOU PERHAPS LEND ME ONE YEN?
I BEG YOUR PARDON?
I-I'M A REPORTER... I LOST MY WALLET...
WHY DON'T YOU JUST GO TO THE POLICE, THEN?
I-IT'S VERY C-COMPLICATED
I CAN'T GO TO THE POLICE. IT'S JUST SO TERRIBLY COMPLICATED...
IF I COULD JUST GET ENOUGH MONEY FOR TRANSPORTATION, I COULD RETURN TO MY OFFICE AND-
I'M ON MY WAY TO CHURCH, SO IF YOU'LL EXCUSE ME...
I UNDERSTAND YOUR RELUCTANCE, BUT I'M NOT A BEGGAR, AND I'M NO CON ARTIST EITHER. PLEASE BELIEVE ME...
MY NAME IS TOGE. I WORK AT THE KYOGO NEWS AGENCY.
FRANKLY, NONE OF THIS REALLY CONCERNS ME!
W-WAIT.

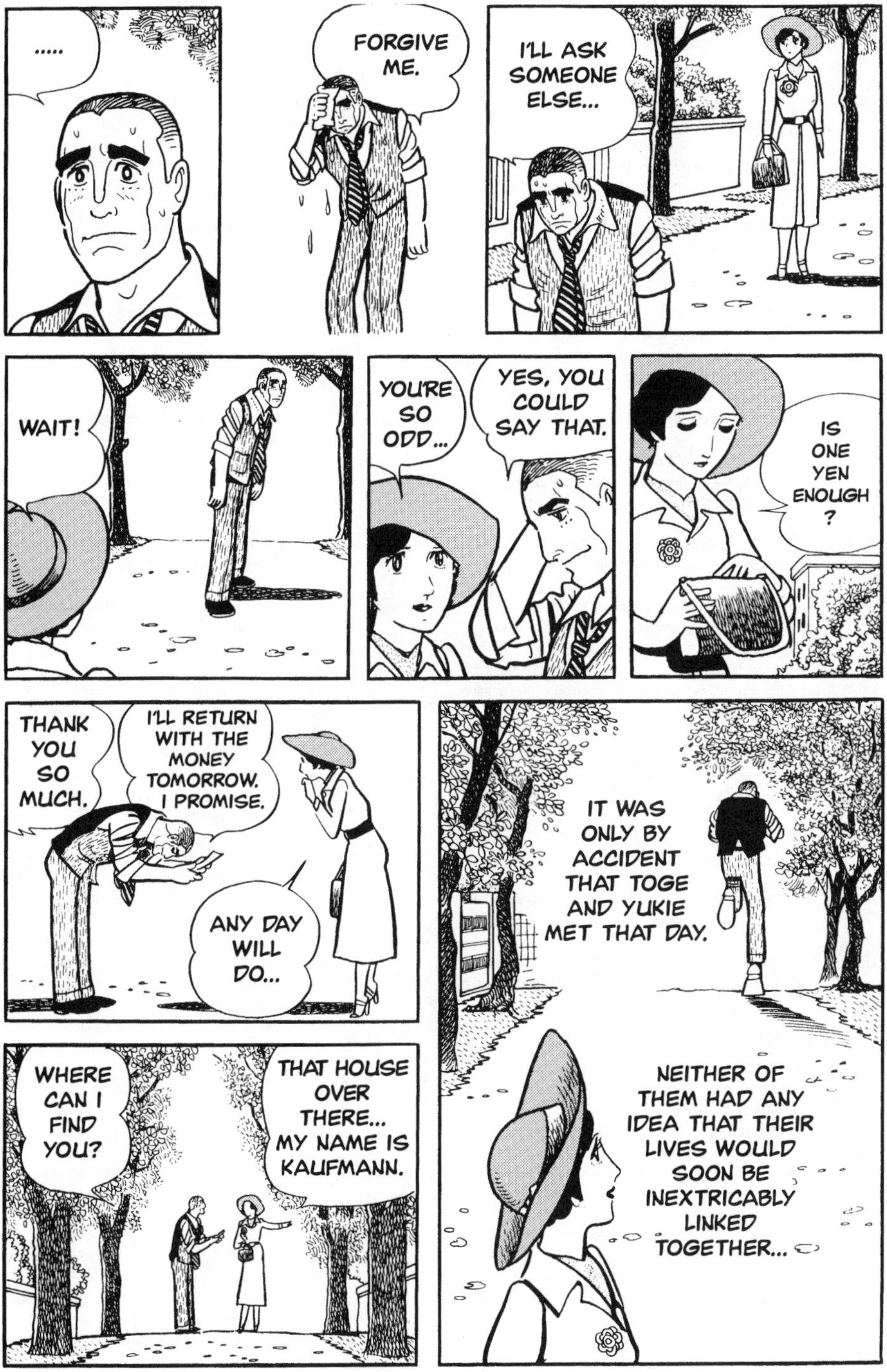
.....
FORGIVE ME.
I'LL ASK SOMEONE ELSE...
WAIT!
YOU'RE SO ODD...
YES, YOU COULD SAY THAT.
IS ONE YEN ENOUGH?
THANK YOU SO MUCH.
I'LL RETURN WITH THE MONEY TOMORROW. I PROMISE.
ANY DAY WILL DO...
WHERE CAN I FIND YOU?
THAT HOUSE OVER THERE... MY NAME IS KAUFMANN.
IT WAS ONLY BY ACCIDENT THAT TOGE AND YUKIE MET THAT DAY.
NEITHER OF THEM HAD ANY IDEA THAT THEIR LIVES WOULD SOON BE INEXTRICABLY LINKED TOGETHER...

1938 TIMELINE

January 13	Japan sets up an autonomous government in North China.
January 12	Austria and Hungary recognize the fascist Franco regime in Spain.
January 15	The Japanese Air Force begins systematic bombing of Chungking, seat of the Chinese government.
February 4	Hitler assumes direct control of the military under a newly formed High Command of the Armed Forces (OKW).
February 20	Hitler recognizes the Japanese puppet government in Manchuria, China, and reveals that he doesn't find Japanese expansionism abhorrent: "Even the greatest victory gained by Japan would be infinitely less dangerous for civilization and world peace than any success achieved by Bolshevism."
March 26	The National Mobilization Bill is passed, authorizing the Japanese government to assume absolute control of the nation's economy.
March 28	Japan establishes the "Reformed Government of the Republic of China" in Nanking.
April 26	In Germany, Jews are required to officially register all personal property valued at more than 5,000 marks. This is the first of a series of regulations that serve to create a record of all Jewish-owned domestic and foreign property, as a prelude to confiscation by the state.
May 4	The Hungarian government introduces numerous clauses restricting Jewish entry into administration, commerce, industry and the liberal professions.
May 13	Béla Imredy, an advocate of anti-Semitic policies, becomes premier of Hungary.
May 14	The League Council condemns Japan for using poison gas in China.
June 10	The Japanese Central China Expeditionary Force launches Japan's largest offensive yet in an attempt to crush the Chinese military and impose a settlement.
July 6-15	The Evian Conference on Refugees, held in France, fails to find a solution to the Jewish refugee problem precipitated by the *Anschluss*, the incorporation of Austria into a Greater Germany. The Federal Representation of German Jews (who attend the conference with Berlin's blessing) propose that other nations open their lands to Jews fleeing persecution. The results of the conference are hardly encouraging. The U.S. agree to accept only the 27,370 Jews from Germany and Austria permitted under its current restrictive immigration quota system. Britain claims it possesses no territory suitable for the resettlement of large groups from any country. Australia announces: "As we have no real racial problem, we are not desirous of importing one." New Zealand con-
	curs. Canada, Columbia, Uruguay, and Venezuela agree to accept only farmers. Nicaragua, Honduras, Costa Rica, and Panama jointly announce they cannot accept "traders or intellectuals." Argentina and France declare they have already reached a saturation point in accepting refugees. Peru commends the U.S. for its policy of "caution and wisdom" in establishing a quota. Only Denmark and the Netherlands show any sensitivity to the plight of the Jews, agreeing to open their borders without qualification.
August 3	Italy enacts sweeping anti-Semitic laws.
September 29-30	The fate of Czechoslovakia is decided in Munich at a meeting between Hitler and the leaders of France, Italy, and Britain. Not a single Czech representative is present. The Sudetenland becomes part of Germany.
October 4	The French Popular Front, a Communist organization, collapses when it refuses to support the Munich Agreement.
October 21	Canton is occupied by the Japanese.
October 28	Thousands of Polish Jews are arrested in Germany and deported to Poland.
November 2	Japan formally resigns from the League of Nations, claiming the organization has been "slandering at every turn Japan's activities in China."
November 3	Japan claims China has been "a victim of the rivalry between powers whose imperialistic ambitions have constantly imperiled her tranquillity and independence." Tokyo proposes the establishment of a "new order" in east Asia, with Japan, Manchukuo, and China tied together economically and in "a joint defense against communism."
November 7	Herschel Grynszpan, a Jew, assassinates a minor German official in retaliation for the deportation of his parents to Poland.
November 9-10	A Nazi-organized campaign of violence is waged, resulting in the destruction of 191 synagogues, 814 Jewish-owned shops, 171 homes, and leaving at least 91 dead. This pogrom comes to be known as Kristallnacht, or "Crystal Night," after all the glass littering the streets from smashed windows. Ironically, Jews are held accountable for the destruction. Approximately 25,000 Jews are sent to concentration camps and 1,000 million marks in "reparations" are levied from Jews.
November 16	Jewish children are forbidden to attend German schools.
December 31	The U.S. State Department rejects Japan's "new order," declaring, "There is no need or warrant for any one power to take upon itself to prescribe what shall be the terms and conditions of a 'new order' in areas not under its sovereignty and to constitute itself the repository of authority and the agent of destiny."

CHAPTER TWO

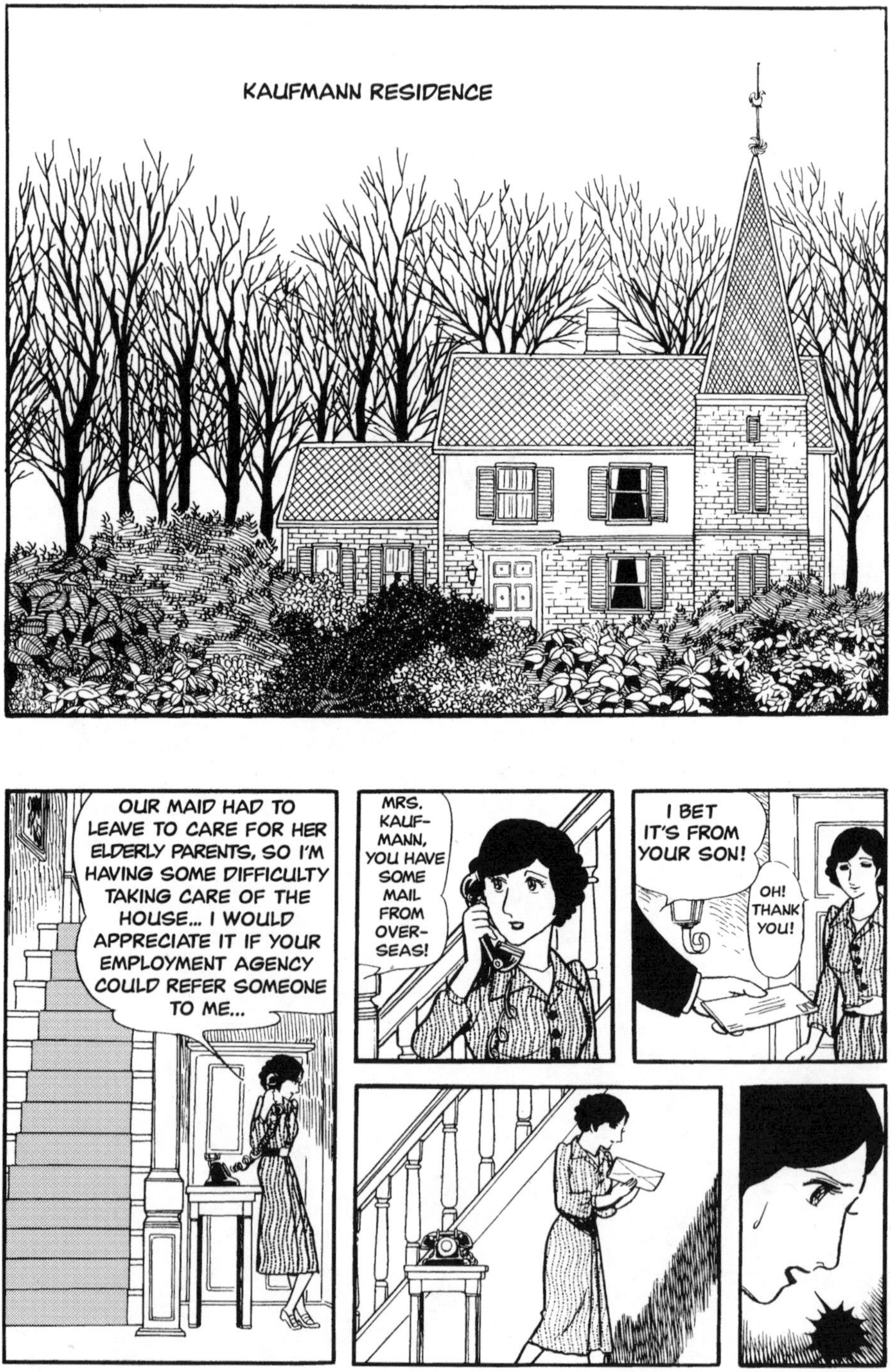
KAUFMANN RESIDENCE
OUR MAID HAD TO LEAVE TO CARE FOR HER ELDERLY PARENTS, SO I'M HAVING SOME DIFFICULTY TAKING CARE OF THE HOUSE... I WOULD APPRECIATE IT IF YOUR EMPLOYMENT AGENCY COULD REFER SOMEONE TO ME...
MRS. KAUF-MANN, YOU HAVE SOME MAIL FROM OVER-SEAS!
I BET IT'S FROM YOUR SON!
OH! THANK YOU!

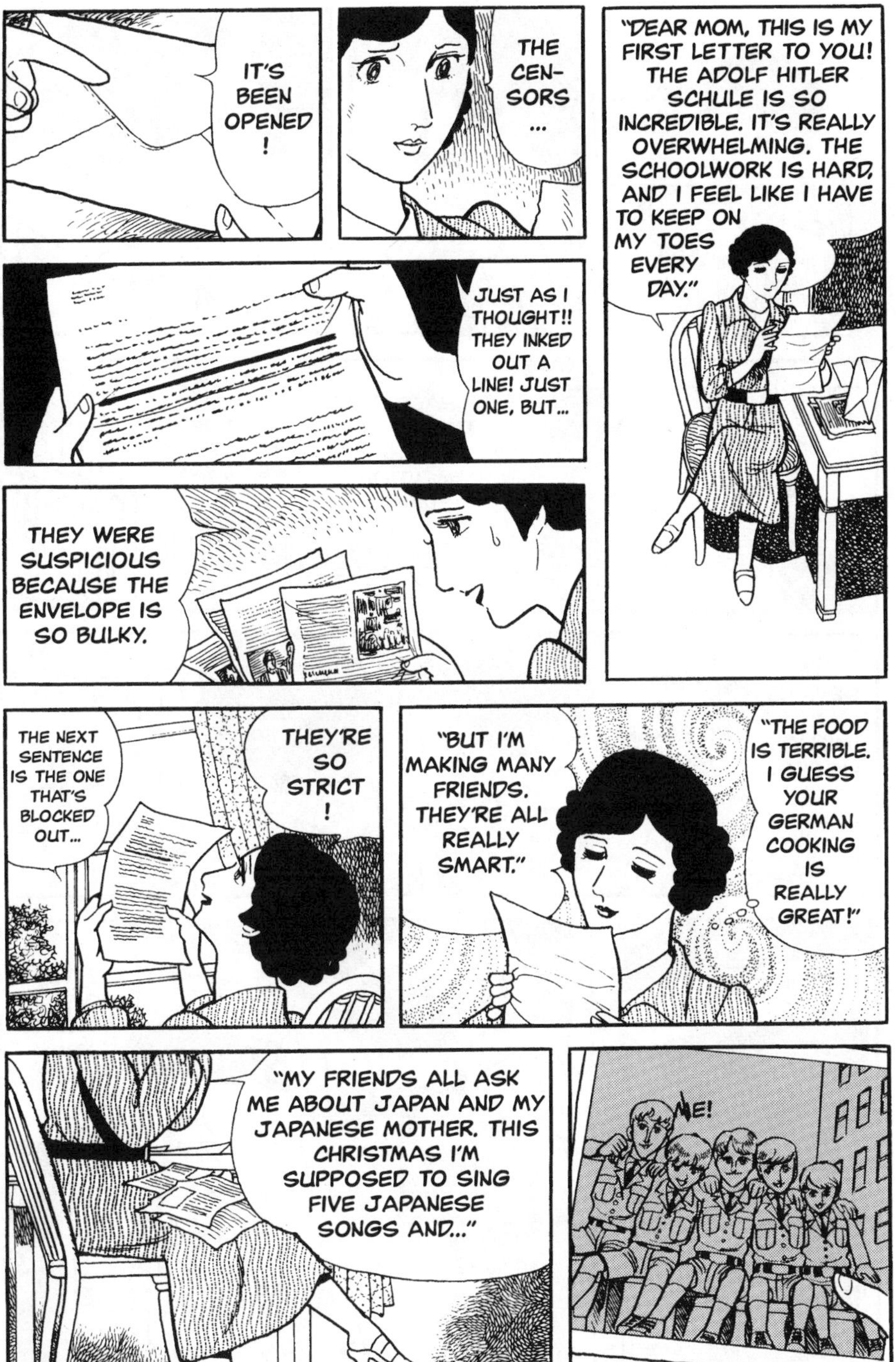
IT'S BEEN OPENED!
THE CENSORS...
JUST AS I THOUGHT!! THEY INKED OUT A LINE! JUST ONE, BUT...
THEY WERE SUSPICIOUS BECAUSE THE ENVELOPE IS SO BULKY.
"DEAR MOM, THIS IS MY FIRST LETTER TO YOU! THE ADOLF HITLER SCHULE IS SO INCREDIBLE. IT'S REALLY OVERWHELMING. THE SCHOOLWORK IS HARD, AND I FEEL LIKE I HAVE TO KEEP ON MY TOES EVERY DAY."
THE NEXT SENTENCE IS THE ONE THAT'S BLOCKED OUT...
THEY'RE SO STRICT!
"BUT I'M MAKING MANY FRIENDS. THEY'RE ALL REALLY SMART."
"THE FOOD IS TERRIBLE. I GUESS YOUR GERMAN COOKING IS REALLY GREAT!"
"MY FRIENDS ALL ASK ME ABOUT JAPAN AND MY JAPANESE MOTHER. THIS CHRISTMAS I'M SUPPOSED TO SING FIVE JAPANESE SONGS AND..."
ME!

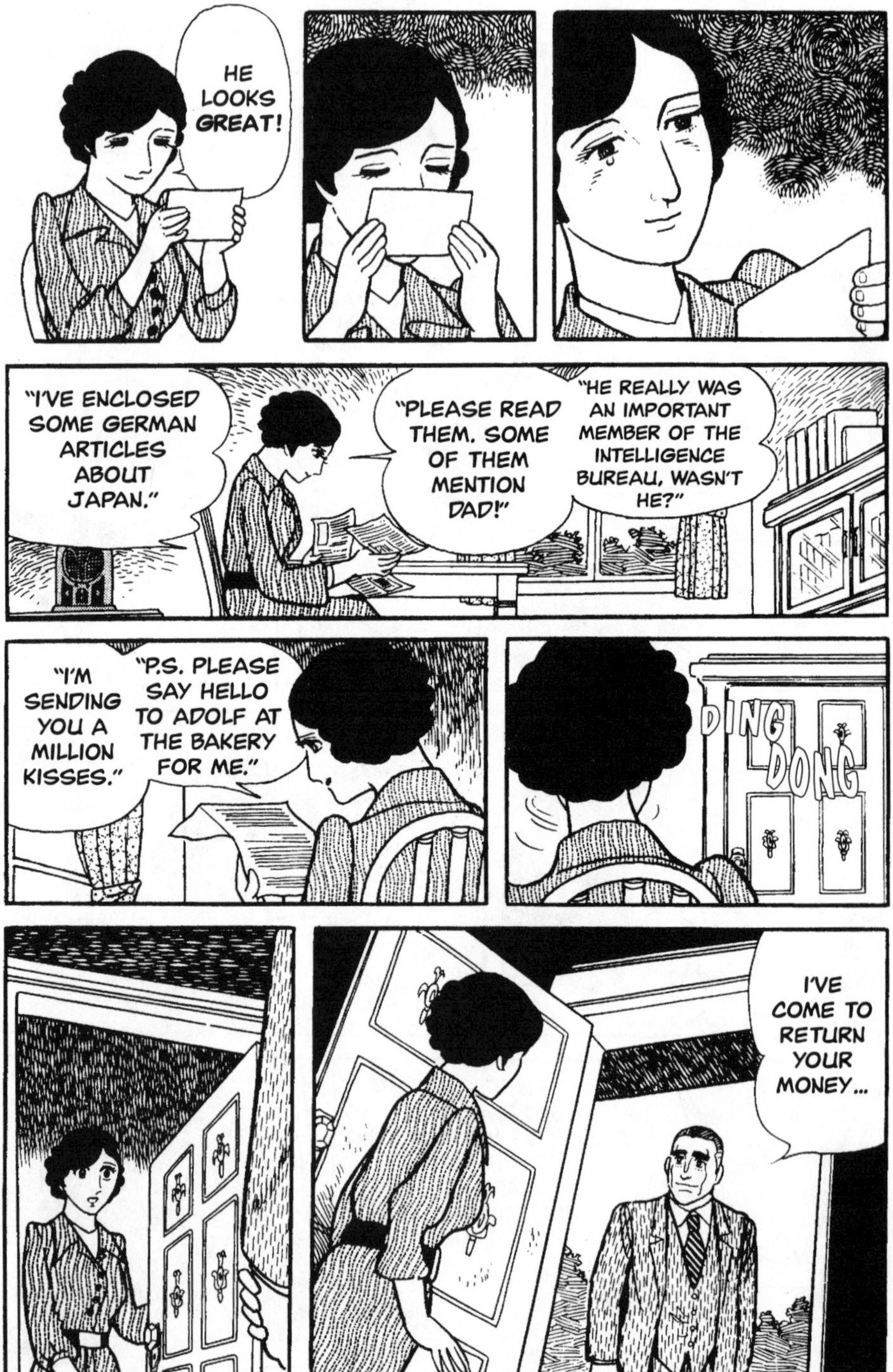
HE LOOKS GREAT!
"I'VE ENCLOSED SOME GERMAN ARTICLES ABOUT JAPAN."
"PLEASE READ THEM. SOME OF THEM MENTION DAD!"
"HE REALLY WAS AN IMPORTANT MEMBER OF THE INTELLIGENCE BUREAU, WASN'T HE?"
"I'M SENDING YOU A MILLION KISSES."
"P.S. PLEASE SAY HELLO TO ADOLF AT THE BAKERY FOR ME."
DING DONG
I'VE COME TO RETURN YOUR MONEY...

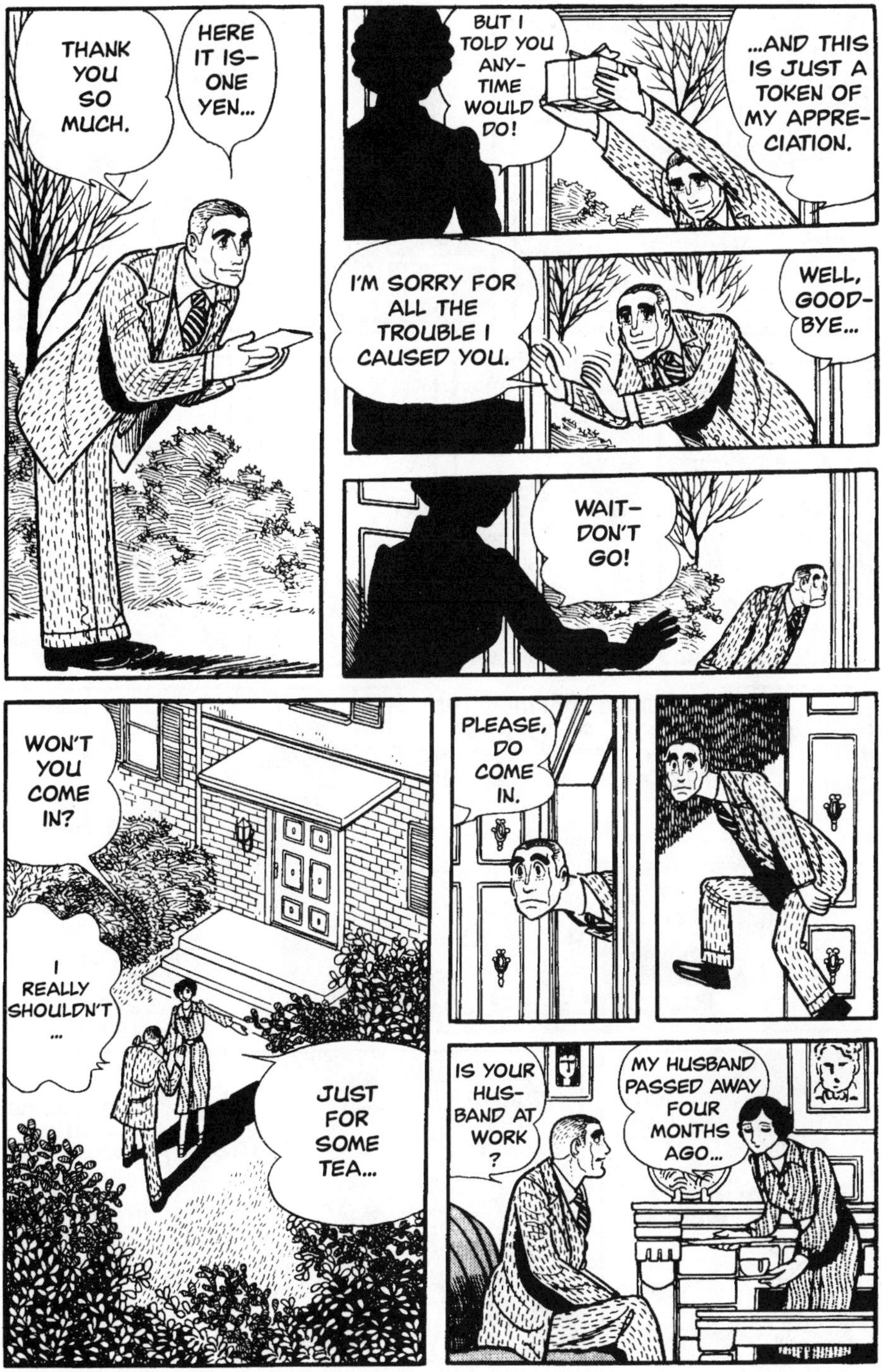
THANK YOU SO MUCH.
HERE IT IS—ONE YEN...
BUT I TOLD YOU ANY-TIME WOULD DO!
...AND THIS IS JUST A TOKEN OF MY APPRE-CIATION.
I'M SORRY FOR ALL THE TROUBLE I CAUSED YOU.
WELL, GOOD-BYE...
WAIT—DON'T GO!
WON'T YOU COME IN?
I REALLY SHOULDN'T ...
JUST FOR SOME TEA...
PLEASE, DO COME IN.
IS YOUR HUS-BAND AT WORK ?
MY HUSBAND PASSED AWAY FOUR MONTHS AGO...

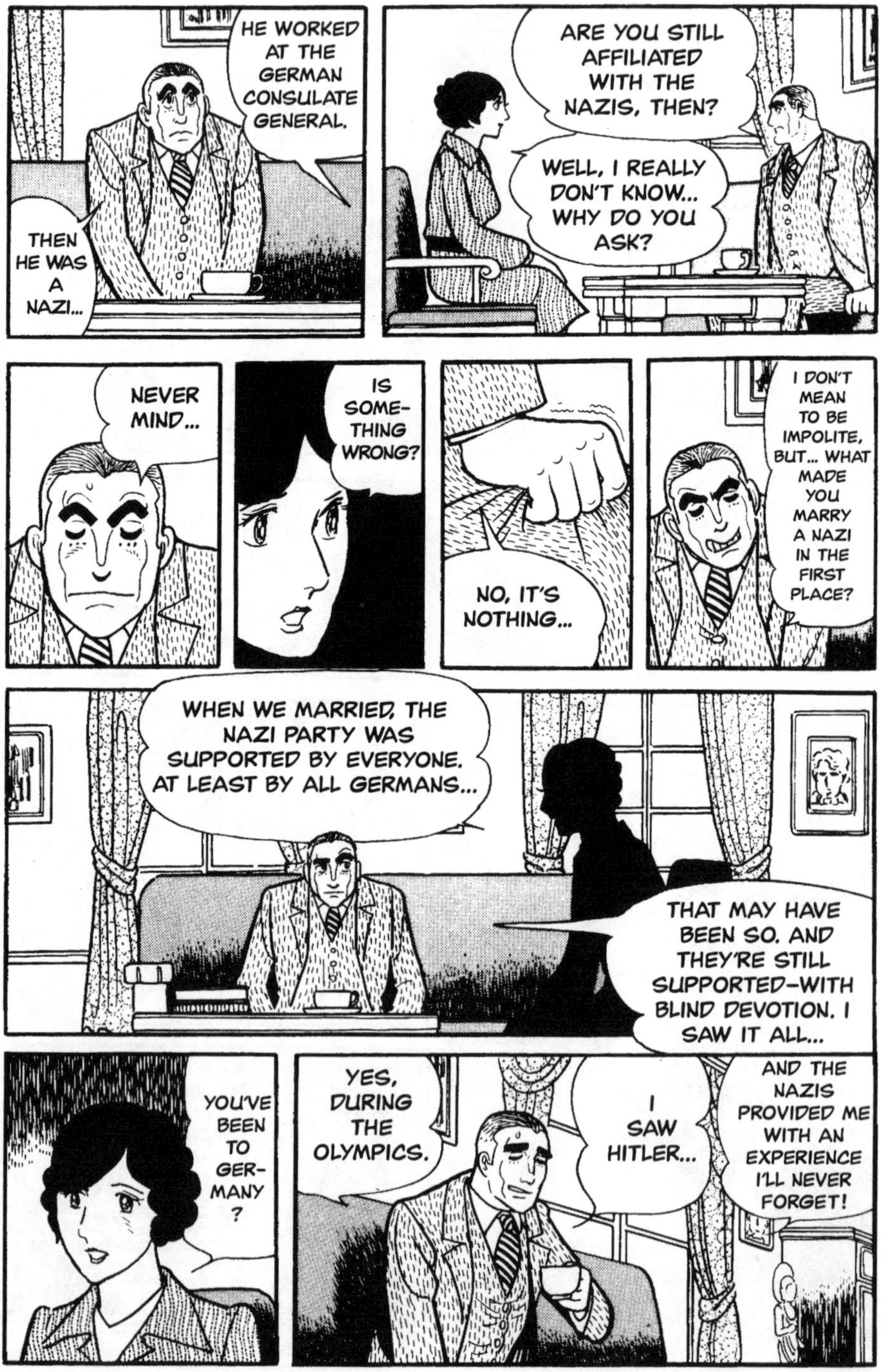
HE WORKED AT THE GERMAN CONSULATE GENERAL.
THEN HE WAS A NAZI...
ARE YOU STILL AFFILIATED WITH THE NAZIS, THEN?
WELL, I REALLY DON'T KNOW... WHY DO YOU ASK?
NEVER MIND...
IS SOME-THING WRONG?
NO, IT'S NOTHING...
I DON'T MEAN TO BE IMPOLITE, BUT... WHAT MADE YOU MARRY A NAZI IN THE FIRST PLACE?
WHEN WE MARRIED, THE NAZI PARTY WAS SUPPORTED BY EVERYONE. AT LEAST BY ALL GERMANS...
THAT MAY HAVE BEEN SO. AND THEY'RE STILL SUPPORTED—WITH BLIND DEVOTION. I SAW IT ALL...
YOU'VE BEEN TO GER-MANY?
YES, DURING THE OLYMPICS.
I SAW HITLER...
AND THE NAZIS PROVIDED ME WITH AN EXPERIENCE I'LL NEVER FORGET!

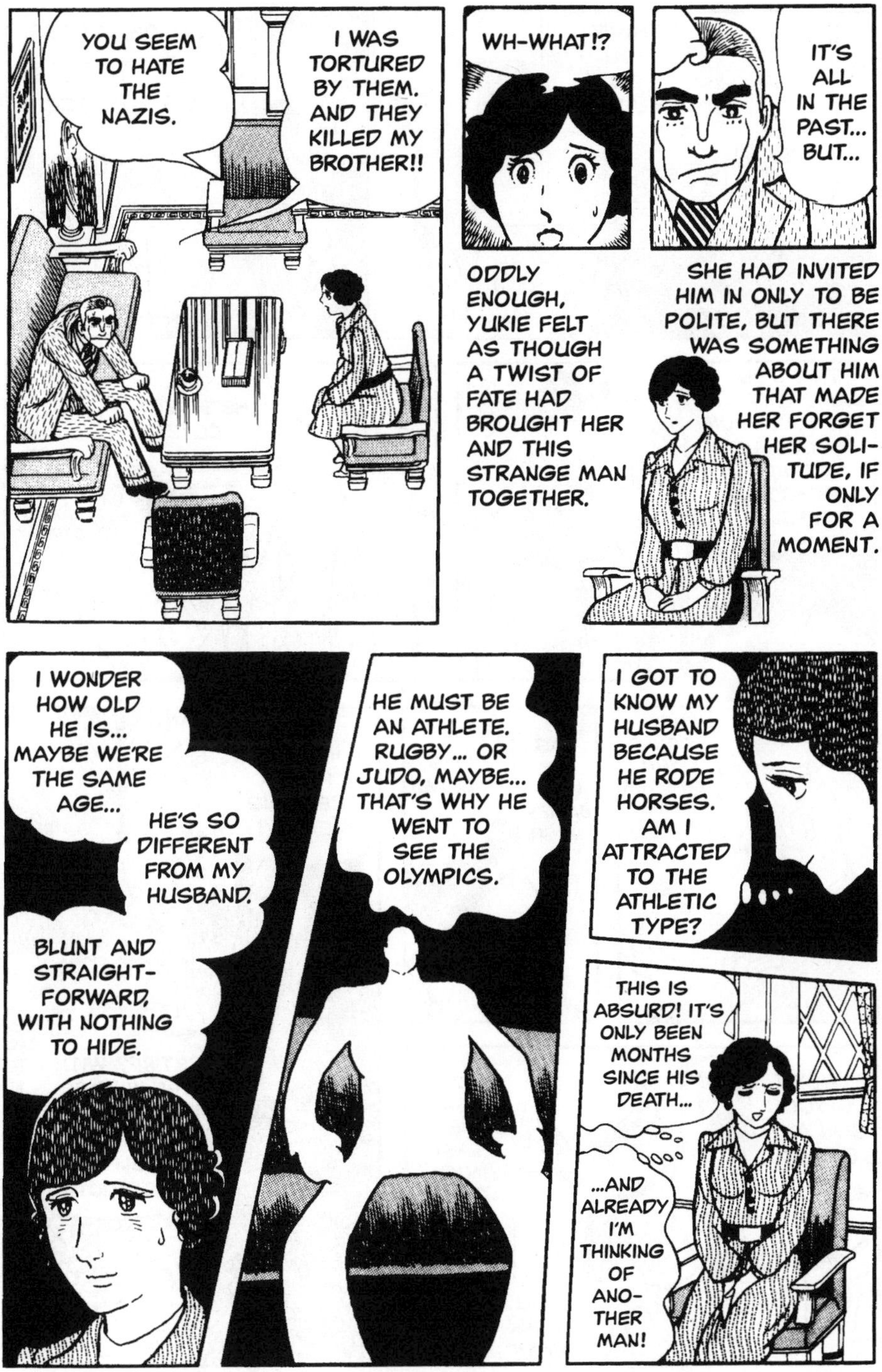
YOU SEEM TO HATE THE NAZIS.
I WAS TORTURED BY THEM. AND THEY KILLED MY BROTHER!!
WH-WHAT!?
IT'S ALL IN THE PAST... BUT...
ODDLY ENOUGH, YUKIE FELT AS THOUGH A TWIST OF FATE HAD BROUGHT HER AND THIS STRANGE MAN TOGETHER.
SHE HAD INVITED HIM IN ONLY TO BE POLITE, BUT THERE WAS SOMETHING ABOUT HIM THAT MADE HER FORGET HER SOLI-TUDE, IF ONLY FOR A MOMENT.
I WONDER HOW OLD HE IS... MAYBE WE'RE THE SAME AGE...
HE'S SO DIFFERENT FROM MY HUSBAND.
BLUNT AND STRAIGHT-FORWARD, WITH NOTHING TO HIDE.
HE MUST BE AN ATHLETE. RUGBY... OR JUDO, MAYBE... THAT'S WHY HE WENT TO SEE THE OLYMPICS.
I GOT TO KNOW MY HUSBAND BECAUSE HE RODE HORSES. AM I ATTRACTED TO THE ATHLETIC TYPE?
THIS IS ABSURD! IT'S ONLY BEEN MONTHS SINCE HIS DEATH...
...AND ALREADY I'M THINKING OF ANO-THER MAN!

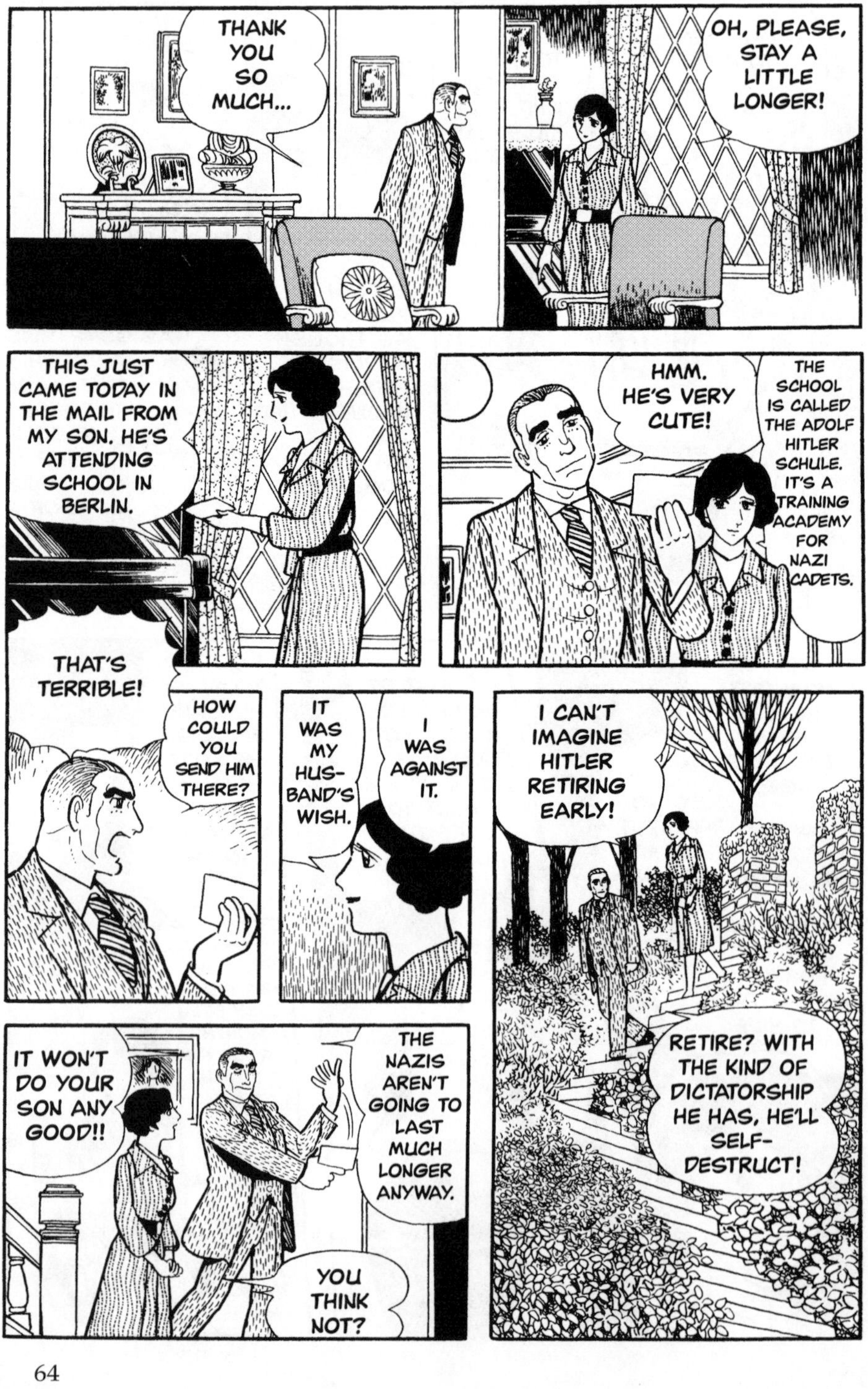
THANK YOU SO MUCH...
OH, PLEASE, STAY A LITTLE LONGER!
THIS JUST CAME TODAY IN THE MAIL FROM MY SON. HE'S ATTENDING SCHOOL IN BERLIN.
HMM. HE'S VERY CUTE!
THE SCHOOL IS CALLED THE ADOLF HITLER SCHULE. IT'S A TRAINING ACADEMY FOR NAZI CADETS.
THAT'S TERRIBLE!
HOW COULD YOU SEND HIM THERE?
IT WAS MY HUS-BAND'S WISH.
I WAS AGAINST IT.
IT WON'T DO YOUR SON ANY GOOD!!
THE NAZIS AREN'T GOING TO LAST MUCH LONGER ANYWAY.
YOU THINK NOT?
I CAN'T IMAGINE HITLER RETIRING EARLY!
RETIRE? WITH THE KIND OF DICTATORSHIP HE HAS, HE'LL SELF-DESTRUCT!

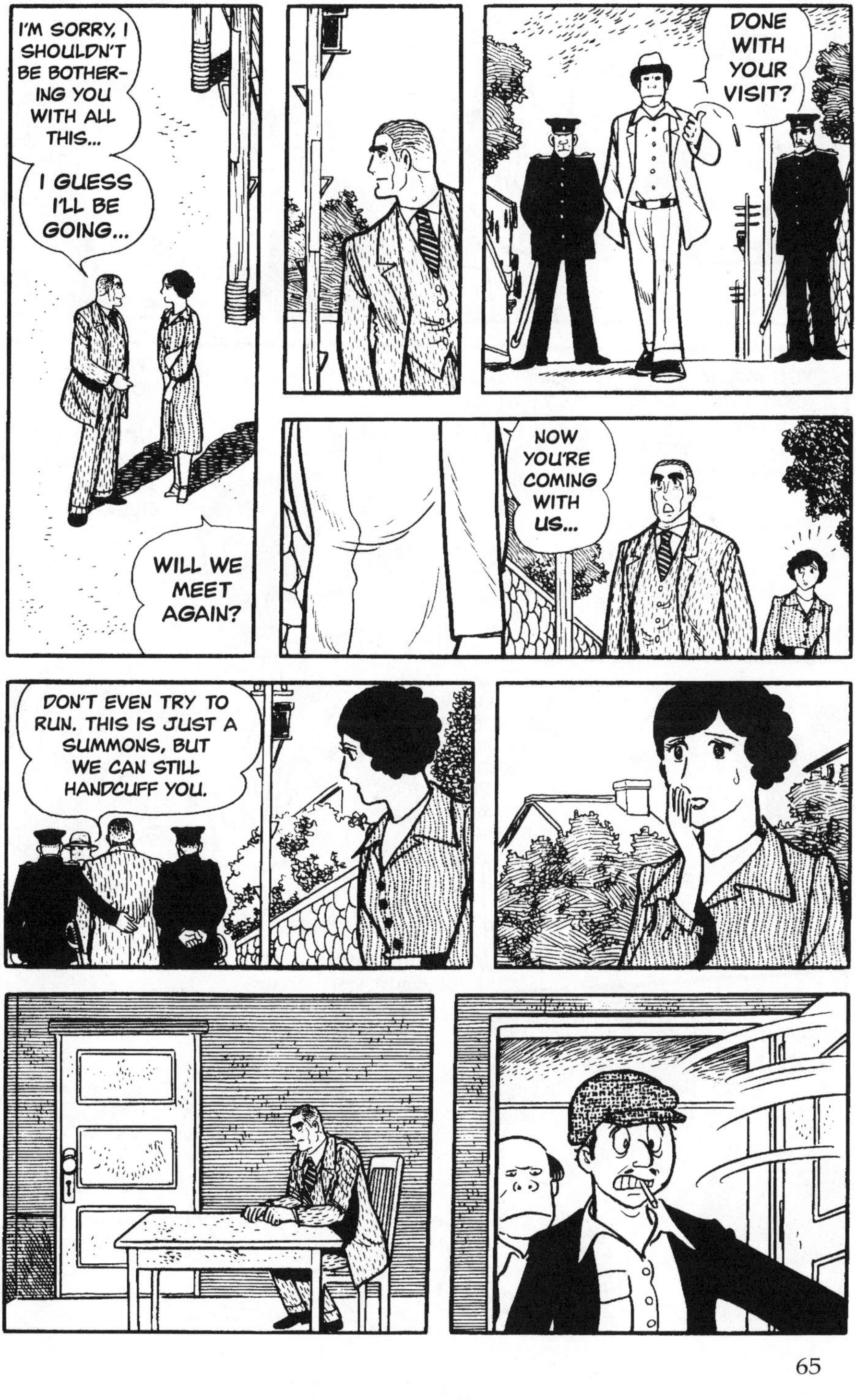
I'M SORRY, I SHOULDN'T BE BOTHERING YOU WITH ALL THIS...
I GUESS I'LL BE GOING...
WILL WE MEET AGAIN?
DONE WITH YOUR VISIT?
NOW YOU'RE COMING WITH US...
DON'T EVEN TRY TO RUN. THIS IS JUST A SUMMONS, BUT WE CAN STILL HANDCUFF YOU.

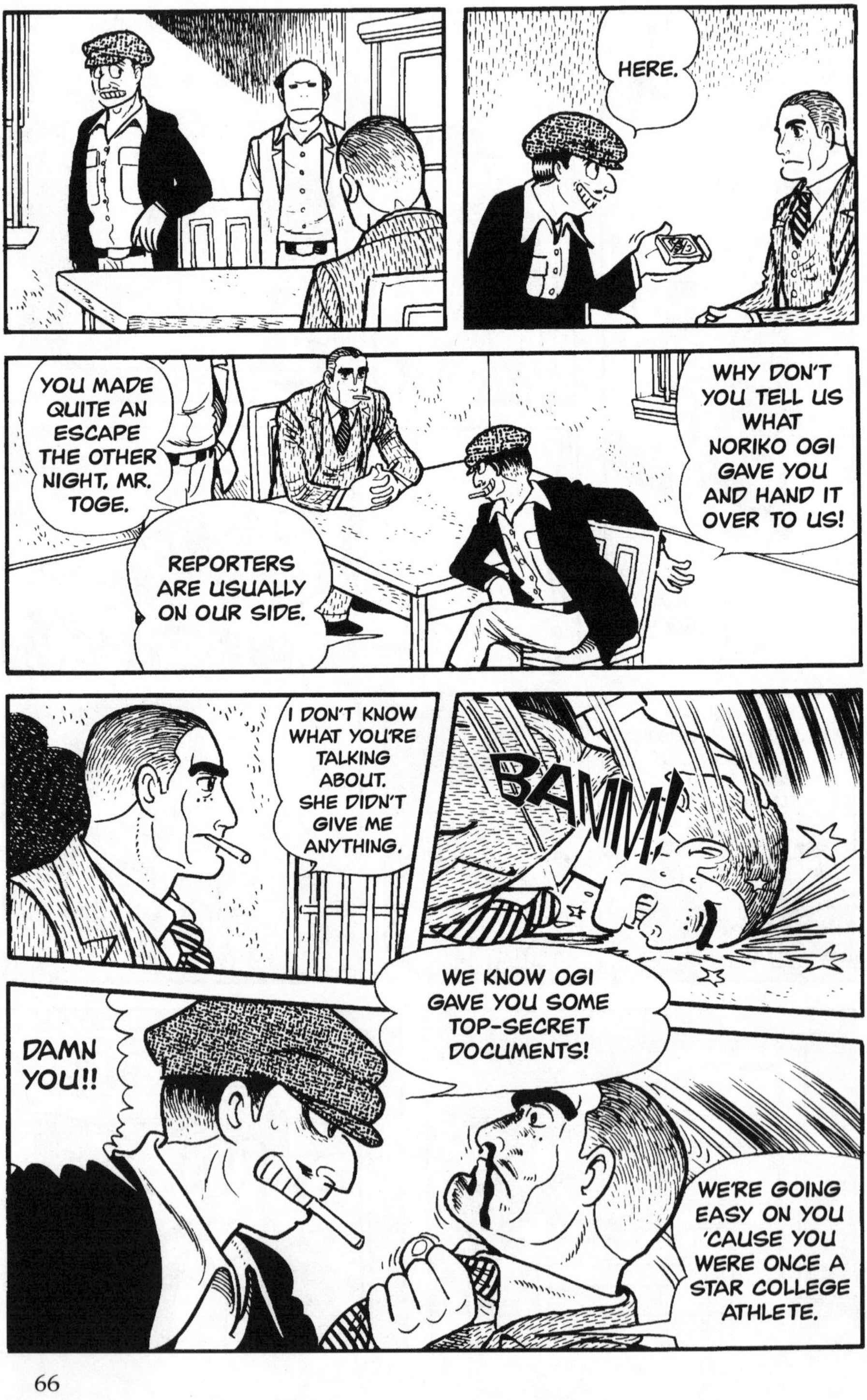
HERE.
YOU MADE QUITE AN ESCAPE THE OTHER NIGHT, MR. TOGE.
REPORTERS ARE USUALLY ON OUR SIDE.
WHY DON'T YOU TELL US WHAT NORIKO OGI GAVE YOU AND HAND IT OVER TO US!
I DON'T KNOW WHAT YOU'RE TALKING ABOUT. SHE DIDN'T GIVE ME ANYTHING.
BAMM!
DAMN YOU!!
WE KNOW OGI GAVE YOU SOME TOP-SECRET DOCUMENTS!
WE'RE GOING EASY ON YOU 'CAUSE YOU WERE ONCE A STAR COLLEGE ATHLETE.

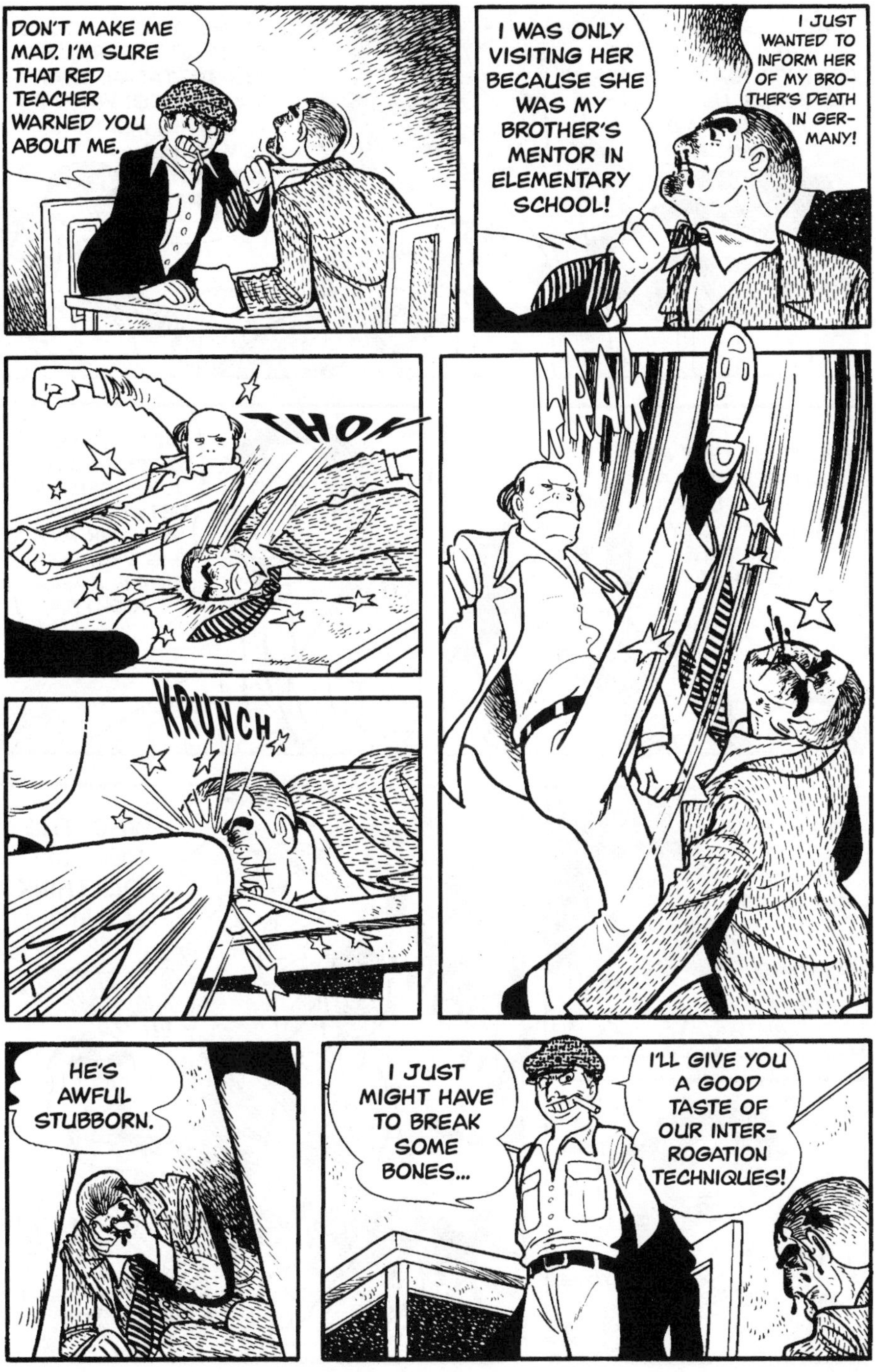
DON'T MAKE ME MAD. I'M SURE THAT RED TEACHER WARNED YOU ABOUT ME.
I WAS ONLY VISITING HER BECAUSE SHE WAS MY BROTHER'S MENTOR IN ELEMENTARY SCHOOL!
I JUST WANTED TO INFORM HER OF MY BROTHER'S DEATH IN GERMANY!
THOK
KRUNCH
KRAK
HE'S AWFUL STUBBORN.
I JUST MIGHT HAVE TO BREAK SOME BONES...
I'LL GIVE YOU A GOOD TASTE OF OUR INTERROGATION TECHNIQUES!

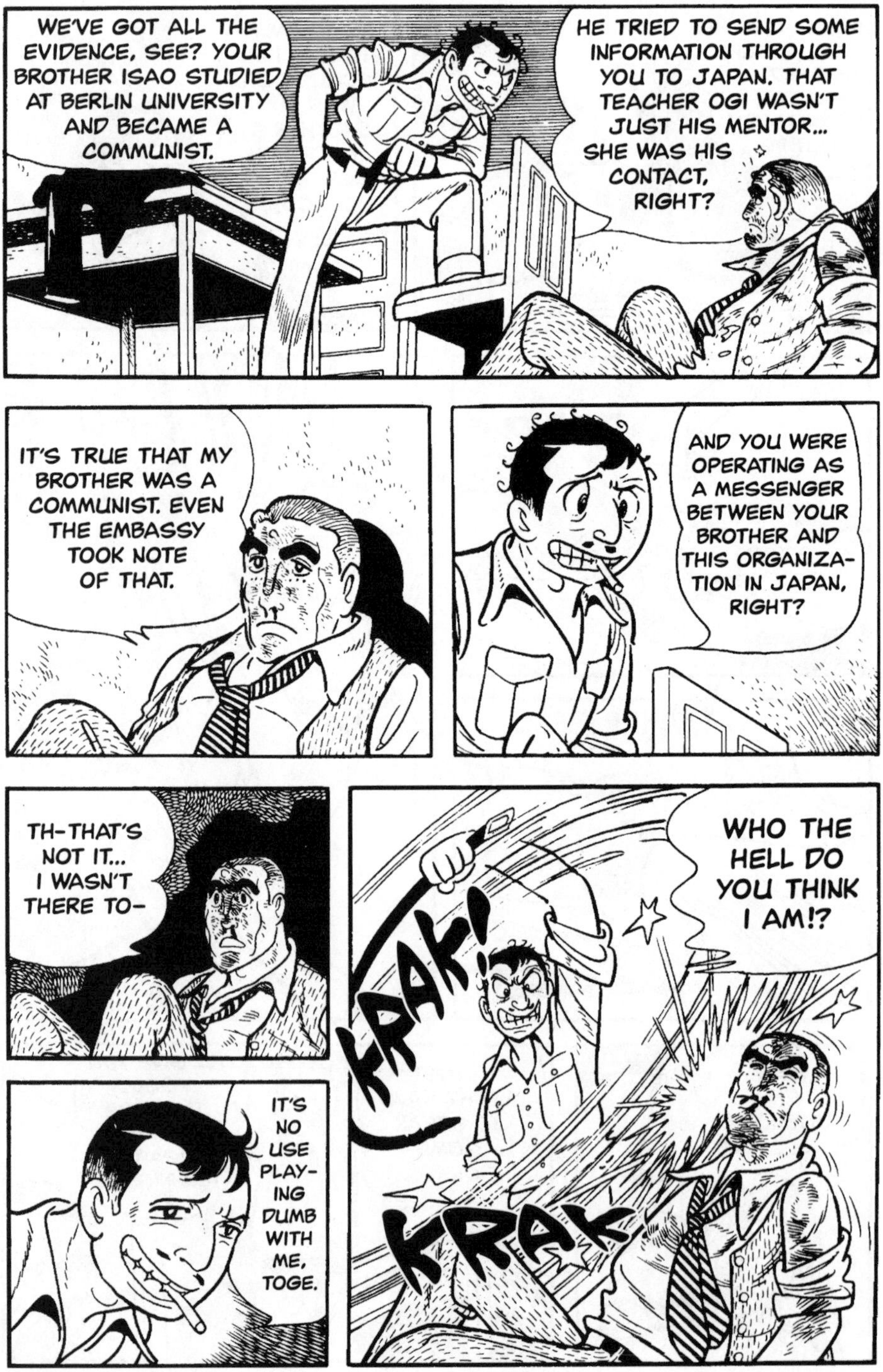
WE'VE GOT ALL THE EVIDENCE, SEE? YOUR BROTHER ISAO STUDIED AT BERLIN UNIVERSITY AND BECAME A COMMUNIST.
HE TRIED TO SEND SOME INFORMATION THROUGH YOU TO JAPAN. THAT TEACHER OGI WASN'T JUST HIS MENTOR... SHE WAS HIS CONTACT, RIGHT?
IT'S TRUE THAT MY BROTHER WAS A COMMUNIST. EVEN THE EMBASSY TOOK NOTE OF THAT.
AND YOU WERE OPERATING AS A MESSENGER BETWEEN YOUR BROTHER AND THIS ORGANIZA-TION IN JAPAN, RIGHT?
TH-THAT'S NOT IT... I WASN'T THERE TO-
IT'S NO USE PLAY-ING DUMB WITH ME, TOGE.
WHO THE HELL DO YOU THINK I AM!?
KRAK!
KRAK

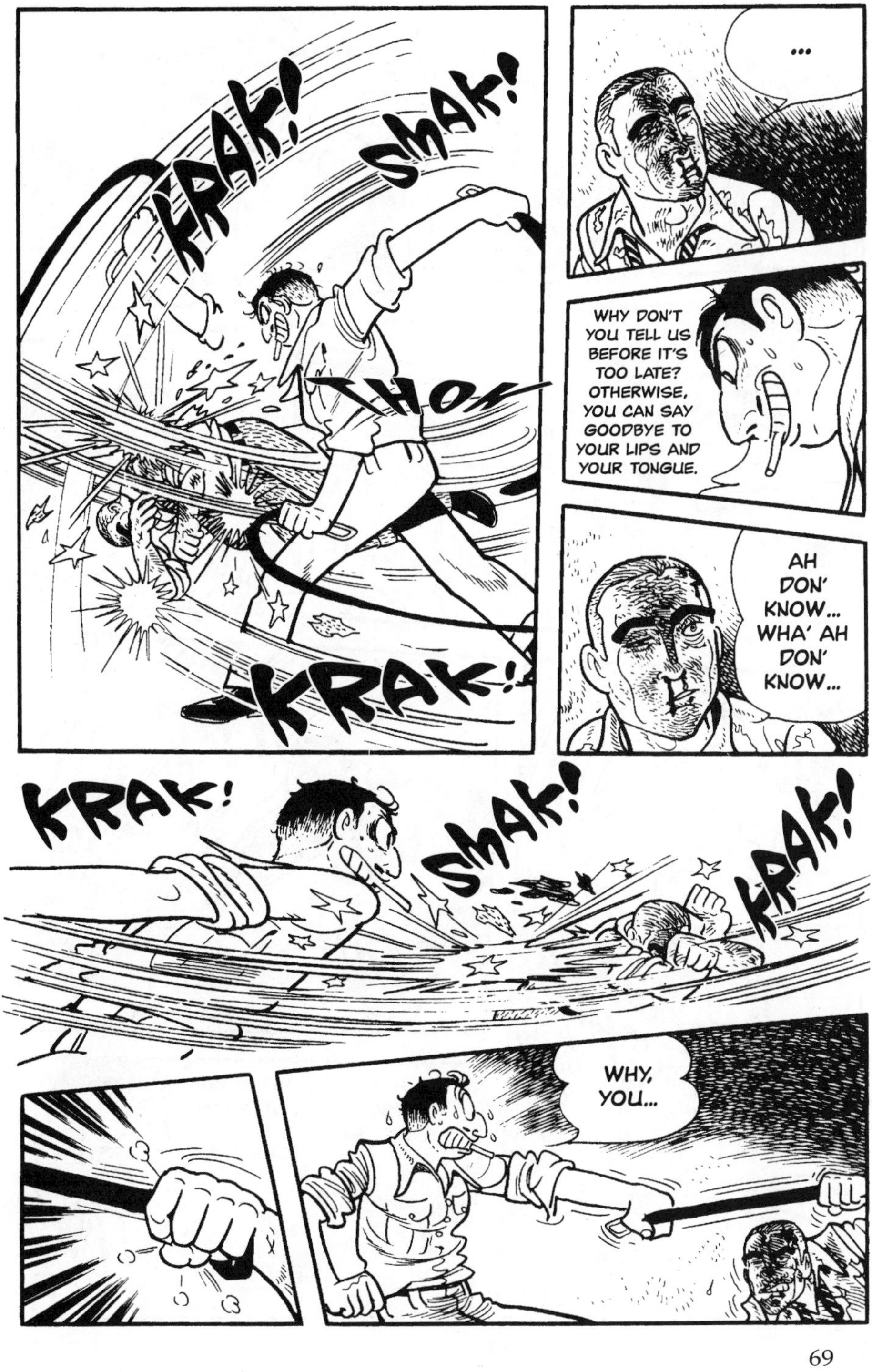
KRAK!
SHAK!
THOK
KRAK!
...
WHY DON'T YOU TELL US BEFORE IT'S TOO LATE? OTHERWISE, YOU CAN SAY GOODBYE TO YOUR LIPS AND YOUR TONGUE.
AH DON' KNOW... WHA' AH DON' KNOW...
KRAK!
SHAK!
KRAK!
WHY, YOU...

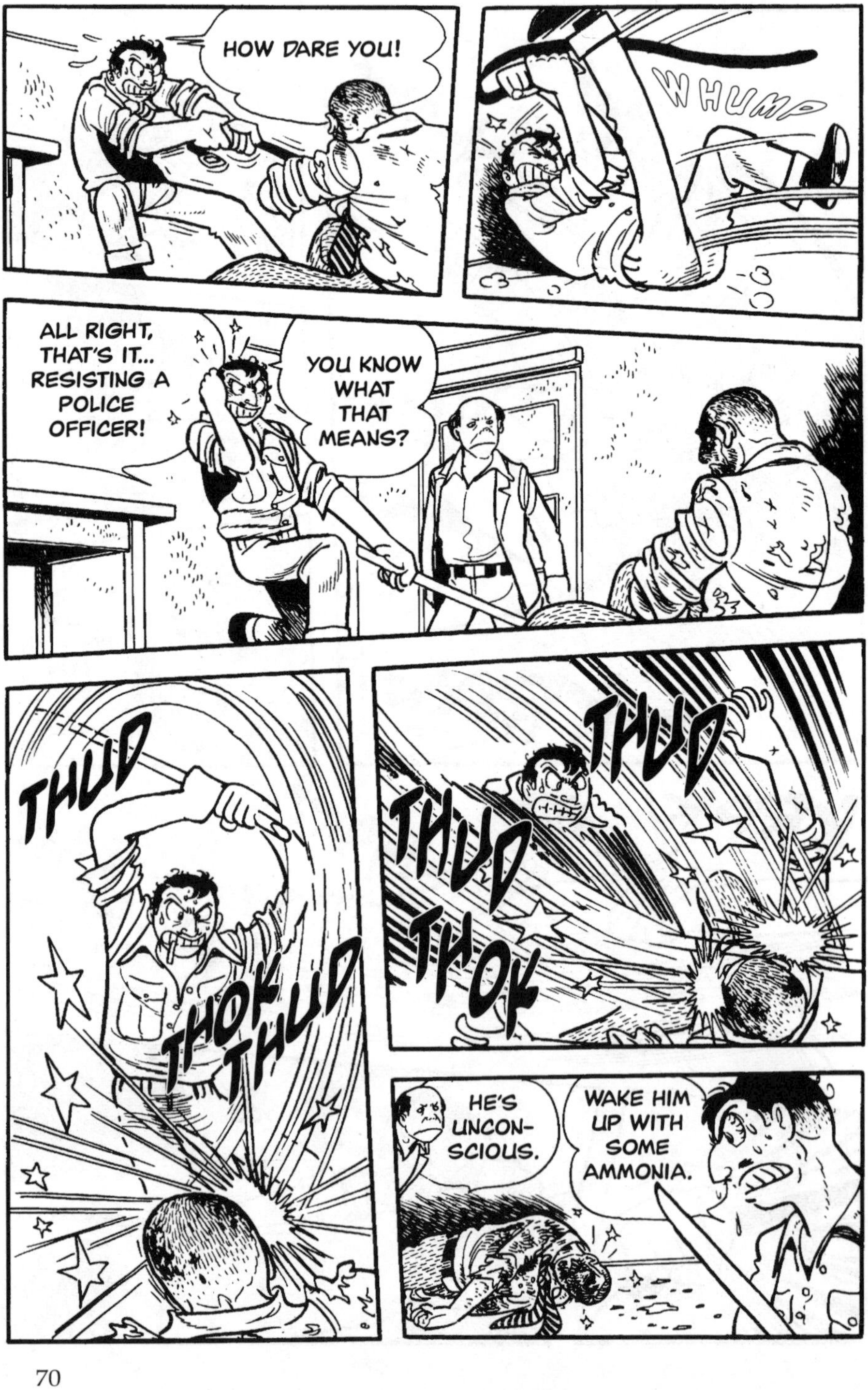
HOW DARE YOU!
WHUMP
ALL RIGHT, THAT'S IT... RESISTING A POLICE OFFICER!
YOU KNOW WHAT THAT MEANS?
THUD
THOK
THUD
THUD
THUD
THOK
HE'S UNCON-SCIOUS.
WAKE HIM UP WITH SOME AMMONIA.

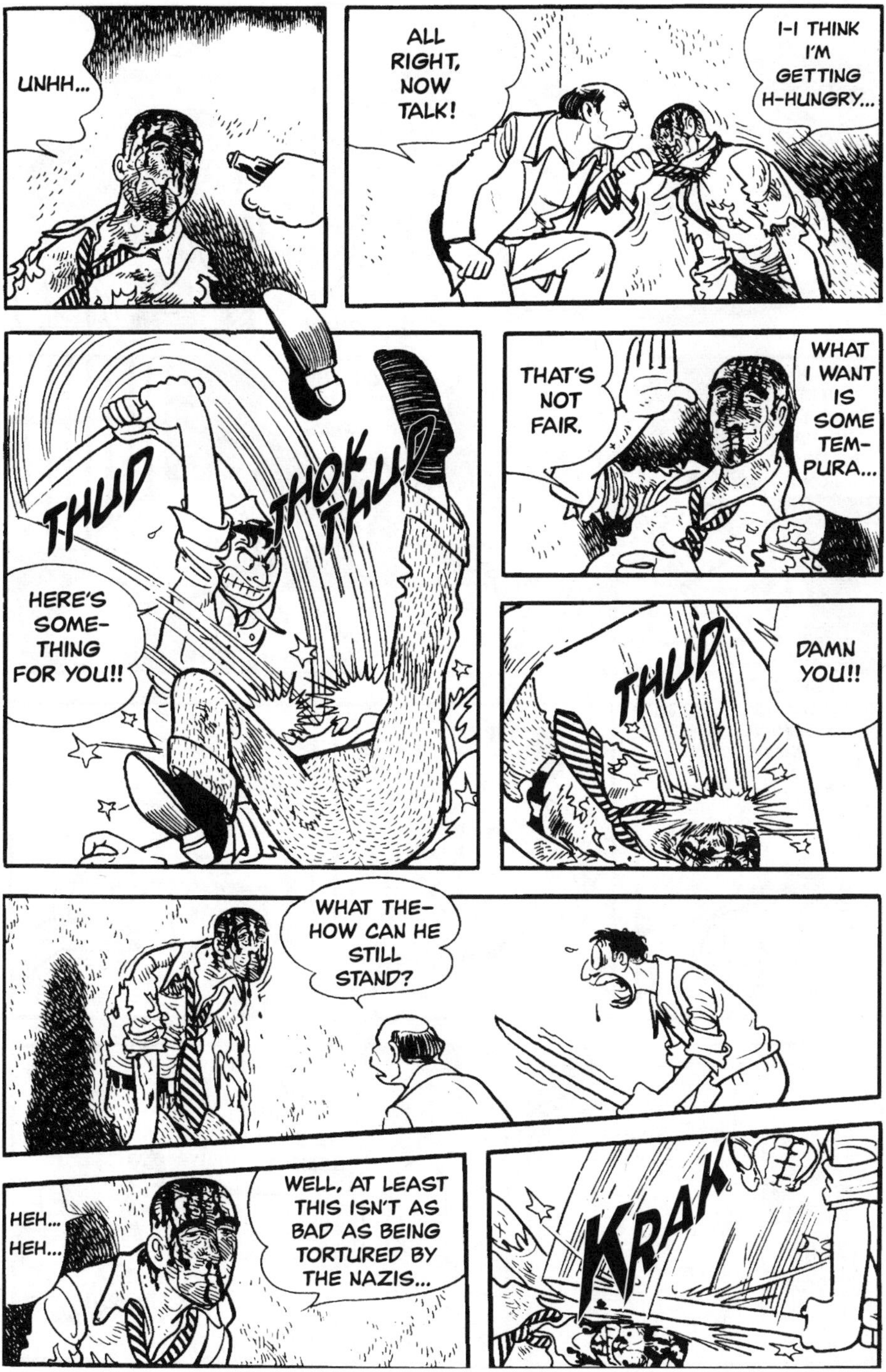
UNHH...
ALL RIGHT, NOW TALK!
I-I THINK I'M GETTING H-HUNGRY...
THUD
THOK
THUD
HERE'S SOME-THING FOR YOU!!
THAT'S NOT FAIR.
WHAT I WANT IS SOME TEM-PURA...
THUD
DAMN YOU!!
WHAT THE- HOW CAN HE STILL STAND?
HEH... HEH...
WELL, AT LEAST THIS ISN'T AS BAD AS BEING TORTURED BY THE NAZIS...
KRAK

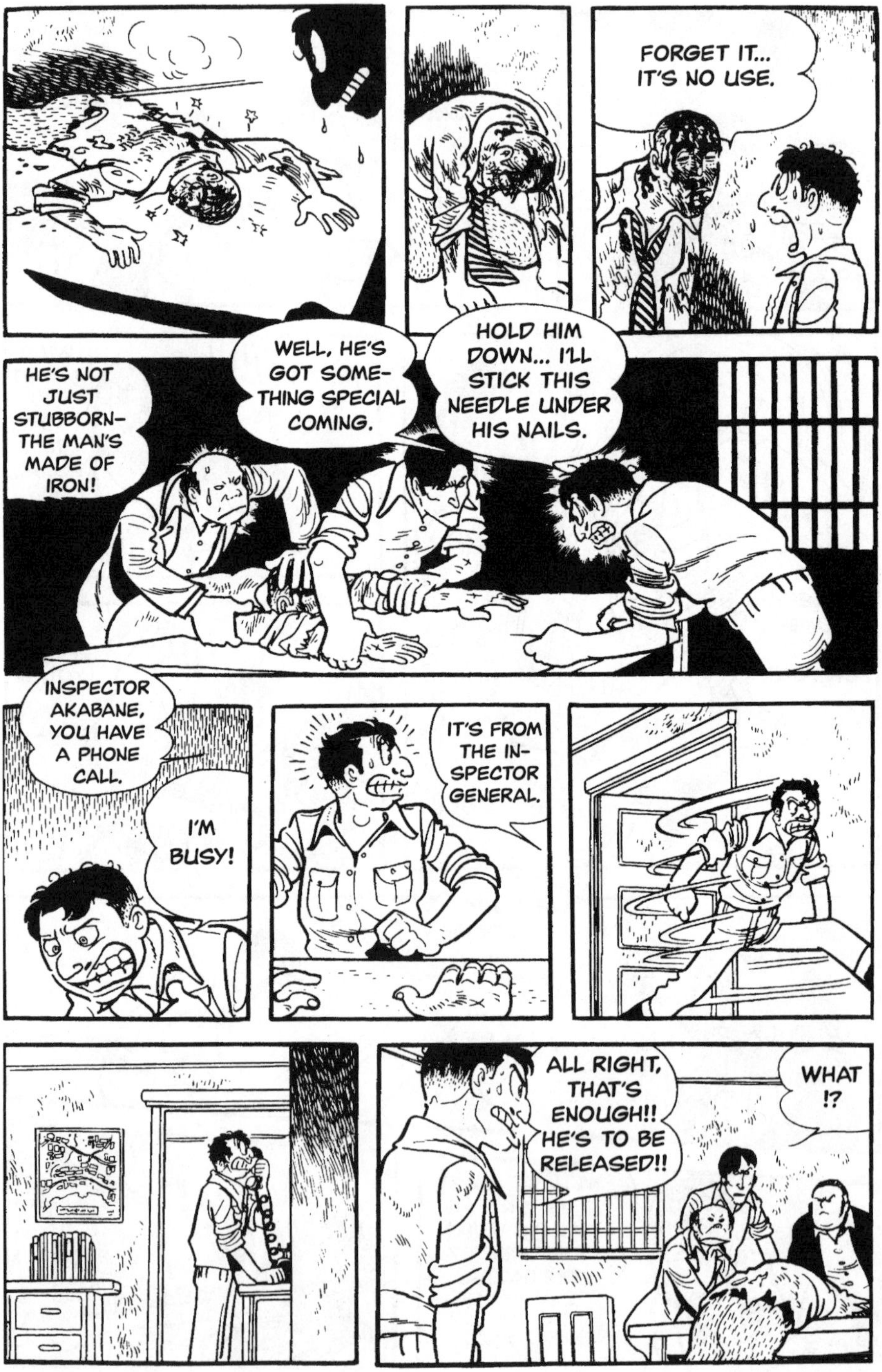
FORGET IT... IT'S NO USE.
HE'S NOT JUST STUBBORN– THE MAN'S MADE OF IRON!
WELL, HE'S GOT SOME-THING SPECIAL COMING.
HOLD HIM DOWN... I'LL STICK THIS NEEDLE UNDER HIS NAILS.
INSPECTOR AKABANE, YOU HAVE A PHONE CALL.
I'M BUSY!
IT'S FROM THE IN-SPECTOR GENERAL.
ALL RIGHT, THAT'S ENOUGH!! HE'S TO BE RELEASED!!
WHAT !?

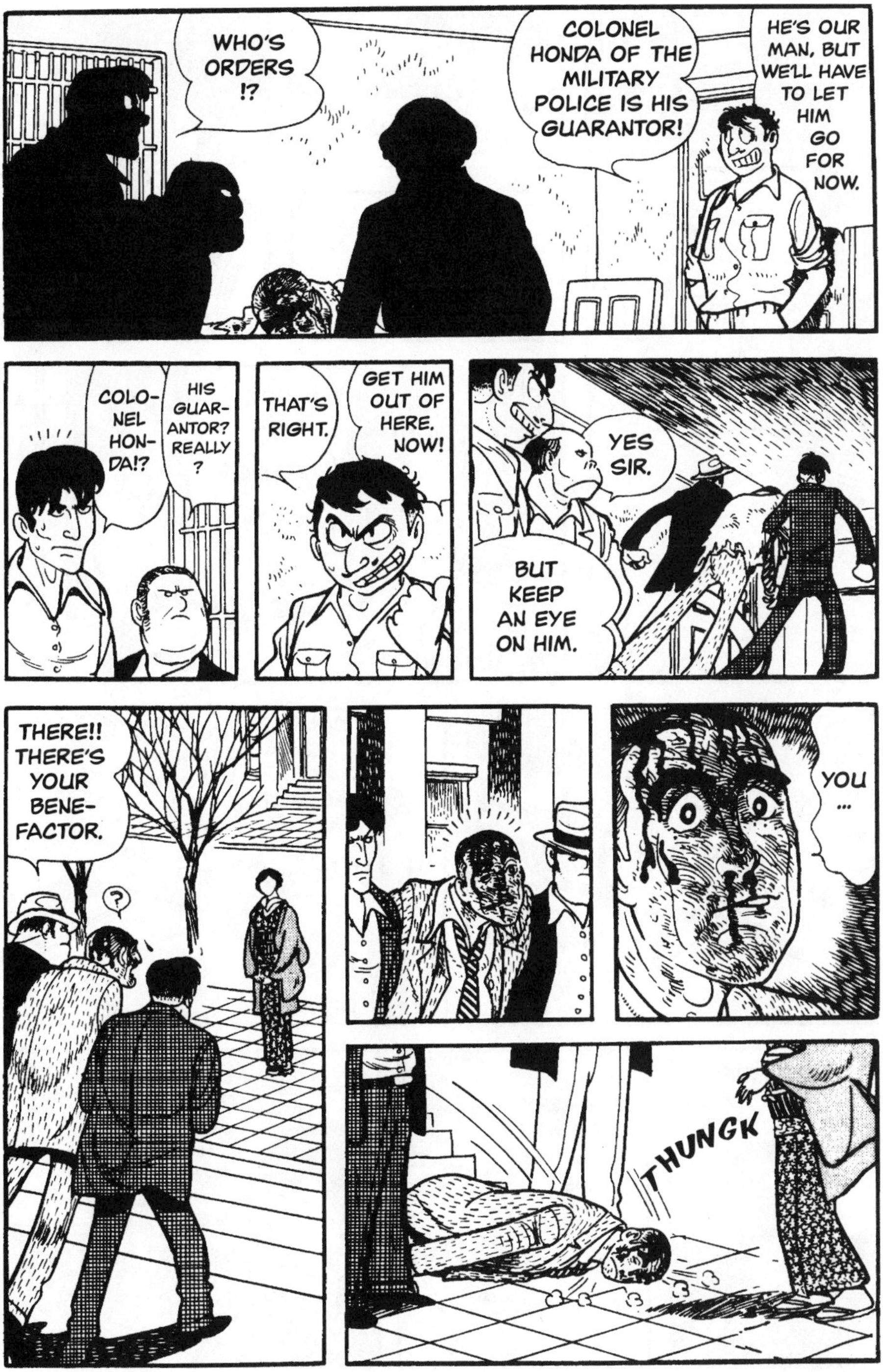
WHO'S ORDERS !?
COLONEL HONDA OF THE MILITARY POLICE IS HIS GUARANTOR!
HE'S OUR MAN, BUT WE'LL HAVE TO LET HIM GO FOR NOW.
COLO-NEL HON-DA!?
HIS GUAR-ANTOR? REALLY ?
THAT'S RIGHT.
GET HIM OUT OF HERE. NOW!
YES SIR.
BUT KEEP AN EYE ON HIM.
THERE!! THERE'S YOUR BENE-FACTOR.
?
YOU ...
THUNGK

Adolf

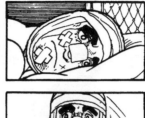

IT'S YOU!

HOW ARE YOU FEELING?

SO YOU'RE THE ONE WHO SAV-ED ME...

SAVED ME FROM THE POLICE... AND THE TORTURE...

I DON'T HAVE THAT KIND OF POWER.

COLONEL HONDA ACTED AS YOUR GUARAN-TOR.

COLONEL HONDA? WHO'S TH-THAT...

UNH...

AN OLD FRIEND OF MINE. HE'LL BE HERE SOON.

WH-WHY ARE YOU HELPING ME?

PLEASE DON'T ASK ME THAT.

WHY? THERE MUST BE SOME REASON !!

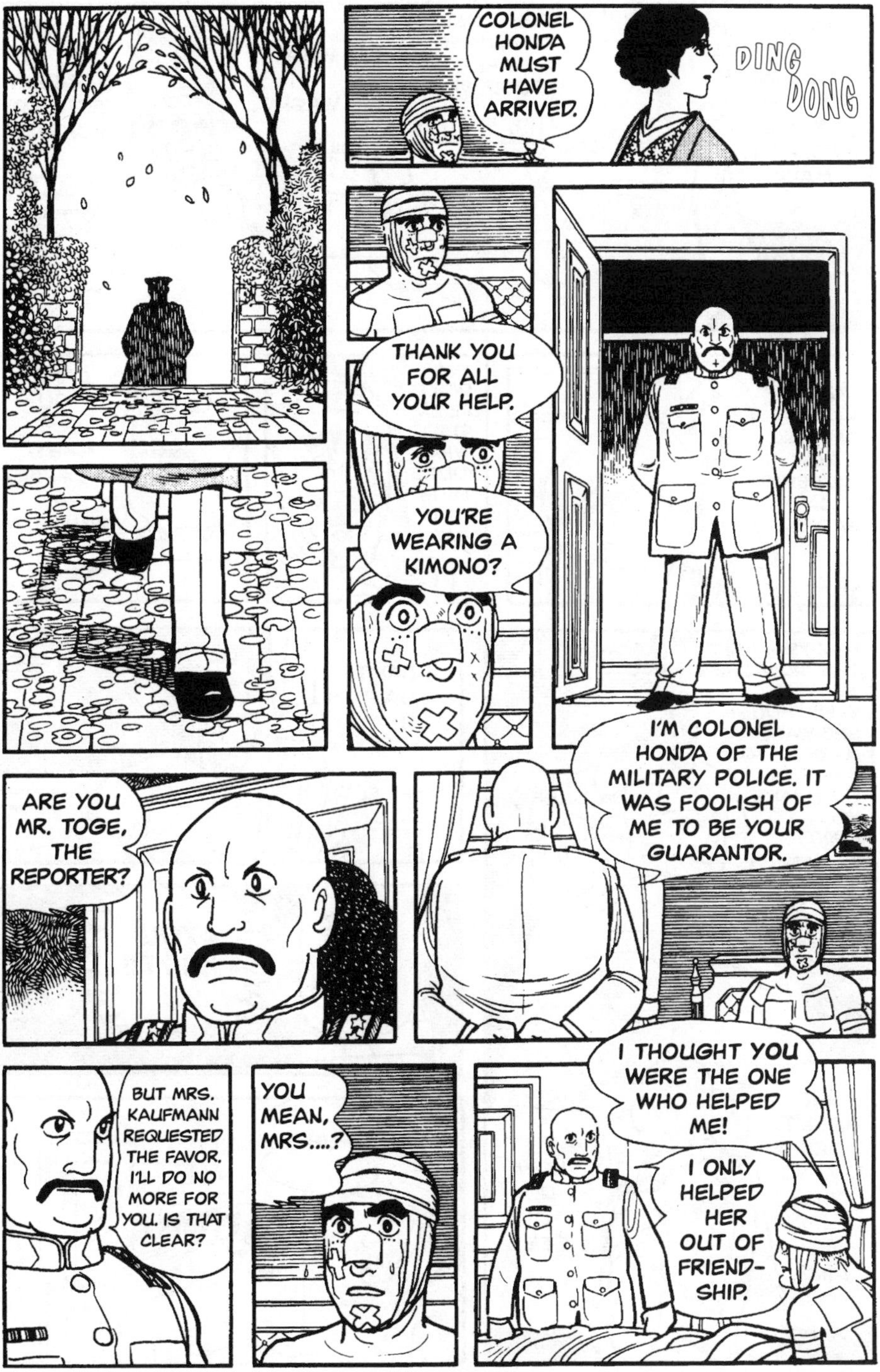
COLONEL HONDA MUST HAVE ARRIVED.
DING DONG
THANK YOU FOR ALL YOUR HELP.
YOU'RE WEARING A KIMONO?
I'M COLONEL HONDA OF THE MILITARY POLICE. IT WAS FOOLISH OF ME TO BE YOUR GUARANTOR.
ARE YOU MR. TOGE, THE REPORTER?
BUT MRS. KAUFMANN REQUESTED THE FAVOR. I'LL DO NO MORE FOR YOU. IS THAT CLEAR?
YOU MEAN, MRS....?
I THOUGHT YOU WERE THE ONE WHO HELPED ME!
I ONLY HELPED HER OUT OF FRIEND-SHIP.

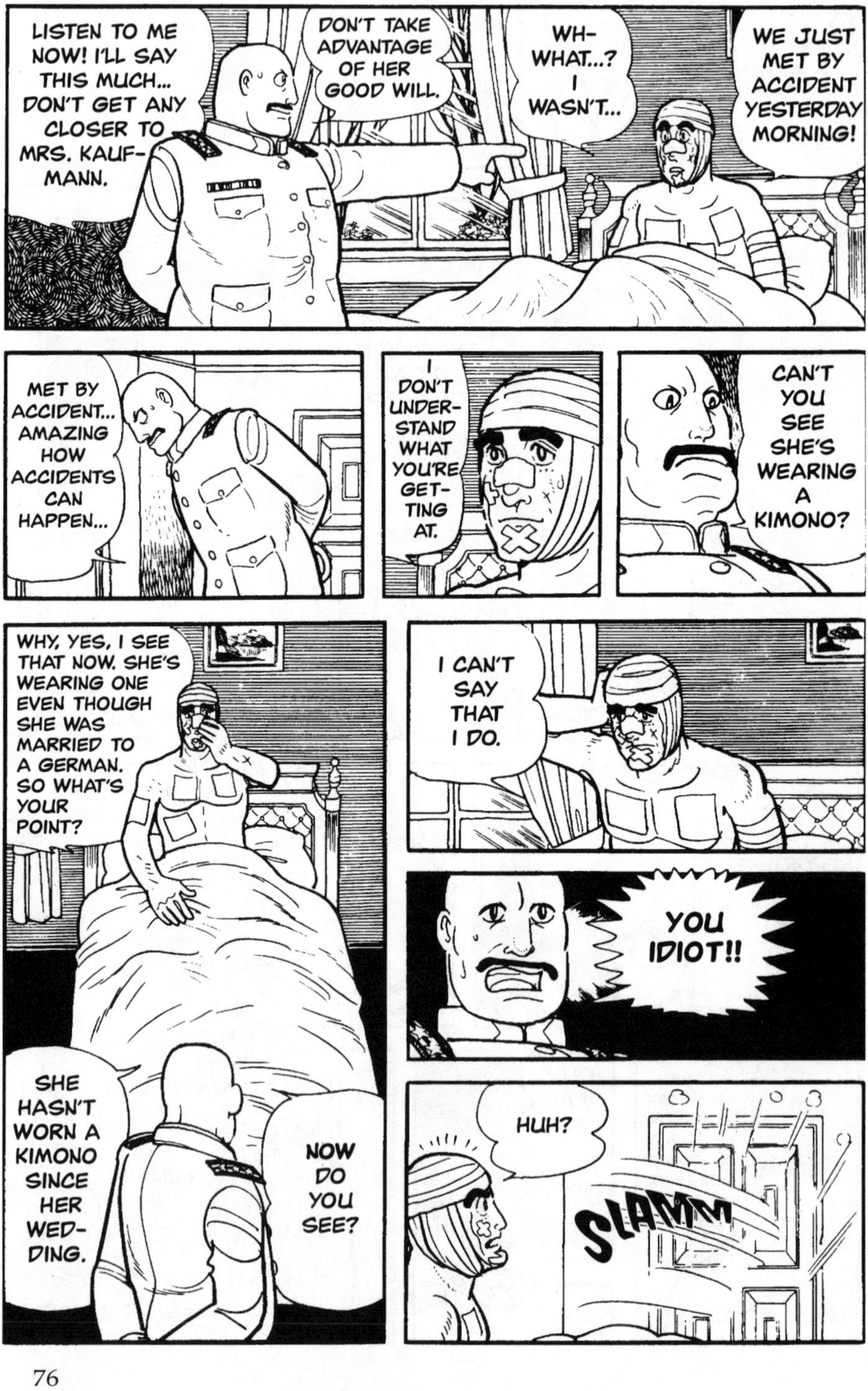
LISTEN TO ME NOW! I'LL SAY THIS MUCH... DON'T GET ANY CLOSER TO MRS. KAUFMANN.
DON'T TAKE ADVANTAGE OF HER GOOD WILL.
WH-WHAT...? I WASN'T...
WE JUST MET BY ACCIDENT YESTERDAY MORNING!
MET BY ACCIDENT... AMAZING HOW ACCIDENTS CAN HAPPEN...
I DON'T UNDERSTAND WHAT YOU'RE GETTING AT.
CAN'T YOU SEE SHE'S WEARING A KIMONO?
WHY, YES, I SEE THAT NOW. SHE'S WEARING ONE EVEN THOUGH SHE WAS MARRIED TO A GERMAN. SO WHAT'S YOUR POINT?
SHE HASN'T WORN A KIMONO SINCE HER WEDDING.
NOW DO YOU SEE?
I CAN'T SAY THAT I DO.
YOU IDIOT!!
HUH?
SLAMM

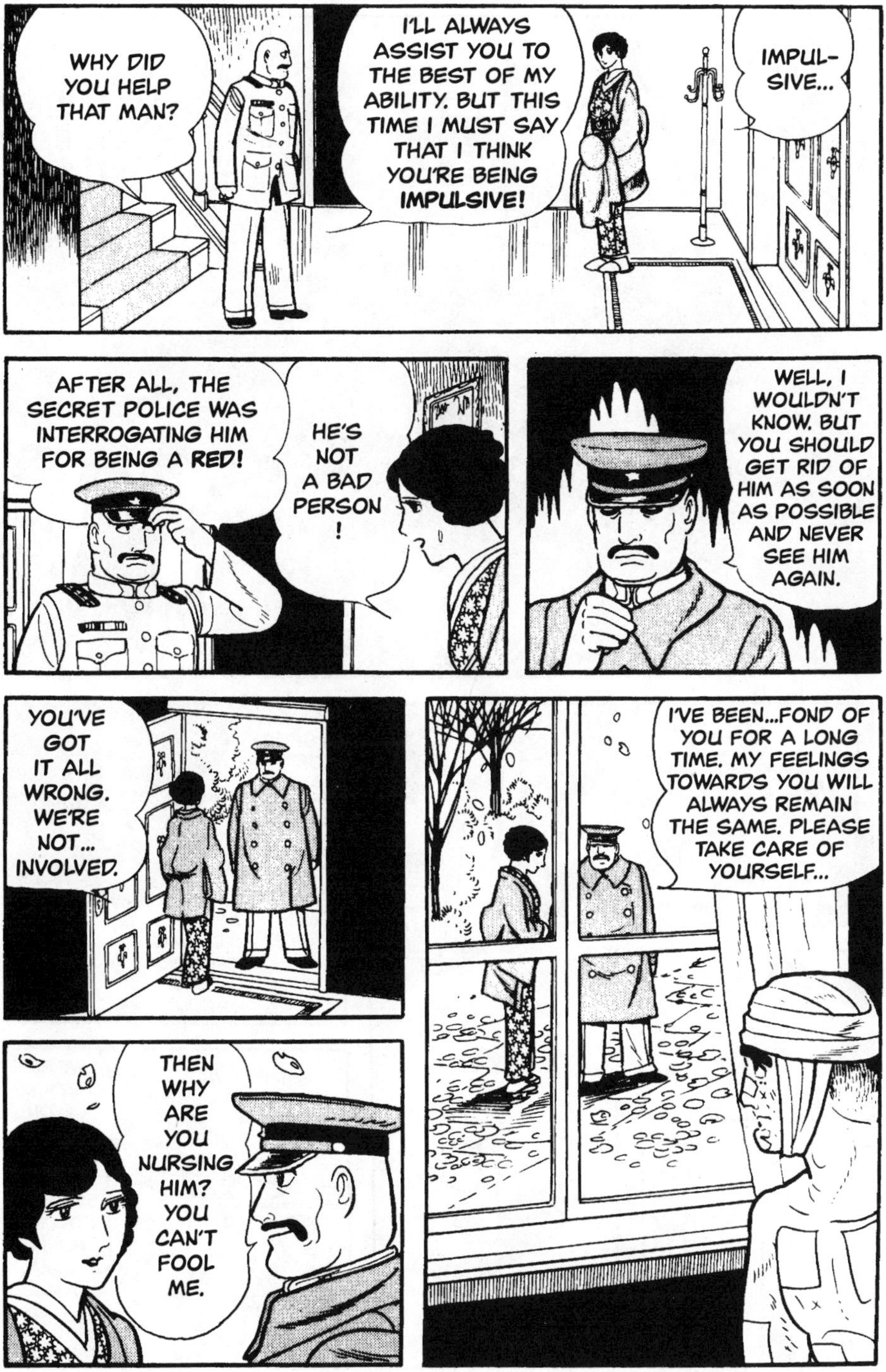
WHY DID YOU HELP THAT MAN?
I'LL ALWAYS ASSIST YOU TO THE BEST OF MY ABILITY. BUT THIS TIME I MUST SAY THAT I THINK YOU'RE BEING IMPULSIVE!
IMPUL-SIVE...
AFTER ALL, THE SECRET POLICE WAS INTERROGATING HIM FOR BEING A RED!
HE'S NOT A BAD PERSON!
WELL, I WOULDN'T KNOW. BUT YOU SHOULD GET RID OF HIM AS SOON AS POSSIBLE AND NEVER SEE HIM AGAIN.
YOU'VE GOT IT ALL WRONG. WE'RE NOT... INVOLVED.
THEN WHY ARE YOU NURSING HIM? YOU CAN'T FOOL ME.
I'VE BEEN...FOND OF YOU FOR A LONG TIME. MY FEELINGS TOWARDS YOU WILL ALWAYS REMAIN THE SAME. PLEASE TAKE CARE OF YOURSELF...

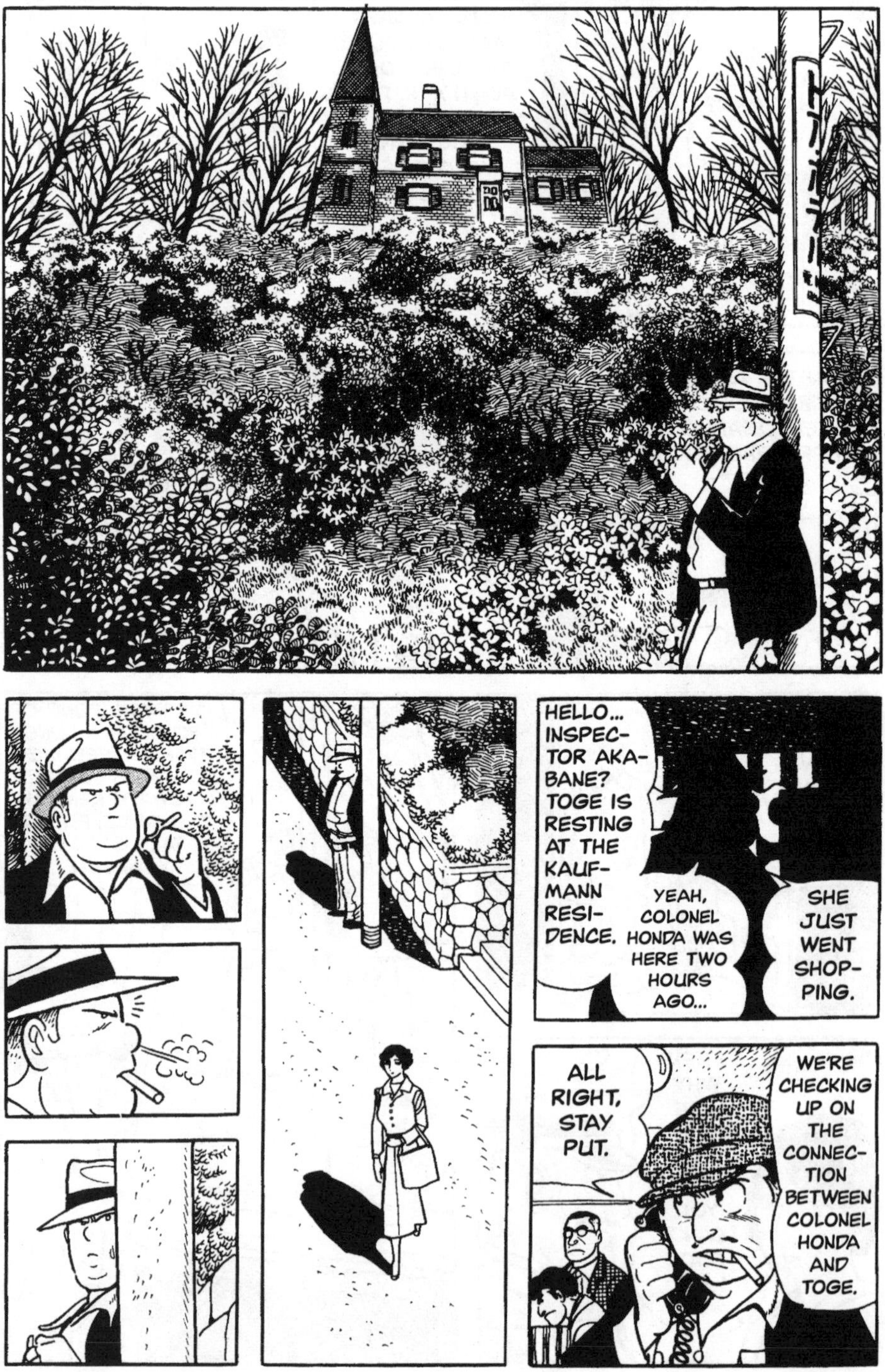
HELLO... INSPECTOR AKABANE? TOGE IS RESTING AT THE KAUFMANN RESIDENCE.
YEAH, COLONEL HONDA WAS HERE TWO HOURS AGO...
SHE JUST WENT SHOPPING.
ALL RIGHT, STAY PUT.
WE'RE CHECKING UP ON THE CONNECTION BETWEEN COLONEL HONDA AND TOGE.

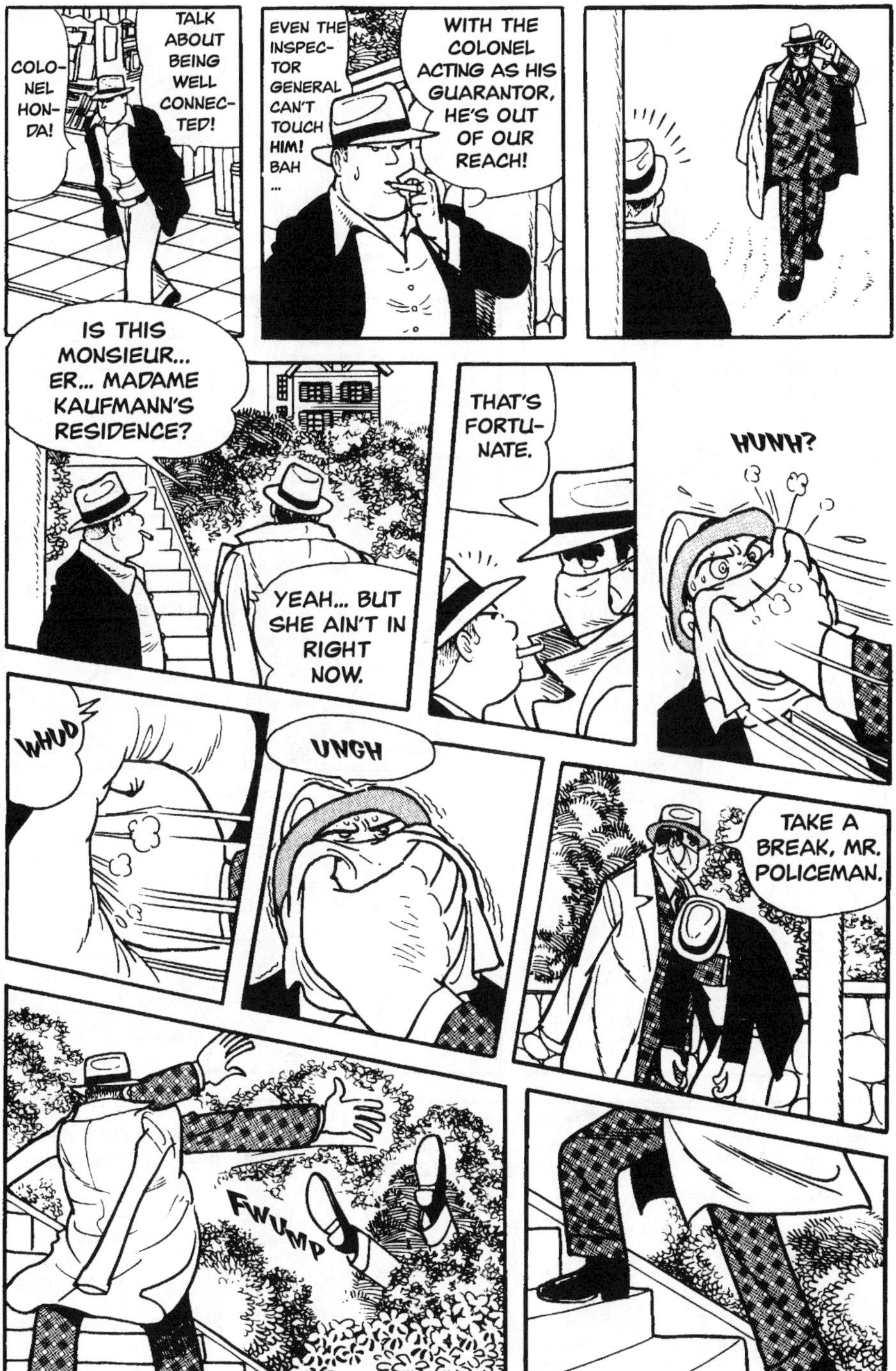
COLONEL HONDA!
TALK ABOUT BEING WELL CONNECTED!
EVEN THE INSPECTOR GENERAL CAN'T TOUCH HIM! BAH ...
WITH THE COLONEL ACTING AS HIS GUARANTOR, HE'S OUT OF OUR REACH!
IS THIS MONSIEUR... ER... MADAME KAUFMANN'S RESIDENCE?
YEAH... BUT SHE AIN'T IN RIGHT NOW.
THAT'S FORTUNATE.
HUNH?
WHUD
UNGH
TAKE A BREAK, MR. POLICEMAN.
FWUMP

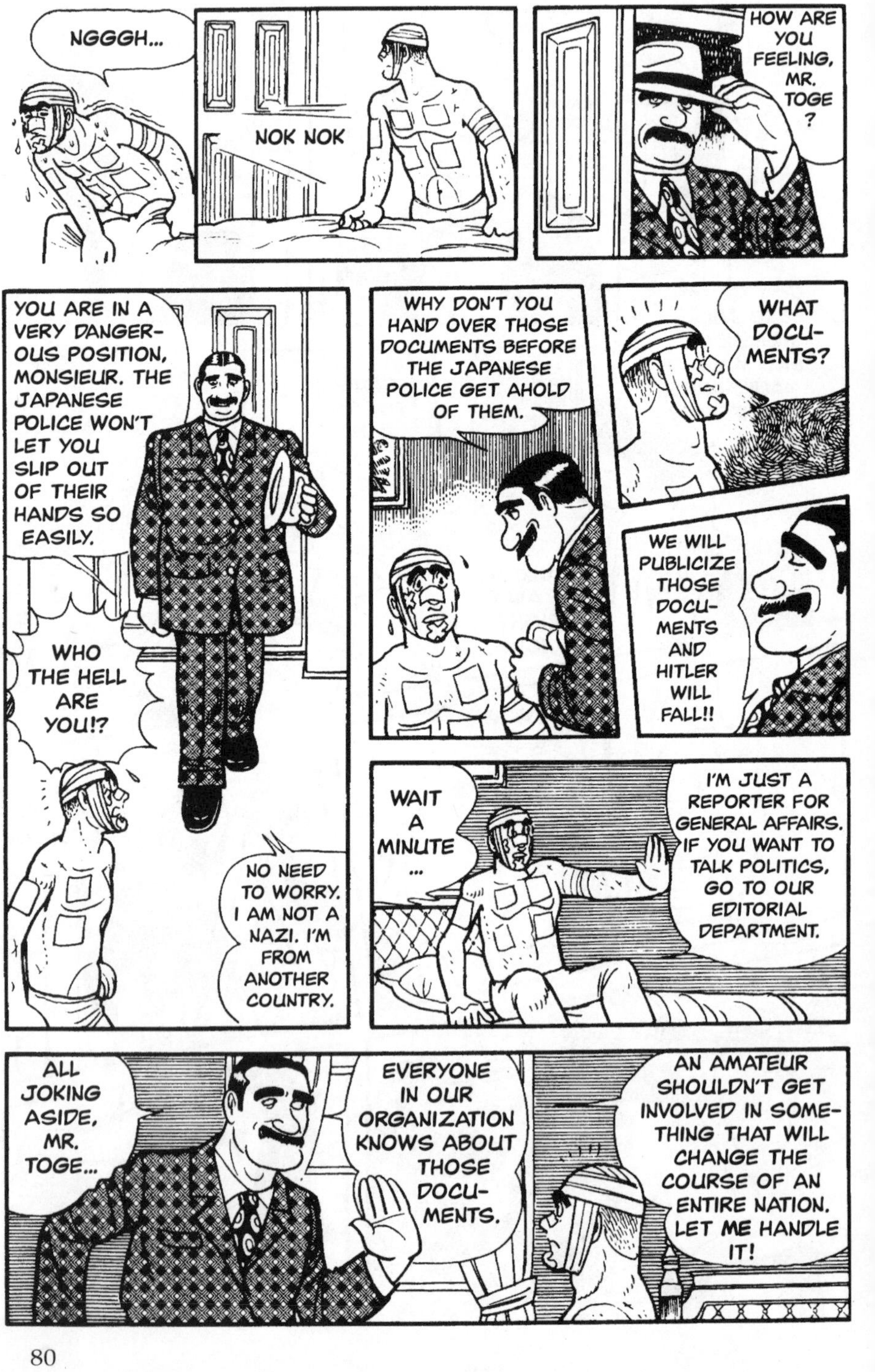
NGGGH...
NOK NOK
HOW ARE YOU FEELING, MR. TOGE?
YOU ARE IN A VERY DANGER-OUS POSITION, MONSIEUR. THE JAPANESE POLICE WON'T LET YOU SLIP OUT OF THEIR HANDS SO EASILY.
WHO THE HELL ARE YOU!?
NO NEED TO WORRY. I AM NOT A NAZI. I'M FROM ANOTHER COUNTRY.
WHY DON'T YOU HAND OVER THOSE DOCUMENTS BEFORE THE JAPANESE POLICE GET AHOLD OF THEM.
WHAT DOCU-MENTS?
WE WILL PUBLICIZE THOSE DOCU-MENTS AND HITLER WILL FALL!!
WAIT A MINUTE ...
I'M JUST A REPORTER FOR GENERAL AFFAIRS. IF YOU WANT TO TALK POLITICS, GO TO OUR EDITORIAL DEPARTMENT.
ALL JOKING ASIDE, MR. TOGE...
EVERYONE IN OUR ORGANIZATION KNOWS ABOUT THOSE DOCU-MENTS.
AN AMATEUR SHOULDN'T GET INVOLVED IN SOME-THING THAT WILL CHANGE THE COURSE OF AN ENTIRE NATION. LET ME HANDLE IT!

GET OUT OF HERE!

I HAVE NOTHING TO GIVE YOU!!

WE ARE NOT FANATICS LIKE THE JAPANESE POLICE, NOR ARE WE CRUEL LIKE THE GESTAPO.

WE ARE OPEN TO NEGOTIATION. WE WILL BUY THOSE DOCUMENTS FOR 50,000 YEN. WE'LL PAY IMMEDIATELY, IN CASH.

50,000 YEN!?

OUI!! YOU'LL MAKE MONEY, AND, I ASSURE YOU, YOU'LL FEEL MUCH SAFER.

WHAT A SHAME...

YOU DON'T SEEM TO UNDERSTAND. WELL THEN...

OW, OW, OW. MY HEAD'S GONNA SPLIT. ALL THE BLOOD'S GOING TO MY HEAD. I CAN FEEL THE WOUNDS.

THAT'S TOO BAD.

IF YOU LOSE YOUR MIND, YOU'LL LOSE THE DOCUMENTS, AND ALL WILL BE TIED IN KNOTS.

YOU MEAN ALL WILL BE FOR NAUGHT!!

OUI, FOR KNOT.

WELL THEN, CALL ME WHEN YOU FEEL BETTER. PLEASE THINK IT OVER... YOU'RE SMART ENOUGH TO KNOW WHAT'S IN YOUR BEST INTEREST.

AU REVOIR, MONSIEUR.

THOK
THOK
THOK

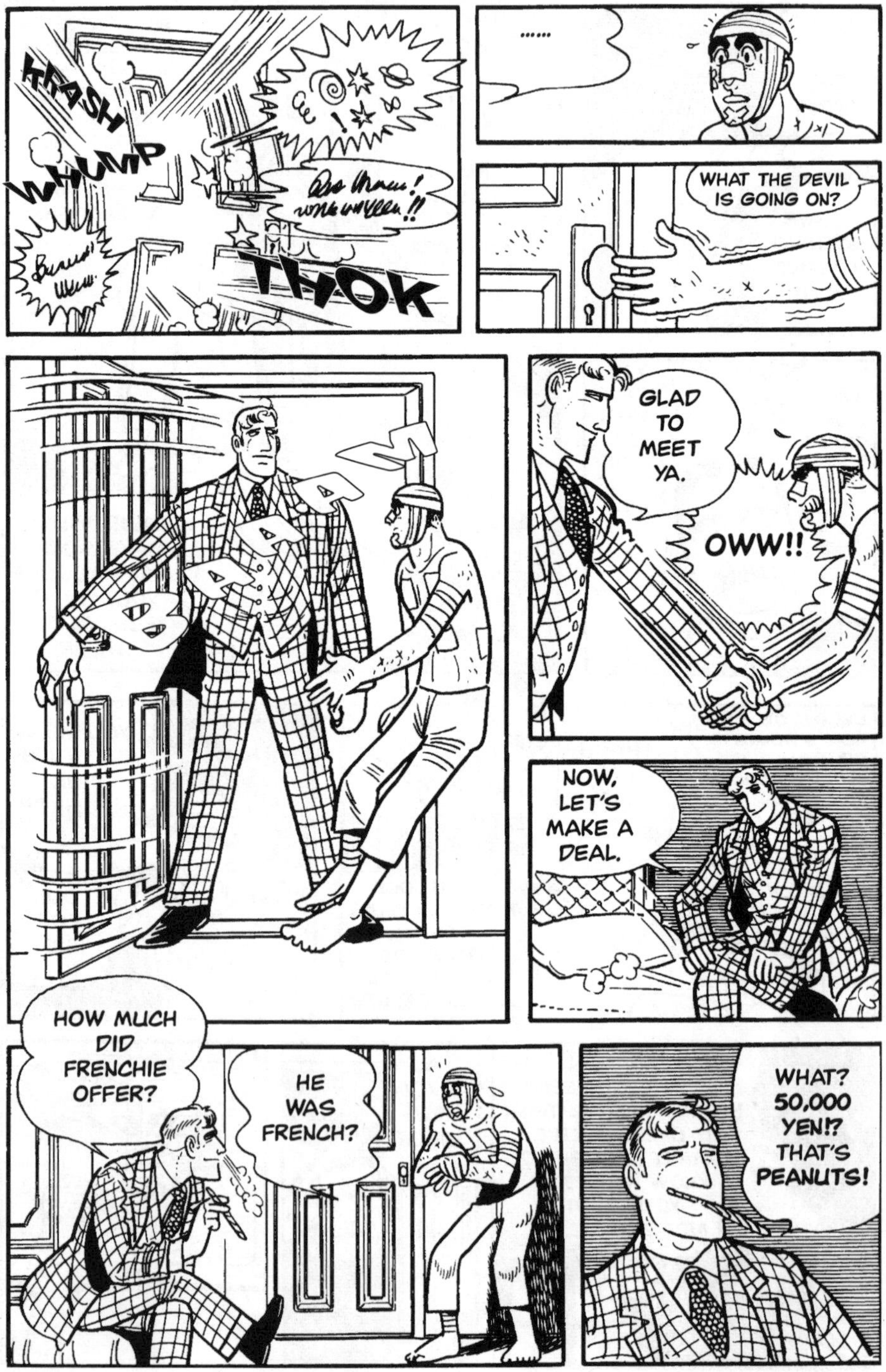
KRASH
WHUMP
THOK
......
WHAT THE DEVIL IS GOING ON?
GLAD TO MEET YA.
OWW!!
NOW, LET'S MAKE A DEAL.
HOW MUCH DID FRENCHIE OFFER?
HE WAS FRENCH?
WHAT? 50,000 YEN!? THAT'S PEANUTS!

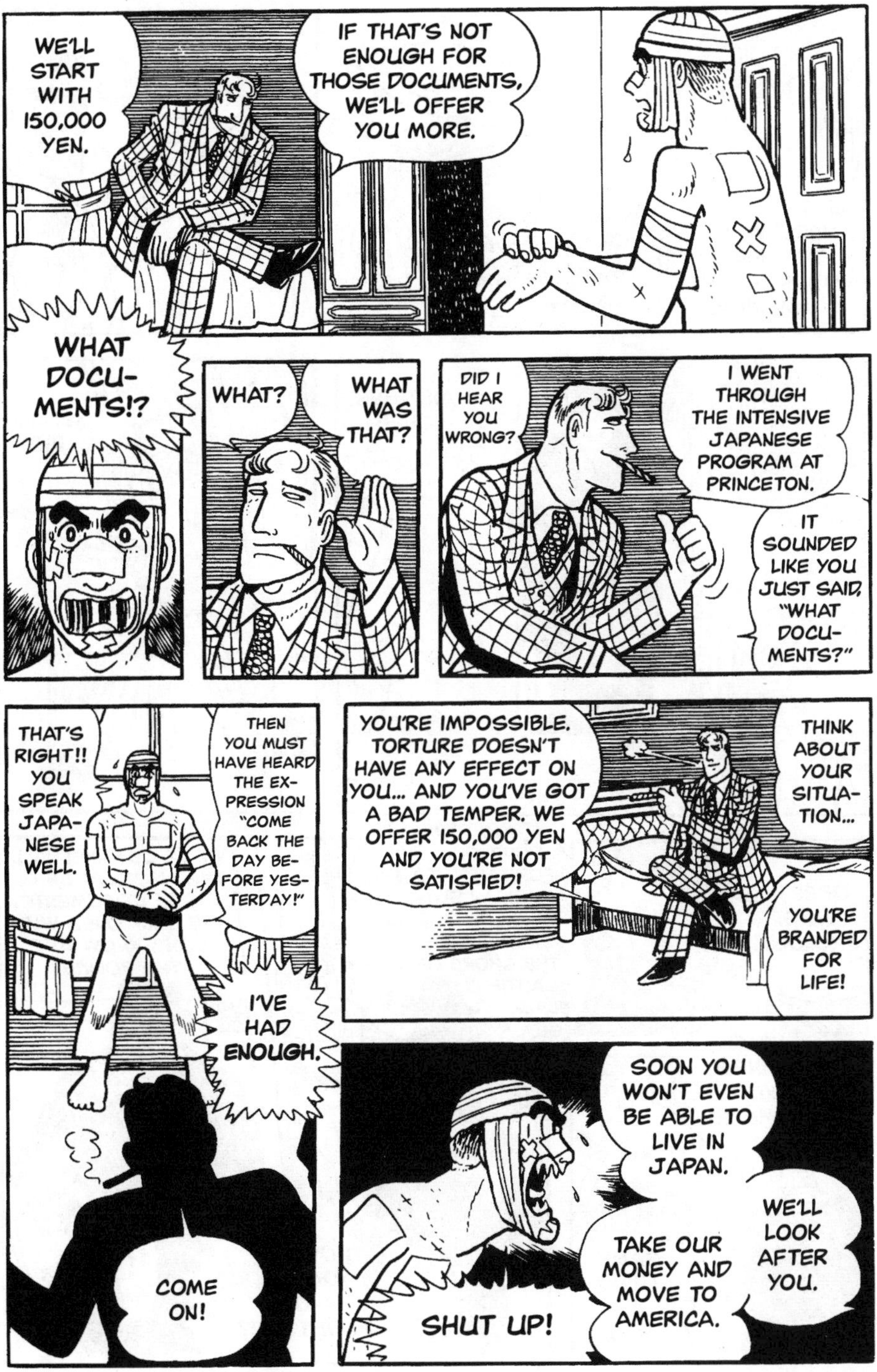
WE'LL START WITH 150,000 YEN.
IF THAT'S NOT ENOUGH FOR THOSE DOCUMENTS, WE'LL OFFER YOU MORE.
WHAT DOCU-MENTS!?
WHAT?
WHAT WAS THAT?
DID I HEAR YOU WRONG?
I WENT THROUGH THE INTENSIVE JAPANESE PROGRAM AT PRINCETON.
IT SOUNDED LIKE YOU JUST SAID, "WHAT DOCU-MENTS?"
THAT'S RIGHT!! YOU SPEAK JAPA-NESE WELL.
THEN YOU MUST HAVE HEARD THE EX-PRESSION "COME BACK THE DAY BE-FORE YES-TERDAY!"
I'VE HAD ENOUGH.
COME ON!
YOU'RE IMPOSSIBLE. TORTURE DOESN'T HAVE ANY EFFECT ON YOU... AND YOU'VE GOT A BAD TEMPER. WE OFFER 150,000 YEN AND YOU'RE NOT SATISFIED!
THINK ABOUT YOUR SITUA-TION...
YOU'RE BRANDED FOR LIFE!
SOON YOU WON'T EVEN BE ABLE TO LIVE IN JAPAN.
SHUT UP!
TAKE OUR MONEY AND MOVE TO AMERICA.
WE'LL LOOK AFTER YOU.

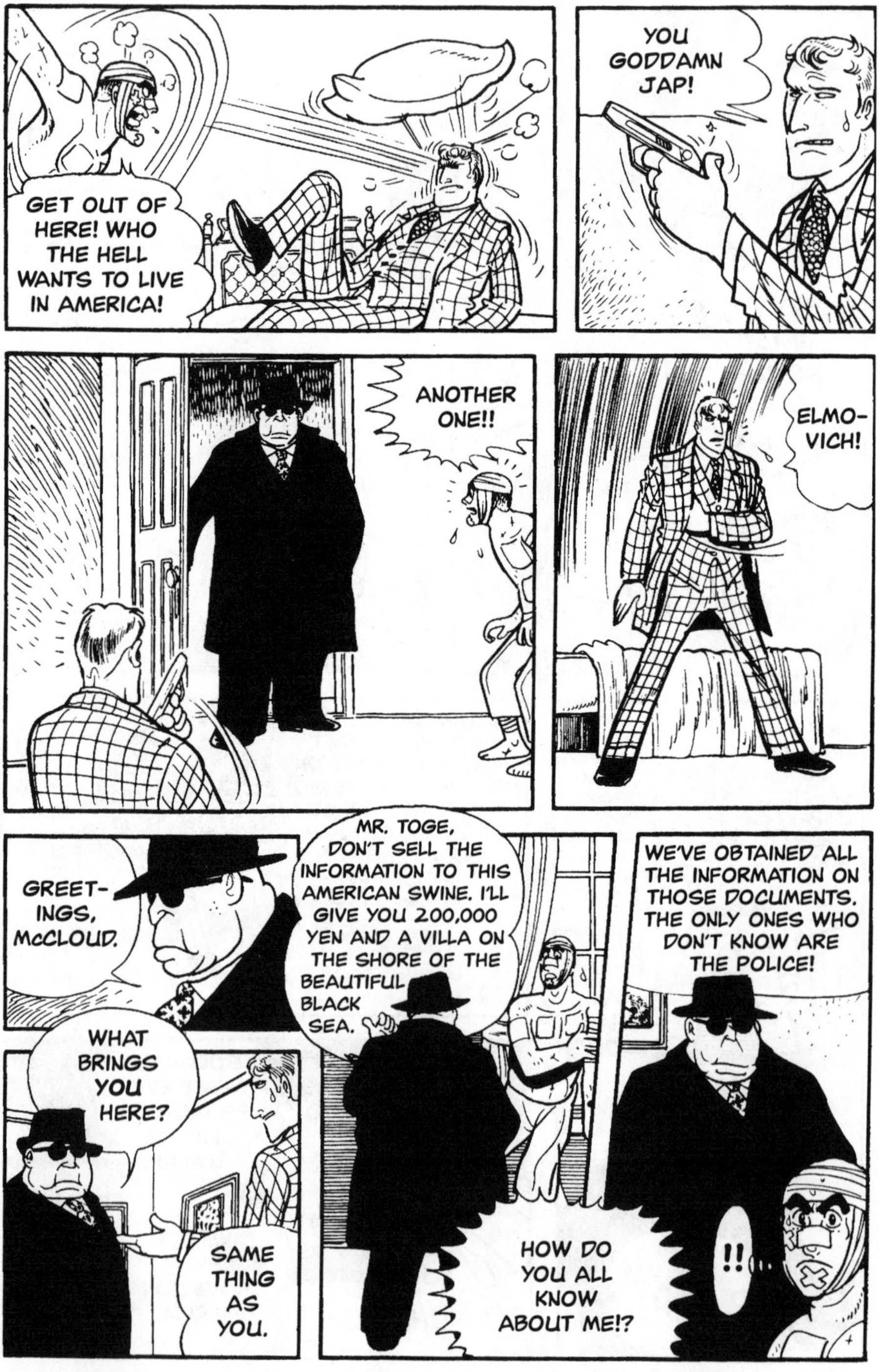
GET OUT OF HERE! WHO THE HELL WANTS TO LIVE IN AMERICA!
YOU GODDAMN JAP!
ANOTHER ONE!!
ELMO-VICH!
GREET-INGS, McCLOUD.
WHAT BRINGS YOU HERE?
SAME THING AS YOU.
MR. TOGE, DON'T SELL THE INFORMATION TO THIS AMERICAN SWINE. I'LL GIVE YOU 200,000 YEN AND A VILLA ON THE SHORE OF THE BEAUTIFUL BLACK SEA.
WE'VE OBTAINED ALL THE INFORMATION ON THOSE DOCUMENTS. THE ONLY ONES WHO DON'T KNOW ARE THE POLICE!
!!
HOW DO YOU ALL KNOW ABOUT ME!?

GET OUT OF HERE— NOW!

MRS. KAUFMANN IS COMING BACK SOON. YOU DON'T WANT TO CAUSE A SCENE, DO YOU!?

THAT'S RIGHT.

IT WOULDN'T LOOK GOOD FOR SPIES TO BE CAUGHT QUARRELING OUT IN THE OPEN. I'LL COME BACK LATER.

I'LL MAKE MY OFFER ONCE MORE, MR. TOGE. GIVE US THE DOCUMENTS. DOSVIDANYA.

PHEW. WHAT A RELIEF.

I CAN'T BELIEVE THEY ALL KNOW ABOUT THOSE DOCUMENTS!

I'VE GOT TO GET OUT OF HERE! I'VE CAUSED MRS. KAUFMANN ENOUGH TROUBLE...

"I FEEL THAT I CANNOT TAKE ADVANTAGE OF YOUR GENEROUS HOSPITALITY ANY LONGER..."

GOODBYE...

1939 TIMELINE

January 4-5	Japan's premier, Prince Konoye, resigns, and Baron Kiichiro Hiranuma is named his successor.
January 12	President Roosevelt outlines a U.S. rearmament program costing $552 million.
January 24	Göring directs the SS to accelerate the emigration and evacuation of Jews from Germany as a solution to the "Jewish problem."
February 21	The German government demands Jews surrender all their gold and silver.
February 27	Britain and France recognize the Franco government in Spain, sounding the final death knell for the Loyalist cause.
March 15	German troops enter Prague and absorb Bohemia and Moravia into Greater Germany, leading to the mass flight of Czech Jews.
March 28	The Spanish Civil War ends.
May 3	Hungary enacts highly restrictive anti-Semitic laws and plans to expel all Jews within five years.
May 17	Britain announces its intention to establish a unified independent Palestine, with Jewish immigration limited to 75,000 over the next five years and none thereafter, unless agreed to by the Arabs.
May 22	The Pact of Steel, a military alliance, is forged between Germany and Italy.
August 20-25	The Soviet Far Eastern Army and the Japanese Kwantung Army engage in battle in Outer Mongolia. The Japanese suffer their worst military setback in modern history.
August 23	The German-Russian Nonaggression Pact is signed in Moscow. Japan renounces the Anti-Comintern Pact to oppose Communism.
September 1	Germany invades Poland, thereby beginning World War II. German Jews are placed under curfew and their radios are confiscated.
September 3	Britain and France declare war on Germany.
September 14	Moscow and Japan agree to a cease-fire.

September 17	Russia invades Poland.
September 21	The dissolution of Polish Jewish communities begins. Jews are forced to resettle in overcrowded ghettos cut off from the outside world. Jews and gypsies are expelled from areas of Poland annexed to Greater Germany.
September 29	Germany and the Soviet Union sign a boundary and friendship treaty, formally dividing Poland.
October 6	Hitler delivers a Reichstag speech in which he indicates Germany is now content with its conquests and willing to make peace with the Allies: "Germany has no further claims against France....nowhere have I ever acted contrary to British interest."
October 7	Hitler issues his "Strengthening of Germanhood Decree," providing for "the elimination of the harmful influence of nationally alien populations, which constitute a danger to the Reich and the German community."
November 4	The United States Congress repeals the U.S. Neutrality Law.
November 23	Jews in occupied Poland are forced to wear Star of David identification badges.
November 30	Russia invades Finland.
December 12	Jewish labor camps are set up throughout German-occupied Poland. All Jewish males between the ages of 14 and 60 are compelled to report for forced labor.
December 14	The League of Nations expels Russia.
December 30	Hitler vows to continue the war: "The Jewish reactionary warmongers have awaited this hour for years. They have prepared and are unwilling to cancel their plans for the destruction of Germany. Those warmongers want war. They shall have it."

CHAPTER
THREE

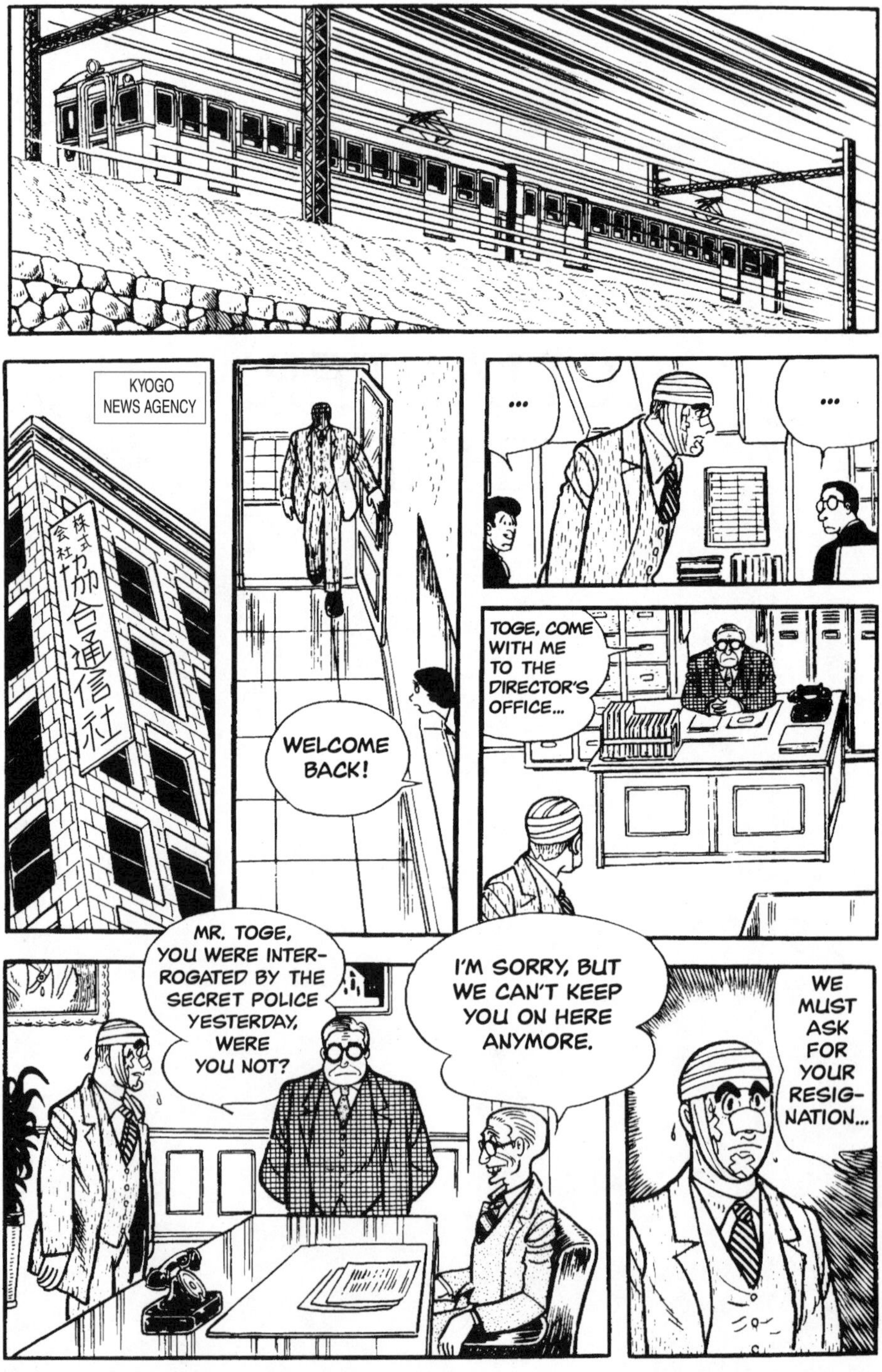
KYOGO
NEWS AGENCY
株式会社 協合通信社
WELCOME BACK!
...
...
TOGE, COME WITH ME TO THE DIRECTOR'S OFFICE...
MR. TOGE, YOU WERE INTER-ROGATED BY THE SECRET POLICE YESTERDAY, WERE YOU NOT?
I'M SORRY, BUT WE CAN'T KEEP YOU ON HERE ANYMORE.
WE MUST ASK FOR YOUR RESIG-NATION...

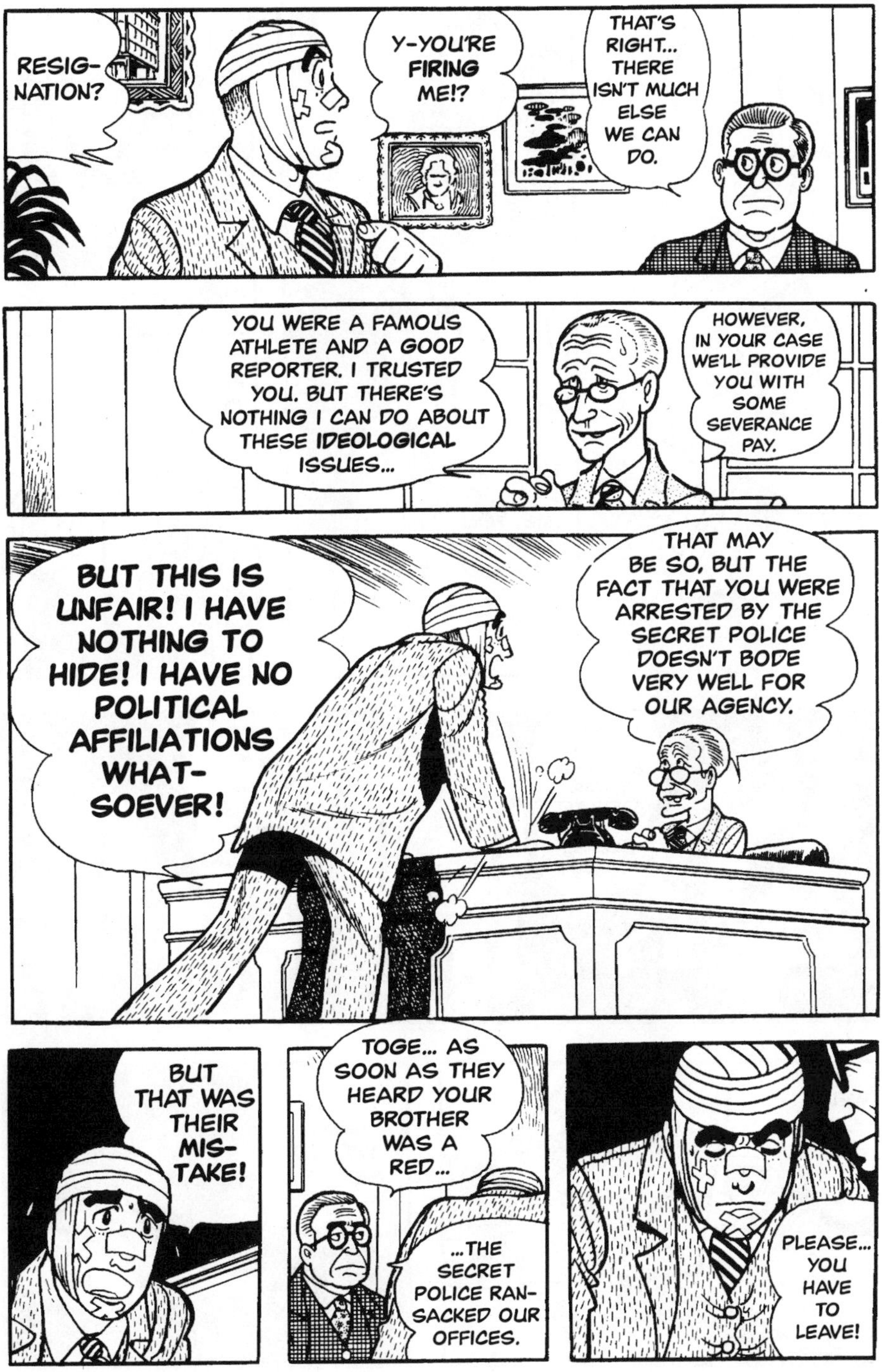
RESIG-NATION?
Y-YOU'RE FIRING ME!?
THAT'S RIGHT... THERE ISN'T MUCH ELSE WE CAN DO.
YOU WERE A FAMOUS ATHLETE AND A GOOD REPORTER. I TRUSTED YOU. BUT THERE'S NOTHING I CAN DO ABOUT THESE IDEOLOGICAL ISSUES...
HOWEVER, IN YOUR CASE WE'LL PROVIDE YOU WITH SOME SEVERANCE PAY.
BUT THIS IS UNFAIR! I HAVE NOTHING TO HIDE! I HAVE NO POLITICAL AFFILIATIONS WHAT-SOEVER!
THAT MAY BE SO, BUT THE FACT THAT YOU WERE ARRESTED BY THE SECRET POLICE DOESN'T BODE VERY WELL FOR OUR AGENCY.
BUT THAT WAS THEIR MIS-TAKE!
TOGE... AS SOON AS THEY HEARD YOUR BROTHER WAS A RED...
...THE SECRET POLICE RAN-SACKED OUR OFFICES.
PLEASE... YOU HAVE TO LEAVE!

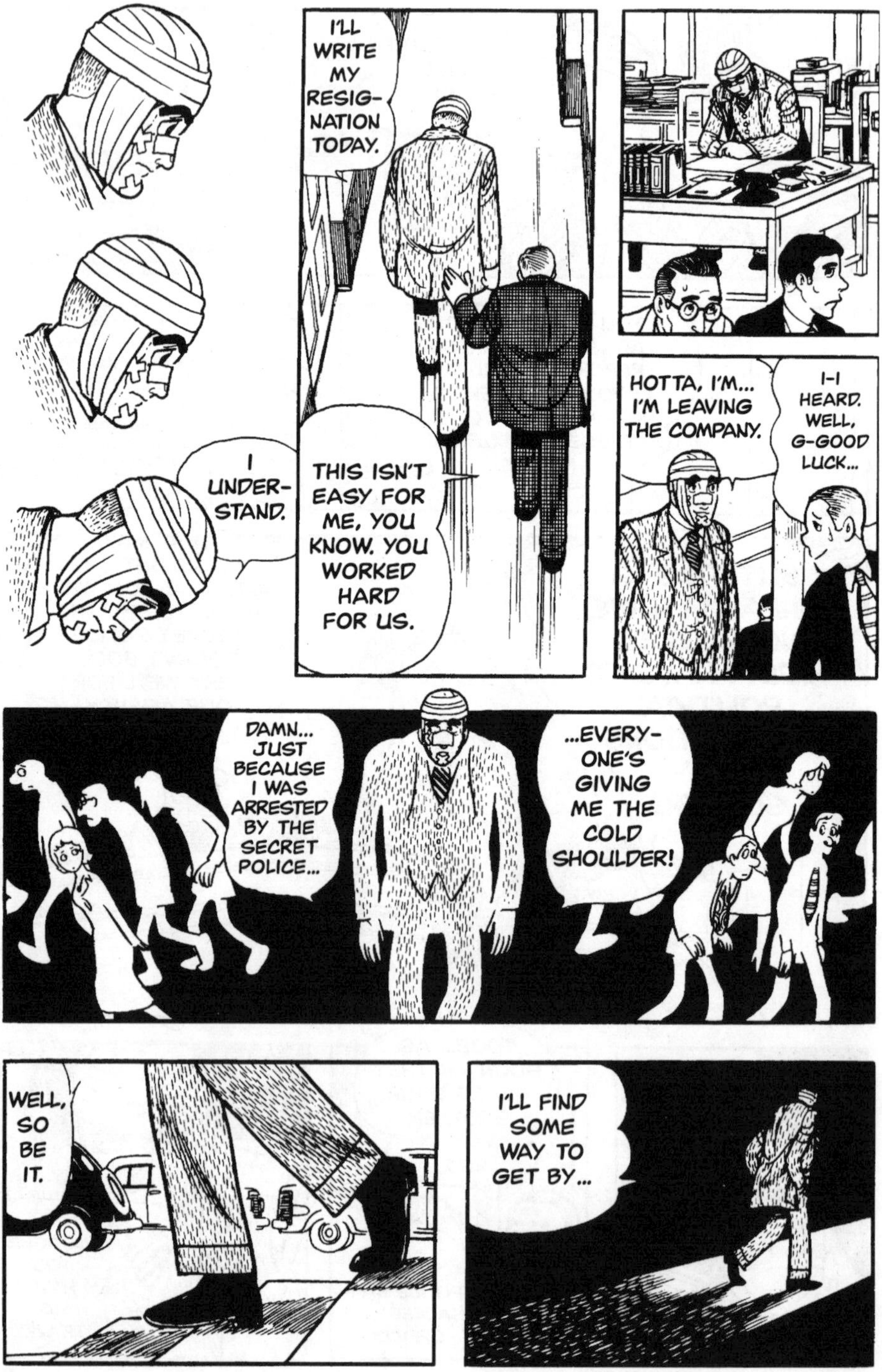
I UNDERSTAND.
I'LL WRITE MY RESIGNATION TODAY.
THIS ISN'T EASY FOR ME, YOU KNOW. YOU WORKED HARD FOR US.
HOTTA, I'M... I'M LEAVING THE COMPANY.
I-I HEARD. WELL, G-GOOD LUCK...
DAMN... JUST BECAUSE I WAS ARRESTED BY THE SECRET POLICE...
...EVERYONE'S GIVING ME THE COLD SHOULDER!
WELL, SO BE IT.
I'LL FIND SOME WAY TO GET BY...

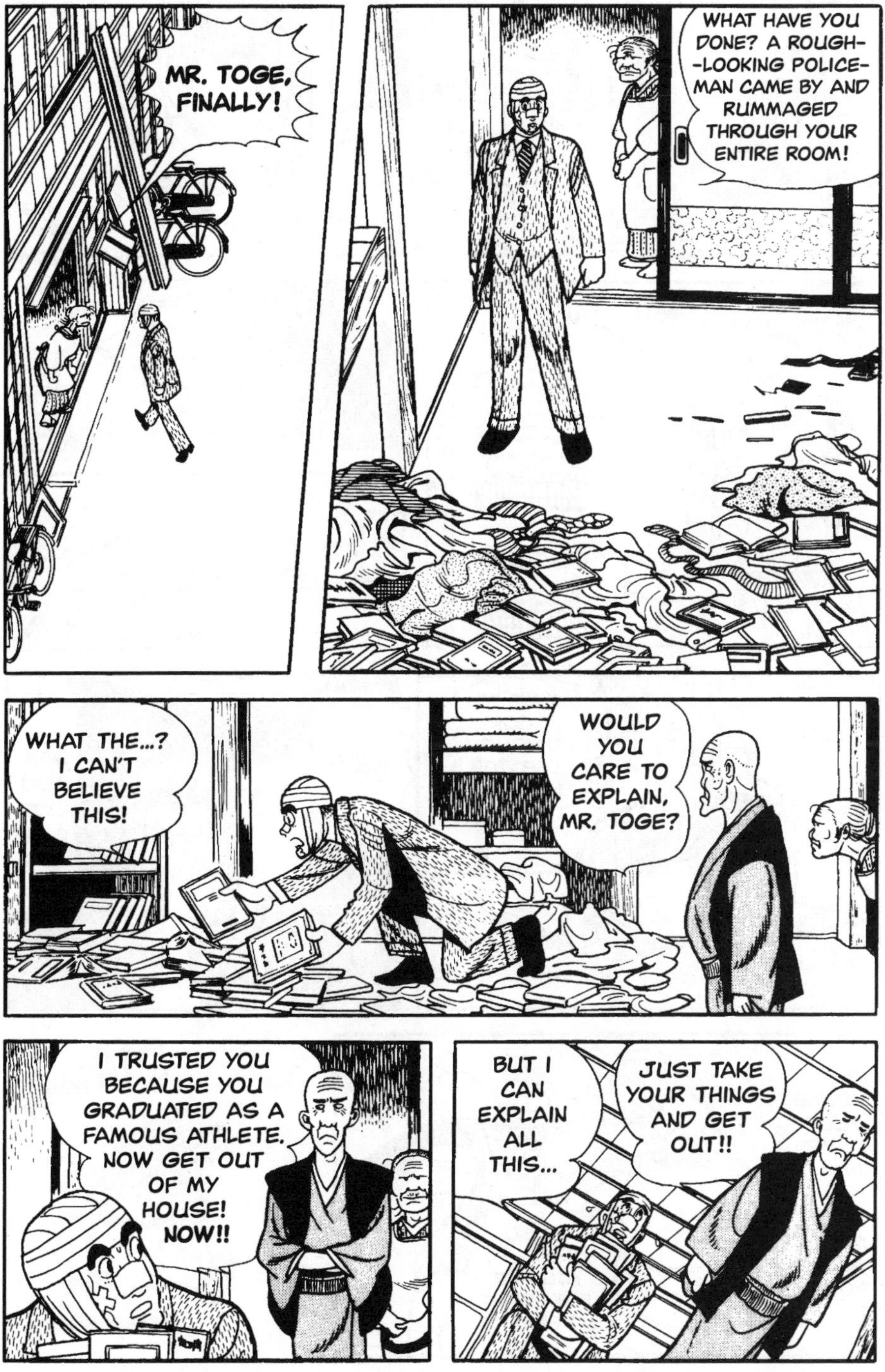
MR. TOGE, FINALLY!
WHAT HAVE YOU DONE? A ROUGH--LOOKING POLICEMAN CAME BY AND RUMMAGED THROUGH YOUR ENTIRE ROOM!
WHAT THE...? I CAN'T BELIEVE THIS!
WOULD YOU CARE TO EXPLAIN, MR. TOGE?
I TRUSTED YOU BECAUSE YOU GRADUATED AS A FAMOUS ATHLETE. NOW GET OUT OF MY HOUSE! NOW!!
BUT I CAN EXPLAIN ALL THIS...
JUST TAKE YOUR THINGS AND GET OUT!!

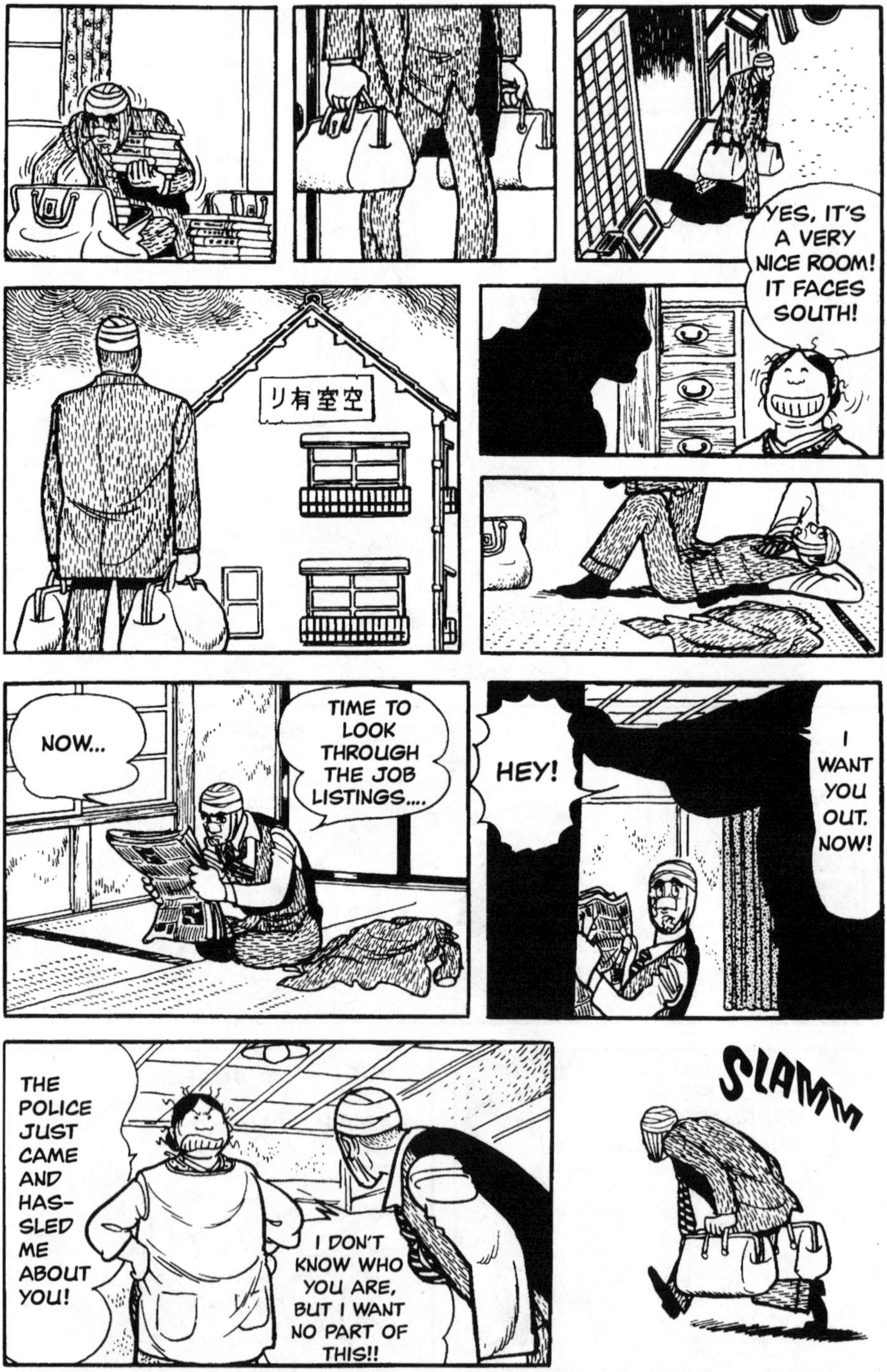
空室有リ
YES, IT'S A VERY NICE ROOM! IT FACES SOUTH!
NOW...
TIME TO LOOK THROUGH THE JOB LISTINGS....
HEY!
I WANT YOU OUT. NOW!
THE POLICE JUST CAME AND HAS-SLED ME ABOUT YOU!
I DON'T KNOW WHO YOU ARE, BUT I WANT NO PART OF THIS!!
SLAMM

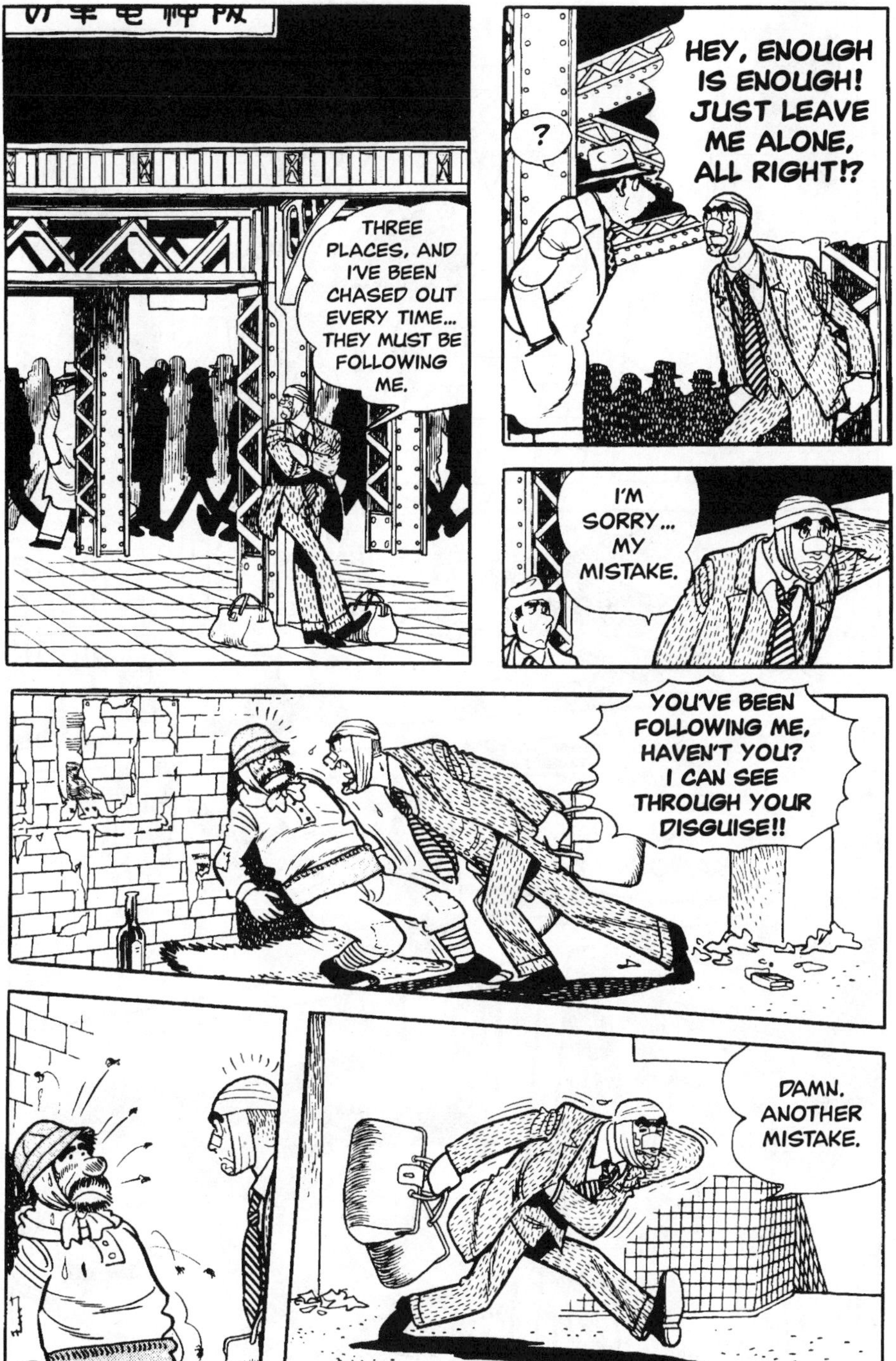
THREE PLACES, AND I'VE BEEN CHASED OUT EVERY TIME... THEY MUST BE FOLLOWING ME.
?
HEY, ENOUGH IS ENOUGH! JUST LEAVE ME ALONE, ALL RIGHT!?
I'M SORRY... MY MISTAKE.
YOU'VE BEEN FOLLOWING ME, HAVEN'T YOU? I CAN SEE THROUGH YOUR DISGUISE!!
DAMN. ANOTHER MISTAKE.

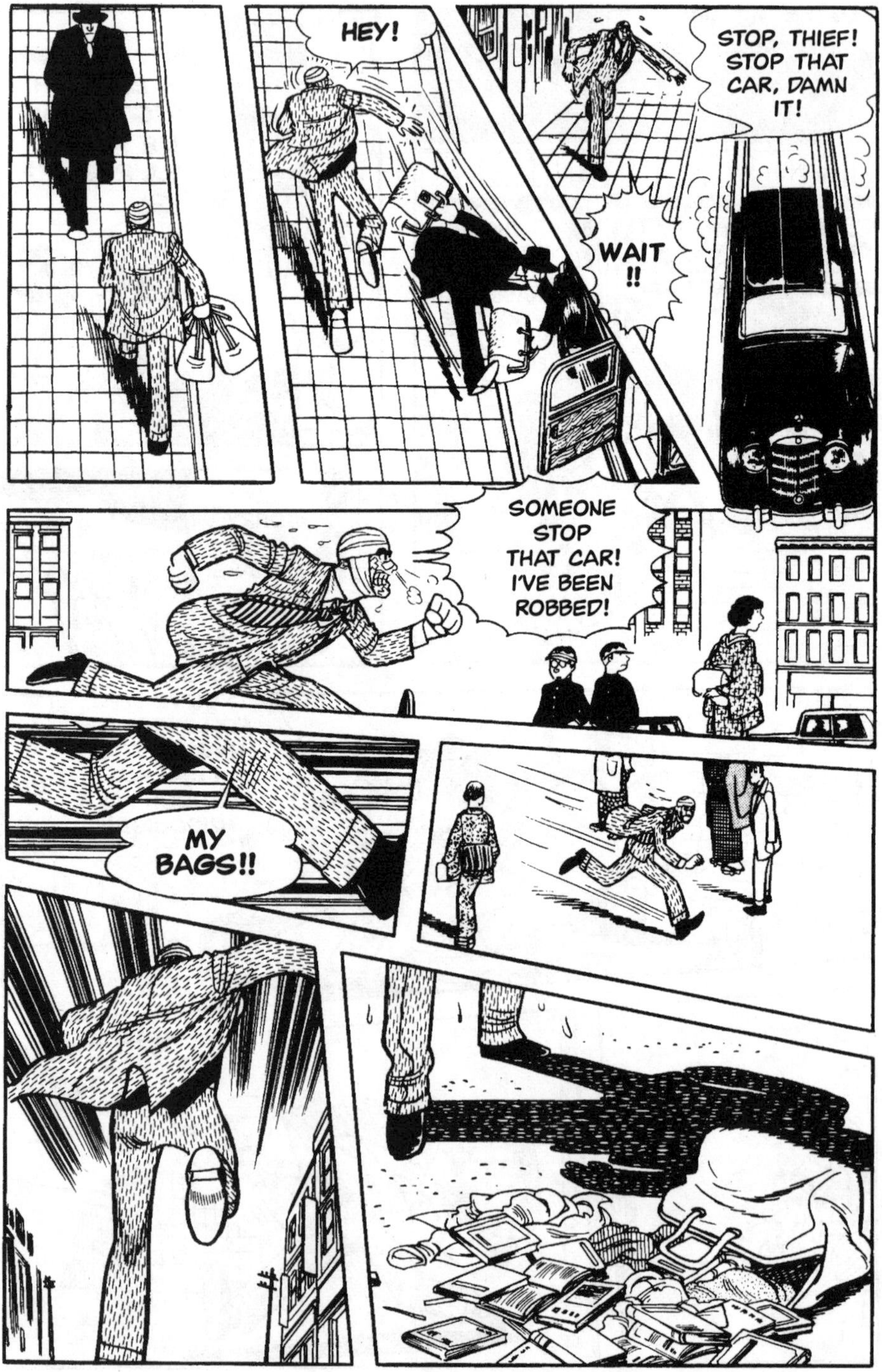
HEY!
STOP, THIEF! STOP THAT CAR, DAMN IT!
WAIT !!
SOMEONE STOP THAT CAR! I'VE BEEN ROBBED!
MY BAGS!!

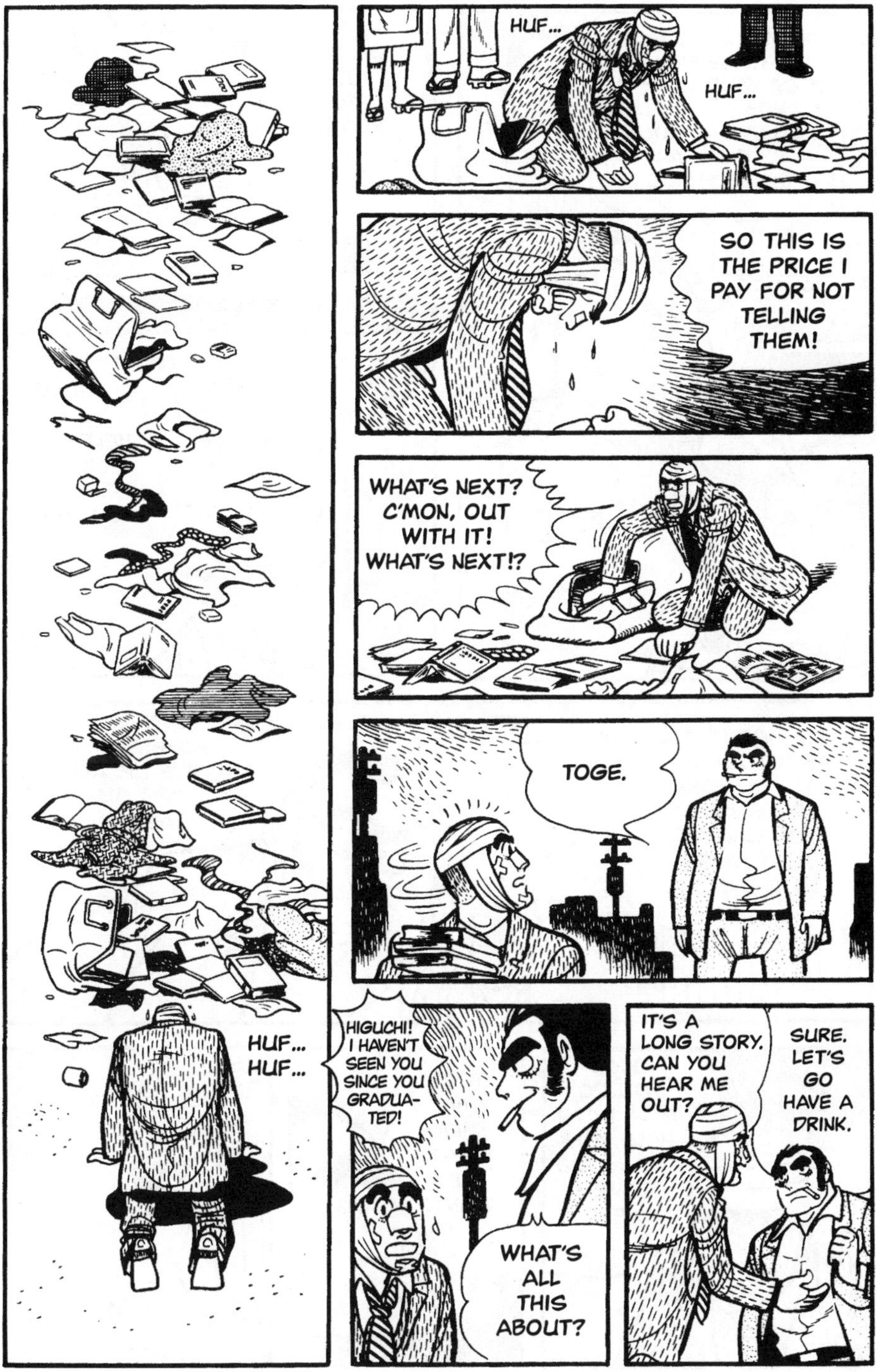
HUF...
HUF...
HUF...
HUF...
SO THIS IS THE PRICE I PAY FOR NOT TELLING THEM!
WHAT'S NEXT? C'MON, OUT WITH IT! WHAT'S NEXT!?
TOGE.
HIGUCHI! I HAVEN'T SEEN YOU SINCE YOU GRADUA-TED!
WHAT'S ALL THIS ABOUT?
IT'S A LONG STORY. CAN YOU HEAR ME OUT?
SURE. LET'S GO HAVE A DRINK.

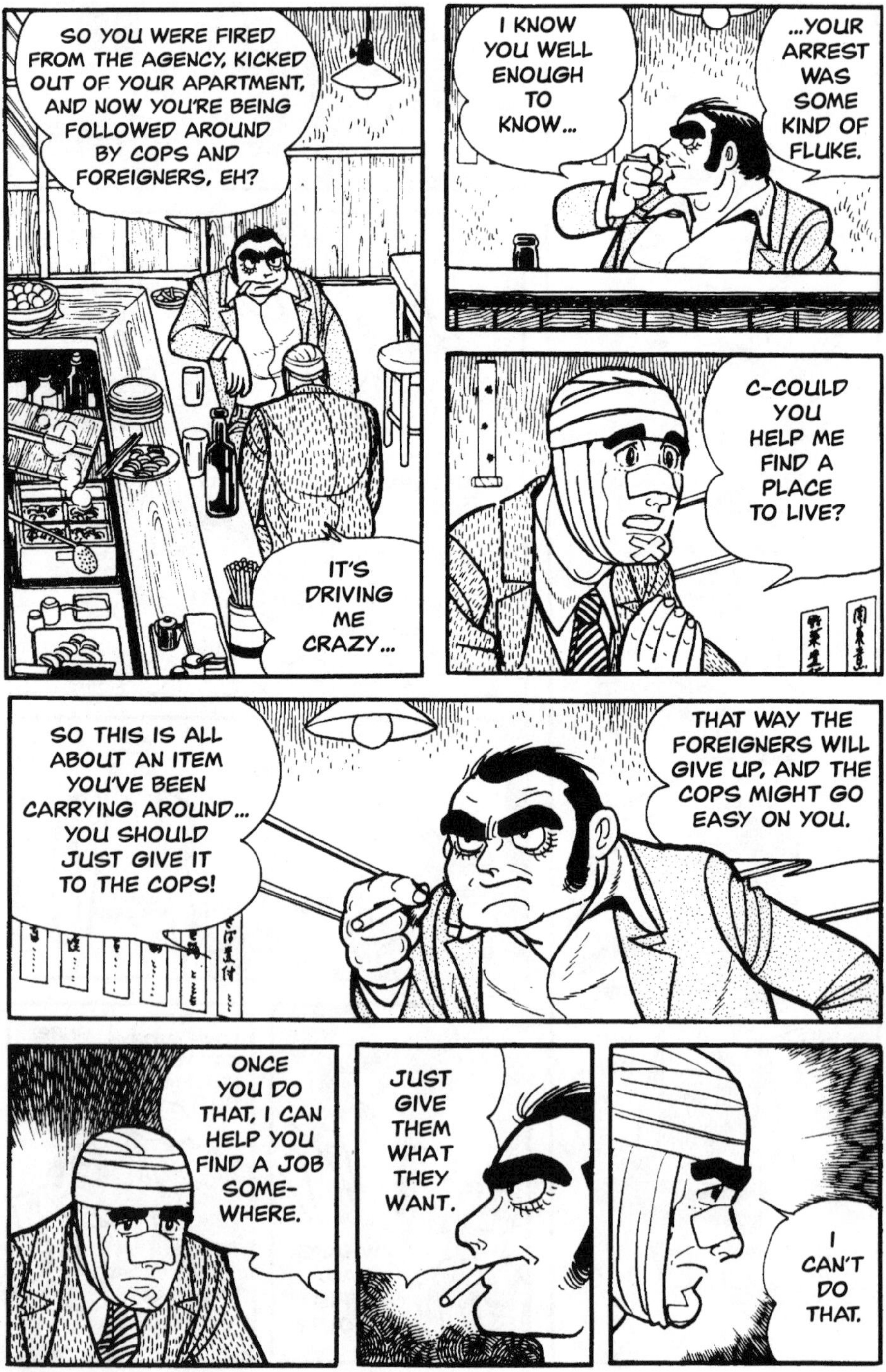
SO YOU WERE FIRED FROM THE AGENCY, KICKED OUT OF YOUR APARTMENT, AND NOW YOU'RE BEING FOLLOWED AROUND BY COPS AND FOREIGNERS, EH?
IT'S DRIVING ME CRAZY...
I KNOW YOU WELL ENOUGH TO KNOW...
...YOUR ARREST WAS SOME KIND OF FLUKE.
C-COULD YOU HELP ME FIND A PLACE TO LIVE?
SO THIS IS ALL ABOUT AN ITEM YOU'VE BEEN CARRYING AROUND... YOU SHOULD JUST GIVE IT TO THE COPS!
THAT WAY THE FOREIGNERS WILL GIVE UP, AND THE COPS MIGHT GO EASY ON YOU.
ONCE YOU DO THAT, I CAN HELP YOU FIND A JOB SOME-WHERE.
JUST GIVE THEM WHAT THEY WANT.
I CAN'T DO THAT.

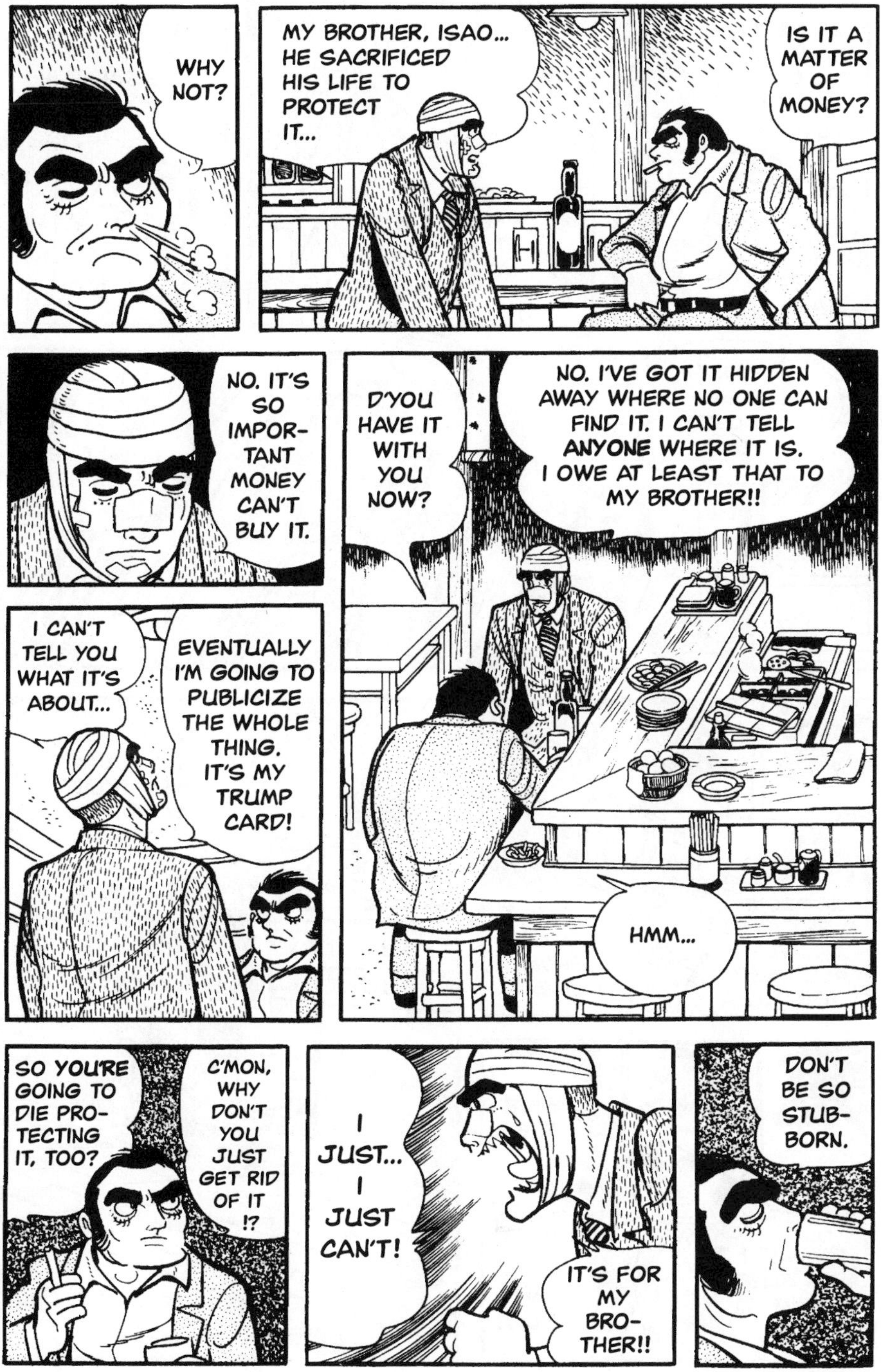
WHY NOT?
MY BROTHER, ISAO... HE SACRIFICED HIS LIFE TO PROTECT IT...
IS IT A MATTER OF MONEY?
NO. IT'S SO IMPOR-TANT MONEY CAN'T BUY IT.
I CAN'T TELL YOU WHAT IT'S ABOUT...
EVENTUALLY I'M GOING TO PUBLICIZE THE WHOLE THING. IT'S MY TRUMP CARD!
D'YOU HAVE IT WITH YOU NOW?
NO. I'VE GOT IT HIDDEN AWAY WHERE NO ONE CAN FIND IT. I CAN'T TELL ANYONE WHERE IT IS. I OWE AT LEAST THAT TO MY BROTHER!!
HMM...
SO YOU'RE GOING TO DIE PRO-TECTING IT, TOO?
C'MON, WHY DON'T YOU JUST GET RID OF IT !?
I JUST... I JUST CAN'T!
IT'S FOR MY BRO-THER!!
DON'T BE SO STUB-BORN.

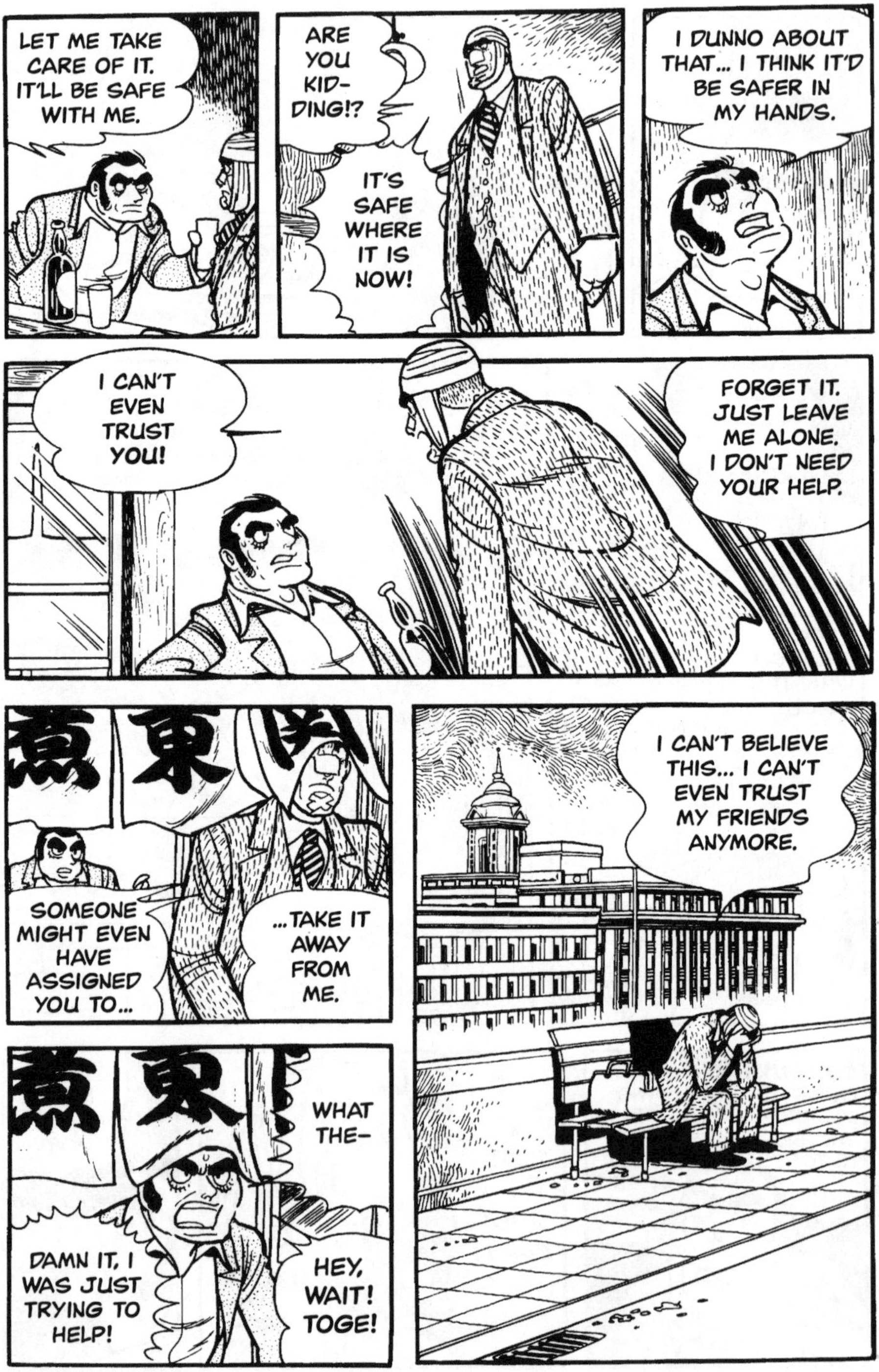
LET ME TAKE CARE OF IT. IT'LL BE SAFE WITH ME.
ARE YOU KID-DING!?
IT'S SAFE WHERE IT IS NOW!
I DUNNO ABOUT THAT... I THINK IT'D BE SAFER IN MY HANDS.
I CAN'T EVEN TRUST YOU!
FORGET IT. JUST LEAVE ME ALONE. I DON'T NEED YOUR HELP.
関東煮
SOMEONE MIGHT EVEN HAVE ASSIGNED YOU TO...
...TAKE IT AWAY FROM ME.
WHAT THE-
DAMN IT, I WAS JUST TRYING TO HELP!
HEY, WAIT! TOGE!
I CAN'T BELIEVE THIS... I CAN'T EVEN TRUST MY FRIENDS ANYMORE.

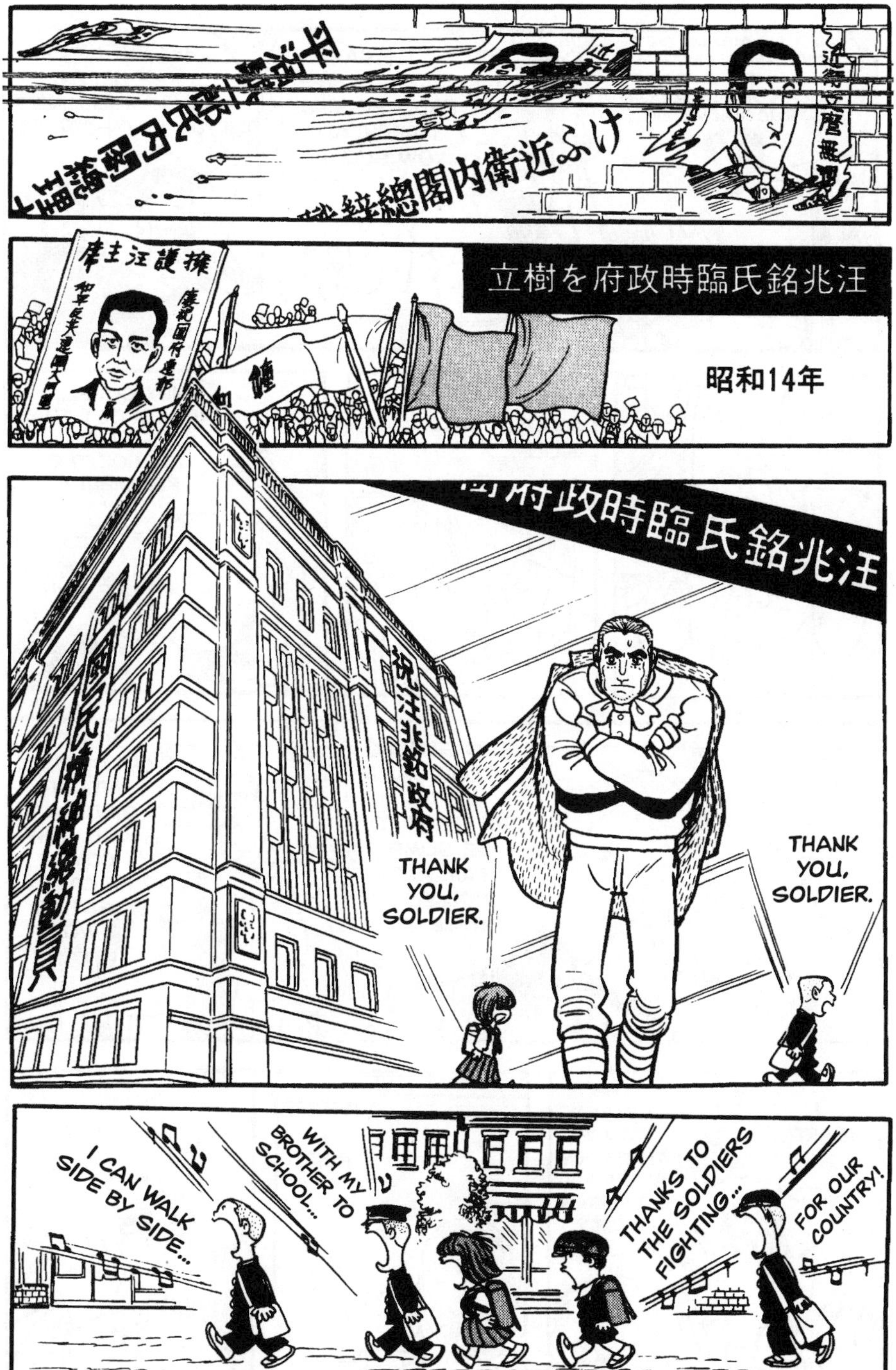
汪兆銘氏臨時政府を樹立
昭和14年
祝汪兆銘政府
THANK YOU, SOLDIER.
THANK YOU, SOLDIER.
I CAN WALK SIDE BY SIDE...
WITH MY BROTHER TO SCHOOL...
THANKS TO THE SOLDIERS FIGHTING...
FOR OUR COUNTRY!

Adolf

IF OUR MEALS GET ANY SMALLER THAN THIS, WE WON'T LAST MUCH LONGER IN CONSTRUCTION WORK...

I'LL SAY. RICE HAS BEEN RATIONED SINCE MARCH, AND NOW SUGAR...

HEY, PUT UP OR SHUT UP! ANY COMPLAINING MAKES YOU A NON-CITIZEN!

COME IN!!

ONE NOODLE SOUP.

HEY, SOHEI... DID YOU GET THAT CONSTRUCTION JOB FOR THE REGIMENT?

NOPE.

HE'S STAYING AT THE SAME PLACE AS ME. HE USED TO BE SOME FAMOUS COLLEGE ATHLETE...

SO HE'S ONE OF THEM "INTELLIGENTSIA," HUH? HOW COME HE CAN'T GET NO WORK?

I HEARD...

THE SECRET POLICE THREW HIM IN THE PEN FOR BEING A RED!

WHAT? A RED?

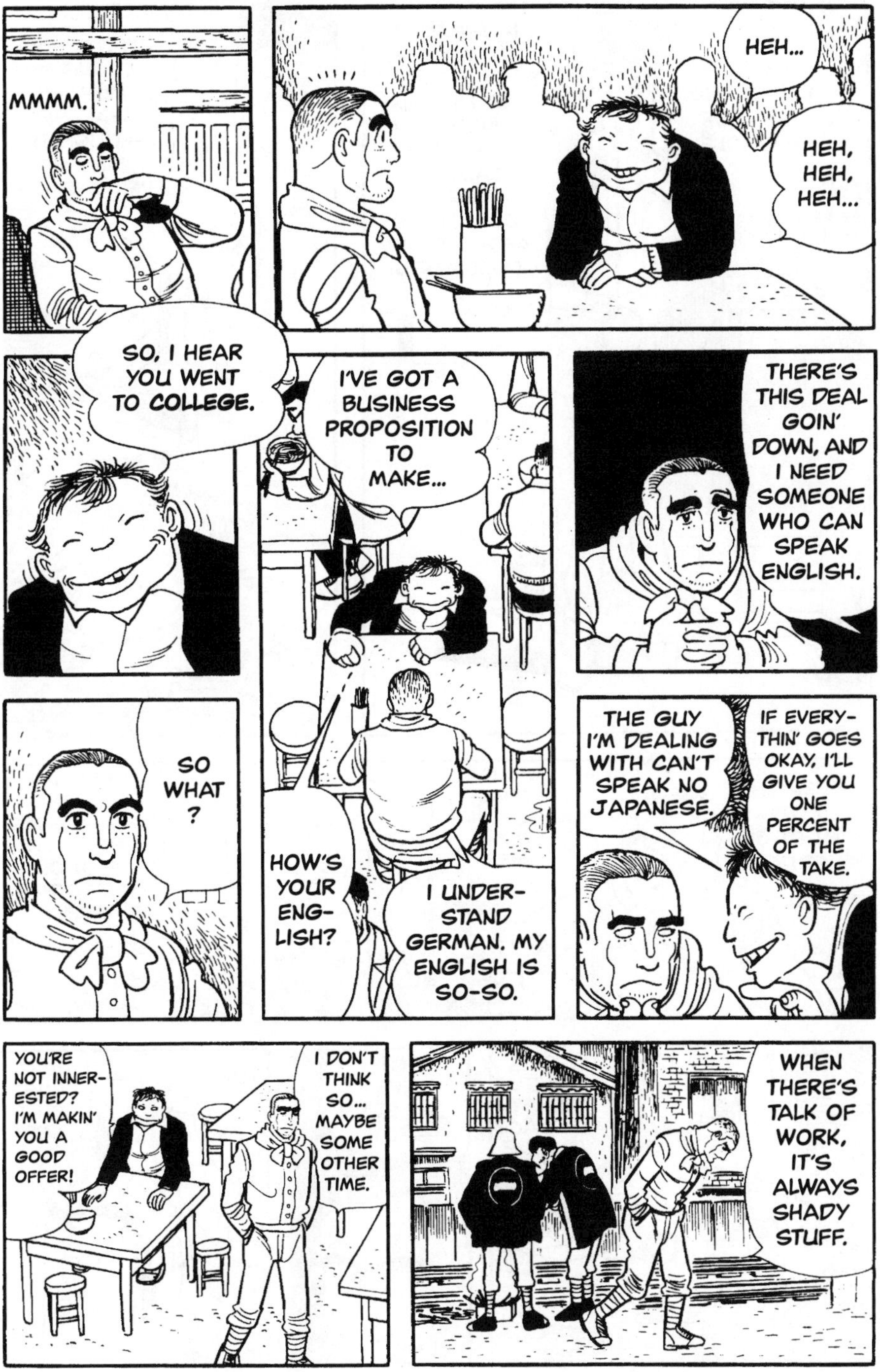
MMMM.
HEH...
HEH, HEH, HEH...
SO, I HEAR YOU WENT TO COLLEGE.
I'VE GOT A BUSINESS PROPOSITION TO MAKE...
THERE'S THIS DEAL GOIN' DOWN, AND I NEED SOMEONE WHO CAN SPEAK ENGLISH.
SO WHAT ?
HOW'S YOUR ENG-LISH?
I UNDER-STAND GERMAN. MY ENGLISH IS SO-SO.
THE GUY I'M DEALING WITH CAN'T SPEAK NO JAPANESE.
IF EVERY-THIN' GOES OKAY, I'LL GIVE YOU ONE PERCENT OF THE TAKE.
YOU'RE NOT INNER-ESTED? I'M MAKIN' YOU A GOOD OFFER!
I DON'T THINK SO... MAYBE SOME OTHER TIME.
WHEN THERE'S TALK OF WORK, IT'S ALWAYS SHADY STUFF.

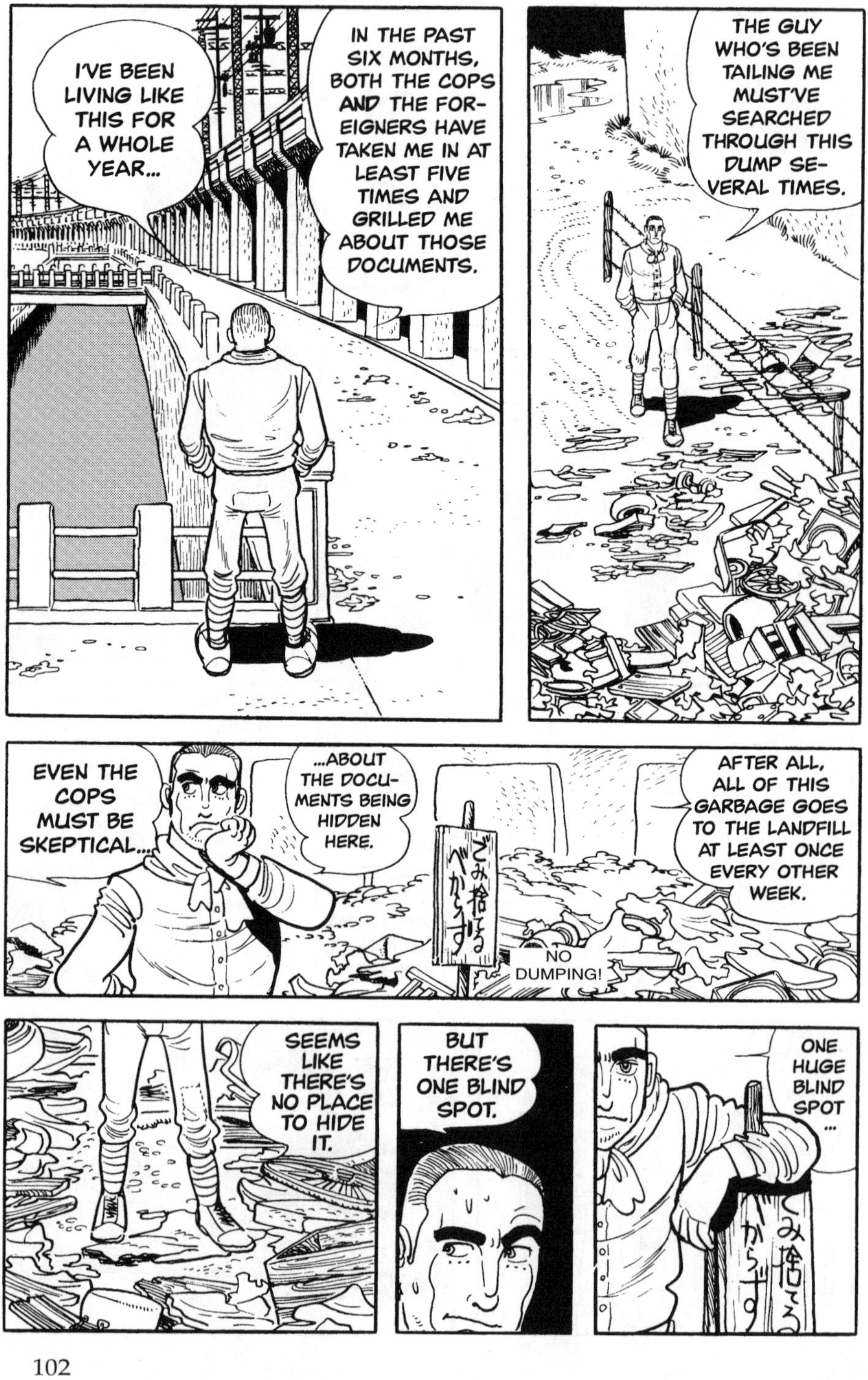
I'VE BEEN LIVING LIKE THIS FOR A WHOLE YEAR...
IN THE PAST SIX MONTHS, BOTH THE COPS AND THE FOR-EIGNERS HAVE TAKEN ME IN AT LEAST FIVE TIMES AND GRILLED ME ABOUT THOSE DOCUMENTS.
THE GUY WHO'S BEEN TAILING ME MUST'VE SEARCHED THROUGH THIS DUMP SE-VERAL TIMES.
EVEN THE COPS MUST BE SKEPTICAL...
...ABOUT THE DOCU-MENTS BEING HIDDEN HERE.
ごみ捨てるべからず
NO DUMPING!
AFTER ALL, ALL OF THIS GARBAGE GOES TO THE LANDFILL AT LEAST ONCE EVERY OTHER WEEK.
SEEMS LIKE THERE'S NO PLACE TO HIDE IT.
BUT THERE'S ONE BLIND SPOT.
ONE HUGE BLIND SPOT ...
ごみ捨てるべからず

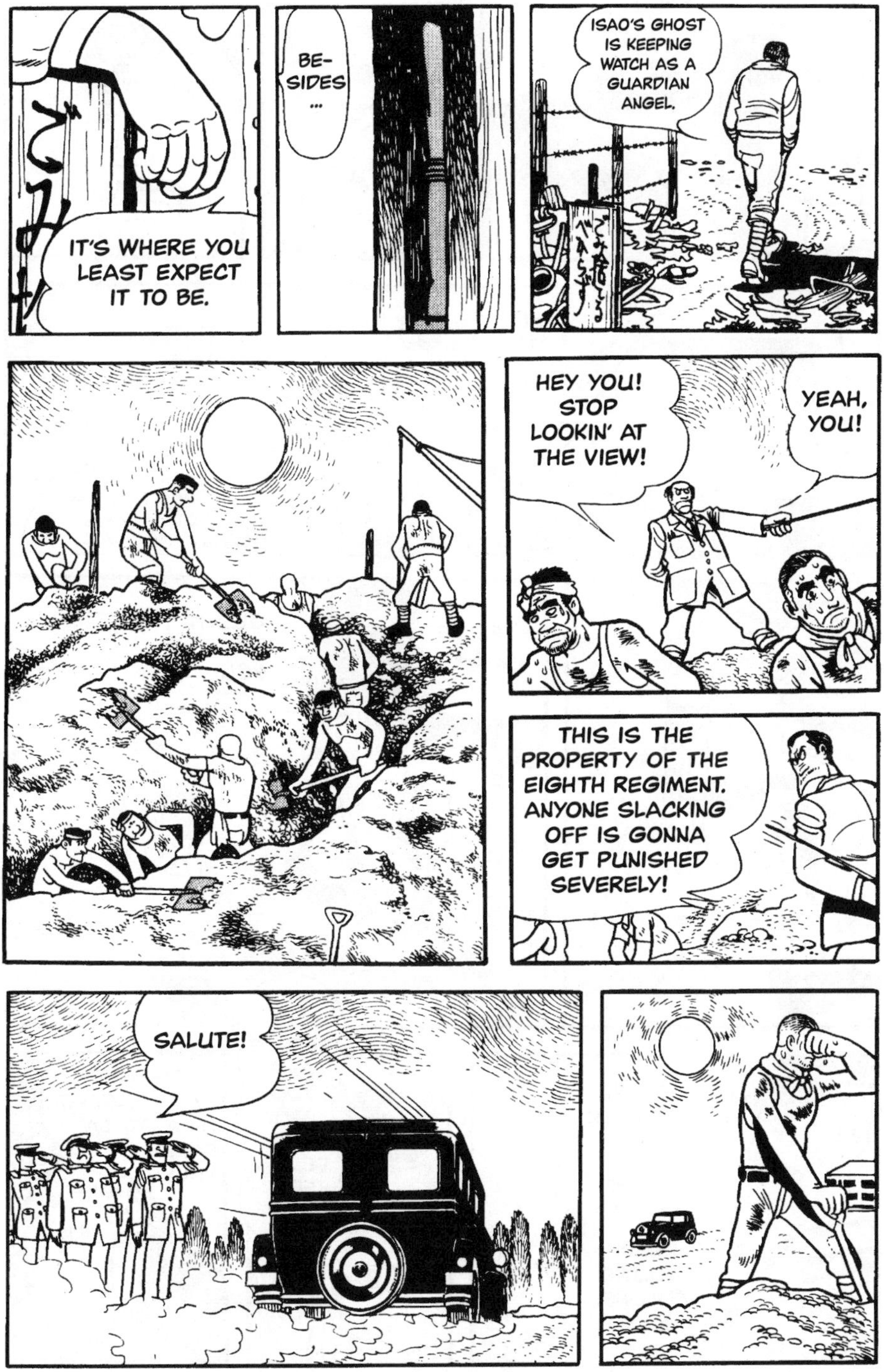
IT'S WHERE YOU LEAST EXPECT IT TO BE.
BE-SIDES ...
ISAO'S GHOST IS KEEPING WATCH AS A GUARDIAN ANGEL.
ごみ捨てるべからず
HEY YOU! STOP LOOKIN' AT THE VIEW!
YEAH, YOU!
THIS IS THE PROPERTY OF THE EIGHTH REGIMENT. ANYONE SLACKING OFF IS GONNA GET PUNISHED SEVERELY!
SALUTE!

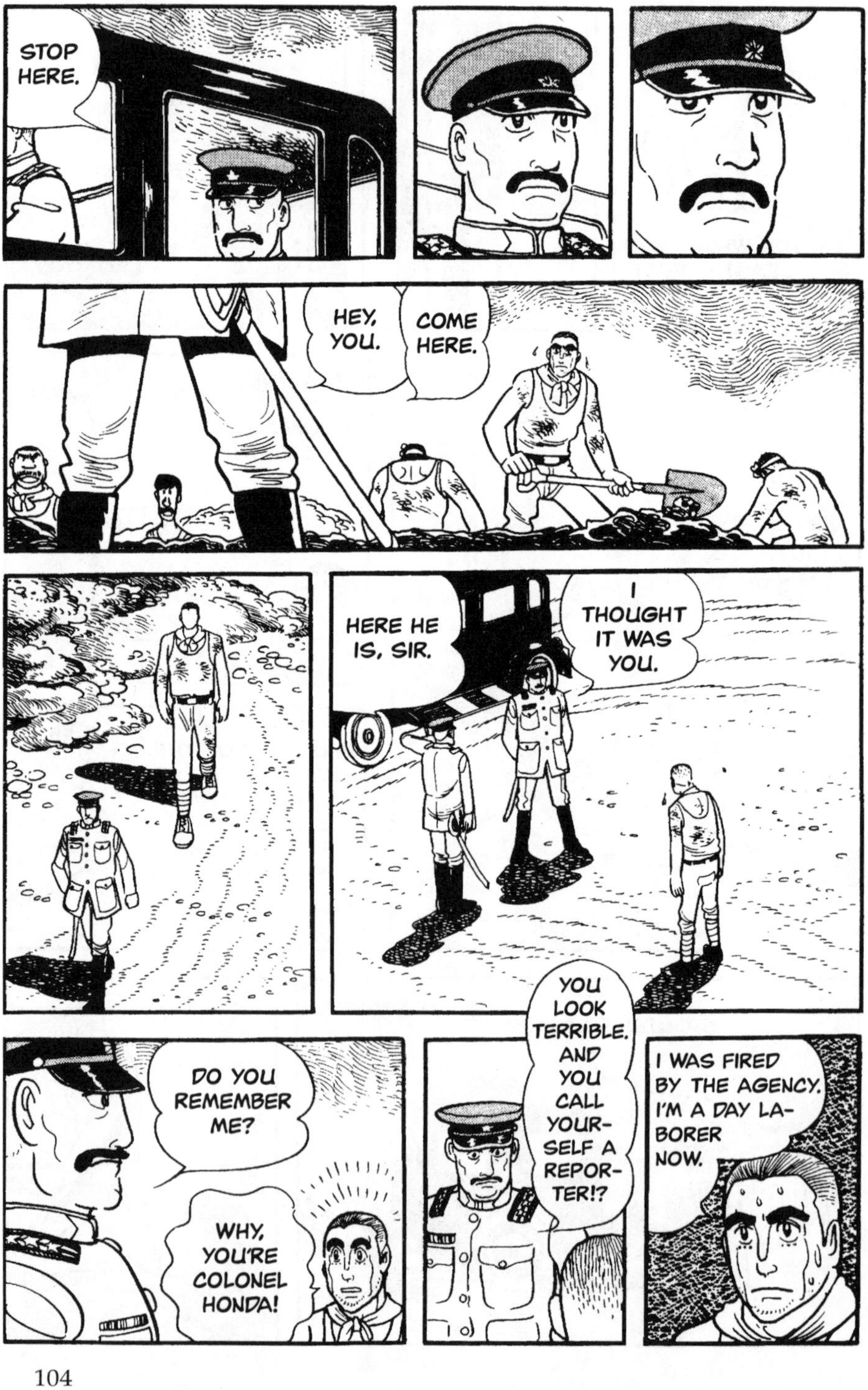
STOP HERE.
HEY, YOU.
COME HERE.
HERE HE IS, SIR.
I THOUGHT IT WAS YOU.
DO YOU REMEMBER ME?
WHY, YOU'RE COLONEL HONDA!
YOU LOOK TERRIBLE. AND YOU CALL YOURSELF A REPORTER!?
I WAS FIRED BY THE AGENCY. I'M A DAY LABORER NOW.

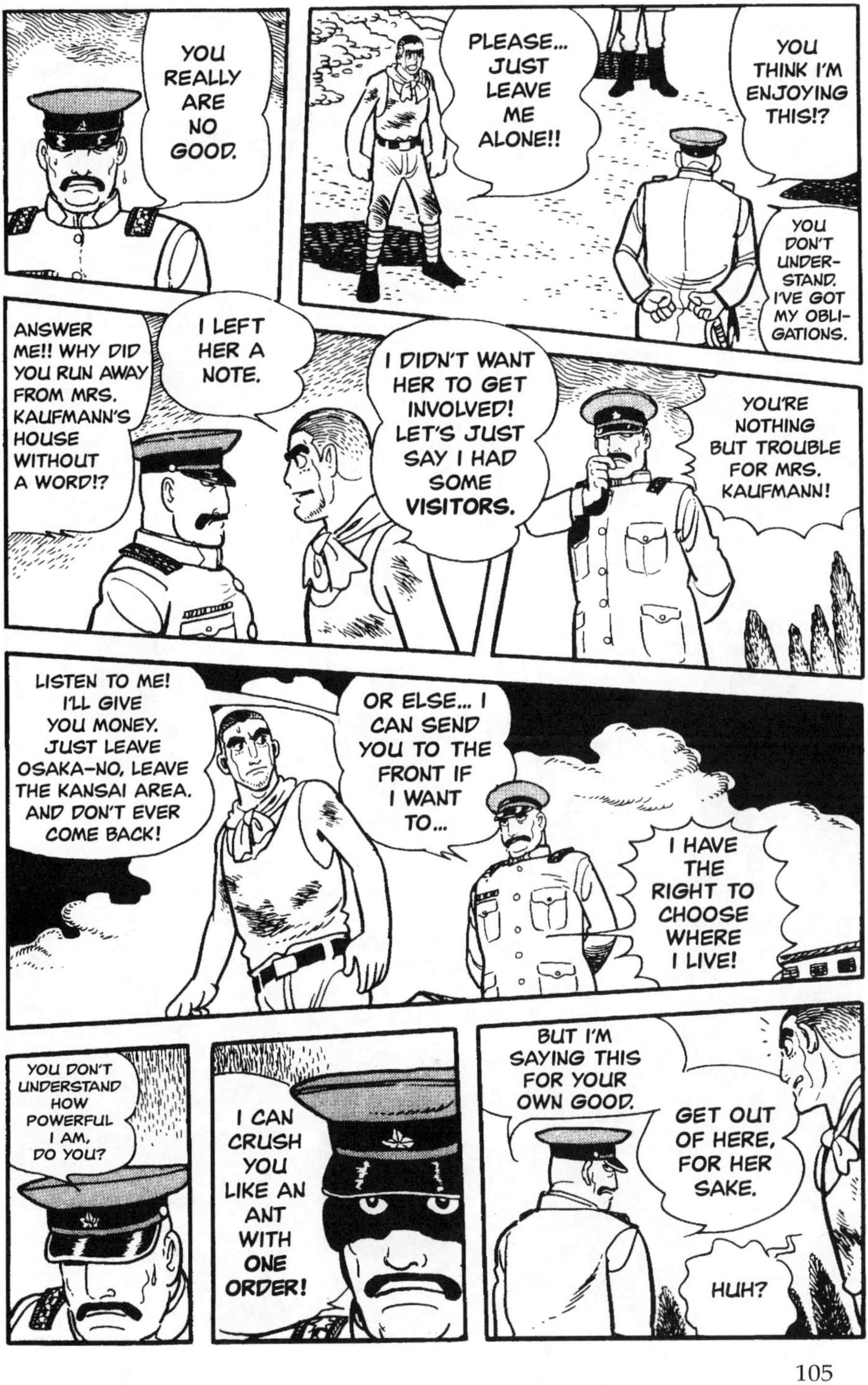
YOU REALLY ARE NO GOOD.
PLEASE... JUST LEAVE ME ALONE!!
YOU THINK I'M ENJOYING THIS!?
YOU DON'T UNDER-STAND. I'VE GOT MY OBLI-GATIONS.
ANSWER ME!! WHY DID YOU RUN AWAY FROM MRS. KAUFMANN'S HOUSE WITHOUT A WORD!?
I LEFT HER A NOTE.
I DIDN'T WANT HER TO GET INVOLVED! LET'S JUST SAY I HAD SOME **VISITORS.**
YOU'RE NOTHING BUT TROUBLE FOR MRS. KAUFMANN!
LISTEN TO ME! I'LL GIVE YOU MONEY. JUST LEAVE OSAKA—NO, LEAVE THE KANSAI AREA. AND DON'T EVER COME BACK!
OR ELSE... I CAN SEND YOU TO THE FRONT IF I WANT TO...
I HAVE THE RIGHT TO CHOOSE WHERE I LIVE!
YOU DON'T UNDERSTAND HOW POWERFUL I AM, DO YOU?
I CAN CRUSH YOU LIKE AN ANT WITH **ONE ORDER!**
BUT I'M SAYING THIS FOR YOUR OWN GOOD.
GET OUT OF HERE, FOR HER SAKE.
HUH?

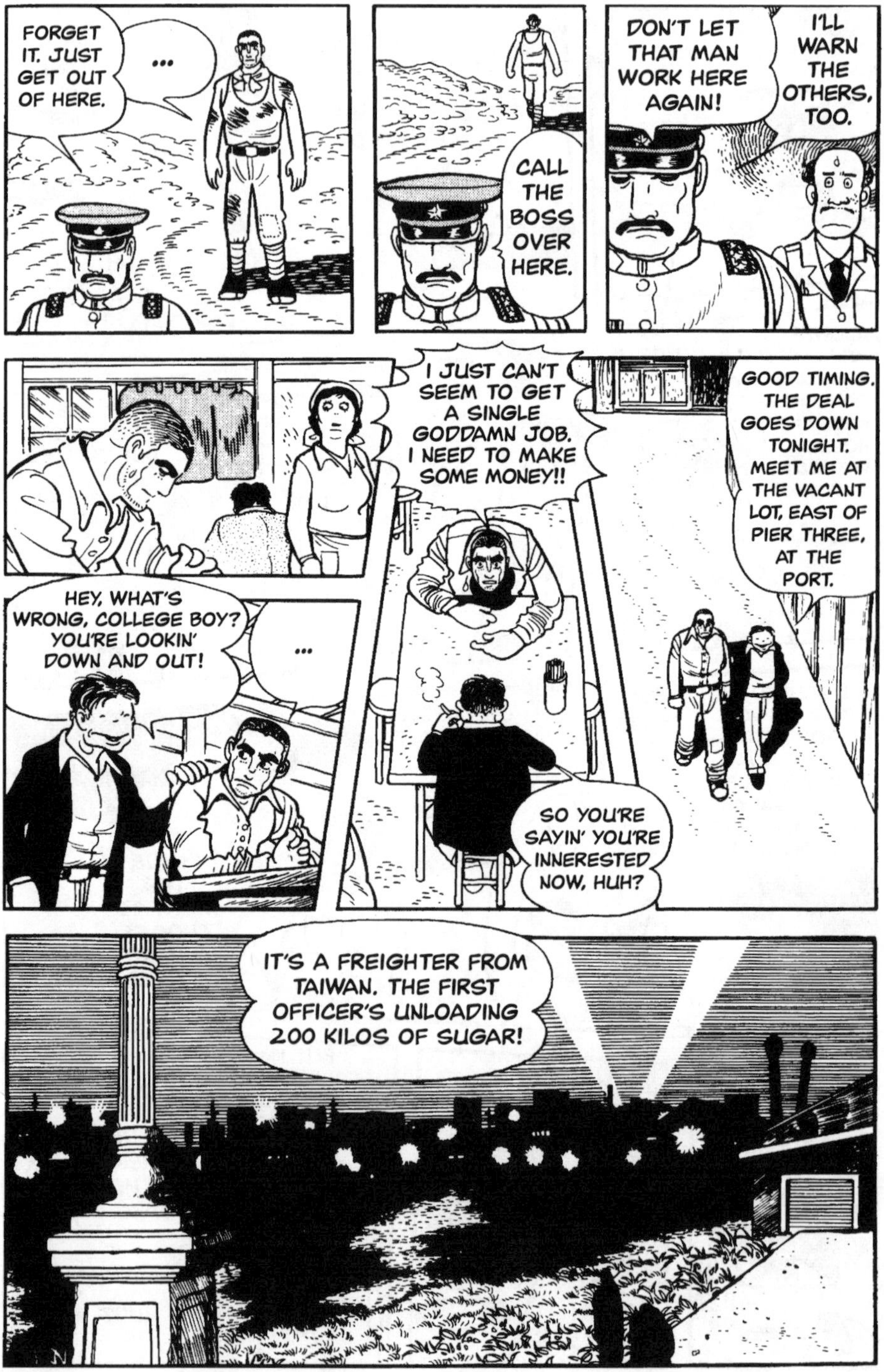
FORGET IT. JUST GET OUT OF HERE.
...
CALL THE BOSS OVER HERE.
DON'T LET THAT MAN WORK HERE AGAIN!
I'LL WARN THE OTHERS, TOO.
HEY, WHAT'S WRONG, COLLEGE BOY? YOU'RE LOOKIN' DOWN AND OUT!
...
I JUST CAN'T SEEM TO GET A SINGLE GODDAMN JOB. I NEED TO MAKE SOME MONEY!!
SO YOU'RE SAYIN' YOU'RE INNERESTED NOW, HUH?
GOOD TIMING. THE DEAL GOES DOWN TONIGHT. MEET ME AT THE VACANT LOT, EAST OF PIER THREE, AT THE PORT.
IT'S A FREIGHTER FROM TAIWAN. THE FIRST OFFICER'S UNLOADING 200 KILOS OF SUGAR!

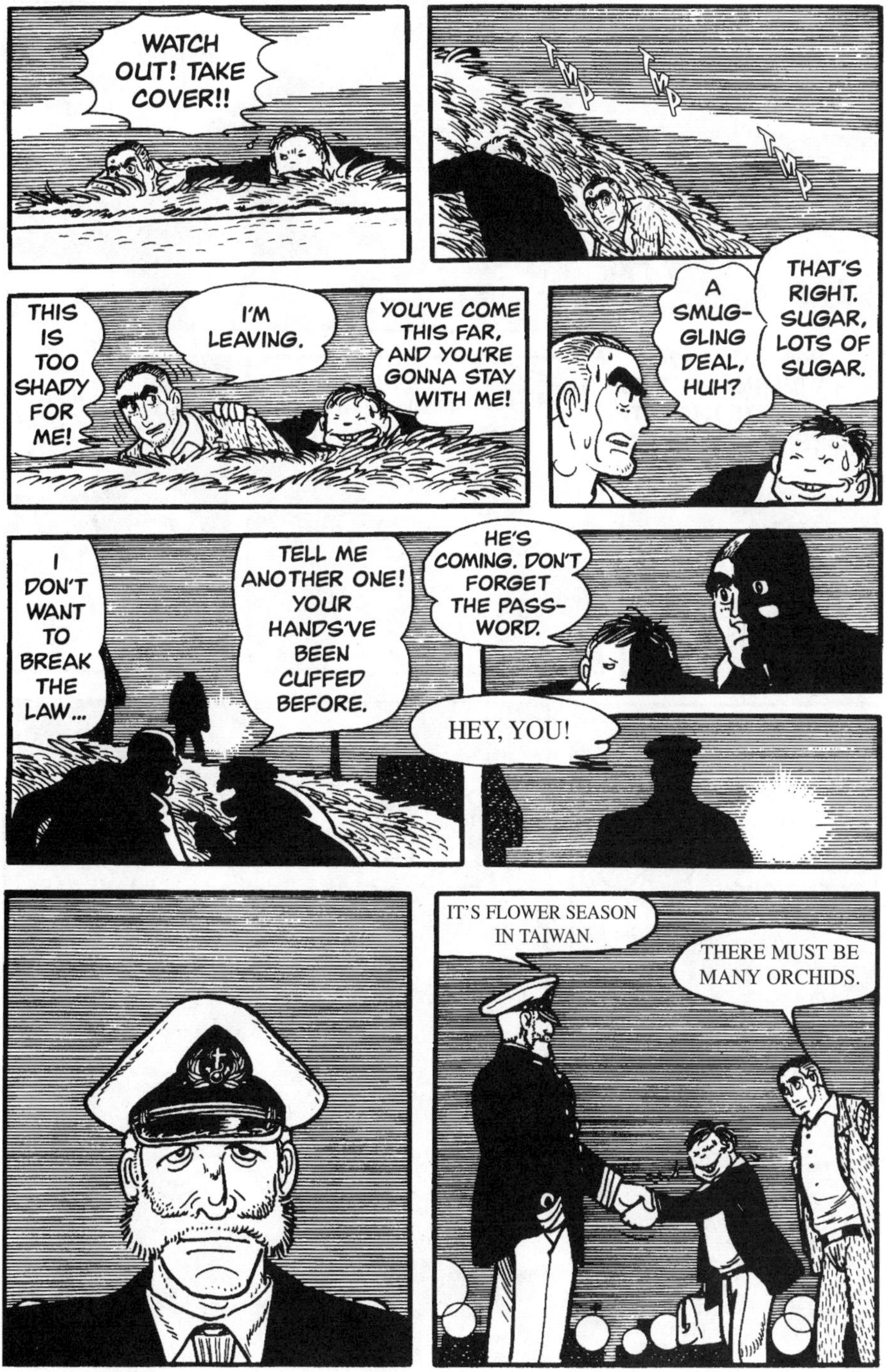
WATCH OUT! TAKE COVER!!
TMP
TMP
TMP
THIS IS TOO SHADY FOR ME!
I'M LEAVING.
YOU'VE COME THIS FAR, AND YOU'RE GONNA STAY WITH ME!
A SMUG-GLING DEAL, HUH?
THAT'S RIGHT. SUGAR, LOTS OF SUGAR.
I DON'T WANT TO BREAK THE LAW...
TELL ME ANOTHER ONE! YOUR HANDS'VE BEEN CUFFED BEFORE.
HE'S COMING. DON'T FORGET THE PASS-WORD.
HEY, YOU!
IT'S FLOWER SEASON IN TAIWAN.
THERE MUST BE MANY ORCHIDS.

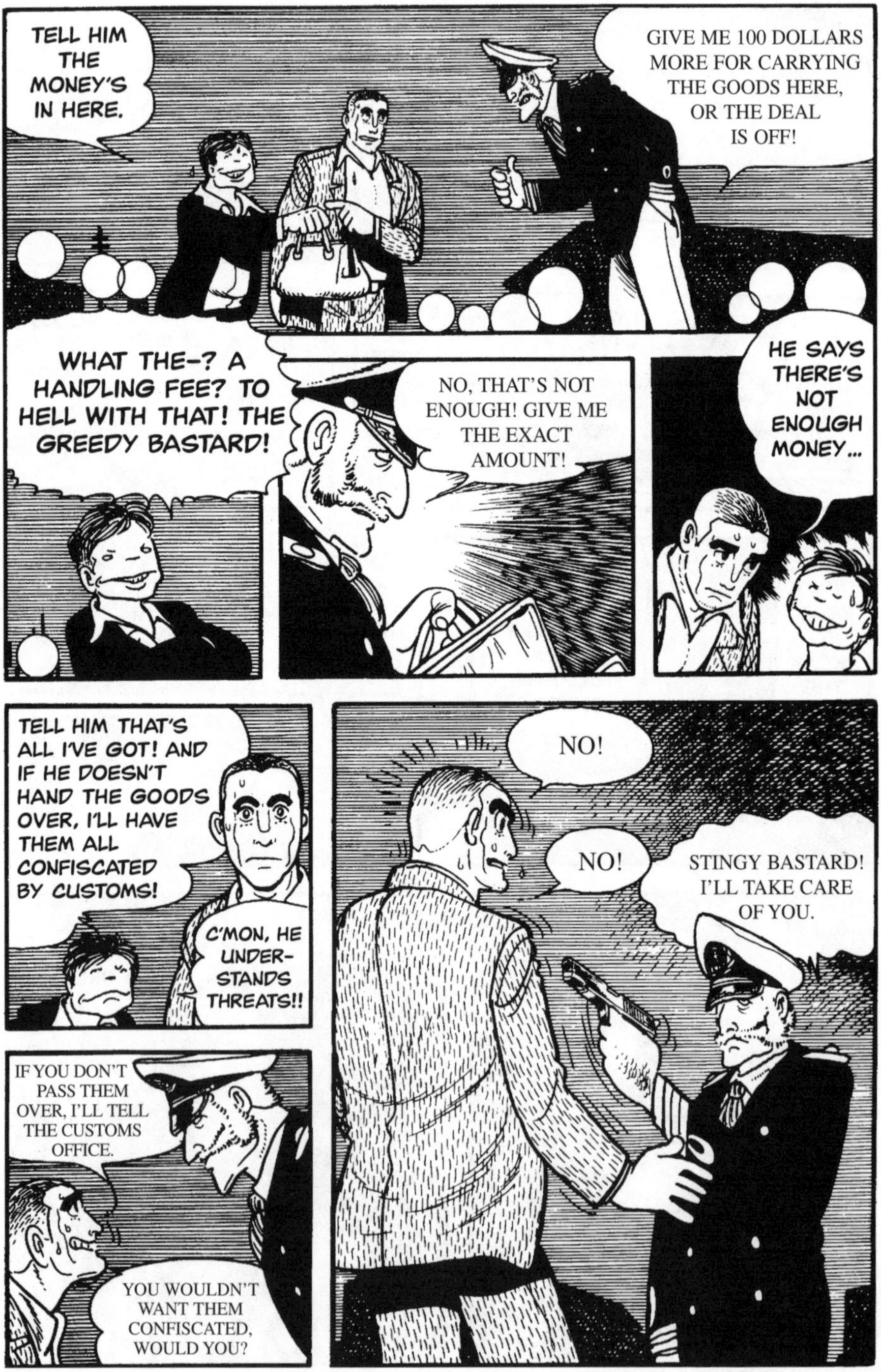
TELL HIM THE MONEY'S IN HERE.
GIVE ME 100 DOLLARS MORE FOR CARRYING THE GOODS HERE, OR THE DEAL IS OFF!
WHAT THE-? A HANDLING FEE? TO HELL WITH THAT! THE GREEDY BASTARD!
NO, THAT'S NOT ENOUGH! GIVE ME THE EXACT AMOUNT!
HE SAYS THERE'S NOT ENOUGH MONEY...
TELL HIM THAT'S ALL I'VE GOT! AND IF HE DOESN'T HAND THE GOODS OVER, I'LL HAVE THEM ALL CONFISCATED BY CUSTOMS!
C'MON, HE UNDER-STANDS THREATS!!
IF YOU DON'T PASS THEM OVER, I'LL TELL THE CUSTOMS OFFICE.
YOU WOULDN'T WANT THEM CONFISCATED, WOULD YOU?
NO!
NO!
STINGY BASTARD! I'LL TAKE CARE OF YOU.

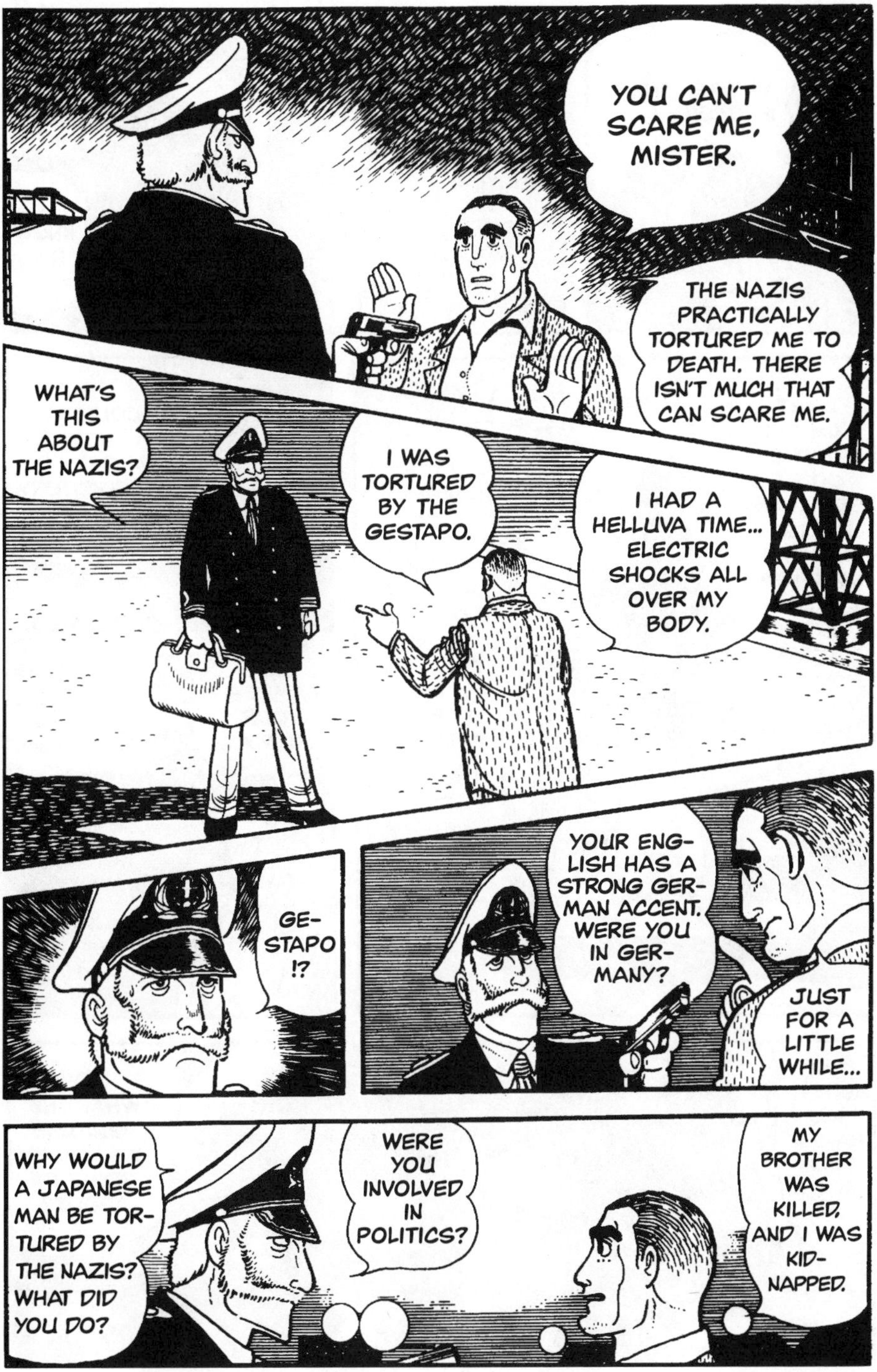
YOU CAN'T SCARE ME, MISTER.
THE NAZIS PRACTICALLY TORTURED ME TO DEATH. THERE ISN'T MUCH THAT CAN SCARE ME.
WHAT'S THIS ABOUT THE NAZIS?
I WAS TORTURED BY THE GESTAPO.
I HAD A HELLUVA TIME... ELECTRIC SHOCKS ALL OVER MY BODY.
GE-STAPO !?
YOUR ENG-LISH HAS A STRONG GER-MAN ACCENT. WERE YOU IN GER-MANY?
JUST FOR A LITTLE WHILE...
WHY WOULD A JAPANESE MAN BE TOR-TURED BY THE NAZIS? WHAT DID YOU DO?
WERE YOU INVOLVED IN POLITICS?
MY BROTHER WAS KILLED, AND I WAS KID-NAPPED.

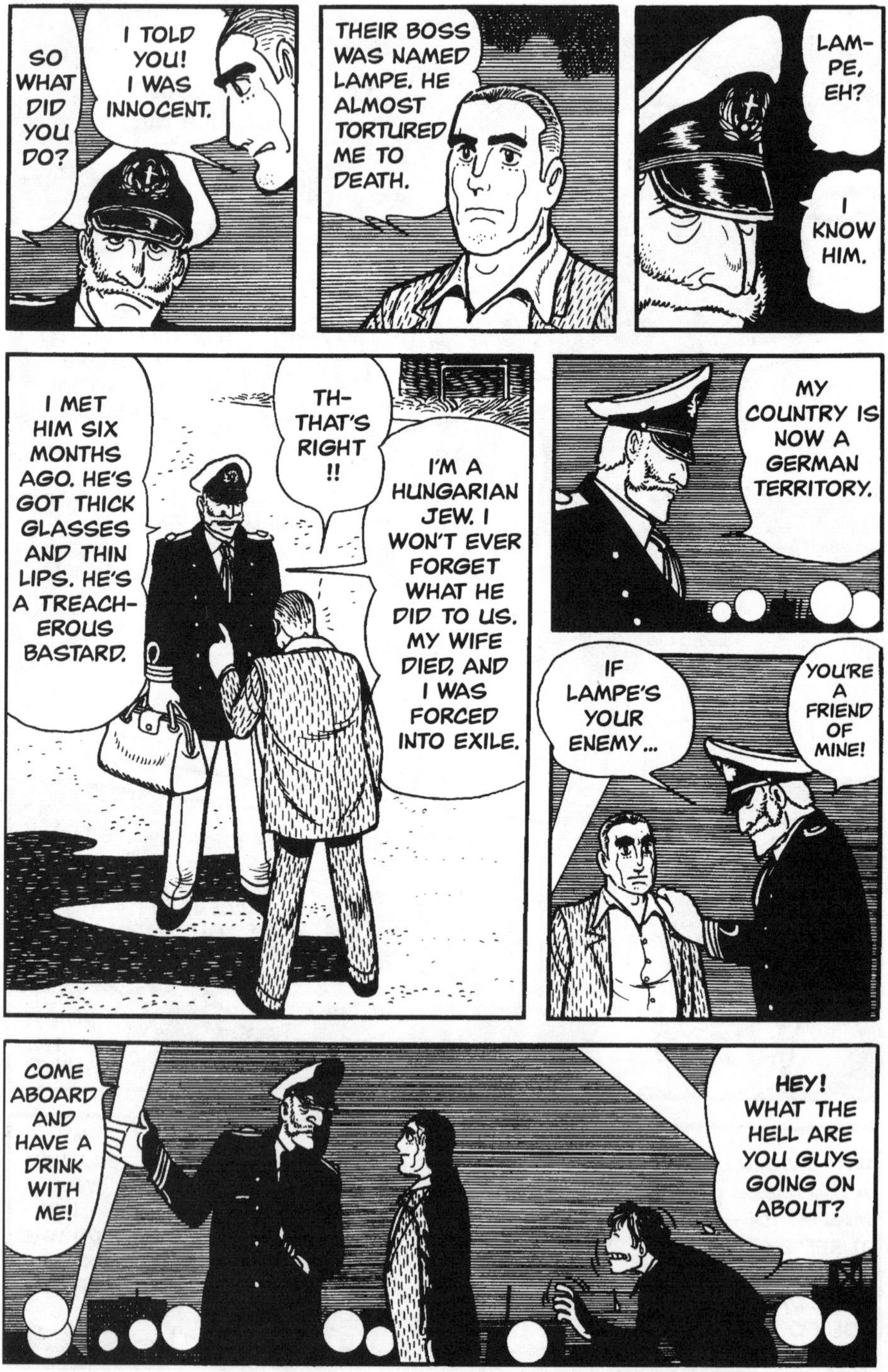
SO WHAT DID YOU DO?
I TOLD YOU! I WAS INNOCENT.
THEIR BOSS WAS NAMED LAMPE. HE ALMOST TORTURED ME TO DEATH.
LAM-PE, EH?
I KNOW HIM.
I MET HIM SIX MONTHS AGO. HE'S GOT THICK GLASSES AND THIN LIPS. HE'S A TREACH-EROUS BASTARD.
TH-THAT'S RIGHT !!
I'M A HUNGARIAN JEW. I WON'T EVER FORGET WHAT HE DID TO US. MY WIFE DIED, AND I WAS FORCED INTO EXILE.
MY COUNTRY IS NOW A GERMAN TERRITORY.
IF LAMPE'S YOUR ENEMY...
YOU'RE A FRIEND OF MINE!
COME ABOARD AND HAVE A DRINK WITH ME!
HEY! WHAT THE HELL ARE YOU GUYS GOING ON ABOUT?

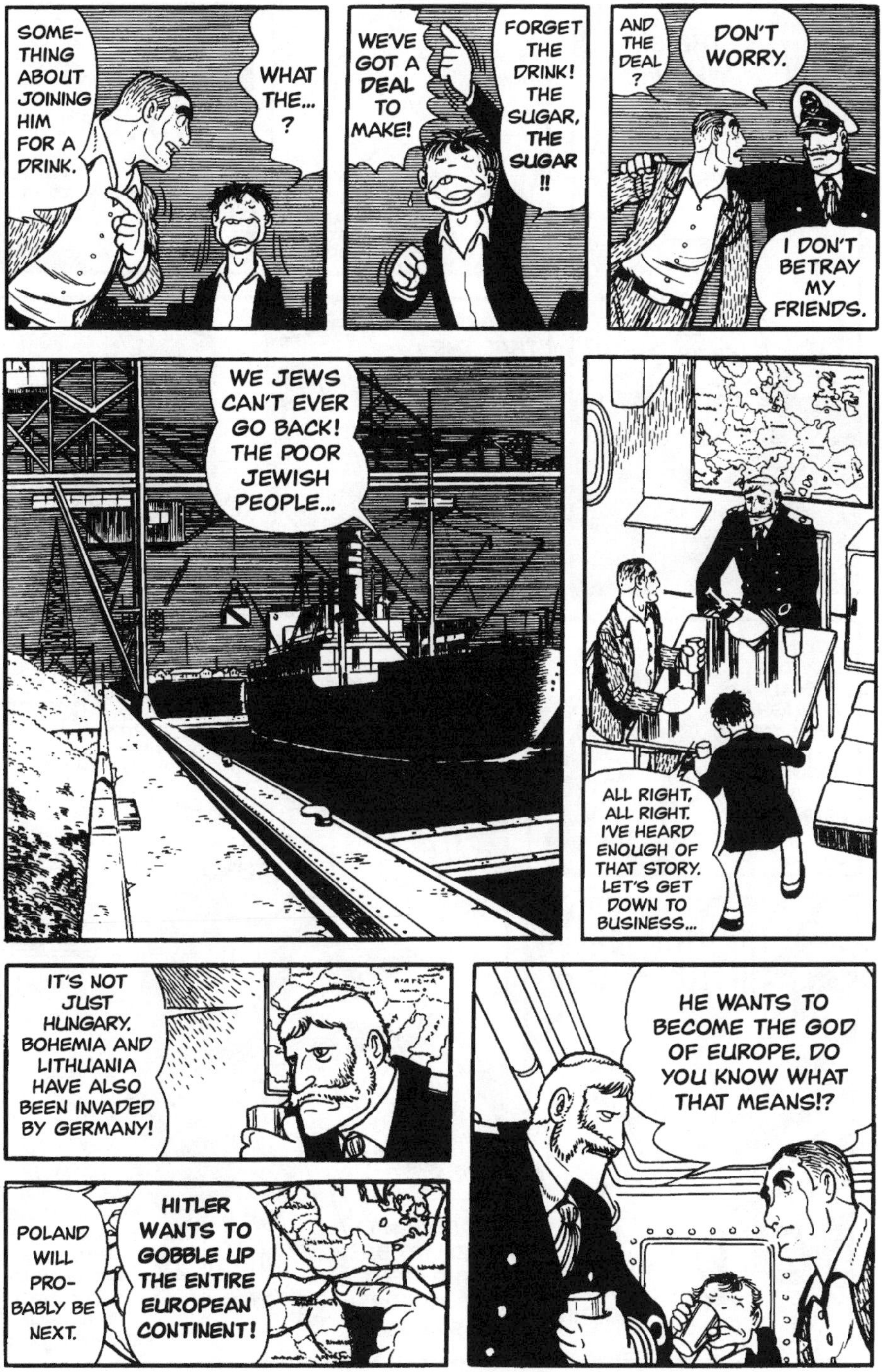
SOME-THING ABOUT JOINING HIM FOR A DRINK.
WHAT THE... ?
WE'VE GOT A DEAL TO MAKE!
FORGET THE DRINK! THE SUGAR, THE SUGAR!!
AND THE DEAL?
DON'T WORRY.
I DON'T BETRAY MY FRIENDS.
WE JEWS CAN'T EVER GO BACK! THE POOR JEWISH PEOPLE...
ALL RIGHT, ALL RIGHT. I'VE HEARD ENOUGH OF THAT STORY. LET'S GET DOWN TO BUSINESS...
IT'S NOT JUST HUNGARY. BOHEMIA AND LITHUANIA HAVE ALSO BEEN INVADED BY GERMANY!
POLAND WILL PRO-BABLY BE NEXT.
HITLER WANTS TO GOBBLE UP THE ENTIRE EUROPEAN CONTINENT!
HE WANTS TO BECOME THE GOD OF EUROPE. DO YOU KNOW WHAT THAT MEANS!?

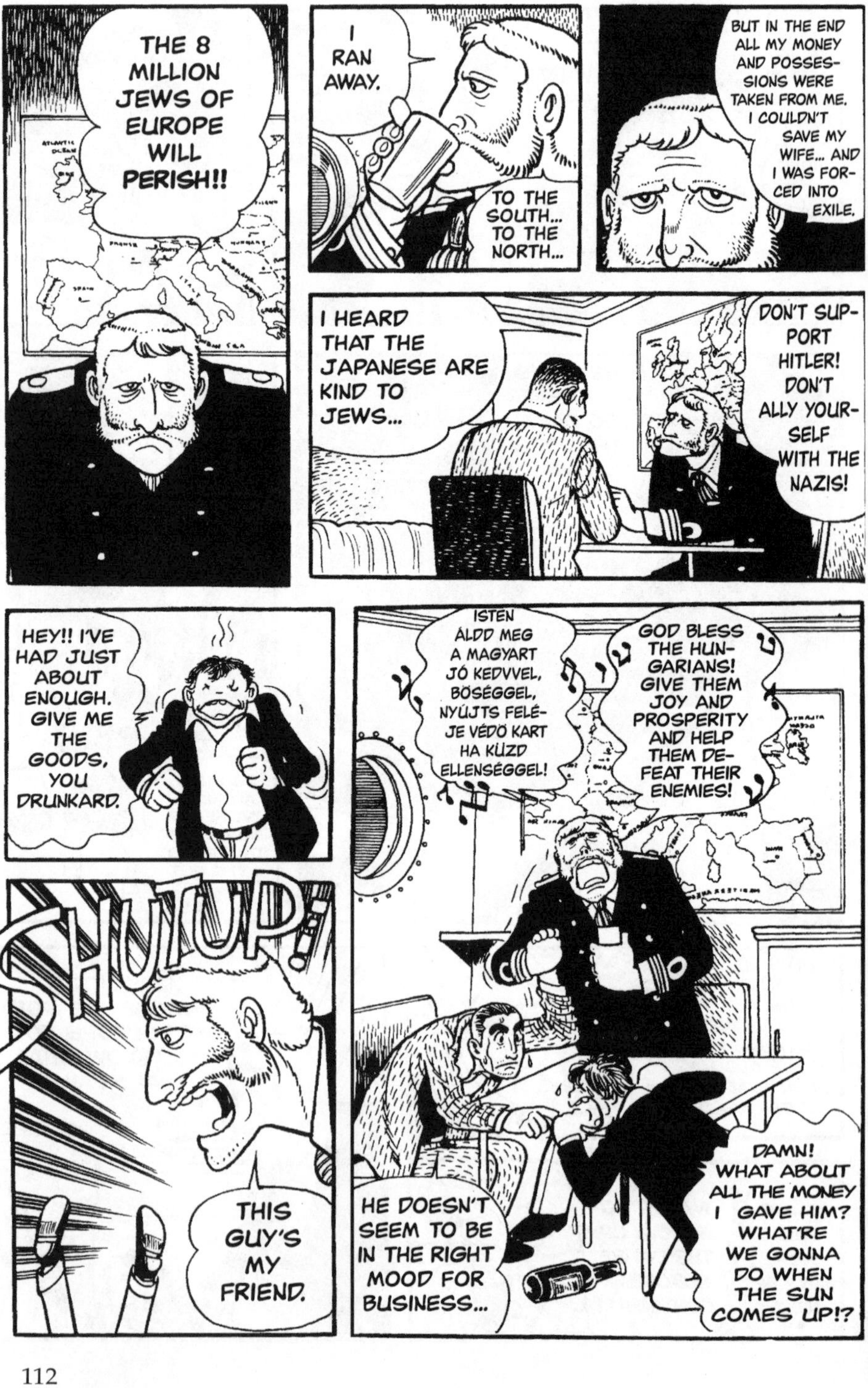
THE 8 MILLION JEWS OF EUROPE WILL PERISH!!
I RAN AWAY.
TO THE SOUTH... TO THE NORTH...
BUT IN THE END ALL MY MONEY AND POSSESSIONS WERE TAKEN FROM ME. I COULDN'T SAVE MY WIFE... AND I WAS FORCED INTO EXILE.
I HEARD THAT THE JAPANESE ARE KIND TO JEWS...
DON'T SUPPORT HITLER! DON'T ALLY YOURSELF WITH THE NAZIS!
HEY!! I'VE HAD JUST ABOUT ENOUGH. GIVE ME THE GOODS, YOU DRUNKARD.
SHUT UP!
THIS GUY'S MY FRIEND.
ISTEN ÁLDD MEG A MAGYART JÓ KEDVVEL, BÖSÉGGEL, NYÚJTS FELÉJE VÉDÖ KART HA KÜZD ELLENSÉGGEL!
GOD BLESS THE HUNGARIANS! GIVE THEM JOY AND PROSPERITY AND HELP THEM DEFEAT THEIR ENEMIES!
HE DOESN'T SEEM TO BE IN THE RIGHT MOOD FOR BUSINESS...
DAMN! WHAT ABOUT ALL THE MONEY I GAVE HIM? WHAT'RE WE GONNA DO WHEN THE SUN COMES UP!?

CHAPTER
FOUR

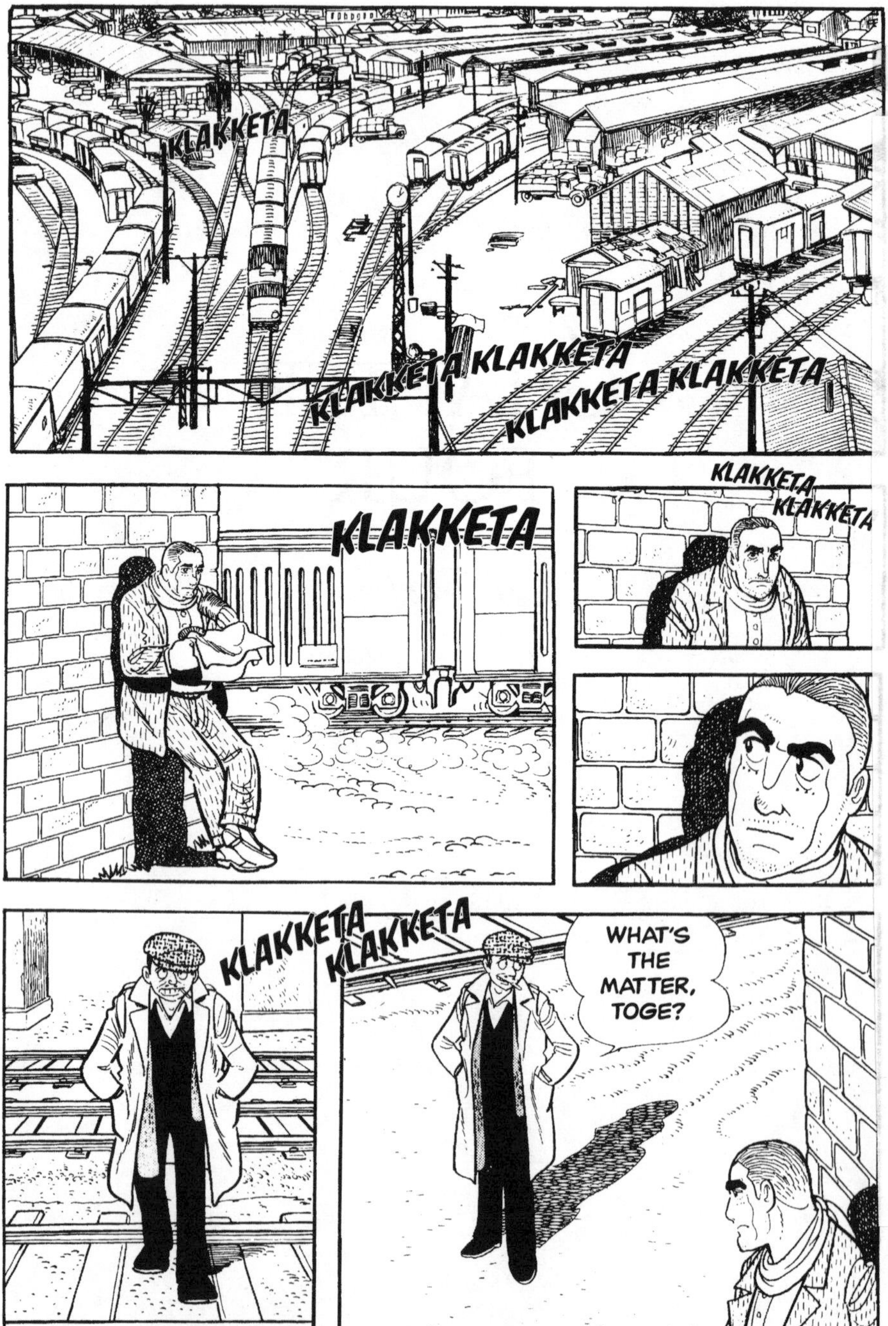
KLAKKETA
KLAKKETA KLAKKETA
KLAKKETA KLAKKETA
KLAKKETA
KLAKKETA
KLAKKETA
KLAKKETA
KLAKKETA
WHAT'S THE MATTER, TOGE?

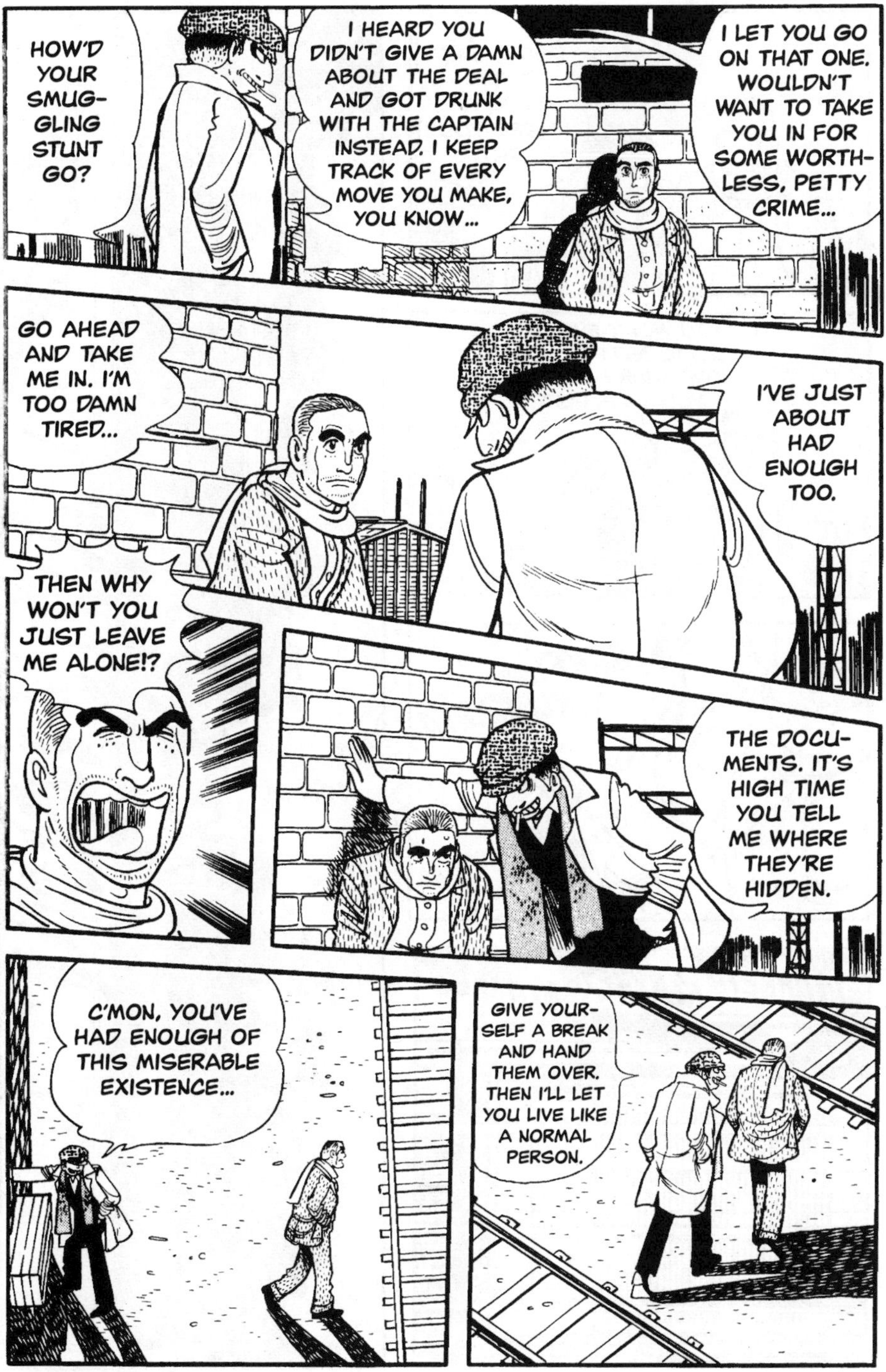
HOW'D YOUR SMUG-GLING STUNT GO?
I HEARD YOU DIDN'T GIVE A DAMN ABOUT THE DEAL AND GOT DRUNK WITH THE CAPTAIN INSTEAD. I KEEP TRACK OF EVERY MOVE YOU MAKE, YOU KNOW...
I LET YOU GO ON THAT ONE. WOULDN'T WANT TO TAKE YOU IN FOR SOME WORTH-LESS, PETTY CRIME...
GO AHEAD AND TAKE ME IN. I'M TOO DAMN TIRED...
I'VE JUST ABOUT HAD ENOUGH TOO.
THEN WHY WON'T YOU JUST LEAVE ME ALONE!?
THE DOCU-MENTS. IT'S HIGH TIME YOU TELL ME WHERE THEY'RE HIDDEN.
C'MON, YOU'VE HAD ENOUGH OF THIS MISERABLE EXISTENCE...
GIVE YOUR-SELF A BREAK AND HAND THEM OVER. THEN I'LL LET YOU LIVE LIKE A NORMAL PERSON.

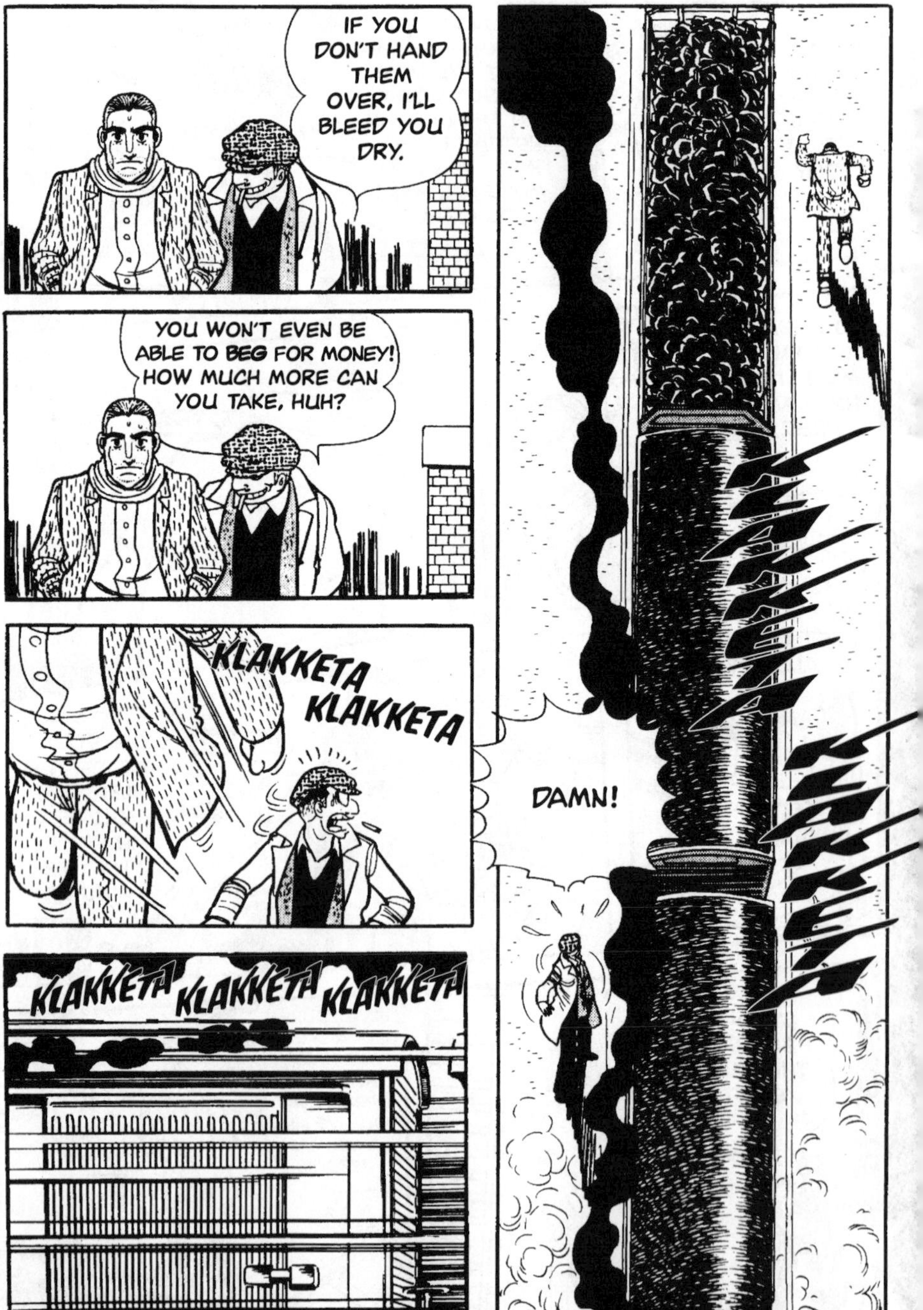
IF YOU DON'T HAND THEM OVER, I'LL BLEED YOU DRY.
YOU WON'T EVEN BE ABLE TO BEG FOR MONEY! HOW MUCH MORE CAN YOU TAKE, HUH?
KLAKKETA KLAKKETA
KLAKKETA KLAKKETA KLAKKETA
KLAKKETA KLAKKETA
DAMN!

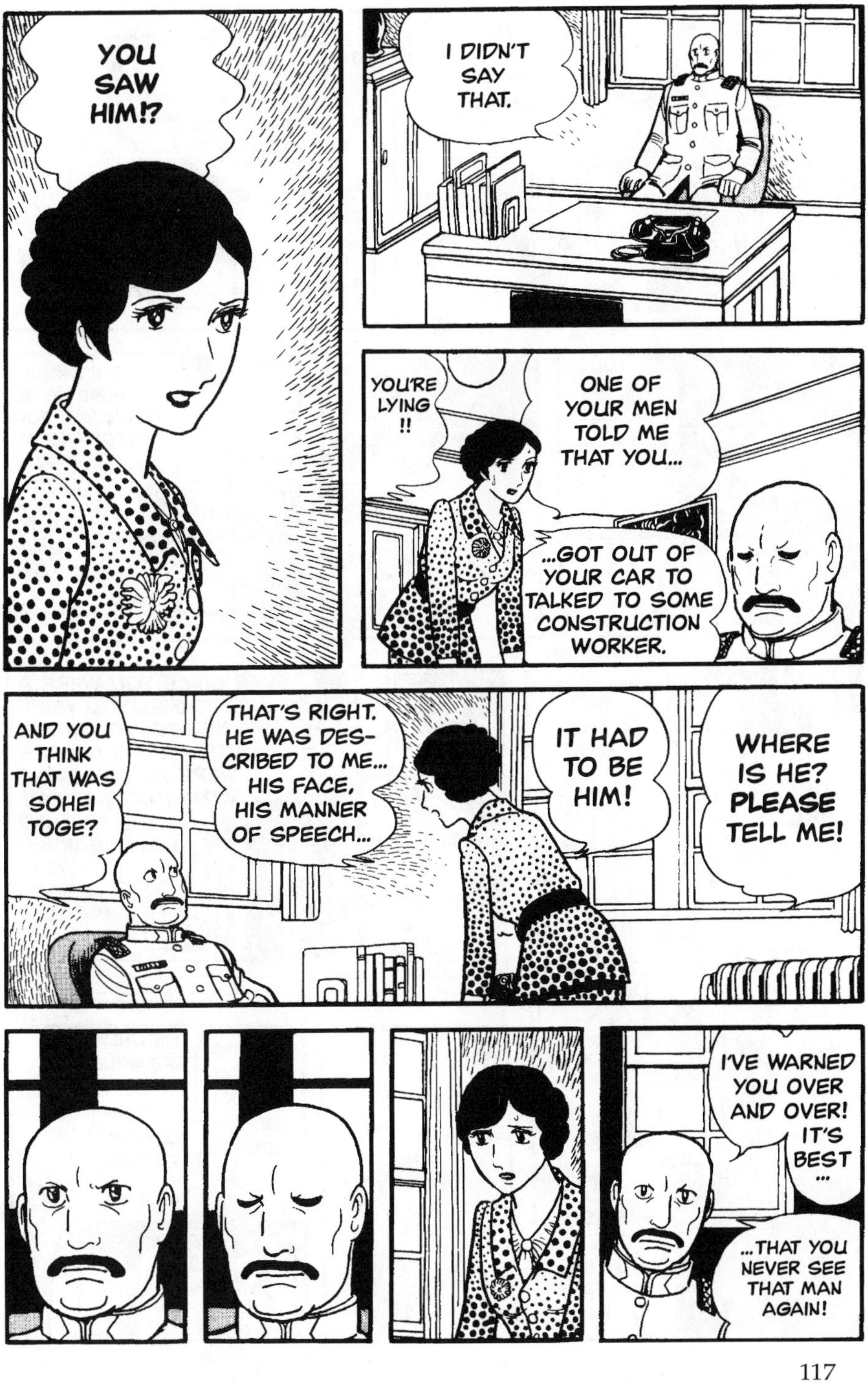
YOU SAW HIM!?
I DIDN'T SAY THAT.
YOU'RE LYING !!
ONE OF YOUR MEN TOLD ME THAT YOU...
...GOT OUT OF YOUR CAR TO TALKED TO SOME CONSTRUCTION WORKER.
AND YOU THINK THAT WAS SOHEI TOGE?
THAT'S RIGHT. HE WAS DES-CRIBED TO ME... HIS FACE, HIS MANNER OF SPEECH...
IT HAD TO BE HIM!
WHERE IS HE? PLEASE TELL ME!
I'VE WARNED YOU OVER AND OVER! IT'S BEST ...
...THAT YOU NEVER SEE THAT MAN AGAIN!

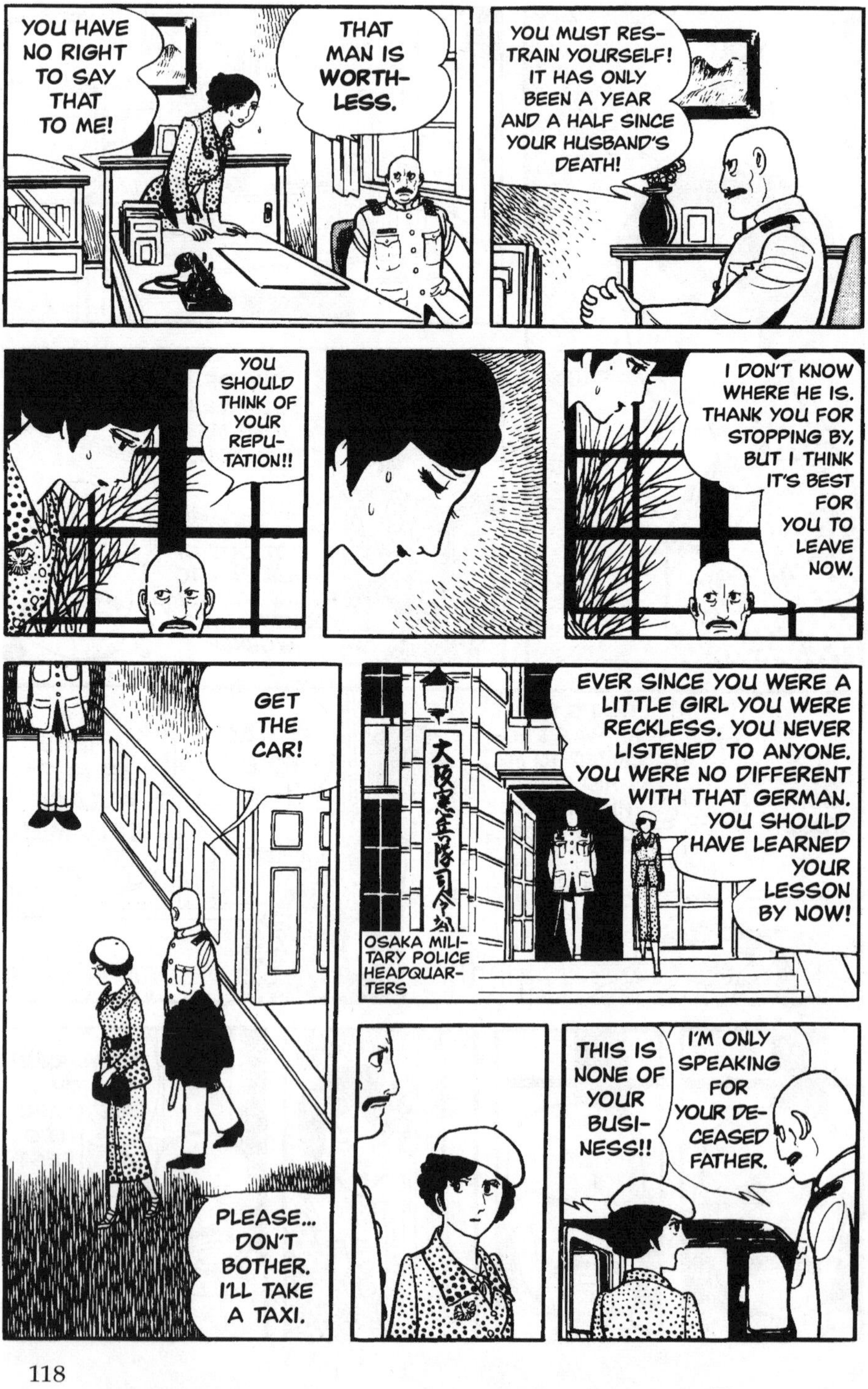
YOU HAVE NO RIGHT TO SAY THAT TO ME!
THAT MAN IS WORTHLESS.
YOU MUST RESTRAIN YOURSELF! IT HAS ONLY BEEN A YEAR AND A HALF SINCE YOUR HUSBAND'S DEATH!
YOU SHOULD THINK OF YOUR REPUTATION!!
I DON'T KNOW WHERE HE IS. THANK YOU FOR STOPPING BY, BUT I THINK IT'S BEST FOR YOU TO LEAVE NOW.
GET THE CAR!
PLEASE... DON'T BOTHER. I'LL TAKE A TAXI.
大阪憲兵隊司令部
OSAKA MILITARY POLICE HEADQUARTERS
EVER SINCE YOU WERE A LITTLE GIRL YOU WERE RECKLESS. YOU NEVER LISTENED TO ANYONE. YOU WERE NO DIFFERENT WITH THAT GERMAN. YOU SHOULD HAVE LEARNED YOUR LESSON BY NOW!
THIS IS NONE OF YOUR BUSINESS!!
I'M ONLY SPEAKING FOR YOUR DECEASED FATHER.

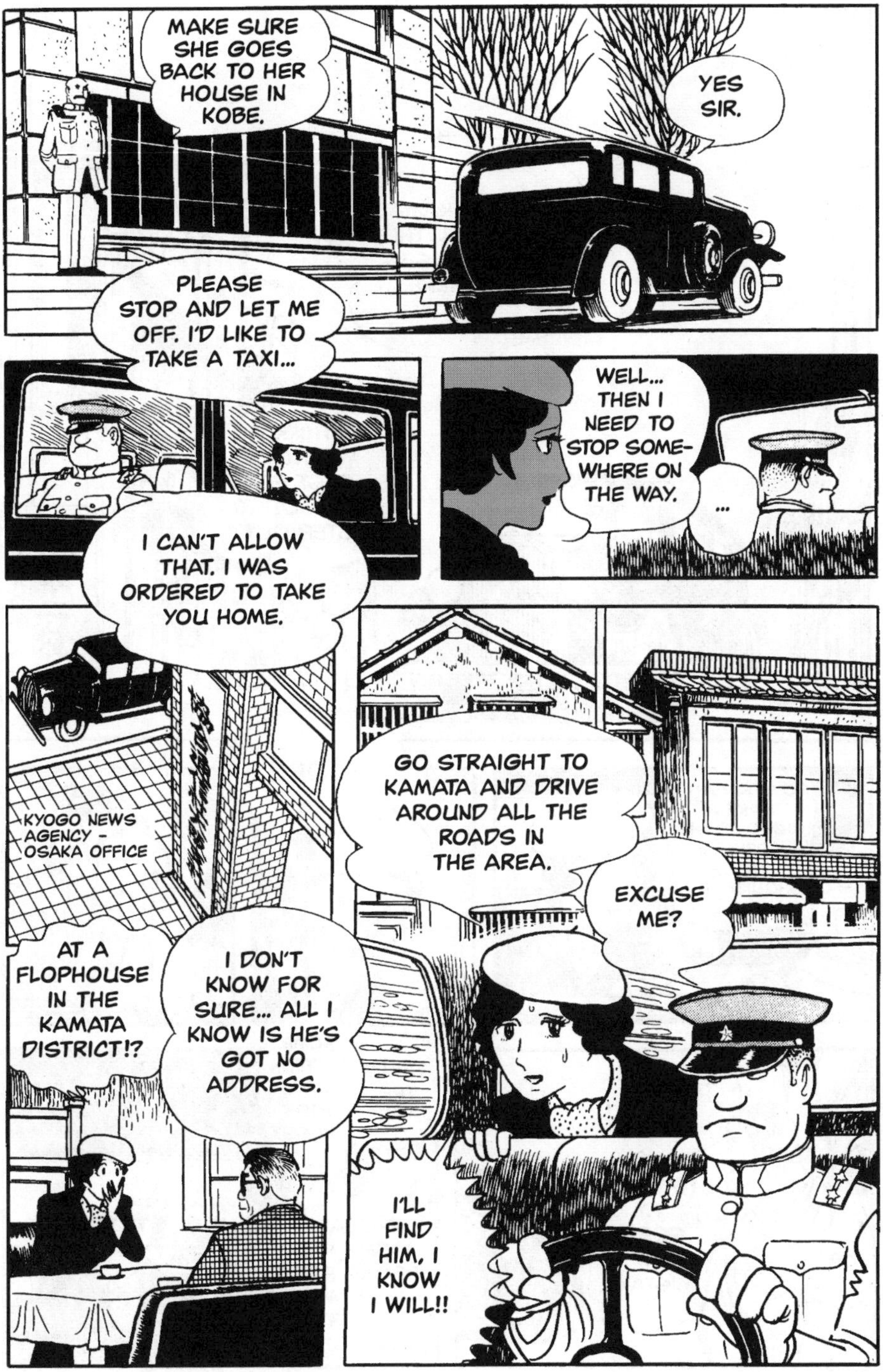
MAKE SURE SHE GOES BACK TO HER HOUSE IN KOBE.
YES SIR.
PLEASE STOP AND LET ME OFF. I'D LIKE TO TAKE A TAXI...
I CAN'T ALLOW THAT. I WAS ORDERED TO TAKE YOU HOME.
WELL... THEN I NEED TO STOP SOME-WHERE ON THE WAY.
...
KYOGO NEWS AGENCY - OSAKA OFFICE
AT A FLOPHOUSE IN THE KAMATA DISTRICT!?
I DON'T KNOW FOR SURE... ALL I KNOW IS HE'S GOT NO ADDRESS.
GO STRAIGHT TO KAMATA AND DRIVE AROUND ALL THE ROADS IN THE AREA.
EXCUSE ME?
I'LL FIND HIM, I KNOW I WILL!!

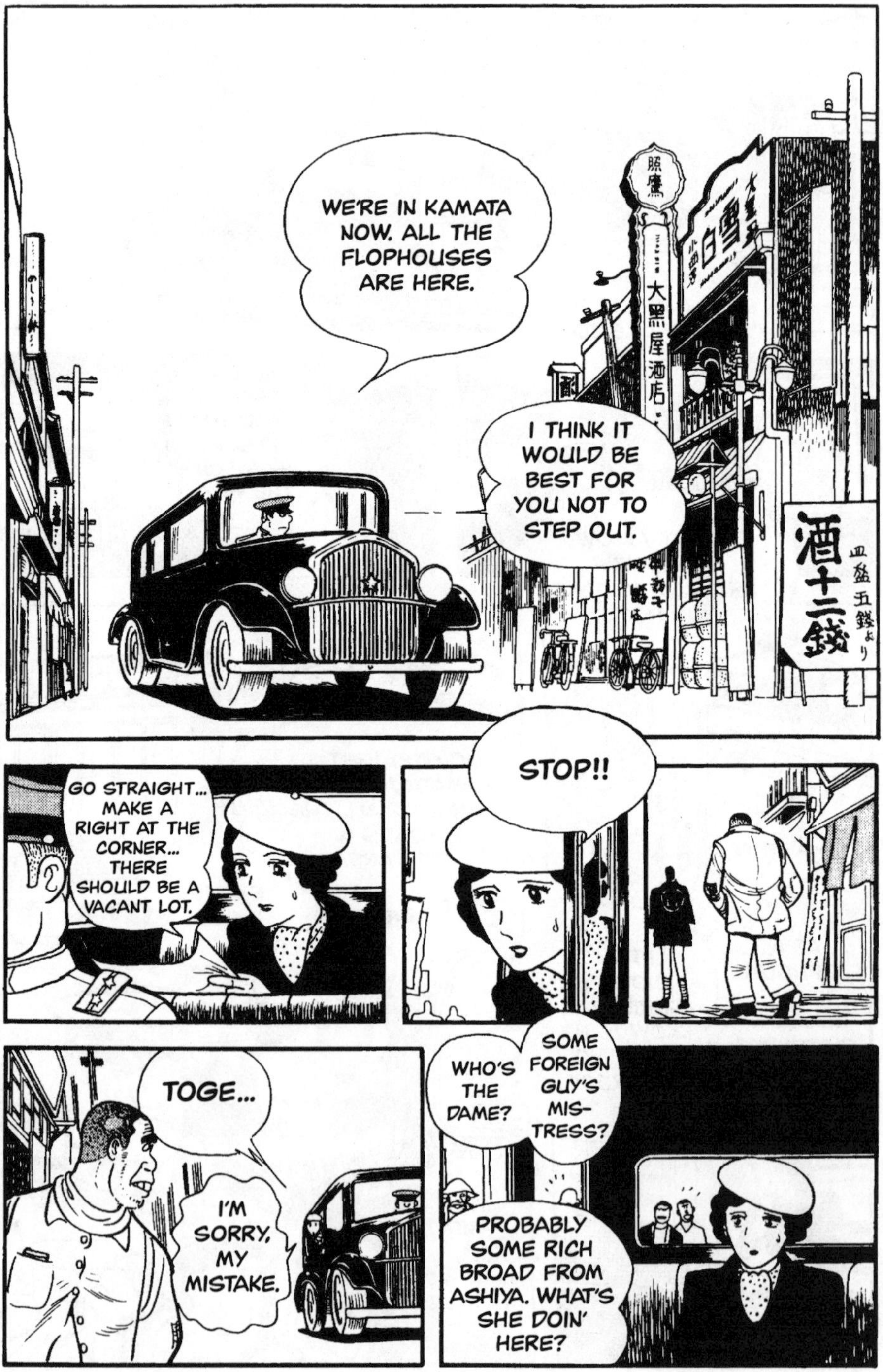
WE'RE IN KAMATA NOW. ALL THE FLOPHOUSES ARE HERE.
大黒屋酒店
白雪
酒十二銭
皿盃五銭より
I THINK IT WOULD BE BEST FOR YOU NOT TO STEP OUT.
GO STRAIGHT... MAKE A RIGHT AT THE CORNER... THERE SHOULD BE A VACANT LOT.
STOP!!
TOGE...
I'M SORRY, MY MISTAKE.
WHO'S THE DAME?
SOME FOREIGN GUY'S MIS-TRESS?
PROBABLY SOME RICH BROAD FROM ASHIYA. WHAT'S SHE DOIN' HERE?

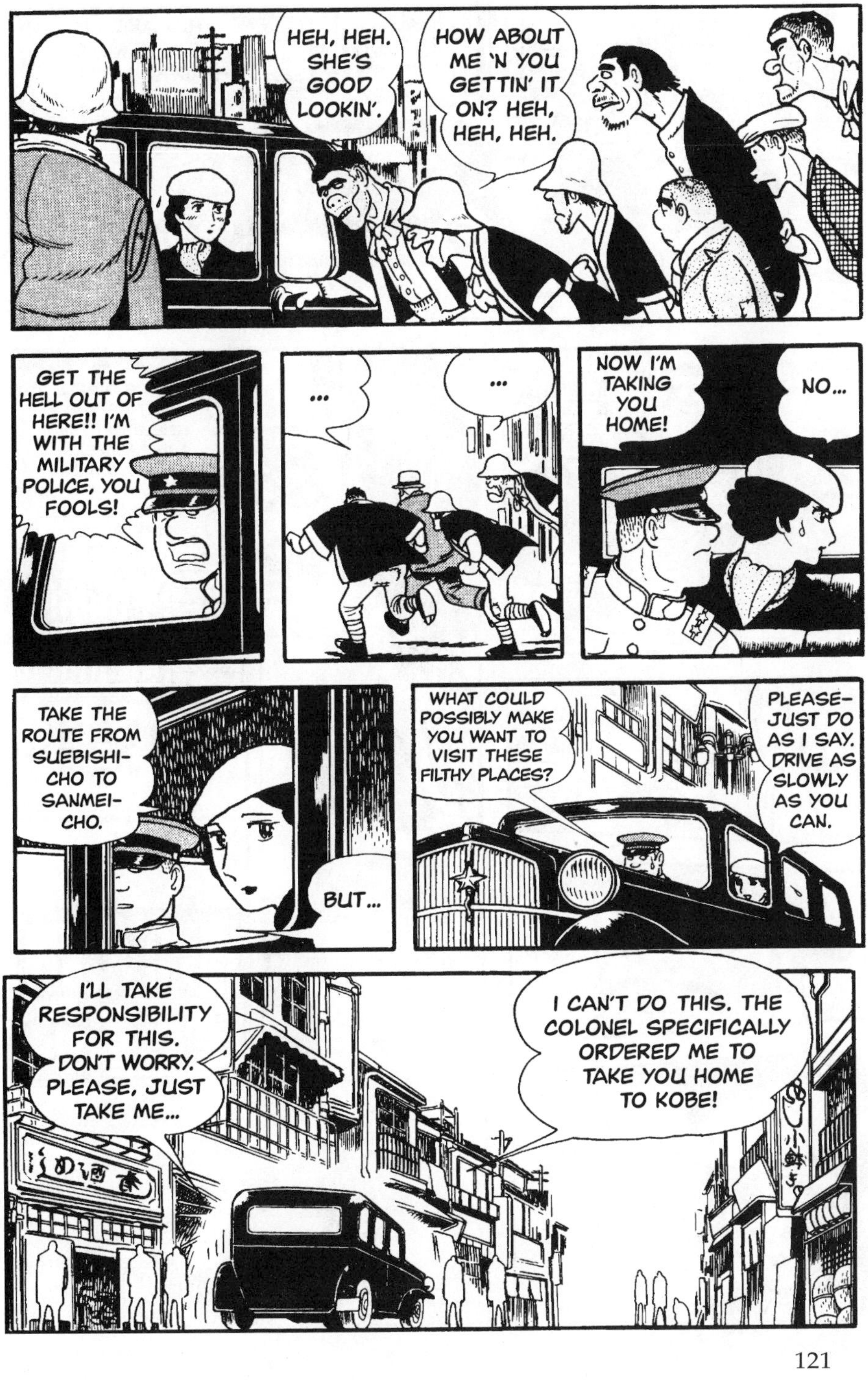
HEH, HEH. SHE'S GOOD LOOKIN'.
HOW ABOUT ME 'N YOU GETTIN' IT ON? HEH, HEH, HEH.
GET THE HELL OUT OF HERE!! I'M WITH THE MILITARY POLICE, YOU FOOLS!
...
...
NOW I'M TAKING YOU HOME!
NO...
TAKE THE ROUTE FROM SUEBISHI-CHO TO SANMEI-CHO.
BUT...
WHAT COULD POSSIBLY MAKE YOU WANT TO VISIT THESE FILTHY PLACES?
PLEASE- JUST DO AS I SAY. DRIVE AS SLOWLY AS YOU CAN.
I'LL TAKE RESPONSIBILITY FOR THIS. DON'T WORRY. PLEASE, JUST TAKE ME...
I CAN'T DO THIS. THE COLONEL SPECIFICALLY ORDERED ME TO TAKE YOU HOME TO KOBE!

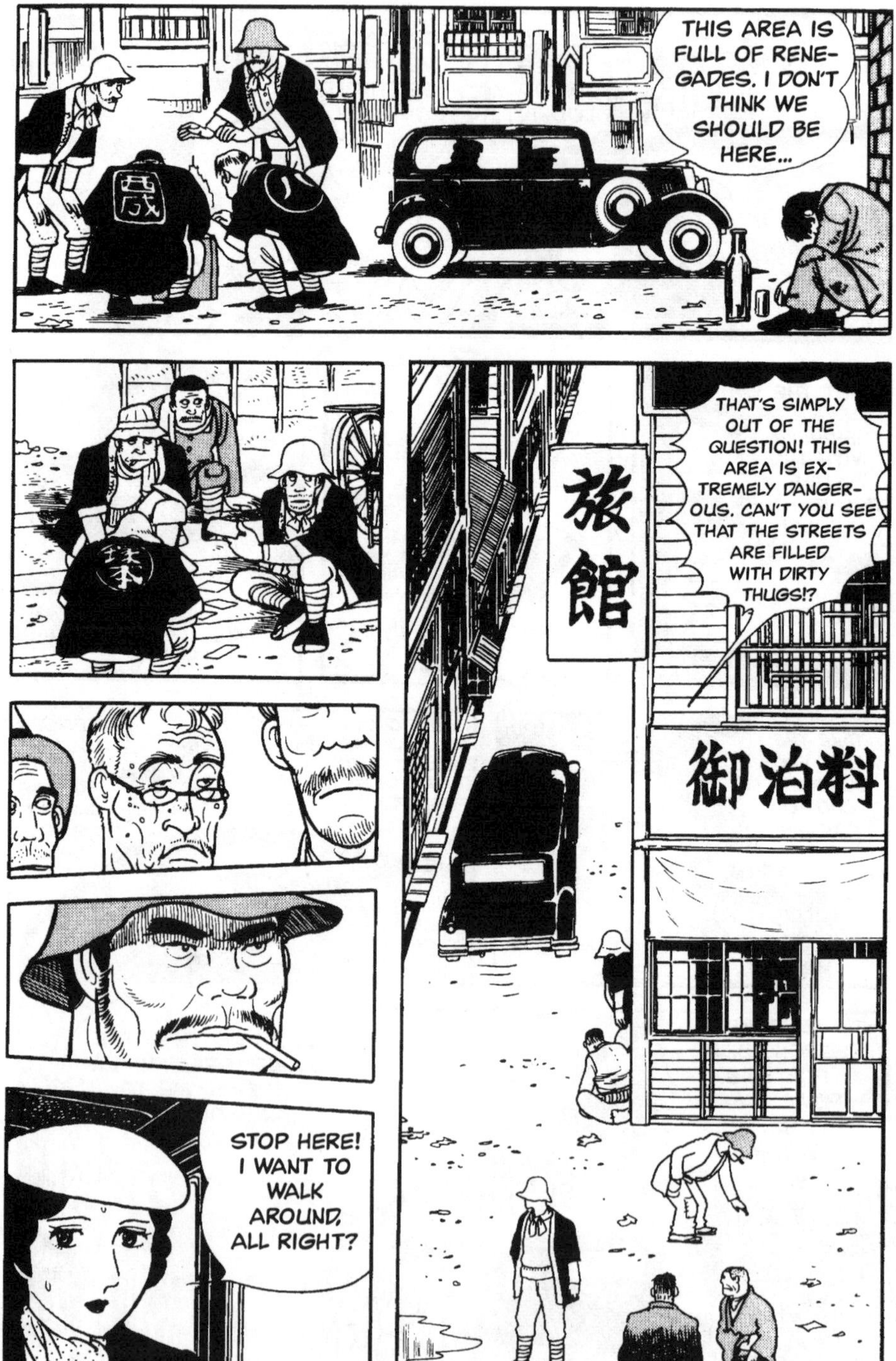
THIS AREA IS FULL OF RENE-GADES. I DON'T THINK WE SHOULD BE HERE...
STOP HERE! I WANT TO WALK AROUND, ALL RIGHT?
旅館
THAT'S SIMPLY OUT OF THE QUESTION! THIS AREA IS EX-TREMELY DANGER-OUS. CAN'T YOU SEE THAT THE STREETS ARE FILLED WITH DIRTY THUGS!?
御泊料

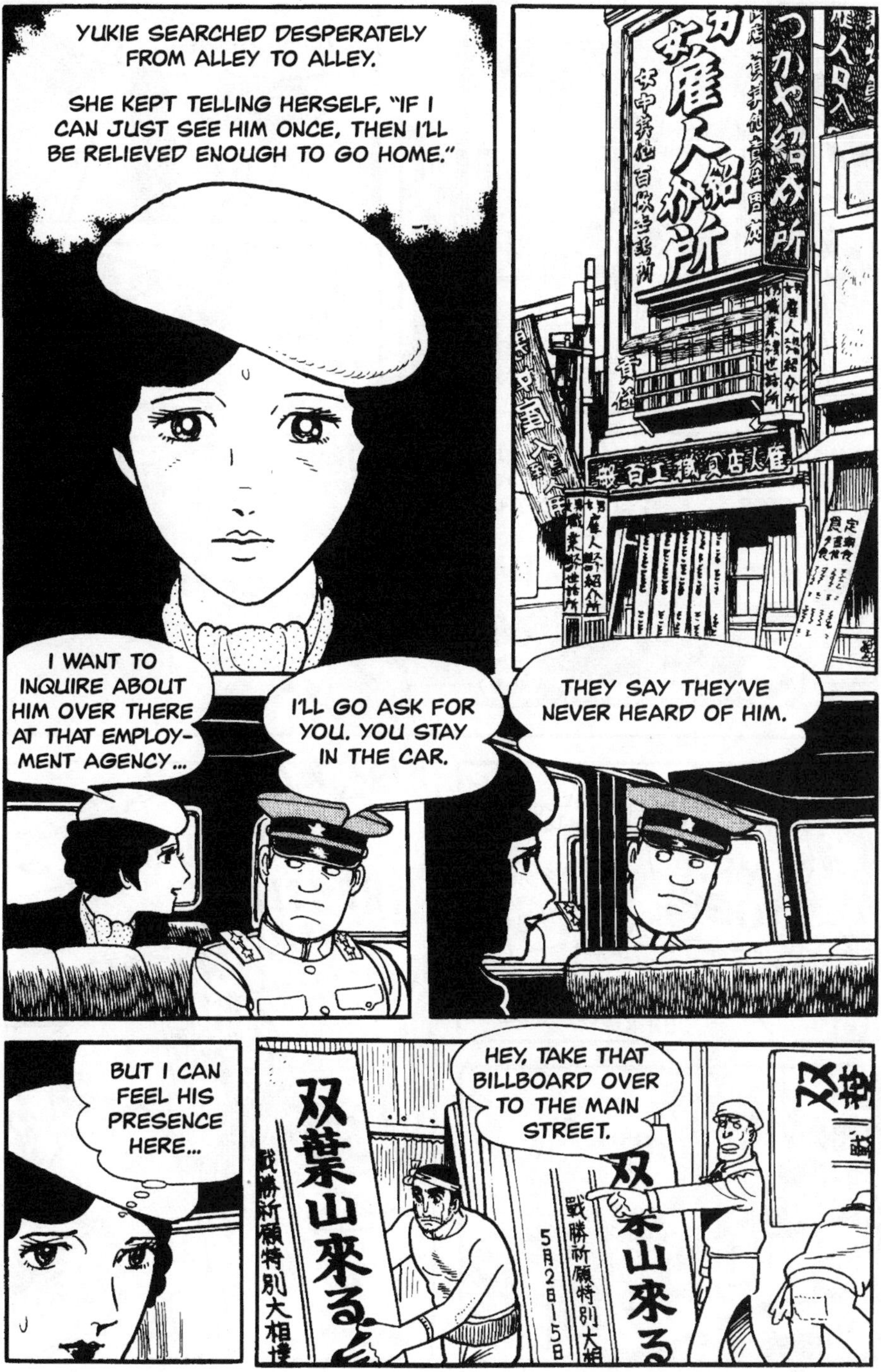
YUKIE SEARCHED DESPERATELY FROM ALLEY TO ALLEY.
SHE KEPT TELLING HERSELF, "IF I CAN JUST SEE HIM ONCE, THEN I'LL BE RELIEVED ENOUGH TO GO HOME."
I WANT TO INQUIRE ABOUT HIM OVER THERE AT THAT EMPLOY-MENT AGENCY...
I'LL GO ASK FOR YOU. YOU STAY IN THE CAR.
THEY SAY THEY'VE NEVER HEARD OF HIM.
BUT I CAN FEEL HIS PRESENCE HERE...
双葉山來る
戰勝祈願特別大相撲
HEY, TAKE THAT BILLBOARD OVER TO THE MAIN STREET.
5月2日—5日

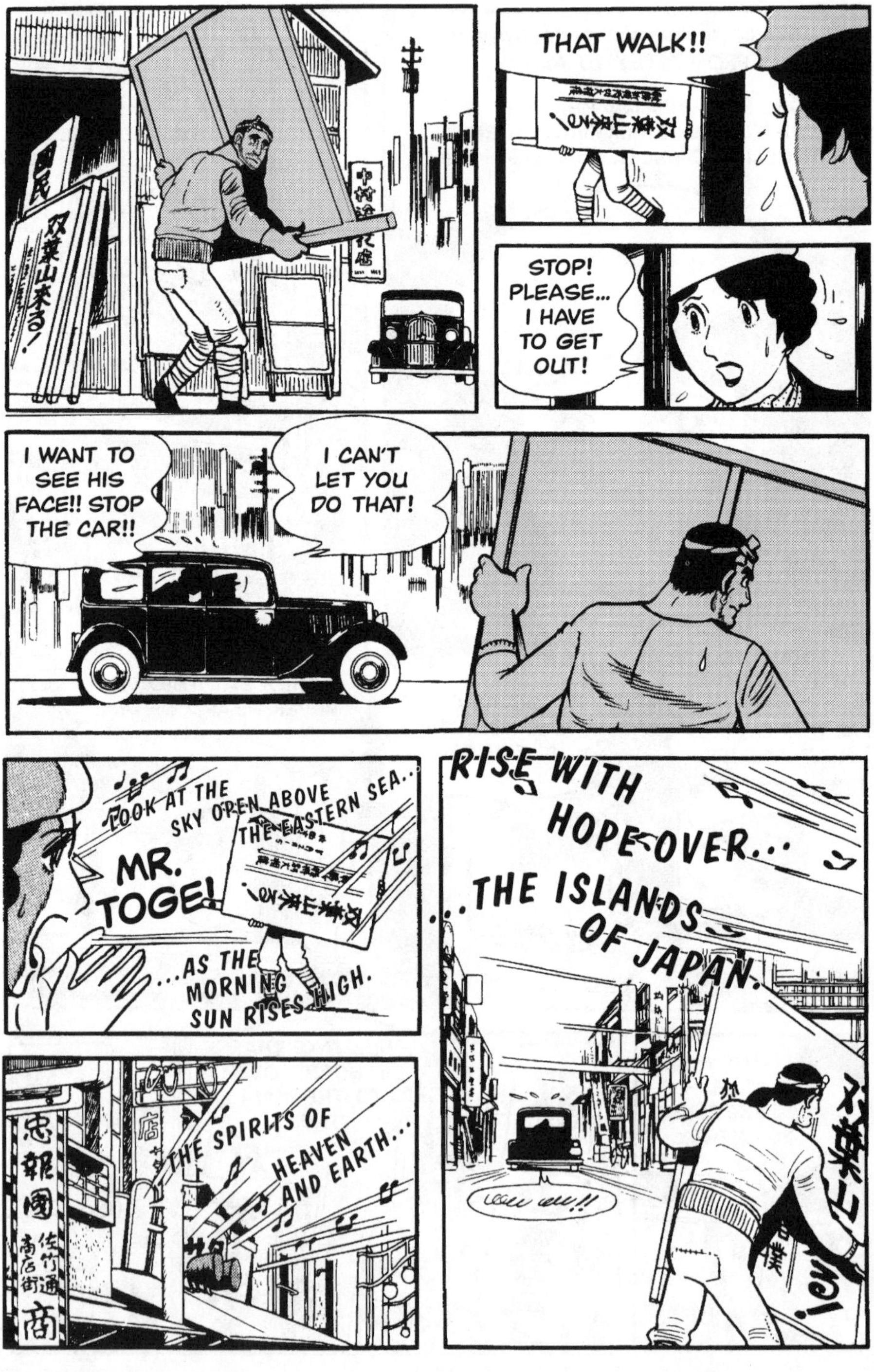
THAT WALK!!
STOP! PLEASE... I HAVE TO GET OUT!
I WANT TO SEE HIS FACE!! STOP THE CAR!!
I CAN'T LET YOU DO THAT!
LOOK AT THE SKY OPEN ABOVE THE EASTERN SEA...
MR. TOGE!
...AS THE MORNING SUN RISES HIGH.
THE SPIRITS OF HEAVEN AND EARTH...
RISE WITH HOPE OVER...
...THE ISLANDS OF JAPAN.

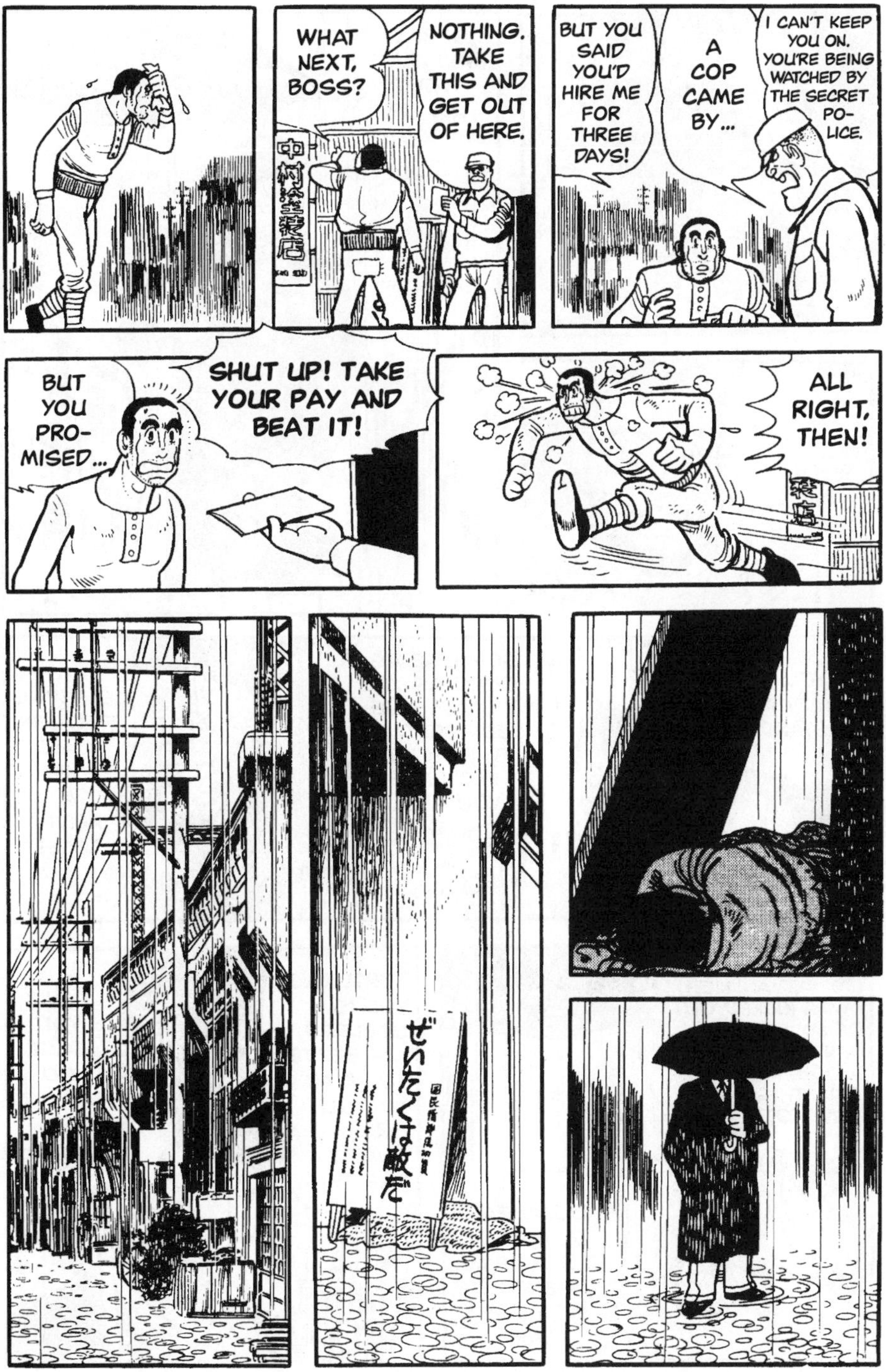
WHAT NEXT, BOSS?
NOTHING. TAKE THIS AND GET OUT OF HERE.
BUT YOU SAID YOU'D HIRE ME FOR THREE DAYS!
A COP CAME BY...
I CAN'T KEEP YOU ON. YOU'RE BEING WATCHED BY THE SECRET PO-LICE.
BUT YOU PRO-MISED...
SHUT UP! TAKE YOUR PAY AND BEAT IT!
ALL RIGHT, THEN!
ぜいたくは敵だ

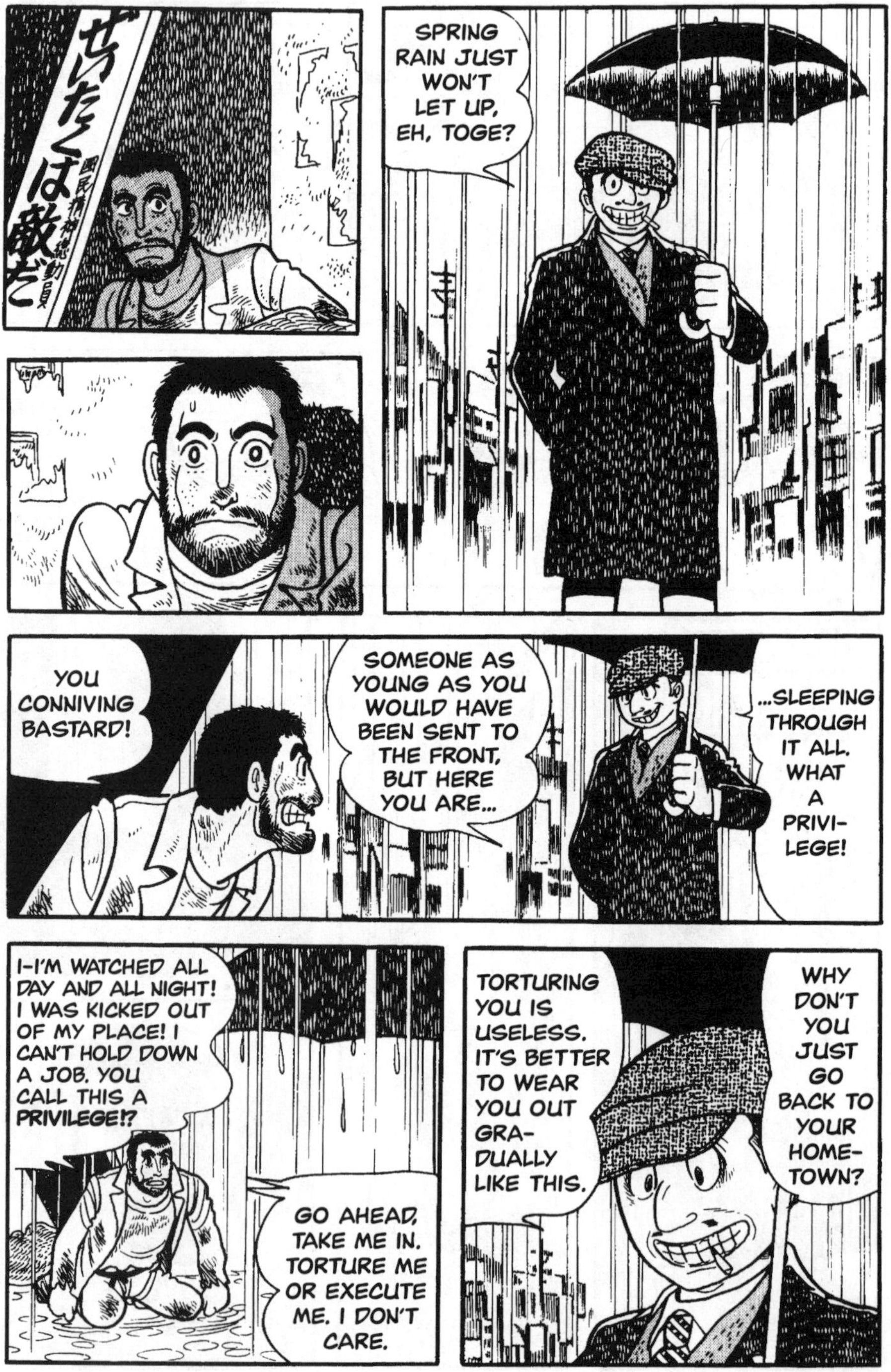
ぜいたくは敵だ
国民精神総動員
SPRING RAIN JUST WON'T LET UP, EH, TOGE?
YOU CONNIVING BASTARD!
SOMEONE AS YOUNG AS YOU WOULD HAVE BEEN SENT TO THE FRONT, BUT HERE YOU ARE...
...SLEEPING THROUGH IT ALL. WHAT A PRIVI-LEGE!
I-I'M WATCHED ALL DAY AND ALL NIGHT! I WAS KICKED OUT OF MY PLACE! I CAN'T HOLD DOWN A JOB. YOU CALL THIS A PRIVILEGE!?
GO AHEAD, TAKE ME IN. TORTURE ME OR EXECUTE ME. I DON'T CARE.
TORTURING YOU IS USELESS. IT'S BETTER TO WEAR YOU OUT GRA-DUALLY LIKE THIS.
WHY DON'T YOU JUST GO BACK TO YOUR HOME-TOWN?

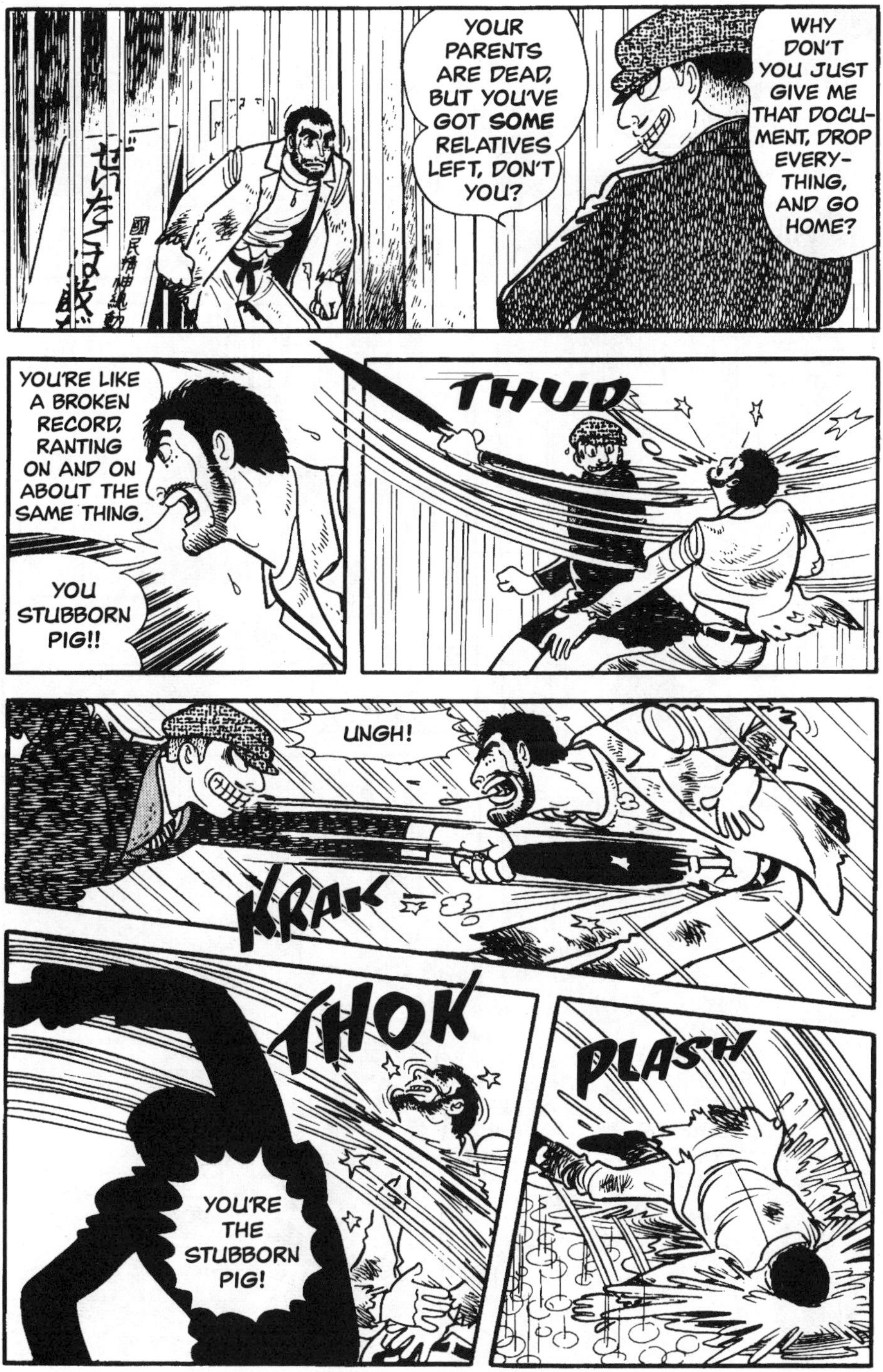
YOUR PARENTS ARE DEAD, BUT YOU'VE GOT SOME RELATIVES LEFT, DON'T YOU?
WHY DON'T YOU JUST GIVE ME THAT DOCUMENT, DROP EVERYTHING, AND GO HOME?
YOU'RE LIKE A BROKEN RECORD, RANTING ON AND ON ABOUT THE SAME THING.
YOU STUBBORN PIG!!
THUD
UNGH!
KRAK
THOK
YOU'RE THE STUBBORN PIG!
PLASH

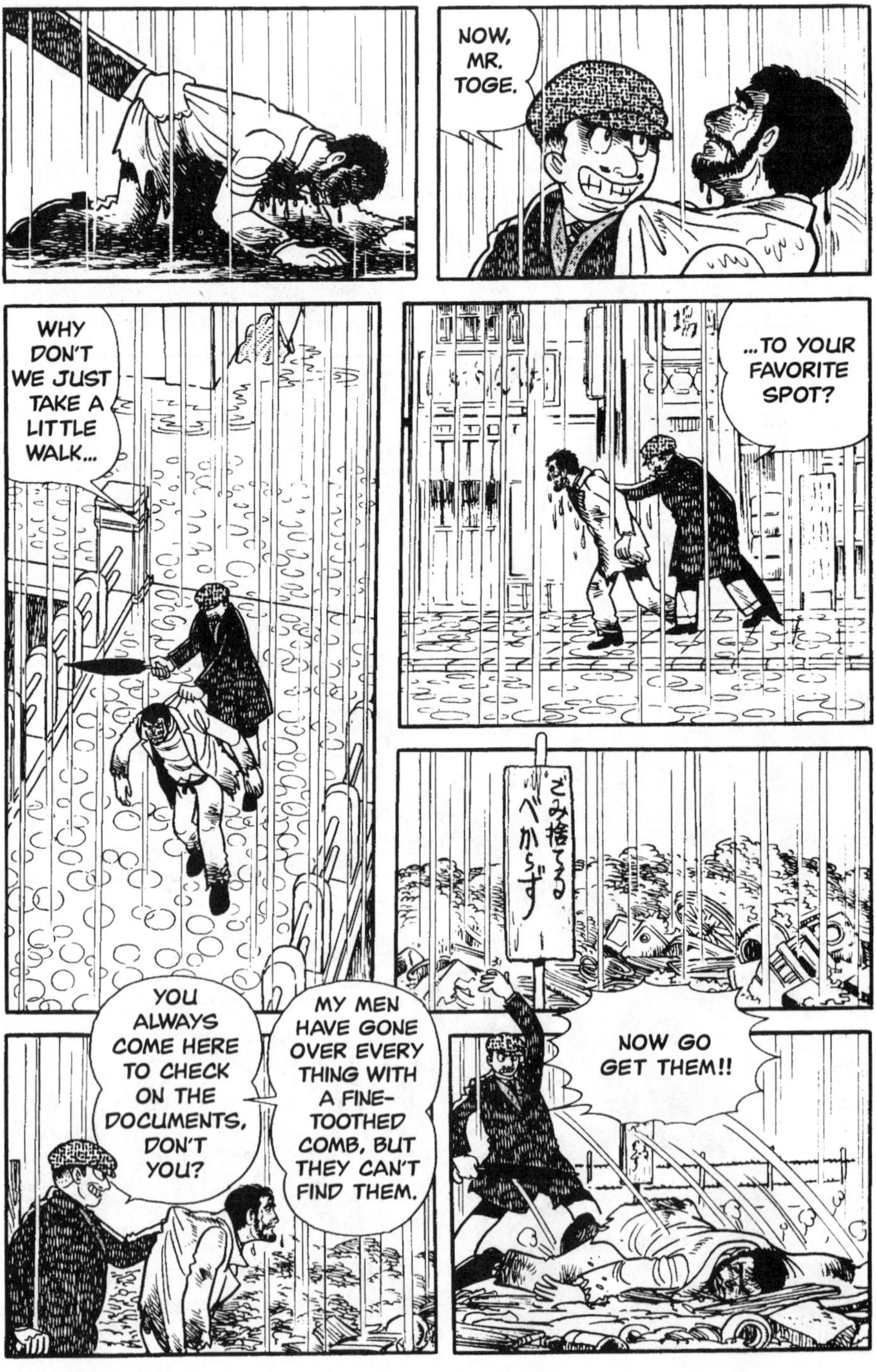
NOW, MR. TOGE.
WHY DON'T WE JUST TAKE A LITTLE WALK...
場
...TO YOUR FAVORITE SPOT?
ごみ捨てるべからず
YOU ALWAYS COME HERE TO CHECK ON THE DOCUMENTS, DON'T YOU?
MY MEN HAVE GONE OVER EVERY THING WITH A FINE-TOOTHED COMB, BUT THEY CAN'T FIND THEM.
NOW GO GET THEM!!

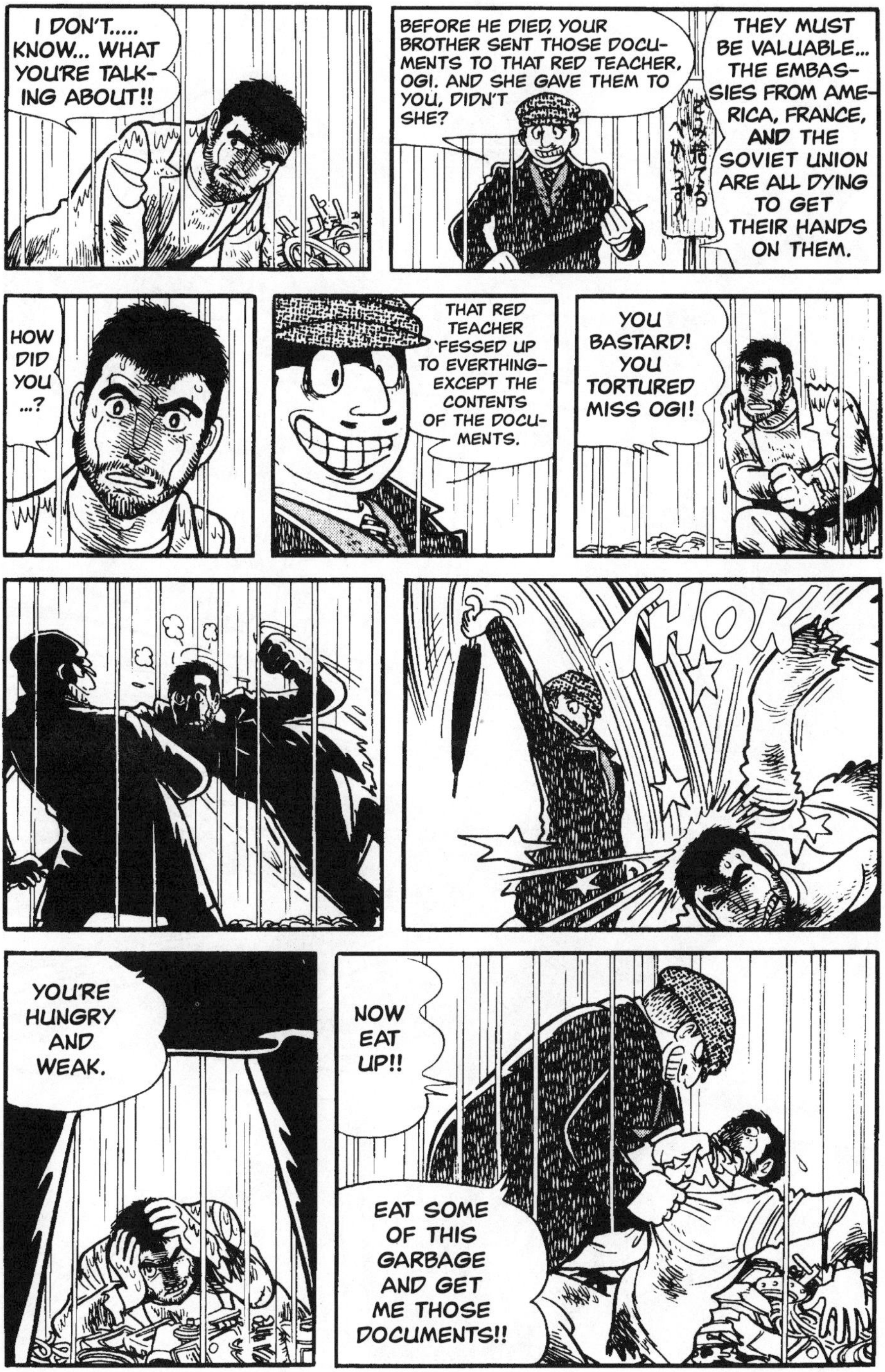
I DON'T..... KNOW... WHAT YOU'RE TALKING ABOUT!!
BEFORE HE DIED, YOUR BROTHER SENT THOSE DOCUMENTS TO THAT RED TEACHER, OGI. AND SHE GAVE THEM TO YOU, DIDN'T SHE?
THEY MUST BE VALUABLE... THE EMBASSIES FROM AMERICA, FRANCE, AND THE SOVIET UNION ARE ALL DYING TO GET THEIR HANDS ON THEM.
HOW DID YOU ...?
THAT RED TEACHER 'FESSED UP TO EVERTHING- EXCEPT THE CONTENTS OF THE DOCUMENTS.
YOU BASTARD! YOU TORTURED MISS OGI!
THOK
YOU'RE HUNGRY AND WEAK.
NOW EAT UP!!
EAT SOME OF THIS GARBAGE AND GET ME THOSE DOCUMENTS!!

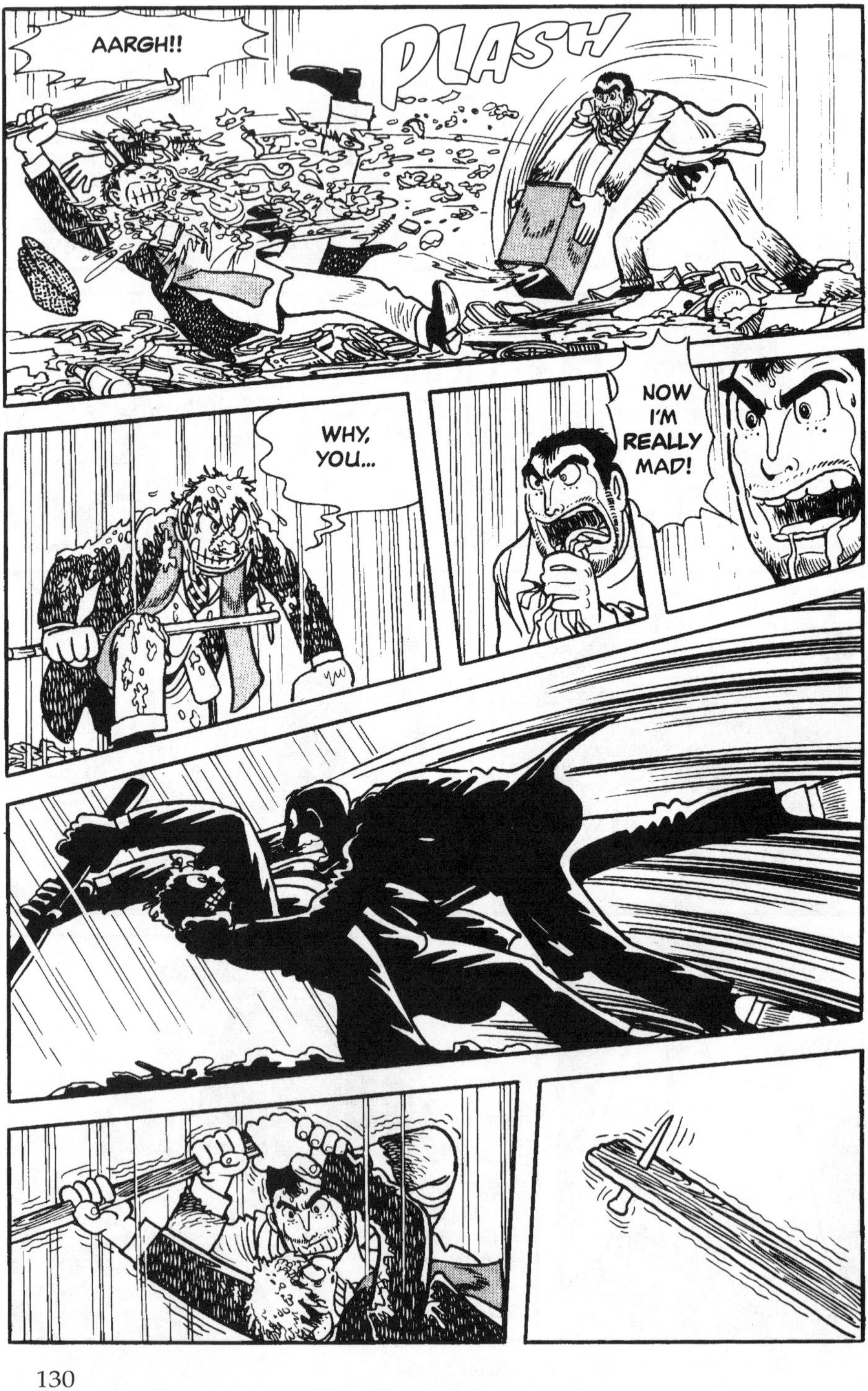
AARGH!!
PLASH
WHY, YOU...
NOW I'M REALLY MAD!

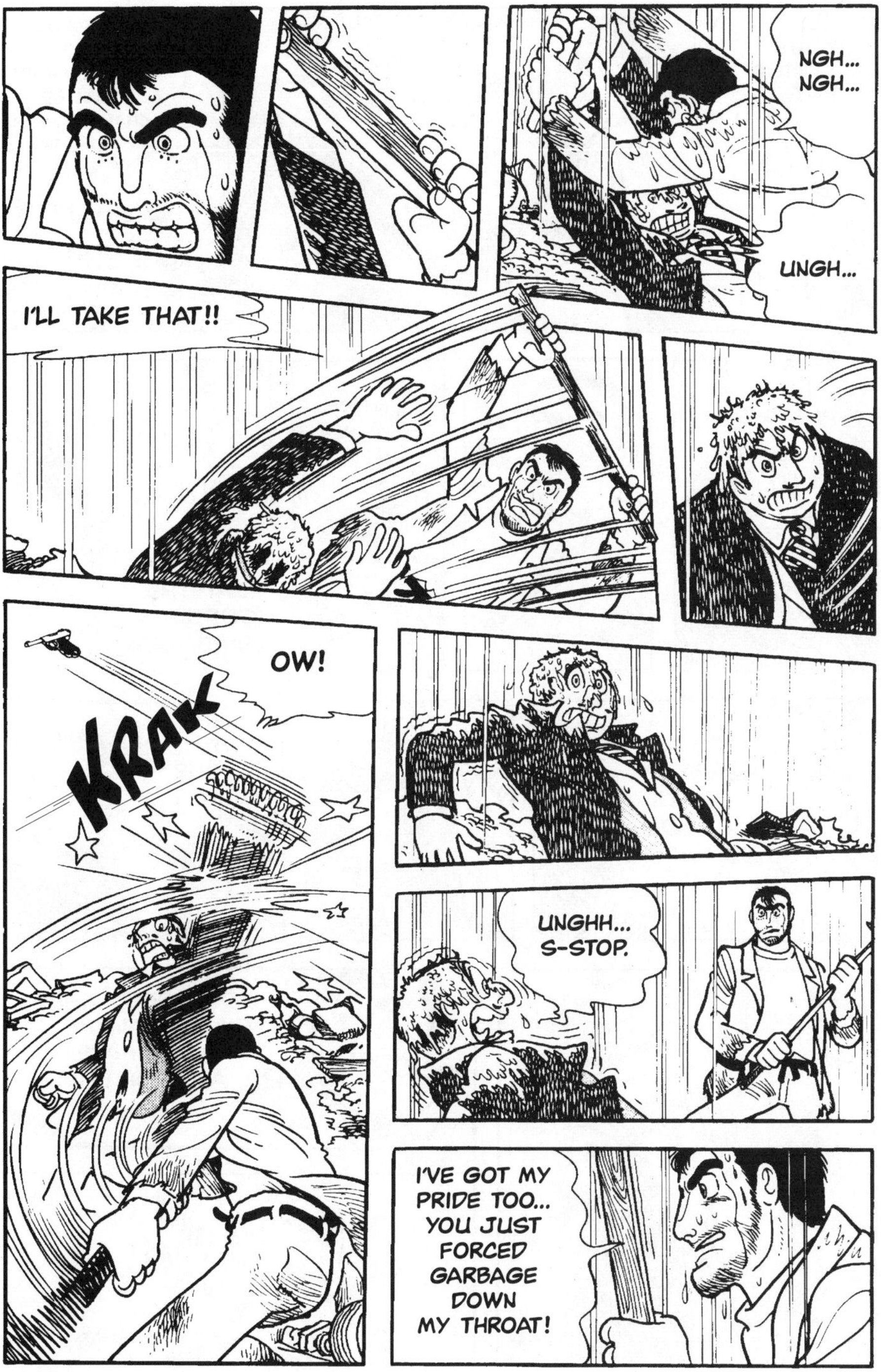
NGH... NGH...
UNGH...
I'LL TAKE THAT!!
OW!
KRAK
UNGHH... S-STOP.
I'VE GOT MY PRIDE TOO... YOU JUST FORCED GARBAGE DOWN MY THROAT!

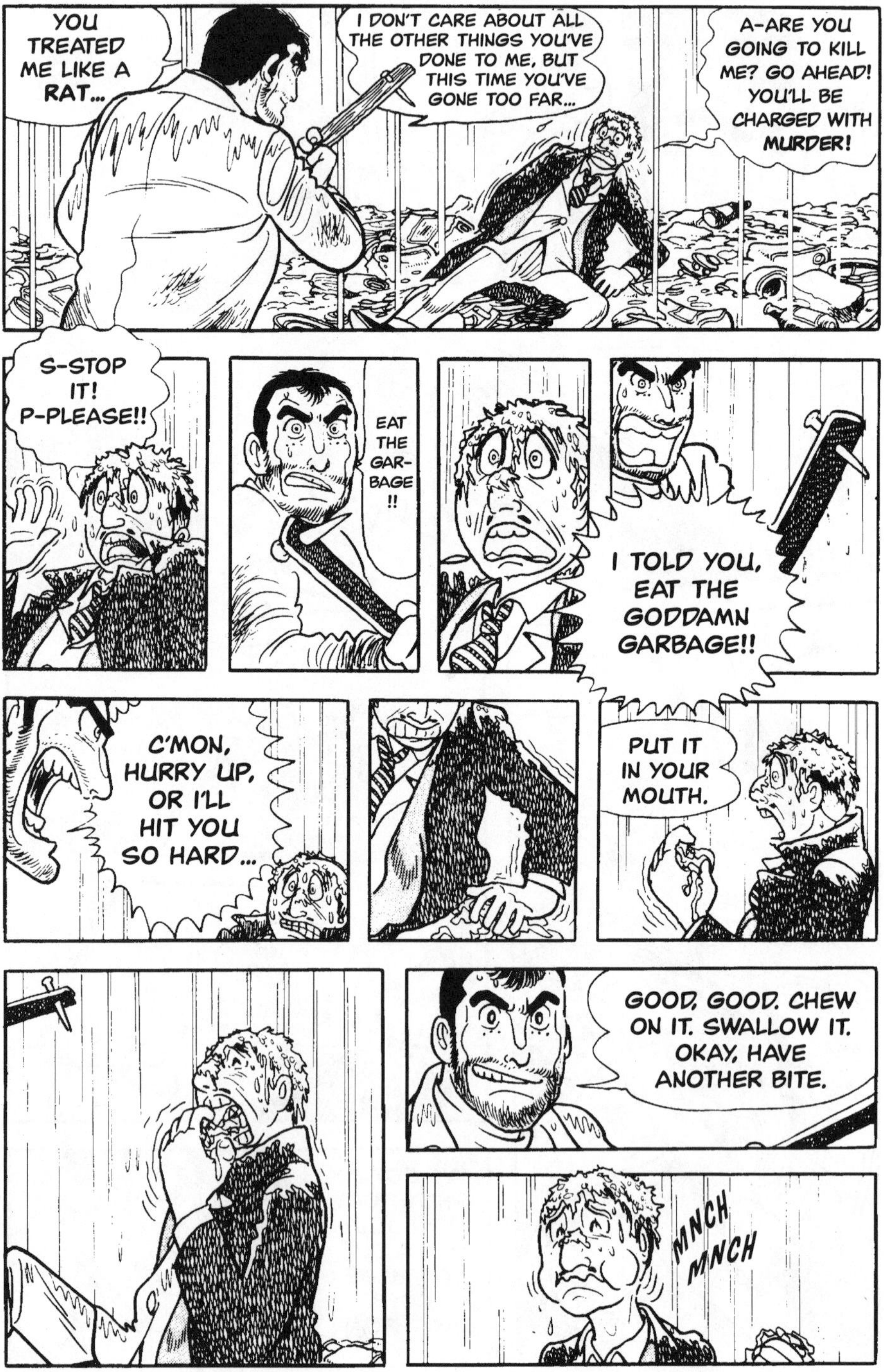
YOU TREATED ME LIKE A RAT...
I DON'T CARE ABOUT ALL THE OTHER THINGS YOU'VE DONE TO ME, BUT THIS TIME YOU'VE GONE TOO FAR...
A-ARE YOU GOING TO KILL ME? GO AHEAD! YOU'LL BE CHARGED WITH MURDER!
S-STOP IT! P-PLEASE!!
EAT THE GAR-BAGE !!
I TOLD YOU, EAT THE GODDAMN GARBAGE!!
C'MON, HURRY UP, OR I'LL HIT YOU SO HARD...
PUT IT IN YOUR MOUTH.
GOOD, GOOD. CHEW ON IT. SWALLOW IT. OKAY, HAVE ANOTHER BITE.
MNCH MNCH

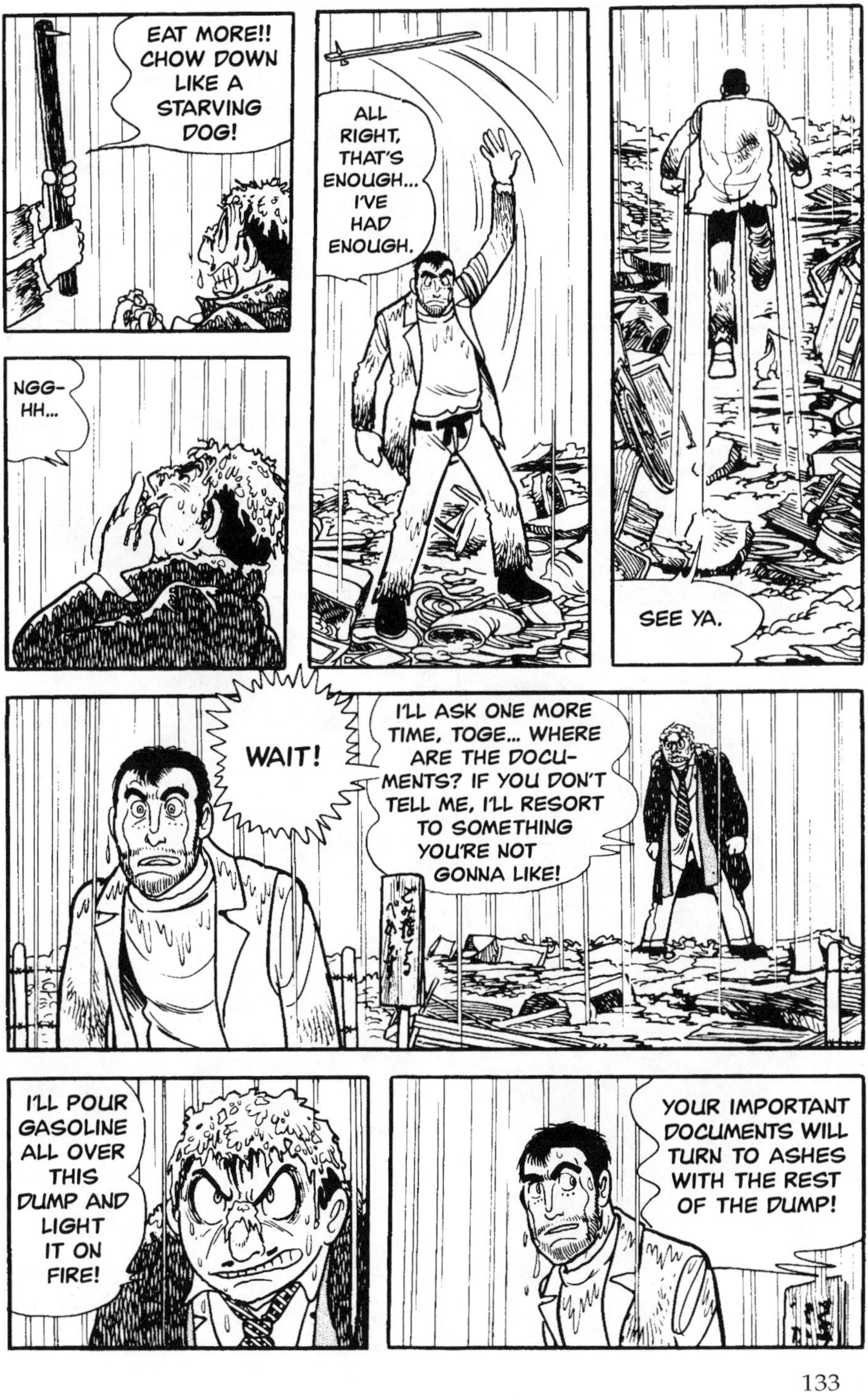
EAT MORE!! CHOW DOWN LIKE A STARVING DOG!
NGG-HH...
ALL RIGHT, THAT'S ENOUGH... I'VE HAD ENOUGH.
SEE YA.
WAIT!
I'LL ASK ONE MORE TIME, TOGE... WHERE ARE THE DOCU-MENTS? IF YOU DON'T TELL ME, I'LL RESORT TO SOMETHING YOU'RE NOT GONNA LIKE!
I'LL POUR GASOLINE ALL OVER THIS DUMP AND LIGHT IT ON FIRE!
YOUR IMPORTANT DOCUMENTS WILL TURN TO ASHES WITH THE REST OF THE DUMP!

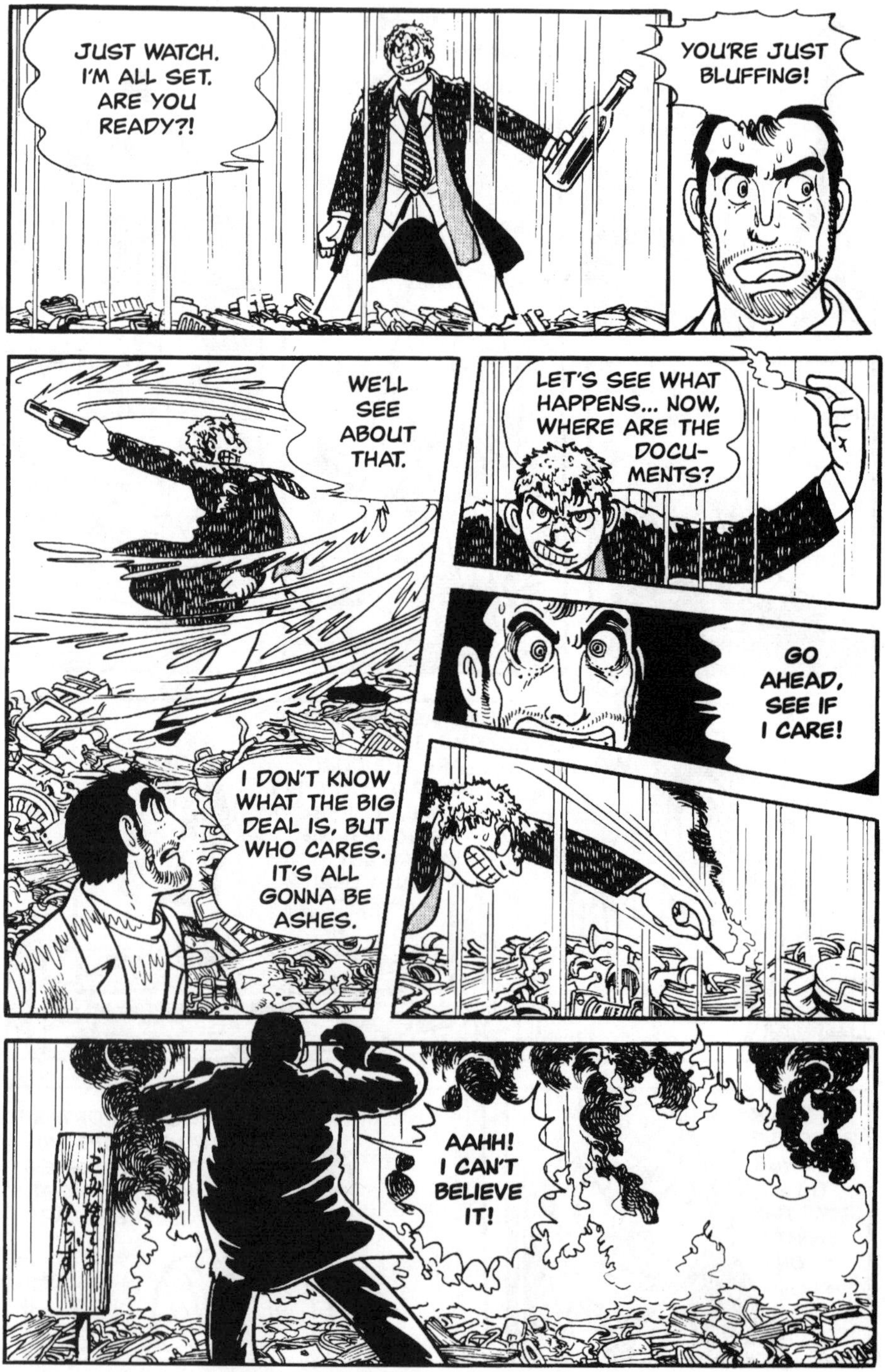
JUST WATCH. I'M ALL SET. ARE YOU READY?!
YOU'RE JUST BLUFFING!
WE'LL SEE ABOUT THAT.
I DON'T KNOW WHAT THE BIG DEAL IS, BUT WHO CARES. IT'S ALL GONNA BE ASHES.
LET'S SEE WHAT HAPPENS... NOW, WHERE ARE THE DOCUMENTS?
GO AHEAD, SEE IF I CARE!
AAHH! I CAN'T BELIEVE IT!

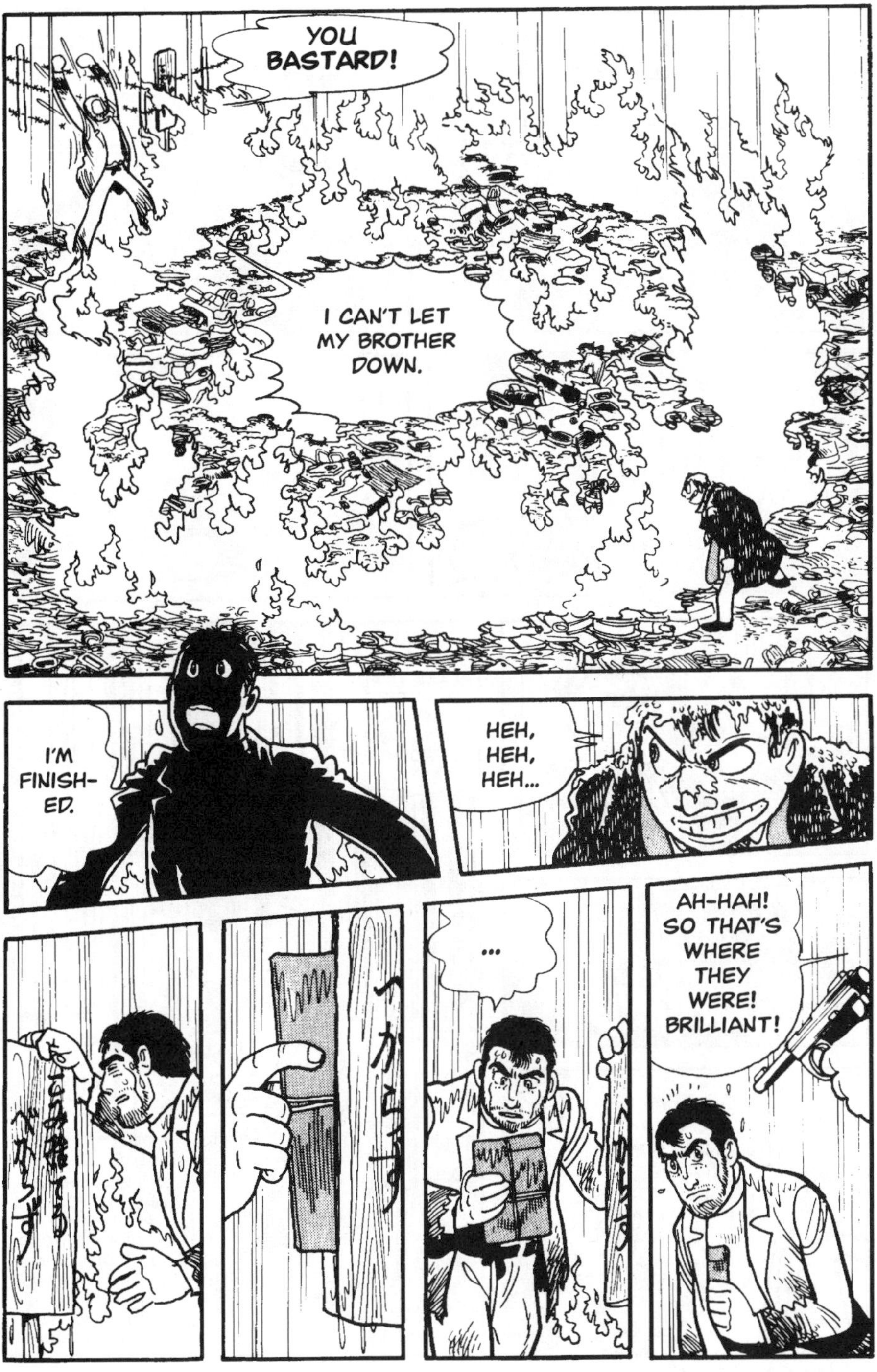
YOU BASTARD!
I CAN'T LET MY BROTHER DOWN.
I'M FINISH-ED.
HEH, HEH, HEH...
...
AH-HAH! SO THAT'S WHERE THEY WERE! BRILLIANT!

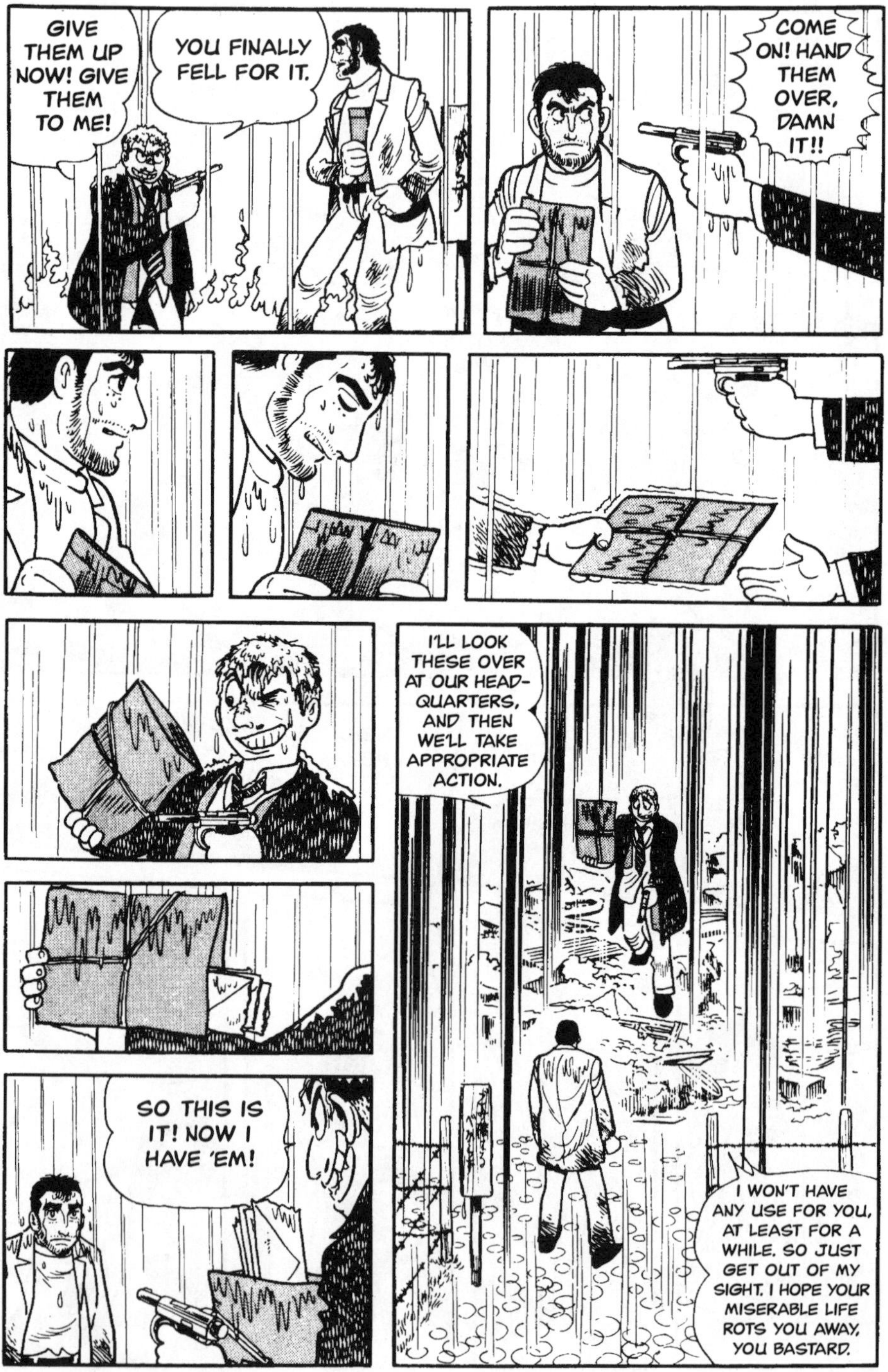
GIVE THEM UP NOW! GIVE THEM TO ME!
YOU FINALLY FELL FOR IT.
COME ON! HAND THEM OVER, DAMN IT!!
SO THIS IS IT! NOW I HAVE 'EM!
I'LL LOOK THESE OVER AT OUR HEAD-QUARTERS, AND THEN WE'LL TAKE APPROPRIATE ACTION.
I WON'T HAVE ANY USE FOR YOU, AT LEAST FOR A WHILE. SO JUST GET OUT OF MY SIGHT. I HOPE YOUR MISERABLE LIFE ROTS YOU AWAY, YOU BASTARD.

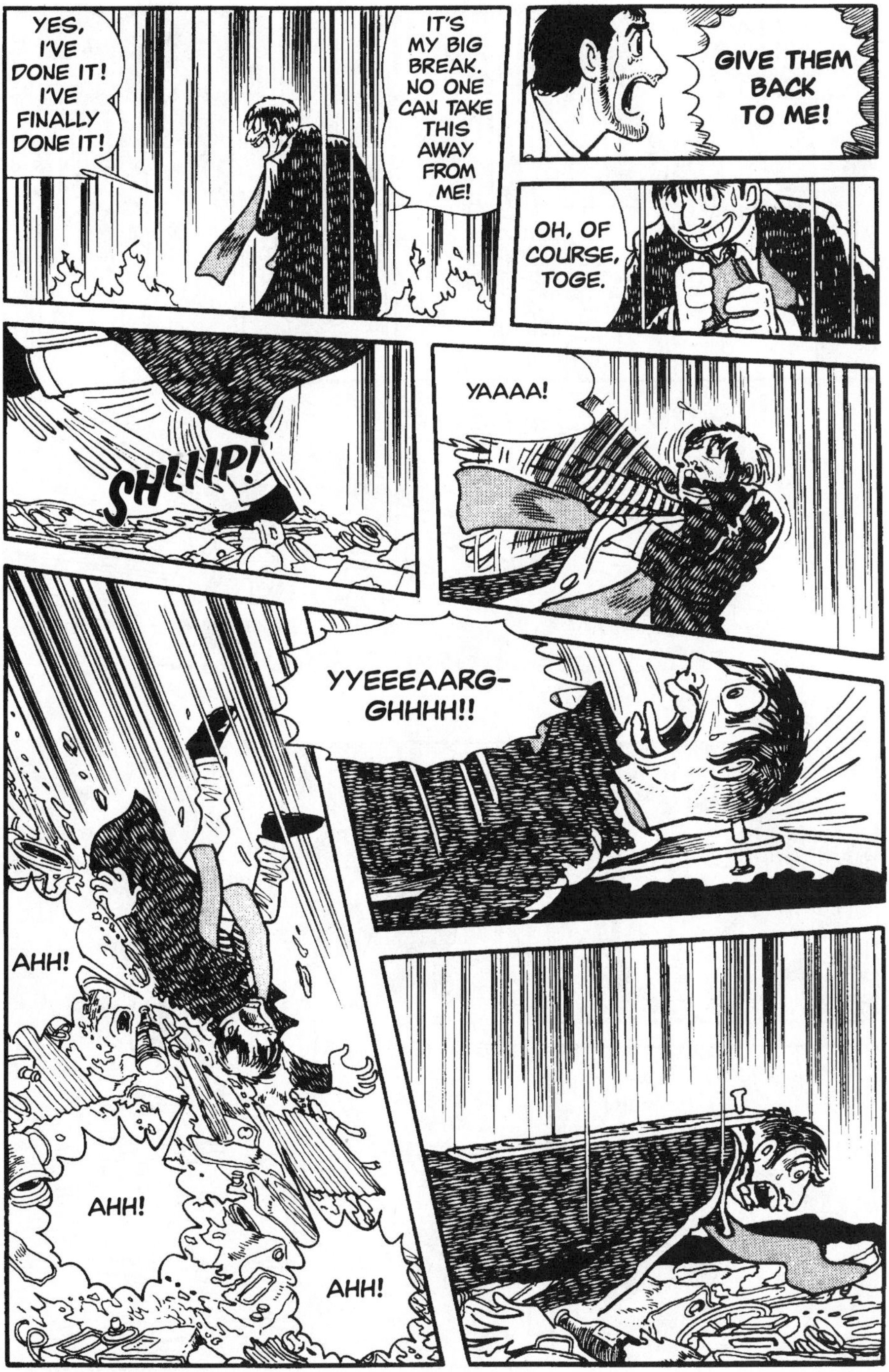
YES, I'VE DONE IT! I'VE FINALLY DONE IT!
IT'S MY BIG BREAK. NO ONE CAN TAKE THIS AWAY FROM ME!
GIVE THEM BACK TO ME!
OH, OF COURSE, TOGE.
SHLLLP!
YAAAA!
AHH!
AHH!
AHH!
YYEEEAARG-GHHHH!!

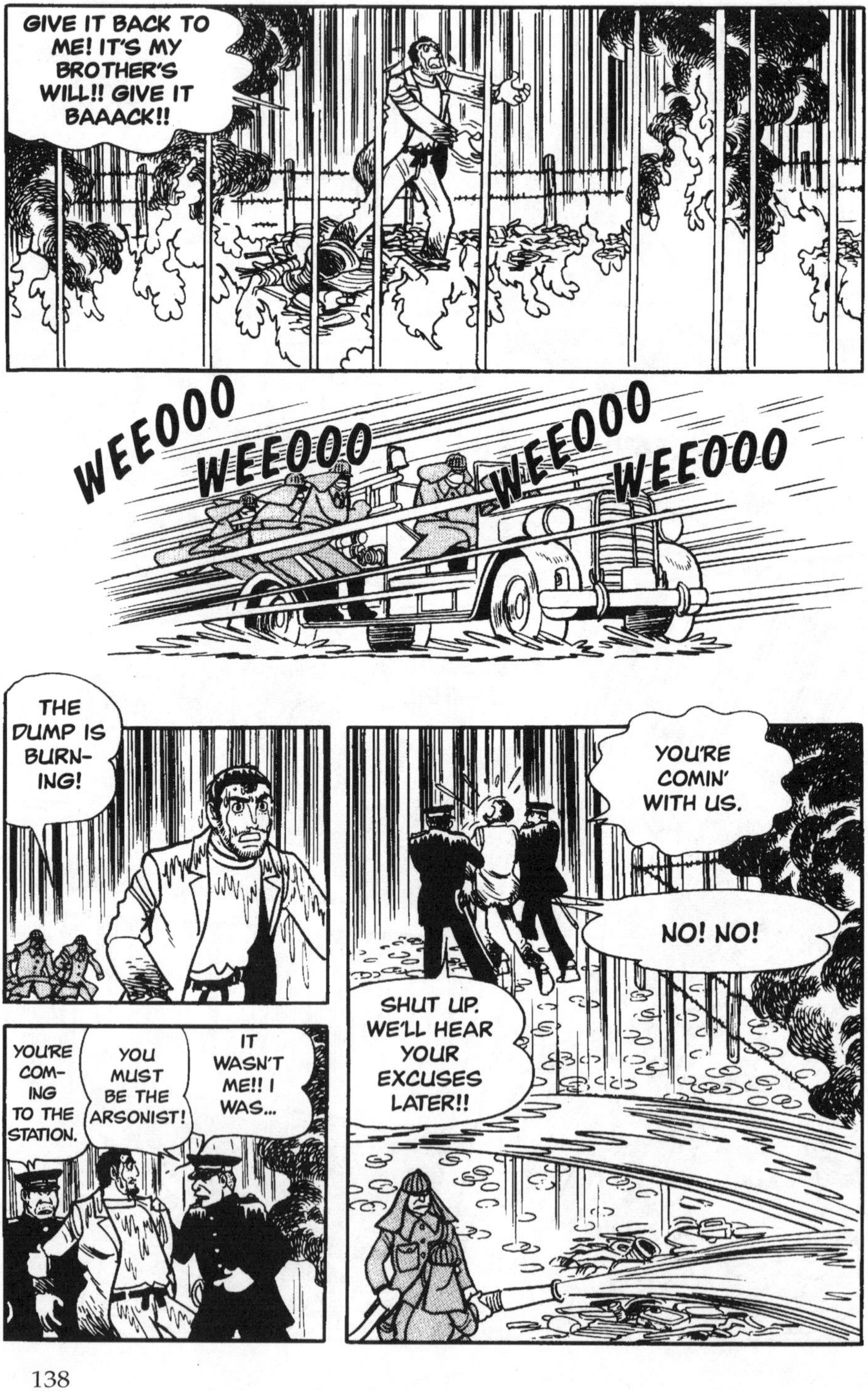
GIVE IT BACK TO ME! IT'S MY BROTHER'S WILL!! GIVE IT BAAACK!!
WEEOOO
WEEOOO
WEEOOO
WEEOOO
THE DUMP IS BURNING!
YOU'RE COMING TO THE STATION.
YOU MUST BE THE ARSONIST!
IT WASN'T ME!! I WAS...
YOU'RE COMIN' WITH US.
NO! NO!
SHUT UP. WE'LL HEAR YOUR EXCUSES LATER!!

CHAPTER
FIVE

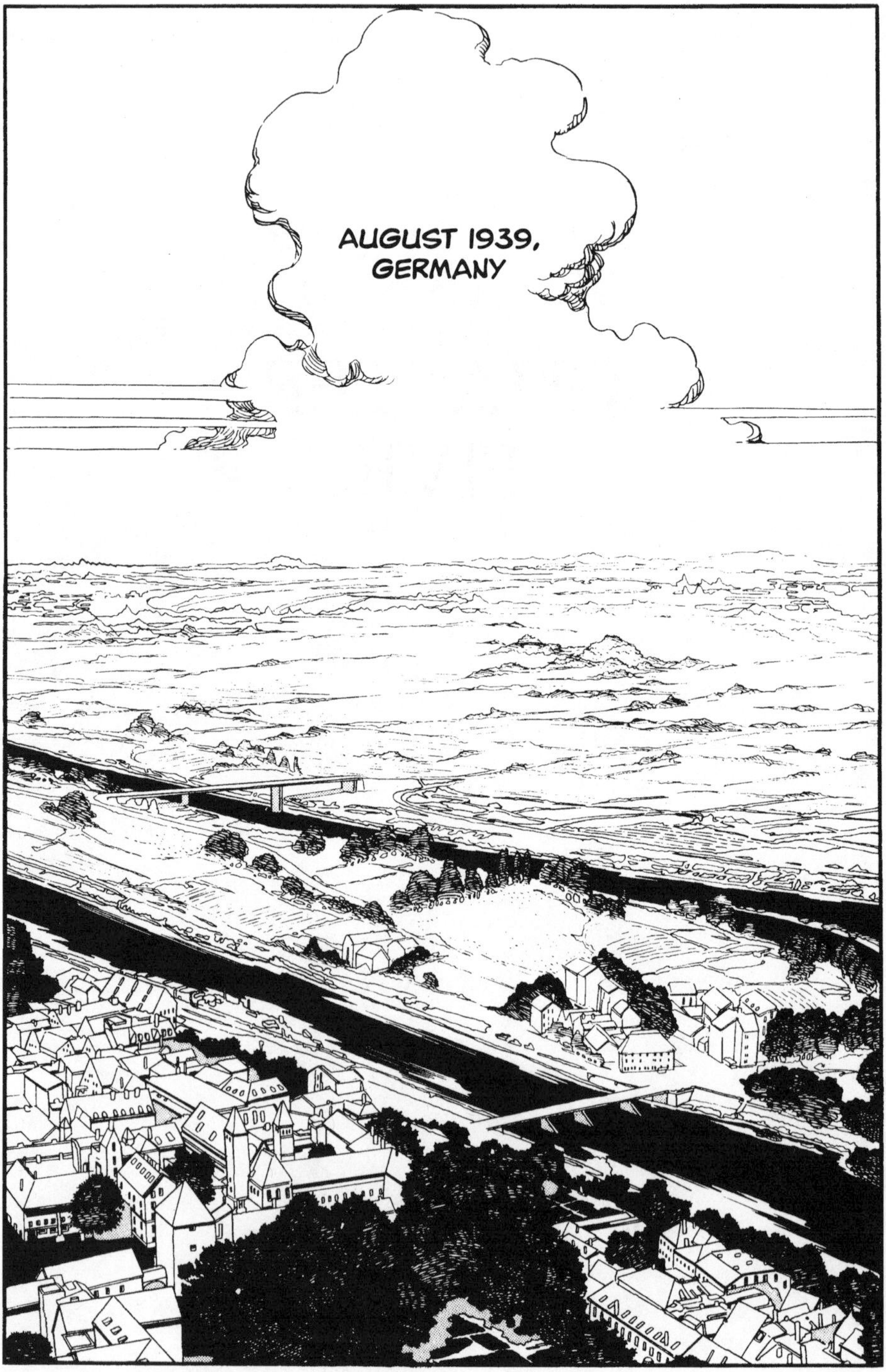
AUGUST 1939,
GERMANY

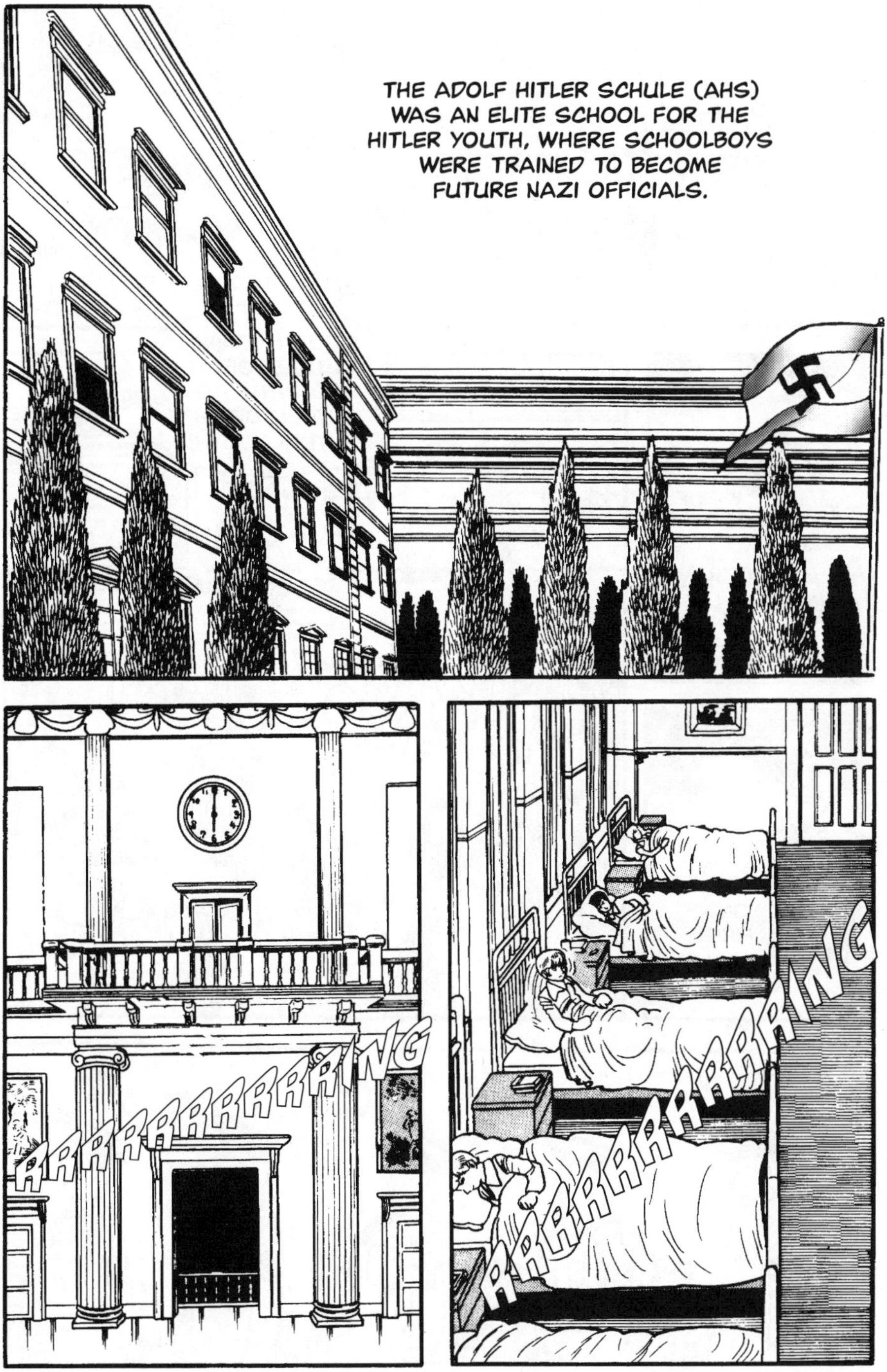
THE ADOLF HITLER SCHULE (AHS) WAS AN ELITE SCHOOL FOR THE HITLER YOUTH, WHERE SCHOOLBOYS WERE TRAINED TO BECOME FUTURE NAZI OFFICIALS.
RRRRRRRRRRING
RRRRRRRRRRRING

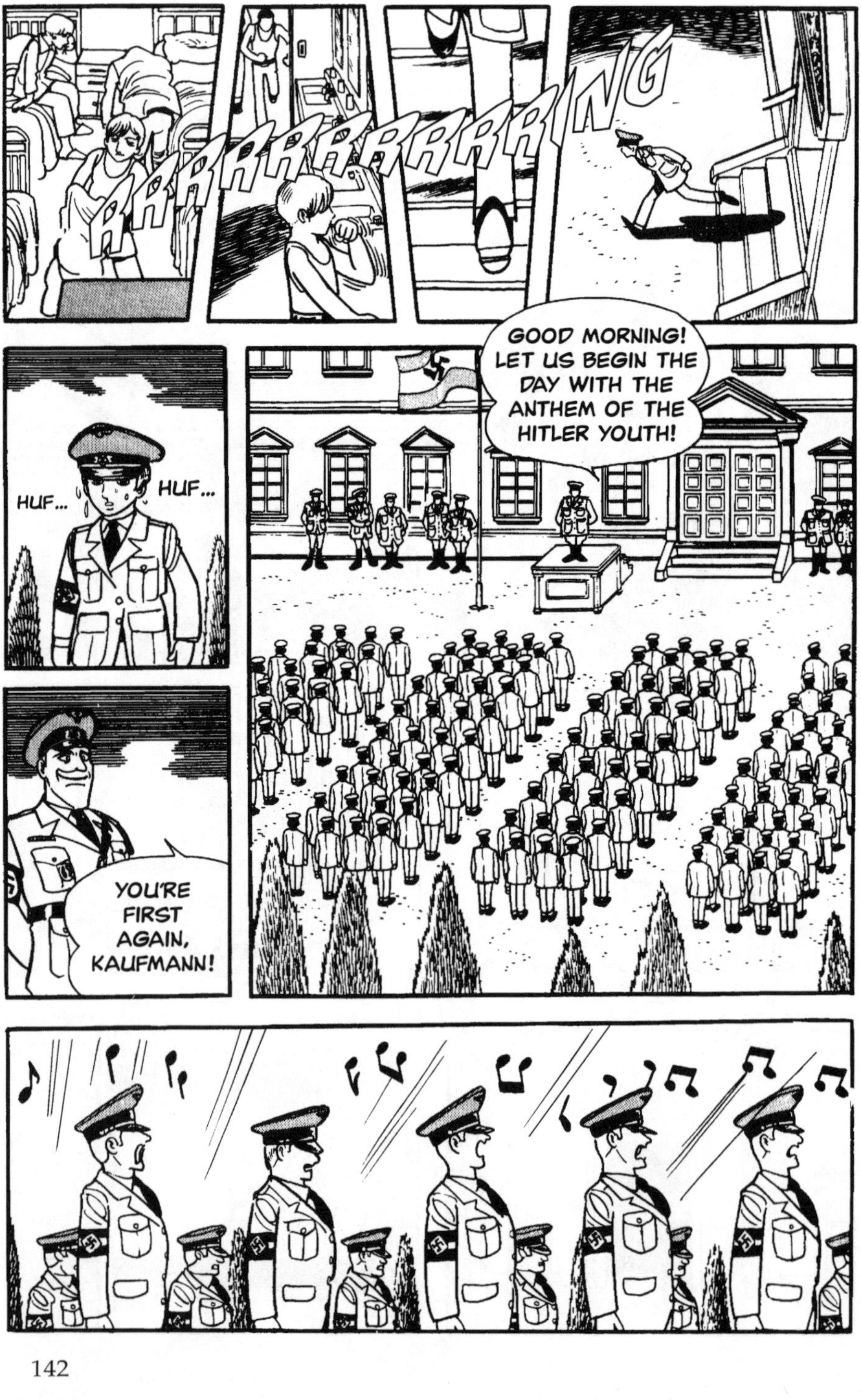
RRRRRRRRRRRRRING
HUF... HUF...
GOOD MORNING! LET US BEGIN THE DAY WITH THE ANTHEM OF THE HITLER YOUTH!
YOU'RE FIRST AGAIN, KAUFMANN!

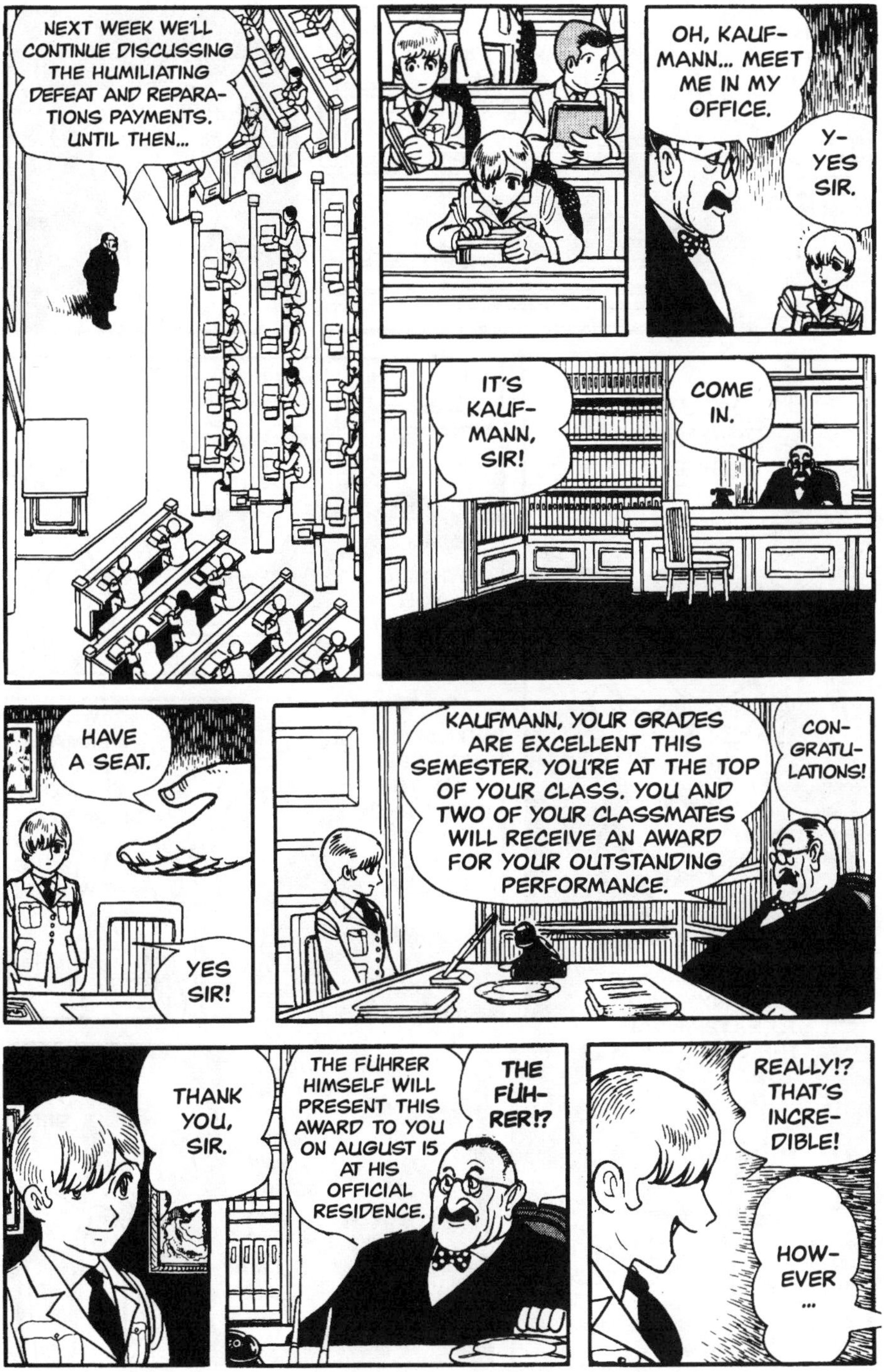
NEXT WEEK WE'LL CONTINUE DISCUSSING THE HUMILIATING DEFEAT AND REPARATIONS PAYMENTS. UNTIL THEN...
OH, KAUFMANN... MEET ME IN MY OFFICE.
Y-YES SIR.
IT'S KAUFMANN, SIR!
COME IN.
HAVE A SEAT.
YES SIR!
KAUFMANN, YOUR GRADES ARE EXCELLENT THIS SEMESTER. YOU'RE AT THE TOP OF YOUR CLASS. YOU AND TWO OF YOUR CLASSMATES WILL RECEIVE AN AWARD FOR YOUR OUTSTANDING PERFORMANCE.
CONGRATULATIONS!
THANK YOU, SIR.
THE FÜHRER HIMSELF WILL PRESENT THIS AWARD TO YOU ON AUGUST 15 AT HIS OFFICIAL RESIDENCE.
THE FÜHRER!?
REALLY!? THAT'S INCREDIBLE!
HOWEVER ...

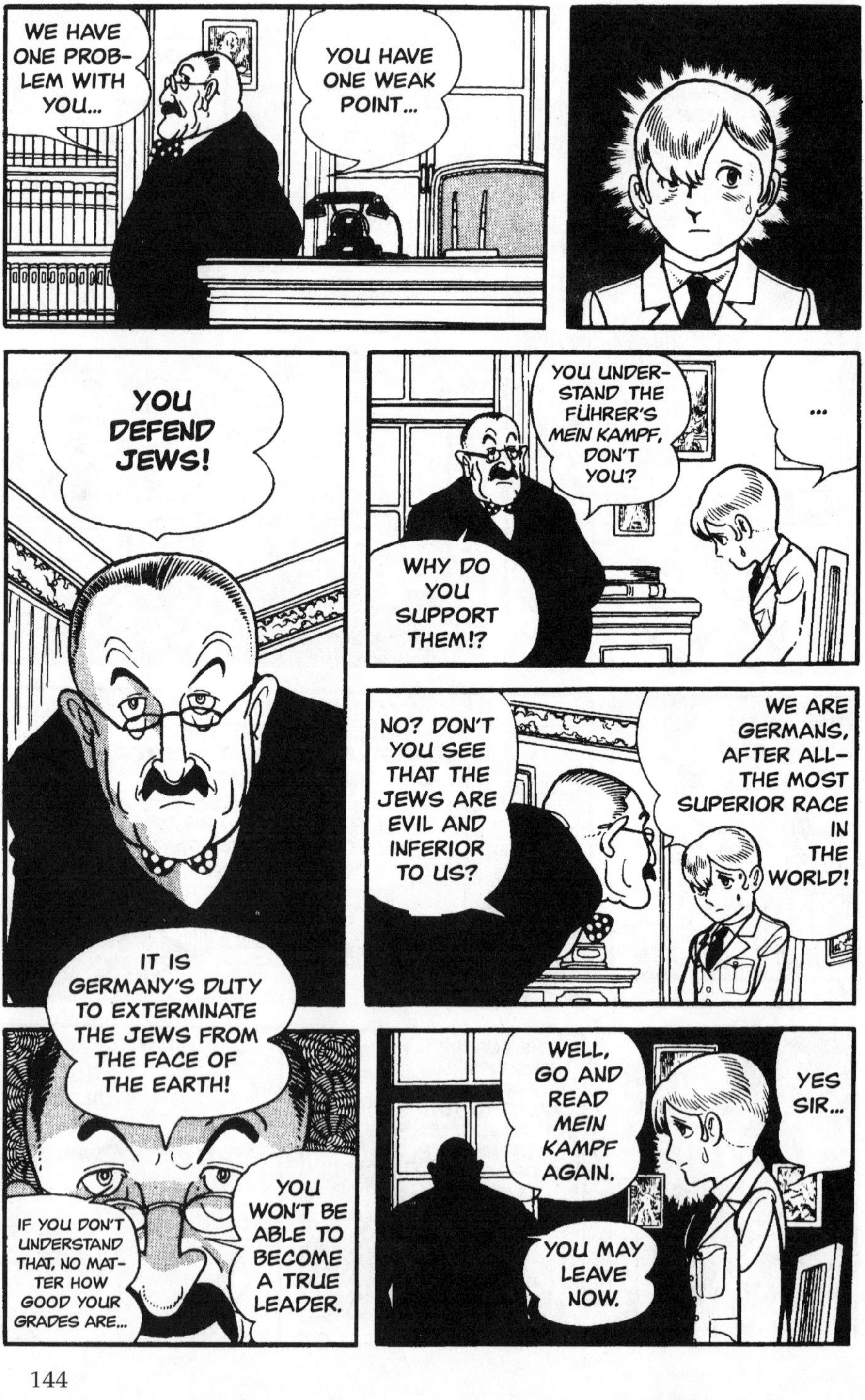
WE HAVE ONE PROB- LEM WITH YOU...
YOU HAVE ONE WEAK POINT...
YOU DEFEND JEWS!
YOU UNDER- STAND THE FÜHRER'S MEIN KAMPF, DON'T YOU?
...
WHY DO YOU SUPPORT THEM!?
NO? DON'T YOU SEE THAT THE JEWS ARE EVIL AND INFERIOR TO US?
WE ARE GERMANS, AFTER ALL– THE MOST SUPERIOR RACE IN THE WORLD!
IT IS GERMANY'S DUTY TO EXTERMINATE THE JEWS FROM THE FACE OF THE EARTH!
IF YOU DON'T UNDERSTAND THAT, NO MAT- TER HOW GOOD YOUR GRADES ARE...
YOU WON'T BE ABLE TO BECOME A TRUE LEADER.
WELL, GO AND READ MEIN KAMPF AGAIN.
YES SIR...
YOU MAY LEAVE NOW.

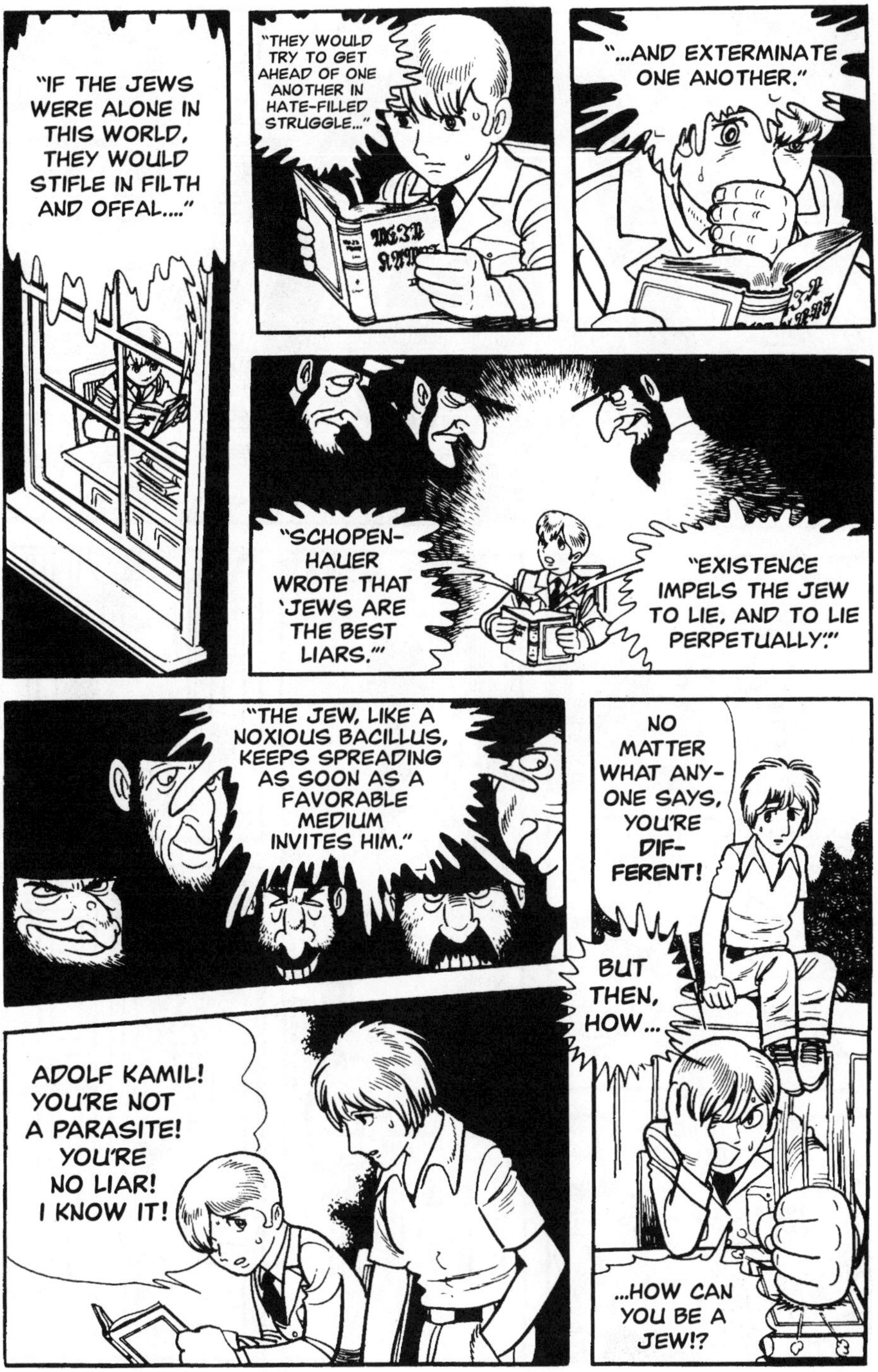
"IF THE JEWS WERE ALONE IN THIS WORLD, THEY WOULD STIFLE IN FILTH AND OFFAL...."
"THEY WOULD TRY TO GET AHEAD OF ONE ANOTHER IN HATE-FILLED STRUGGLE..."
"...AND EXTERMINATE ONE ANOTHER."
"SCHOPEN-HAUER WROTE THAT 'JEWS ARE THE BEST LIARS.'"
"EXISTENCE IMPELS THE JEW TO LIE, AND TO LIE PERPETUALLY."
"THE JEW, LIKE A NOXIOUS BACILLUS, KEEPS SPREADING AS SOON AS A FAVORABLE MEDIUM INVITES HIM."
ADOLF KAMIL! YOU'RE NOT A PARASITE! YOU'RE NO LIAR! I KNOW IT!
NO MATTER WHAT ANY-ONE SAYS, YOU'RE DIF-FERENT!
BUT THEN, HOW...
...HOW CAN YOU BE A JEW!?

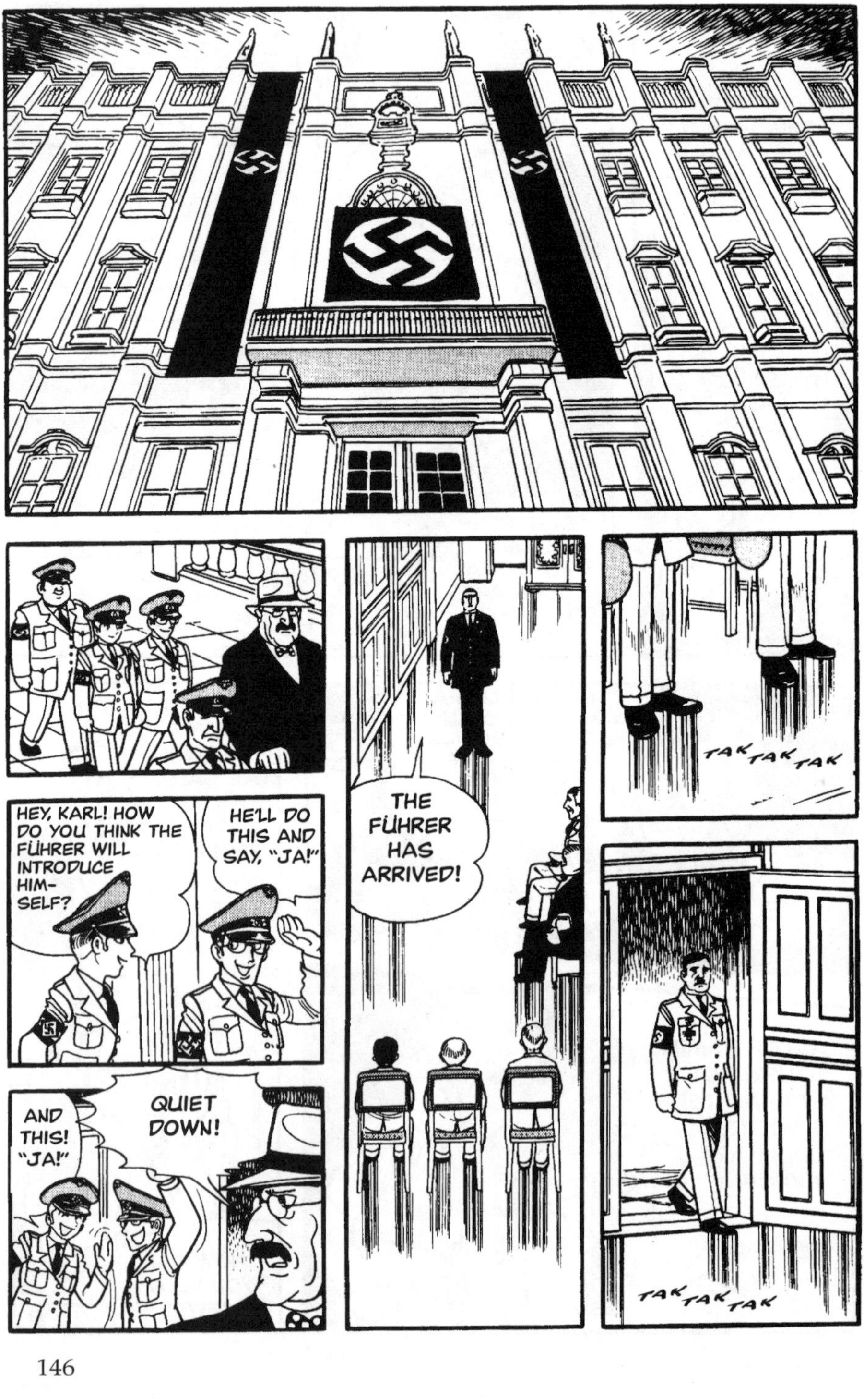
HEY, KARL! HOW DO YOU THINK THE FÜHRER WILL INTRODUCE HIM-SELF?
HE'LL DO THIS AND SAY, "JA!"
AND THIS! "JA!"
QUIET DOWN!
THE FÜHRER HAS ARRIVED!
TAK TAK TAK
TAK TAK TAK

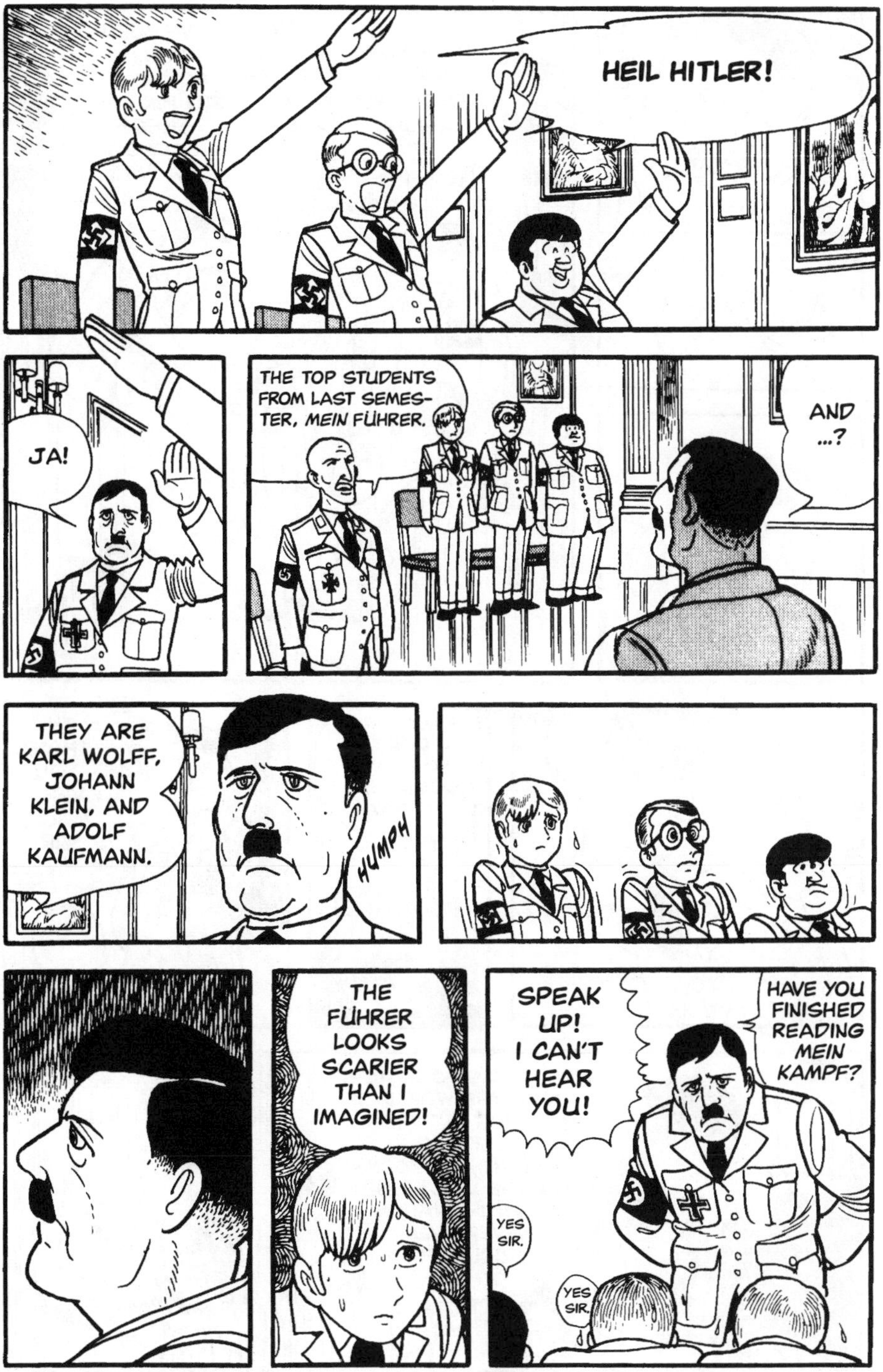
HEIL HITLER!
JA!
THE TOP STUDENTS FROM LAST SEMES-TER, MEIN FÜHRER.
AND ...?
THEY ARE KARL WOLFF, JOHANN KLEIN, AND ADOLF KAUFMANN.
HUMPH
THE FÜHRER LOOKS SCARIER THAN I IMAGINED!
SPEAK UP! I CAN'T HEAR YOU!
HAVE YOU FINISHED READING MEIN KAMPF?
YES SIR.
YES SIR.

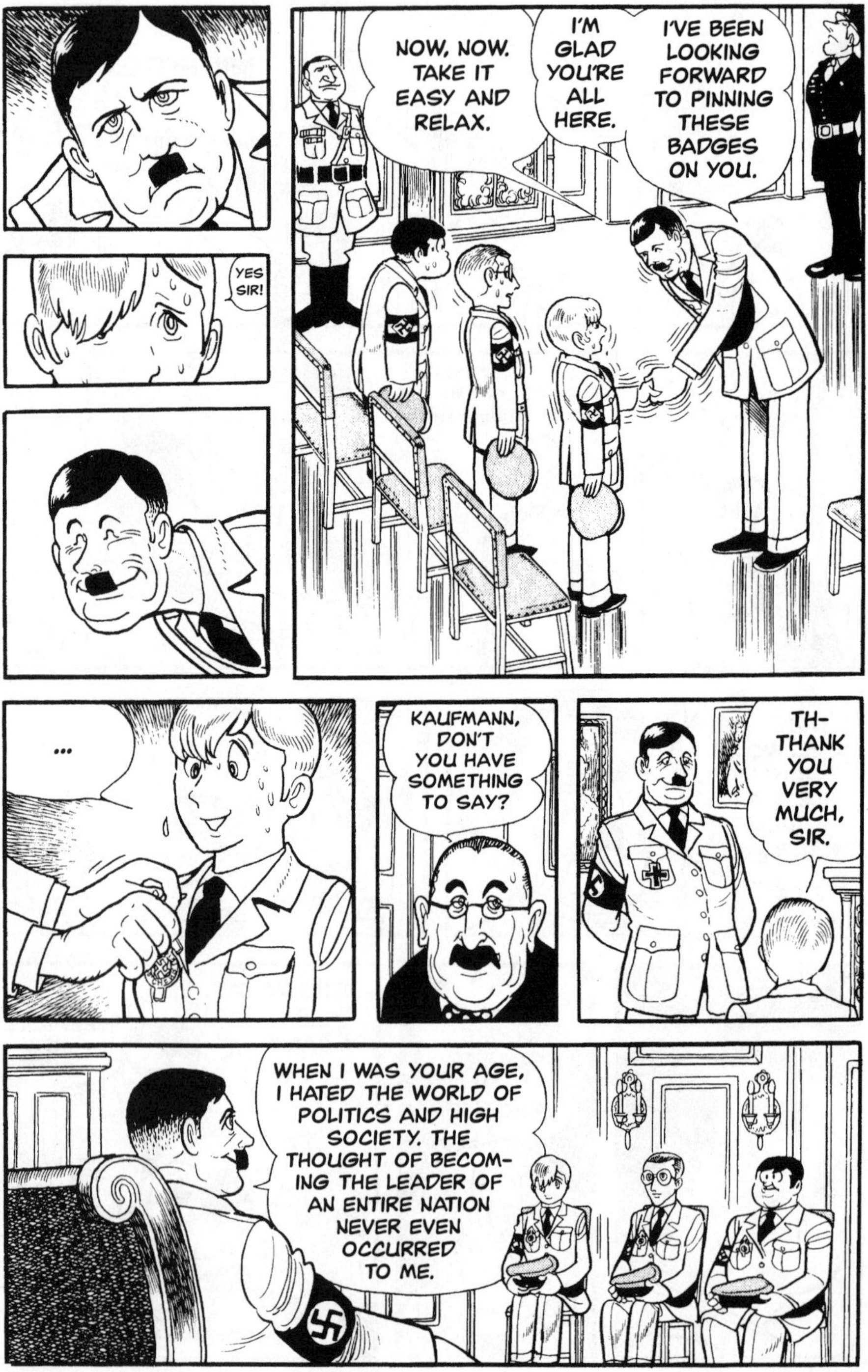
YES SIR!
NOW, NOW. TAKE IT EASY AND RELAX.
I'M GLAD YOU'RE ALL HERE.
I'VE BEEN LOOKING FORWARD TO PINNING THESE BADGES ON YOU.
...
KAUFMANN, DON'T YOU HAVE SOMETHING TO SAY?
TH-THANK YOU VERY MUCH, SIR.
WHEN I WAS YOUR AGE, I HATED THE WORLD OF POLITICS AND HIGH SOCIETY. THE THOUGHT OF BECOMING THE LEADER OF AN ENTIRE NATION NEVER EVEN OCCURRED TO ME.

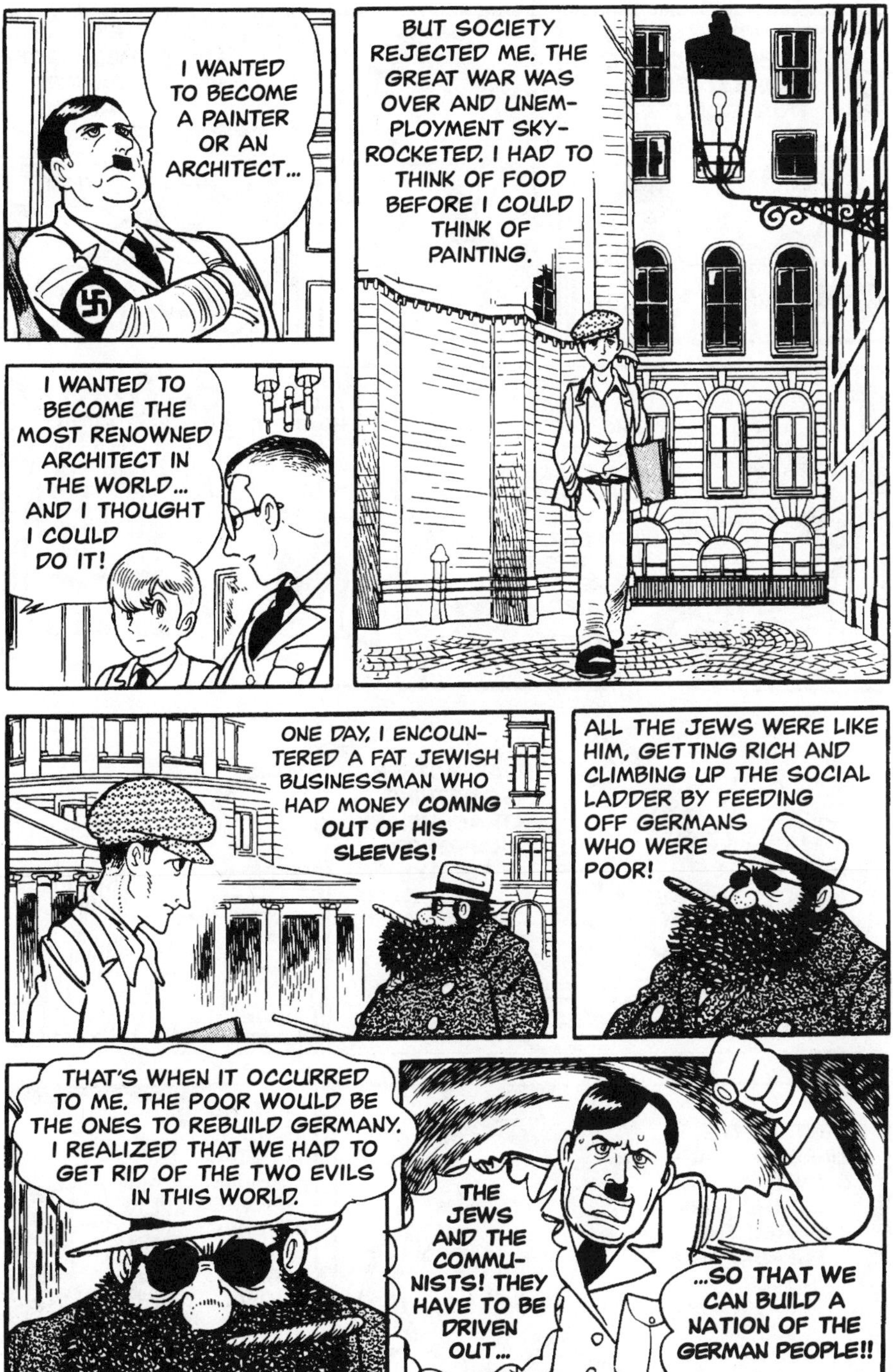
I WANTED TO BECOME A PAINTER OR AN ARCHITECT...
BUT SOCIETY REJECTED ME. THE GREAT WAR WAS OVER AND UNEMPLOYMENT SKYROCKETED. I HAD TO THINK OF FOOD BEFORE I COULD THINK OF PAINTING.
I WANTED TO BECOME THE MOST RENOWNED ARCHITECT IN THE WORLD... AND I THOUGHT I COULD DO IT!
ONE DAY, I ENCOUNTERED A FAT JEWISH BUSINESSMAN WHO HAD MONEY COMING OUT OF HIS SLEEVES!
ALL THE JEWS WERE LIKE HIM, GETTING RICH AND CLIMBING UP THE SOCIAL LADDER BY FEEDING OFF GERMANS WHO WERE POOR!
THAT'S WHEN IT OCCURRED TO ME. THE POOR WOULD BE THE ONES TO REBUILD GERMANY. I REALIZED THAT WE HAD TO GET RID OF THE TWO EVILS IN THIS WORLD.
THE JEWS AND THE COMMUNISTS! THEY HAVE TO BE DRIVEN OUT...
...SO THAT WE CAN BUILD A NATION OF THE GERMAN PEOPLE!!

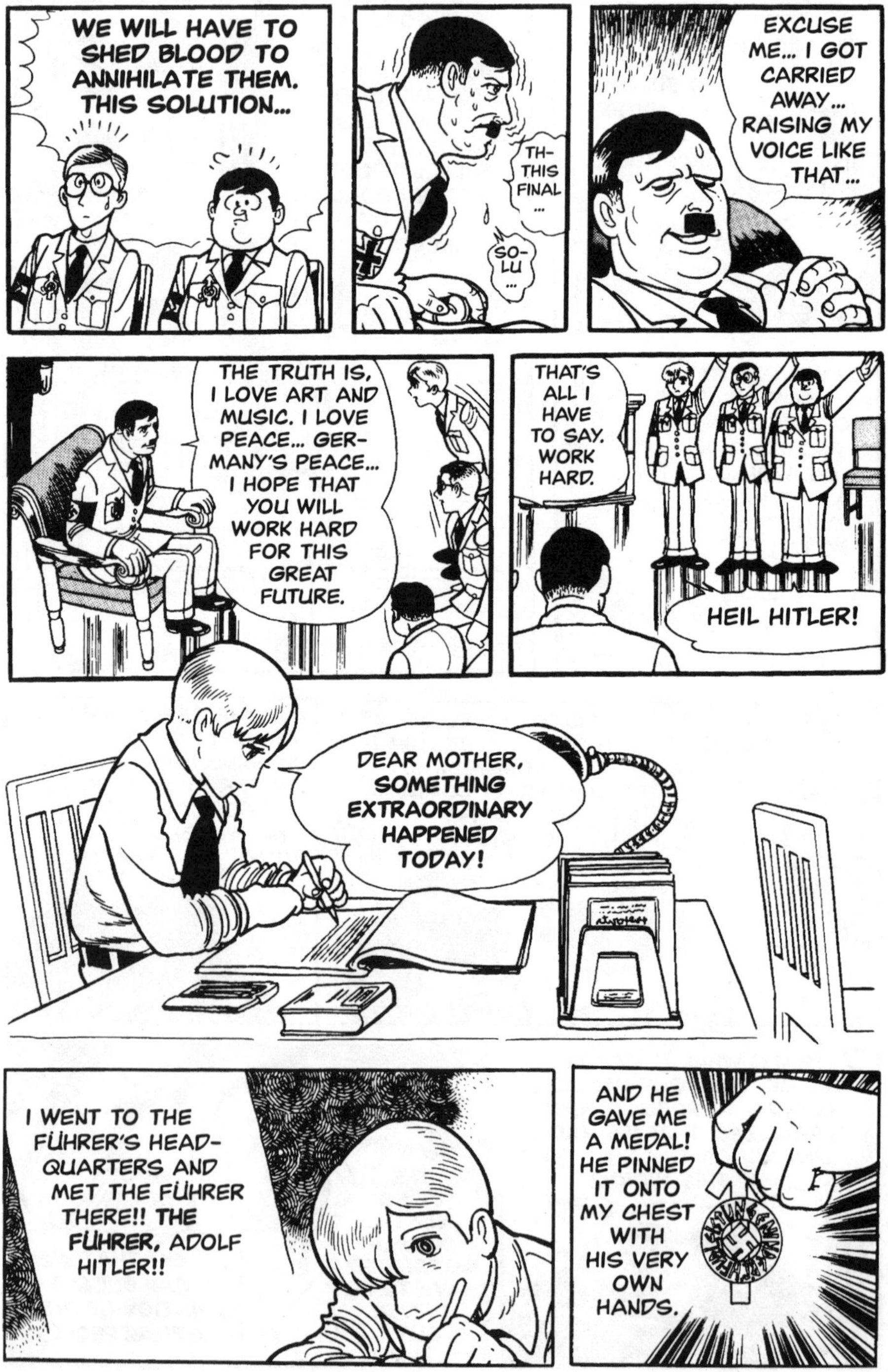
WE WILL HAVE TO SHED BLOOD TO ANNIHILATE THEM. THIS SOLUTION...
TH-THIS FINAL ...
SO-LU ...
EXCUSE ME... I GOT CARRIED AWAY... RAISING MY VOICE LIKE THAT...
THE TRUTH IS, I LOVE ART AND MUSIC. I LOVE PEACE... GER-MANY'S PEACE... I HOPE THAT YOU WILL WORK HARD FOR THIS GREAT FUTURE.
THAT'S ALL I HAVE TO SAY. WORK HARD.
HEIL HITLER!
DEAR MOTHER, SOMETHING EXTRAORDINARY HAPPENED TODAY!
I WENT TO THE FÜHRER'S HEAD-QUARTERS AND MET THE FÜHRER THERE!! THE FÜHRER, ADOLF HITLER!!
AND HE GAVE ME A MEDAL! HE PINNED IT ONTO MY CHEST WITH HIS VERY OWN HANDS.

HE EVEN SHOOK MY HAND! I WAS SO NERVOUS AND STIFF...

I WAS GLUED TO MY SEAT! THE FÜHRER SPOKE OF HIS CHILDHOOD.

MOTHER, THE FÜHRER ACTUALLY HAS REALLY CHARMING EYES. I DIDN'T EXPECT HIM TO BE LIKE THIS. I HEARD HE LIKES KIDS...

AT FIRST I DIDN'T WANT TO COME TO GERMANY, BUT NOW I DON'T FEEL THAT WAY. I'LL GRADUATE FROM THE AHS WITH HIGH HONORS, AND THEN I'LL BE A NAZI CADET! IT'LL TAKE FIVE YEARS... I CAN'T WAIT!

ONE THING THAT REALLY BOTHERS ME THOUGH IS THAT MY FRIENDS DON'T KNOW MUCH ABOUT JAPAN. ACTUALLY, THEY DON'T UNDERSTAND JAPAN AT ALL.

THEY THINK THAT JAPANESE WOMEN ALL BECOME GEISHAS WHEN THEY GROW UP!

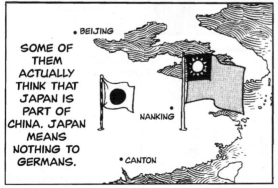

SOME OF THEM ACTUALLY THINK THAT JAPAN IS PART OF CHINA. JAPAN MEANS NOTHING TO GERMANS.

BEIJING / NANKING / CANTON

MOTHER, AM I JAPANESE? OR AM I GERMAN? I'D LIKE TO BE GERMAN, IF IT'S AT ALL POSSIBLE...

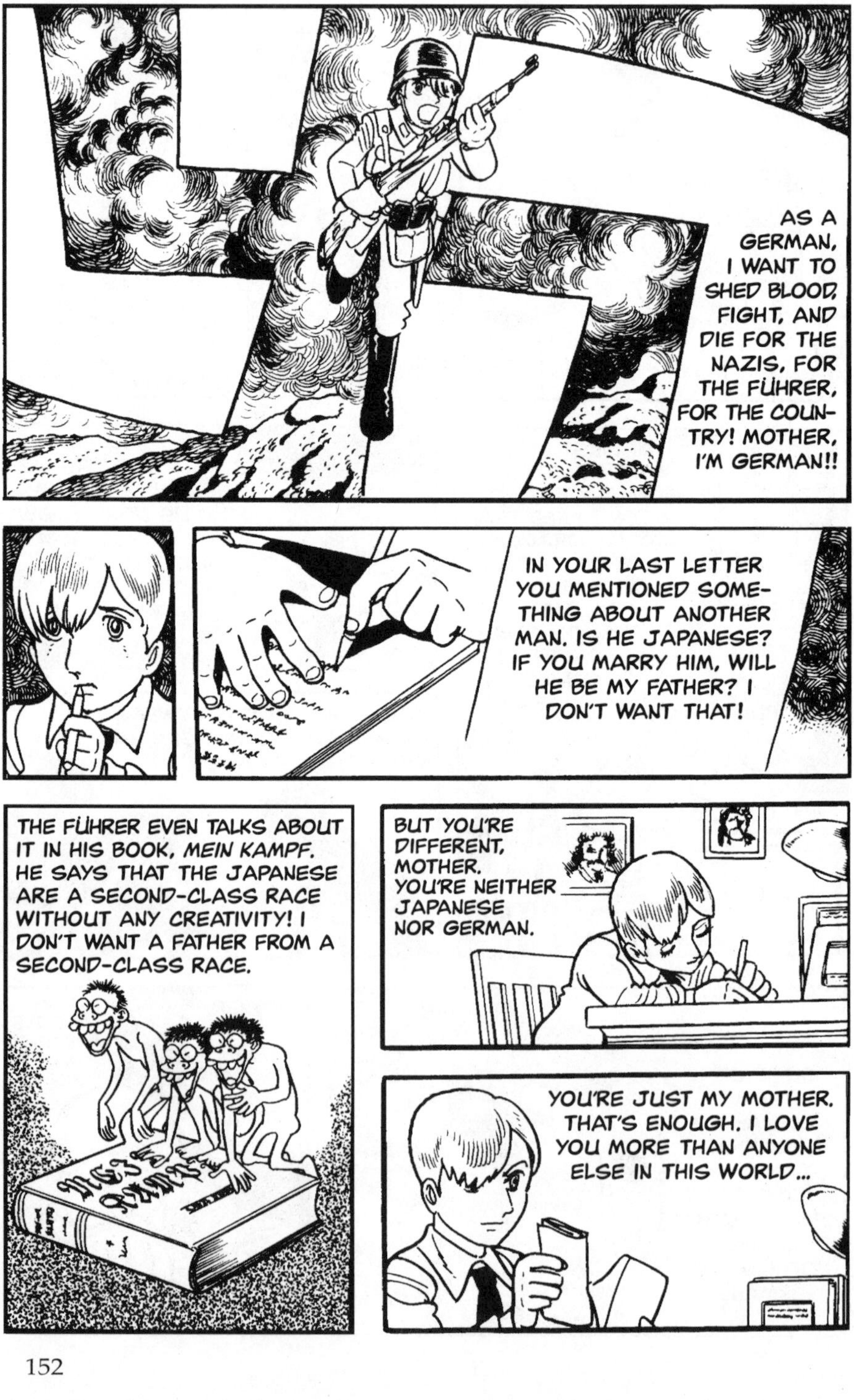
AS A GERMAN, I WANT TO SHED BLOOD, FIGHT, AND DIE FOR THE NAZIS, FOR THE FÜHRER, FOR THE COUNTRY! MOTHER, I'M GERMAN!!
IN YOUR LAST LETTER YOU MENTIONED SOMETHING ABOUT ANOTHER MAN. IS HE JAPANESE? IF YOU MARRY HIM, WILL HE BE MY FATHER? I DON'T WANT THAT!
THE FÜHRER EVEN TALKS ABOUT IT IN HIS BOOK, *MEIN KAMPF*. HE SAYS THAT THE JAPANESE ARE A SECOND-CLASS RACE WITHOUT ANY CREATIVITY! I DON'T WANT A FATHER FROM A SECOND-CLASS RACE.
BUT YOU'RE DIFFERENT, MOTHER. YOU'RE NEITHER JAPANESE NOR GERMAN.
YOU'RE JUST MY MOTHER. THAT'S ENOUGH. I LOVE YOU MORE THAN ANYONE ELSE IN THIS WORLD...

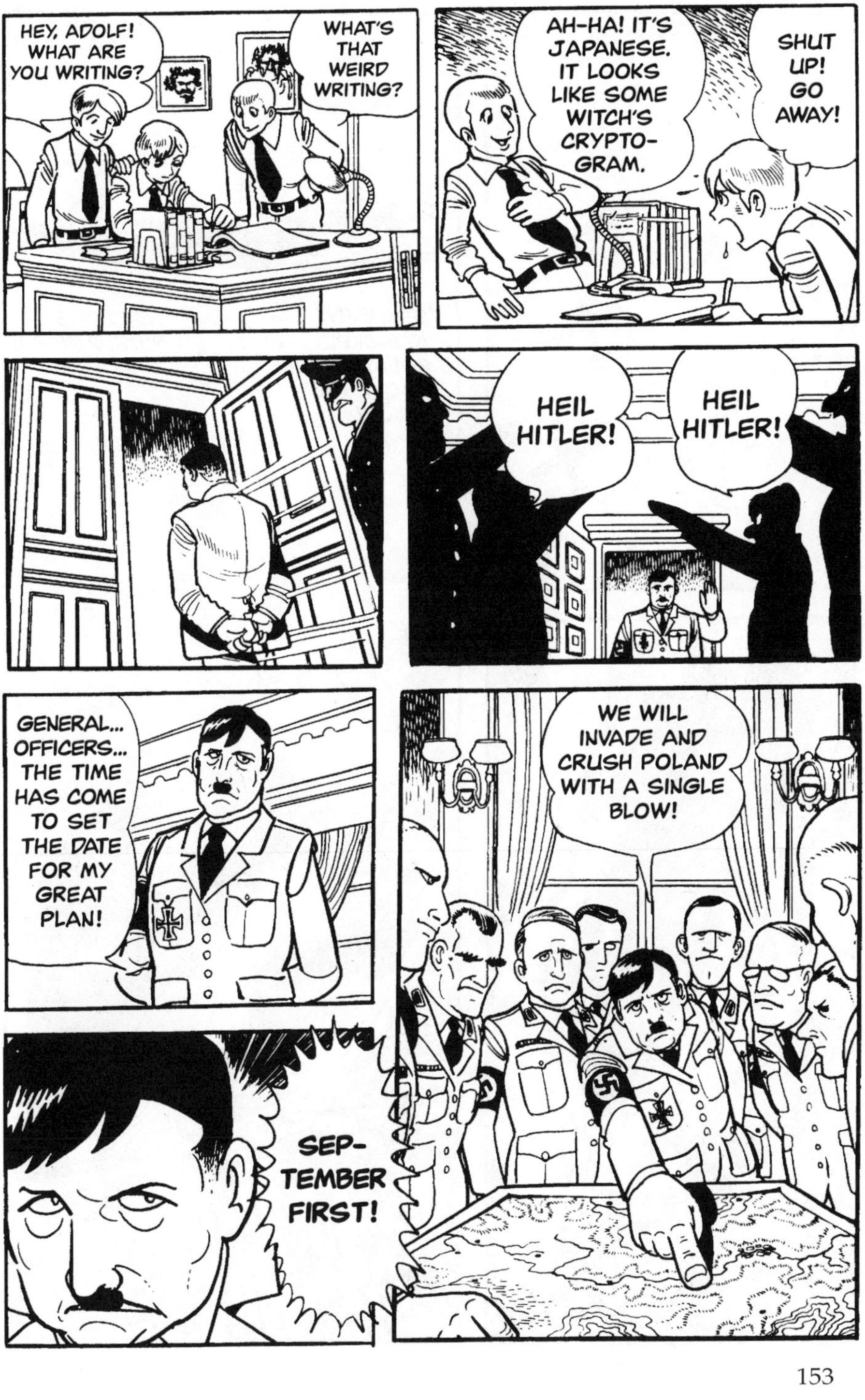
HEY, ADOLF! WHAT ARE YOU WRITING?
WHAT'S THAT WEIRD WRITING?
AH-HA! IT'S JAPANESE. IT LOOKS LIKE SOME WITCH'S CRYPTO-GRAM.
SHUT UP! GO AWAY!
HEIL HITLER!
HEIL HITLER!
GENERAL... OFFICERS... THE TIME HAS COME TO SET THE DATE FOR MY GREAT PLAN!
WE WILL INVADE AND CRUSH POLAND WITH A SINGLE BLOW!
SEP-TEMBER FIRST!

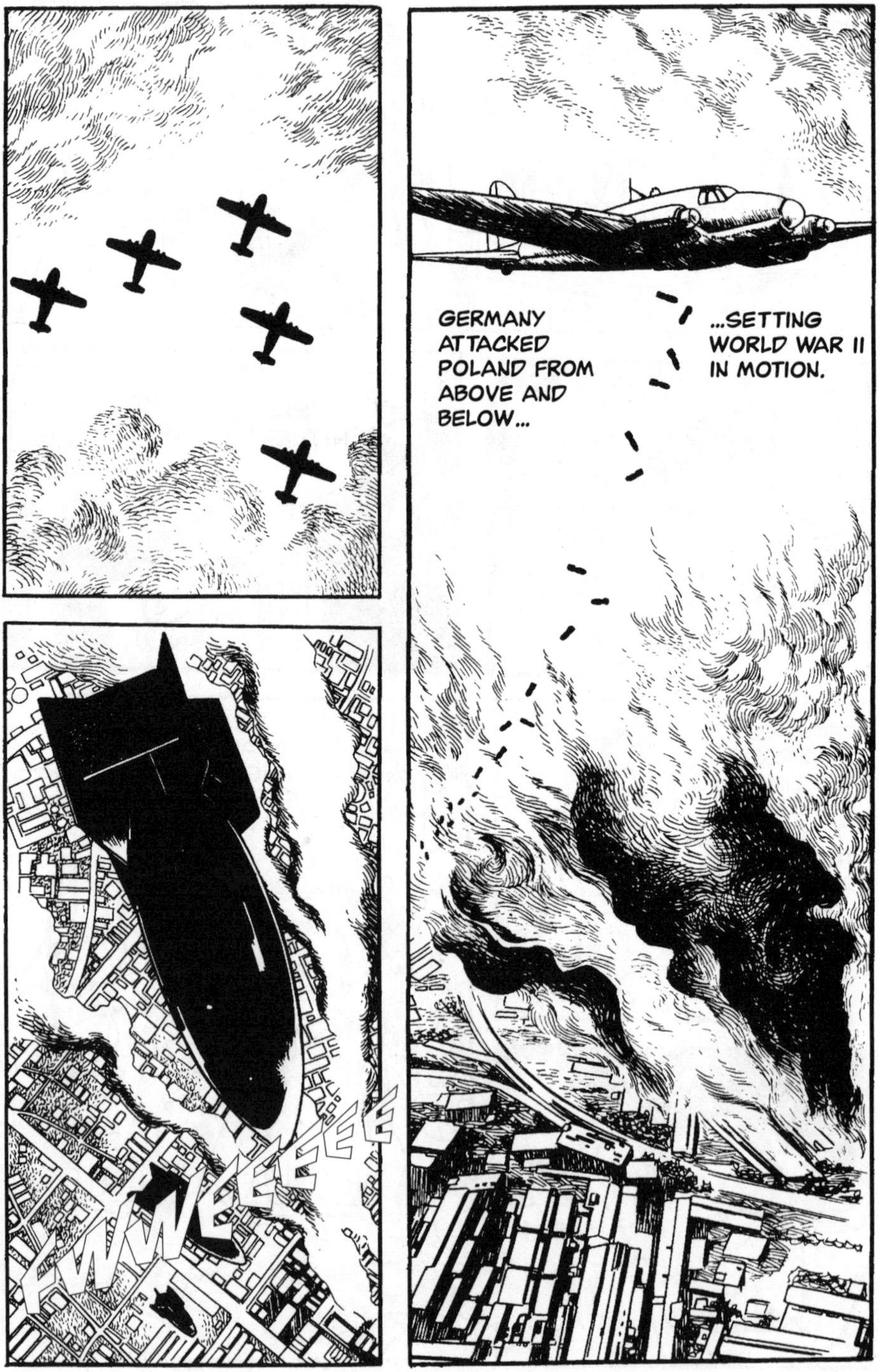
FWWEEEEEE
GERMANY ATTACKED POLAND FROM ABOVE AND BELOW...
...SETTING WORLD WAR II IN MOTION.

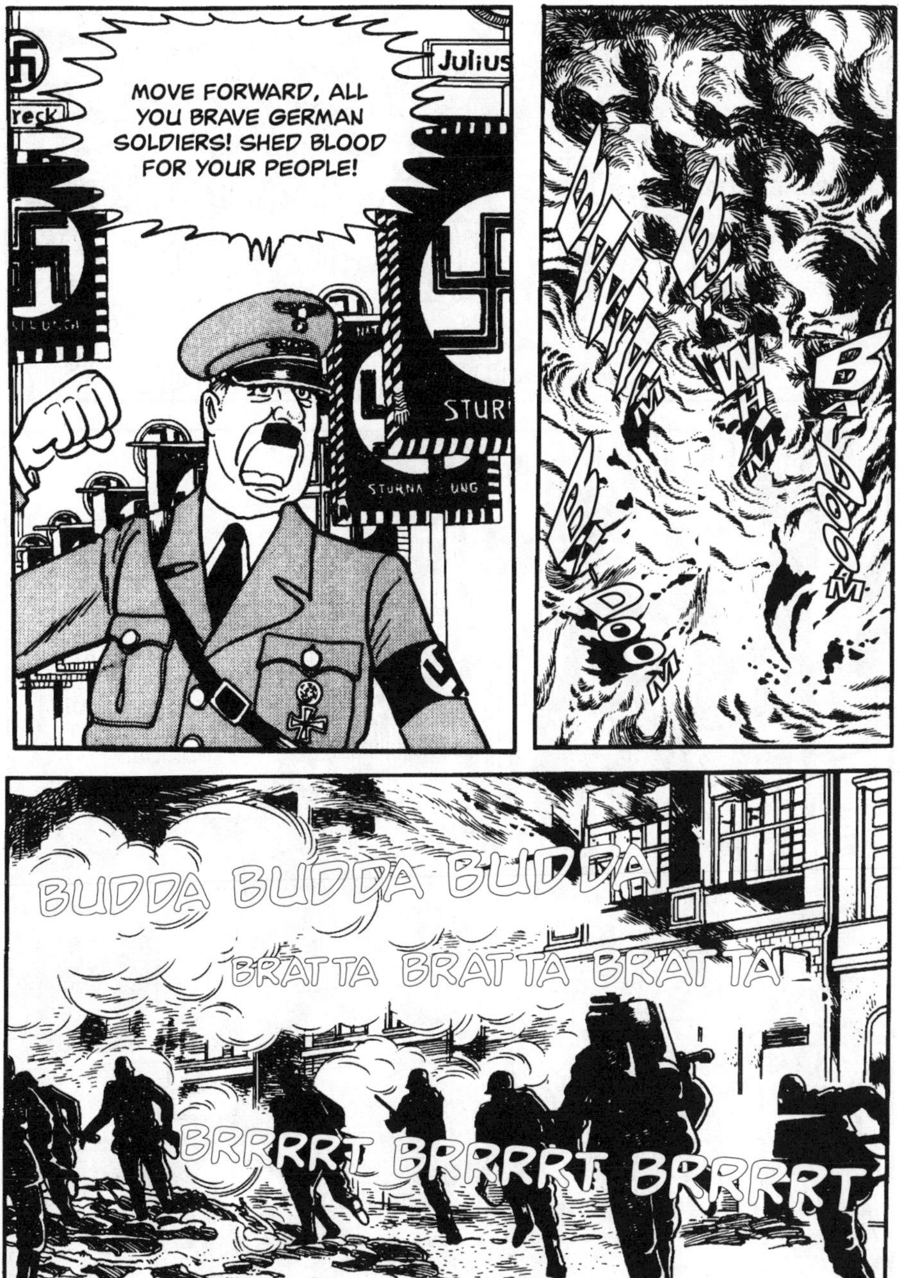
Julius
MOVE FORWARD, ALL YOU BRAVE GERMAN SOLDIERS! SHED BLOOD FOR YOUR PEOPLE!
BADOOOM
DOOM
BUDDA BUDDA BUDDA
BRATTA BRATTA BRATTA
BRRRRT BRRRRT BRRRRT

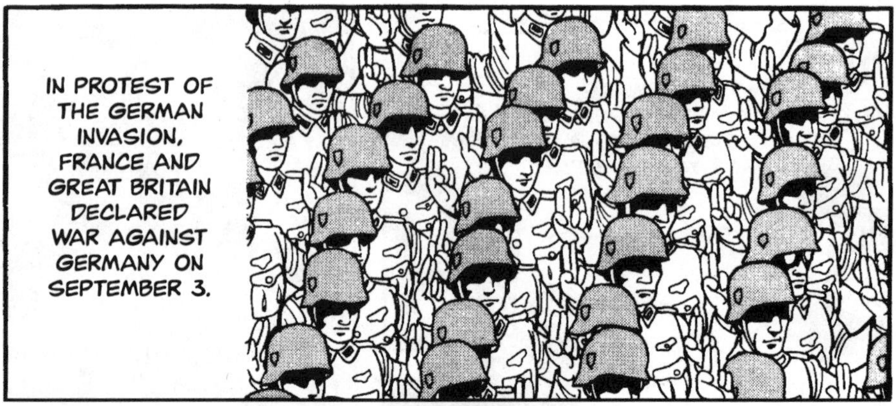
IN PROTEST OF THE GERMAN INVASION, FRANCE AND GREAT BRITAIN DECLARED WAR AGAINST GERMANY ON SEPTEMBER 3.

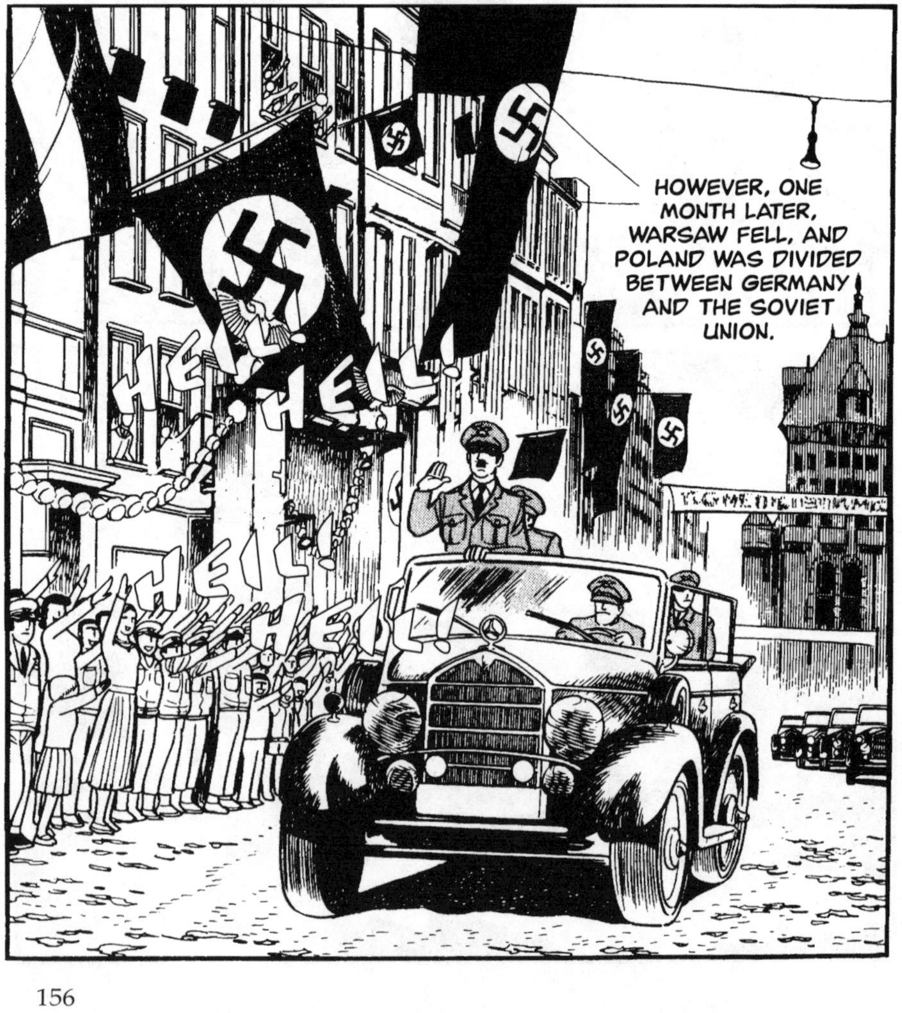
HOWEVER, ONE MONTH LATER, WARSAW FELL, AND POLAND WAS DIVIDED BETWEEN GERMANY AND THE SOVIET UNION.
HEIL! HEIL!
HEIL! HEIL!

CHAPTER
SIX

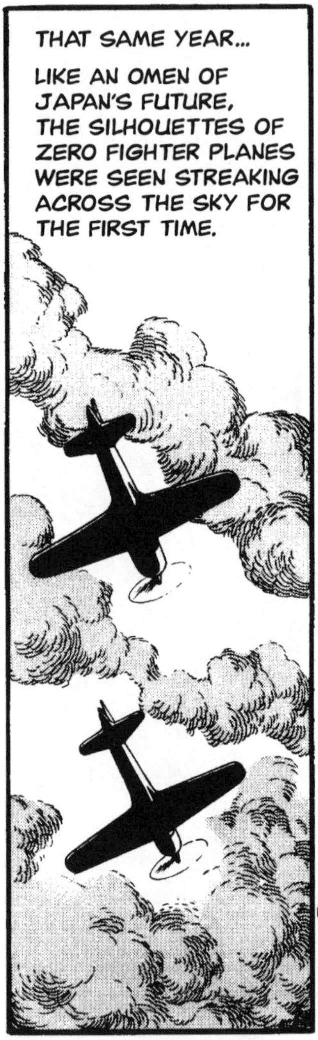
THAT SAME YEAR...
LIKE AN OMEN OF JAPAN'S FUTURE, THE SILHOUETTES OF ZERO FIGHTER PLANES WERE SEEN STREAKING ACROSS THE SKY FOR THE FIRST TIME.

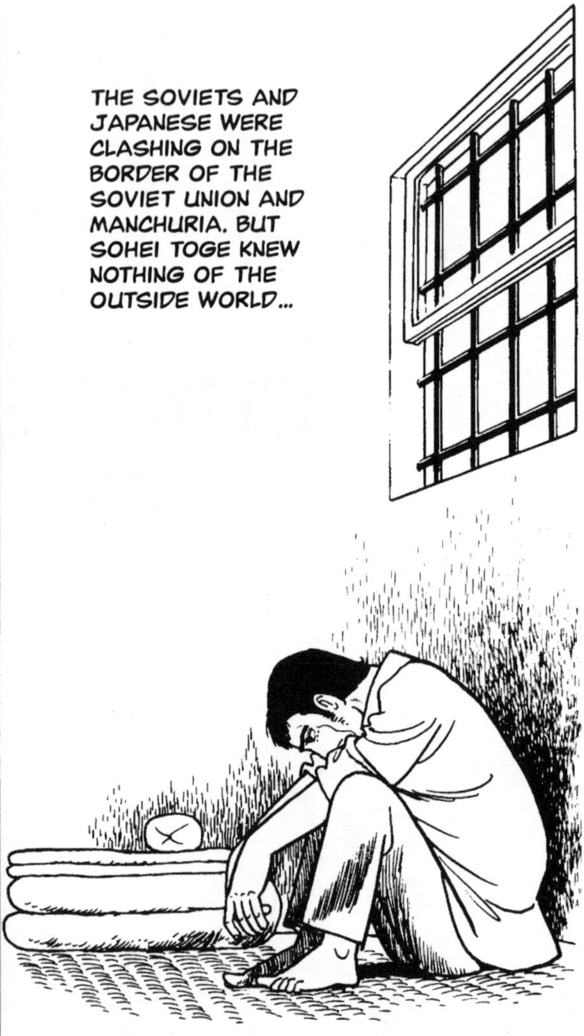
THE SOVIETS AND JAPANESE WERE CLASHING ON THE BORDER OF THE SOVIET UNION AND MANCHURIA. BUT SOHEI TOGE KNEW NOTHING OF THE OUTSIDE WORLD...

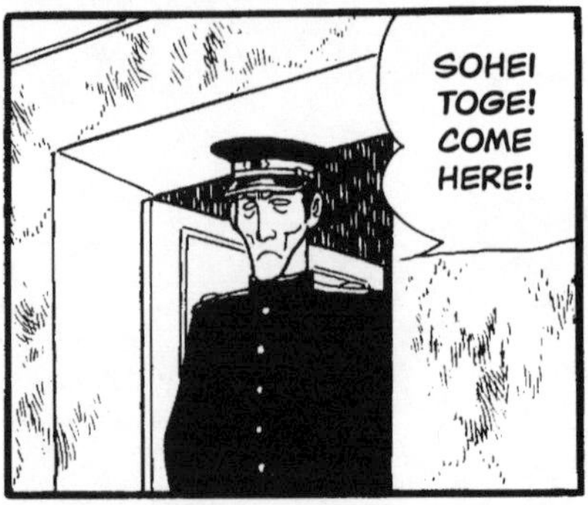
SOHEI TOGE! COME HERE!

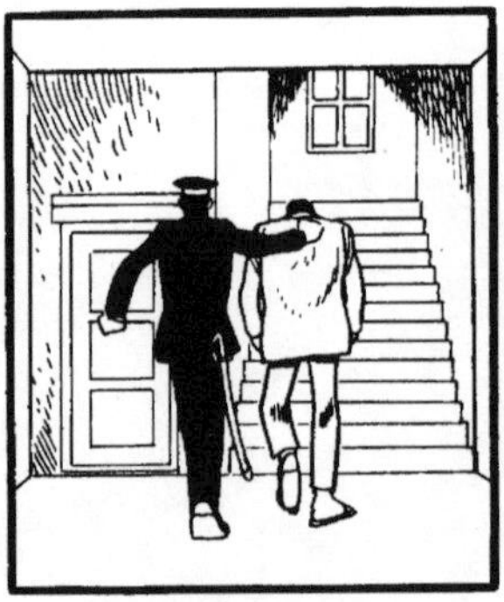

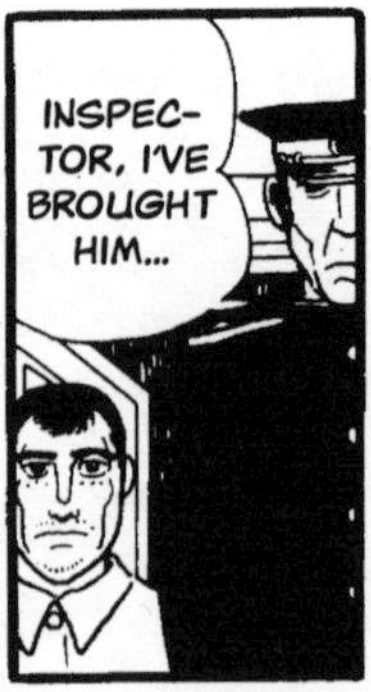
INSPECTOR, I'VE BROUGHT HIM...

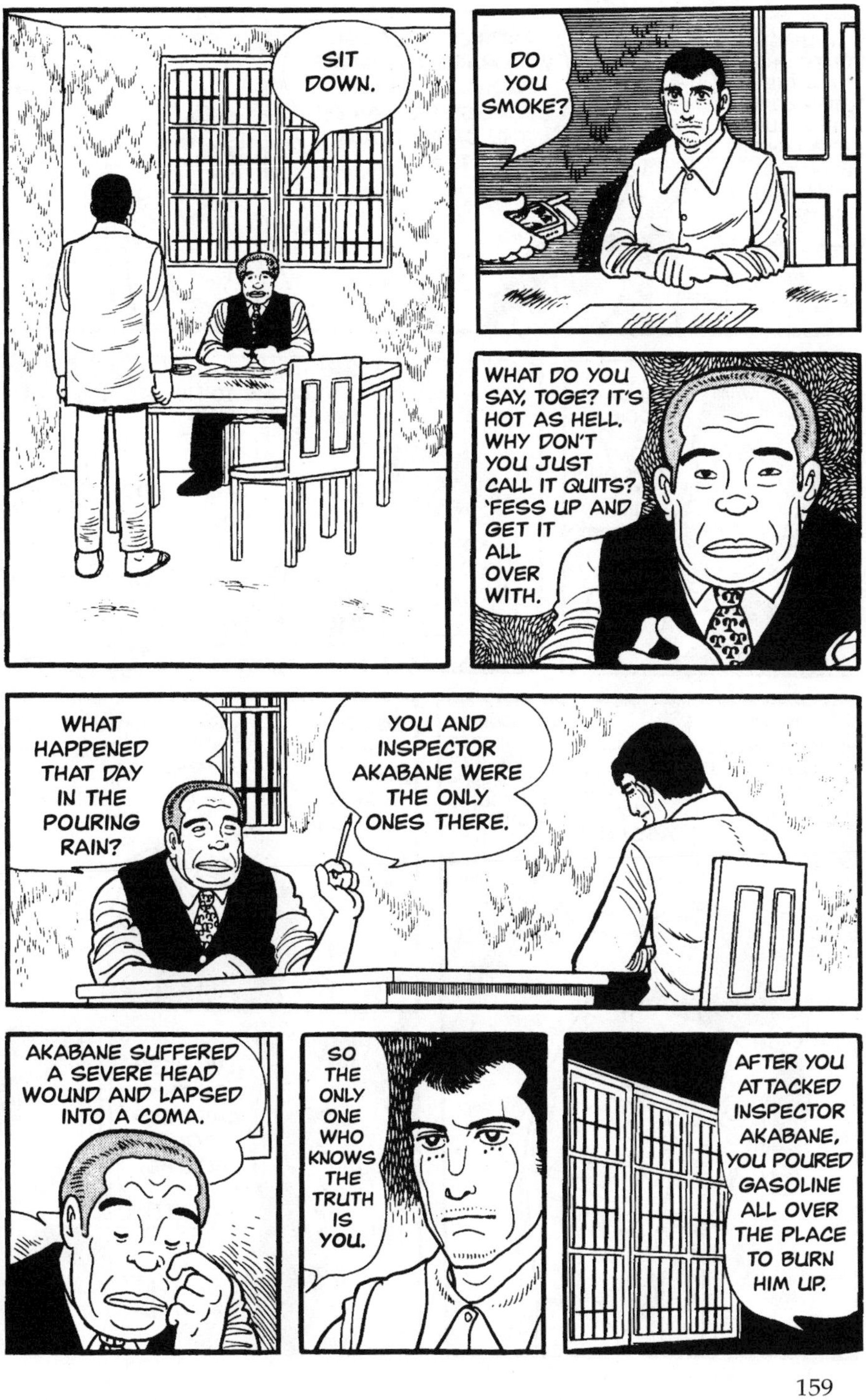
SIT DOWN.
DO YOU SMOKE?
WHAT DO YOU SAY, TOGE? IT'S HOT AS HELL. WHY DON'T YOU JUST CALL IT QUITS? 'FESS UP AND GET IT ALL OVER WITH.
WHAT HAPPENED THAT DAY IN THE POURING RAIN?
YOU AND INSPECTOR AKABANE WERE THE ONLY ONES THERE.
AKABANE SUFFERED A SEVERE HEAD WOUND AND LAPSED INTO A COMA.
SO THE ONLY ONE WHO KNOWS THE TRUTH IS YOU.
AFTER YOU ATTACKED INSPECTOR AKABANE, YOU POURED GASOLINE ALL OVER THE PLACE TO BURN HIM UP.

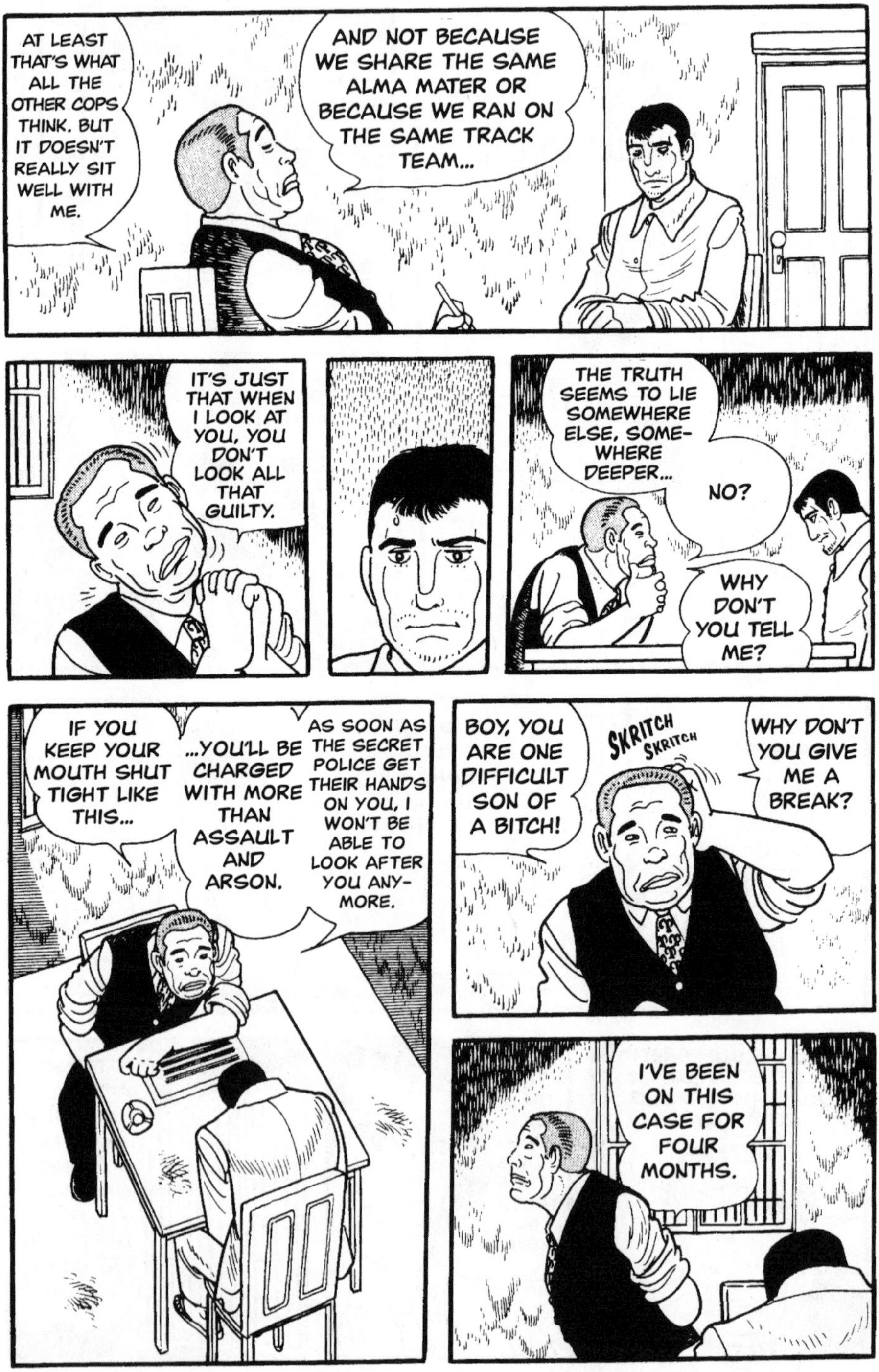
AT LEAST THAT'S WHAT ALL THE OTHER COPS THINK. BUT IT DOESN'T REALLY SIT WELL WITH ME.
AND NOT BECAUSE WE SHARE THE SAME ALMA MATER OR BECAUSE WE RAN ON THE SAME TRACK TEAM...
IT'S JUST THAT WHEN I LOOK AT YOU, YOU DON'T LOOK ALL THAT GUILTY.
THE TRUTH SEEMS TO LIE SOMEWHERE ELSE, SOME-WHERE DEEPER...
NO?
WHY DON'T YOU TELL ME?
IF YOU KEEP YOUR MOUTH SHUT TIGHT LIKE THIS...
...YOU'LL BE CHARGED WITH MORE THAN ASSAULT AND ARSON.
AS SOON AS THE SECRET POLICE GET THEIR HANDS ON YOU, I WON'T BE ABLE TO LOOK AFTER YOU ANY-MORE.
BOY, YOU ARE ONE DIFFICULT SON OF A BITCH!
SKRITCH
SKRITCH
WHY DON'T YOU GIVE ME A BREAK?
I'VE BEEN ON THIS CASE FOR FOUR MONTHS.

I JUST DON'T CARE ANYMORE! I...

PLEASE... JUST DO AS YOU SEE FIT.

DON'T GIVE UP SO EASILY...

I BROKE MY PROMISE TO MY BROTHER...

...SO I DON'T CARE WHAT HAPPENS TO ME ANYMORE.

YOU ALWAYS BRING THAT UP...

WHAT IS THIS PROMISE ABOUT, ANYWAY?

I CAN'T TELL YOU.

YOU ARE SO STUBBORN! COME ON, RELAX...

SKRITCH

INSPECTOR NIKAWA, PLEASE GO AHEAD AND CHARGE ME WITH ATTEMPTED MURDER... OR ARSON... I REALLY DON'T CARE ANYMORE!

YOU'RE TAKING THE EASY WAY OUT. NOW LISTEN TO ME, WHAT I WANT IS THE TRUTH, YOU HEAR ME? THE TRUTH!!

I SWEAR, THESE DAYS NO ONE IS INTERESTED IN THE TRUTH.

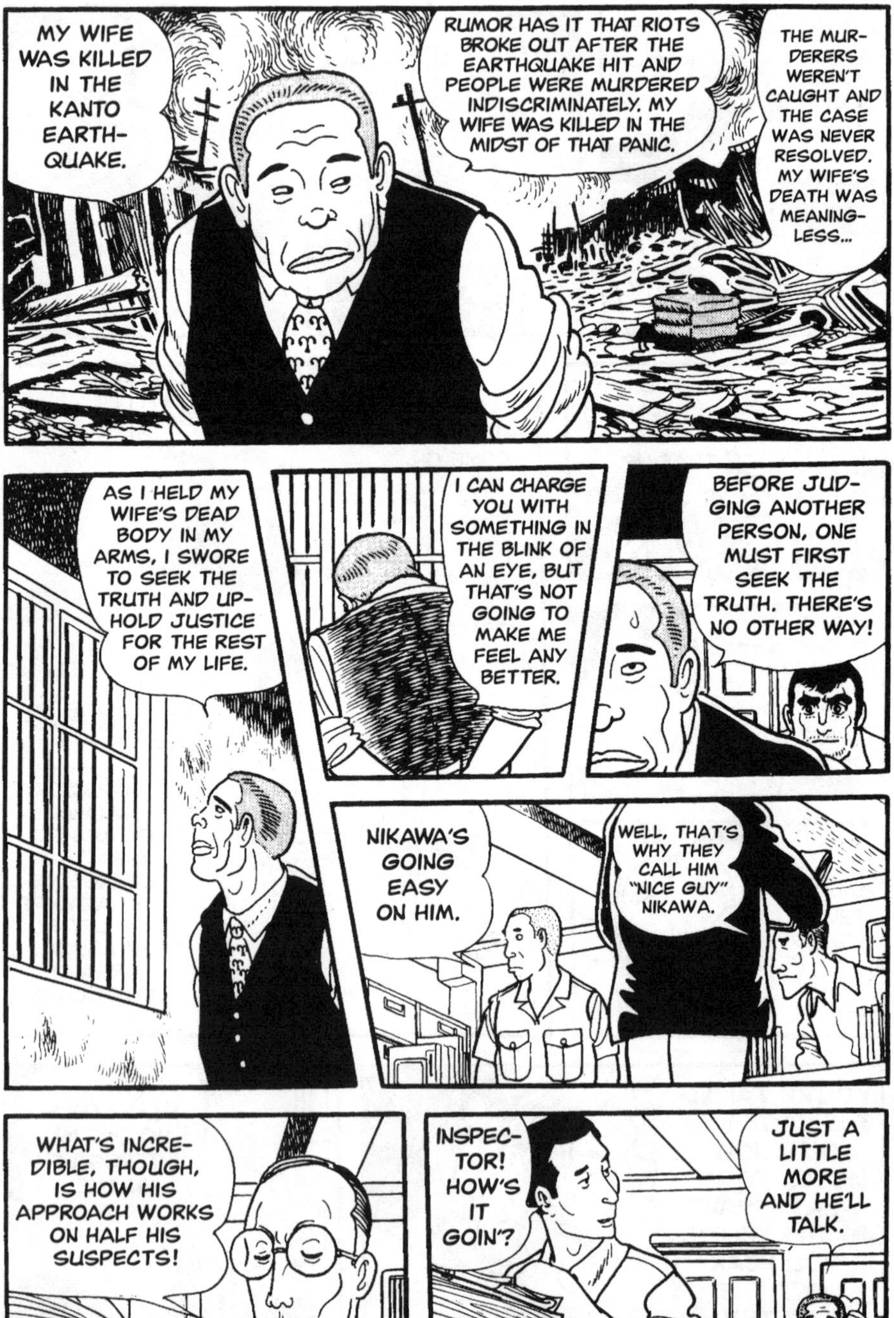
MY WIFE WAS KILLED IN THE KANTO EARTHQUAKE.
RUMOR HAS IT THAT RIOTS BROKE OUT AFTER THE EARTHQUAKE HIT AND PEOPLE WERE MURDERED INDISCRIMINATELY. MY WIFE WAS KILLED IN THE MIDST OF THAT PANIC.
THE MURDERERS WEREN'T CAUGHT AND THE CASE WAS NEVER RESOLVED. MY WIFE'S DEATH WAS MEANINGLESS...
AS I HELD MY WIFE'S DEAD BODY IN MY ARMS, I SWORE TO SEEK THE TRUTH AND UPHOLD JUSTICE FOR THE REST OF MY LIFE.
I CAN CHARGE YOU WITH SOMETHING IN THE BLINK OF AN EYE, BUT THAT'S NOT GOING TO MAKE ME FEEL ANY BETTER.
BEFORE JUDGING ANOTHER PERSON, ONE MUST FIRST SEEK THE TRUTH. THERE'S NO OTHER WAY!
NIKAWA'S GOING EASY ON HIM.
WELL, THAT'S WHY THEY CALL HIM "NICE GUY" NIKAWA.
WHAT'S INCREDIBLE, THOUGH, IS HOW HIS APPROACH WORKS ON HALF HIS SUSPECTS!
INSPECTOR! HOW'S IT GOIN'?
JUST A LITTLE MORE AND HE'LL TALK.

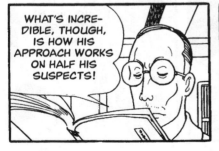

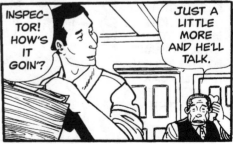

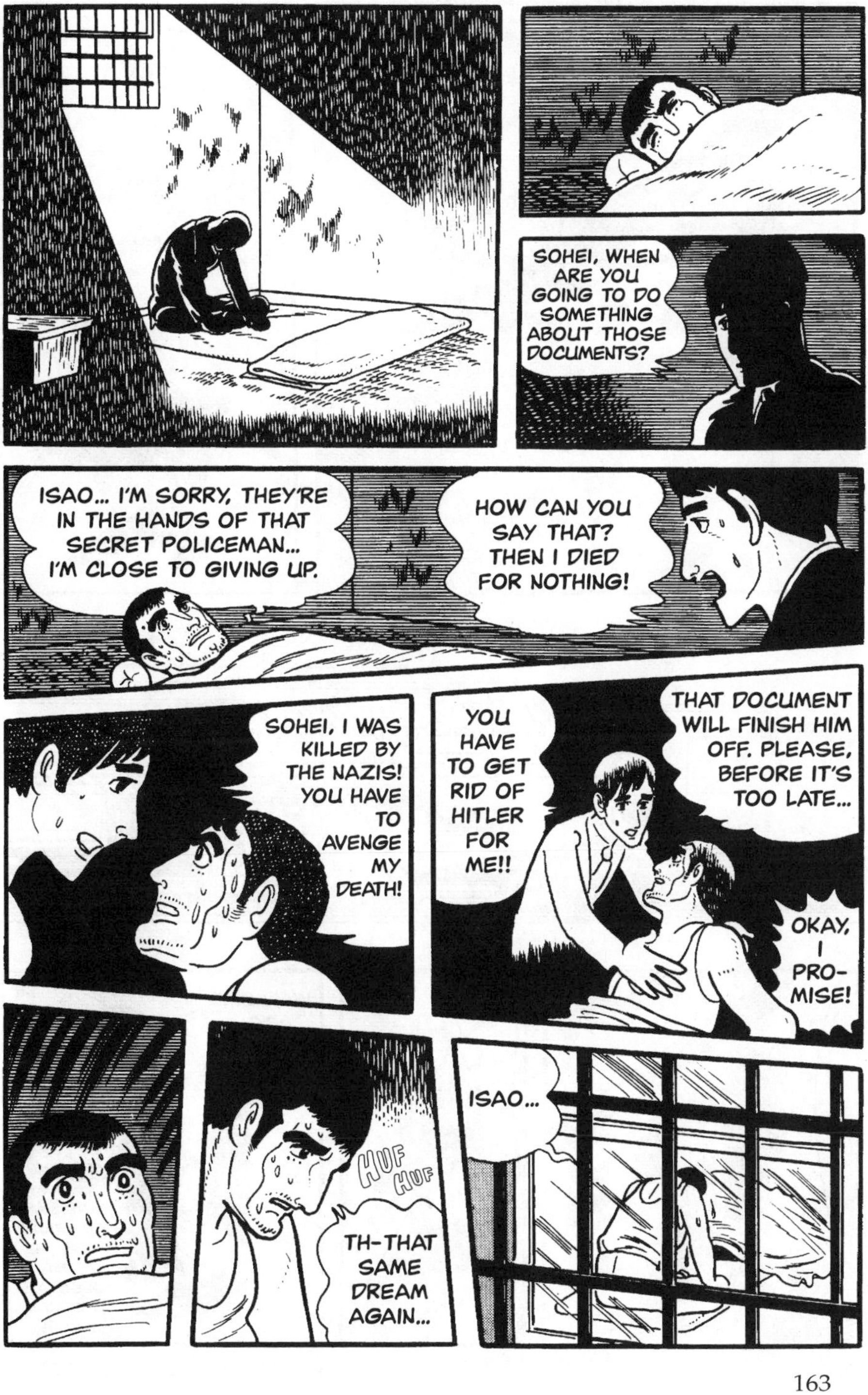
SOHEI, WHEN ARE YOU GOING TO DO SOMETHING ABOUT THOSE DOCUMENTS?
ISAO... I'M SORRY, THEY'RE IN THE HANDS OF THAT SECRET POLICEMAN... I'M CLOSE TO GIVING UP.
HOW CAN YOU SAY THAT? THEN I DIED FOR NOTHING!
SOHEI, I WAS KILLED BY THE NAZIS! YOU HAVE TO AVENGE MY DEATH!
YOU HAVE TO GET RID OF HITLER FOR ME!!
THAT DOCUMENT WILL FINISH HIM OFF. PLEASE, BEFORE IT'S TOO LATE...
OKAY, I PRO-MISE!
HUF HUF
TH-THAT SAME DREAM AGAIN...
ISAO...

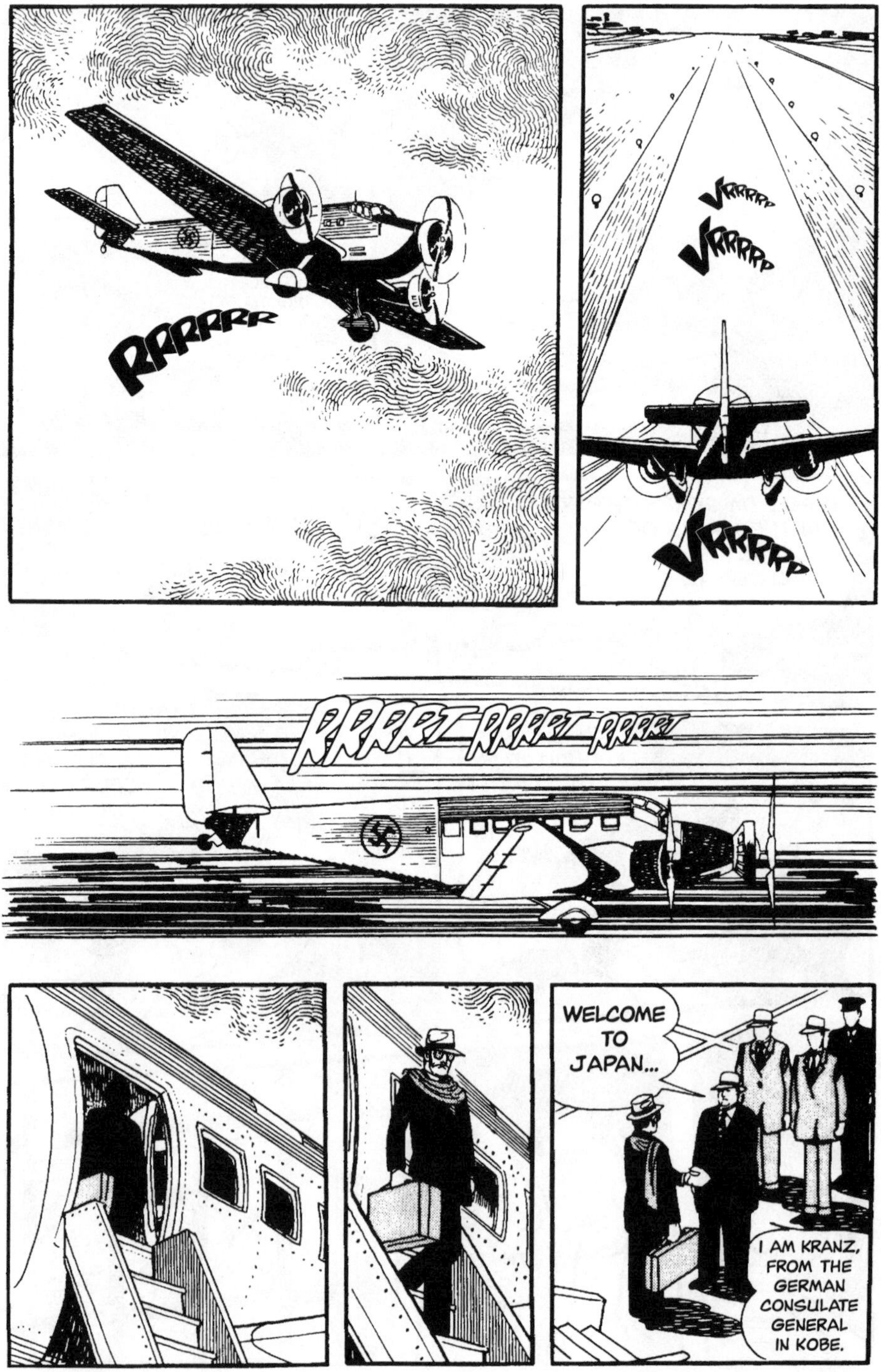
RRRRRR
VRRRRP
VRRRRP
VRRRRP
RRRRRT RRRRT RRRRT
WELCOME TO JAPAN...
I AM KRANZ, FROM THE GERMAN CONSULATE GENERAL IN KOBE.

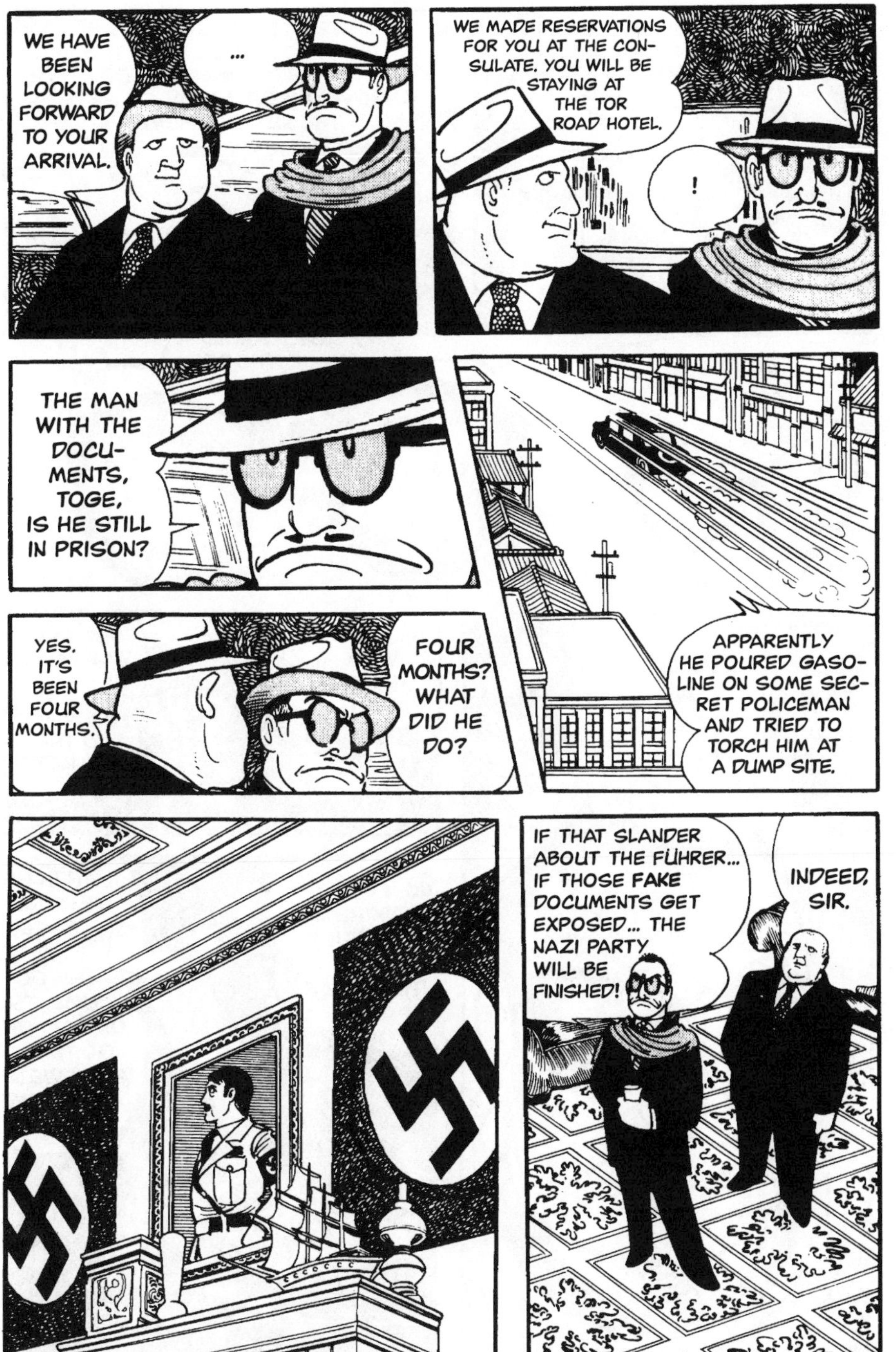
WE HAVE BEEN LOOKING FORWARD TO YOUR ARRIVAL.
...
WE MADE RESERVATIONS FOR YOU AT THE CONSULATE. YOU WILL BE STAYING AT THE TOR ROAD HOTEL.
!
THE MAN WITH THE DOCUMENTS, TOGE, IS HE STILL IN PRISON?
YES. IT'S BEEN FOUR MONTHS.
FOUR MONTHS? WHAT DID HE DO?
APPARENTLY HE POURED GASOLINE ON SOME SECRET POLICEMAN AND TRIED TO TORCH HIM AT A DUMP SITE.
IF THAT SLANDER ABOUT THE FÜHRER... IF THOSE FAKE DOCUMENTS GET EXPOSED... THE NAZI PARTY WILL BE FINISHED!
INDEED, SIR.

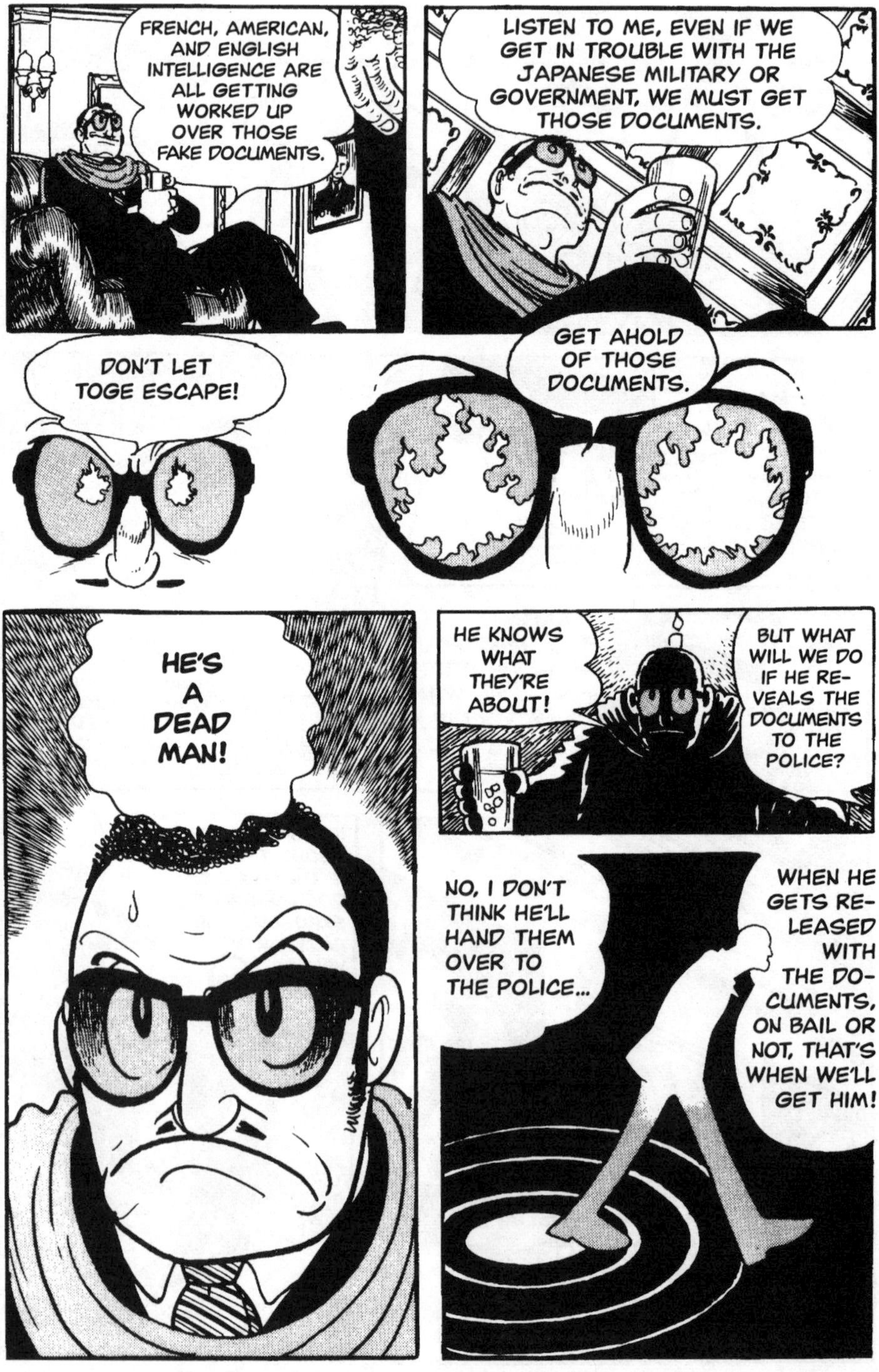
FRENCH, AMERICAN, AND ENGLISH INTELLIGENCE ARE ALL GETTING WORKED UP OVER THOSE FAKE DOCUMENTS.
LISTEN TO ME, EVEN IF WE GET IN TROUBLE WITH THE JAPANESE MILITARY OR GOVERNMENT, WE MUST GET THOSE DOCUMENTS.
DON'T LET TOGE ESCAPE!
GET AHOLD OF THOSE DOCUMENTS.
HE'S A DEAD MAN!
HE KNOWS WHAT THEY'RE ABOUT!
BUT WHAT WILL WE DO IF HE RE-VEALS THE DOCUMENTS TO THE POLICE?
NO, I DON'T THINK HE'LL HAND THEM OVER TO THE POLICE...
WHEN HE GETS RE-LEASED WITH THE DO-CUMENTS, ON BAIL OR NOT, THAT'S WHEN WE'LL GET HIM!

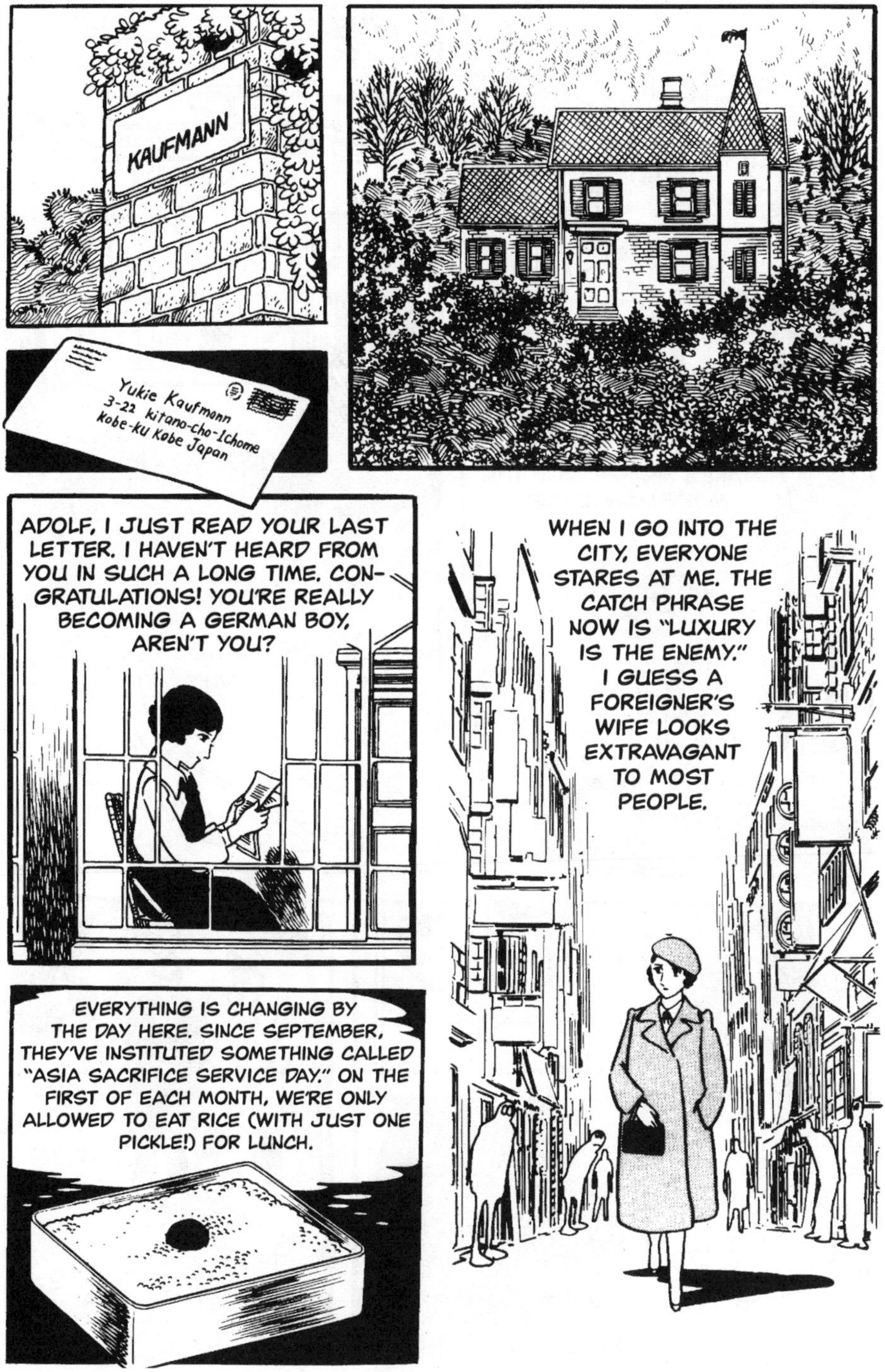
KAUFMANN
Yukie Kaufmann
3-22 kitano-cho-1chome
Kobe-ku Kobe Japan
ADOLF, I JUST READ YOUR LAST LETTER. I HAVEN'T HEARD FROM YOU IN SUCH A LONG TIME. CONGRATULATIONS! YOU'RE REALLY BECOMING A GERMAN BOY, AREN'T YOU?
EVERYTHING IS CHANGING BY THE DAY HERE. SINCE SEPTEMBER, THEY'VE INSTITUTED SOMETHING CALLED "ASIA SACRIFICE SERVICE DAY." ON THE FIRST OF EACH MONTH, WE'RE ONLY ALLOWED TO EAT RICE (WITH JUST ONE PICKLE!) FOR LUNCH.
WHEN I GO INTO THE CITY, EVERYONE STARES AT ME. THE CATCH PHRASE NOW IS "LUXURY IS THE ENEMY." I GUESS A FOREIGNER'S WIFE LOOKS EXTRAVAGANT TO MOST PEOPLE.

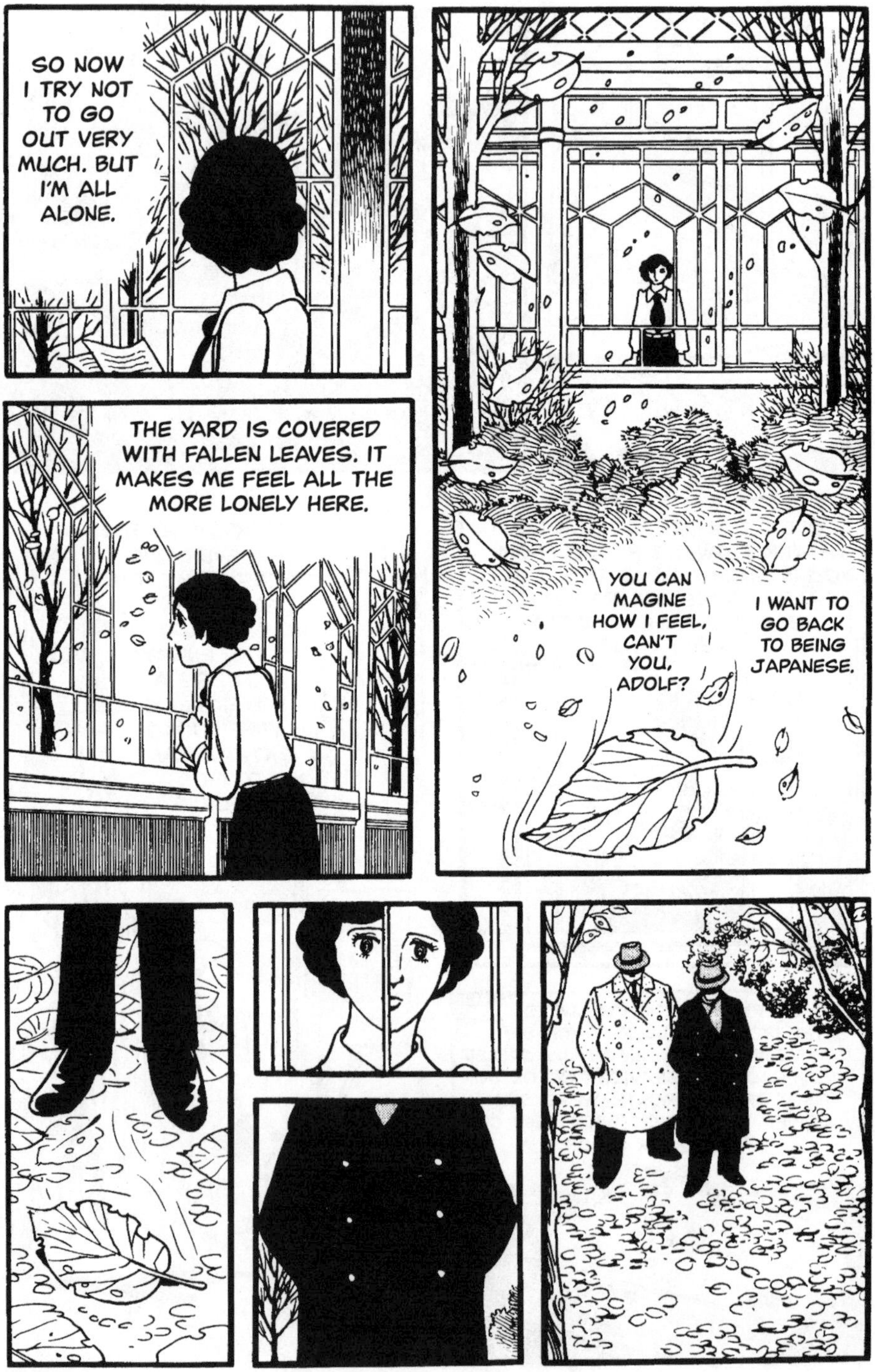
SO NOW I TRY NOT TO GO OUT VERY MUCH. BUT I'M ALL ALONE.
THE YARD IS COVERED WITH FALLEN LEAVES. IT MAKES ME FEEL ALL THE MORE LONELY HERE.
YOU CAN MAGINE HOW I FEEL, CAN'T YOU, ADOLF?
I WANT TO GO BACK TO BEING JAPANESE.

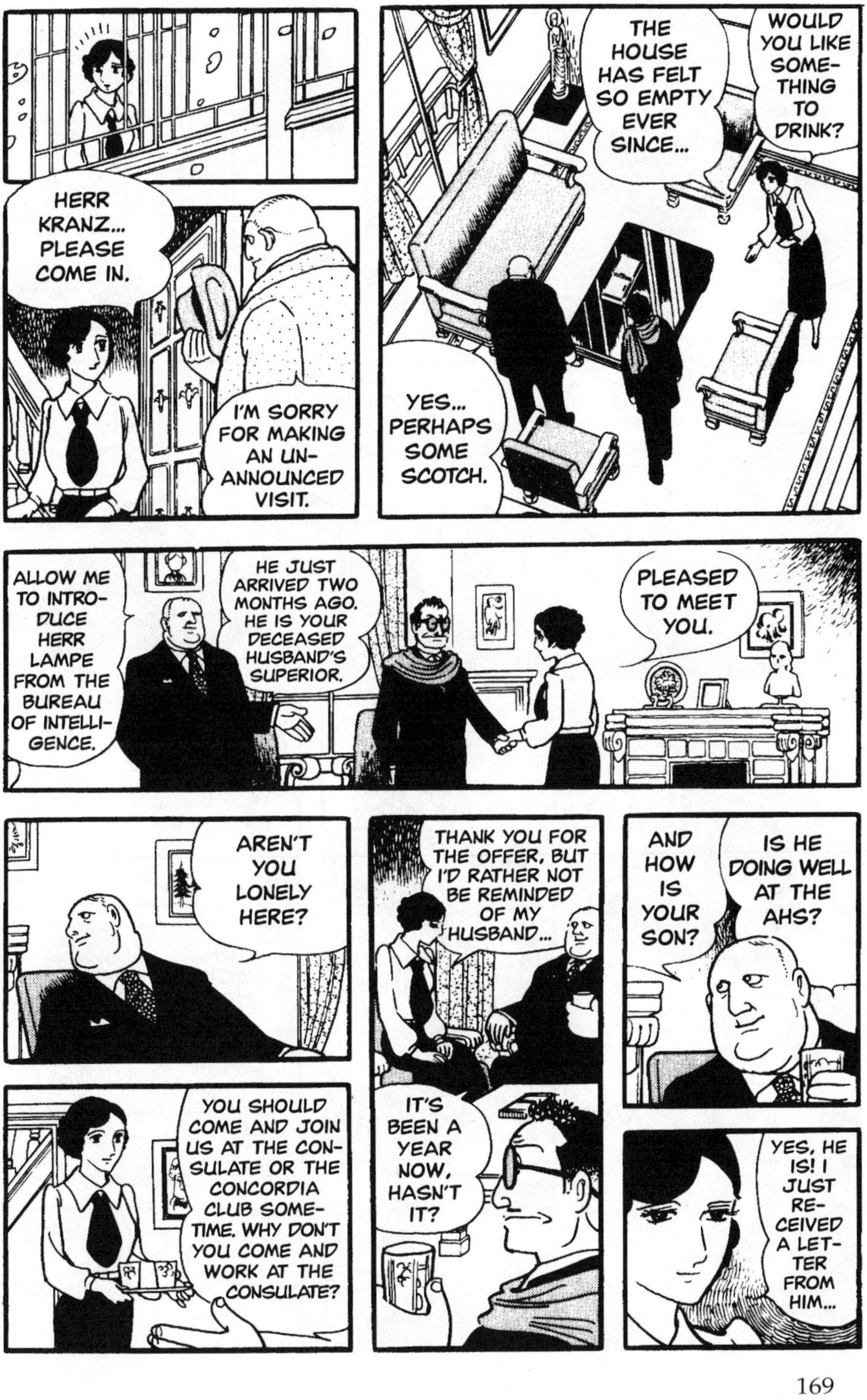
HERR KRANZ... PLEASE COME IN.
I'M SORRY FOR MAKING AN UN-ANNOUNCED VISIT.
THE HOUSE HAS FELT SO EMPTY EVER SINCE...
WOULD YOU LIKE SOME-THING TO DRINK?
YES... PERHAPS SOME SCOTCH.
ALLOW ME TO INTRO-DUCE HERR LAMPE FROM THE BUREAU OF INTELLI-GENCE.
HE JUST ARRIVED TWO MONTHS AGO. HE IS YOUR DECEASED HUSBAND'S SUPERIOR.
PLEASED TO MEET YOU.
AREN'T YOU LONELY HERE?
THANK YOU FOR THE OFFER, BUT I'D RATHER NOT BE REMINDED OF MY HUSBAND...
IT'S BEEN A YEAR NOW, HASN'T IT?
AND HOW IS YOUR SON?
IS HE DOING WELL AT THE AHS?
YES, HE IS! I JUST RE-CEIVED A LET-TER FROM HIM...
YOU SHOULD COME AND JOIN US AT THE CON-SULATE OR THE CONCORDIA CLUB SOME-TIME. WHY DON'T YOU COME AND WORK AT THE CONSULATE?

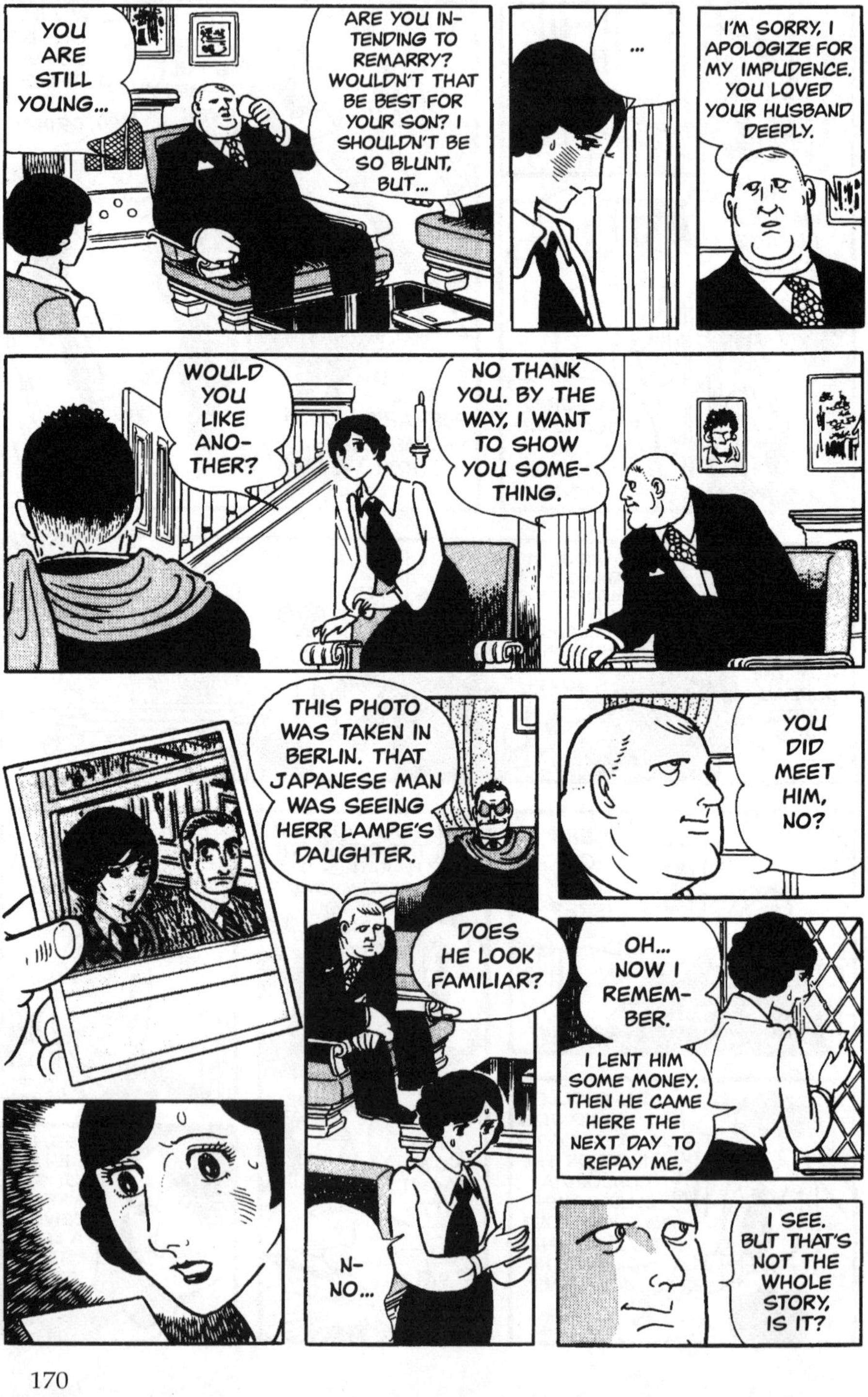
YOU ARE STILL YOUNG...
ARE YOU INTENDING TO REMARRY? WOULDN'T THAT BE BEST FOR YOUR SON? I SHOULDN'T BE SO BLUNT, BUT...
...
I'M SORRY, I APOLOGIZE FOR MY IMPUDENCE. YOU LOVED YOUR HUSBAND DEEPLY.
WOULD YOU LIKE ANOTHER?
NO THANK YOU. BY THE WAY, I WANT TO SHOW YOU SOMETHING.
THIS PHOTO WAS TAKEN IN BERLIN. THAT JAPANESE MAN WAS SEEING HERR LAMPE'S DAUGHTER.
DOES HE LOOK FAMILIAR?
N-NO...
YOU DID MEET HIM, NO?
OH... NOW I REMEMBER.
I LENT HIM SOME MONEY. THEN HE CAME HERE THE NEXT DAY TO REPAY ME.
I SEE. BUT THAT'S NOT THE WHOLE STORY, IS IT?

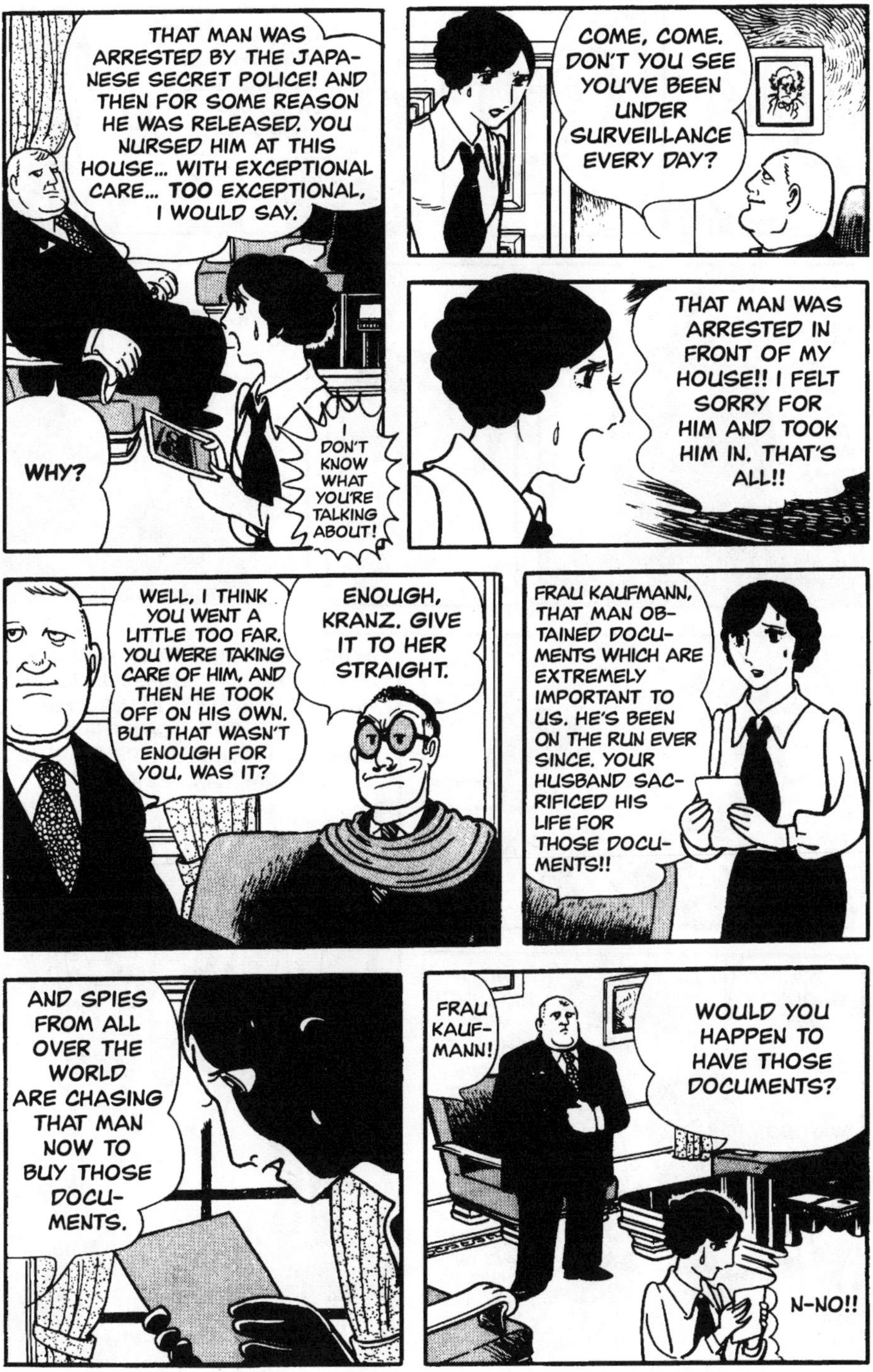
THAT MAN WAS ARRESTED BY THE JAPANESE SECRET POLICE! AND THEN FOR SOME REASON HE WAS RELEASED. YOU NURSED HIM AT THIS HOUSE... WITH EXCEPTIONAL CARE... **TOO** EXCEPTIONAL, I WOULD SAY.
WHY?
I DON'T KNOW WHAT YOU'RE TALKING ABOUT!
COME, COME. DON'T YOU SEE YOU'VE BEEN UNDER SURVEILLANCE EVERY DAY?
THAT MAN WAS ARRESTED IN FRONT OF MY HOUSE!! I FELT SORRY FOR HIM AND TOOK HIM IN. THAT'S ALL!!
WELL, I THINK YOU WENT A LITTLE TOO FAR. YOU WERE TAKING CARE OF HIM, AND THEN HE TOOK OFF ON HIS OWN. BUT THAT WASN'T ENOUGH FOR YOU, WAS IT?
ENOUGH, KRANZ. GIVE IT TO HER STRAIGHT.
FRAU KAUFMANN, THAT MAN OBTAINED DOCUMENTS WHICH ARE EXTREMELY IMPORTANT TO US. HE'S BEEN ON THE RUN EVER SINCE. YOUR HUSBAND SACRIFICED HIS LIFE FOR THOSE DOCUMENTS!!
AND SPIES FROM ALL OVER THE WORLD ARE CHASING THAT MAN NOW TO BUY THOSE DOCUMENTS.
FRAU KAUFMANN!
WOULD YOU HAPPEN TO HAVE THOSE DOCUMENTS?
N-NO!!

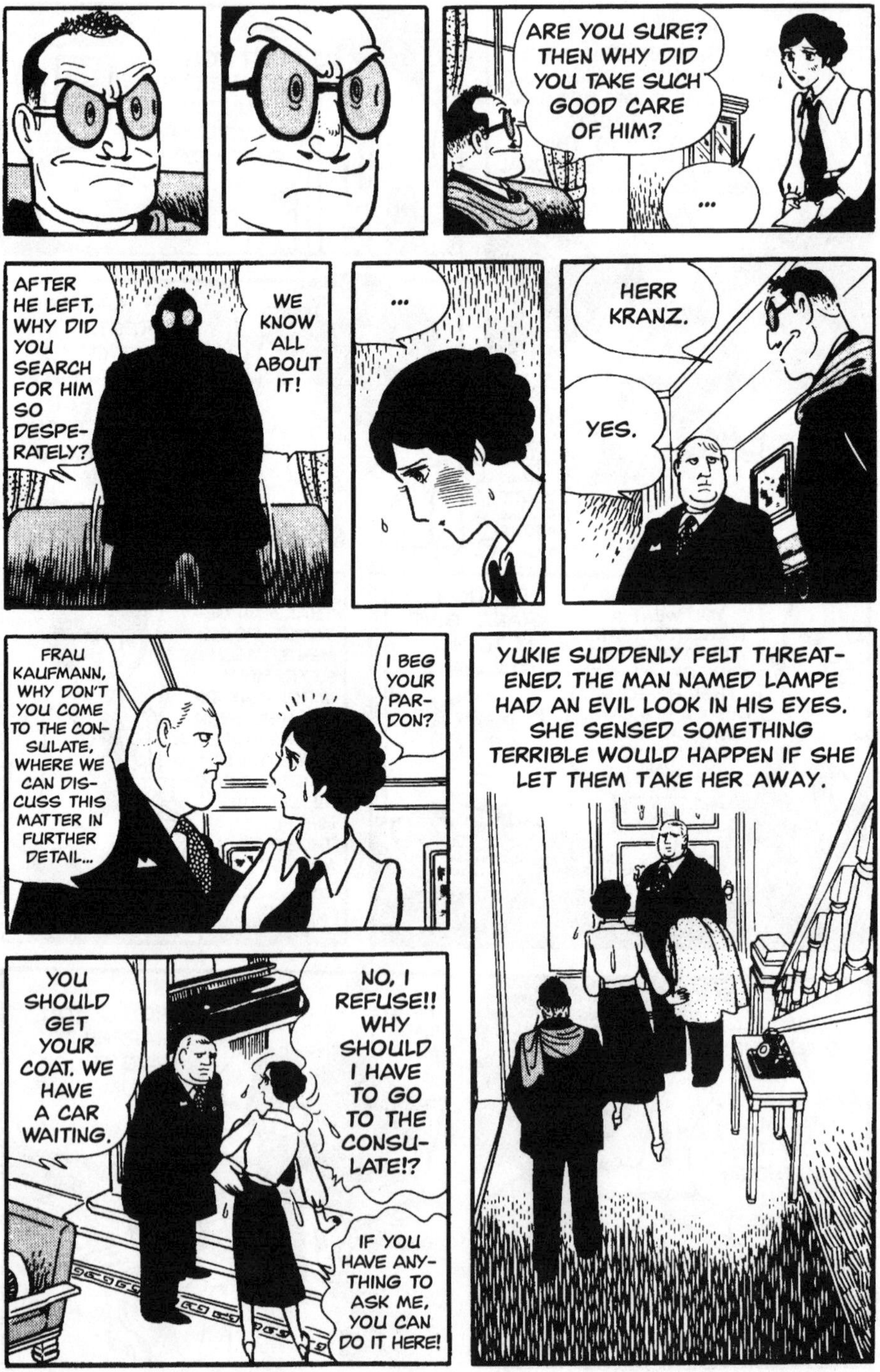
ARE YOU SURE? THEN WHY DID YOU TAKE SUCH GOOD CARE OF HIM?
...
AFTER HE LEFT, WHY DID YOU SEARCH FOR HIM SO DESPERATELY?
WE KNOW ALL ABOUT IT!
...
HERR KRANZ.
YES.
FRAU KAUFMANN, WHY DON'T YOU COME TO THE CONSULATE, WHERE WE CAN DISCUSS THIS MATTER IN FURTHER DETAIL...
I BEG YOUR PARDON?
YOU SHOULD GET YOUR COAT. WE HAVE A CAR WAITING.
NO, I REFUSE!! WHY SHOULD I HAVE TO GO TO THE CONSULATE!?
IF YOU HAVE ANYTHING TO ASK ME, YOU CAN DO IT HERE!
YUKIE SUDDENLY FELT THREATENED. THE MAN NAMED LAMPE HAD AN EVIL LOOK IN HIS EYES. SHE SENSED SOMETHING TERRIBLE WOULD HAPPEN IF SHE LET THEM TAKE HER AWAY.

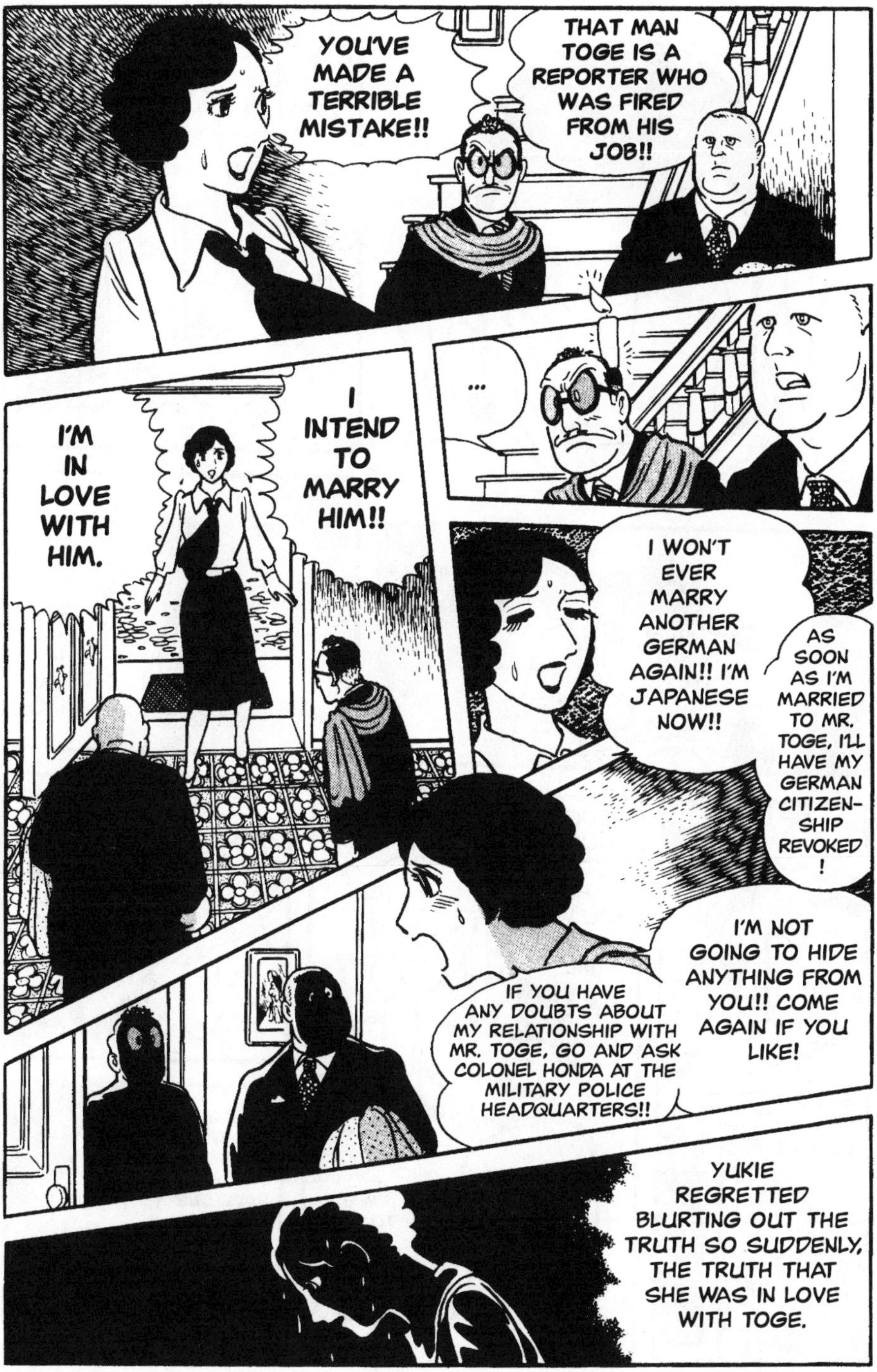
YOU'VE MADE A TERRIBLE MISTAKE!!
THAT MAN TOGE IS A REPORTER WHO WAS FIRED FROM HIS JOB!!
I'M IN LOVE WITH HIM.
I INTEND TO MARRY HIM!!
...
I WON'T EVER MARRY ANOTHER GERMAN AGAIN!! I'M JAPANESE NOW!!
AS SOON AS I'M MARRIED TO MR. TOGE, I'LL HAVE MY GERMAN CITIZEN-SHIP REVOKED!
IF YOU HAVE ANY DOUBTS ABOUT MY RELATIONSHIP WITH MR. TOGE, GO AND ASK COLONEL HONDA AT THE MILITARY POLICE HEADQUARTERS!!
I'M NOT GOING TO HIDE ANYTHING FROM YOU!! COME AGAIN IF YOU LIKE!
YUKIE REGRETTED BLURTING OUT THE TRUTH SO SUDDENLY, THE TRUTH THAT SHE WAS IN LOVE WITH TOGE.

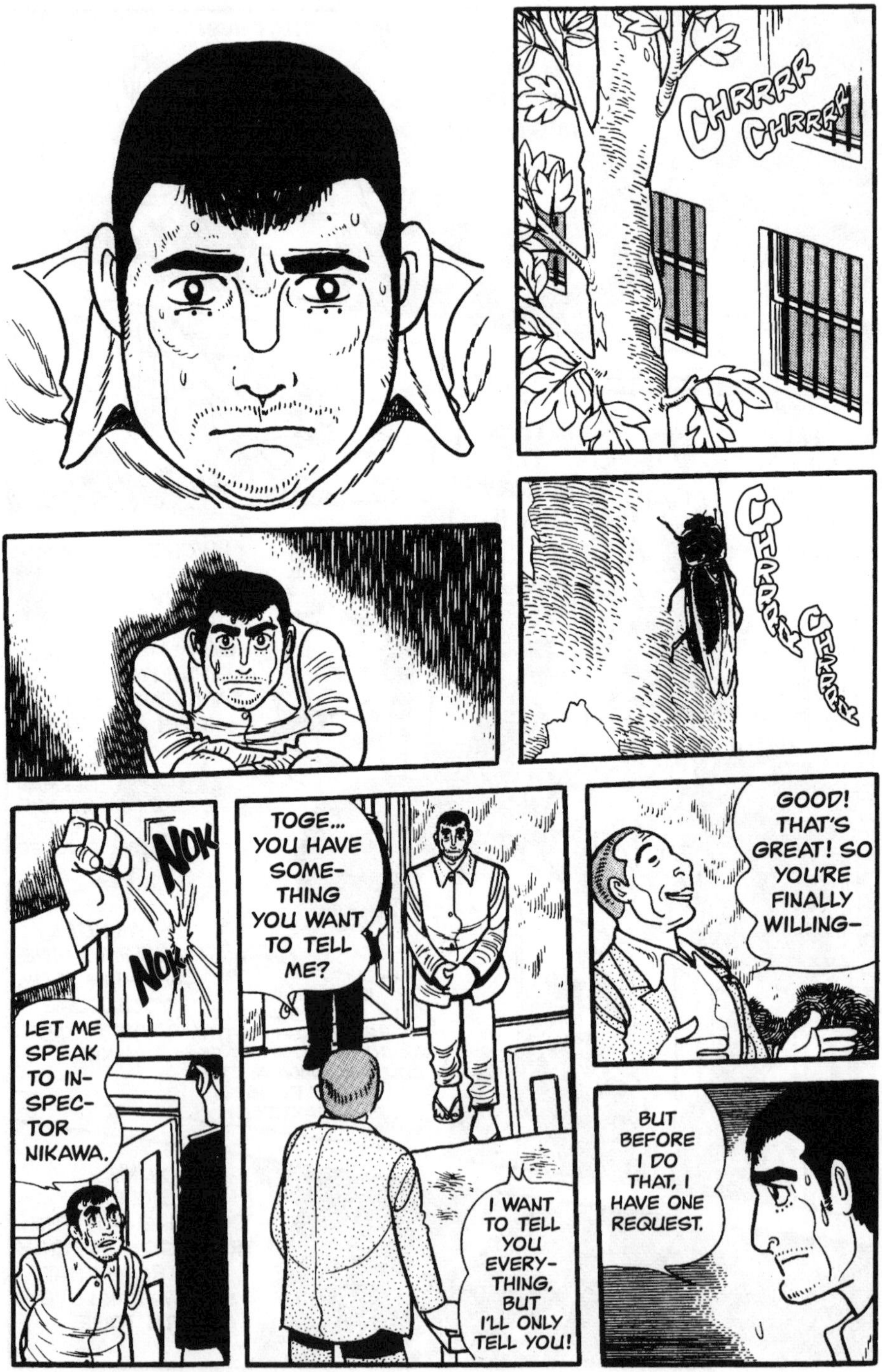
CHRRRR
CHRRRR
CHRRRR
CHRRRR
NOK
NOK
LET ME SPEAK TO IN-SPECTOR NIKAWA.
TOGE... YOU HAVE SOME-THING YOU WANT TO TELL ME?
I WANT TO TELL YOU EVERY-THING, BUT I'LL ONLY TELL YOU!
GOOD! THAT'S GREAT! SO YOU'RE FINALLY WILLING—
BUT BEFORE I DO THAT, I HAVE ONE REQUEST.

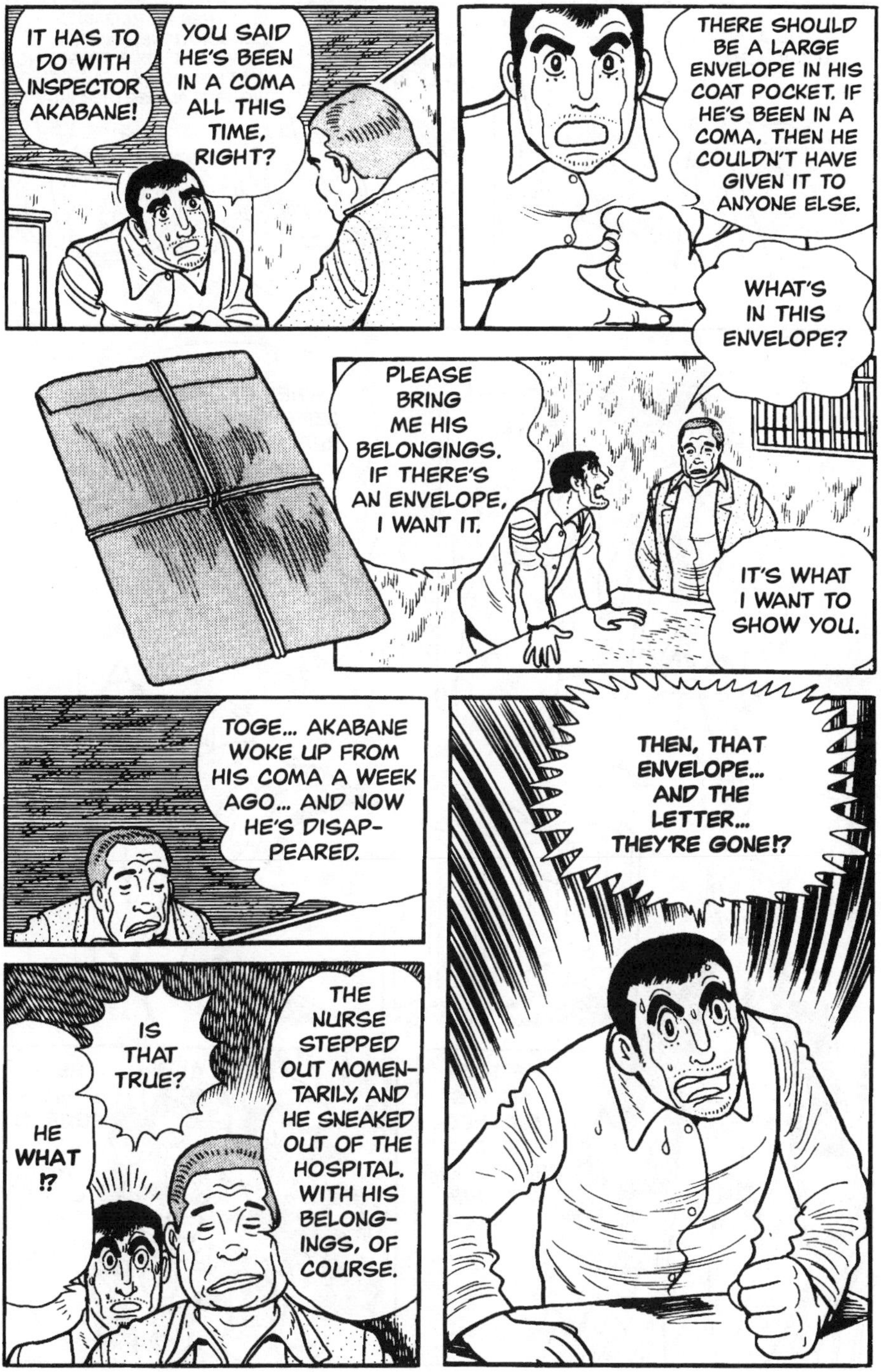
IT HAS TO DO WITH INSPECTOR AKABANE!
YOU SAID HE'S BEEN IN A COMA ALL THIS TIME, RIGHT?
THERE SHOULD BE A LARGE ENVELOPE IN HIS COAT POCKET. IF HE'S BEEN IN A COMA, THEN HE COULDN'T HAVE GIVEN IT TO ANYONE ELSE.
WHAT'S IN THIS ENVELOPE?
PLEASE BRING ME HIS BELONGINGS. IF THERE'S AN ENVELOPE, I WANT IT.
IT'S WHAT I WANT TO SHOW YOU.
TOGE... AKABANE WOKE UP FROM HIS COMA A WEEK AGO... AND NOW HE'S DISAP-PEARED.
IS THAT TRUE?
HE WHAT!?
THE NURSE STEPPED OUT MOMEN-TARILY, AND HE SNEAKED OUT OF THE HOSPITAL. WITH HIS BELONG-INGS, OF COURSE.
THEN, THAT ENVELOPE... AND THE LETTER... THEY'RE GONE!?

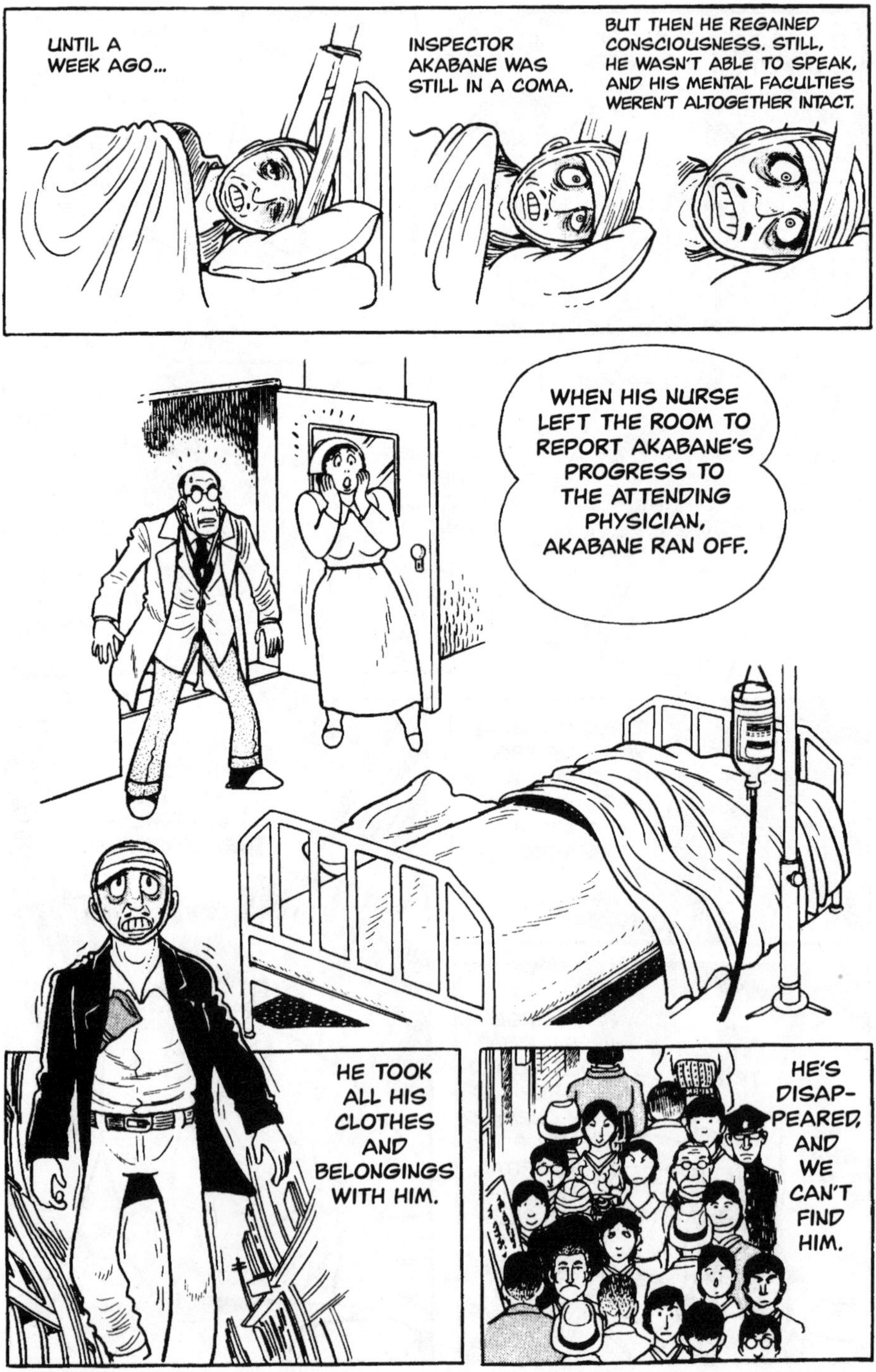
UNTIL A WEEK AGO...
INSPECTOR AKABANE WAS STILL IN A COMA.
BUT THEN HE REGAINED CONSCIOUSNESS. STILL, HE WASN'T ABLE TO SPEAK, AND HIS MENTAL FACULTIES WEREN'T ALTOGETHER INTACT.
WHEN HIS NURSE LEFT THE ROOM TO REPORT AKABANE'S PROGRESS TO THE ATTENDING PHYSICIAN, AKABANE RAN OFF.
HE TOOK ALL HIS CLOTHES AND BELONGINGS WITH HIM.
HE'S DISAP-PEARED, AND WE CAN'T FIND HIM.

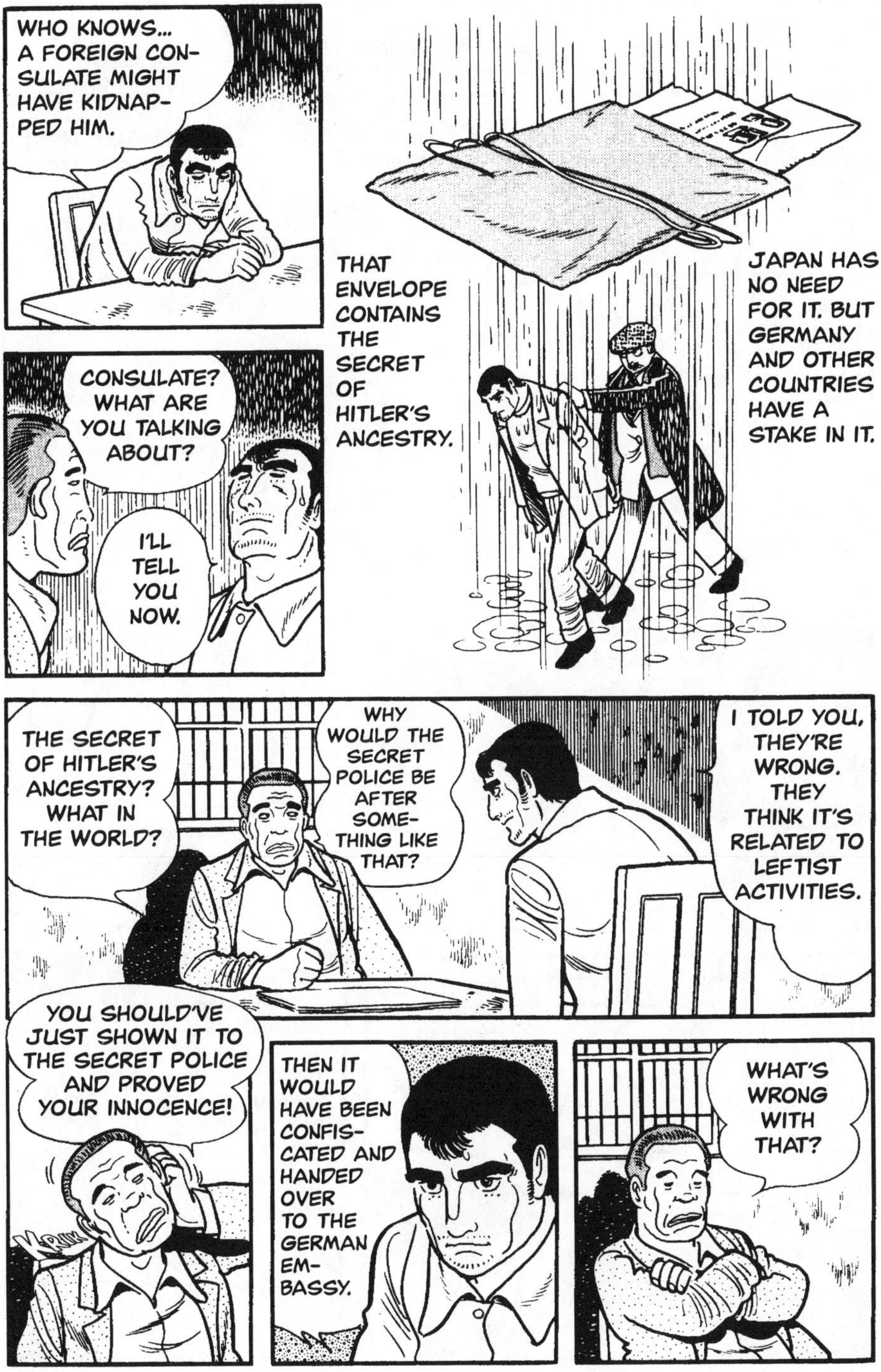
WHO KNOWS... A FOREIGN CONSULATE MIGHT HAVE KIDNAPPED HIM.
CONSULATE? WHAT ARE YOU TALKING ABOUT?
I'LL TELL YOU NOW.
THAT ENVELOPE CONTAINS THE SECRET OF HITLER'S ANCESTRY.
JAPAN HAS NO NEED FOR IT. BUT GERMANY AND OTHER COUNTRIES HAVE A STAKE IN IT.
THE SECRET OF HITLER'S ANCESTRY? WHAT IN THE WORLD?
WHY WOULD THE SECRET POLICE BE AFTER SOMETHING LIKE THAT?
I TOLD YOU, THEY'RE WRONG. THEY THINK IT'S RELATED TO LEFTIST ACTIVITIES.
YOU SHOULD'VE JUST SHOWN IT TO THE SECRET POLICE AND PROVED YOUR INNOCENCE!
THEN IT WOULD HAVE BEEN CONFISCATED AND HANDED OVER TO THE GERMAN EMBASSY.
WHAT'S WRONG WITH THAT?

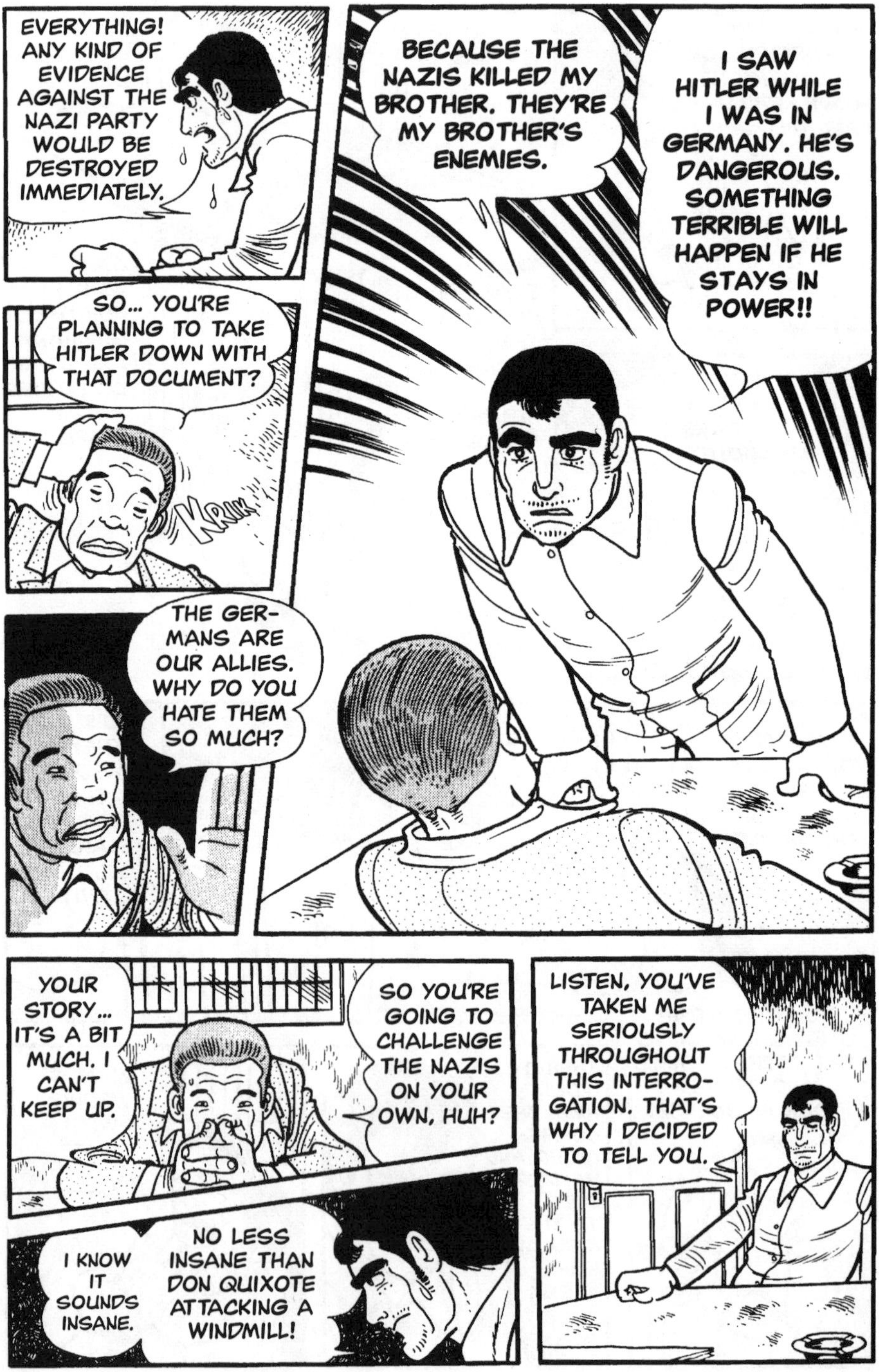
EVERYTHING! ANY KIND OF EVIDENCE AGAINST THE NAZI PARTY WOULD BE DESTROYED IMMEDIATELY.
SO... YOU'RE PLANNING TO TAKE HITLER DOWN WITH THAT DOCUMENT?
KRIK
THE GERMANS ARE OUR ALLIES. WHY DO YOU HATE THEM SO MUCH?
BECAUSE THE NAZIS KILLED MY BROTHER. THEY'RE MY BROTHER'S ENEMIES.
I SAW HITLER WHILE I WAS IN GERMANY. HE'S DANGEROUS. SOMETHING TERRIBLE WILL HAPPEN IF HE STAYS IN POWER!!
YOUR STORY... IT'S A BIT MUCH. I CAN'T KEEP UP.
SO YOU'RE GOING TO CHALLENGE THE NAZIS ON YOUR OWN, HUH?
I KNOW IT SOUNDS INSANE.
NO LESS INSANE THAN DON QUIXOTE ATTACKING A WINDMILL!
LISTEN, YOU'VE TAKEN ME SERIOUSLY THROUGHOUT THIS INTERROGATION. THAT'S WHY I DECIDED TO TELL YOU.

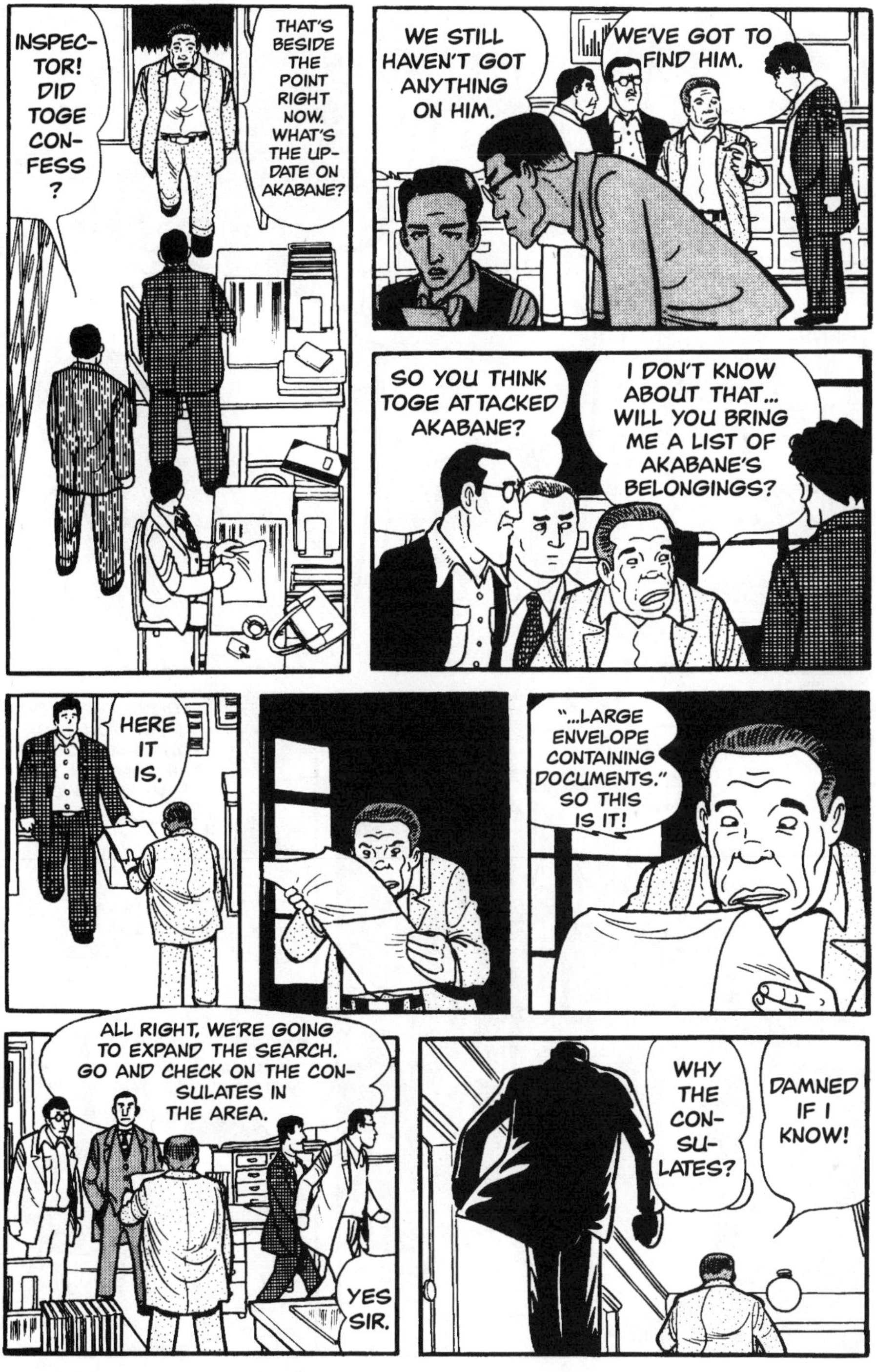
INSPECTOR! DID TOGE CONFESS?
THAT'S BESIDE THE POINT RIGHT NOW. WHAT'S THE UPDATE ON AKABANE?
WE STILL HAVEN'T GOT ANYTHING ON HIM.
WE'VE GOT TO FIND HIM.
SO YOU THINK TOGE ATTACKED AKABANE?
I DON'T KNOW ABOUT THAT... WILL YOU BRING ME A LIST OF AKABANE'S BELONGINGS?
HERE IT IS.
"...LARGE ENVELOPE CONTAINING DOCUMENTS." SO THIS IS IT!
ALL RIGHT, WE'RE GOING TO EXPAND THE SEARCH. GO AND CHECK ON THE CONSULATES IN THE AREA.
YES SIR.
WHY THE CONSULATES?
DAMNED IF I KNOW!

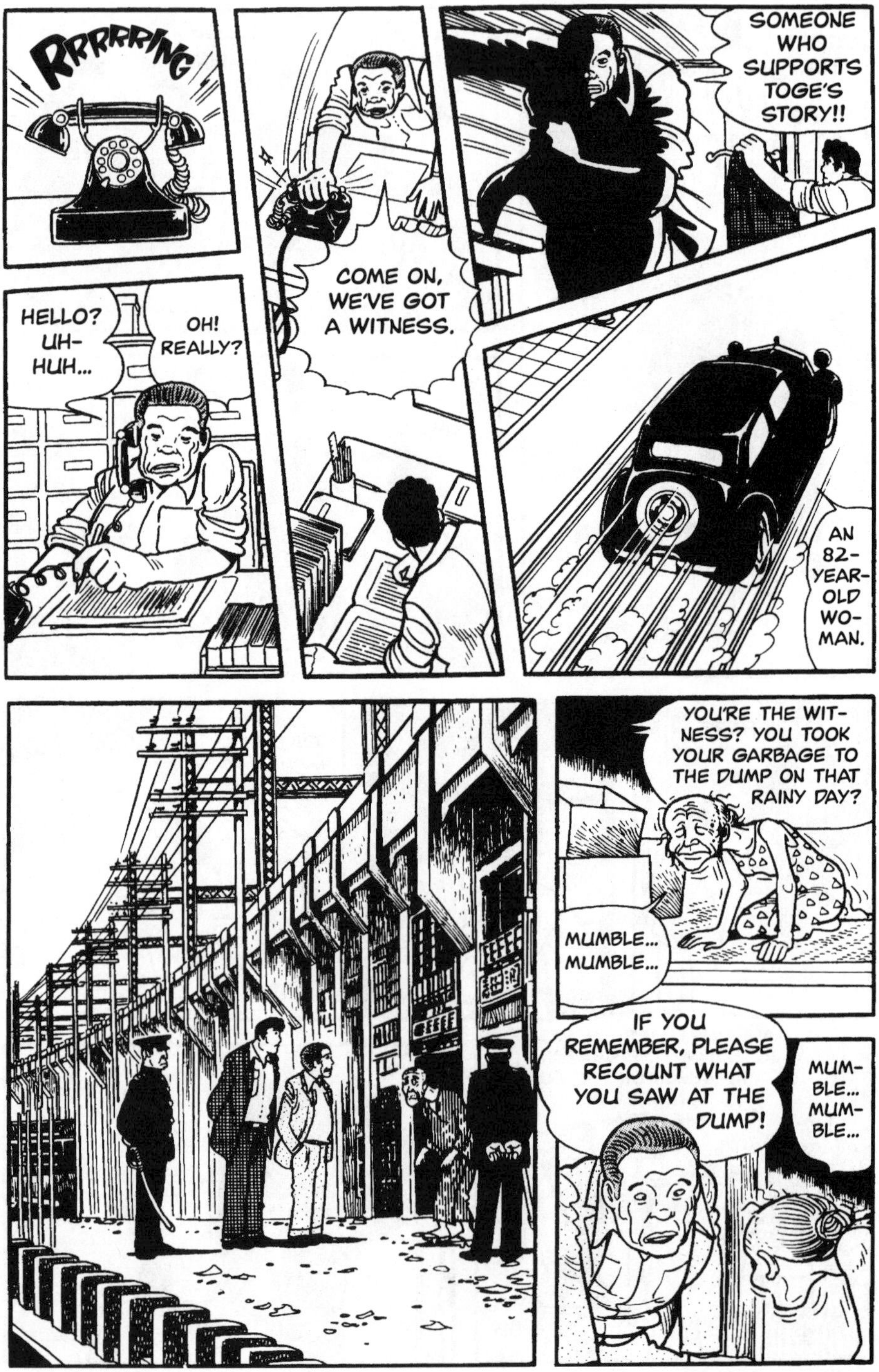
RRRRRING
HELLO? UH-HUH...
OH! REALLY?
COME ON, WE'VE GOT A WITNESS.
SOMEONE WHO SUPPORTS TOGE'S STORY!!
AN 82-YEAR-OLD WO-MAN.
YOU'RE THE WIT-NESS? YOU TOOK YOUR GARBAGE TO THE DUMP ON THAT RAINY DAY?
MUMBLE... MUMBLE...
IF YOU REMEMBER, PLEASE RECOUNT WHAT YOU SAW AT THE DUMP!
MUM-BLE... MUM-BLE...

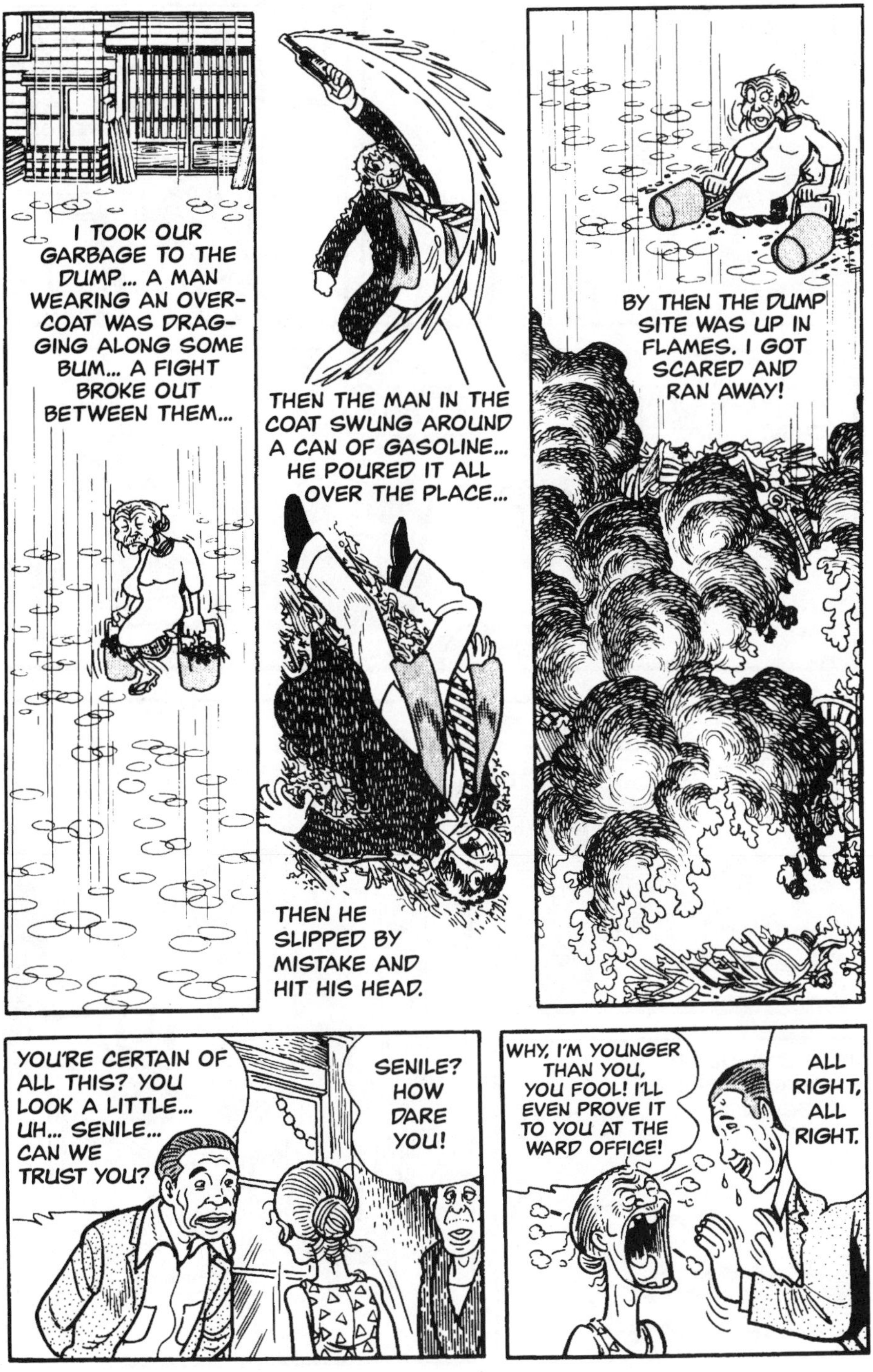
I TOOK OUR GARBAGE TO THE DUMP... A MAN WEARING AN OVER-COAT WAS DRAG-GING ALONG SOME BUM... A FIGHT BROKE OUT BETWEEN THEM...
THEN THE MAN IN THE COAT SWUNG AROUND A CAN OF GASOLINE... HE POURED IT ALL OVER THE PLACE...
THEN HE SLIPPED BY MISTAKE AND HIT HIS HEAD.
BY THEN THE DUMP SITE WAS UP IN FLAMES. I GOT SCARED AND RAN AWAY!
YOU'RE CERTAIN OF ALL THIS? YOU LOOK A LITTLE... UH... SENILE... CAN WE TRUST YOU?
SENILE? HOW DARE YOU!
WHY, I'M YOUNGER THAN YOU, YOU FOOL! I'LL EVEN PROVE IT TO YOU AT THE WARD OFFICE!
ALL RIGHT, ALL RIGHT.

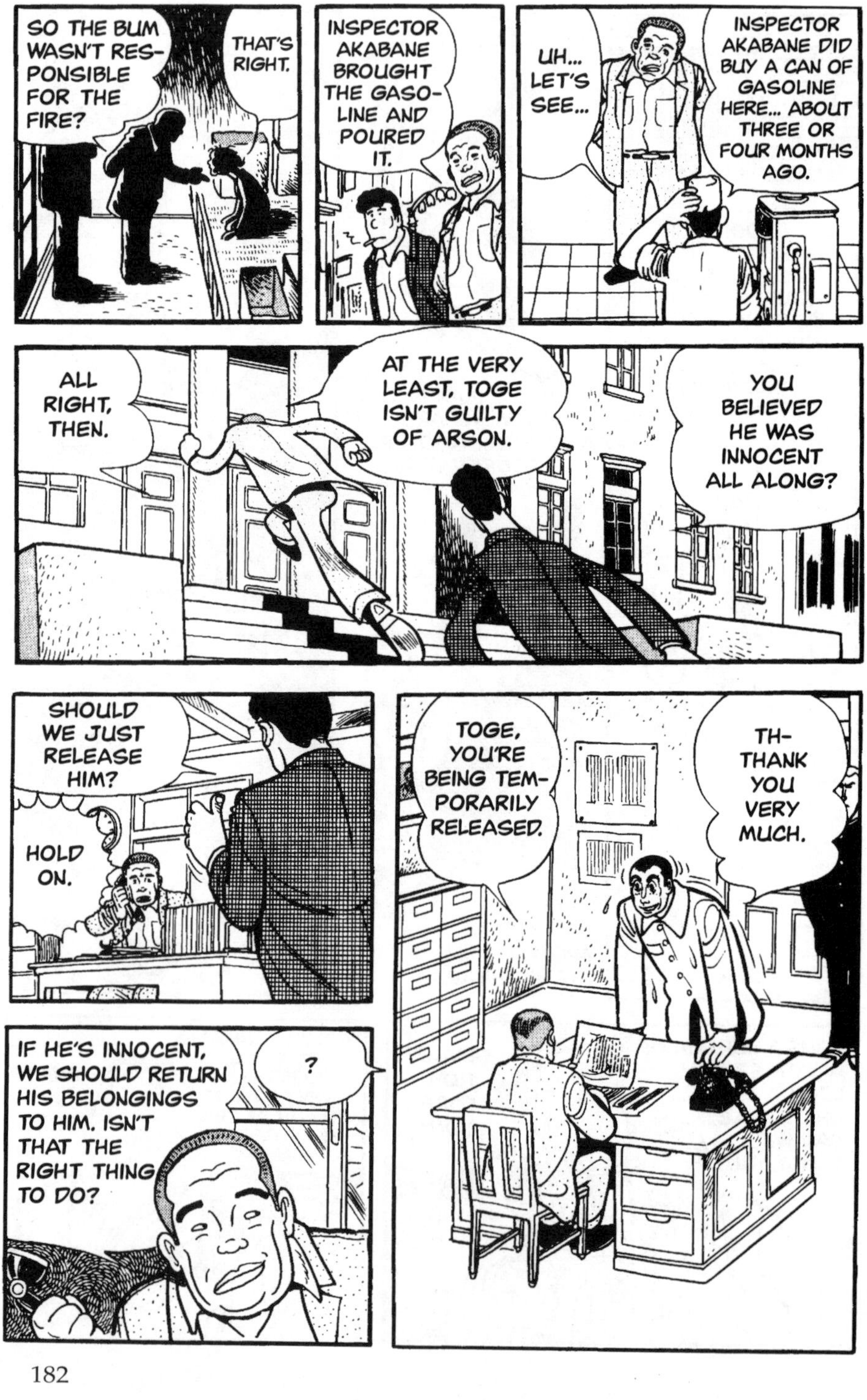
SO THE BUM WASN'T RESPONSIBLE FOR THE FIRE?
THAT'S RIGHT.
INSPECTOR AKABANE BROUGHT THE GASOLINE AND POURED IT.
UH... LET'S SEE...
INSPECTOR AKABANE DID BUY A CAN OF GASOLINE HERE... ABOUT THREE OR FOUR MONTHS AGO.
ALL RIGHT, THEN.
AT THE VERY LEAST, TOGE ISN'T GUILTY OF ARSON.
YOU BELIEVED HE WAS INNOCENT ALL ALONG?
SHOULD WE JUST RELEASE HIM?
HOLD ON.
IF HE'S INNOCENT, WE SHOULD RETURN HIS BELONGINGS TO HIM. ISN'T THAT THE RIGHT THING TO DO?
?
TOGE, YOU'RE BEING TEMPORARILY RELEASED.
TH- THANK YOU VERY MUCH.

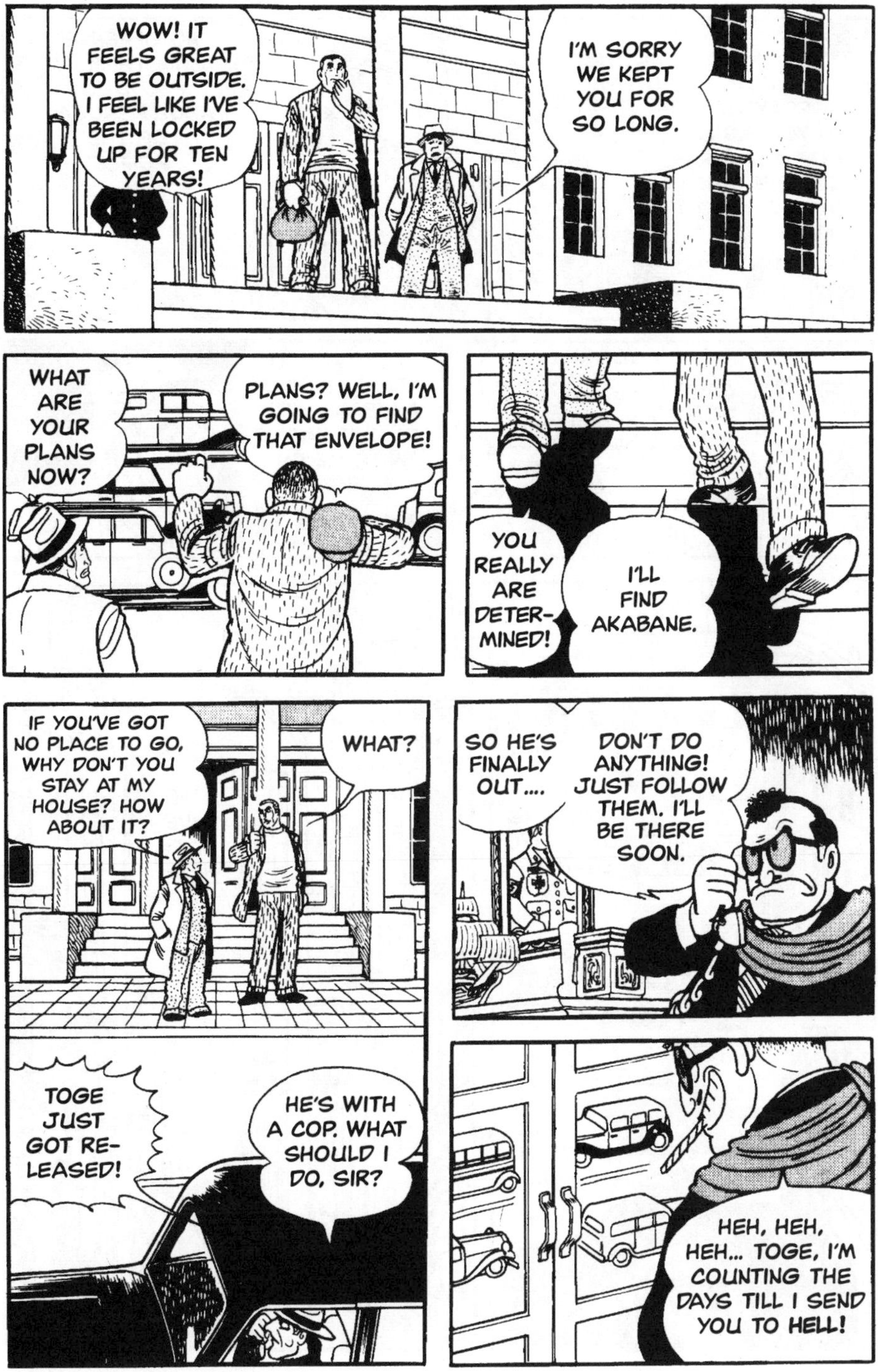
WOW! IT FEELS GREAT TO BE OUTSIDE. I FEEL LIKE I'VE BEEN LOCKED UP FOR TEN YEARS!
I'M SORRY WE KEPT YOU FOR SO LONG.
WHAT ARE YOUR PLANS NOW?
PLANS? WELL, I'M GOING TO FIND THAT ENVELOPE!
YOU REALLY ARE DETER-MINED!
I'LL FIND AKABANE.
IF YOU'VE GOT NO PLACE TO GO, WHY DON'T YOU STAY AT MY HOUSE? HOW ABOUT IT?
WHAT?
SO HE'S FINALLY OUT....
DON'T DO ANYTHING! JUST FOLLOW THEM. I'LL BE THERE SOON.
TOGE JUST GOT RE-LEASED!
HE'S WITH A COP. WHAT SHOULD I DO, SIR?
HEH, HEH, HEH... TOGE, I'M COUNTING THE DAYS TILL I SEND YOU TO HELL!

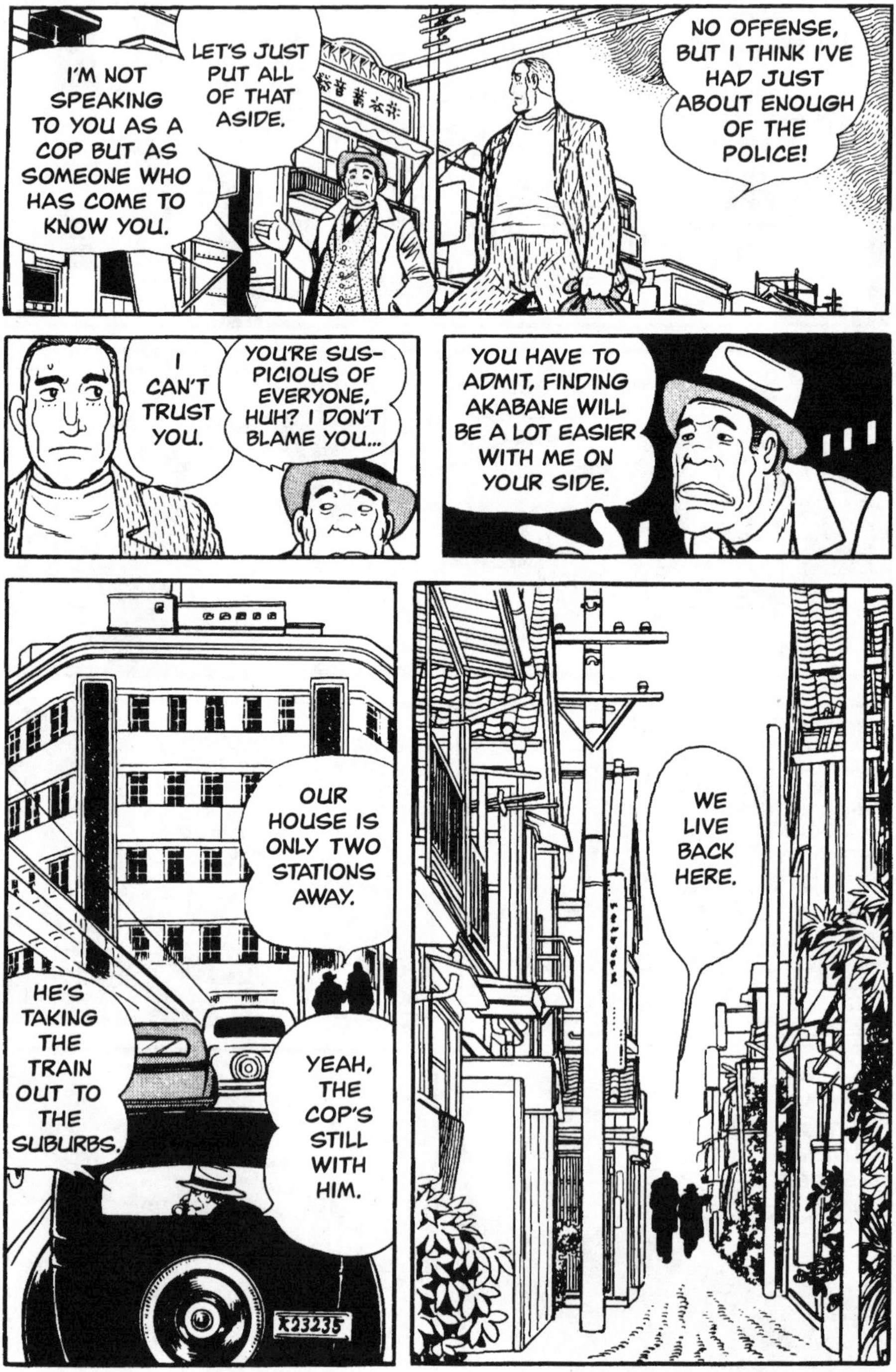
I'M NOT SPEAKING TO YOU AS A COP BUT AS SOMEONE WHO HAS COME TO KNOW YOU.
LET'S JUST PUT ALL OF THAT ASIDE.
NO OFFENSE, BUT I THINK I'VE HAD JUST ABOUT ENOUGH OF THE POLICE!
I CAN'T TRUST YOU.
YOU'RE SUS-PICIOUS OF EVERYONE, HUH? I DON'T BLAME YOU...
YOU HAVE TO ADMIT, FINDING AKABANE WILL BE A LOT EASIER WITH ME ON YOUR SIDE.
OUR HOUSE IS ONLY TWO STATIONS AWAY.
HE'S TAKING THE TRAIN OUT TO THE SUBURBS.
YEAH, THE COP'S STILL WITH HIM.
WE LIVE BACK HERE.

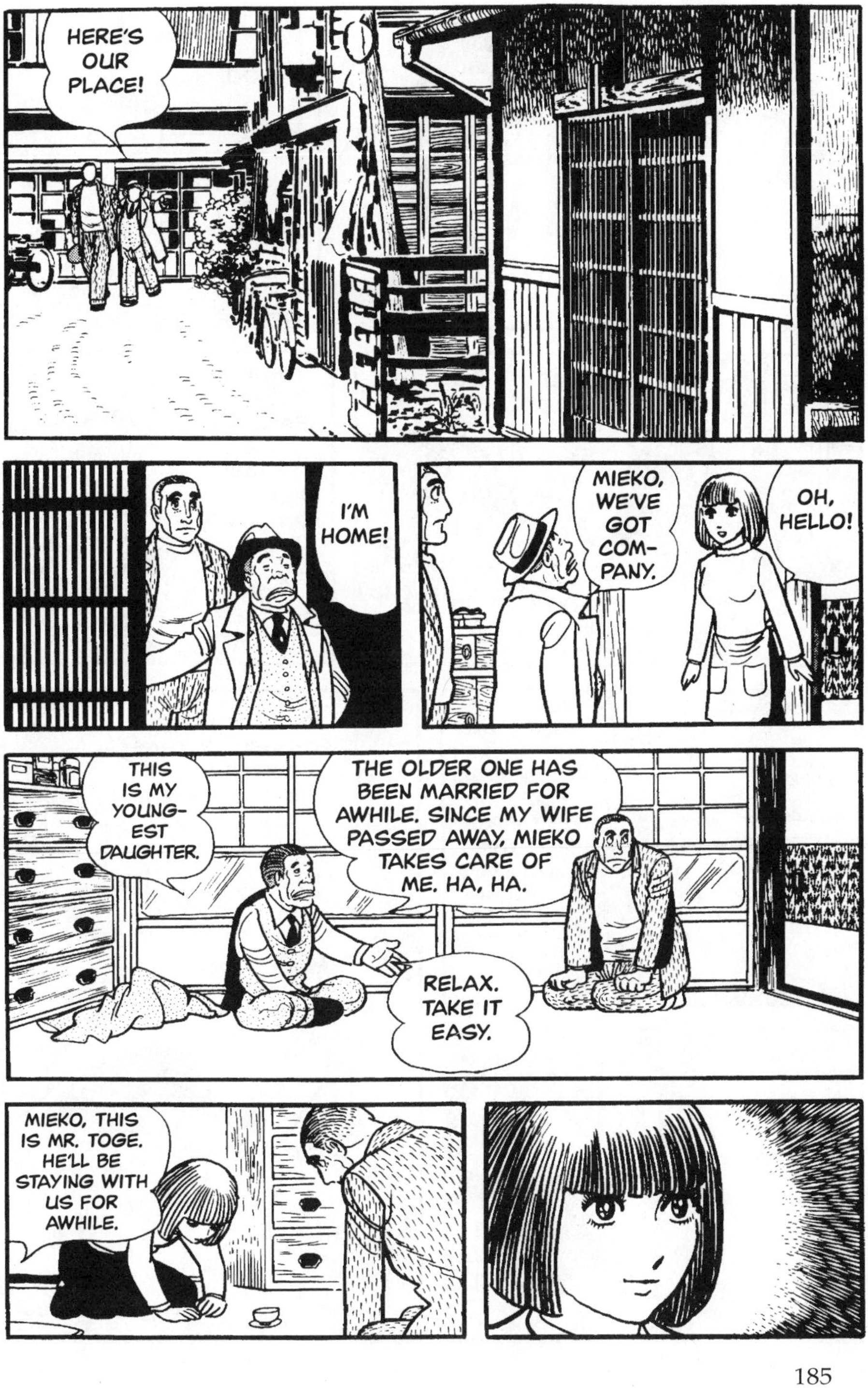
HERE'S OUR PLACE!
I'M HOME!
MIEKO, WE'VE GOT COM-PANY.
OH, HELLO!
THIS IS MY YOUNG-EST DAUGHTER.
THE OLDER ONE HAS BEEN MARRIED FOR AWHILE. SINCE MY WIFE PASSED AWAY, MIEKO TAKES CARE OF ME. HA, HA.
RELAX. TAKE IT EASY.
MIEKO, THIS IS MR. TOGE. HE'LL BE STAYING WITH US FOR AWHILE.

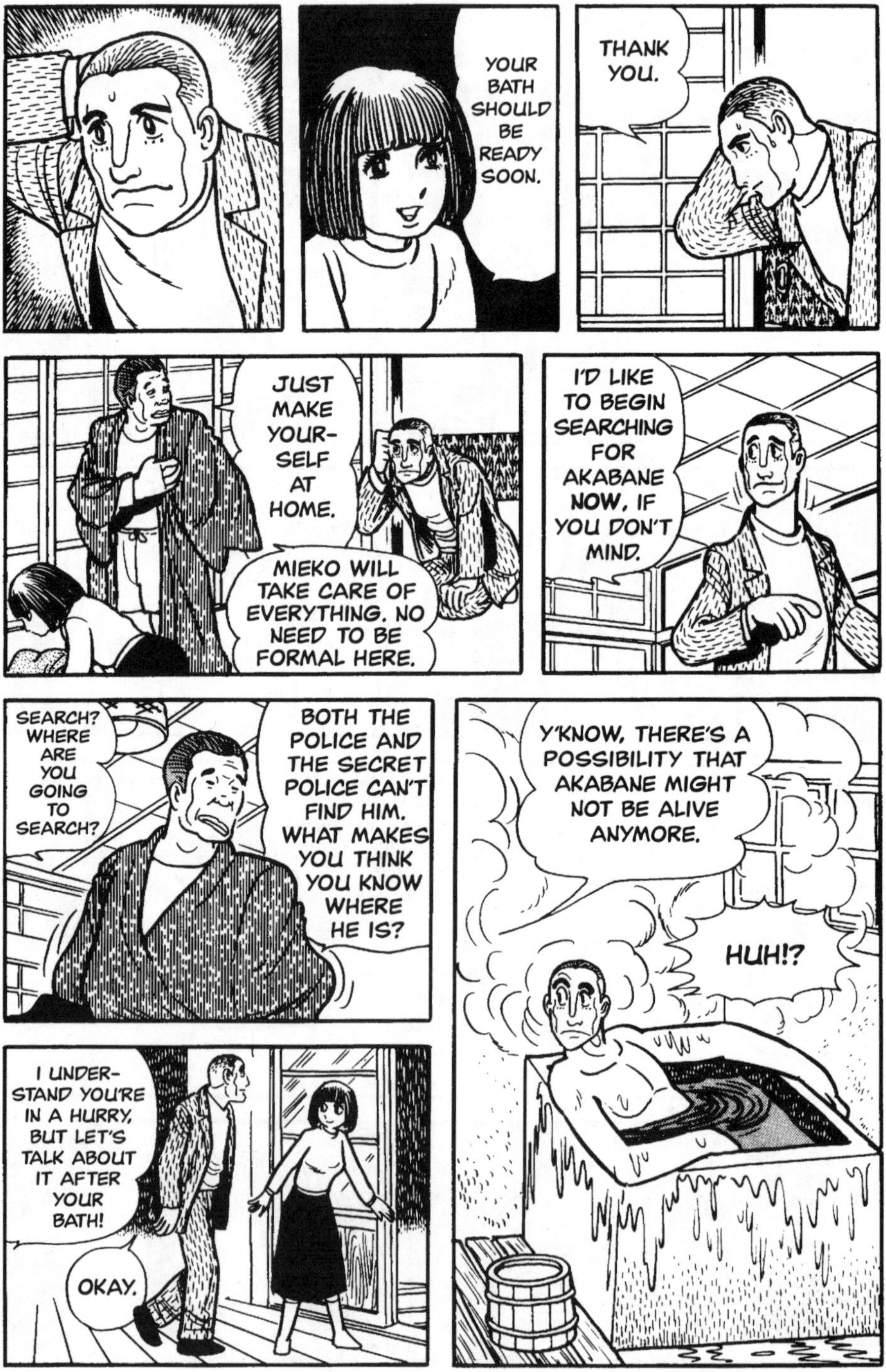
YOUR BATH SHOULD BE READY SOON.
THANK YOU.
JUST MAKE YOUR-SELF AT HOME.
MIEKO WILL TAKE CARE OF EVERYTHING. NO NEED TO BE FORMAL HERE.
I'D LIKE TO BEGIN SEARCHING FOR AKABANE NOW, IF YOU DON'T MIND.
SEARCH? WHERE ARE YOU GOING TO SEARCH?
BOTH THE POLICE AND THE SECRET POLICE CAN'T FIND HIM. WHAT MAKES YOU THINK YOU KNOW WHERE HE IS?
I UNDER-STAND YOU'RE IN A HURRY, BUT LET'S TALK ABOUT IT AFTER YOUR BATH!
OKAY.
Y'KNOW, THERE'S A POSSIBILITY THAT AKABANE MIGHT NOT BE ALIVE ANYMORE.
HUH!?

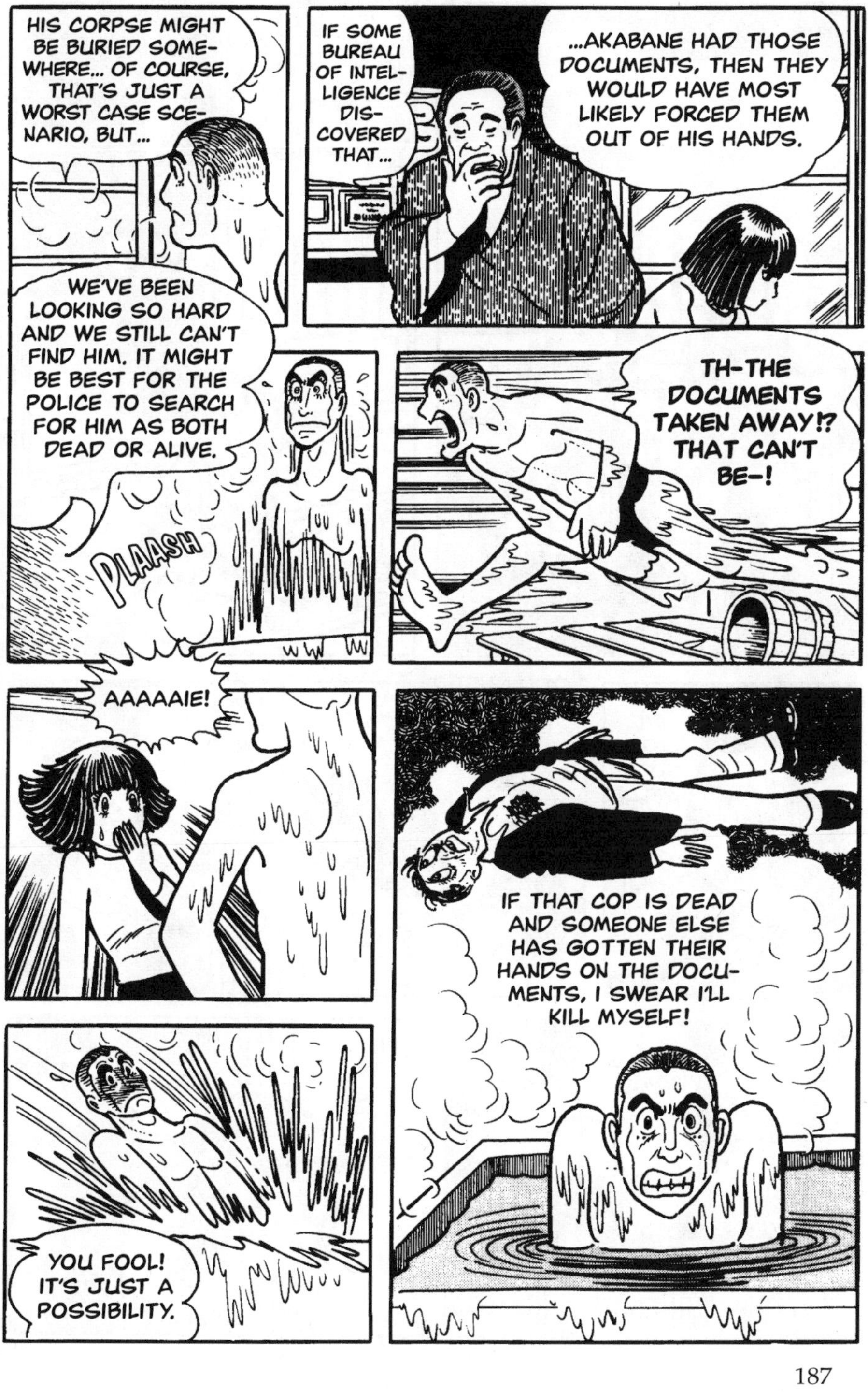
HIS CORPSE MIGHT BE BURIED SOME-WHERE... OF COURSE, THAT'S JUST A WORST CASE SCE-NARIO, BUT...
IF SOME BUREAU OF INTEL-LIGENCE DIS-COVERED THAT...
...AKABANE HAD THOSE DOCUMENTS, THEN THEY WOULD HAVE MOST LIKELY FORCED THEM OUT OF HIS HANDS.
WE'VE BEEN LOOKING SO HARD AND WE STILL CAN'T FIND HIM. IT MIGHT BE BEST FOR THE POLICE TO SEARCH FOR HIM AS BOTH DEAD OR ALIVE.
PLAASH
TH-THE DOCUMENTS TAKEN AWAY!? THAT CAN'T BE-!
AAAAAIE!
YOU FOOL! IT'S JUST A POSSIBILITY.
IF THAT COP IS DEAD AND SOMEONE ELSE HAS GOTTEN THEIR HANDS ON THE DOCU-MENTS, I SWEAR I'LL KILL MYSELF!

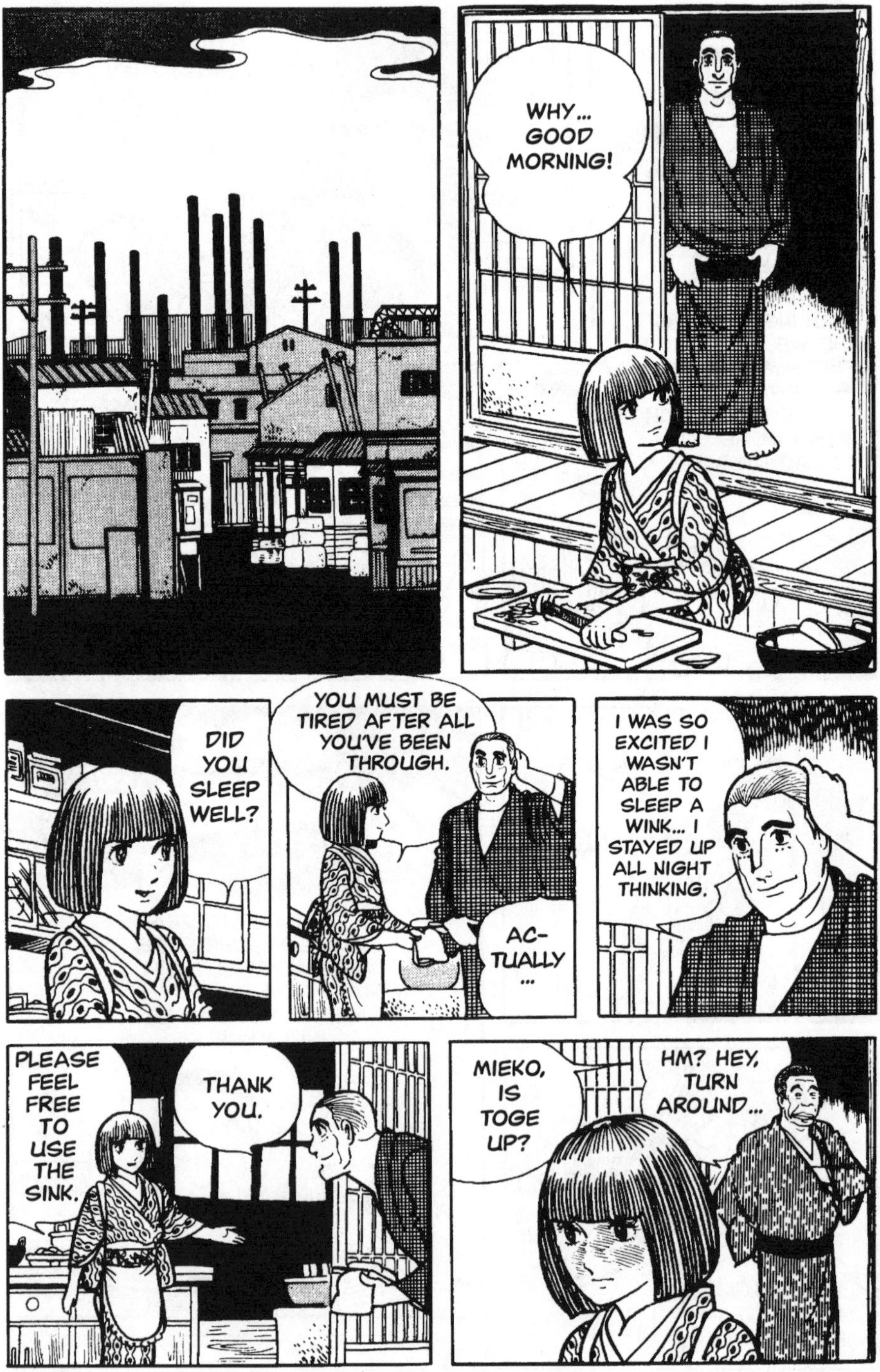
WHY... GOOD MORNING!
DID YOU SLEEP WELL?
YOU MUST BE TIRED AFTER ALL YOU'VE BEEN THROUGH.
AC-TUALLY...
I WAS SO EXCITED I WASN'T ABLE TO SLEEP A WINK... I STAYED UP ALL NIGHT THINKING.
PLEASE FEEL FREE TO USE THE SINK.
THANK YOU.
MIEKO, IS TOGE UP?
HM? HEY, TURN AROUND...

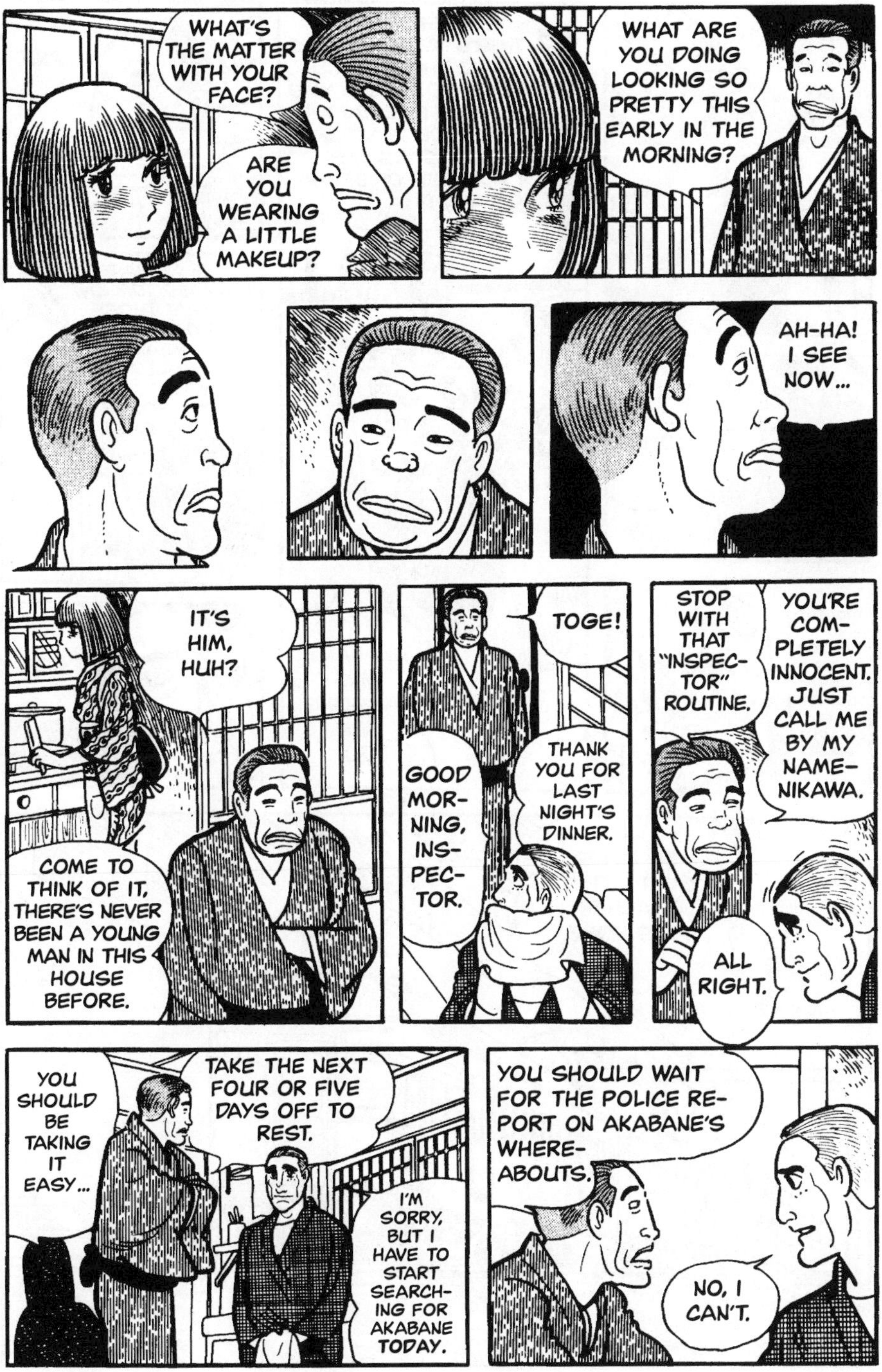
WHAT'S THE MATTER WITH YOUR FACE?
ARE YOU WEARING A LITTLE MAKEUP?
WHAT ARE YOU DOING LOOKING SO PRETTY THIS EARLY IN THE MORNING?
AH-HA! I SEE NOW...
IT'S HIM, HUH?
COME TO THINK OF IT, THERE'S NEVER BEEN A YOUNG MAN IN THIS HOUSE BEFORE.
TOGE!
GOOD MOR-NING, INS-PEC-TOR.
THANK YOU FOR LAST NIGHT'S DINNER.
STOP WITH THAT "INSPEC-TOR" ROUTINE.
YOU'RE COM-PLETELY INNOCENT. JUST CALL ME BY MY NAME-NIKAWA.
ALL RIGHT.
YOU SHOULD BE TAKING IT EASY...
TAKE THE NEXT FOUR OR FIVE DAYS OFF TO REST.
I'M SORRY, BUT I HAVE TO START SEARCH-ING FOR AKABANE TODAY.
YOU SHOULD WAIT FOR THE POLICE RE-PORT ON AKABANE'S WHERE-ABOUTS.
NO, I CAN'T.

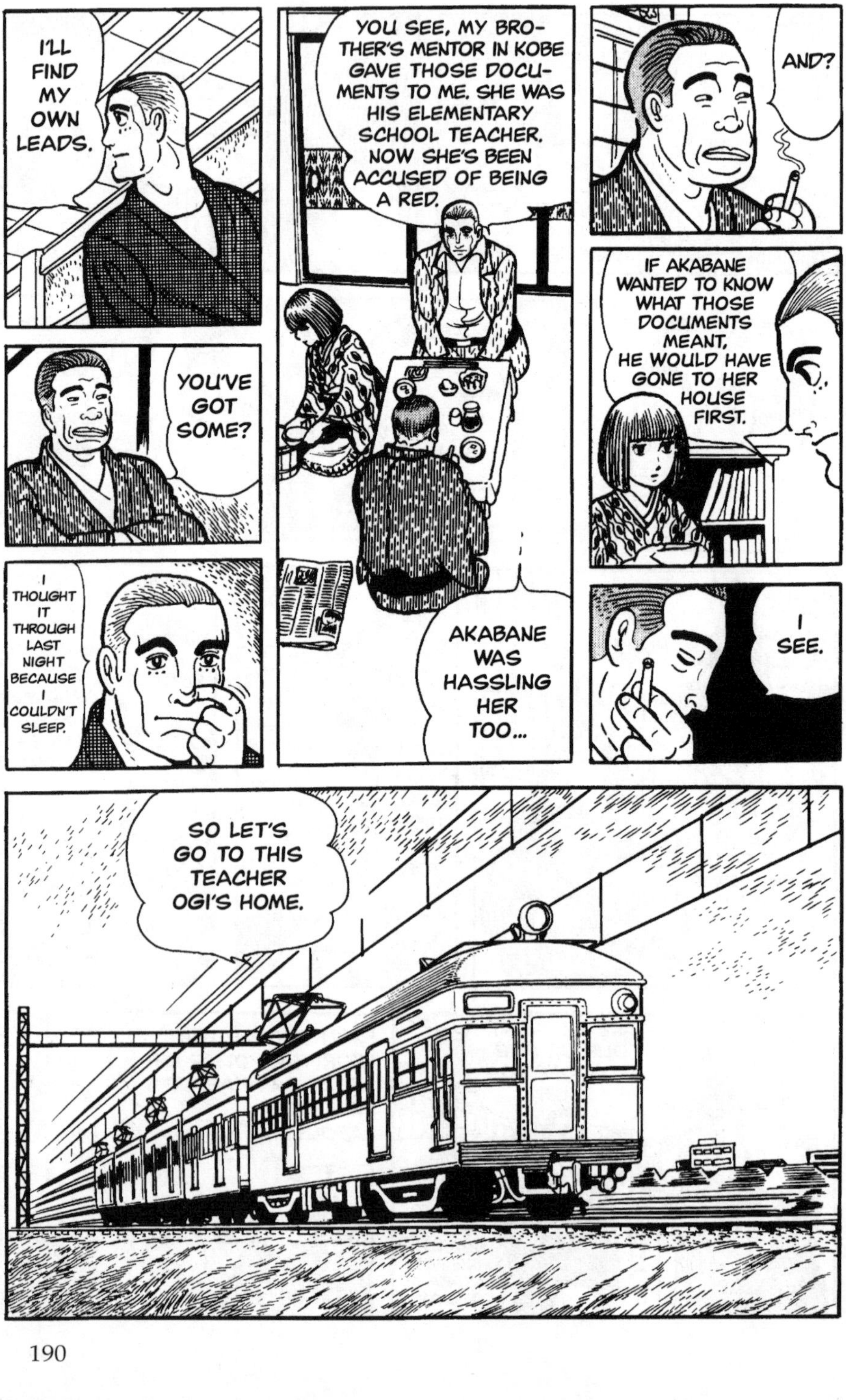
I'LL FIND MY OWN LEADS.
YOU'VE GOT SOME?
I THOUGHT IT THROUGH LAST NIGHT BECAUSE I COULDN'T SLEEP.
YOU SEE, MY BROTHER'S MENTOR IN KOBE GAVE THOSE DOCUMENTS TO ME. SHE WAS HIS ELEMENTARY SCHOOL TEACHER. NOW SHE'S BEEN ACCUSED OF BEING A RED.
AKABANE WAS HASSLING HER TOO...
AND?
IF AKABANE WANTED TO KNOW WHAT THOSE DOCUMENTS MEANT, HE WOULD HAVE GONE TO HER HOUSE FIRST.
I SEE.
SO LET'S GO TO THIS TEACHER OGI'S HOME.

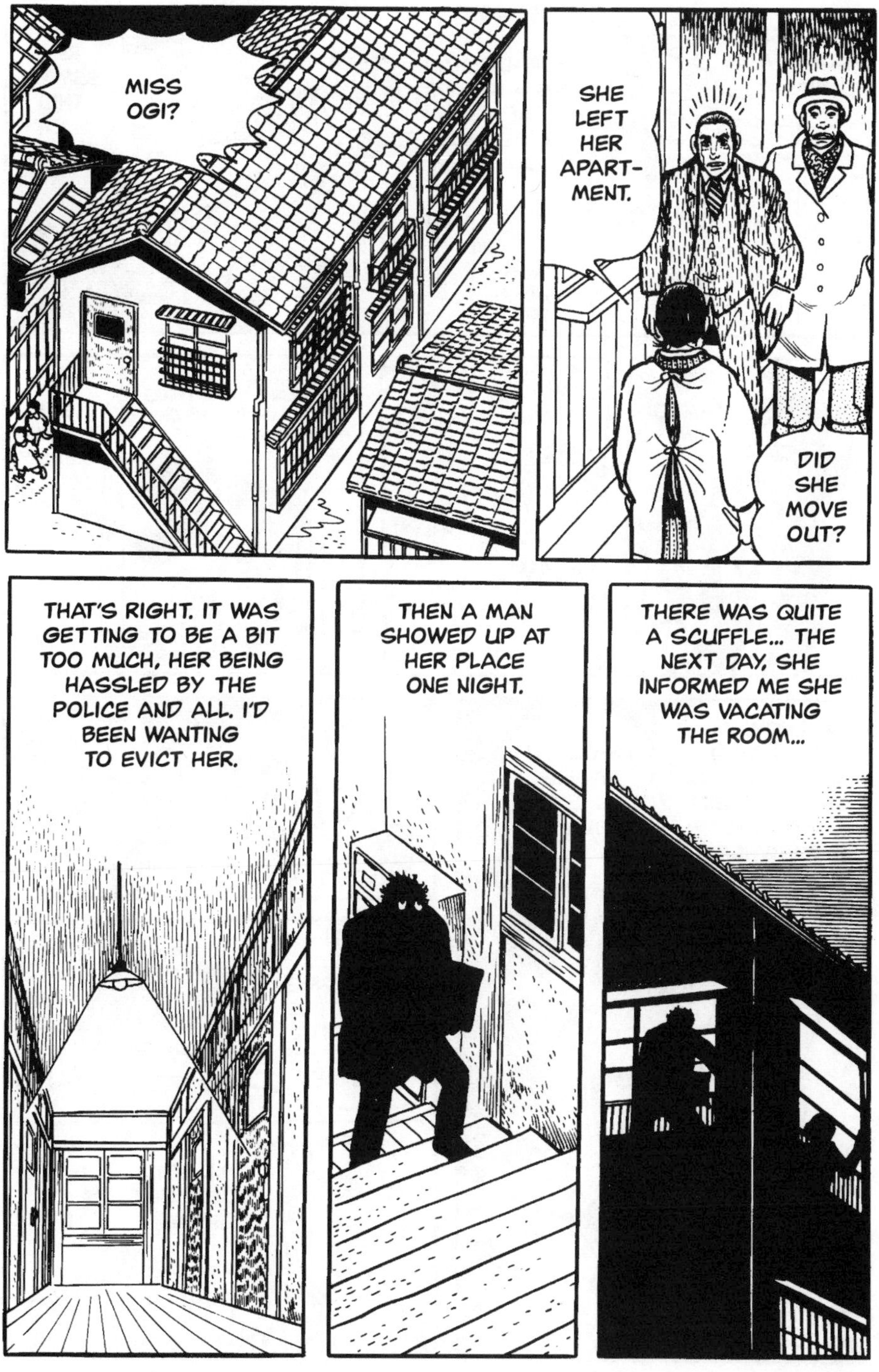
MISS OGI?
SHE LEFT HER APART-MENT.
DID SHE MOVE OUT?
THAT'S RIGHT. IT WAS GETTING TO BE A BIT TOO MUCH, HER BEING HASSLED BY THE POLICE AND ALL. I'D BEEN WANTING TO EVICT HER.
THEN A MAN SHOWED UP AT HER PLACE ONE NIGHT.
THERE WAS QUITE A SCUFFLE... THE NEXT DAY, SHE INFORMED ME SHE WAS VACATING THE ROOM...

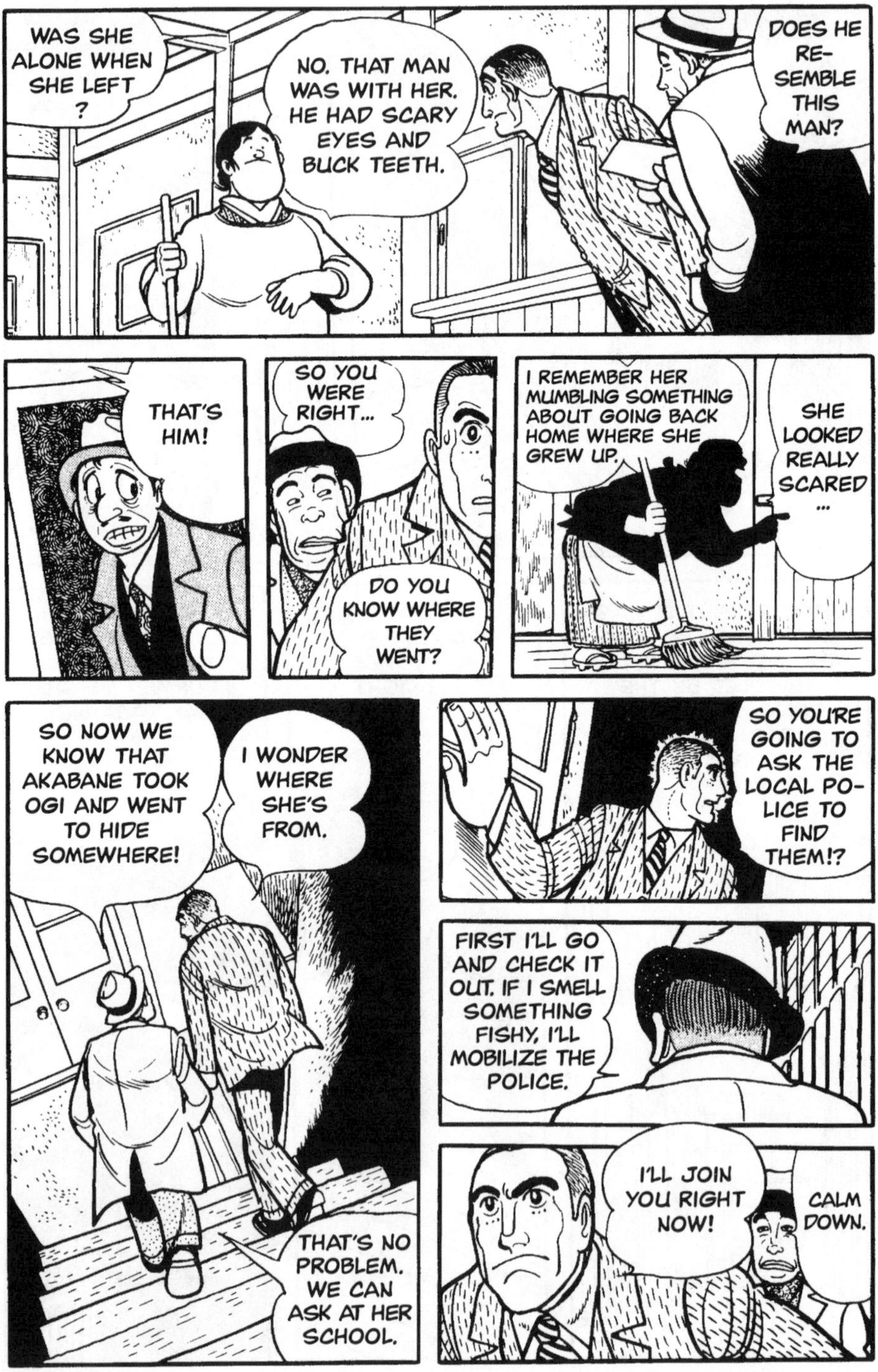
WAS SHE ALONE WHEN SHE LEFT ?
NO. THAT MAN WAS WITH HER. HE HAD SCARY EYES AND BUCK TEETH.
DOES HE RE-SEMBLE THIS MAN?
THAT'S HIM!
SO YOU WERE RIGHT...
DO YOU KNOW WHERE THEY WENT?
I REMEMBER HER MUMBLING SOMETHING ABOUT GOING BACK HOME WHERE SHE GREW UP.
SHE LOOKED REALLY SCARED ...
SO NOW WE KNOW THAT AKABANE TOOK OGI AND WENT TO HIDE SOMEWHERE!
I WONDER WHERE SHE'S FROM.
THAT'S NO PROBLEM. WE CAN ASK AT HER SCHOOL.
SO YOU'RE GOING TO ASK THE LOCAL PO-LICE TO FIND THEM!?
FIRST I'LL GO AND CHECK IT OUT. IF I SMELL SOMETHING FISHY, I'LL MOBILIZE THE POLICE.
I'LL JOIN YOU RIGHT NOW!
CALM DOWN.

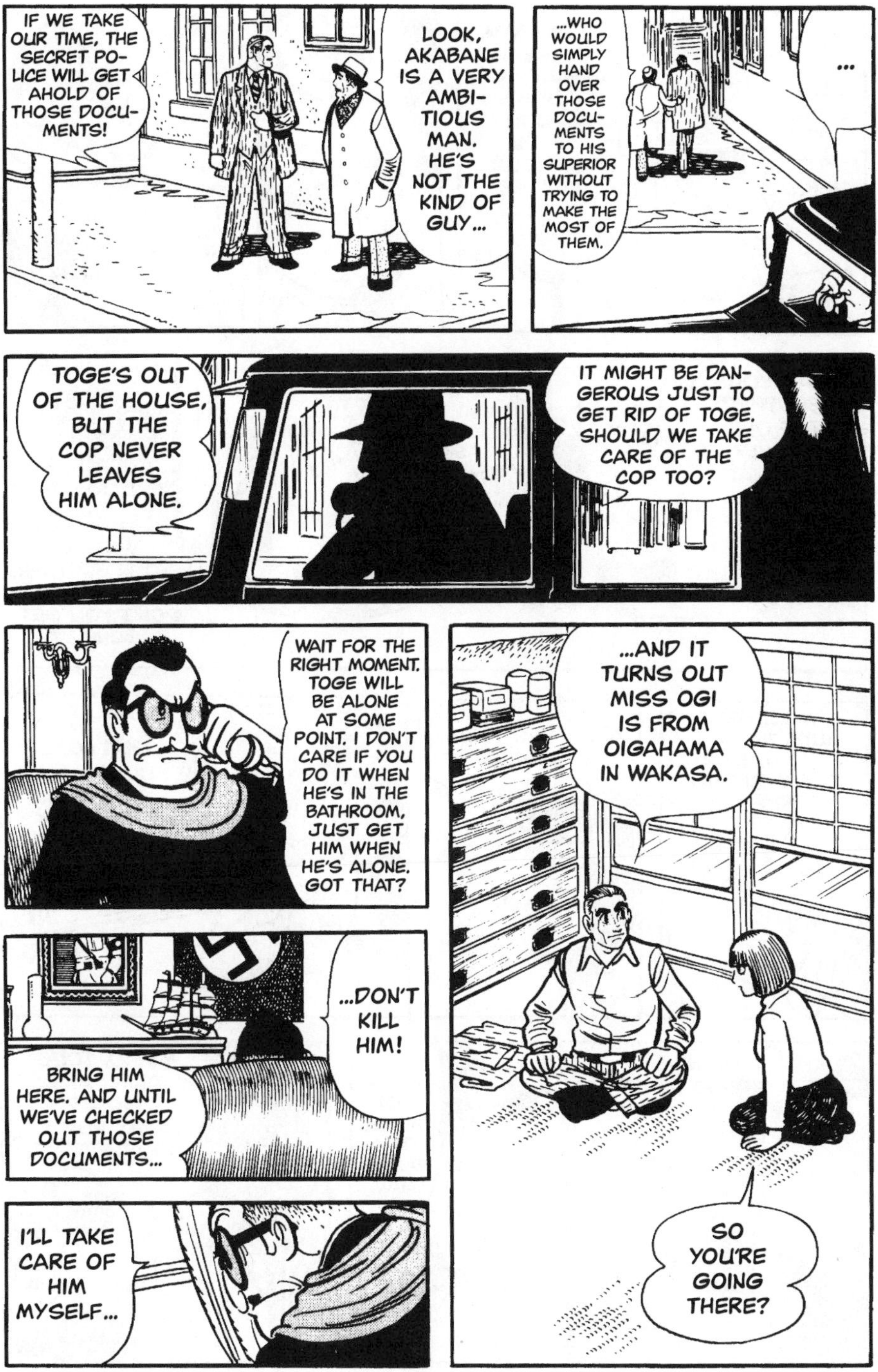
IF WE TAKE OUR TIME, THE SECRET PO-LICE WILL GET AHOLD OF THOSE DOCU-MENTS!
LOOK, AKABANE IS A VERY AMBI-TIOUS MAN. HE'S NOT THE KIND OF GUY...
...WHO WOULD SIMPLY HAND OVER THOSE DOCU-MENTS TO HIS SUPERIOR WITHOUT TRYING TO MAKE THE MOST OF THEM.
...
TOGE'S OUT OF THE HOUSE, BUT THE COP NEVER LEAVES HIM ALONE.
IT MIGHT BE DAN-GEROUS JUST TO GET RID OF TOGE. SHOULD WE TAKE CARE OF THE COP TOO?
WAIT FOR THE RIGHT MOMENT. TOGE WILL BE ALONE AT SOME POINT. I DON'T CARE IF YOU DO IT WHEN HE'S IN THE BATHROOM, JUST GET HIM WHEN HE'S ALONE. GOT THAT?
BRING HIM HERE. AND UNTIL WE'VE CHECKED OUT THOSE DOCUMENTS...
...DON'T KILL HIM!
I'LL TAKE CARE OF HIM MYSELF...
...AND IT TURNS OUT MISS OGI IS FROM OIGAHAMA IN WAKASA.
SO YOU'RE GOING THERE?

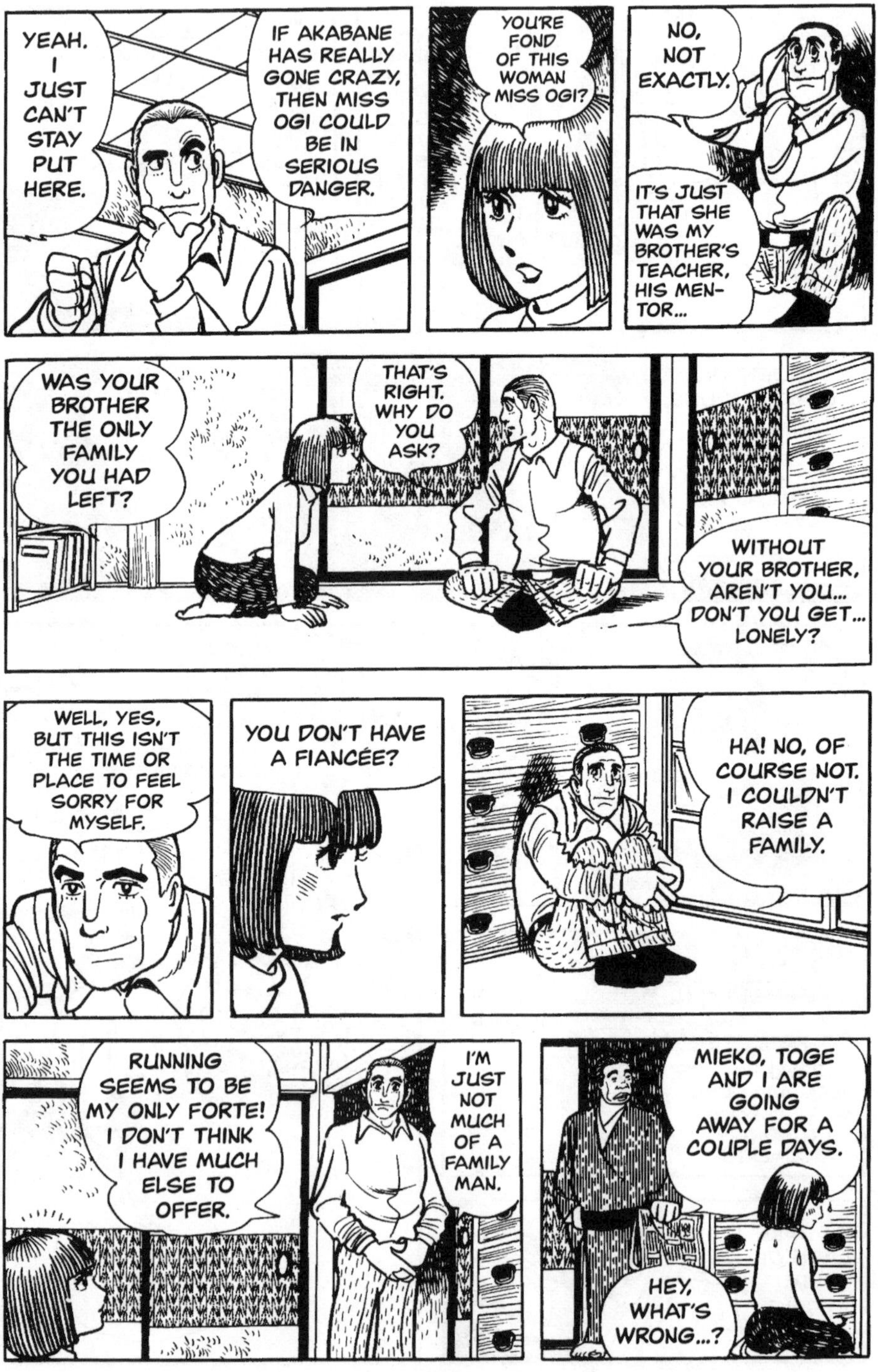
YEAH. I JUST CAN'T STAY PUT HERE.
IF AKABANE HAS REALLY GONE CRAZY, THEN MISS OGI COULD BE IN SERIOUS DANGER.
YOU'RE FOND OF THIS WOMAN MISS OGI?
NO, NOT EXACTLY.
IT'S JUST THAT SHE WAS MY BROTHER'S TEACHER, HIS MEN-TOR...
WAS YOUR BROTHER THE ONLY FAMILY YOU HAD LEFT?
THAT'S RIGHT. WHY DO YOU ASK?
WITHOUT YOUR BROTHER, AREN'T YOU... DON'T YOU GET... LONELY?
WELL, YES, BUT THIS ISN'T THE TIME OR PLACE TO FEEL SORRY FOR MYSELF.
YOU DON'T HAVE A FIANCÉE?
HA! NO, OF COURSE NOT. I COULDN'T RAISE A FAMILY.
RUNNING SEEMS TO BE MY ONLY FORTE! I DON'T THINK I HAVE MUCH ELSE TO OFFER.
I'M JUST NOT MUCH OF A FAMILY MAN.
MIEKO, TOGE AND I ARE GOING AWAY FOR A COUPLE DAYS.
HEY, WHAT'S WRONG...?

CHAPTER
SEVEN

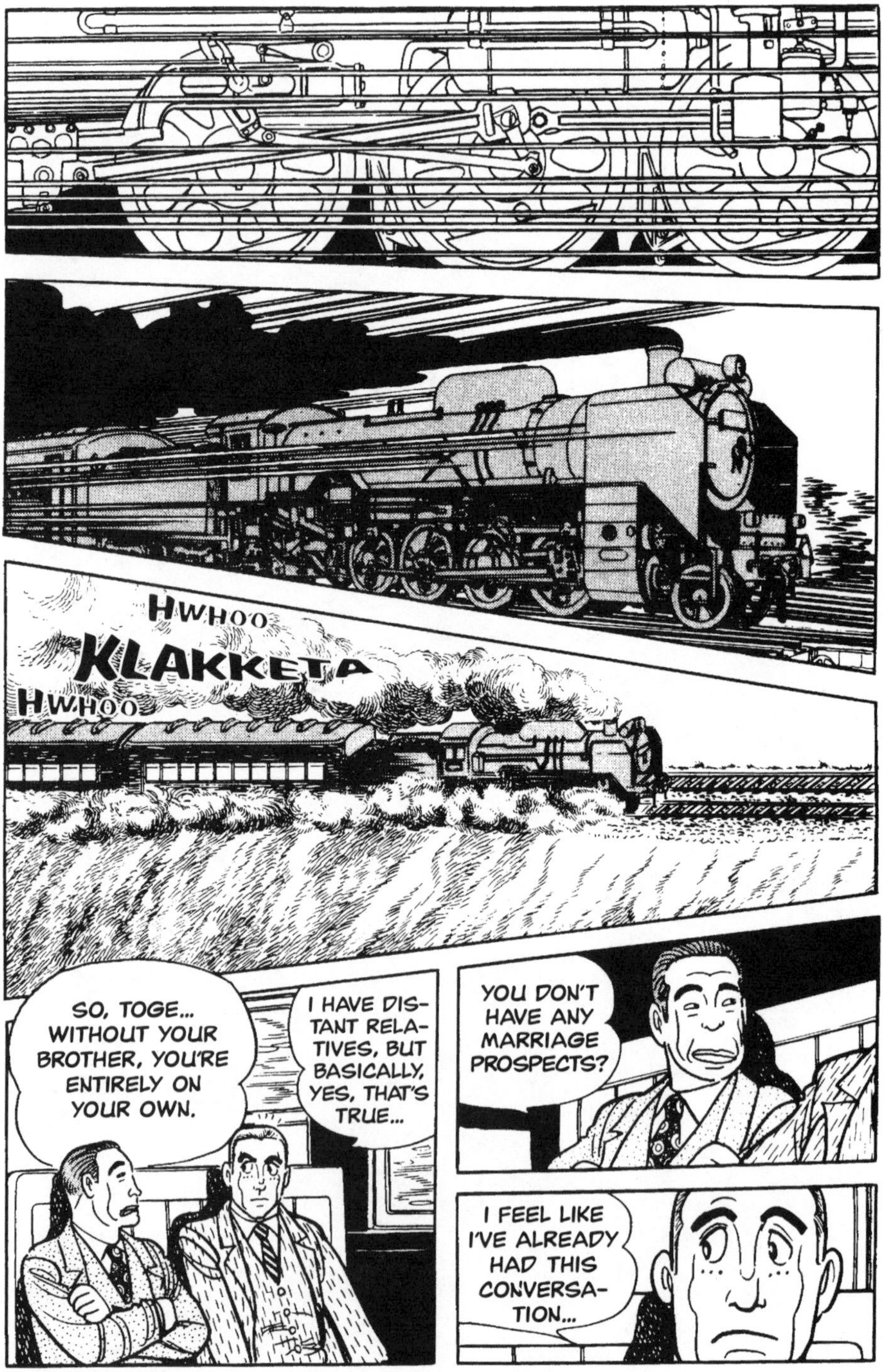
HWHOO
KLAKKETA
HWHOO
SO, TOGE... WITHOUT YOUR BROTHER, YOU'RE ENTIRELY ON YOUR OWN.
I HAVE DISTANT RELATIVES, BUT BASICALLY, YES, THAT'S TRUE...
YOU DON'T HAVE ANY MARRIAGE PROSPECTS?
I FEEL LIKE I'VE ALREADY HAD THIS CONVERSATION...

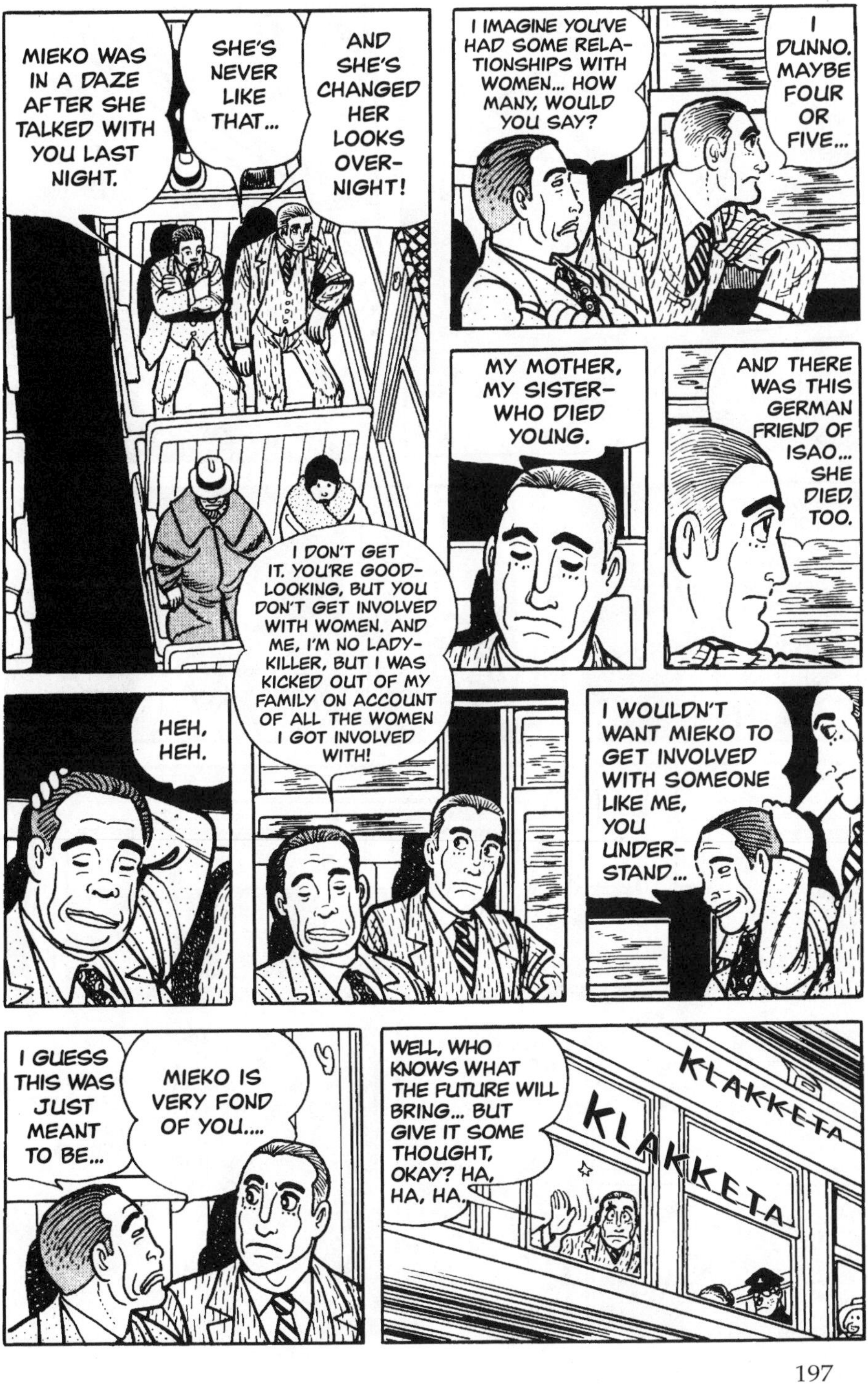
MIEKO WAS IN A DAZE AFTER SHE TALKED WITH YOU LAST NIGHT.
SHE'S NEVER LIKE THAT...
AND SHE'S CHANGED HER LOOKS OVER-NIGHT!
I IMAGINE YOU'VE HAD SOME RELA-TIONSHIPS WITH WOMEN... HOW MANY, WOULD YOU SAY?
I DUNNO. MAYBE FOUR OR FIVE...
MY MOTHER, MY SISTER-WHO DIED YOUNG.
AND THERE WAS THIS GERMAN FRIEND OF ISAO... SHE DIED, TOO.
HEH, HEH.
I DON'T GET IT. YOU'RE GOOD-LOOKING, BUT YOU DON'T GET INVOLVED WITH WOMEN. AND ME, I'M NO LADY-KILLER, BUT I WAS KICKED OUT OF MY FAMILY ON ACCOUNT OF ALL THE WOMEN I GOT INVOLVED WITH!
I WOULDN'T WANT MIEKO TO GET INVOLVED WITH SOMEONE LIKE ME, YOU UNDER-STAND...
I GUESS THIS WAS JUST MEANT TO BE...
MIEKO IS VERY FOND OF YOU....
WELL, WHO KNOWS WHAT THE FUTURE WILL BRING... BUT GIVE IT SOME THOUGHT, OKAY? HA, HA, HA.
KLAKKETA
KLAKKETA

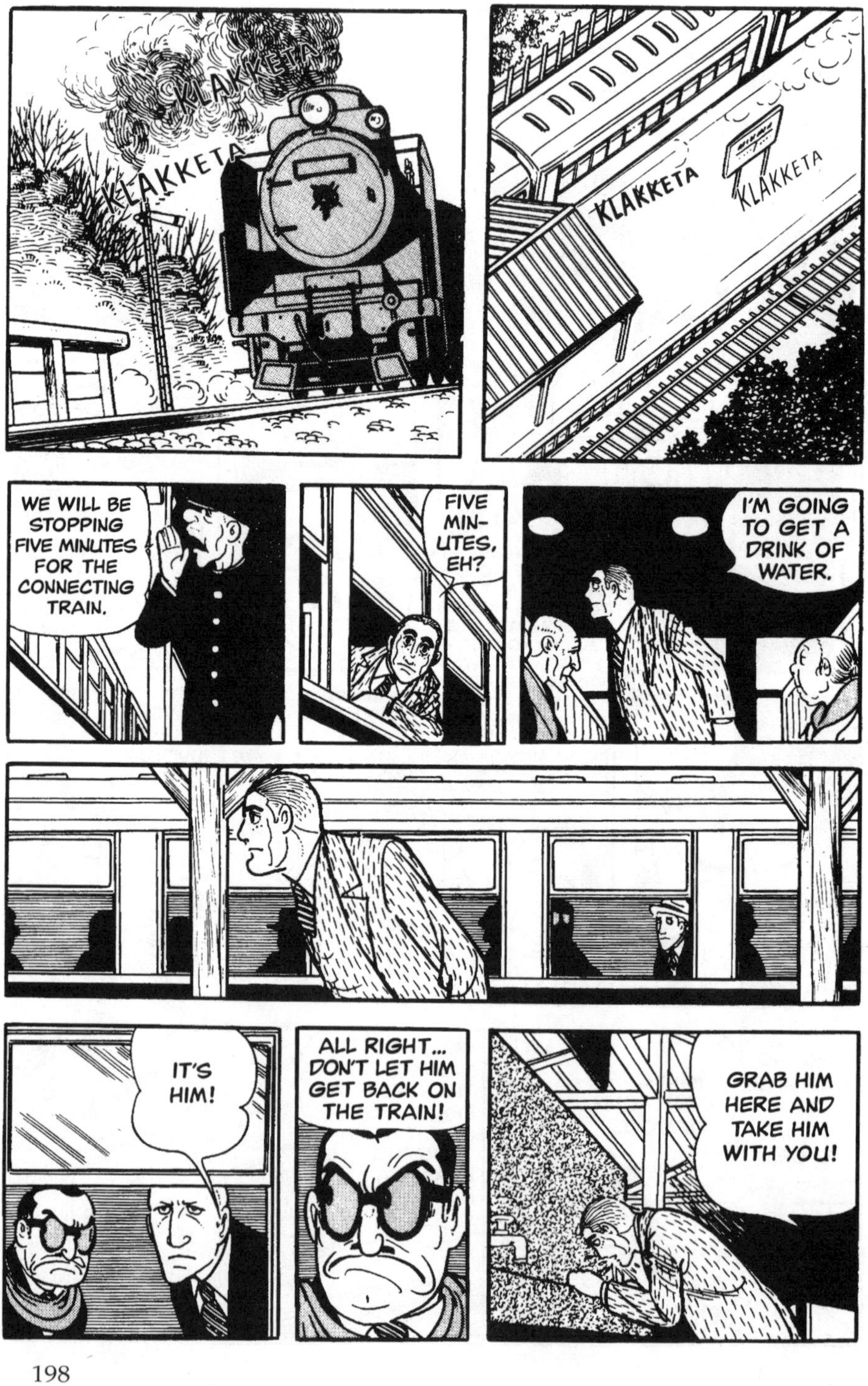
KLAKKETA
KLAKKETA
KLAKKETA
KLAKKETA
WE WILL BE STOPPING FIVE MINUTES FOR THE CONNECTING TRAIN.
FIVE MIN-UTES, EH?
I'M GOING TO GET A DRINK OF WATER.
IT'S HIM!
ALL RIGHT... DON'T LET HIM GET BACK ON THE TRAIN!
GRAB HIM HERE AND TAKE HIM WITH YOU!

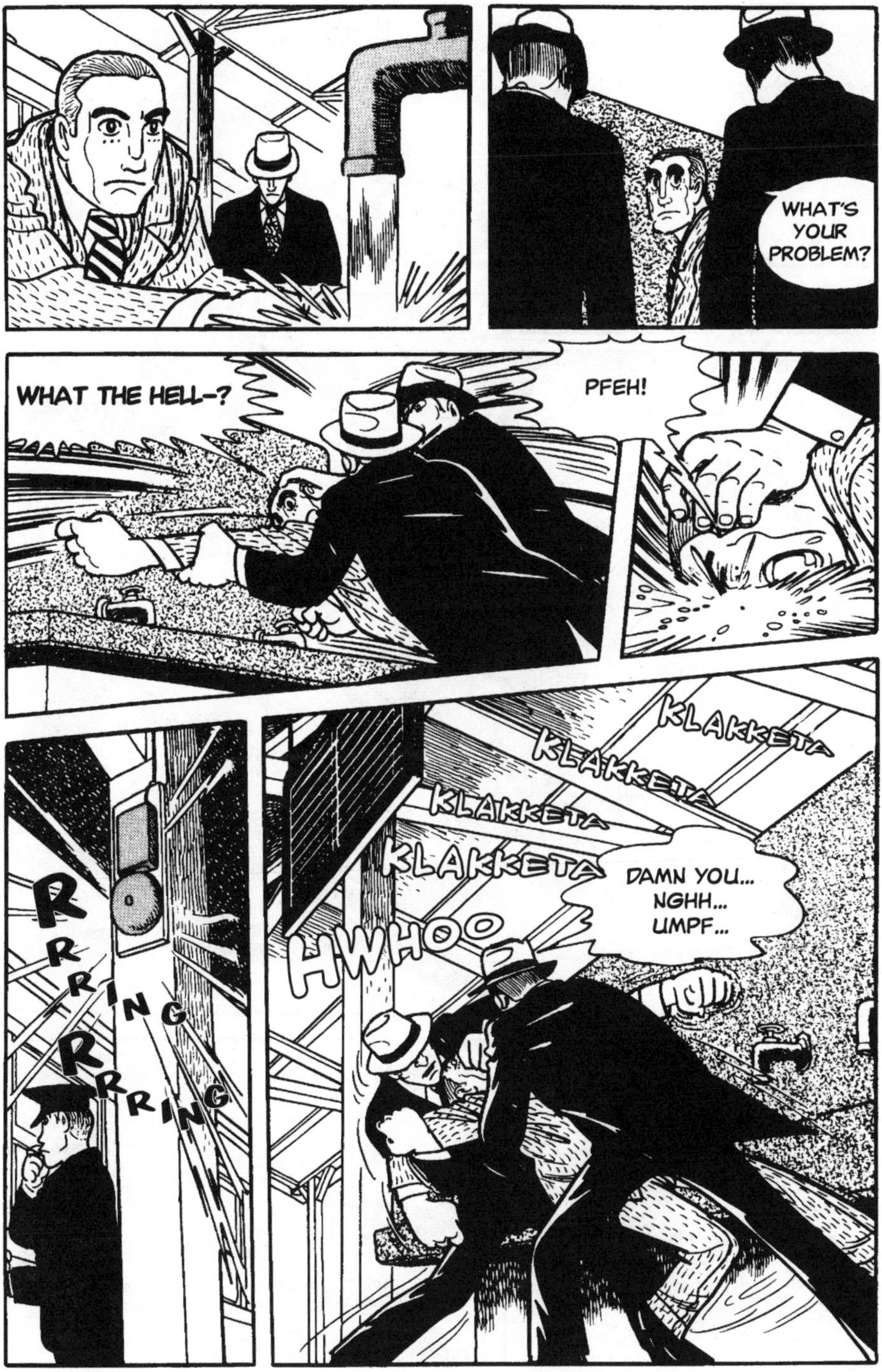
WHAT'S YOUR PROBLEM?
WHAT THE HELL-?
PFEH!
R RRRING RRRRING
KLAKKETA KLAKKETA KLAKKETA KLAKKETA
DAMN YOU... NGHH... UMPF...
HWHOO

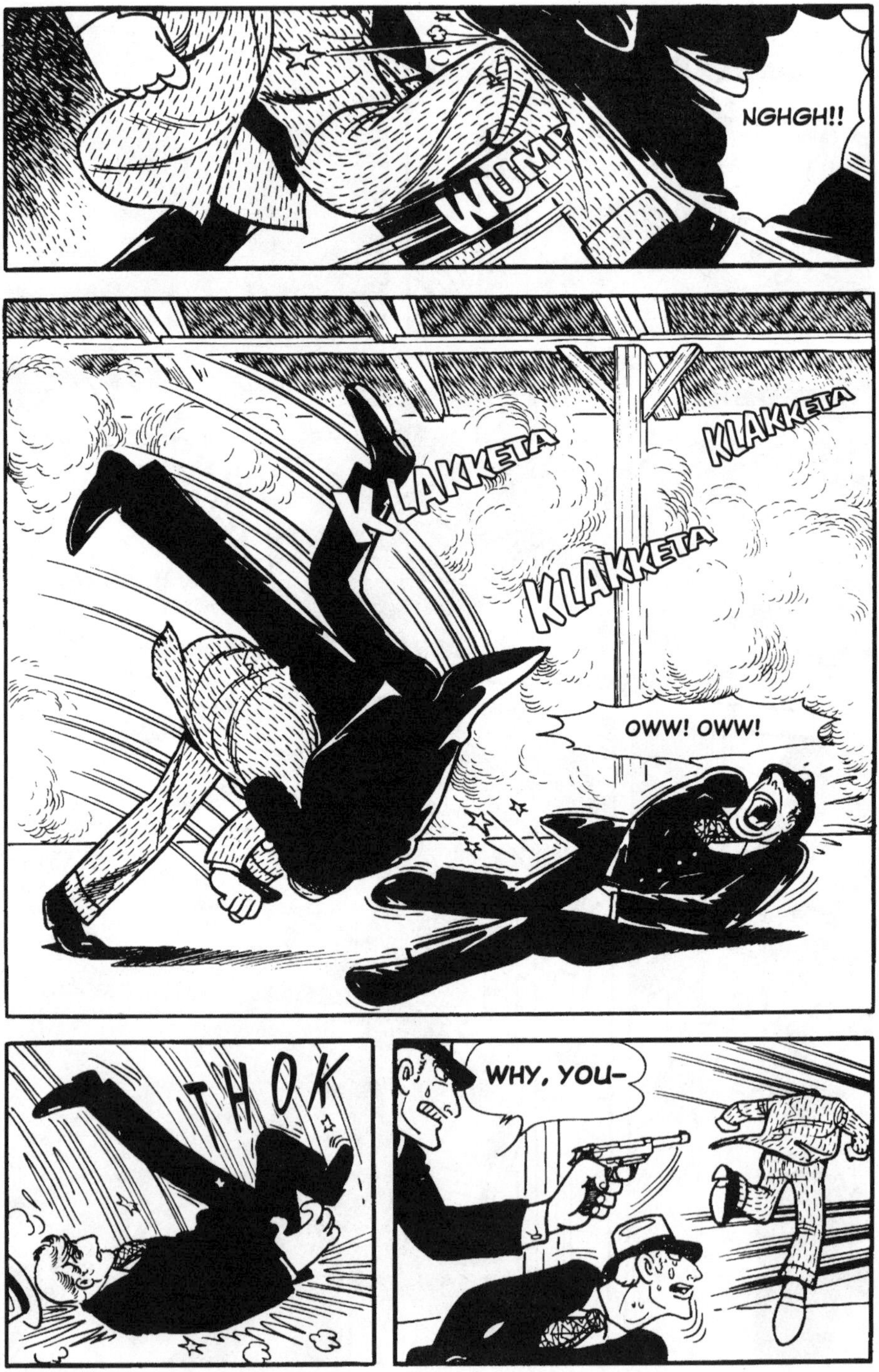
WUMP
NGHGH!!
KLAKKETA
KLAKKETA
KLAKKETA
OWW! OWW!
THOK
WHY, YOU-

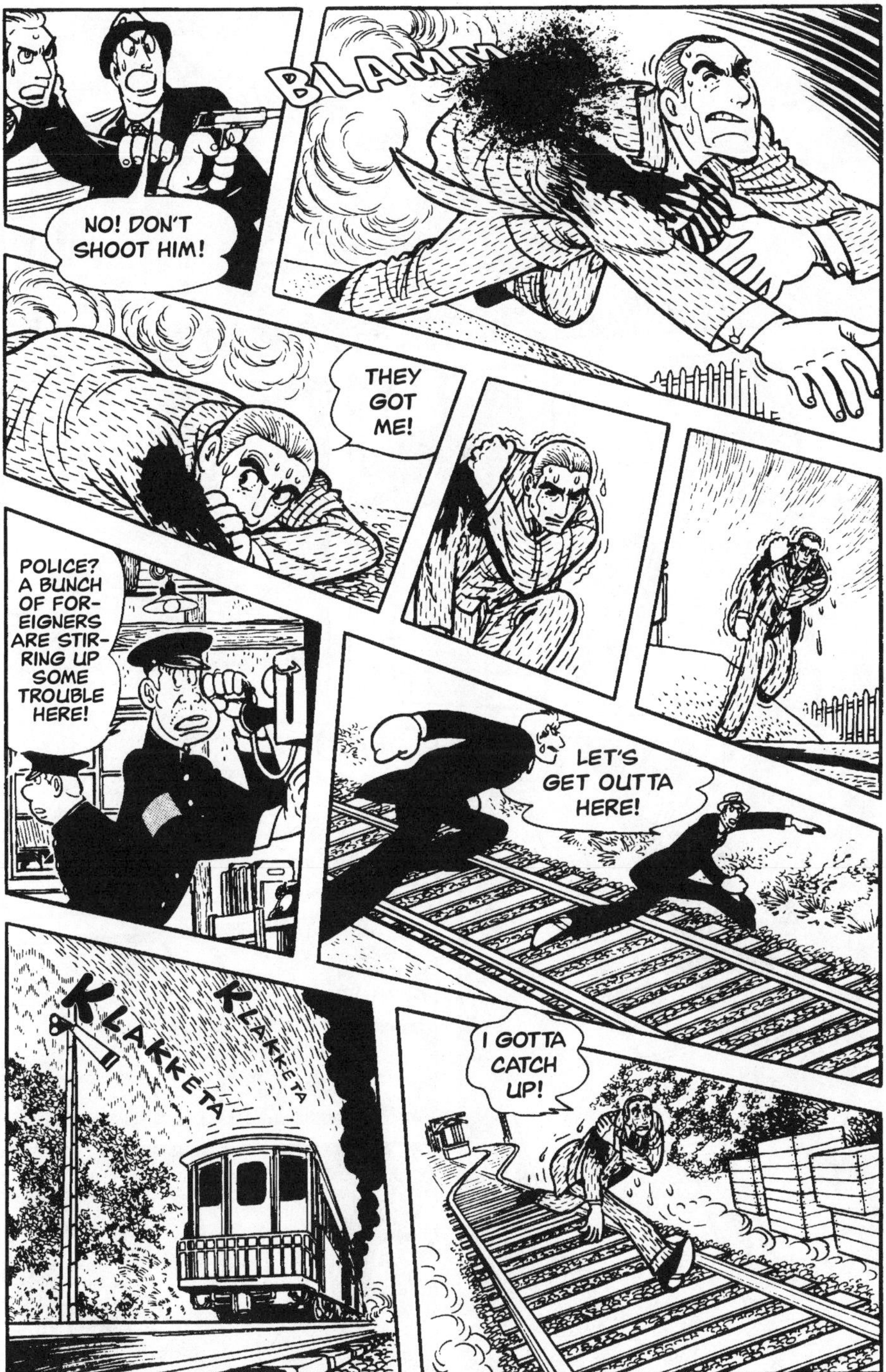
NO! DON'T SHOOT HIM!
BLAMM
THEY GOT ME!
POLICE? A BUNCH OF FOR-EIGNERS ARE STIR-RING UP SOME TROUBLE HERE!
LET'S GET OUTTA HERE!
KLAKKETA
KLAKKETA
I GOTTA CATCH UP!

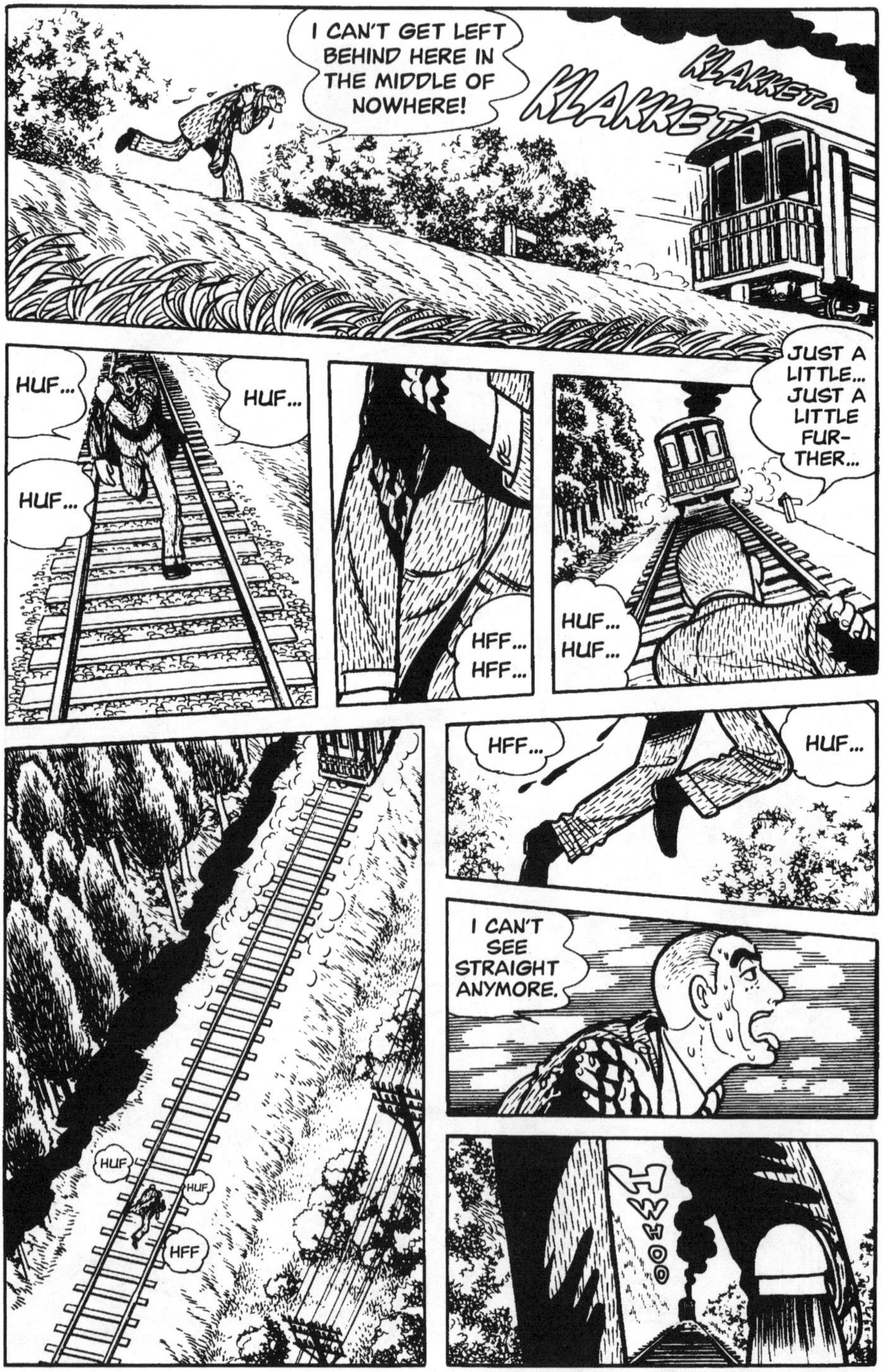
I CAN'T GET LEFT BEHIND HERE IN THE MIDDLE OF NOWHERE!
KLAKKETA
KLAKKETA
HUF...
HUF...
HUF...
HFF...
HFF...
JUST A LITTLE... JUST A LITTLE FUR-THER...
HUF...
HUF...
HUF
HUF
HFF
HFF...
HUF...
I CAN'T SEE STRAIGHT ANYMORE.
HWHOO

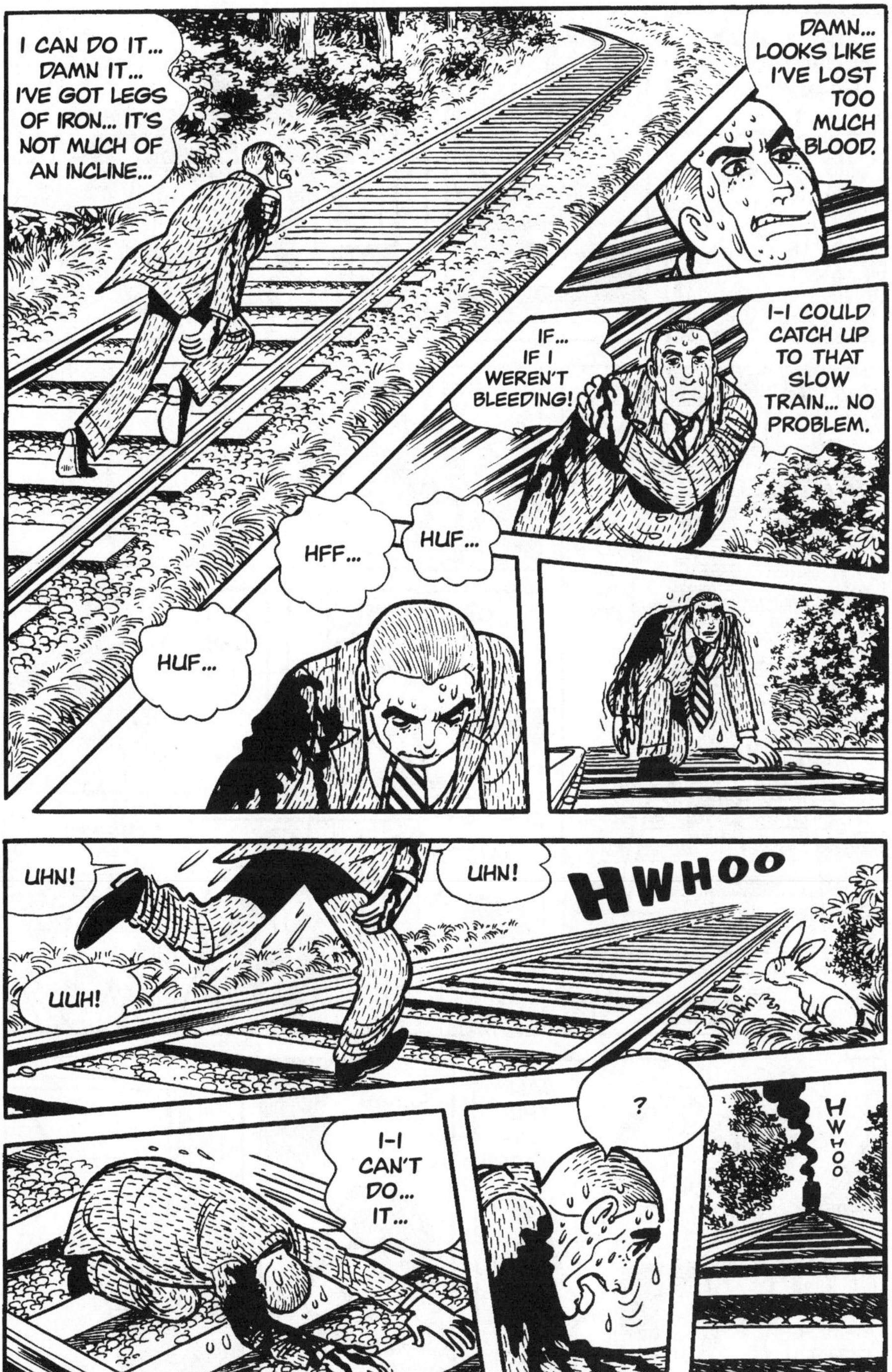
I CAN DO IT... DAMN IT... I'VE GOT LEGS OF IRON... IT'S NOT MUCH OF AN INCLINE...
DAMN... LOOKS LIKE I'VE LOST TOO MUCH BLOOD.
IF... IF I WEREN'T BLEEDING!
I-I COULD CATCH UP TO THAT SLOW TRAIN... NO PROBLEM.
HFF...
HUF...
HUF...
UHN!
UHN!
UUH!
HWHOO
I-I CAN'T DO... IT...
?
HWHOO

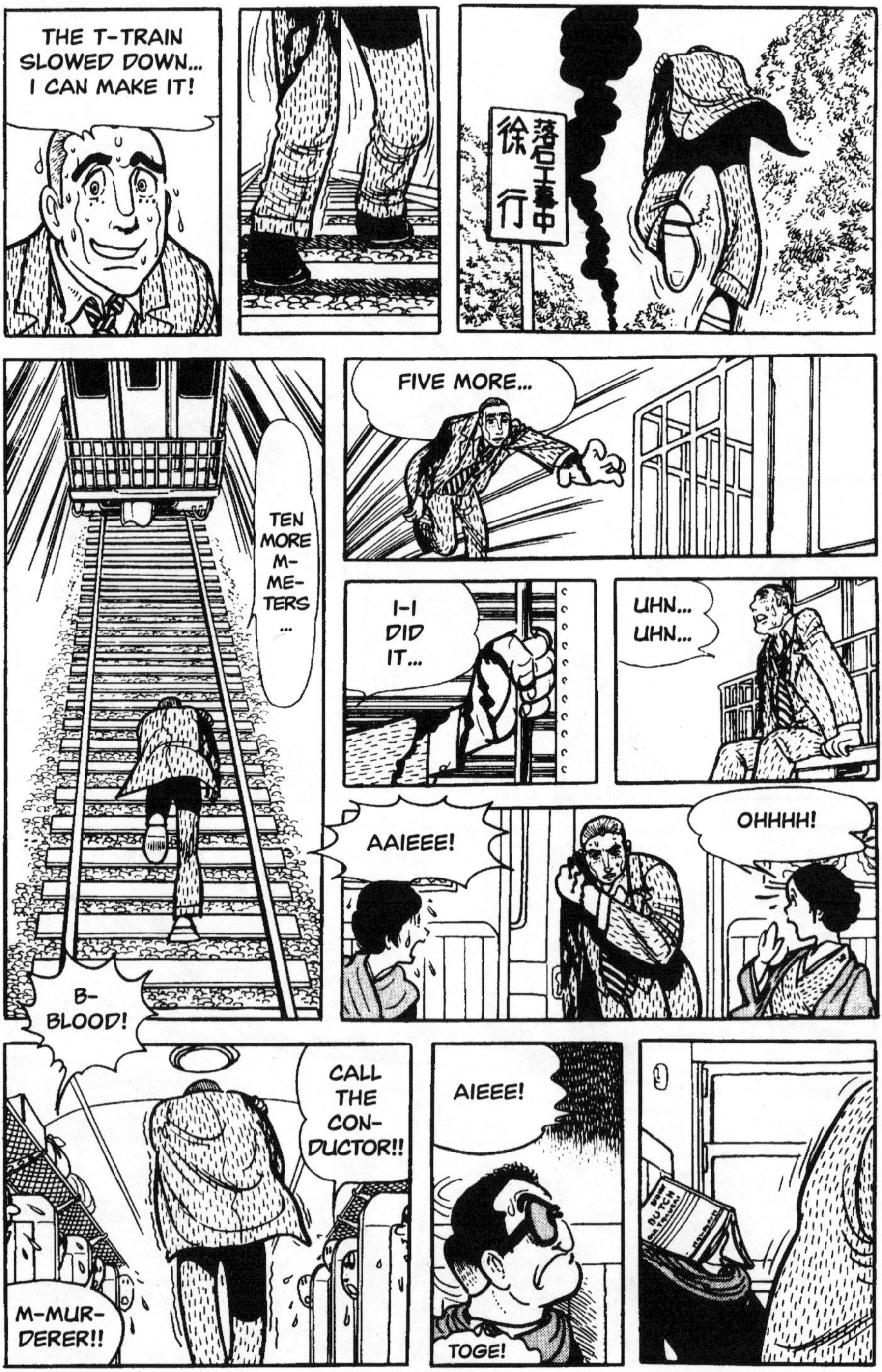
THE T-TRAIN SLOWED DOWN... I CAN MAKE IT!
落石工事中
徐行
TEN MORE M-ME-TERS ...
FIVE MORE...
I-I DID IT...
UHN... UHN...
AAIEEE!
OHHHH!
B-BLOOD!
CALL THE CONDUCTOR!!
M-MURDERER!!
AIEEE!
TOGE!

OH MY GOD!

TOGE, WHAT THE HELL?

TOGE!!

COMPOUND FRACTURES IN THE SHOULDER BLADE FROM THE GUNSHOT WOUND... WORSE, AT LEAST THREE OF HIS NERVES HAVE BEEN SEVERED.

HE SHOULD HAVE BEEN TREATED IMMEDIATELY, BUT INSTEAD HE RAN LIKE A MADMAN UP THAT HILL. NOW HIS WOUND'S A BIG MESS.

YOU HEAR THAT, TOGE? I'M CALLING AN AMBULANCE. WE'LL HAVE TO CONTINUE LATER.

WH-WHAT!?

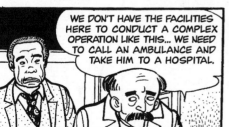

WE DON'T HAVE THE FACILITIES HERE TO CONDUCT A COMPLEX OPERATION LIKE THIS... WE NEED TO CALL AN AMBULANCE AND TAKE HIM TO A HOSPITAL.

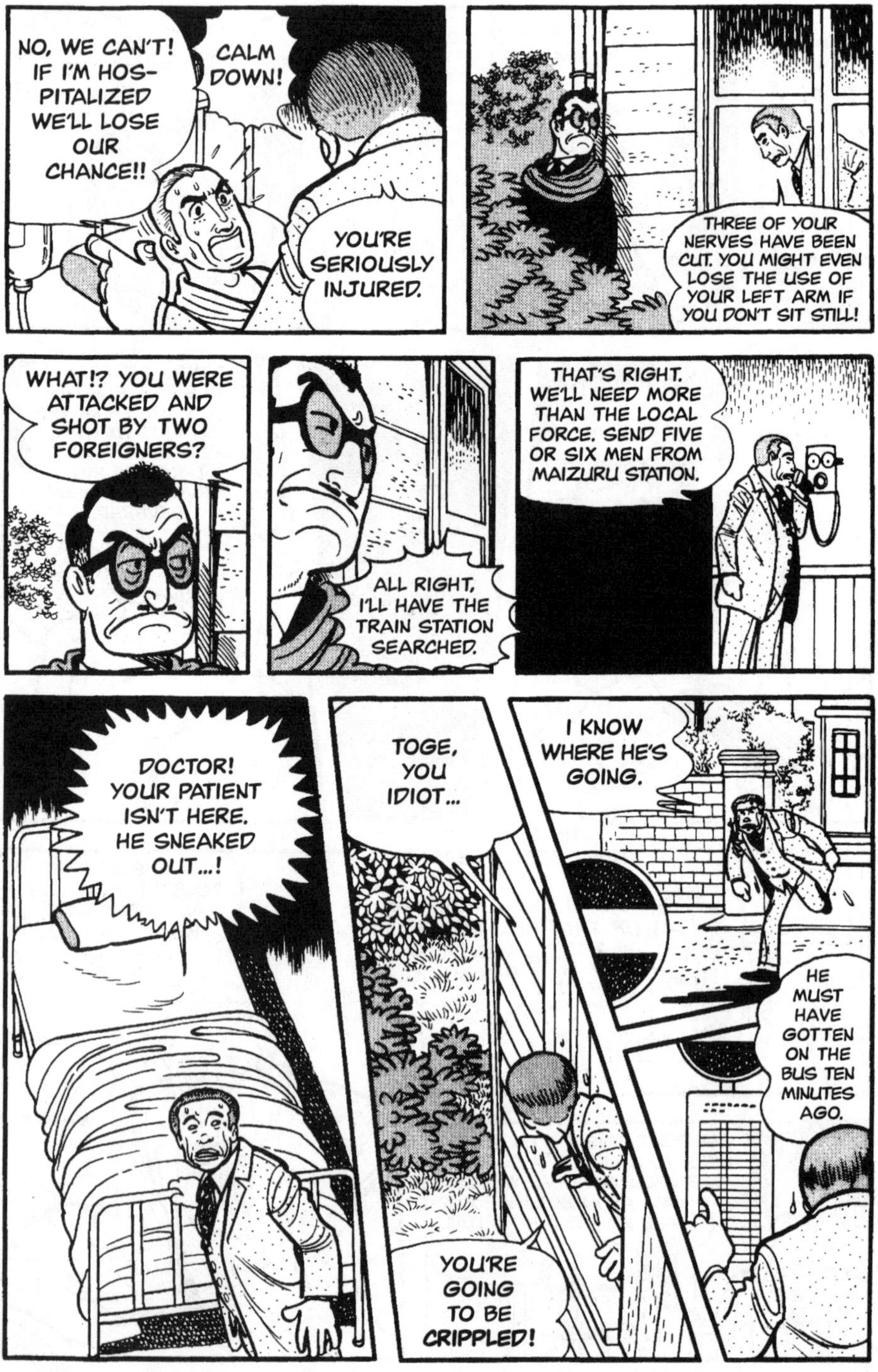
NO, WE CAN'T! IF I'M HOS-PITALIZED WE'LL LOSE OUR CHANCE!!
CALM DOWN!
YOU'RE SERIOUSLY INJURED.
THREE OF YOUR NERVES HAVE BEEN CUT. YOU MIGHT EVEN LOSE THE USE OF YOUR LEFT ARM IF YOU DON'T SIT STILL!
WHAT!? YOU WERE ATTACKED AND SHOT BY TWO FOREIGNERS?
ALL RIGHT, I'LL HAVE THE TRAIN STATION SEARCHED.
THAT'S RIGHT. WE'LL NEED MORE THAN THE LOCAL FORCE. SEND FIVE OR SIX MEN FROM MAIZURU STATION.
DOCTOR! YOUR PATIENT ISN'T HERE. HE SNEAKED OUT...!
TOGE, YOU IDIOT...
YOU'RE GOING TO BE CRIPPLED!
I KNOW WHERE HE'S GOING.
HE MUST HAVE GOTTEN ON THE BUS TEN MINUTES AGO.

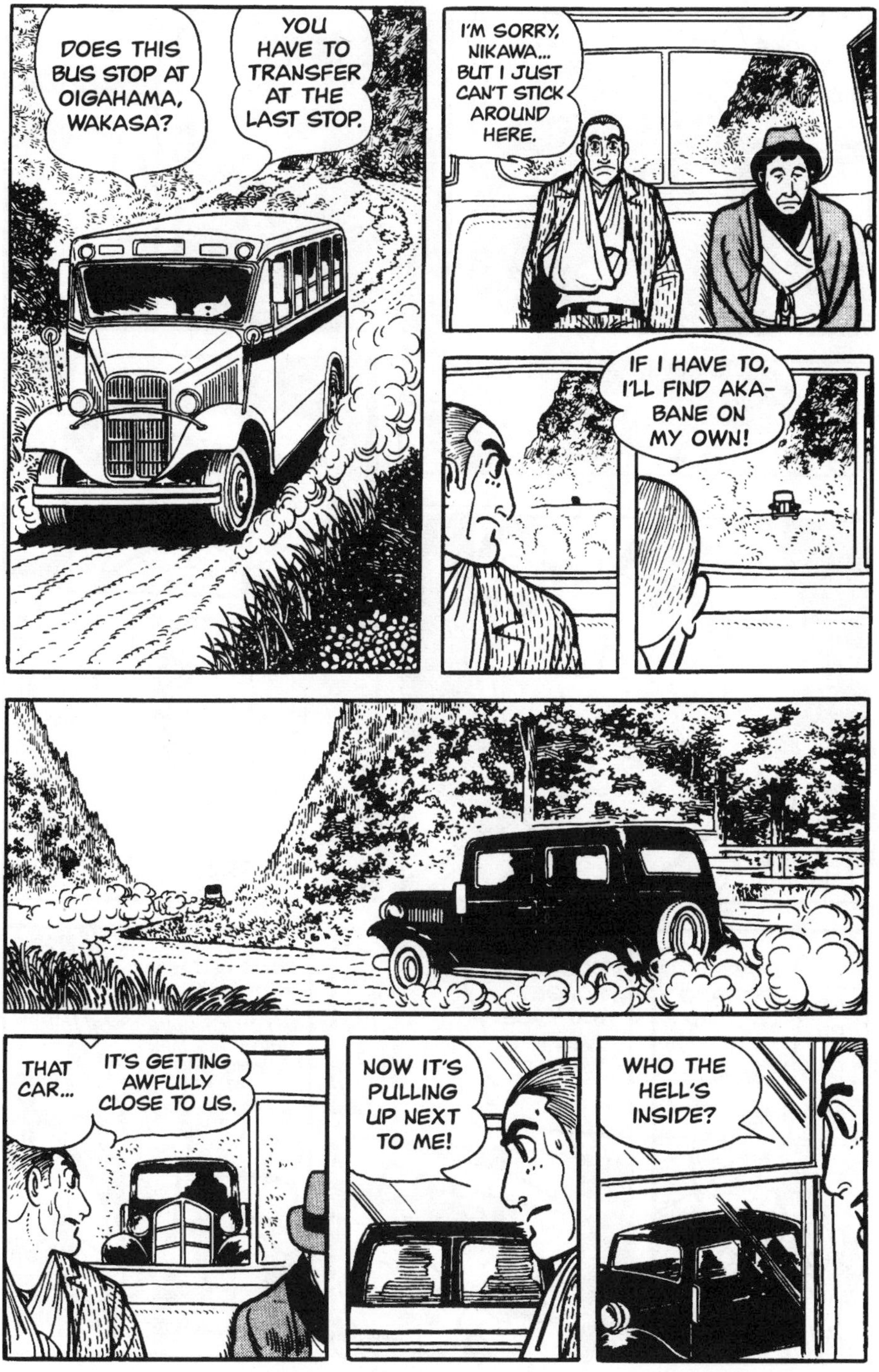
DOES THIS BUS STOP AT OIGAHAMA, WAKASA?
YOU HAVE TO TRANSFER AT THE LAST STOP.
I'M SORRY, NIKAWA... BUT I JUST CAN'T STICK AROUND HERE.
IF I HAVE TO, I'LL FIND AKA-BANE ON MY OWN!
THAT CAR...
IT'S GETTING AWFULLY CLOSE TO US.
NOW IT'S PULLING UP NEXT TO ME!
WHO THE HELL'S INSIDE?

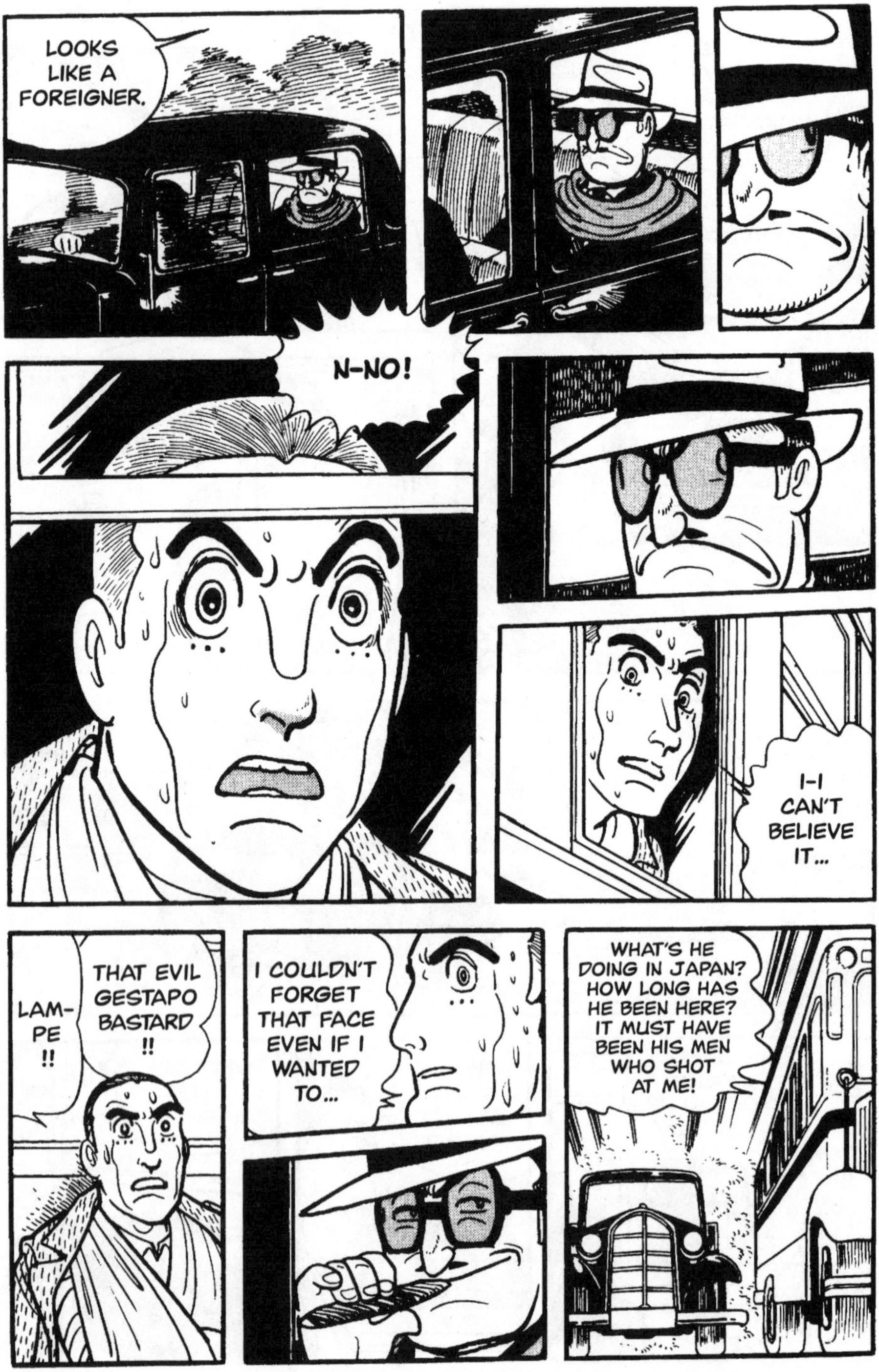
LOOKS LIKE A FOREIGNER.
N-NO!
I-I CAN'T BELIEVE IT...
LAM-PE !!
THAT EVIL GESTAPO BASTARD !!
I COULDN'T FORGET THAT FACE EVEN IF I WANTED TO...
WHAT'S HE DOING IN JAPAN? HOW LONG HAS HE BEEN HERE? IT MUST HAVE BEEN HIS MEN WHO SHOT AT ME!

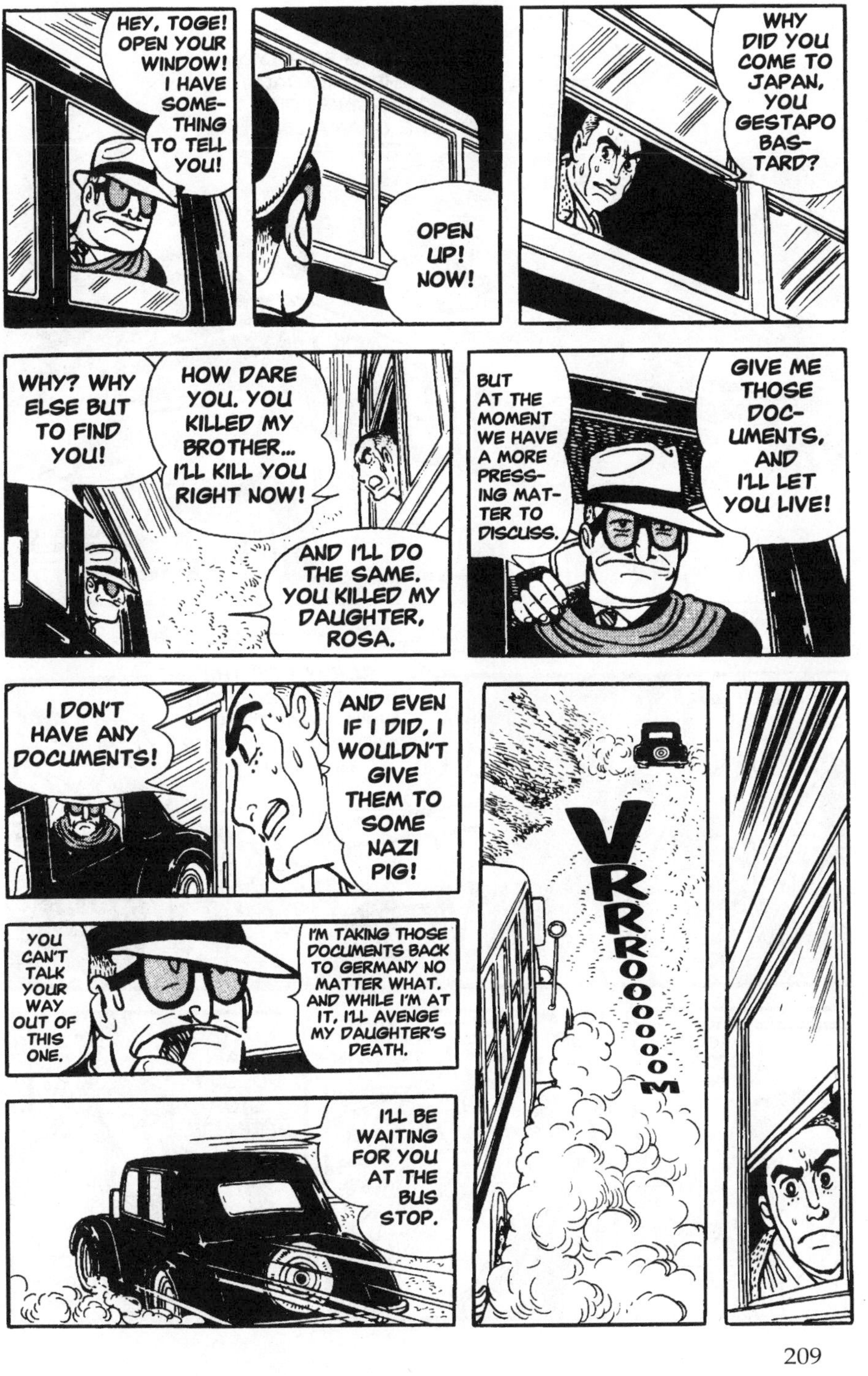
HEY, TOGE! OPEN YOUR WINDOW! I HAVE SOME-THING TO TELL YOU!
OPEN UP! NOW!
WHY DID YOU COME TO JAPAN, YOU GESTAPO BAS-TARD?
WHY? WHY ELSE BUT TO FIND YOU!
HOW DARE YOU. YOU KILLED MY BROTHER... I'LL KILL YOU RIGHT NOW!
AND I'LL DO THE SAME. YOU KILLED MY DAUGHTER, ROSA.
BUT AT THE MOMENT WE HAVE A MORE PRESS-ING MAT-TER TO DISCUSS.
GIVE ME THOSE DOC-UMENTS, AND I'LL LET YOU LIVE!
I DON'T HAVE ANY DOCUMENTS!
AND EVEN IF I DID, I WOULDN'T GIVE THEM TO SOME NAZI PIG!
YOU CAN'T TALK YOUR WAY OUT OF THIS ONE.
I'M TAKING THOSE DOCUMENTS BACK TO GERMANY NO MATTER WHAT. AND WHILE I'M AT IT, I'LL AVENGE MY DAUGHTER'S DEATH.
I'LL BE WAITING FOR YOU AT THE BUS STOP.
VRROOOOOOOM

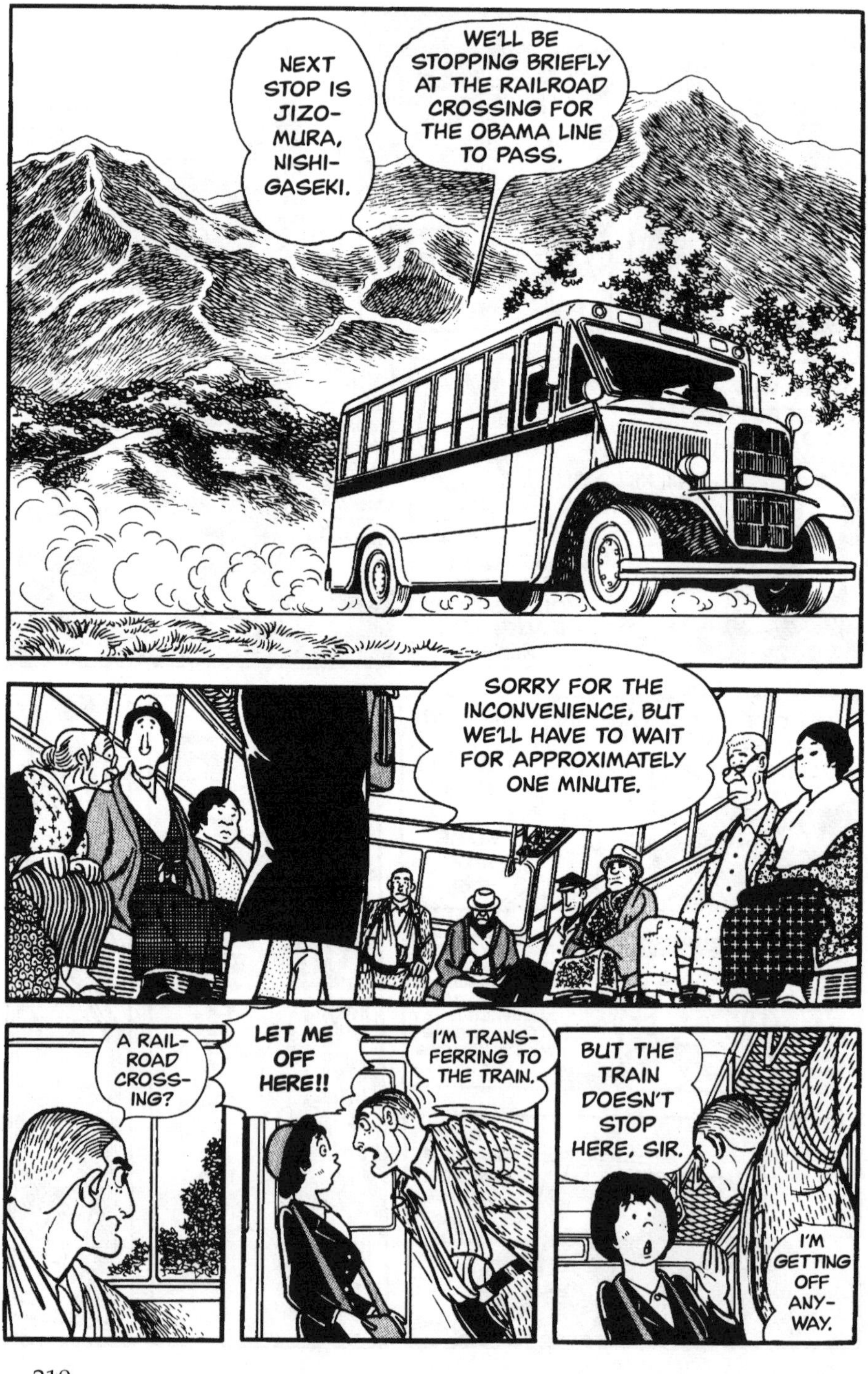
NEXT STOP IS JIZO-MURA, NISHI-GASEKI.
WE'LL BE STOPPING BRIEFLY AT THE RAILROAD CROSSING FOR THE OBAMA LINE TO PASS.
SORRY FOR THE INCONVENIENCE, BUT WE'LL HAVE TO WAIT FOR APPROXIMATELY ONE MINUTE.
A RAIL-ROAD CROSS-ING?
LET ME OFF HERE!!
I'M TRANS-FERRING TO THE TRAIN.
BUT THE TRAIN DOESN'T STOP HERE, SIR.
I'M GETTING OFF ANY-WAY.

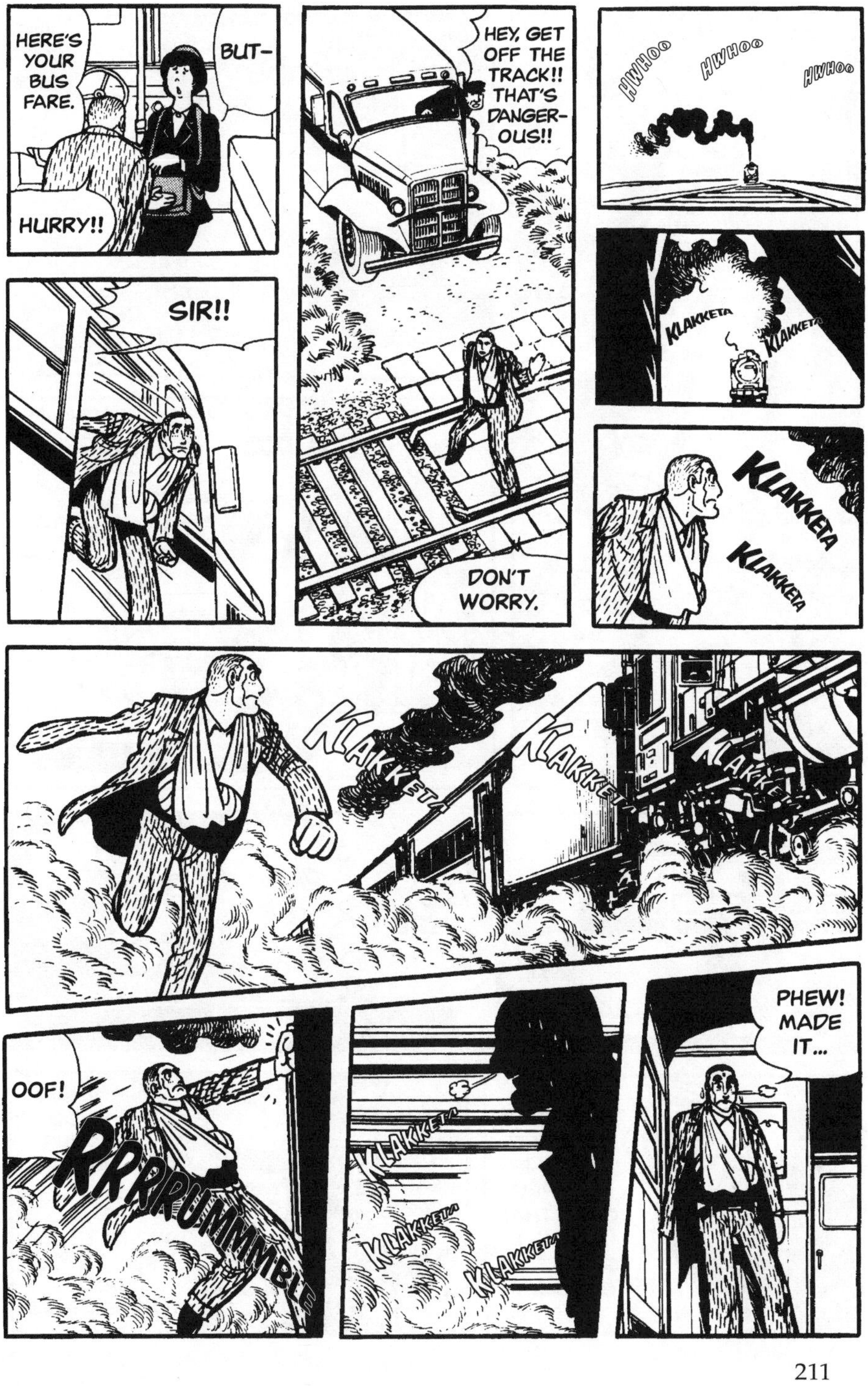
HERE'S YOUR BUS FARE.
BUT-
HURRY!!
SIR!!
HEY, GET OFF THE TRACK!! THAT'S DANGEROUS!!
DON'T WORRY.
HWHOO
HWHOO
HWHOO
KLAKKETA
KLAKKETA
KLAKKETA
KLAKKETA
KLAKKETA
KLAKKETA
KLAKKETA
OOF!
RRRRUMMMBLE
KLAKKETA
KLAKKETA
KLAKKETA
PHEW! MADE IT...

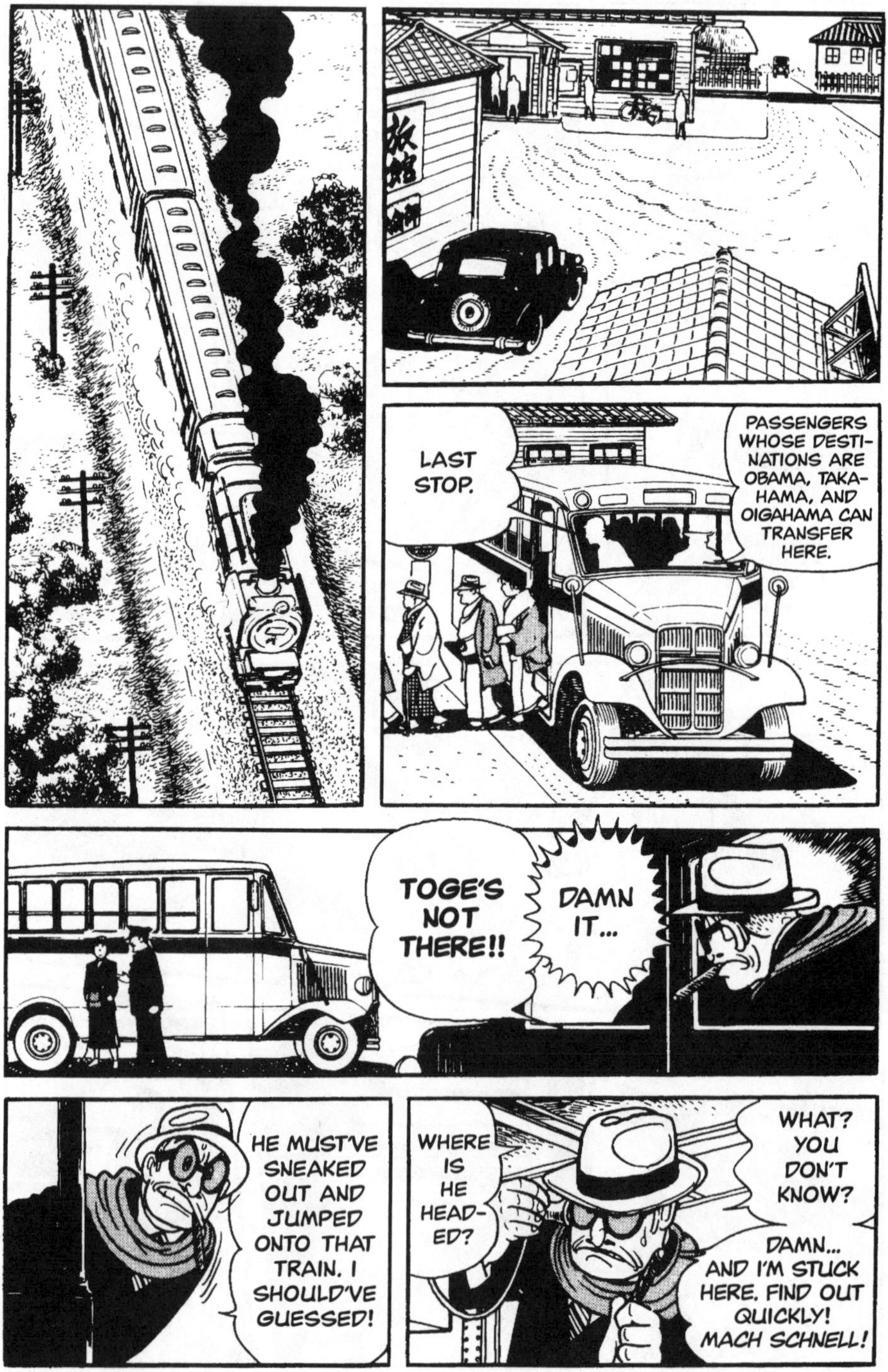
旅館
LAST STOP.
PASSENGERS WHOSE DESTINATIONS ARE OBAMA, TAKAHAMA, AND OIGAHAMA CAN TRANSFER HERE.
TOGE'S NOT THERE!!
DAMN IT...
HE MUST'VE SNEAKED OUT AND JUMPED ONTO THAT TRAIN. I SHOULD'VE GUESSED!
WHERE IS HE HEADED?
WHAT? YOU DON'T KNOW?
DAMN... AND I'M STUCK HERE. FIND OUT QUICKLY! MACH SCHNELL!

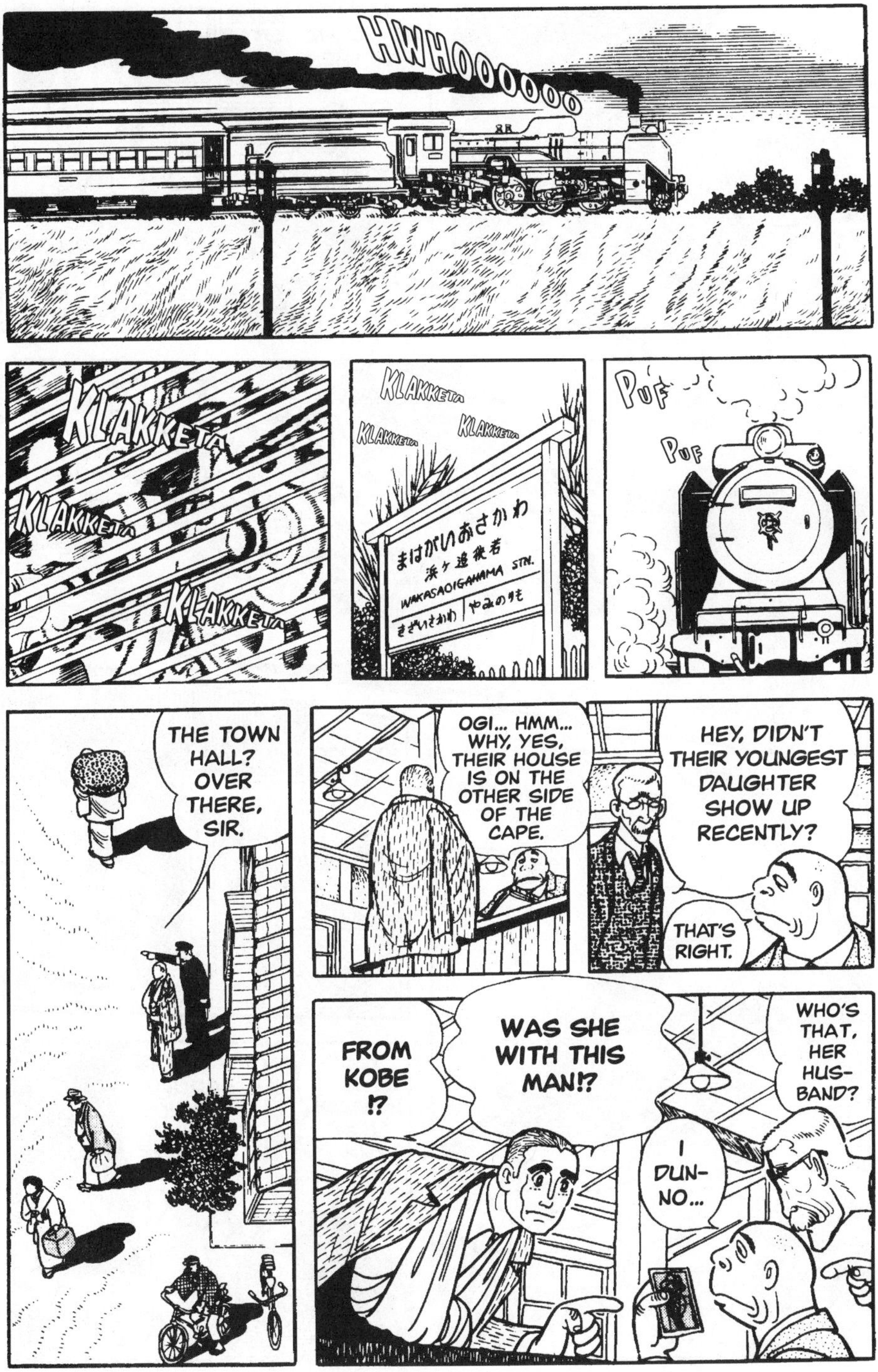
HWHOOOOOOO
KLAKKETA
KLAKKETA
KLAKKETA
KLAKKETA
KLAKKETA
KLAKKETA
WAKASAOIGAHAMA STN.
PUF
PUF
THE TOWN HALL? OVER THERE, SIR.
OGI... HMM... WHY, YES, THEIR HOUSE IS ON THE OTHER SIDE OF THE CAPE.
HEY, DIDN'T THEIR YOUNGEST DAUGHTER SHOW UP RECENTLY?
THAT'S RIGHT.
FROM KOBE!?
WAS SHE WITH THIS MAN!?
WHO'S THAT, HER HUS-BAND?
I DUN-NO...

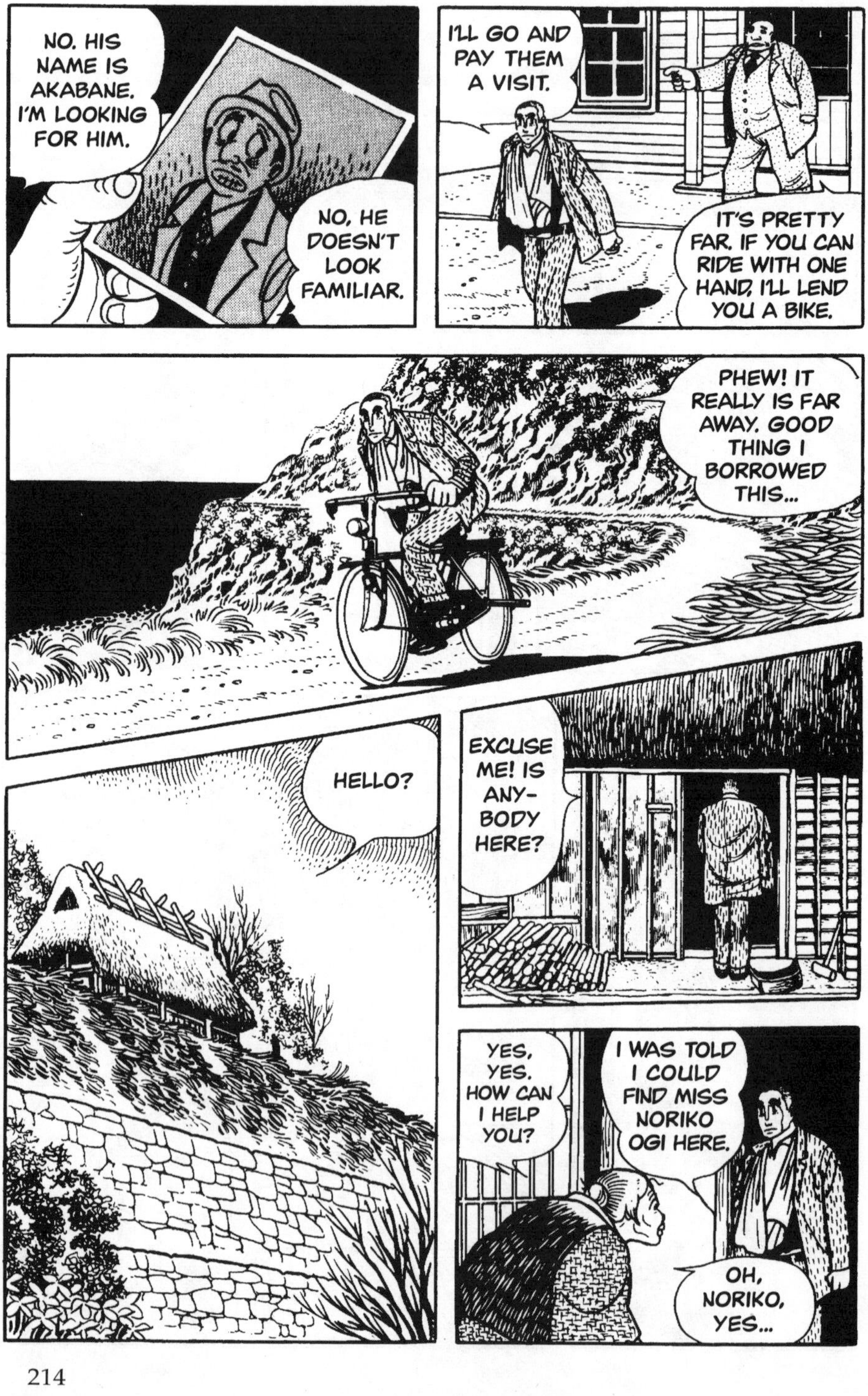
NO. HIS NAME IS AKABANE. I'M LOOKING FOR HIM.
NO, HE DOESN'T LOOK FAMILIAR.
I'LL GO AND PAY THEM A VISIT.
IT'S PRETTY FAR. IF YOU CAN RIDE WITH ONE HAND, I'LL LEND YOU A BIKE.
PHEW! IT REALLY IS FAR AWAY. GOOD THING I BORROWED THIS...
HELLO?
EXCUSE ME! IS ANY-BODY HERE?
YES, YES. HOW CAN I HELP YOU?
I WAS TOLD I COULD FIND MISS NORIKO OGI HERE.
OH, NORIKO, YES...

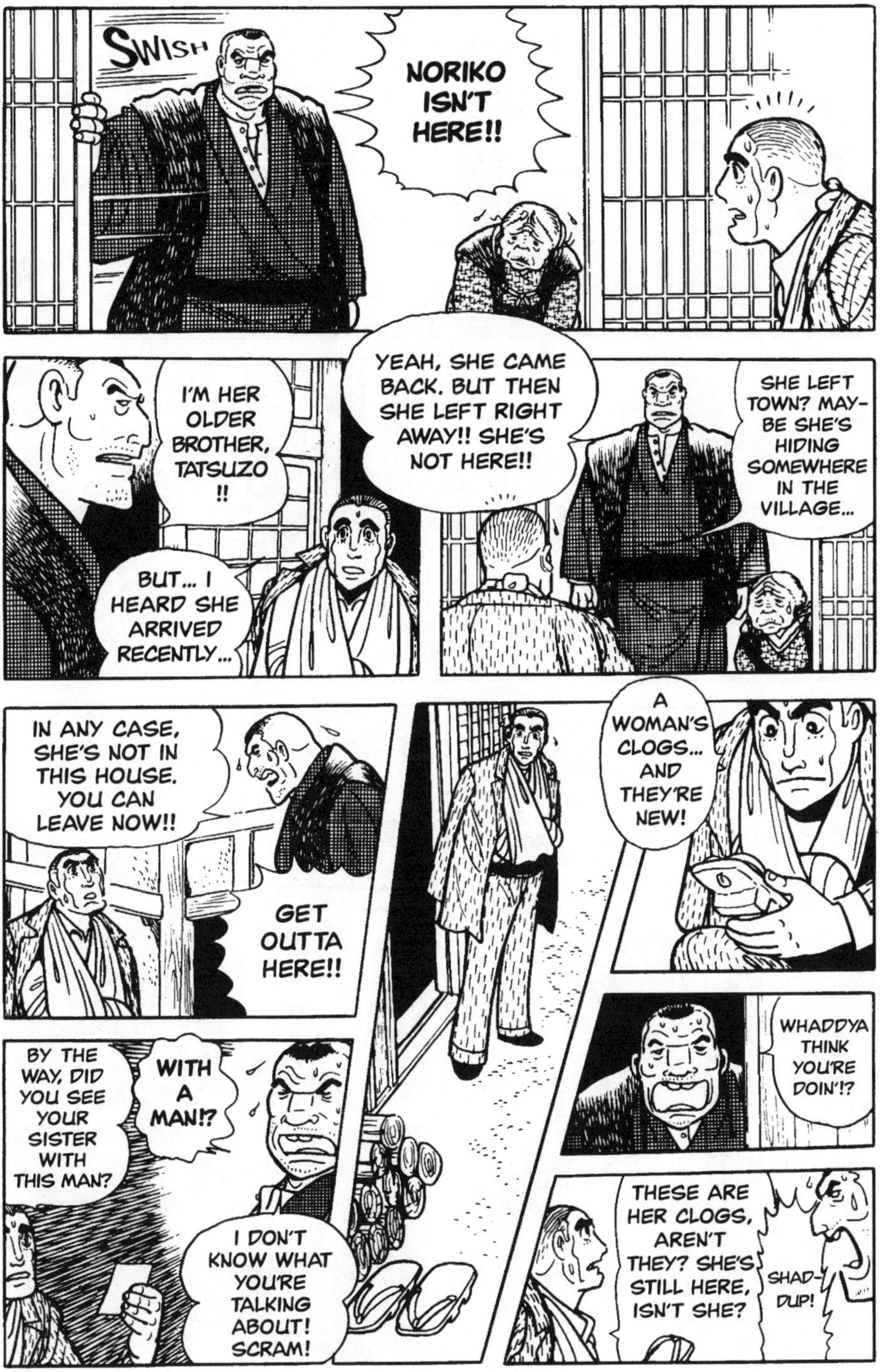
SWISH
NORIKO ISN'T HERE!!
I'M HER OLDER BROTHER, TATSUZO!!
BUT... I HEARD SHE ARRIVED RECENTLY...
YEAH, SHE CAME BACK. BUT THEN SHE LEFT RIGHT AWAY!! SHE'S NOT HERE!!
SHE LEFT TOWN? MAY-BE SHE'S HIDING SOMEWHERE IN THE VILLAGE...
IN ANY CASE, SHE'S NOT IN THIS HOUSE. YOU CAN LEAVE NOW!!
GET OUTTA HERE!!
BY THE WAY, DID YOU SEE YOUR SISTER WITH THIS MAN?
WITH A MAN!?
I DON'T KNOW WHAT YOU'RE TALKING ABOUT! SCRAM!
A WOMAN'S CLOGS... AND THEY'RE NEW!
WHADDYA THINK YOU'RE DOIN'!?
THESE ARE HER CLOGS, AREN'T THEY? SHE'S STILL HERE, ISN'T SHE?
SHAD-DUP!

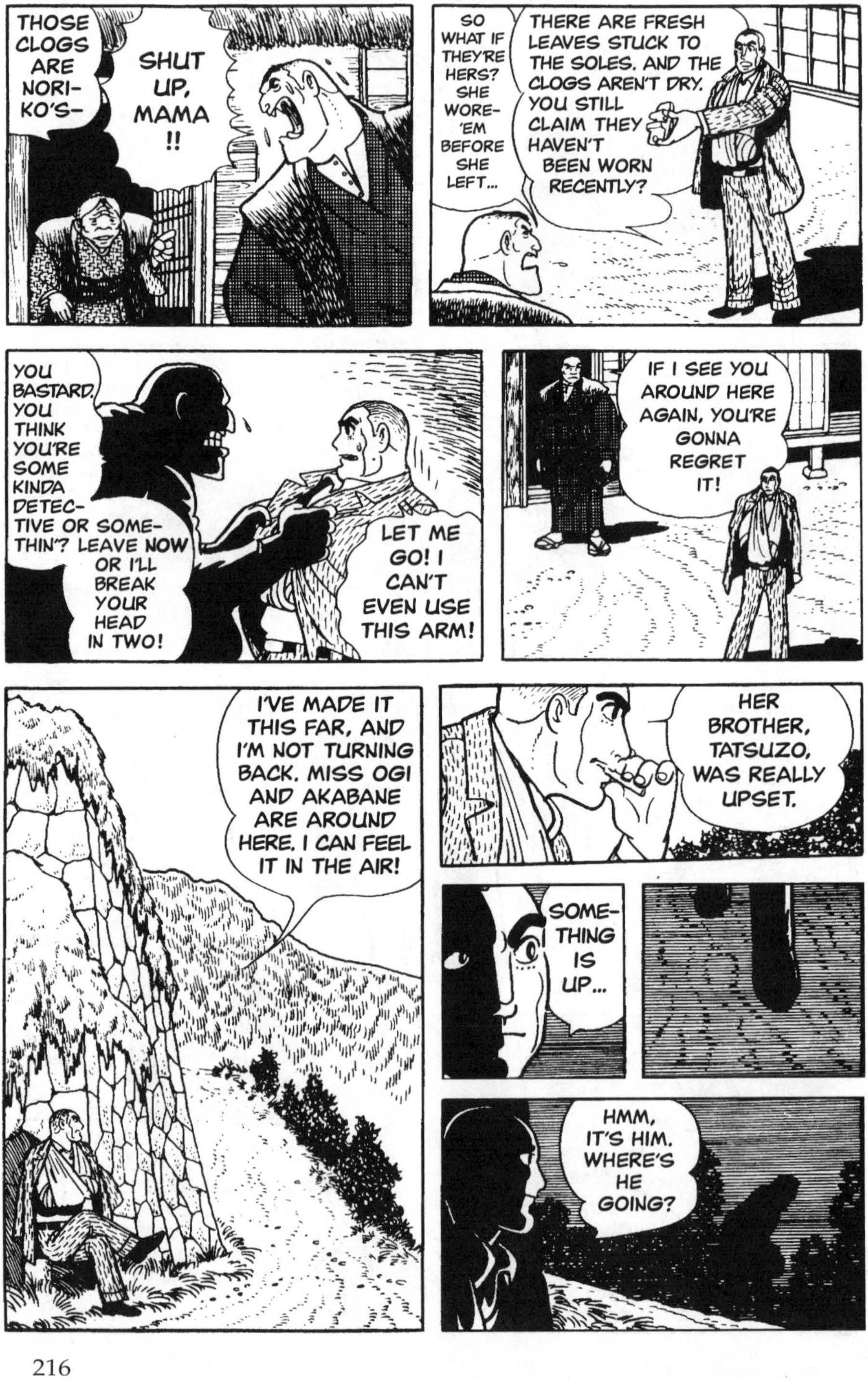
THOSE CLOGS ARE NORI-KO'S-
SHUT UP, MAMA!!
SO WHAT IF THEY'RE HERS? SHE WORE-'EM BEFORE SHE LEFT...
THERE ARE FRESH LEAVES STUCK TO THE SOLES. AND THE CLOGS AREN'T DRY. YOU STILL CLAIM THEY HAVEN'T BEEN WORN RECENTLY?
YOU BASTARD. YOU THINK YOU'RE SOME KINDA DETEC-TIVE OR SOME-THIN'? LEAVE NOW OR I'LL BREAK YOUR HEAD IN TWO!
LET ME GO! I CAN'T EVEN USE THIS ARM!
IF I SEE YOU AROUND HERE AGAIN, YOU'RE GONNA REGRET IT!
I'VE MADE IT THIS FAR, AND I'M NOT TURNING BACK. MISS OGI AND AKABANE ARE AROUND HERE. I CAN FEEL IT IN THE AIR!
HER BROTHER, TATSUZO, WAS REALLY UPSET.
SOME-THING IS UP...
HMM, IT'S HIM. WHERE'S HE GOING?

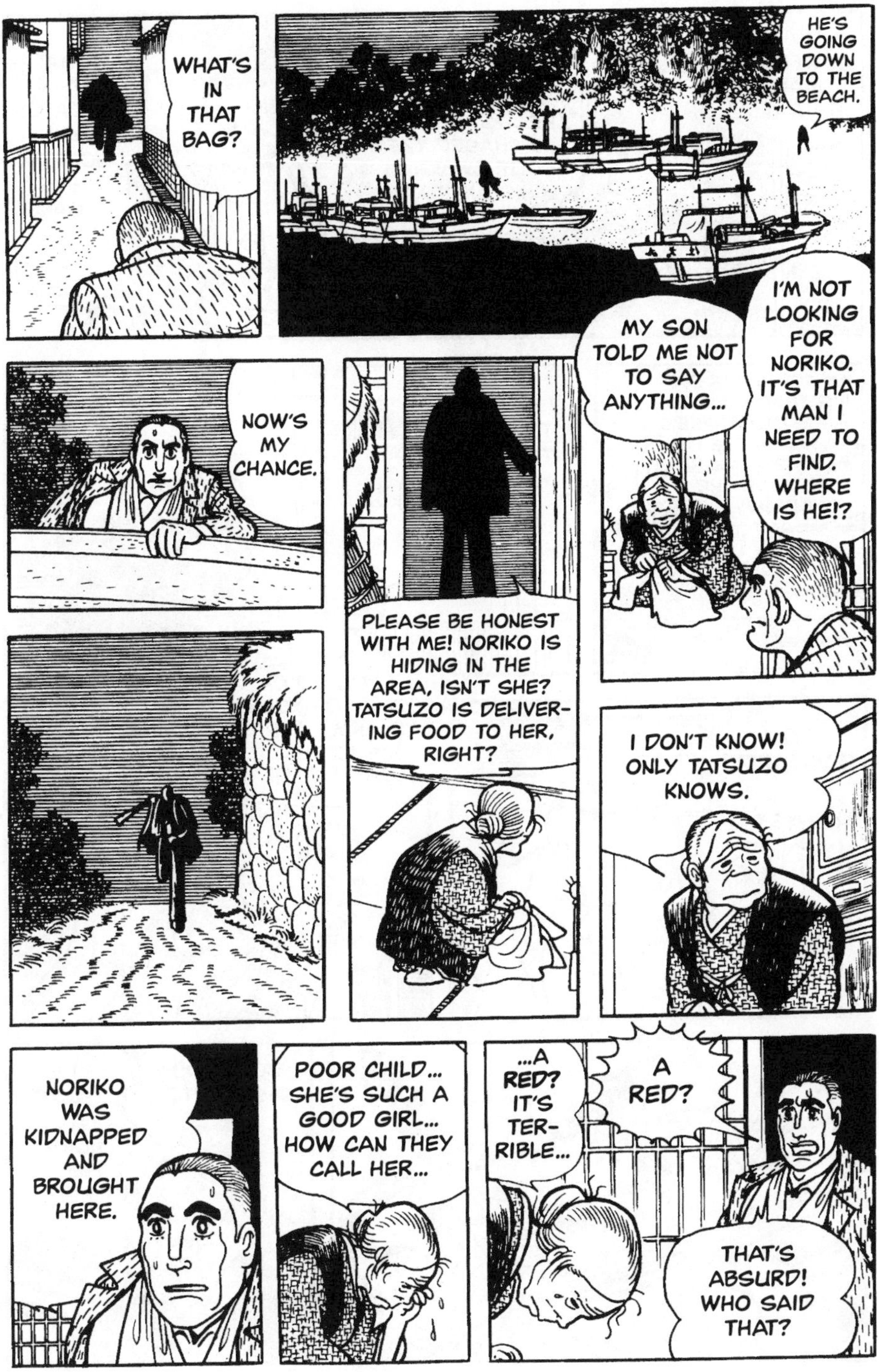
WHAT'S IN THAT BAG?
HE'S GOING DOWN TO THE BEACH.
NOW'S MY CHANCE.
PLEASE BE HONEST WITH ME! NORIKO IS HIDING IN THE AREA, ISN'T SHE? TATSUZO IS DELIVERING FOOD TO HER, RIGHT?
MY SON TOLD ME NOT TO SAY ANYTHING...
I'M NOT LOOKING FOR NORIKO. IT'S THAT MAN I NEED TO FIND. WHERE IS HE!?
I DON'T KNOW! ONLY TATSUZO KNOWS.
NORIKO WAS KIDNAPPED AND BROUGHT HERE.
POOR CHILD... SHE'S SUCH A GOOD GIRL... HOW CAN THEY CALL HER...
...A RED? IT'S TERRIBLE...
A RED?
THAT'S ABSURD! WHO SAID THAT?

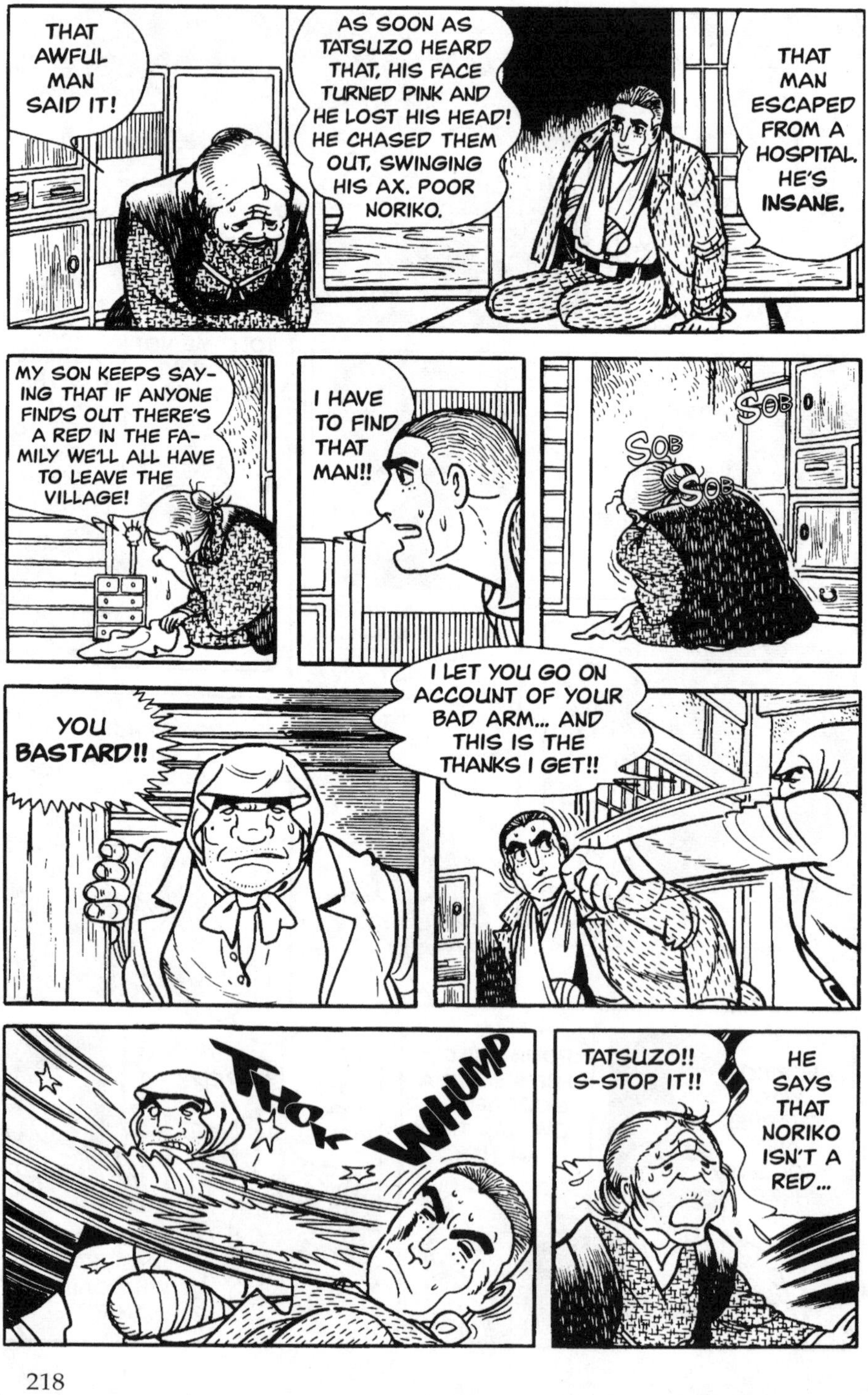
THAT AWFUL MAN SAID IT!
AS SOON AS TATSUZO HEARD THAT, HIS FACE TURNED PINK AND HE LOST HIS HEAD! HE CHASED THEM OUT, SWINGING HIS AX. POOR NORIKO.
THAT MAN ESCAPED FROM A HOSPITAL. HE'S INSANE.
MY SON KEEPS SAYING THAT IF ANYONE FINDS OUT THERE'S A RED IN THE FAMILY WE'LL ALL HAVE TO LEAVE THE VILLAGE!
I HAVE TO FIND THAT MAN!!
SOB
SOB
SOB
YOU BASTARD!!
I LET YOU GO ON ACCOUNT OF YOUR BAD ARM... AND THIS IS THE THANKS I GET!!
THOK
WHUMP
TATSUZO!! S-STOP IT!!
HE SAYS THAT NORIKO ISN'T A RED...

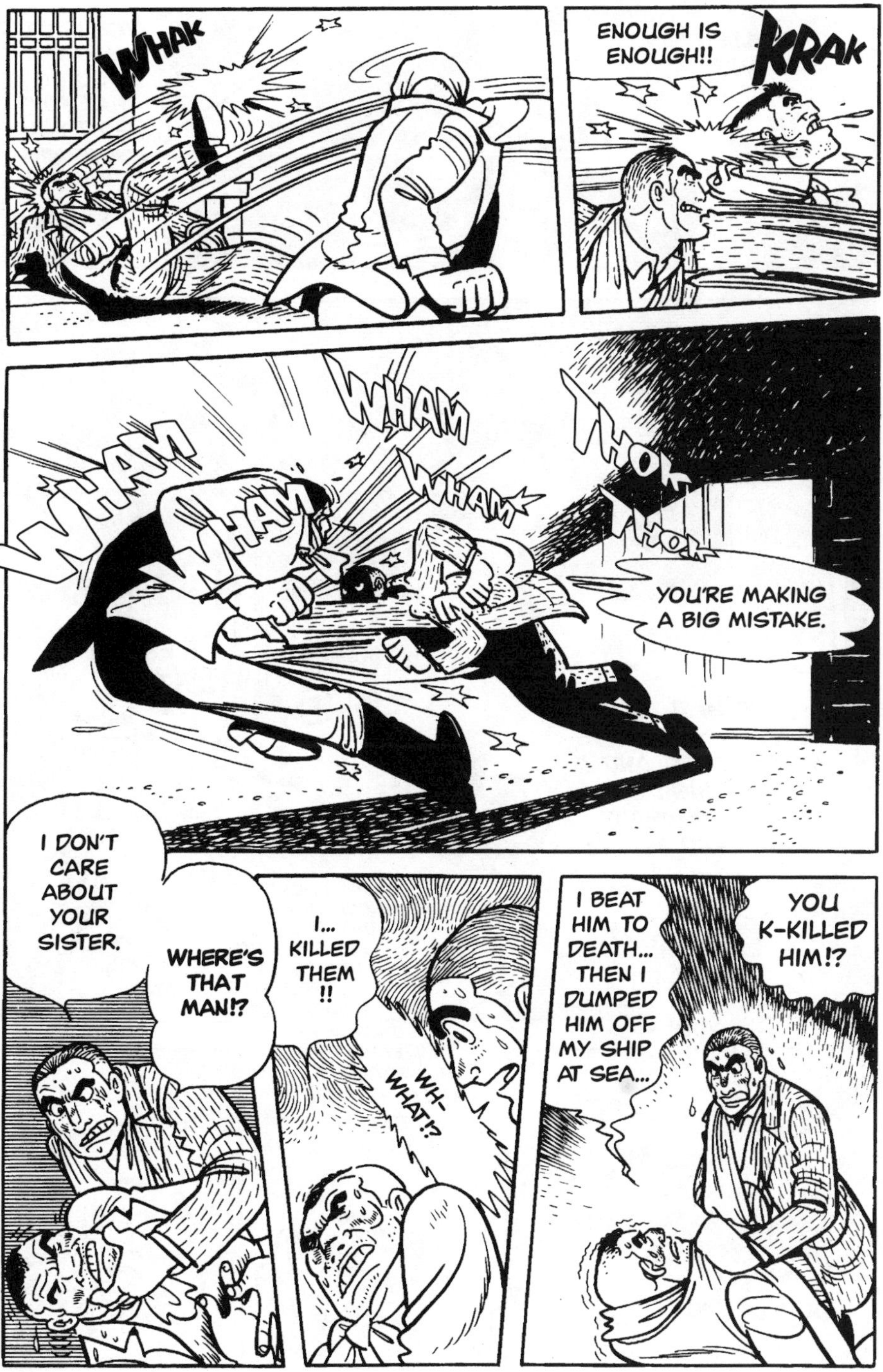
WHAK
ENOUGH IS ENOUGH!!
KRAK
WHAM
WHAM
WHAM
WHAM
WHAM
THOK
THOK
YOU'RE MAKING A BIG MISTAKE.
I DON'T CARE ABOUT YOUR SISTER.
WHERE'S THAT MAN!?
I... KILLED THEM !!
WH-WHAT!?
I BEAT HIM TO DEATH... THEN I DUMPED HIM OFF MY SHIP AT SEA...
YOU K-KILLED HIM!?

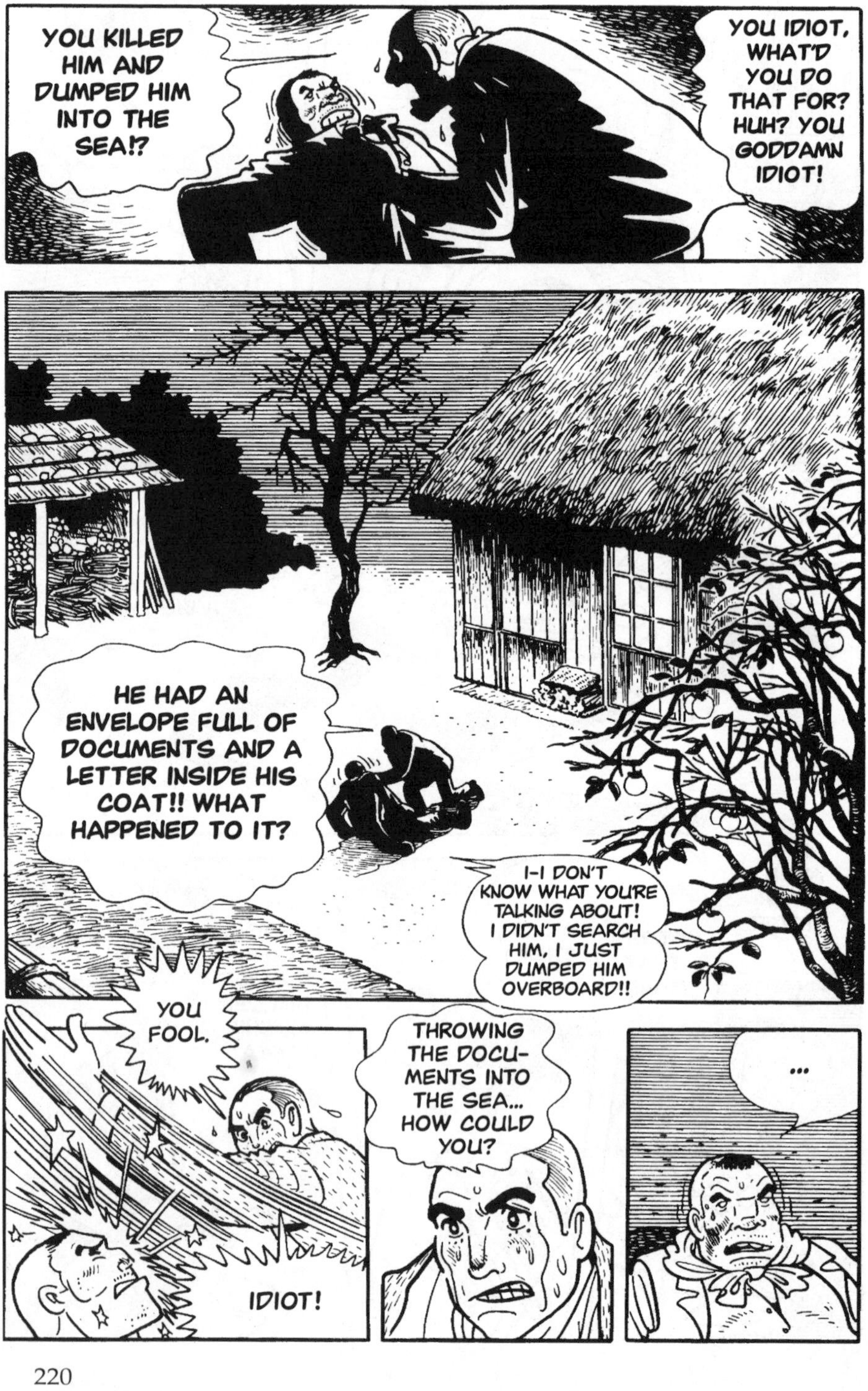
YOU KILLED HIM AND DUMPED HIM INTO THE SEA!?
YOU IDIOT, WHAT'D YOU DO THAT FOR? HUH? YOU GODDAMN IDIOT!
HE HAD AN ENVELOPE FULL OF DOCUMENTS AND A LETTER INSIDE HIS COAT!! WHAT HAPPENED TO IT?
I-I DON'T KNOW WHAT YOU'RE TALKING ABOUT! I DIDN'T SEARCH HIM, I JUST DUMPED HIM OVERBOARD!!
YOU FOOL.
IDIOT!
THROWING THE DOCU-MENTS INTO THE SEA... HOW COULD YOU?
...

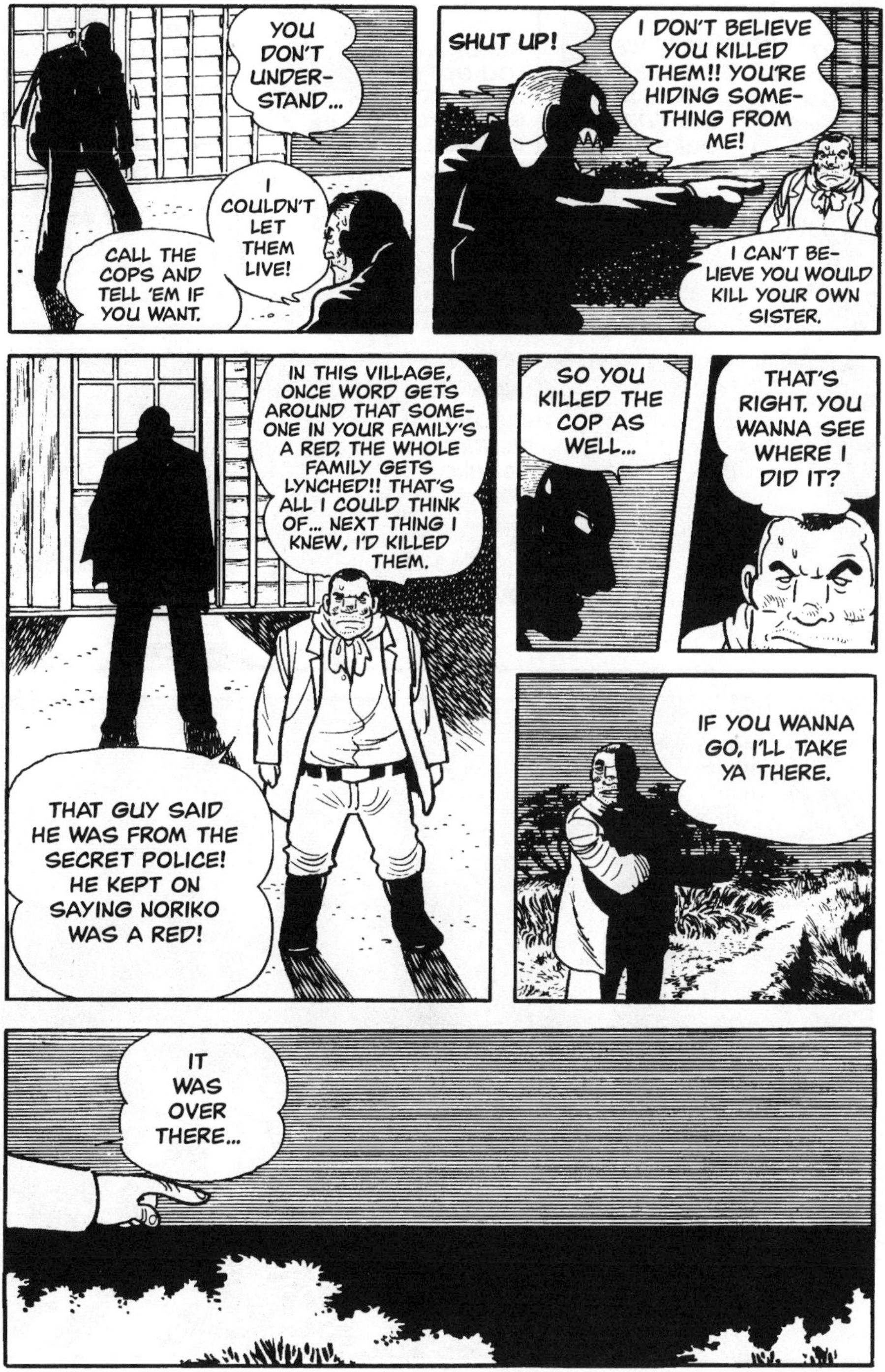
YOU DON'T UNDER-STAND...
I COULDN'T LET THEM LIVE!
CALL THE COPS AND TELL 'EM IF YOU WANT.
SHUT UP!
I DON'T BELIEVE YOU KILLED THEM!! YOU'RE HIDING SOME-THING FROM ME!
I CAN'T BE-LIEVE YOU WOULD KILL YOUR OWN SISTER.
IN THIS VILLAGE, ONCE WORD GETS AROUND THAT SOME-ONE IN YOUR FAMILY'S A RED, THE WHOLE FAMILY GETS LYNCHED!! THAT'S ALL I COULD THINK OF... NEXT THING I KNEW, I'D KILLED THEM.
THAT GUY SAID HE WAS FROM THE SECRET POLICE! HE KEPT ON SAYING NORIKO WAS A RED!
SO YOU KILLED THE COP AS WELL...
THAT'S RIGHT. YOU WANNA SEE WHERE I DID IT?
IF YOU WANNA GO, I'LL TAKE YA THERE.
IT WAS OVER THERE...

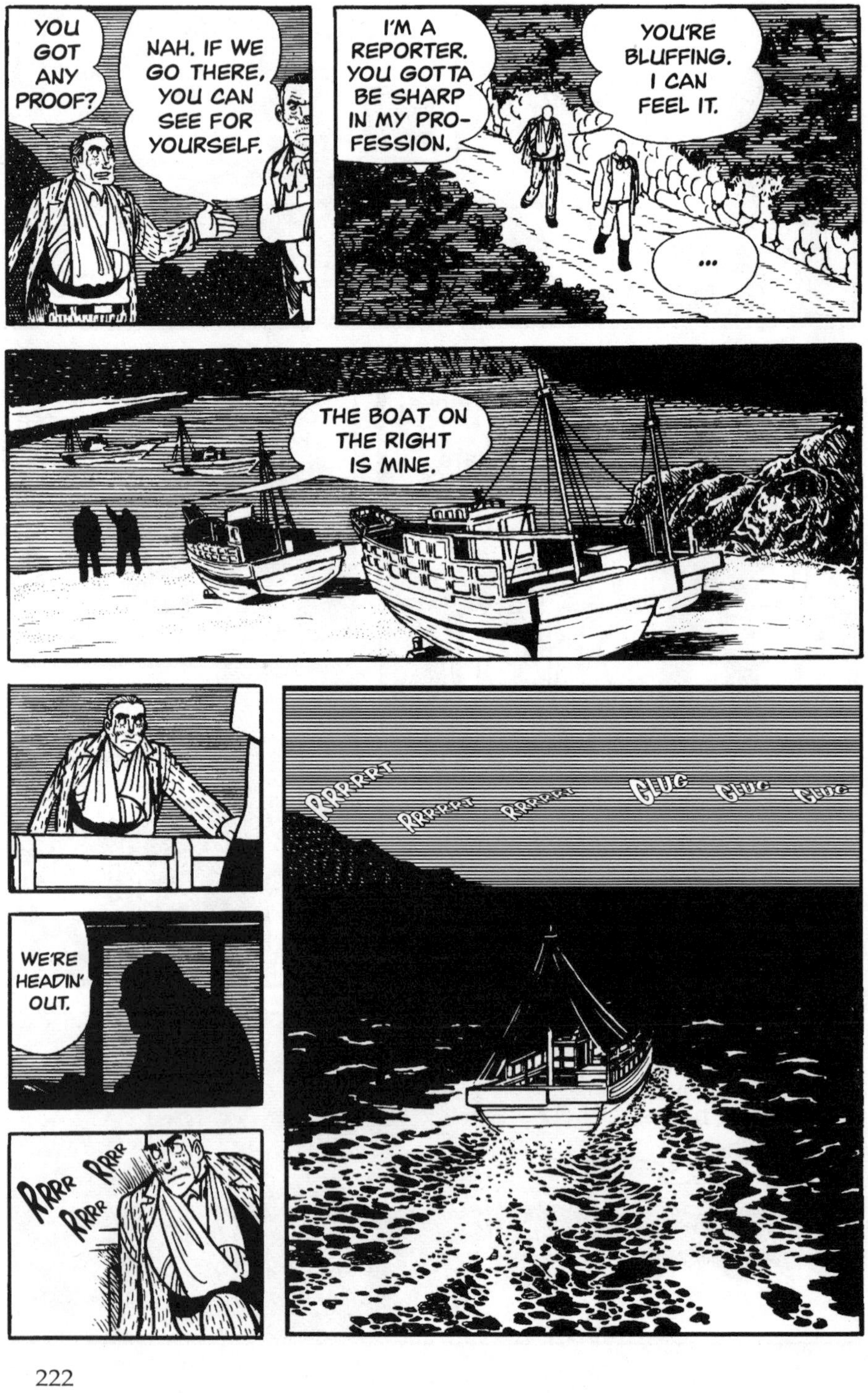
YOU GOT ANY PROOF?
NAH. IF WE GO THERE, YOU CAN SEE FOR YOURSELF.
I'M A REPORTER. YOU GOTTA BE SHARP IN MY PRO-FESSION.
YOU'RE BLUFFING. I CAN FEEL IT.
...
THE BOAT ON THE RIGHT IS MINE.
WE'RE HEADIN' OUT.
RRRR RRRR RRRR
RRRRRT
RRRRRT
RRRRRT
GLUG
GLUG
GLUG

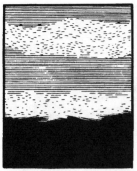

YES, THIS IS THE TOWN HALL...

A YOUNG MAN WEARING A SLING?

YES, HE WAS HERE THIS EVENING...

HE WENT TO VISIT THE OGIS.

HE BORROWED ONE OF OUR BIKES.

MAY I ASK WHO'S CALLING?

HELLO? WHO IS THIS? HELLO?

WHO WOULD CALL ON SUCH A FOGGY NIGHT?

HIS VOICE SOUNDED KINDA FUNNY. AND HE HUNG UP ON ME.

WE'VE FINALLY FOUND HIM.

THE FOG IS REALLY THICK, SIR. SHOULD WE CONTINUE?

KEEP GOING. IT PUTS ME IN THE RIGHT MOOD FOR KILLING.

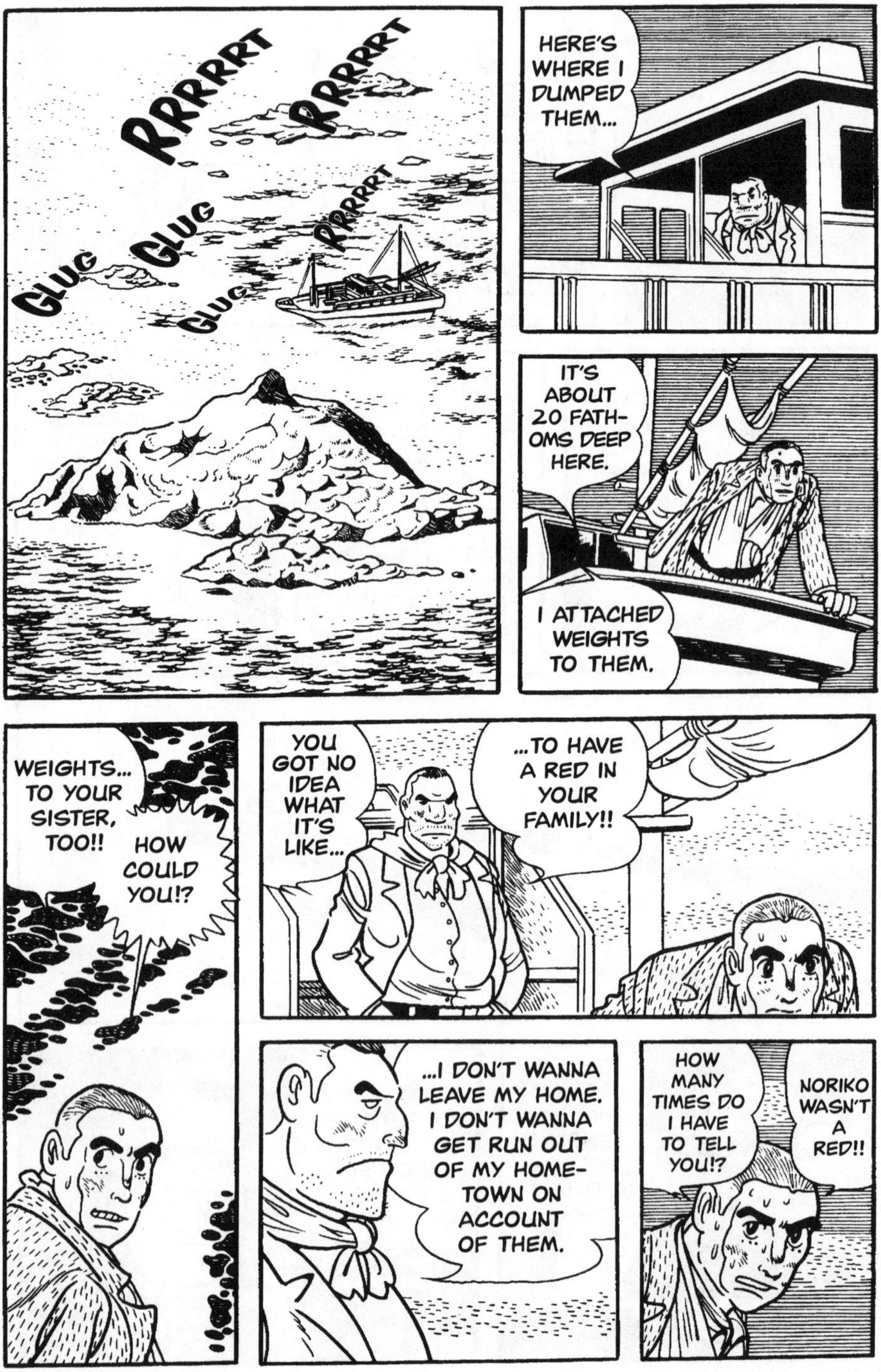
RRRRRT
RRRRRRT
GLUG
GLUG
GLUG
RRRRRT
HERE'S WHERE I DUMPED THEM...
IT'S ABOUT 20 FATHOMS DEEP HERE.
I ATTACHED WEIGHTS TO THEM.
WEIGHTS... TO YOUR SISTER, TOO!!
HOW COULD YOU!?
YOU GOT NO IDEA WHAT IT'S LIKE...
...TO HAVE A RED IN YOUR FAMILY!!
...I DON'T WANNA LEAVE MY HOME. I DON'T WANNA GET RUN OUT OF MY HOME-TOWN ON ACCOUNT OF THEM.
HOW MANY TIMES DO I HAVE TO TELL YOU!?
NORIKO WASN'T A RED!!

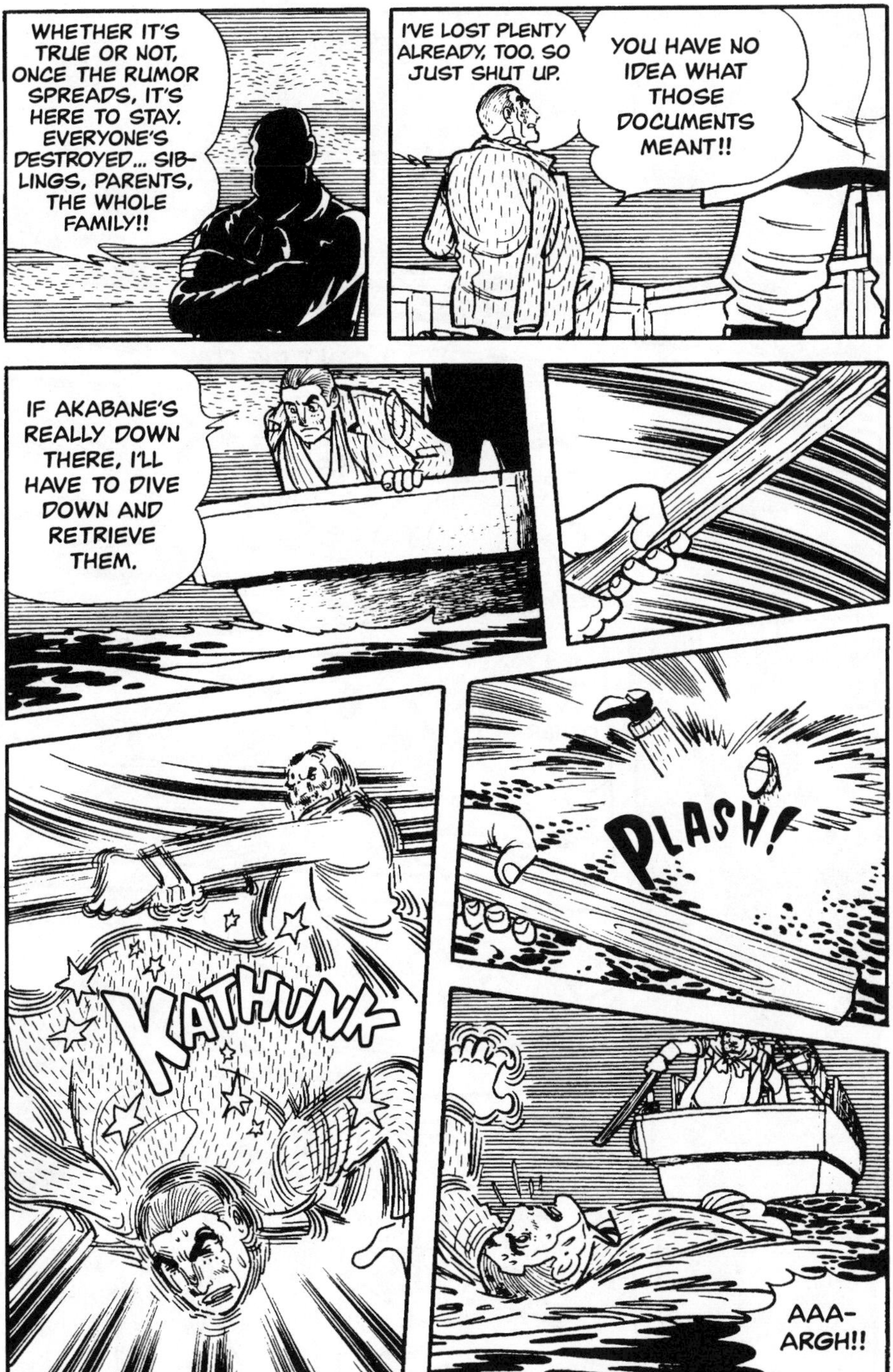
WHETHER IT'S TRUE OR NOT, ONCE THE RUMOR SPREADS, IT'S HERE TO STAY. EVERYONE'S DESTROYED... SIB-LINGS, PARENTS, THE WHOLE FAMILY!!
I'VE LOST PLENTY ALREADY, TOO. SO JUST SHUT UP.
YOU HAVE NO IDEA WHAT THOSE DOCUMENTS MEANT!!
IF AKABANE'S REALLY DOWN THERE, I'LL HAVE TO DIVE DOWN AND RETRIEVE THEM.
KATHUNK
PLASH!
AAA-ARGH!!

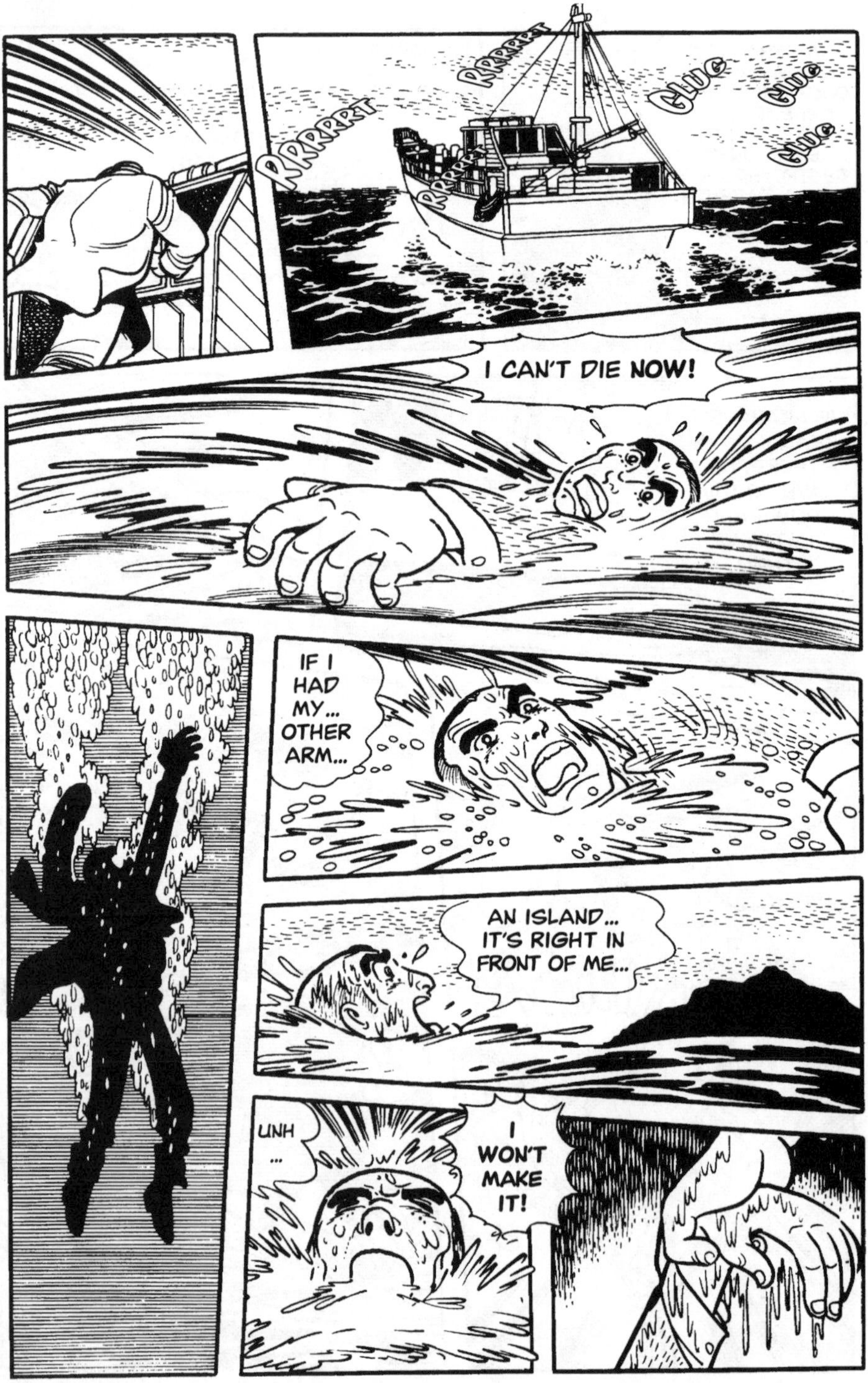
RRRRRT
RRRRRT
RRRRRT
GLUG
GLUG
GLUG
I CAN'T DIE NOW!
IF I HAD MY... OTHER ARM...
AN ISLAND... IT'S RIGHT IN FRONT OF ME...
UNH ...
I WON'T MAKE IT!

JUST IN TIME...

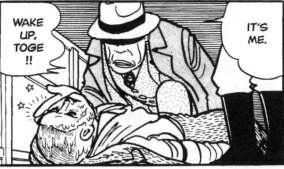

WAKE UP, TOGE!!

IT'S ME.

UHN... INSPECTOR... NIKAWA!

YOU REALLY OUGHT TO TAKE BETTER CARE OF YOURSELF...

H-HOW DID YOU KNOW WHERE TO FIND ME?

I KNEW YOU WERE SOMEWHERE IN THE VILLAGE. SOMEONE REPORTED SEEING YOU AT THE BEACH LATE AT NIGHT. SO I BORROWED A BOAT AND CAME OUT HERE.

IMPRESSIVE... YOU REALLY ARE A PRO.

YEAH, SURE... WHAT'S WITH YOUR ARM NOW? IT MUST BE PERMANENTLY INJURED.

FORGET THAT! THERE ARE SUPPOSED TO BE SOME BODIES AT THE BOTTOM OF THE OCEAN HERE.

BODIES?

YES, INSPECTOR AKABANE AND MISS NORIKO OGI!

AKABANE'S DOWN THERE? HOW'D THAT HAPPEN?

MISS OGI'S BROTHER SAYS HE KILLED THEM! HE THREW ME OVERBOARD TOO.

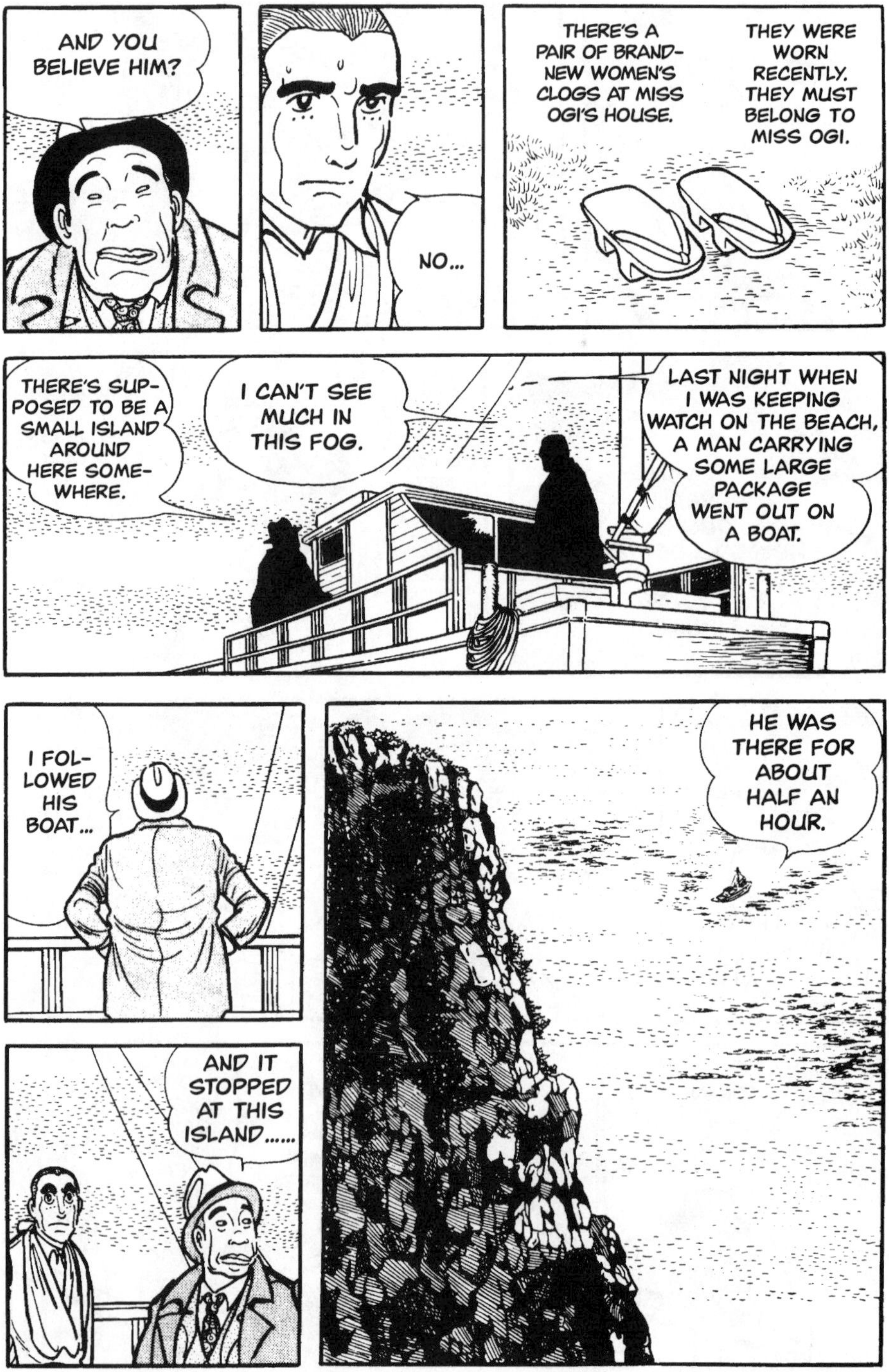
AND YOU BELIEVE HIM?
NO...
THERE'S A PAIR OF BRAND-NEW WOMEN'S CLOGS AT MISS OGI'S HOUSE.
THEY WERE WORN RECENTLY. THEY MUST BELONG TO MISS OGI.
THERE'S SUPPOSED TO BE A SMALL ISLAND AROUND HERE SOMEWHERE.
I CAN'T SEE MUCH IN THIS FOG.
LAST NIGHT WHEN I WAS KEEPING WATCH ON THE BEACH, A MAN CARRYING SOME LARGE PACKAGE WENT OUT ON A BOAT.
I FOLLOWED HIS BOAT...
AND IT STOPPED AT THIS ISLAND......
HE WAS THERE FOR ABOUT HALF AN HOUR.

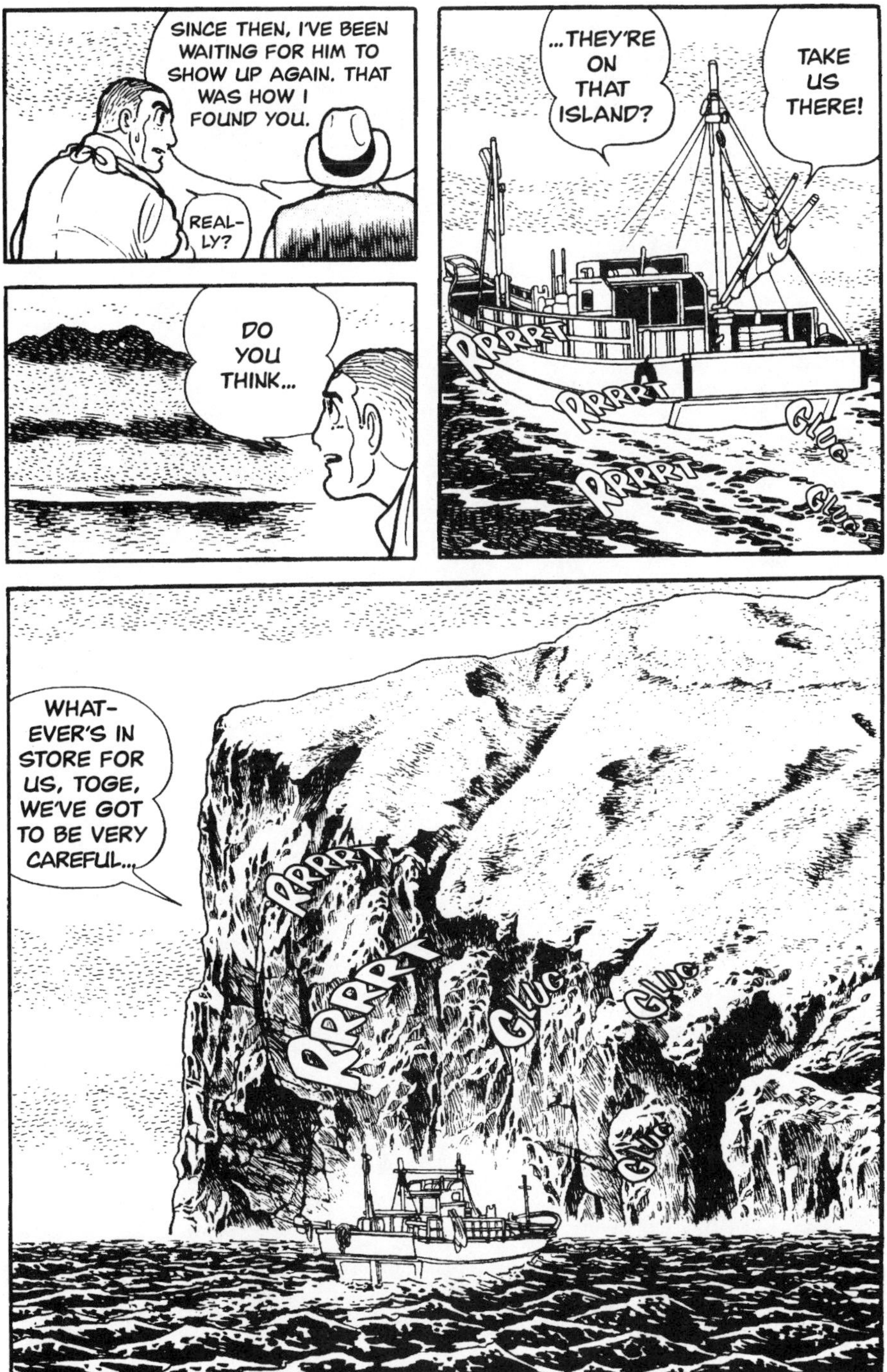
SINCE THEN, I'VE BEEN WAITING FOR HIM TO SHOW UP AGAIN. THAT WAS HOW I FOUND YOU.
REAL-LY?
DO YOU THINK...
...THEY'RE ON THAT ISLAND?
TAKE US THERE!
RRRRT
RRRRT
RRRRT
GLUG
GLUG
WHAT-EVER'S IN STORE FOR US, TOGE, WE'VE GOT TO BE VERY CAREFUL...
RRRRT
RRRRT
GLUG
GLUG
GLUG

CHAPTER
EIGHT

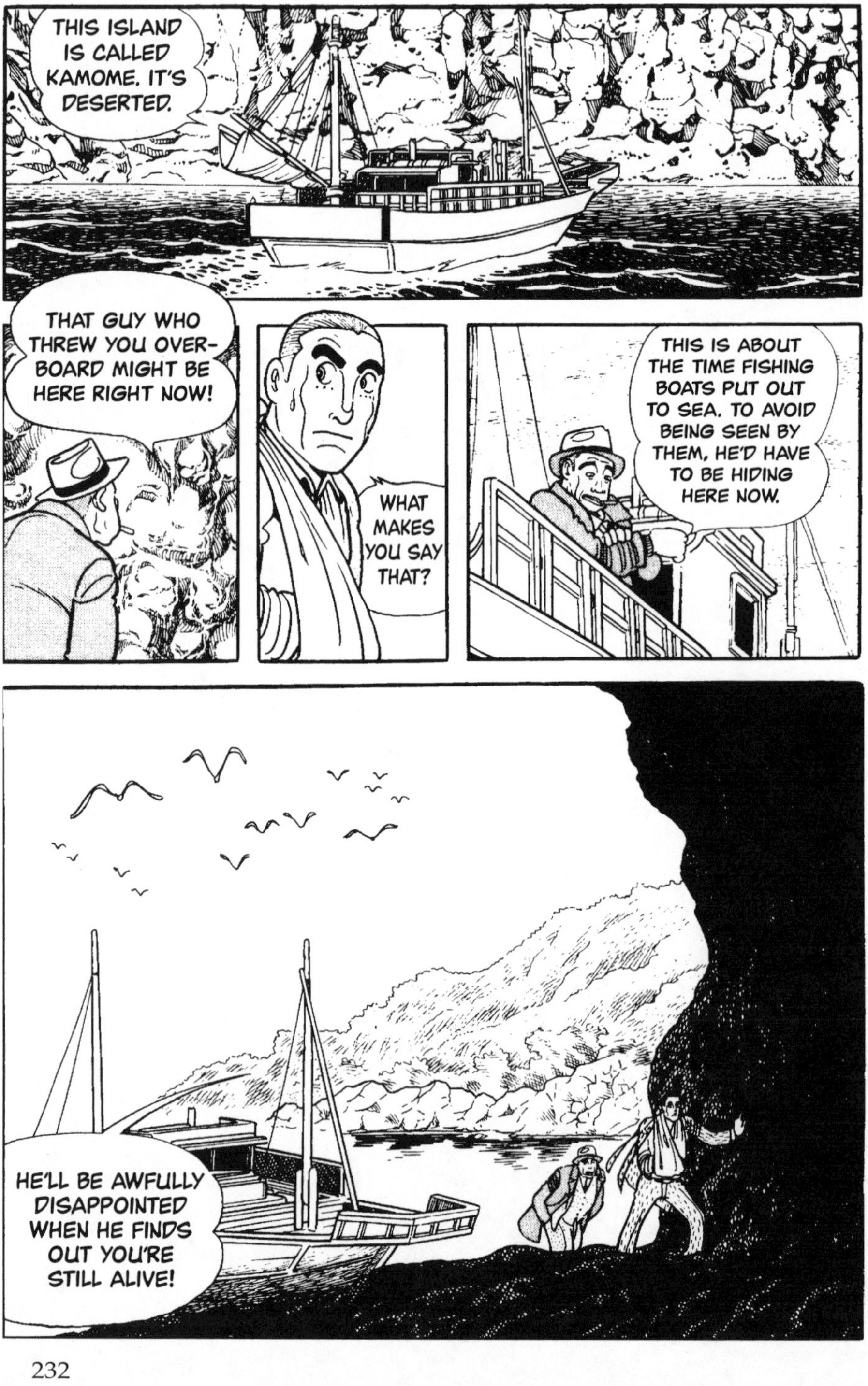
THIS ISLAND IS CALLED KAMOME. IT'S DESERTED.
THAT GUY WHO THREW YOU OVER-BOARD MIGHT BE HERE RIGHT NOW!
WHAT MAKES YOU SAY THAT?
THIS IS ABOUT THE TIME FISHING BOATS PUT OUT TO SEA. TO AVOID BEING SEEN BY THEM, HE'D HAVE TO BE HIDING HERE NOW.
HE'LL BE AWFULLY DISAPPOINTED WHEN HE FINDS OUT YOU'RE STILL ALIVE!

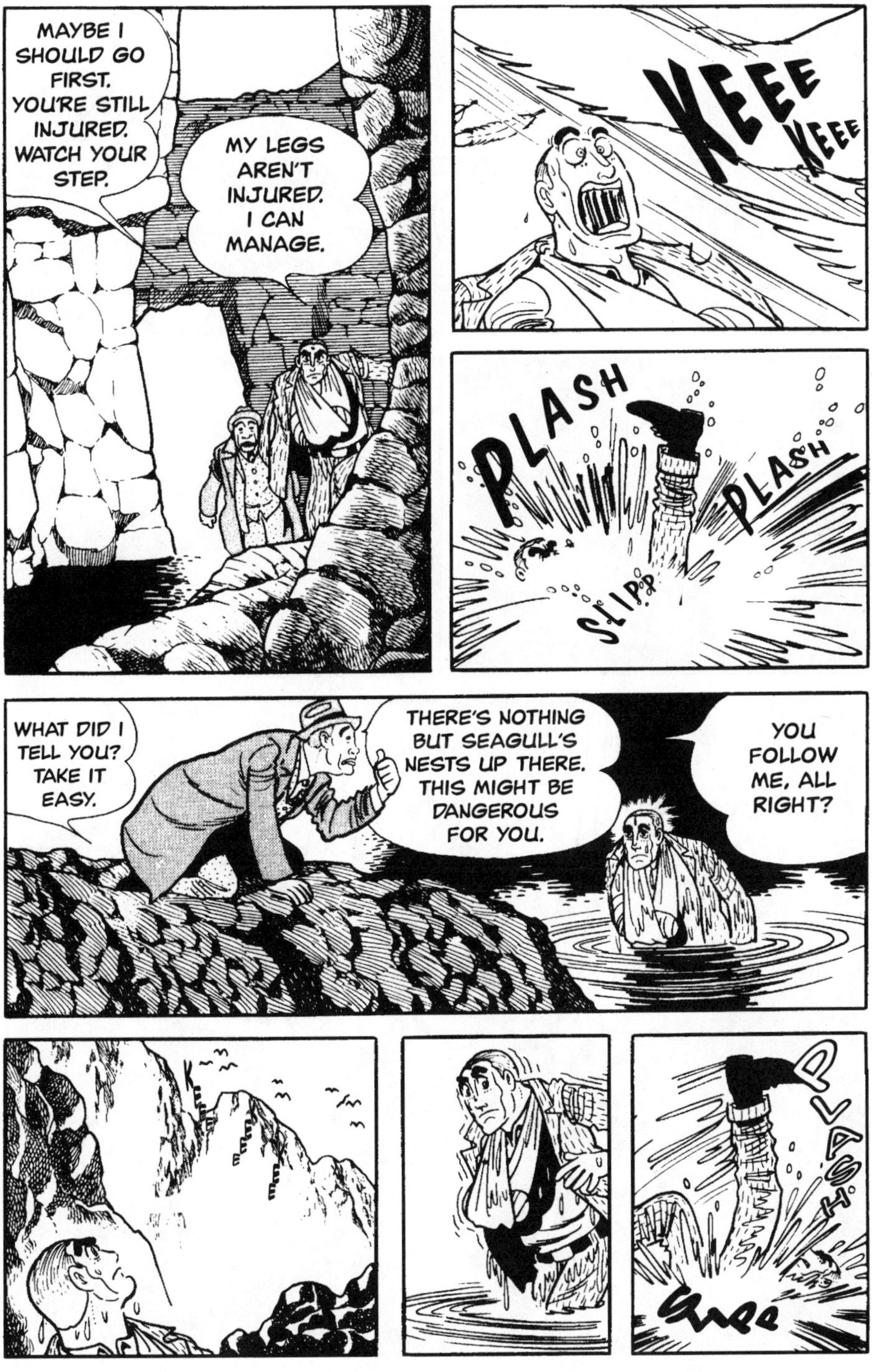
MAYBE I SHOULD GO FIRST. YOU'RE STILL INJURED. WATCH YOUR STEP.
MY LEGS AREN'T INJURED. I CAN MANAGE.
KEEE
KEEE
PLASH
PLASH
SLIPP
WHAT DID I TELL YOU? TAKE IT EASY.
THERE'S NOTHING BUT SEAGULL'S NESTS UP THERE. THIS MIGHT BE DANGEROUS FOR YOU.
YOU FOLLOW ME, ALL RIGHT?
PLASH

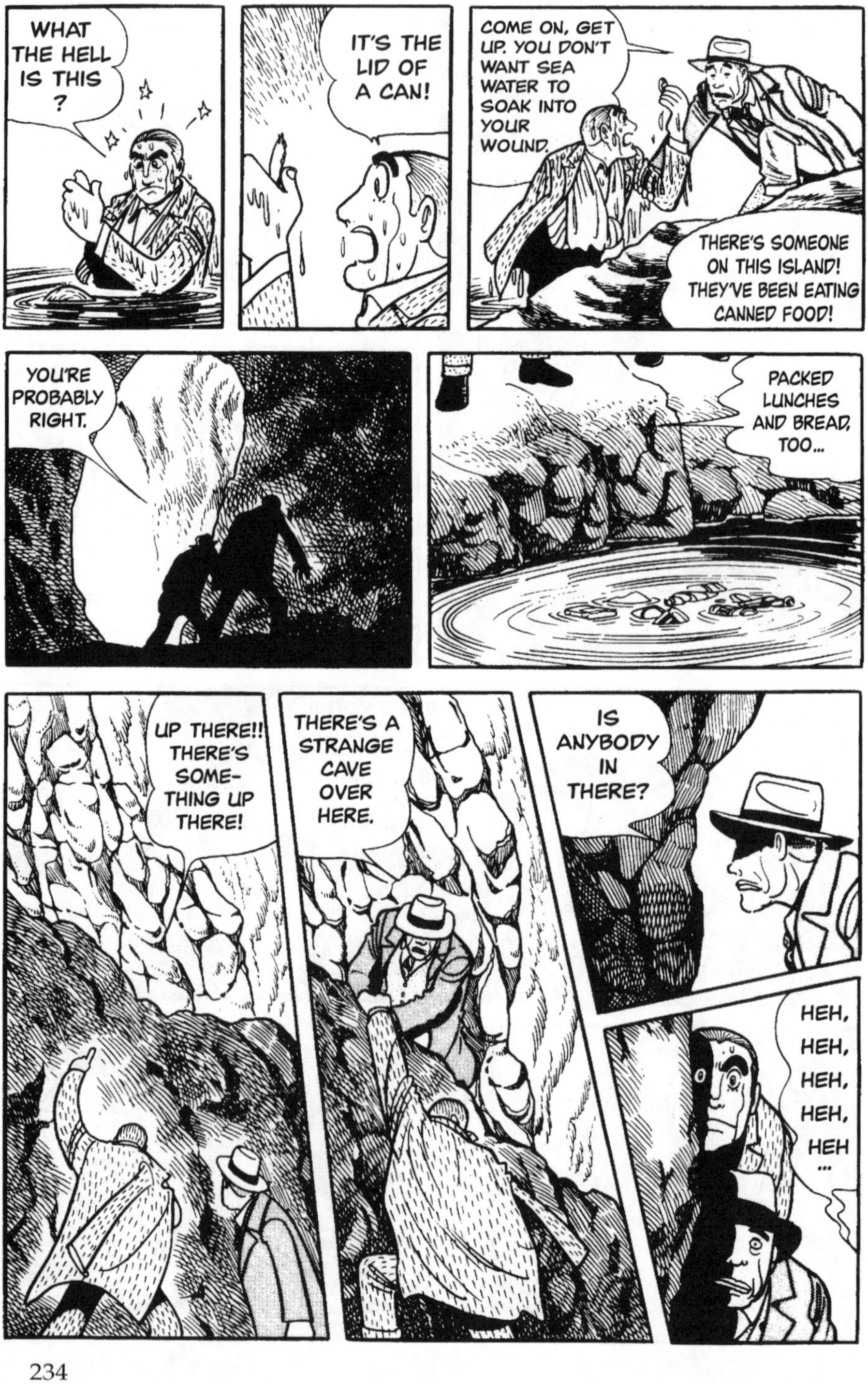
WHAT THE HELL IS THIS ?
IT'S THE LID OF A CAN!
COME ON, GET UP. YOU DON'T WANT SEA WATER TO SOAK INTO YOUR WOUND.
THERE'S SOMEONE ON THIS ISLAND! THEY'VE BEEN EATING CANNED FOOD!
YOU'RE PROBABLY RIGHT.
PACKED LUNCHES AND BREAD, TOO...
UP THERE!! THERE'S SOME-THING UP THERE!
THERE'S A STRANGE CAVE OVER HERE.
IS ANYBODY IN THERE?
HEH, HEH, HEH, HEH, HEH ...

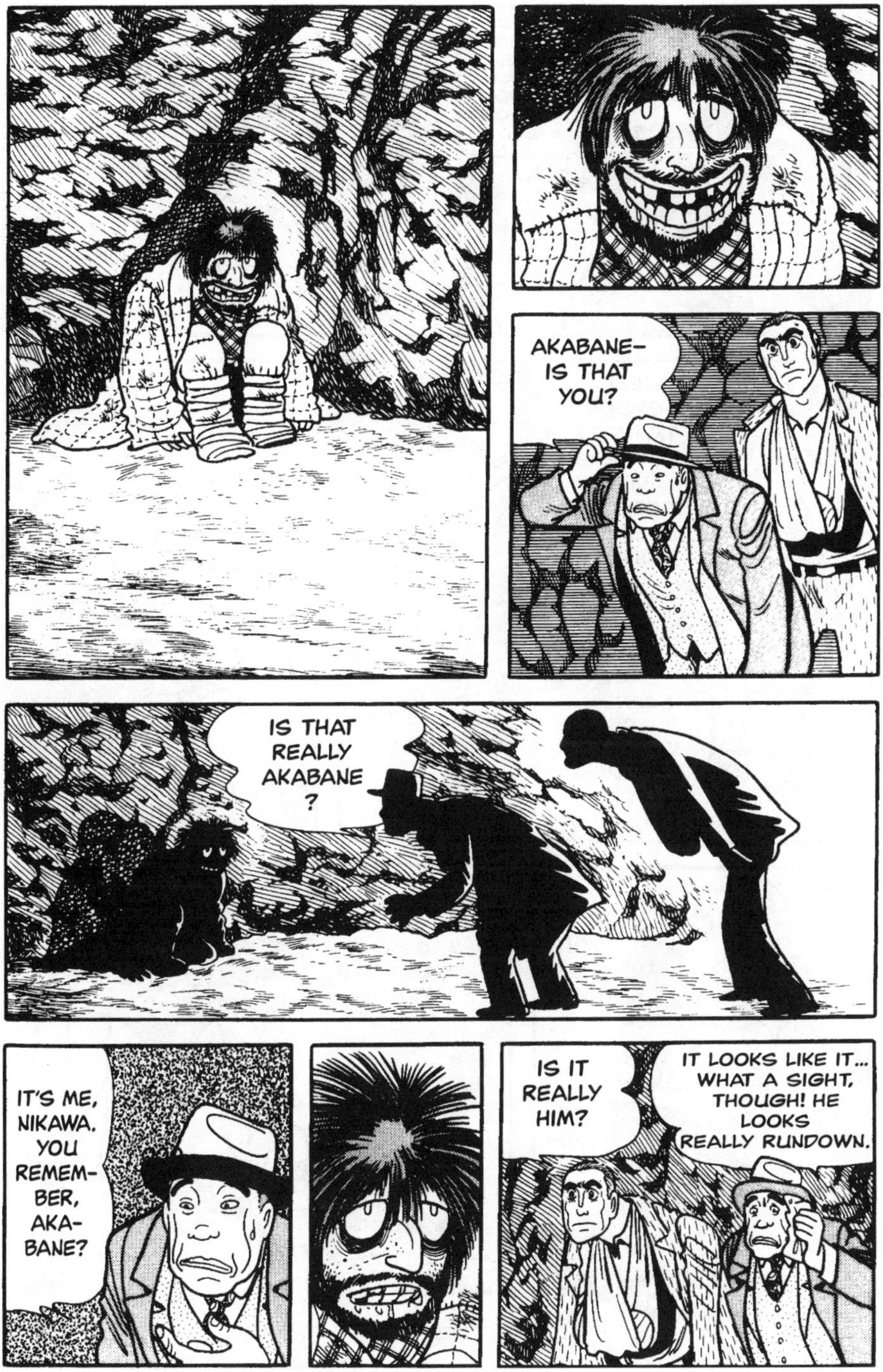
AKABANE– IS THAT YOU?
IS THAT REALLY AKABANE ?
IT'S ME, NIKAWA. YOU REMEMBER, AKABANE?
IS IT REALLY HIM?
IT LOOKS LIKE IT... WHAT A SIGHT, THOUGH! HE LOOKS REALLY RUNDOWN.

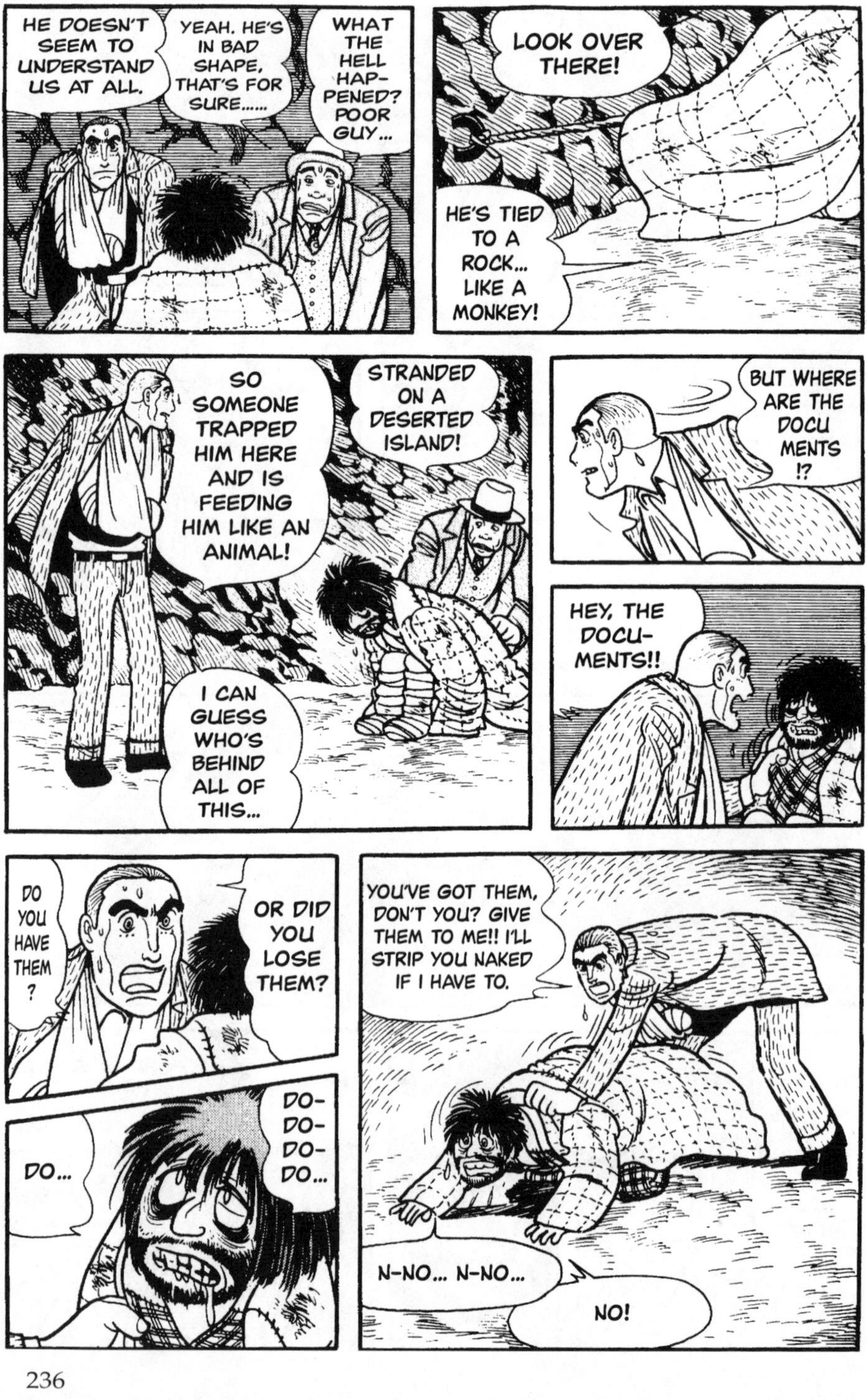
HE DOESN'T SEEM TO UNDERSTAND US AT ALL.
YEAH. HE'S IN BAD SHAPE, THAT'S FOR SURE......
WHAT THE HELL HAP-PENED? POOR GUY...
LOOK OVER THERE!
HE'S TIED TO A ROCK... LIKE A MONKEY!
SO SOMEONE TRAPPED HIM HERE AND IS FEEDING HIM LIKE AN ANIMAL!
STRANDED ON A DESERTED ISLAND!
I CAN GUESS WHO'S BEHIND ALL OF THIS...
BUT WHERE ARE THE DOCU MENTS !?
HEY, THE DOCU-MENTS!!
DO YOU HAVE THEM ?
OR DID YOU LOSE THEM?
DO...
DO-DO-DO-DO...
YOU'VE GOT THEM, DON'T YOU? GIVE THEM TO ME!! I'LL STRIP YOU NAKED IF I HAVE TO.
N-NO... N-NO...
NO!

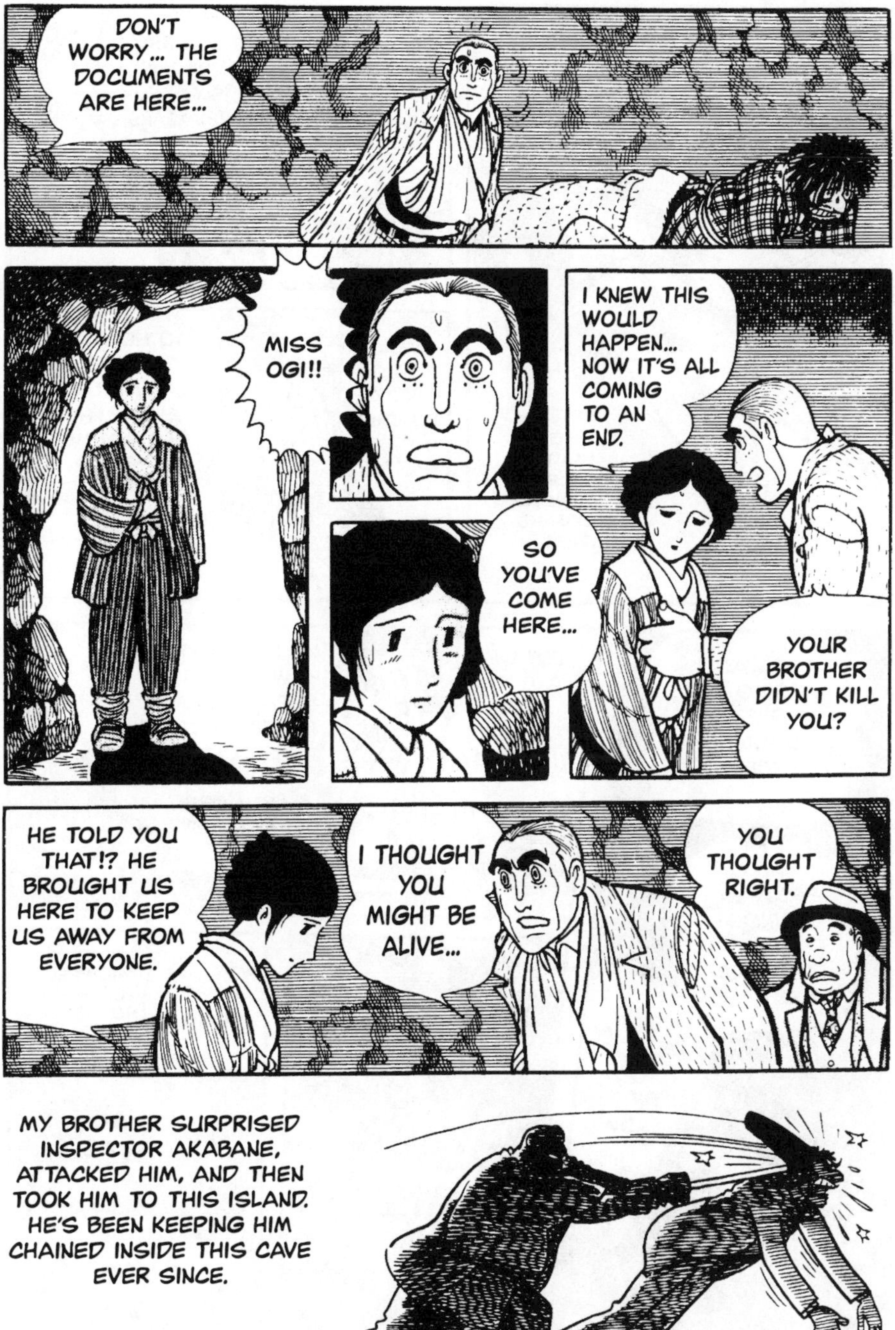
DON'T WORRY... THE DOCUMENTS ARE HERE...
MISS OGI!!
SO YOU'VE COME HERE...
I KNEW THIS WOULD HAPPEN... NOW IT'S ALL COMING TO AN END.
YOUR BROTHER DIDN'T KILL YOU?
HE TOLD YOU THAT!? HE BROUGHT US HERE TO KEEP US AWAY FROM EVERYONE.
I THOUGHT YOU MIGHT BE ALIVE...
YOU THOUGHT RIGHT.
MY BROTHER SURPRISED INSPECTOR AKABANE, ATTACKED HIM, AND THEN TOOK HIM TO THIS ISLAND. HE'S BEEN KEEPING HIM CHAINED INSIDE THIS CAVE EVER SINCE.

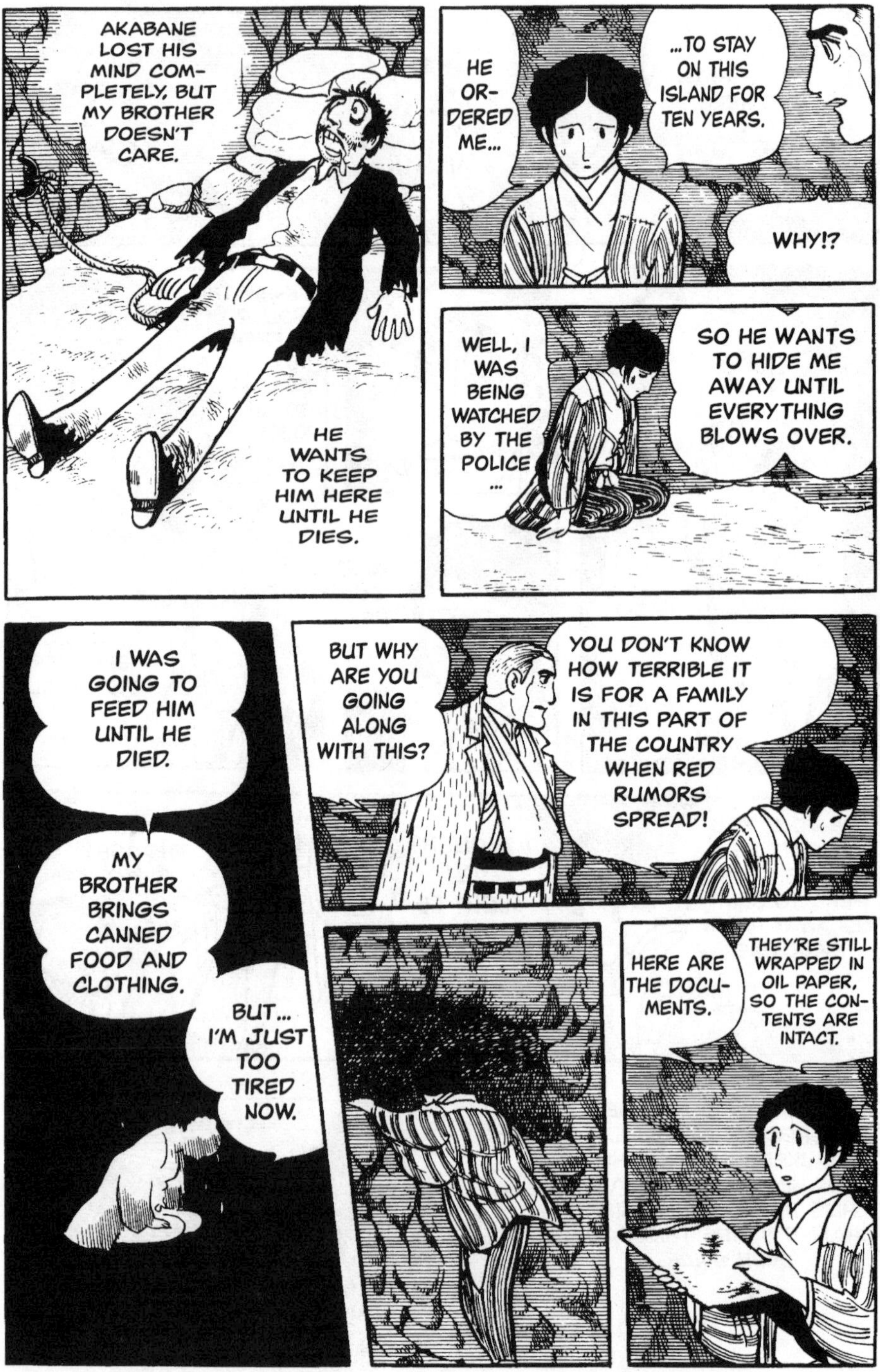
AKABANE LOST HIS MIND COMPLETELY, BUT MY BROTHER DOESN'T CARE.
HE WANTS TO KEEP HIM HERE UNTIL HE DIES.
HE ORDERED ME...
...TO STAY ON THIS ISLAND FOR TEN YEARS.
WHY!?
WELL, I WAS BEING WATCHED BY THE POLICE ...
SO HE WANTS TO HIDE ME AWAY UNTIL EVERYTHING BLOWS OVER.
I WAS GOING TO FEED HIM UNTIL HE DIED.
MY BROTHER BRINGS CANNED FOOD AND CLOTHING.
BUT... I'M JUST TOO TIRED NOW.
BUT WHY ARE YOU GOING ALONG WITH THIS?
YOU DON'T KNOW HOW TERRIBLE IT IS FOR A FAMILY IN THIS PART OF THE COUNTRY WHEN RED RUMORS SPREAD!
HERE ARE THE DOCUMENTS.
THEY'RE STILL WRAPPED IN OIL PAPER, SO THE CONTENTS ARE INTACT.

THIS IS IT!!

Y-YES... TH-THIS IS... IT!

I'M SAVED!

I IMAGINE MY BROTHER WILL BE PUNISHED SEVERELY...

THERE'S NO QUESTION ABOUT THAT. ASSAULT, KIDNAPPING, ILLEGAL DETENTION...

AND HE'LL BE CHARGED WITH ATTEMPTING TO MURDER TOGE.

BUT TOGE... NOW YOU'VE GOT THESE DOCUMENTS BACK! WHAT A MIRACLE!

MR. NIKAWA!! I-I CAN'T BELIEVE IT!!

TATSU-ZO...

TATSUZO OGI, YOU'RE UNDER ARREST! I'LL HAVE HEAD-QUARTERS SEND ME A WARRANT.

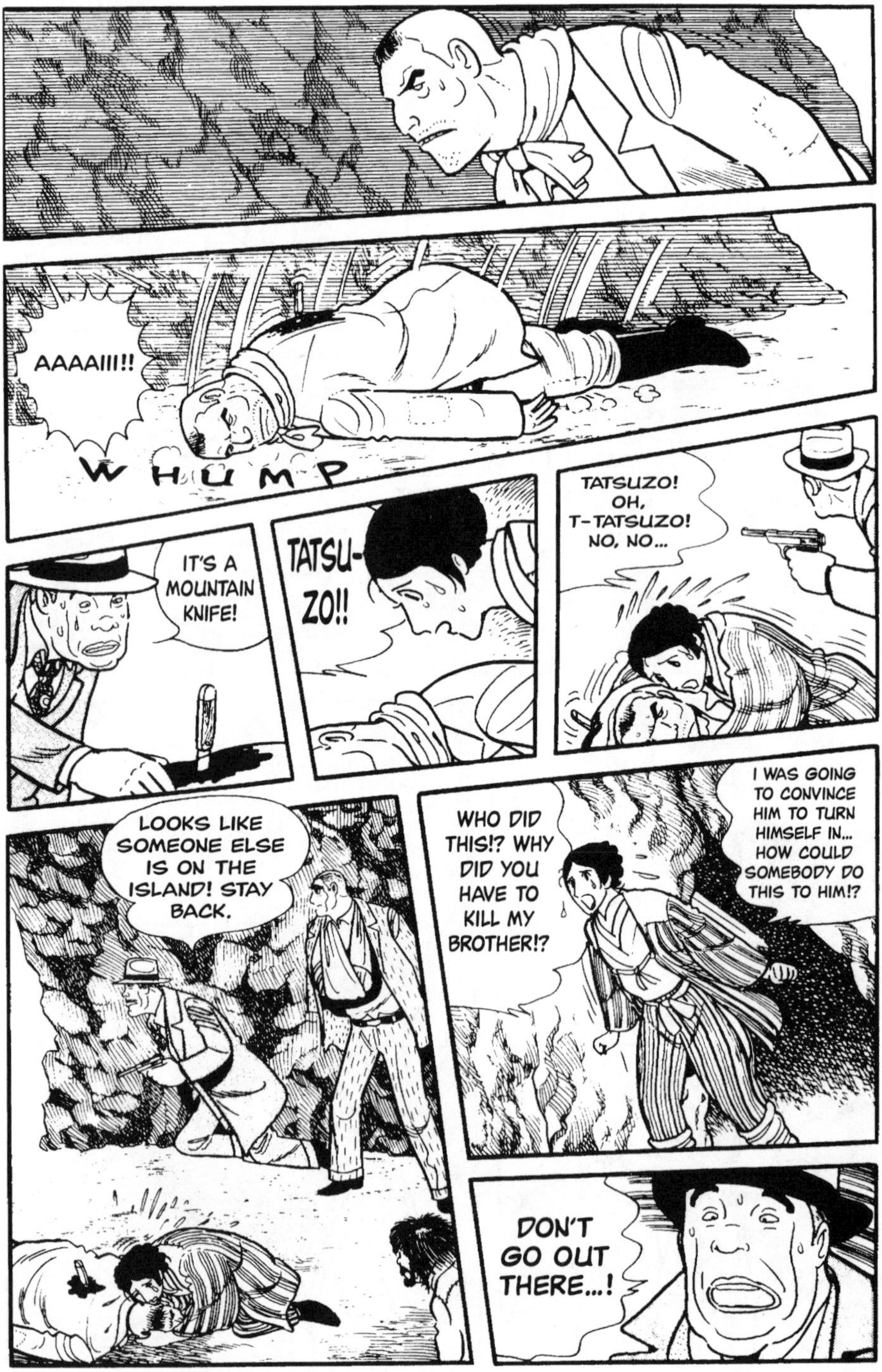
AAAAIII!!
WHUMP
IT'S A MOUNTAIN KNIFE!
TATSU-ZO!!
TATSUZO! OH, T-TATSUZO! NO, NO...
LOOKS LIKE SOMEONE ELSE IS ON THE ISLAND! STAY BACK.
WHO DID THIS!? WHY DID YOU HAVE TO KILL MY BROTHER!?
I WAS GOING TO CONVINCE HIM TO TURN HIMSELF IN... HOW COULD SOMEBODY DO THIS TO HIM!?
DON'T GO OUT THERE...!

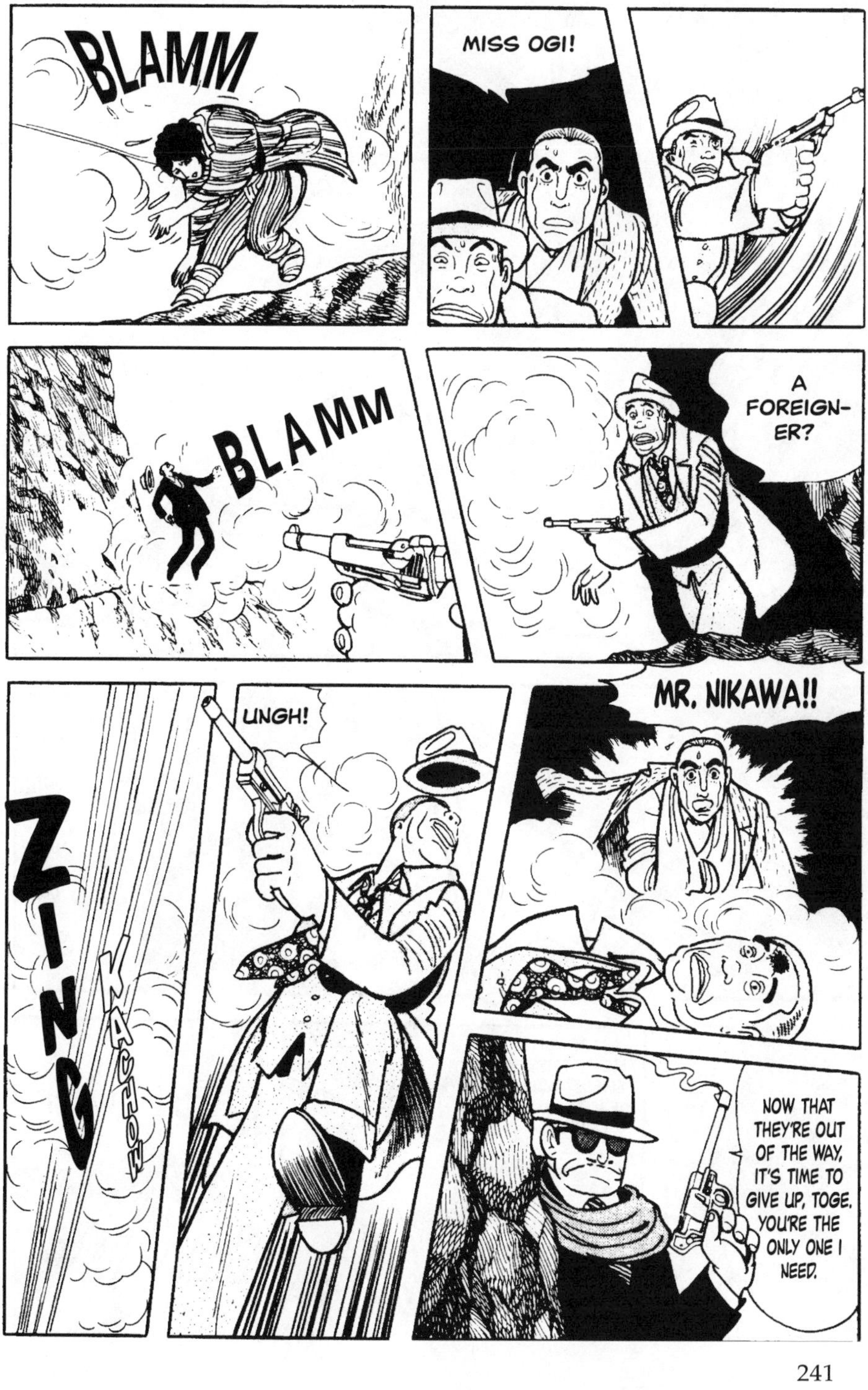
BLAMM
MISS OGI!
BLAMM
A FOREIGN-ER?
ZING
KACHOW
UNGH!
MR. NIKAWA!!
NOW THAT THEY'RE OUT OF THE WAY, IT'S TIME TO GIVE UP, TOGE. YOU'RE THE ONLY ONE I NEED.

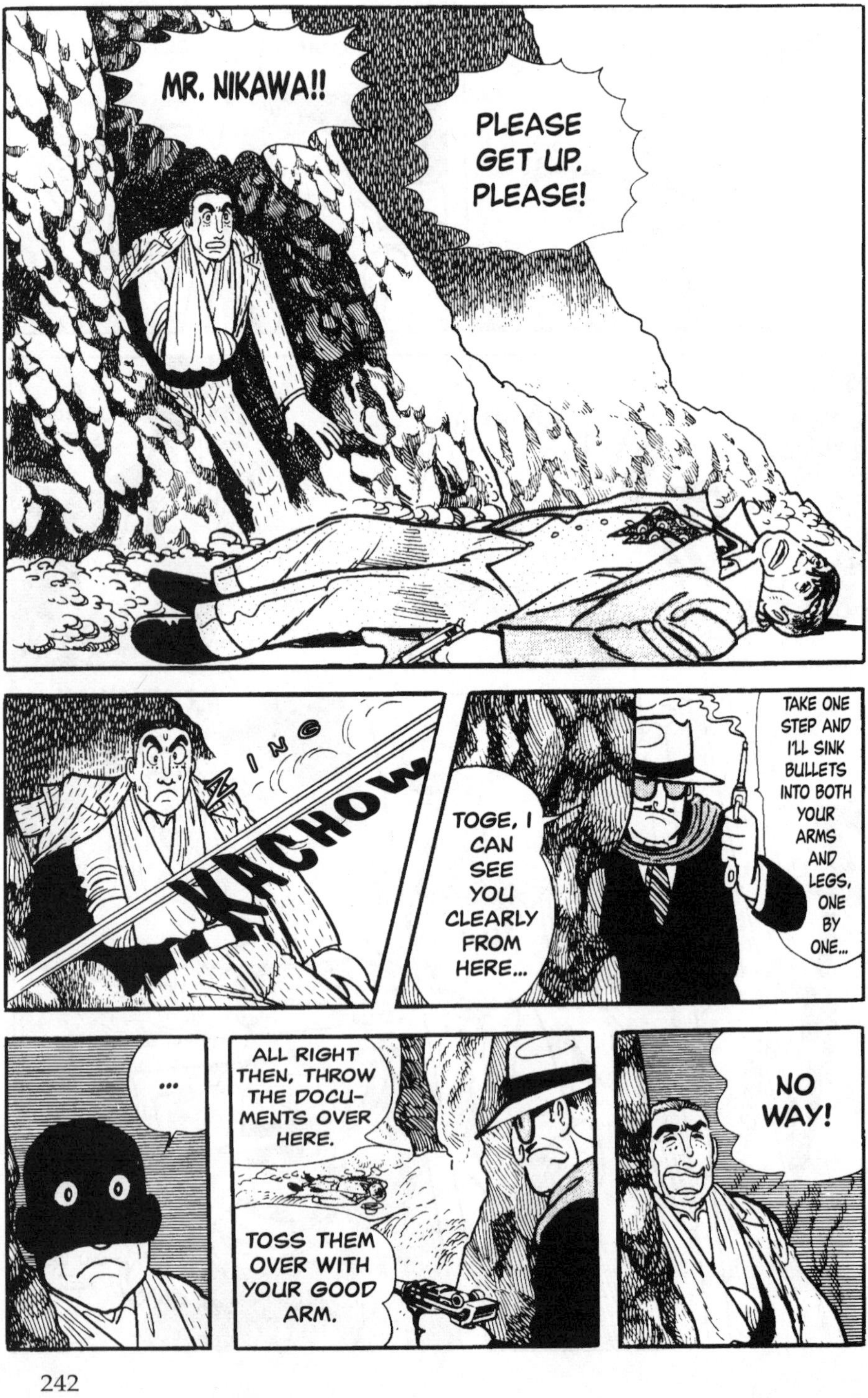
MR. NIKAWA!!
PLEASE GET UP. PLEASE!
ZING
KACHOW
TOGE, I CAN SEE YOU CLEARLY FROM HERE...
TAKE ONE STEP AND I'LL SINK BULLETS INTO BOTH YOUR ARMS AND LEGS, ONE BY ONE...
...
ALL RIGHT THEN, THROW THE DOCU-MENTS OVER HERE.
TOSS THEM OVER WITH YOUR GOOD ARM.
NO WAY!

YOU HAVE NO USE FOR THEM.

YOU REALLY THINK THOSE PAPERS COULD POSE A THREAT TO THE NAZIS? YOU FOOL! HAND THEM OVER TO ME BEFORE YOU DO ANYTHING STUPID WITH THEM.

SHUT UP!

DAMN... IF I COULD JUST GET AHOLD OF NIKAWA'S PISTOL.

YEAH, THEN I COULD DISTRACT HIM...

HEY, AKABANE, I'M RELYING ON YOU.

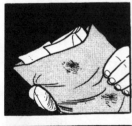

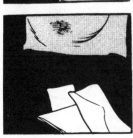

GO AND GIVE THIS EMPTY ENVELOPE TO THAT CRAZY KILLER!

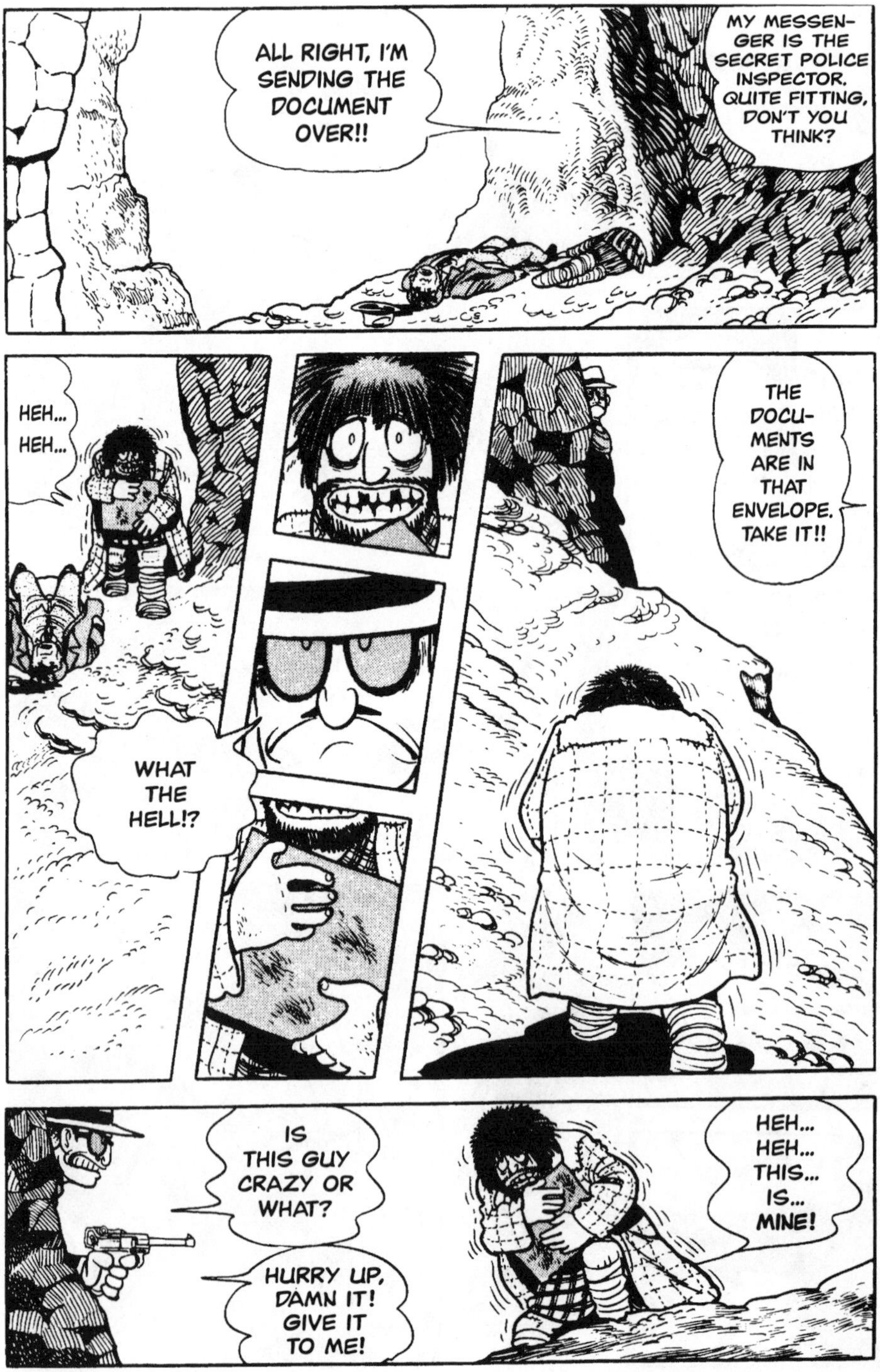
ALL RIGHT, I'M SENDING THE DOCUMENT OVER!!
MY MESSENGER IS THE SECRET POLICE INSPECTOR. QUITE FITTING, DON'T YOU THINK?
HEH... HEH...
WHAT THE HELL!?
THE DOCUMENTS ARE IN THAT ENVELOPE. TAKE IT!!
IS THIS GUY CRAZY OR WHAT?
HURRY UP, DAMN IT! GIVE IT TO ME!
HEH... HEH... THIS... IS... MINE!

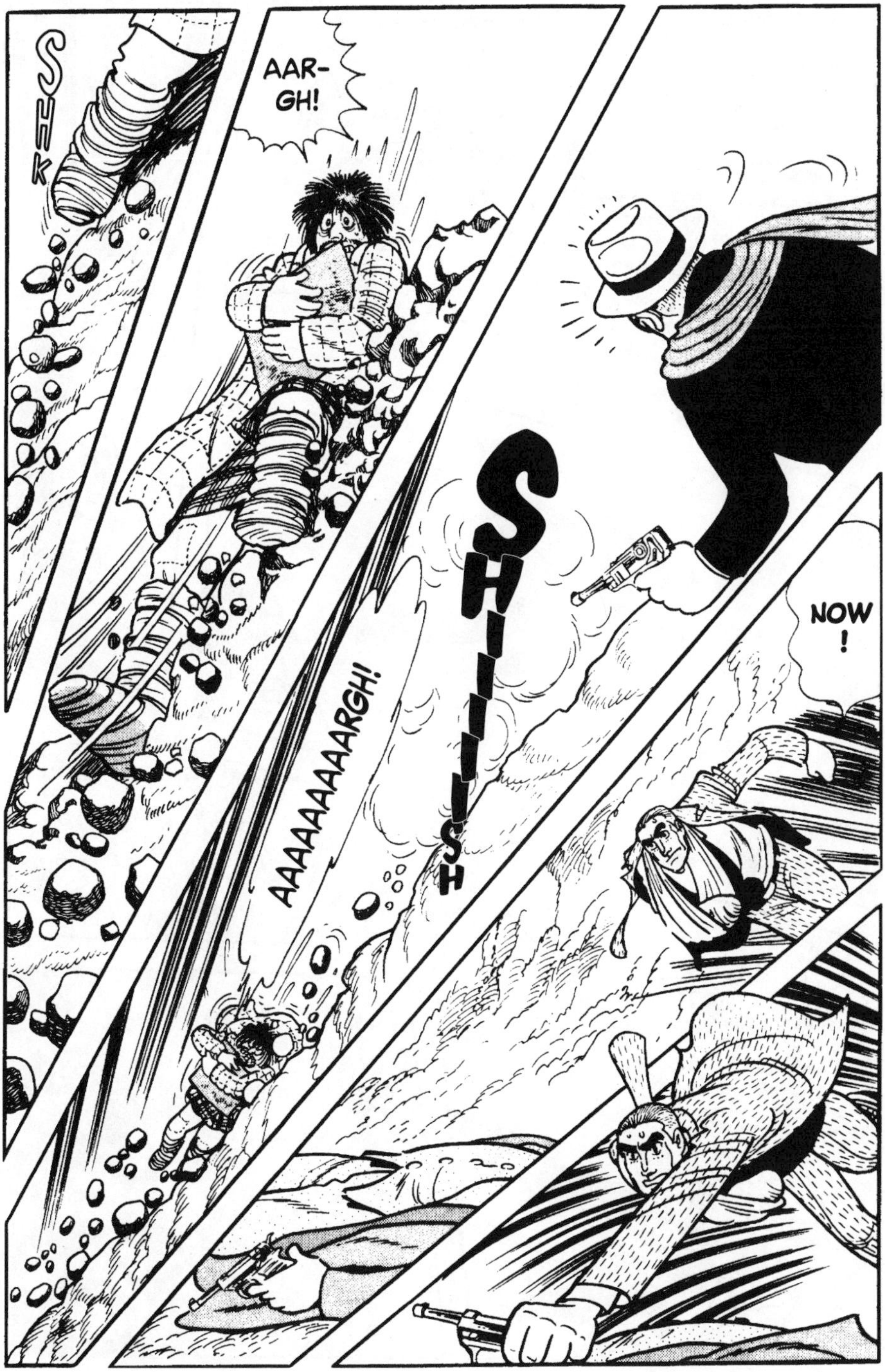
SHHK
AAR-GH!
AAAAAAAAARGH!
SHIIIIISH
NOW!

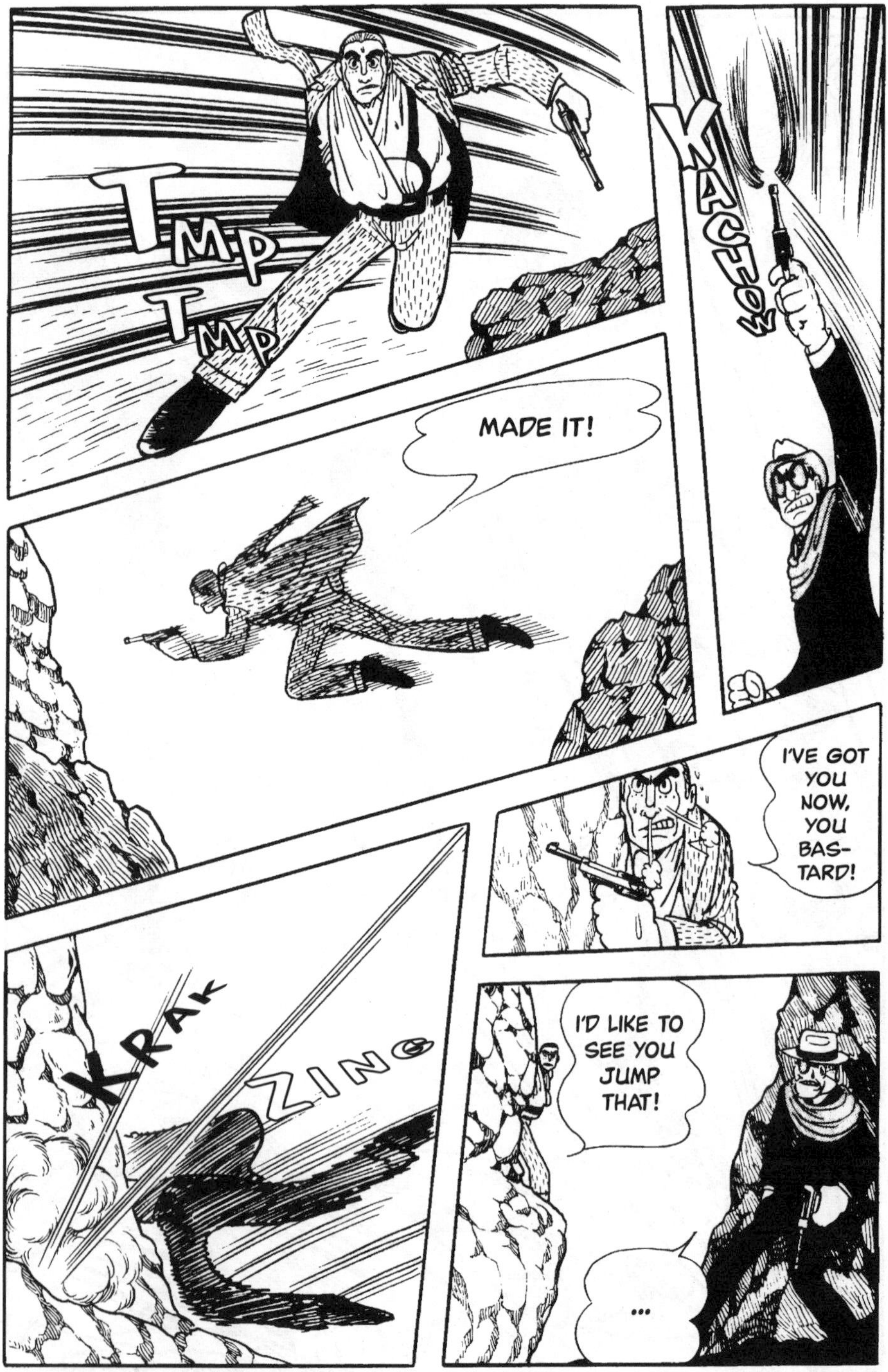
TMP
TMP
MADE IT!
KACHOW
I'VE GOT YOU NOW, YOU BASTARD!
KRAK
ZING
I'D LIKE TO SEE YOU JUMP THAT!
...

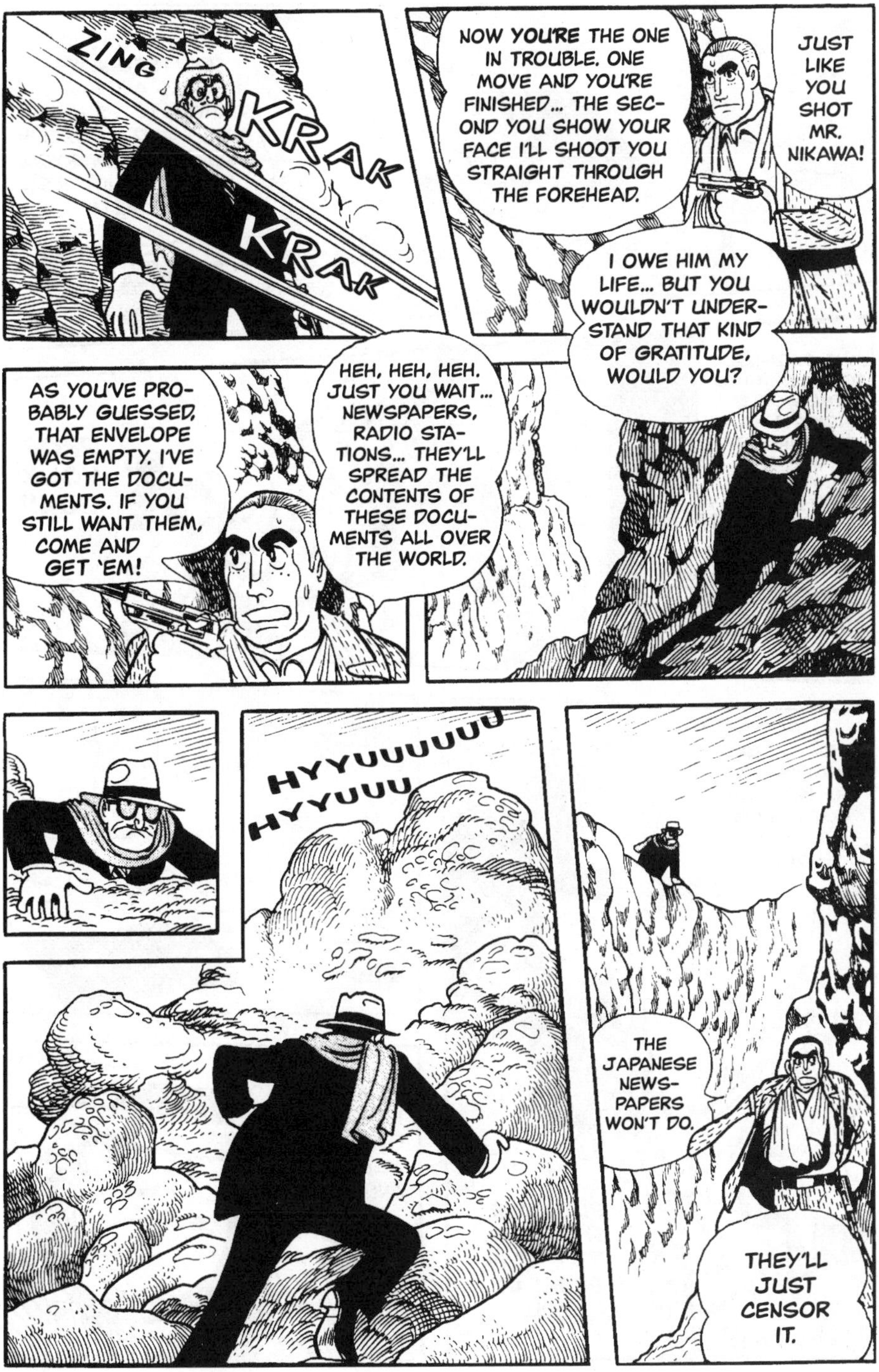
ZING
KRAK
KRAK
NOW YOU'RE THE ONE IN TROUBLE. ONE MOVE AND YOU'RE FINISHED... THE SECOND YOU SHOW YOUR FACE I'LL SHOOT YOU STRAIGHT THROUGH THE FOREHEAD.
JUST LIKE YOU SHOT MR. NIKAWA!
I OWE HIM MY LIFE... BUT YOU WOULDN'T UNDERSTAND THAT KIND OF GRATITUDE, WOULD YOU?
AS YOU'VE PROBABLY GUESSED, THAT ENVELOPE WAS EMPTY. I'VE GOT THE DOCUMENTS. IF YOU STILL WANT THEM, COME AND GET 'EM!
HEH, HEH, HEH. JUST YOU WAIT... NEWSPAPERS, RADIO STATIONS... THEY'LL SPREAD THE CONTENTS OF THESE DOCUMENTS ALL OVER THE WORLD.
HYYUUUUUU
HYYUUU
THE JAPANESE NEWSPAPERS WON'T DO.
THEY'LL JUST CENSOR IT.

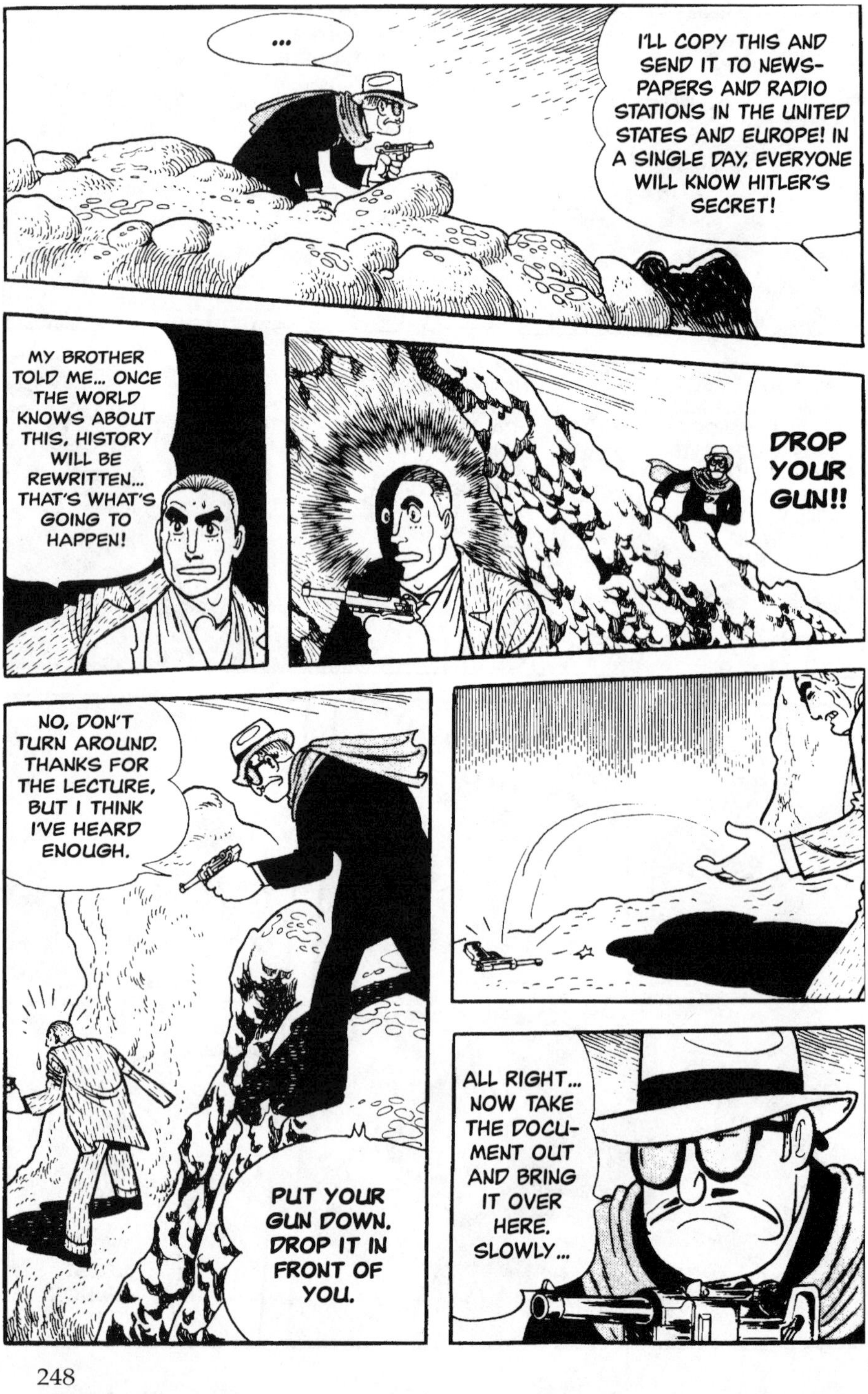
...
I'LL COPY THIS AND SEND IT TO NEWS-PAPERS AND RADIO STATIONS IN THE UNITED STATES AND EUROPE! IN A SINGLE DAY, EVERYONE WILL KNOW HITLER'S SECRET!
MY BROTHER TOLD ME... ONCE THE WORLD KNOWS ABOUT THIS, HISTORY WILL BE REWRITTEN... THAT'S WHAT'S GOING TO HAPPEN!
DROP YOUR GUN!!
NO, DON'T TURN AROUND. THANKS FOR THE LECTURE, BUT I THINK I'VE HEARD ENOUGH.
PUT YOUR GUN DOWN. DROP IT IN FRONT OF YOU.
ALL RIGHT... NOW TAKE THE DOCU-MENT OUT AND BRING IT OVER HERE. SLOWLY...

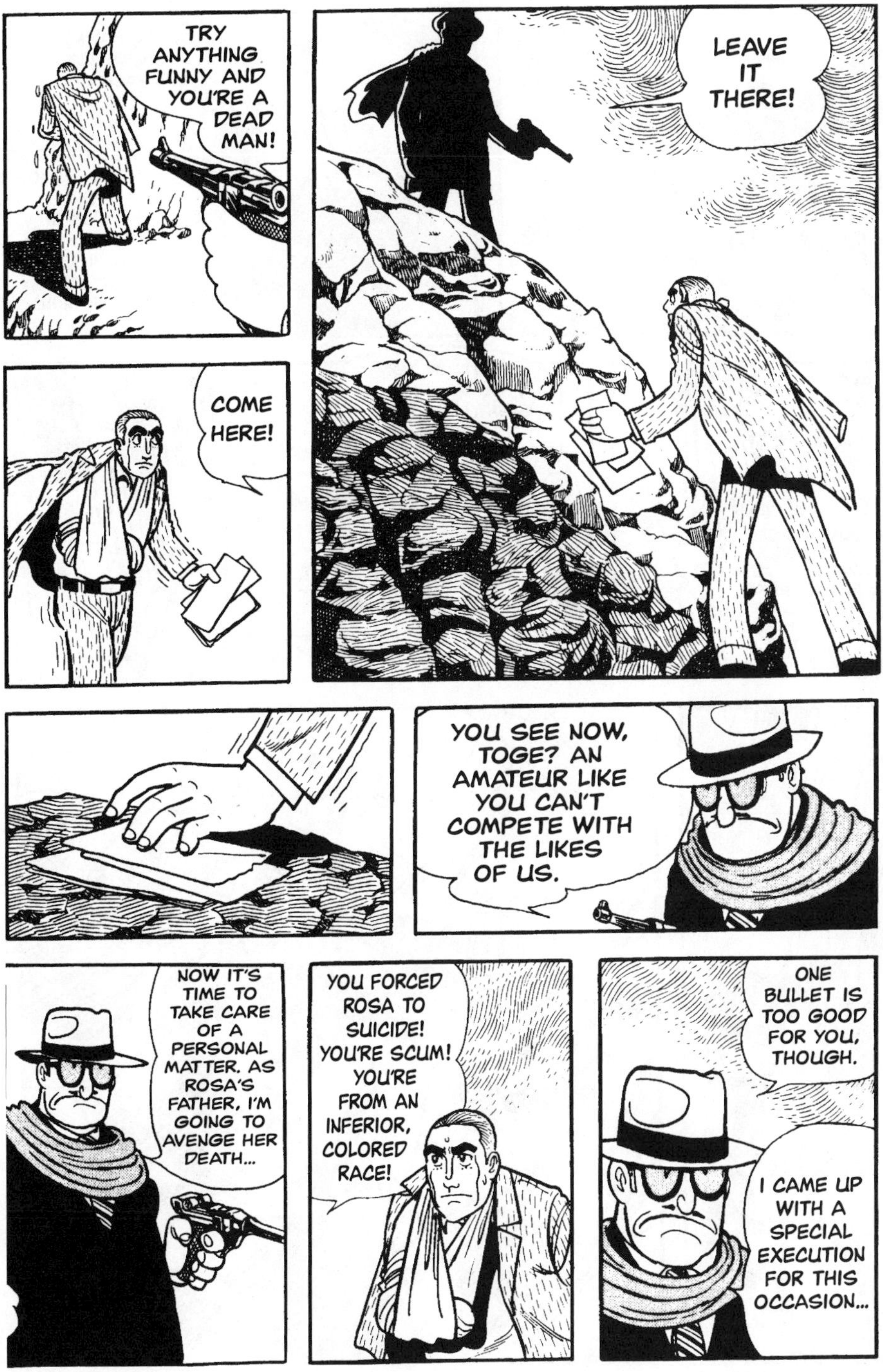
TRY ANYTHING FUNNY AND YOU'RE A DEAD MAN!
LEAVE IT THERE!
COME HERE!
YOU SEE NOW, TOGE? AN AMATEUR LIKE YOU CAN'T COMPETE WITH THE LIKES OF US.
NOW IT'S TIME TO TAKE CARE OF A PERSONAL MATTER. AS ROSA'S FATHER, I'M GOING TO AVENGE HER DEATH...
YOU FORCED ROSA TO SUICIDE! YOU'RE SCUM! YOU'RE FROM AN INFERIOR, COLORED RACE!
ONE BULLET IS TOO GOOD FOR YOU, THOUGH.
I CAME UP WITH A SPECIAL EXECUTION FOR THIS OCCASION...

FIRST, I'LL CUT THE TENDONS IN YOUR ANKLES...

THEN, HAVING COMPLETELY INCAPACITATED YOU...

I'LL MOVE ON TO SOME BIO-LOGICAL EXPERIMENTS. HERE ARE MY TOOLS. I'LL CUT OPEN YOUR SKIN...

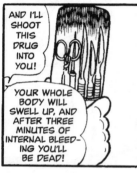

AND I'LL SHOOT THIS DRUG INTO YOU!

YOUR WHOLE BODY WILL SWELL UP, AND AFTER THREE MINUTES OF INTERNAL BLEED-ING YOU'LL BE DEAD!

YOU'LL BE MY GUINEA PIG. EVENTUALLY, WE'LL USE THE SAME METHOD ON JEWS...

WHOOSH

BLAMM

KEEE KEEE KEEE

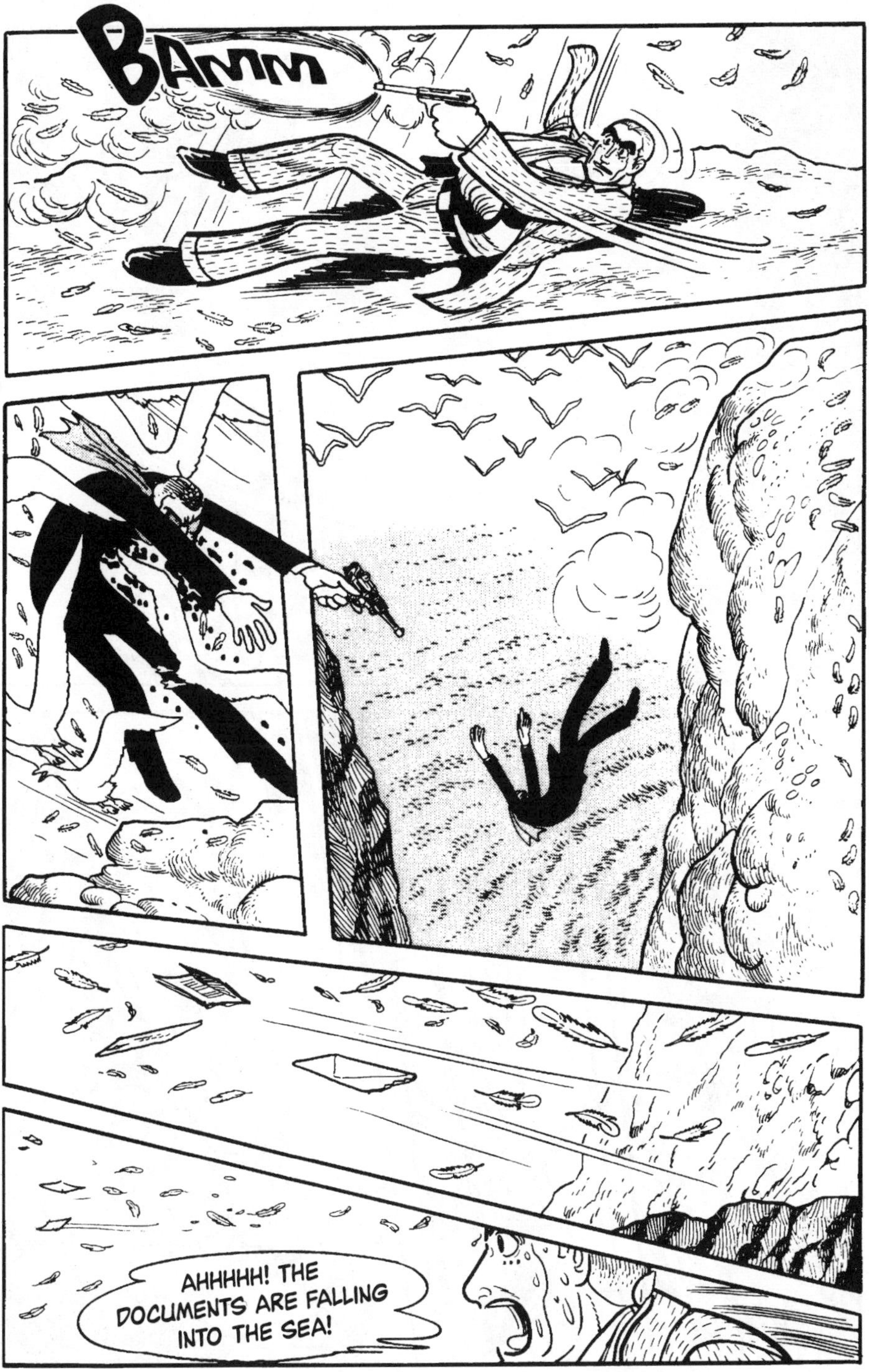
BAMM
AHHHHH! THE DOCUMENTS ARE FALLING INTO THE SEA!

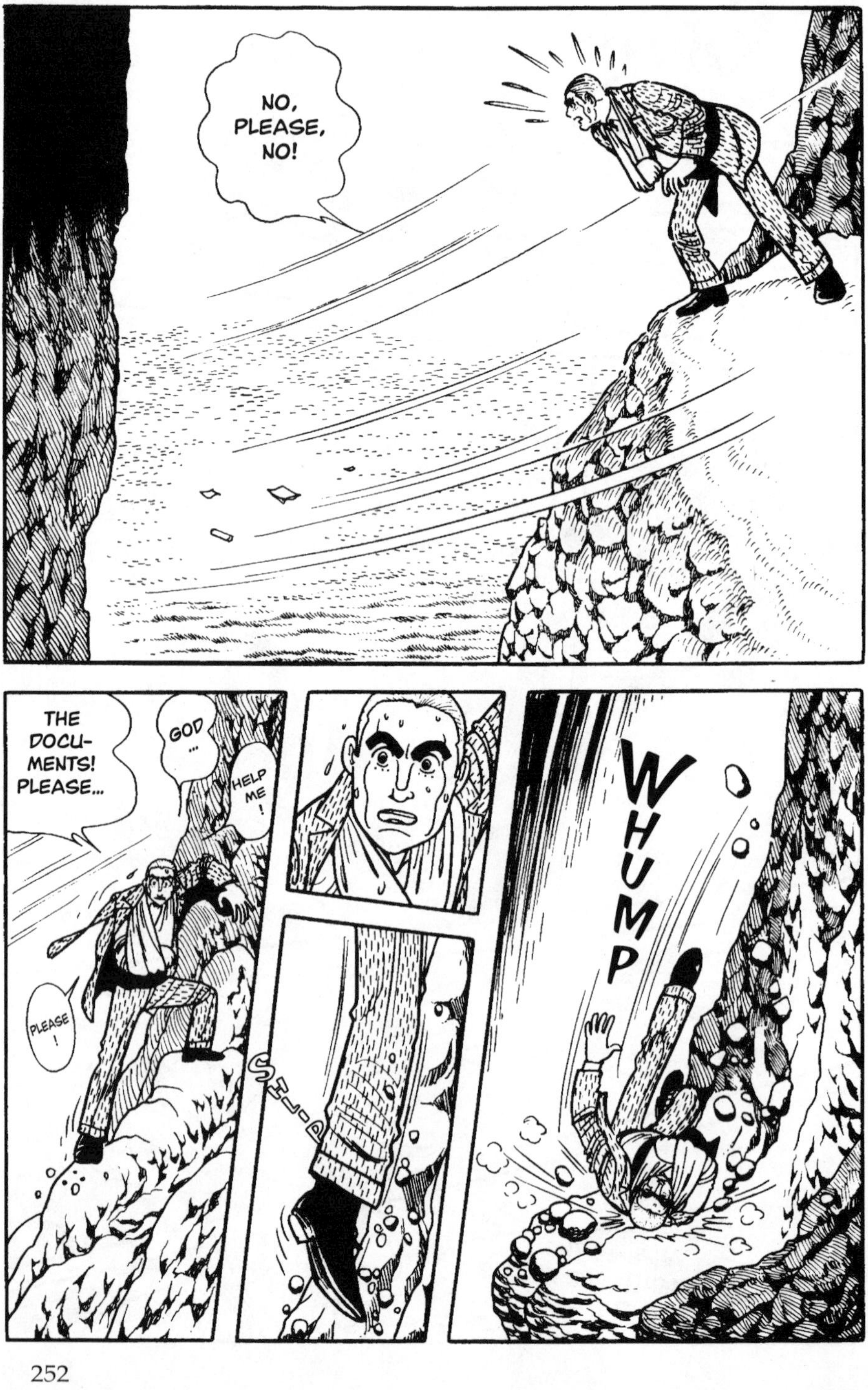
NO, PLEASE, NO!
THE DOCUMENTS! PLEASE...
GOD ...
HELP ME !
PLEASE !
SLIP
WHUMP

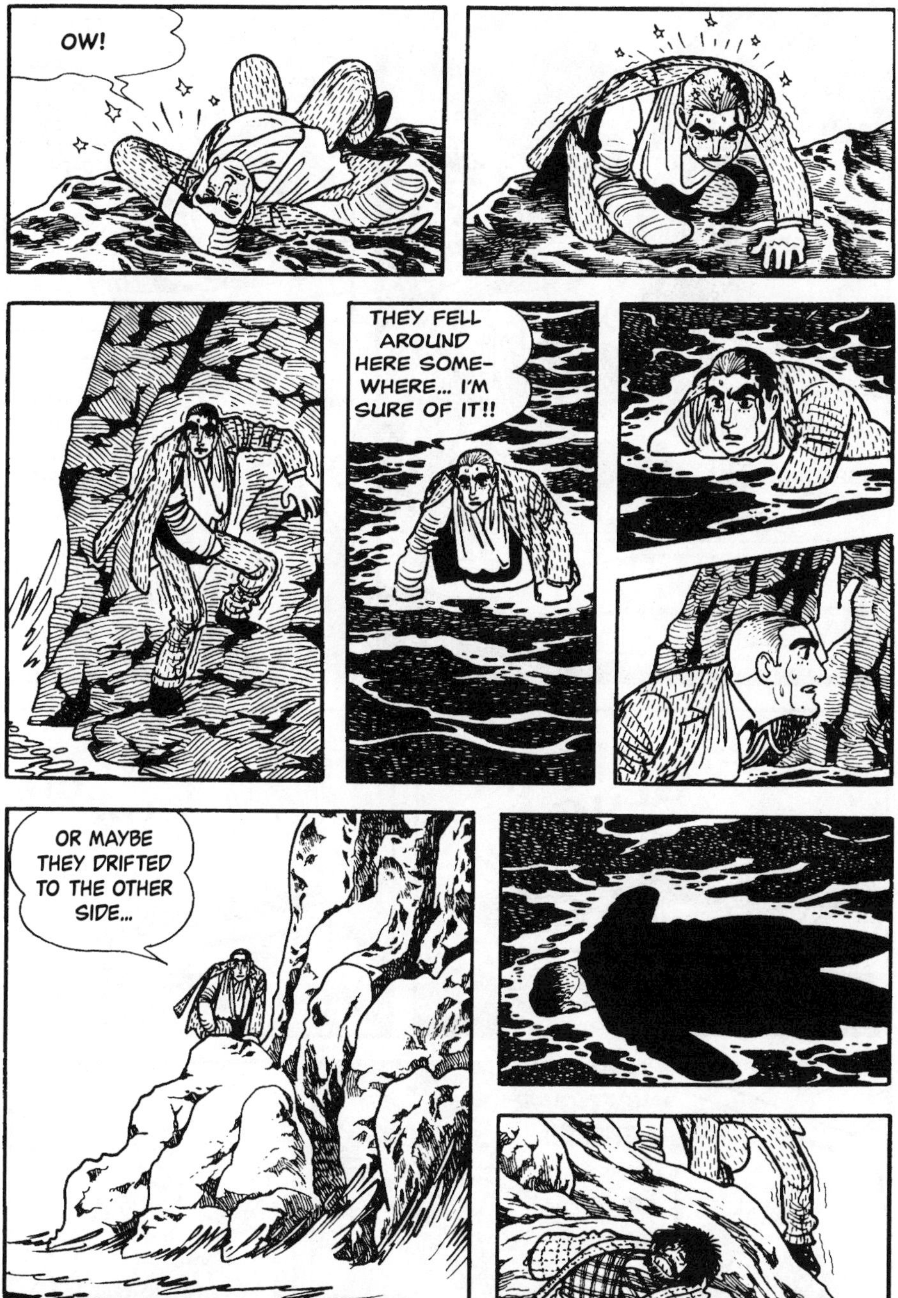
OW!
THEY FELL AROUND HERE SOME-WHERE... I'M SURE OF IT!!
OR MAYBE THEY DRIFTED TO THE OTHER SIDE...

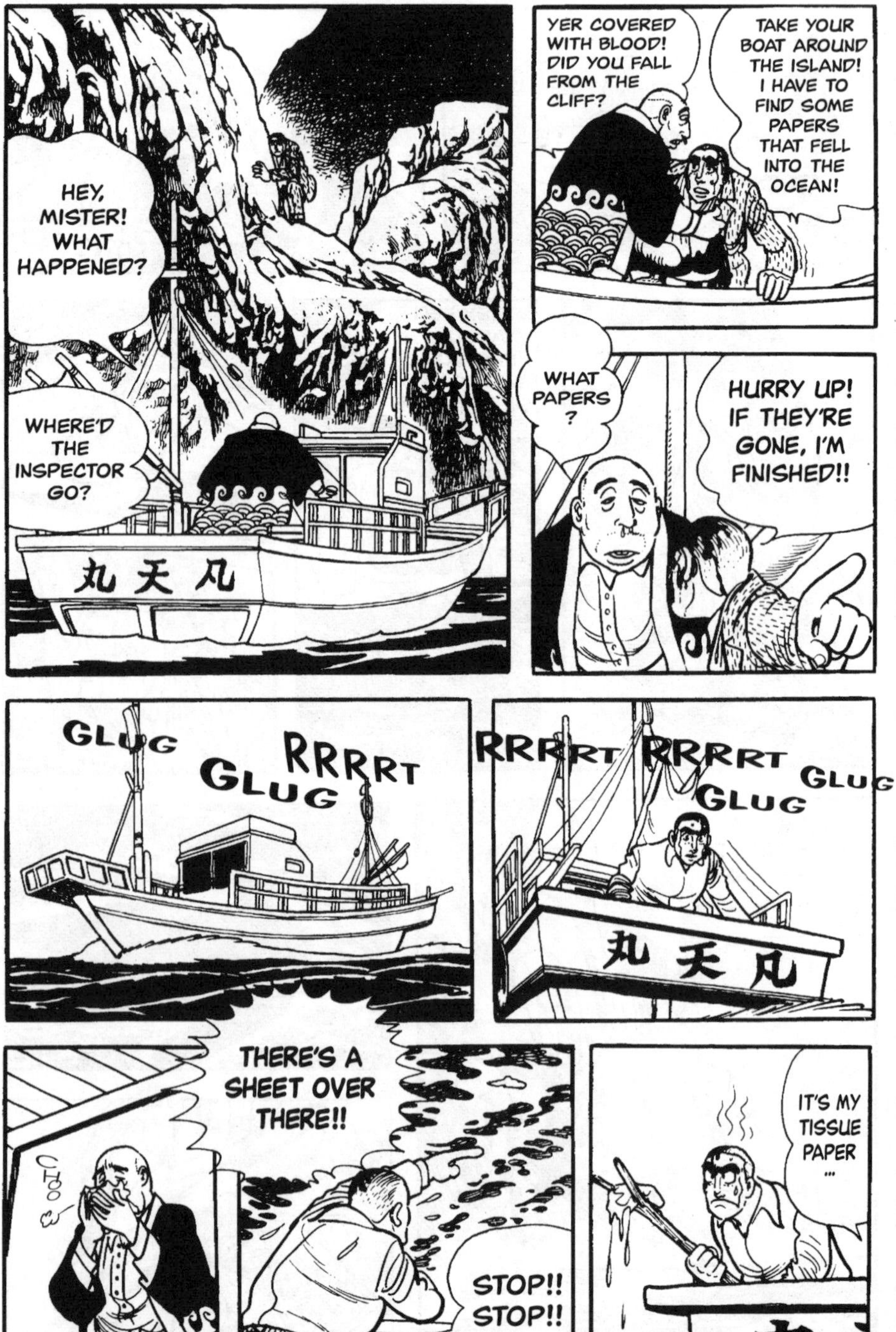
HEY, MISTER! WHAT HAPPENED?
WHERE'D THE INSPECTOR GO?
丸天凡
YER COVERED WITH BLOOD! DID YOU FALL FROM THE CLIFF?
TAKE YOUR BOAT AROUND THE ISLAND! I HAVE TO FIND SOME PAPERS THAT FELL INTO THE OCEAN!
WHAT PAPERS ?
HURRY UP! IF THEY'RE GONE, I'M FINISHED!!
GLUG
GLUG
RRRRT
RRRRT
RRRRT
GLUG
GLUG
丸天凡
CHOO
THERE'S A SHEET OVER THERE!!
STOP!! STOP!!
IT'S MY TISSUE PAPER ...
丸

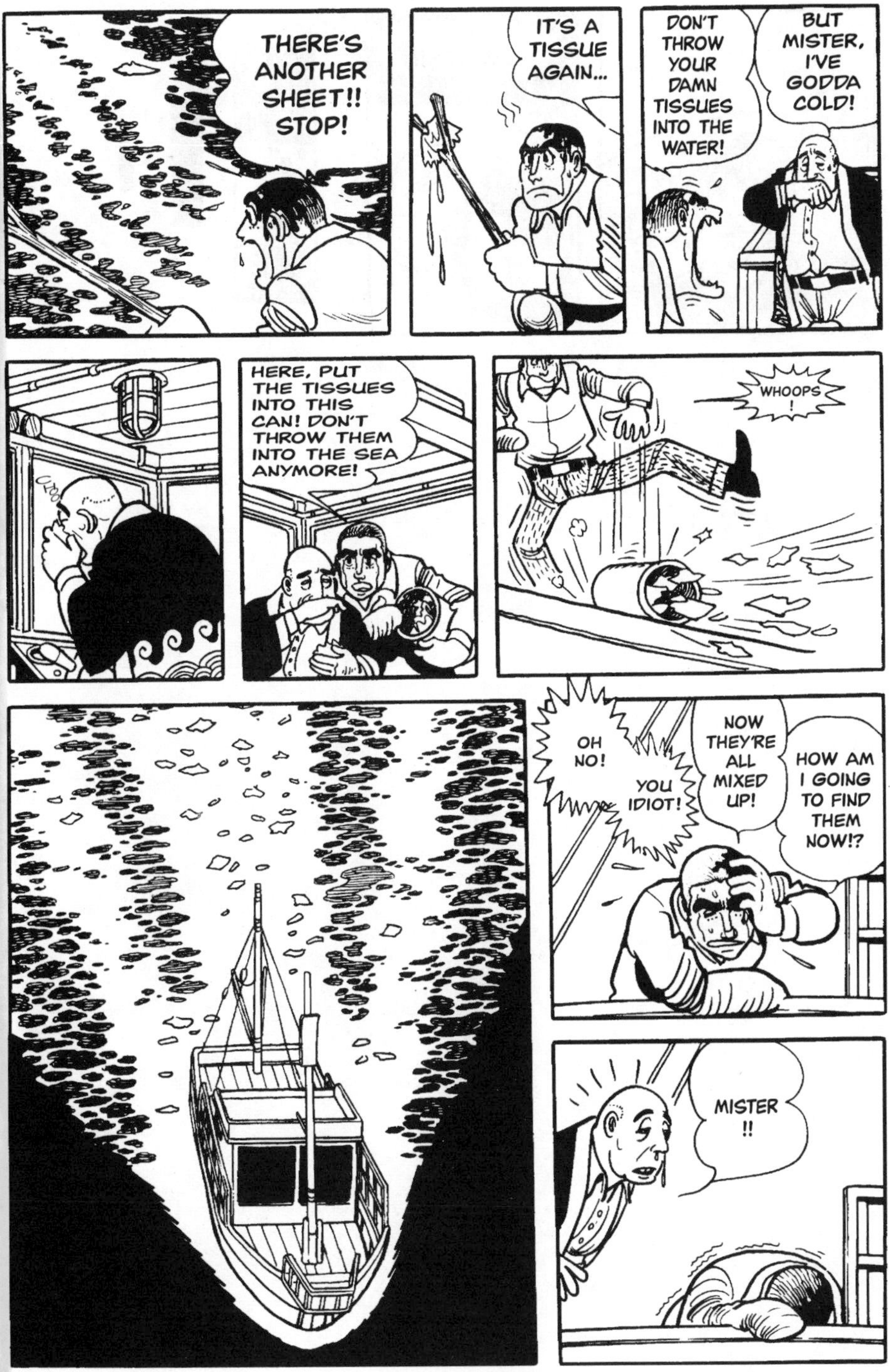
THERE'S ANOTHER SHEET!! STOP!
IT'S A TISSUE AGAIN...
DON'T THROW YOUR DAMN TISSUES INTO THE WATER!
BUT MISTER, I'VE GODDA COLD!
HERE, PUT THE TISSUES INTO THIS CAN! DON'T THROW THEM INTO THE SEA ANYMORE!
WHOOPS !
OH NO!
YOU IDIOT!
NOW THEY'RE ALL MIXED UP!
HOW AM I GOING TO FIND THEM NOW!?
MISTER !!

TO BE CONTINUED IN *ADOLF: THE HALF-ARYAN!*